PRAISE FOR
BELLOW

"You can apply virtually any complimentary adjective to this book: compelling, engrossing, incisive, profoundly enjoyable. . . . In the vast intellectual range of his work, Bellow has been, in many senses, the Mind of America. James Atlas is now our Mind-Reader."
—Scott Turow

"Let me be upfront: Almost everything I know about Bellow that I didn't guess from reading him, I got from the encyclopedic Atlas. I could no more stop reading his biography than I could stop reading Saul Bellow after he blew the blinds off the windows in my head."
—John Leonard, *The New York Times Book Review*

"*Bellow* is not only a compelling story of a great and flawed writer, one who continues to demand our attention, but also a portrait of an extraordinary (and now rapidly receding) epoch in the history of American letters."
—*The New York Times*

"*Bellow* is a masterly model of the biographer's art. It is balanced and even-tempered, composed with intelligence and grace, long enough to encompass its subject, yet not inundated with unnecessary detail. . . . The subject deserves a big, important book, and *Bellow* is equal to the task."
—*Newsday*

"Well worth the wait. Vigorous and incisive . . . a sharp-edged, provocative portrait."
—*Publishers Weekly,* starred review

"James Atlas's biography is a deep, nuanced portrait of the Nobel novelist's life, loves, city, and writings."
—*The Boston Sunday Globe*

"The book is lively, intelligent, and as readable as it is thorough. Its judgments, more often than not, are persuasive. And while it will not please those for whom Bellow can do no wrong, most readers are likely to feel that it is written essentially out of admiration—or out of a struggle to preserve that admiration."

—John Gross, *Commentary*

"*Bellow* is an astonishing, brilliant work. I cannot recall when a living writer was last the subject of such an intimate, full-length portrait."

—Jay Parini, *The Chronicle of Higher Education*

"An intelligent and perceptive, lively and absorbing narrative."

—Jeffrey Meyers, *The New Criterion*

"Magnificent. . . . James Atlas is thoroughly engaged here. This is the book he was born to write."

—James Kaplan, *The New York Observer*

"A magnificent example of the best a literary biography can be: a scrupulously researched narrative of this major American author's life and a truly valuable study of the meaning and importance of the works."

—*Elle*

"*Bellow* is a big book, but all its bulk is muscle. It neither debunks nor canonizes its subject. Thankfully, Atlas the critic is just as probing as Atlas the shrink, and the result is stunning: a full-blooded biography with brains."

—*GQ*

"Bellow, the man and the artist, could not have been more thoroughly or eloquently rendered."

—*Vogue*

"Atlas says it well and with authority in this thoroughly entertaining biography: A."

—*Entertainment Weekly*

BELLOW

A BIOGRAPHY

MODERN LIBRARY ⚘ NEW YORK

BELLOW

JAMES ATLAS

Library of Congress Cataloging-in-Publication Data

Atlas, James.
Bellow : a biography / James Atlas.
p.   cm.
Originally published: New York: Random House, 2000.
Includes bibliographical references and index.
ISBN 0-394-58501-1 (hc.: alk. paper)—ISBN 0-375-75958-1 (pbk.:   )
1. Bellow, Saul.   2. Novelists, American—20th Century—Biography.   I. Title
PS3503.E4488   Z554   2002
813'.52—DC21
[B]   2001056270

Book design by Carole Lowenstein

for Anna, always

INTRODUCTION

"Why don't you write a biography of Saul Bellow?" The question was posed to me by Philip Roth. It came at a difficult moment in my life, when I was between projects and casting about for the next book to write. At the age of twenty-eight, I had published a biography of the poet Delmore Schwartz—the model for the dissolute genius poet in Bellow's novel *Humboldt's Gift*—and had been inexorably identified as a career biographer. Did I want to write on Tennessee Williams? Cyril Connolly? Edmund Wilson? The last suggestion, put to me by Roger W. Straus, the founder of Farrar, Straus & Giroux and publisher of my Schwartz biography, had been so compelling—I was a great admirer of Wilson and had read every word he'd written—that I had signed a contract. How could a writer barely into his thirties turn down the opportunity to write the biography—the *authorized* biography yet—of America's greatest modern man of letters?

Five years later, I hadn't written a word. I hadn't even gone up to Yale to look at Wilson's papers in the Beinecke Library. As Philip Rahv, a founder of *Partisan Review* and one of my literary culture-heroes, used to say, "It wasn't in the cards." Much as I loved Wilson's work, I had a toxic response to his character. The bullying proclamations, the tedious self-revelations, the drinking and philandering—in the end, he just didn't appeal to me as a subject to whose life and work I was willing to apprentice myself for the better part of a decade, the time any conscientious biographer of a major personage can expect to allot. And there was a more nagging disincentive: Wilson had already written it all himself. His copious journals, assembled in five volumes, and his letters, also thoroughly compiled in several fat volumes by his executor, Leon Edel, took up all the literary oxygen in the room; I thought there would be nothing left for me to do except stitch together a dutiful narrative. But the most compelling reason not to write his biography was a deeply personal one: I felt no emotional connection with my subject, no "elective affinity," to borrow Goethe's phrase. As a figure with whom I could identify—or at the very least through whom I could tease out, however subliminally, the hidden themes of my own life—Wilson left me cold. He wasn't my type.

I had learned from my long and solitary work on the life of Delmore Schwartz that biography is a process of immersion. Poring over letters and discarded drafts day after day, interviewing the subject's family, befriending the subject's friends and lovers, the biographer enters into a kind of relationship that's duplicated nowhere else in life—he becomes an instant confidant, privy to the most intimate secrets, a conduit for unresolved and unexpressed feelings; yet at the same time he's supposed to remain emotionally distant, formal, objective. The role verges on the psychoanalytic—in our effort to elicit testimony that will illuminate our subject's life, we experience transference, deceit, repression. It's also a kind of marriage: The more zealously one tries to define the relationship, the more it seems to elude one's grasp. Over the years, the biographer acquires an ever-deepening intimacy with his subject, discovering in the process how contradictory and, in the end, unfathomable we all are, both to others and to ourselves. The relationship isn't always smooth: to disapprove, to feel exasperation, resentment, even hatred, are all parts of it. But to feel a lack of engagement is fatal; witness Mark Schorer, who, in the process of writing his compendious biography of Sinclair Lewis, came to loathe his subject; or Lawrance Thompson, who turned inexorably against Robert Frost. Their identifications with their subjects had created a form of bondage. The two most discerning biographies in English, to my mind, are Boswell's *Life of Samuel Johnson* and Richard Ellmann's *James Joyce*, two books imbued with profound sympathy for their subjects' foibles and failings—imbued, to put it plainly, with love.

Bellow was a natural choice for me; Roth wasn't the only one to suggest him. I had grown up in Chicago; my parents were from the same Northwest Side Jewish milieu that Bellow had rendered so vividly in a succession of books, and they belonged to the same generation; he was *experience-near.* We even knew people in common: The family of my mother's best friend, the Teitelbaums, had sold their bakery to Bellow's uncle, the same uncle who had urged Bellow's father to come to Chicago and had given him a job. The streets on which Bellow had grown up, the schools he had attended, the landmarks of his youth, belonged to the world of Jewish-immigrant Chicago, visible traces of which lingered in my grandmother's home and in my parents' family albums. To write a biography of Saul Bellow would be, in a sense, to write my own autobiography, a generation removed.

This historical connection spoke to me directly through the medium of Bellow's prose. Even now, I can remember my first encounter with his utterly distinctive voice. I was fourteen when I happened upon a worn orange Penguin paperback of *Dangling Man,* Bellow's first novel. The simple, diaristic narrative conveyed to me that literature could be written in a recognizably American idiom; the fact that it was about lower-middle-class Chicago and concerned a bookish (and clearly Jewish) intellectual struggling to find his way in that inhospitable environment suggested that my own experience might be worth writing about, that it, too, possessed the components of literature. Later on, as I read through Bellow's work, I felt—as did so many thousands of others from so many disparate worlds—captivated by his sensibility, which was so capable of encompassing the high and the low, Spengler and pool halls, the Great Books aura of the University of Chicago and the gritty prospect of the Ravenswood El. I could recite by heart the long opening sentence of *The Adventures of Augie March:* "I am an American, Chicago born—Chicago, that somber city—and go at things as I have taught myself, free-style, and will make the record in my own way: first to knock, first admitted; sometimes an innocent knock, sometimes a not so innocent." Now *there* was a credo I could embrace.

None of this meant I could write Bellow's biography. Numerous obstacles presented themselves. For one thing, I was certain Bellow would never authorize it. He had eluded his first biographer, Mark Harris, for a decade, prompting Harris to write *Saul Bellow, Drumlin Woodchuck*, his comic masterpiece about *not* writing Bellow's biography. To authorize a biographer would be to commit himself—and from what I knew of Bellow that was something he never did, preferring to keep his escape hatches open. On the other hand, I didn't *want* him to authorize it. Official biographies, to my mind, are fatally compromised; they can never dispel the suspicion that subject and biographer have colluded. Like Augie, I was determined to make the record in my own way. In practice, this meant getting Bellow to cooperate while leaving me to my own devices—a hard bargain to strike.

Then there was the matter of Bellow's papers. Documents, letters, manuscripts form the heart of biography, especially the biography of a literary figure. They give texture and voice to the narrative. Yet even if a biographer manages to obtain them from libraries and private hands, he's enjoined from quoting them; the words themselves belong to the author. The recent example of the Ian Hamilton/J. D. Salinger debacle—Salinger refused to let Hamilton quote any of his letters and went to court to ensure that his wish was carried out—served as a potential biographical deterrent. Not even the shrewd and masterly biographer Peter Ackroyd, denied permission to quote from T. S. Eliot's letters by the poet's widow, was able to pull it off; his biography of Eliot is informative but monotonous in tone. Clearly, I would need Bellow's permission to quote from his correspondence and unpublished manuscripts if I was to write his biography. And I needed him to let me interview his friends and family—or at least not warn them off when I came calling. I wasn't Kitty Kelley, and he wasn't Frank Sinatra; if he really didn't want me to write the book, I wasn't going to write it.

In the summer of 1987, I wrote Bellow a letter, broaching the matter in a gingerly fashion, then followed it up a few weeks later with a phone call. Had he given any thought to my letter? He had, he said apologetically, and he'd been meaning to write. He professed to be flattered that I thought him worthy of a biography, and he had kind words for my biography of Delmore Schwartz. But he was intending to write a memoir of his own and didn't feel he could both reminisce to me and write. Maybe later on . . . And there we left it.

A year later, I came across both a book of essays by Isaac Rosenfeld that had just been published by a university press with a foreword by Bellow and, fortuitously, a reissue of Rosenfeld's novel, *Passage from Home*. Rosenfeld held a significant place in my personal literary pantheon. He had grown up with Bellow in Chicago; the two were friends and rivals at Tuley High School in the 1920s. At the University of Chicago and later on in New York they were inseparable. But their paths eventually diverged, and Rosenfeld died prematurely of a heart attack at the age of thirty-eight. To me, he was a haunting figure, not only because he'd written a novel about the troubled adolescence of a sensitive Jewish boy in Chicago, a theme dear to my heart, but because he had always represented the obverse of Bellow's startling rise to fame. The obscurity that was Rosenfeld's reward seemed a far more plausible outcome of literary aspiration than winning the Nobel Prize and just as dramatically compelling.

In the spring of 1989, on an impulse, I went to Chicago for a look at Bellow's papers. I didn't know what I would find or even what I was looking for, but as I pored over the extensive bibliography of the holdings on deposit at the Rare Book and Manuscripts Collection of the Regenstein Library at the University of Chicago, I came across an intriguing manuscript entitled "Charm and Death." Bellow published only a portion of what he wrote; he discarded endless drafts of manuscripts, abandoned works in progress without regret; he was exacting about what he added to his oeuvre. Sitting at a table in the rare-books room, I was struck forcibly by the main character's name, written in Bellow's hand at the top of the manuscript: *Zetland*. This was the name he had given to Rosenfeld in a fictional fragment about his dear dead friend that was published in his collection *Him with His Foot in His Mouth and Other Stories*. The manuscript was a chronicle of Rosenfeld's early life in Chicago, his college years in Hyde Park, his triumph and rapid decline in the Greenwich Village of the fifties. It was two hundred pages long and beautifully written. When I got up from the table at the end of a long day, I knew that I would write this book.

I explained my decision in a letter to Bellow, making it clear that I wasn't asking him to authorize the book. I hoped, quoting Samuel Beckett's famous edict to his first biographer, Deirdre Bair, that he would "neither help nor hinder." In the end, he did much more: He gave me permission to examine his papers, with restrictions that were so erratic and intermittent as to constitute virtual authorization; more important, he didn't discourage his friends and associates from seeing me. I often taxed his patience, speculating about his change of name from Solomon to Saul and writing about his son Adam in *The New York Times Magazine*. Yet even when I tested his limits by publishing in *The New Yorker* an account of our relationship, he didn't banish me—or if he did, it was a banishment of brief duration. "I'll tell you a story," he said coldly when I called him up not long afterward: "A wise man is asked, 'What is the difference between ignorance and indifference?' " And what was the answer? "I don't know and I don't care." A year later, we were sitting under a tree in his front yard in Vermont, going over his correspondence.

Still, I had my doubts that I would emerge unscathed by his occasional wrath against biographers. After a decade of collaboration on a book about him, Ruth Miller, Bellow's friend for half a century, found herself talking to his lawyers when he didn't like what she'd written. But when I sent him the last batch of quotations from his letters in the summer of 1998 and followed up with a phone call, he sounded cordial. We agreed to meet in the town a few miles from his Vermont house. Pancho's Wreck, the restaurant Bellow chose for our rendezvous, wasn't open yet, so we walked over to the local hotel and found a table by the window in the empty dining room. Bellow tossed the envelope on the table and said, "I don't have a problem with any of this." I was stunned. We talked for a while, and he noted a few places where I'd gotten contextual information wrong. Finally, I brought myself to say that it would be helpful if he could somehow make official note of the fact that he'd given me permission to quote from his letters. I handed him a pen, and he scrawled, "Okay, except for occasional exceptions. S. Bellow."

"Why did he let me do it?" I asked his son Dan a few weeks later.

"He realized that you weren't going to go away."

BELLOW

*The living man is preoccupied with such questions as who he is,
what he lives for, what he is so keenly and interminably yearning for,
what his human essence is.*

—SAUL BELLOW,
The Jefferson Lectures

"I WAS, IN 1937, a very young, married man who had quickly
lost his first job and who lived with his in-laws. His affectionate, loyal, and pretty wife insisted that he must be given a
chance to write something."

But what? In "Starting Out in Chicago," originally delivered as
a Brandeis commencement address in 1974, Saul Bellow provided
a memorable portrait of his beginnings as a writer. If the year is
wrong—it was 1938, just a year before the outbreak of World War
II in Europe—the details are painfully accurate. This brief memoir,
more than anything else he ever wrote, captures the early stage of
that momentous confrontation in which "American society and
S. Bellow came face to face." He was twenty-two years old.

The job he'd lost was a stint in his older brother Maurice's coalyard, and he was fired for absenteeism. Maurice, not unreason-
ably, expected his brother to keep regular hours; Bellow had other
ideas about how to spend his time: He wanted to write.

His in-laws' apartment on North Virginia Avenue in the Northwest Side neighborhood of Ravenswood was drab and anonymous, one of the thousands of identical brick dwellings that
sprawled mile upon mile across a dull, orderly grid of streets.
While his wife, Anita, attended classes at the School of Social
Service Administration at the university, Bellow sat at a bridge
table in the back bedroom:

My table faced three cement steps that rose from the cellar into the brick gloom of a passageway. Only my mother-in-law was at home. A widow, then in her seventies [actually, her mid-sixties], she wore a heavy white braid down her back. She had been a modern woman and a socialist and suffragette in the old country. She was attractive in a fragile, steely way. You felt Sophie's [Sonya's] strength of will in all things. She kept a neat house. The very plants, the ashtrays, the pedestals, the doilies, the chairs, revealed her mastery. Each object had its military place. Her apartment could easily have been transferred to West Point.

Lunch occurred at half past twelve. The cooking was good. We ate together in the kitchen. The meal was followed by an interval of stone. My mother-in-law took a nap. I went into the street. Ravenswood was utterly empty. I walked about with something like a large stone in my belly. I often turned into Lawrence Avenue and stood on the bridge looking into the drainage canal. If I had been a dog I would have howled.

American writers are largely self-made. William Faulkner emerged out of the somnolent town of Oxford, Mississippi; Ernest Hemingway was brought up in the bland suburb of Oak Park, just a few miles from Ravenswood; Sinclair Lewis hailed from Sauk Centre, Minnesota. They simply "materialized somehow," as Bellow put it. But even by the folkloric standards of American literature, Bellow's remoteness from the centers of culture was extreme. "Bernanos, the French religious novelist, said that his soul could not bear to be cut off from its kind, and that was why he did his work in cafés," Bellow noted enviously: "Cafés indeed! I would have kissed the floor of a café. There were no cafés in Chicago. There were greasy-spoon cafeterias, one-arm joints, taverns. I never yet heard of a writer who brought his manuscripts into a tavern."

Over the years, he collected a virtual anthology of disparaging observations that visitors had made about the city: Oscar Wilde found the Water Tower, one of the few buildings to survive the great Chicago fire of 1871, an offense against good taste; "he was amazed that people could so abuse Gothic art." Rudyard Kipling was appalled by the Palmer House, "a gilded and mirrored rabbit-warren crammed with people talking about money and spitting about everywhere." Edmund Wilson was oppressed by the canyons of La Salle Street: "In the morning, the winter sun does not seem to give any light: it leaves the streets dull. It is more like a forge which has just been started up, and is beginning to burn red in an atmosphere darkened by coal-fumes."

It would have been hard to deny the truth of what they saw: Culture in Chicago was a marginal enterprise. Dominated by the brute forces of industry, by stockyards and farm-machinery works and automobile assembly lines, it was the city, in Sandburg's famous line, of "big shoulders." Yet it was also true that Chicago possessed an indigenous literature. In the decades just before and after 1900, novels by Chicago writers crowded the shelves: Frank Norris's *The Pit* (1903), about wheat speculators on the floor of the Chicago Board of Trade; Willa Cather's *The Song of the Lark* (1915), about a young lady from Nebraska who came to study music in the city; Upton Sinclair's *The Jungle* (1906), a raw depiction of the harsh existence of a Lithuanian immigrant family in the South Side stockyards; Theodore Dreiser's Frank Cowperwood trilogy, based on the career of Charles T. Yerkes, the Chicago railroad financier; the works of Sherwood Anderson. The Chicago Renaissance was a fact. "Find a writer who is indubitably an American in every pulse-beat, snort and adenoid, an American who has something new and peculiarly American to say and who says it in an unmistakable American way," H. L. Mencken declared, "and nine times out of ten you will find that he has some sort of connection with the gargantuan and inordinate abattoir by Lake Michigan."

What nineteenth-century Paris had been to Lucien de Rubempré, the hero of Balzac's *Lost Illusions*, twentieth-century Chicago was to young men and women from Terre Haute or Valparaiso: "*the* place," wrote Bellow, "the incredible, vital, sinful, fascinating big city." If there were no cafés, there was still a tremendous concentration of vivid private experience—evidence, Bellow contended in his memoir, "that the life lived in great manufacturing, shipping, and banking centers, with their slaughter stink, their great slums, prisons, hospitals, and schools, was also a human life." Milton Friedman, who brought honor to the university by winning a Nobel Prize in economics in 1976 (the same year that

Bellow won in literature), has speculated that the city's reputation for nurturing literary and intellectual talent can be traced to the same geographical centrality that made it a great industrial power. Chicago, Friedman noted, was "a new, raw city bursting with energy, far less sophisticated than New York, but for that very reason far more tolerant of diversity, of heterodox ideas." New York looked east, to the Old World. Chicago looked west, to the frontier—in effect, inventing its own frontiers.

This energy was the catalyst of Bellow's art. In his hands, the city would become a character in its own right, the center of both his life and his work. The shelf of books he produced over the course of a career sustained for more than half a century was to make "Bellow's Chicago" as familiar a locale in literature as Joyce's Dublin. It wasn't an achievement that his circumstances preordained; the absence of encouragement, of community, of any plausible way to make a living would have provoked a person far sturdier than Bellow to despair. But he was armored against disappointment by a stubborn belief in his destiny—a belief he maintained in the absence of both proof and reason. The sociologist Edward Shils, for many years his colleague at the University of Chicago and one of the most incisive interpreters of his character, noted, "For Bellow, an artist was the same as being a saint, an 'unacknowledged legislator of mankind,' one who was consecrated to the highest function of which any human being is capable, namely, to be an artist." It was a belief that enabled him to prevail.

At the turn of the century, it was illegal for Jews in Russia to live outside the Pale of Settlement—the area from the Black Sea to the Baltic—without a permit. But Abraham Belo bribed the authorities, and for eight years after his marriage to Lescha Gordin, in 1905, the Belos resided in Saint Petersburg. At twenty-four, Abraham was an importer of Turkish figs and Egyptian onions—a "produce broker," as his son the novelist liked to put it. Once a rabbinical student in Vilnius, "the Jerusalem of Lithuania," Abraham was a romantic, self-dramatizing figure who read Pushkin and played the violin. For one family photograph, he posed with some business partners while wearing a heavy winter overcoat and a fur hat, gazing at the camera with large, soulful eyes—"a sharpie circa 1905," according to his son. In truth, Abraham Belo didn't have much of a head for business. His wife's parents were convinced that she had made a poor match. The Gordins weren't shtetl folk like the Belos; Lescha's father was a rabbi, and the family was well-off, even with twelve children. In the village of Dagda, near Riga, they ran the local post office and owned a small bakery. But it was Lescha's brothers who made what a later generation would describe as real money. One went off to South Africa and returned with his pockets full of diamonds. Another opened a prosperous restaurant—Gordin's—in Saint Petersburg. They were generous to their sister; the Belos kept servants and a governess for the children and had a dacha in the countryside.

But in 1912, the police cracked down on Abraham. He was convicted of illegal residence and nearly deported to Siberia. Lescha's brother managed to smuggle him out of the country with forged papers—"the best papers he could buy," Bellow used to joke. In November 1913, Abraham brought his family by boat to Canada, where his sister Rosa had settled in 1908 with her husband, Max Gameroff. Two of their other siblings, Hannah and Willie, were already there. Lescha and the three small children traveled under a passport separate from Abraham's:

> *Lescha Belo avec ses enfants*
> *Zelda, 7 ans*
> *Movscha, 5 ans*
> *Samuel, 2 ans*
> *Se rendent à l'étranger de St. Petersburg*
> *Signé*
> *Conte Adlersberg*

"I am not yet part of that family," Bellow liked to say when he showed visitors the old, yellowing permit to emigrate. It predated his own birth by two years.

In Canada, Lescha officially became Liza, a name she had adopted in Saint Petersburg. And Belo—the name derives from *byelo*, "white" in Russian—became, through a Halifax customs official's haphazard transliteration, Bellow.

Lachine, a working-class town on the outskirts of Montreal, was a melting pot; Ukrainians and Russians, Greeks and Italians, Hungarians and Poles were packed in side by side, drawn there by its thriving industries. The Dominion Bridge Company employed virtually the whole town. Bellow lovingly evoked these laborers, "their gold-capped teeth, the greenhorn outfits they had been sold at Halifax, the spectacular outfits they would need to begin a new life in the New World." There were only three hundred Jews in the whole town.

The Bellows moved into the cramped ground-floor apartment of a two-story brick house at 130 Eighth Avenue, just a block from Nôtre-Dame, the main commercial thoroughfare. Upstairs lived the Gameroffs with their four children, Lena, Sam, Louis, and Meyer. In the summer of 1915, two years after their arrival in Canada, Abraham and Liza had a fourth child of their own: Solomon Bellow, known as Shloime or Shloimke and later as Saul. He was the first—and last—of their children born in the New World—an accident of fate that was to shape his life. It gave him a huge advantage, enabling him to harness the raw cultural power of this world to his own developing genius, but it also made him different. "I never belonged to my own family," he lamented in later life. "I was always the one apart."

On the morning of his birth—or so Bellow later claimed—one of the Gameroff boys was dispatched to find the bibulous obstetrician. "Sam made the rounds of the saloons until finally he found him, slumped over the bar counter, dead drunk. He dragged the doctor outside, cranked up his Model T, and drove him home to my poor mother, who'd been in Canada two years and couldn't speak a word of English or French. There she was, in the midst of labor, being tended to by a dead-drunk French-Canadian who could barely stand up." (Ruth Gameroff, Sam's wife, told a less scandalous version of this episode: The doctor, named Dixon, was "not a drinking man," she maintained. But Bellow's made a better story.)

On Bellow's birth certificate, the date of birth is listed as July 10, but subsequent biographical and reference works list his birth

date as June 10, 1915. Lachine's city hall burned down in the
1920s, and Bellow's birth certificate was reconstructed from other
documents. It is also possible that Bellow's mother could have
been going by the Jewish calendar; immigrants were habitually
negligent about such details, and Jews were often unfamiliar with
the Christian calendar. (Lescha Gordin didn't even know her own
birthday; on her death certificate, her date of birth is listed as
"about 1883.") "My mother insisted that it *was* June, and I must
acknowledge her claim," Bellow explained to a Canadian scholar
who was doing research on his early life. Yet on his application for
a Guggenheim Foundation Fellowship, he himself entered the July
date. Thus did a writer renowned for his elusiveness, his resistance
to biography, throw into question even the first, most basic fact
about his life.

There was a Yiddish song that circulated in eastern Europe at the
time of the great emigration: *Geyt, yidelekh, in der vayter velt; in
kanade vet ir ferdinen gelt* ("Go, little Jews, into the wide world;
in Canada, you will earn a living"). And so it had been for the
Gameroffs of Dvinsk. Max Gameroff, Bellow's paternal uncle,
was industrious. He worked for the Canadian Pacific Railway,
sold used furniture, did carpentry—"anything he could to make a
dollar and put food on the table," said his daughter-in-law Ruth.
Eventually, he got into the scrap business.

Max was a religious man and would have been content to spend
his days in the synagogue. His wife, Rosa, was more ambitious.
She speculated in real estate, buying up vacant lots on the outskirts
of Lachine. The Gameroffs were never exactly well-to-do, but they
were comfortable. "Their apartment was roomier than ours, and
they had a bigger coal stove," Bellow recalled. "Uncle Max used to
sit on the porch up there and read his sons the matrimonial advertisements from the Yiddish newspapers: 'Young widow, well endowed, looking for a husband.' "

Abram—as the family called him—was a more improvident
sort. "My father was violent, strong, authoritarian," Bellow wrote
in a memoir of his early life. "He had what the French call a *soupe-
au-lait* temper, boiling over like a pot of milk, sinking quickly

when the flame was turned off." He failed at one enterprise after another. On his son's birth certificate, he was listed as a junk dealer; he was also in the dry-goods business for a time. He invested in a bakery with another greener, as the greenhorns were called, and delivered bread in the middle of the night. He sold cemetery lots. He squandered thousands of rubles that had been smuggled over from Russia on some land in Valleyfield, Quebec, and tried his hand at farming. "They were out in the bush somewhere," said Bellow. "There weren't enough Jews for a *minyan*"—the congregation of ten males required for public worship. "The wolves howled at night." For Liza Bellow, her mythologizing son insisted, Canada represented a "fall" in the world. Bellow liked to depict his mother as an educated woman who devoured the Russian classics, though she also wept over the sentimental novels of Jewish life on the Lower East Side that were serialized in the *Daily Forward*. That the daughter of an eminent rabbi, a person who had lived in the cosmopolitan city of Saint Petersburg and dined at the Café Chantant, should end up in this raucous industrial port was a profound humiliation. "We were exotic," Bellow recalled. "The trunks my parents traveled with were exotic—the taffeta petticoats, the ostrich plumes, the long gloves, the buttoned boots, and all the rest of those family treasures made me feel that I'd come from another world."

If Abram had trouble making ends meet, it was partly his own fault—or at least that was how the Gameroffs saw it. The Bellows "put on airs" and "acted as if the world owed them a living." Abram preferred to borrow money from his sister rather than have his children work in their uncle's junkyard. Poor as he was, he could afford to keep a piano in the house, and to pay a Mr. Poirier three dollars a month for his daughter Janey's lessons.* "*Jenke, shpil epes*," Abram commanded when guests came to the house. "Play something." Culture was more important than money. Liza's own father had spent his days immersed in books, depending on his wife to support the family. In the shtetl world from which they had come—at least for those who thought of them-

---

*Just as Shloimke became Solomon, Movscha became Maurice, and Zelda became Jane—another stage in the process of assimilation.

selves as intellectuals—to be unemployed was less a sign of indolence than of some higher calling. "He never did a day's work in his life," Bellow said, "except the very hardest." (No doubt it was this feature of Russian-Jewish life that made it natural for Bellow to sit at home with his mother-in-law as a young man just out of college and pursue his dream of writing while his wife went off to work: He was reproducing the pattern of his ancestral home.)

Bellow remembered his birthplace as a pastoral, idyllic village where the barges on the Lachine Canal were so slow that he used to hop off and get a haircut while the locks were filling up. His Iroquois nurse, a girl from the Caughnawaga reservation on the opposite bank of the Saint Lawrence, chewed his meat for him and put it in his mouth. Lachine was "paradise," Bellow rhapsodized in old age: "I can remember Mr. Goldwater's movie house burning on Nôtre-Dame Street; I can remember my Uncle William in his fruit store on the same street flipping open brown bags with a smart crack, or my late cousin, Sam Gameroff, setting the spark of his Model T Ford before cranking the engine. . . . This was the world as I first knew it."

Rather, as he remembered it. In reality, the Bellows' Canadian years were as gritty and filled with struggle as those of most immigrants. In 1918, when Bellow was three, the family moved to Montreal, hoping to make a fresh start. Their new home, on the second floor at 1092 Saint Dominique Street—in "a row of dowdy low brick buildings"—was in the heart of the Jewish ghetto, the city's poorest neighborhood. Rats foraged in the dirt-packed yards. Across the way lived the Polish tailor, Mr. Gottheil, who every year built in his backyard a *sukkah*, a crude wooden shack made of old doors and covered with cornstalks. On Succoth, the Festival of Tabernacles, the tailor slept in his homemade booth "to earn another *mitzvah*"—a good deed. Mr. Gottheil's wife lowered his dinner from the third floor in a bucket.

The Bellows had a boarder, a pitiful drunkard named Daitch who worked in a fruit store in Rachel Market. On Sundays, Daitch would finish off a bottle of cheap red wine and stagger home, loudly berating "that s.o.b., mein boss." Lachrymose and self-pitying, Daitch drank away the money he was supposed to be saving up to bring his family over from the Old Country. (In

Herzog, Daitch became Ravitch, "like a tragic actor of the Yiddish stage, with a straight drunken nose and a bowler pressing on the veins of his forehead.")

If Bellow mythologized his early childhood, he also saw it as a battleground of sibling rivalry. Even as a child, he claimed, he was different from his brothers, marked out for a more exalted destiny. A sickly child, afflicted with respiratory ailments, he was his mother's favorite; she treated him like an invalid. But in the patriarchal dynasty of family life, he ranked at the bottom. The two older brothers whose bed he shared, Moishe and Schmule—in their New World incarnations Maurice and Sam—were healthy, vigorous, dynamic; no one in the family was surprised when they went on to become big deal makers in Chicago real estate.

In family portraits, the resemblance between generations is almost eerily pronounced. "I was upright on my grandfather's bones and the bones of those before him on a temporary loan," Bellow wrote in *Dangling Man* of a yellowing photograph from the family album. The same wide, liquid eyes, sensuous mouth, and patrician nose recur in photographs of his grandfather in rabbinical garb, a long beard streaming down his tunic; in those of his father, the produce merchant; and in the remarkable family portrait taken when Bellow was five years old, which shows him in a tunic and bangs, standing beside his two older brothers and his sister, Jane, with his parents in the background.

It was in temperament that Bellow diverged from the family line. He was the designated "nostalgia-man," as he described himself, the keeper of warm memories; the brothers were aggressive and practical. Idealized versions of them showed up in Bellow's books: the wealthy, satisfied Amos in *Dangling Man;* the woman-hungry, larger-than-life Simon in *The Adventures of Augie March;* the Cadillac-driving, capable Will in *Herzog;* the rich, brutish entrepreneur Ulick in *Humboldt's Gift.* Likewise, the heroes of these books were all versions of Bellow—variously depicted as a dreamer, a bookish, head-in-the-clouds intellectual, a confused soul in need of guidance from his fraternal "reality instructors." "Our serious Old World parents certainly had produced a pair of American clowns—one a demonic millionaire clown, and the other one a higher-thought clown," he wrote of Ulick Citrine and his cerebral, mysticism-inclined brother, Charlie.

In life, the two older brothers loomed over the youngest one. While even in middle age Bellow had trouble patching together the rent, their empire-building feats—and, on occasion, their criminal deeds—were reported regularly in the Chicago newspapers: Sam's nursing homes, Maurice's hotels and landfill ventures. Their worldly success was a persistent rebuke to the impecuniousness of their intermittently broke and never wealthy brother. Together with Abram, who at last became a prosperous businessman in his forties, they formed a triumvirate from whose judgmental gaze the novelist struggled to free himself—without much success—throughout his days.

If Bellow didn't inherit the family's business gene, he surely inherited its narrative gifts. Abram, especially, was "a good raconteur," recalled Willie Greenberg, whose family lived next door to the Bellows in Montreal. Often out of work, Abram hung around the Greenbergs' kitchen, smoking foul Caporals and entertaining Willie's mother with tales of the Old Country. It was widely known in the neighborhood that you couldn't keep a secret around Abram—or his son. Shloimke was the world's biggest storyteller, Greenberg's mother would say, shaking her head: "*Oi, is dos kind a bluffer!*" "Is this kid a liar!" (Seven decades later, Bellow summed up his genetic inheritance with another Yiddish adage: *from meshuggeneh genz meshugenneh gribbenes.* "Crazy giblets from crazy geese.")

The stories Bellow listened to at the dinner table formed a counterpoint to the books he pored over in the basement classroom on Milton Street where he studied Hebrew, translating the Pentateuch for his teacher, Mr. Stein. "He was yellowish, tiny, snubnosed, and his moustache was short and black," in Bellow's description. "In his tiny carpet slippers he walked rapidly and had a distinct way of lifting his feet. His pants were cylindrical, neat and brief, and his chest was clad in a woolen long-sleeved undershirt manufactured by the Penman Company. Iridescent buttons fastened it."

By the time he was four, Bellow could recite whole pages of the book of Genesis, in both Yiddish and Hebrew. "*Vayehi,*" he would repeat after Reb Stein: " 'And it came to pass.' *Bereshith boro Elohim:* 'God created heaven and earth.' " The text seemed literal. "I couldn't readily distinguish between a parent and the heroic ancestors." Abraham was Abram, his own father, "the primal Patriarch"; Isaac and Jacob could have been his brothers. Shloime himself was named after Shloime Hamelech, King Solomon in the Bible. "The most ordinary Yiddish conversation is full of the grandest historical, mythological, and religious allusions," Bellow observed many years later in a review of *Adventures of Mottel, the Cantor's Son*, a collection of Sholem Aleichem stories: "The Creation, the fall, the flood, Egypt, Alexander, Titus, Napoleon, the Rothschilds, the Sages, and the Laws may get into the discussion of an egg, a clothes-line, or a pair of pants."

It was a rich culture. "In the streets of Montreal, on cold winter days, you could meet, in the 1920's, characters wrapped in great coats, their breath exhaled in vapor, walking out of the 19th century," wrote the biographer Leon Edel, himself a Canadian, "in Westmount out of Dickens or Thackeray, in Montreal East out of Balzac. And in between, figures Biblical, or characters created by say Israel Zangwill—a glimpse of the Galician or Rumanian, the Lithuanian, or the Russian."

It was out of this aggregate of languages and cultures that Bellow was to fashion his unique literary idiom. His parents spoke to each other in Russian and Yiddish; he and his three siblings spoke English and Yiddish at home; on the streets of Montreal they spoke French, and in public school they spoke English. "I didn't even know they were different languages," Bellow wrote. At home, in the fetid water closet on the landing, he hesitated to tear up the Yiddish newspaper that served for toilet paper "because of those sacred characters." His prose reflects the animated cadences of his origins—what the critic Irving Howe described as "the jabbing interchange of ironies, the intimate vulgarities, the blend of sardonic and sentimental" characteristic of Yiddish. "If your mother called you an angel, it meant you were a devil," Bellow said. "If she said that your hands were clean, it meant that your hands were filthy; if your nose was running, you were complimented on your well-wiped nose."

Liza Bellow was "minutely observant" of Jewish ritual; she lit the Shabbos candles on Friday night, kept kosher, and baked a loaf of challah once a week for each member of the family. Abram and the boys wore *tsitsit*, the fringed undergarments of the Orthodox.

Bellow later called the neighborhood "a medieval ghetto." Visiting Kraków in the 1970s, he was reminded instantly of Saint Dominique Street—"the synagogues, the ritual baths, the gloomy yards, the muddy streets, the yellow pages of prayer books."

The Bellows' world was a microcosm of the one they'd fled, but the New World also imposed its ways. On Saint Dominique Street, Orthodox Jews mingled with kilted Highlanders and nuns from the parish school. "We read British books and sang God Save the King and recited the Lord's Prayer and all the rest of it." Bellow attended the Strathearn School on Jeanne-Mance, just west of Saint Lawrence Main, an elegant boulevard of mansions with bay windows, gardens in the back, and wrought-iron staircases. Students marched to class accompanied by a drummer in a Boy Scout uniform.

One of Bellow's earliest memories was of Armistice Day 1918: "It was a tremendous noise, and I didn't really know what it was all about, but the kids were standing on the front steps and everybody was yelling, 'Peace!' " That same year he sat by the window with his brother Sam during the flu epidemic as the horse-drawn funeral corteges went by. Every house on the street had a wreath on the door, even their own. The landlord's young son died of tuberculosis; Bellow got a glimpse of the boy, white-faced in his coffin, surrounded by flowers.

Bellow nearly ended up in a coffin himself. In the winter of 1923, when he was eight years old, he developed peritonitis and pneumonia after an emergency appendectomy and was rushed to the Royal Victoria Hospital, a castlelike fortress atop a hill in Mont Royal Park. He stayed there for six months; the doctors feared tuberculosis. A Christian lady from the Bible Society visited his bedside in high-button boots, an ankle-length skirt, and a huge-brimmed hat laden with wax fruit and flowers. Bellow read aloud to her from the New Testament. "Jesus overwhelmed me," he wrote in an extraordinary letter to the biblical scholar Stephen Mitchell in 1991, his memory of that traumatic winter still vivid nearly seventy years later:

> I had heard about him, of course—marginal information, unfriendly (why should it have been friendly?). But I was moved when I read the Gospels. It wasn't a sentimental reaction. I

wasn't one for crying. I had to get through this crisis, I had made up my mind about that. But I was moved out of myself by Jesus, by "suffer little children to come unto me," by the lilies of the field. Jesus moved me beyond all bounds by his deeds and his words, gospels against the Jews, my people, Pharisees and Sadducees. In the ward, too, Jews were hated. My thought was (I tell it as it came to me then): How could it be my fault? I am in the hospital.

Alone in Ward H, the boy read *Uncle Tom's Cabin, Raggedy Ann, Black Beauty.* He also read the funny papers: Boob McNutt and Barney Google; the Katzenjammer Kids; Mutt and Jeff. He stood at the foot of the bed and studied his own chart: "I knew it was very unpromising." Children died in the night. A screen was pulled around a bed; nurses bustled about with flashlights. In the morning, that bed was empty. "My belly was haggled open—it was draining, I stank," he recalled in his letter to Mitchell: "I understood that I might die. I was pretty steady about this, I think. I didn't cry when my mother came and went."

Bellow later claimed that he discovered his unique sense of destiny in Ward H: "Anyone who's faced death at that age is likely to feel something of what I felt—that it was a triumph, that I had gotten away with it." Time and again, he returned to this episode in his fiction. "Each man has his batch of poems," says Moses Herzog, referring to the self-generated mythology of our lives that we order into stories. In that novel, Bellow rehearsed the months he spent in the hospital with eidetic clarity: "From the hospital roof hung icicles like the teeth of fish, clear drops burning at their tips"; in *Humboldt's Gift,* Charlie Citrine thinks back to the year he spent in a tuberculosis sanatorium when he was eight: "I became very thoughtful here and I think that my disease of the lungs passed over into an emotional disorder," he says. "Owing to the TB I connected breathing with joy, and owing to the gloom of the ward I connected joy with light, and owing to my irrationality I related light on the walls to light inside me."

But there was a darker legacy as well, one that Bellow only touched on in his fiction, so often a screen for painful memories rather than a revelation of their meaning. The void created by his long separation from his family remained with him all his life—

like "the topography of scars" on his abdomen, later described by a girlfriend. "It was his crucible, the primary life experience that defined him. It gave him an absolute standard of truth—raw truth—of values and priorities. It showed him there was no one to count on." To face, on his own, not only separation from his family, from the comforts of his familiar Jewish world, but the real prospect of death was a formative experience. It made Bellow at once clear-eyed about the precariousness of the human condition and imbued him with a longing to be parented. It also convinced him that he was alone in the world—that he would have to save himself.

When he got out of the hospital, his father gave him a violin: "It was a cheap little quarter-size," Bellow recalled, "and he carved the bridge himself."

Near the end of 1923, the Bellows were in dire financial straits. Abram had to beg Mr. Stein, the Hebrew teacher, to forgive the three dollars he was owed for Shloime's tuition. "Everything in Canada had failed for Pa," wrote Bellow in an early version of *Herzog:* "The bakery, the sacks, peddling, jobbing, buying produce in the country and selling it door to door, the dry goods store was a failure; matchmaking, insurance schemes, selling cemetery lots—all failed."

One day, Liza Bellow hurried next door to the Greenbergs' house in great agitation. In her arms was a pile of rugs. Would Mrs. Greenberg keep them for a while? "My mother started to shake," recalled her son Willie. "She was an accessory to the crime. But what else could she do?" Soon afterward, the police showed up and searched the Bellows' apartment.

Abram became a bootlegger. "Well, boys, what'll it be tonight?" he'd say, setting up shop at the kitchen table with a paste pot and forged labels. "White Horse or Haig and Haig?" Shloimke himself was enlisted to make the occasional delivery, stashing bottles in his violin case. Sometimes, he went along for the ride when Abram tore off in a dilapidated Ford, down back roads to the Saint Lawrence River, where smugglers waited in boats. Once, the hapless bootlegger was hijacked on the road to Verdun and robbed of his shipment at gunpoint by thugs who beat him up and left him in a ditch. He stumbled home bloody.

In desperation, Abram got in touch with his cousin Louis Dworkin in Chicago. Within a decade of his arrival from Riga, Louis had saved enough money to buy a bakery on the city's Northwest Side. He offered Abram a job. In the winter of 1924, Abram arrived in Chicago and went to work for Dworkin's Imperial Baking Company, on the corner of Marshfield and Augusta. Louis's sister and her husband put him up in their small bungalow on Hamlin Avenue, where he slept in the kitchen on a folding cot.

It was six months before he could afford to send for his family. On a boiling afternoon in July 1924, Liza and her four children were smuggled across the border by one of Abram's bootlegger associates, and they boarded a train for Chicago. In the baggage car was their steamer trunk with the curved lid, a relic from Saint Petersburg. Inside it were the Bellows' Old World possessions: the bulbous samovar; embroidered table linen; black taffeta petticoats and elbow-length gloves and ostrich plumes; family photographs of bearded great-uncles and relatives in military uniforms; envelopes with locks of children's hair.

They owed their landlord in Montreal ten dollars.

2

There is in America an incredible city named Chicago:
a rain-coloured city of topless marble towers that stand among waste
plots knee-high with tawny grasses beside a lake that has grey waves
like the sea. It has a shopping and office district that for miles round
is a darkness laid on the eyes, so high are the buildings, so cluttered up
are the narrow streets with a gauntly striding elevated railway, and a
stockyards district that for miles round is a stench in the nostrils.

—REBECCA WEST,
The Selected Poems of Carl Sandburg

The Chicago Jew is practically a newcomer in the realm of Art.

—H. L. MEITES,
A History of the Jews of Chicago

COUSIN LOUIS MET LIZA and the children at Union Station in a big Dodge touring car driven by his new bride, Rose—"the first woman I had ever seen behind the wheel of a car," Bellow recalled in "The Chicago Book," an unpublished memoir about growing up in the city.

It was the Fourth of July—an auspicious day for the arrival of a novelist who was to make the process of becoming American one of his major themes. As they drove up Milwaukee Avenue in Cousin Louis's fancy car, the new arrivals were deafened by the sound of explosive caps (known as sonofaguns) that had been laid on trolley tracks. An acrid smell of firecrackers hung in the air.

Their destination was the bungalow of Louis's sister, Flora, on Hamlin, where Abram had been living while he looked for another place. "Cousin Flora was like her brother," wrote Bellow: "large, handsomely expressive, much moved by our coming. The table was set for us, the beds were ready. She and her round, bald, smiling husband Baron with his blinking tic—these large people gave us tacit assurances that we had come to a place where human qualities were what they were elsewhere."

A few weeks later, the family moved into an apartment that Rose Dworkin had found for them at 2629 West Augusta Boulevard, the top floor of a redbrick two-flat between Rockwell and Washtenaw, on the city's Northwest Side. It consisted of five small rooms: three bedrooms, a parlor, and a kitchen dominated by a huge iron-and-nickel coal range. The boys shared a bedroom in the back. There was also a roomer, as they were called in those days: Ezra Davis, a punch-press operator who had known the family in Montreal. "The place always seemed full," said Herbert Passin, a neighborhood boy who didn't help matters by sleeping over at the Bellows' on a cot in the kitchen.

The landlord, a Polish laborer named Lusczowiak, occupied the apartment below. Next door lived the August boys, Charlie and Morris, with their mother and an imperious old lady by the name of Rebecca Reich, who had moved in after Mr. August vanished from the scene. A widow from Odessa who rolled her own cigarettes and made the children address her as "Madame," Rebecca ran the August household "with an iron hand," according to her grandson Charles. She was to become, with little alteration, the conniving, autocratic Grandma Lausch, "one of those Machiavellis of small street and neighborhood," who presides with bullying energy over the feeble, distracted Mrs. March and her high-spirited boys in *The Adventures of Augie March.*

The city was a shock at first. "Everything was louder, rawer, cruder, noisier, hotter, bigger than anything I had seen in Canada," Bellow wrote in "The Chicago Book." There was something crude and elemental about it—"animal-flavored," to use Bellow's epithet: "You knew what its big industry was when the wind blew from the Yards. Along Cermak Road and other South Side streets red cattle cars waited on the sidings, cows and sheep staring through the slats in brute innocence, death-bound. The odor of blood, manure, bacon-making, soap- and fertilizer-manufacture became a weight lying on your heart."

The Bellows' apartment was east of Humboldt Park, in a modest neighborhood of wooden bungalows and brick six-flats with marble stoops. Originally settled by Germans, Irish, and Scandinavians who flocked to the city in great numbers during the 1860s and 1870s, it had gradually absorbed the influx of Ashkenazim from central and eastern Europe who fled to America in the wake of the repressive "May Laws" promulgated by Czar Alexander III: Polish Jews, Hungarians, Estonians, Yiddish-speaking émigrés from the old Russian empire, Latvians, and Lithuanians. By 1924, when the Bellows arrived, there were close to three hundred thousand Jews in Chicago.

The neighborhood inhabitants were mostly Polish and Jewish, intermingled with the older immigrant groups. The Old Neighborhood, as people who grew up there called it, was "quiet, almost countrylike," remembered Fred Glotzer, whose family had come over from Russia. "We were born into gaslight and horse and wagons." Horse-drawn wagons delivered bread and, in the summer, sweating blocks of ice. The gas street lamps flared brightly on the wide boulevards after the lamplighter made his rounds at dusk. On hot summer nights, whole families spread out their blankets on the grassy knolls of Humboldt Park, the green oasis at the neighborhood center. A balalaika orchestra performed beneath the leafy trees. For a quarter, you could rent a boat at the pagoda-roofed boathouse and go out on the lagoon.

The Jews were a highly visible presence in Humboldt Park. Up and down North Avenue were lodges, congregations, relief associations, and *landsmannshaften*—clubs for people from various communities in eastern Europe. On high holidays, the Austro-Galician Congregation at California and Hirsch—"a beautiful synagogue, with stained-glass windows and a balcony for women," as one of its members described it—was filled to capacity. *The Chicago Israelite* enjoyed wide circulation in the neighborhood.

In Chicago, the Bellows maintained their old ways. Abram attended shul on Saturday, and he made sure that his sons had a traditional Jewish education. Bellow studied the Talmud in a basement on Rockwell Street and attended Sunday school at the Jewish People's Institute. He was bar mitzvahed at the Spaulding Avenue synagogue.

"A new world!" marveled one of Bellow's childhood friends: "Chicago was like a magical circus." Division Street was lined with ornate new movie palaces: the Crystal and the Harmony, the Biltmore and the Crown. The Crystal's chandelier "startled and amazed the neighborhood." Bellow saw Ramon Novarro as Ben-

Hur; he saw Lon Chaney throw knives with his feet in *The Unknown*. "One of us would go into the Biltmore Theatre on Division Street or the Vision Theatre on Washtenaw and pay and go open the side fire door and the others would pour in," explained Bellow's friend Dave Peltz.

"*Bliss was it in that dawn to be alive, / But to be young was very heaven!*": Bellow often invoked Wordsworth's lines when he was remembering those days. "On summer nights," he wrote in "The Chicago Book,"

> you sat on the back porch, your neighbors on their back porches all down the line, the graceless cottonwoods reaching toward you and you listened to the accordions and player pianos and harmonicas below, across the way, down the street, playing mazurkas. You spoke in low voices; your father smoked in a corner, your mother in her housedress folded her housewifely arms after the driving day. One of the children was sent to the corner to bring home a pitcherful of soda pop (the druggist called it a phosphate). Over every drugstore in Chicago there swung a large mortar and pestle outlined in electric bulbs and every summer the sandflies with green light transparent wings covered the windows.

In his work, Bellow recorded the physical details of Chicago with a preternaturally observant eye. The rubbery urban foliage, the rows of burgundy-brick three-flats, the tiny yards and cracked sidewalks: All this fell under his keen scrutiny. It was the emotional dynamics that tended to elude him—or that he chose to gloss over with a sentimental patina. The cozily domestic father and mother evoked in his memoir bore little resemblance to the stormy, histrionic parents who loomed over his childhood. At his best—most notably in *Herzog*—Bellow afforded a vivid glimpse of the high-strung, quick-tempered Abram, contemptuous of his bookish son and capable, when his temper flared, of raising a hand against his boys. In Bellow's fictional but accurate portrait of him, Abram, "one of the small-boned Herzogs," was "fine-made, round-headed, keen, nervous, handsome." He was also tyrannical and vain—traits exacerbated by the tensions of adapting to the New

World. For immigrant Jews, life in America, especially in the early years of their transplantation, was difficult, perplexing, even shameful. Abram was a proud man who—in his own estimation—had lost status. In Russia, he had considered himself a gentleman; in America, he was a laborer. Like his wife, he felt he'd come down in the world.

In 1926, the Bellows moved to the ground floor of a three-flat at 2226 Cortez, a quiet, tree-lined street just east of Oakley Boulevard. The three boys still shared a room. But there was a sunporch, a yard with a garden, and sturdy furniture, which they had bought from the departing tenants. In the kitchen was a telephone with a coin box that a man came and emptied once a month, counting out the nickels on the dining-room table.

Abram worked hard to support his family. Hired as a shipping clerk at the Imperial Baking Company, he quickly became a "man of all work" on the night shift; he fermented dough for rye bread, stoked ovens, loaded bread boxes onto wagons. "At night, while the bakers worked," Bellow wrote in his memoir, "he napped on the flour sacks while rats walked about on the rafters." In the morning, he came home, hung his flour-caked overalls behind the bathroom door, and went to bed.

With four children to support, there was no money to spare. Abram earned twenty-five dollars a week. Whom to pay first? The landlord or the man who supplied their coal? Abram busied himself with phantom calculations, obsessed over the money he could have made *if only* . . . "I always associated my father with figures, with long curving swaying columns of numbers jotted with Russian flourishes, like angry poems." By the time Abram had finished his calculations, translating from rubles to dollars, adjusting for inflation since 1912 and writing off the expense involved in raising a family, it was clear that, had it not been for a run of bad luck, he would have been a millionaire.

Liza was embarrassed by her husband's job. "She felt he was too knowledgeable to work in a factory," according to Bellow's sister, Jane. "At the table he would tell us, this really *is* the land of opportunity; you're free to do whatever you like, within the law, and you're free either to run yourself into the ground or improve your chances."

Bellow's mother was an equally devout believer in the gospel of self-improvement. That her husband had failed only intensified her aspirations for her youngest son—a common dynamic in immigrant households. She wanted Sol, as he was called in America, to be a rabbi, like *her* father, or, failing that, a concert violinist. She was always nagging him to practice—a typical scenario on the Northwest Side of Chicago circa 1927. "That was the era of the Jascha/Mischa/Toscha craze," said Fred Glotzer, referring to the distinguished musical trio of Jascha Heifetz, Mischa Mishakoff (concertmaster of the Chicago Symphony), and violinist Toscha Seidel, "when all these Russian fiddlers came over to this country and knocked everyone cold." Every Jewish child was a potential prodigy. Once a week, Bellow got on the trolley with his violin and made the long trip down to the Fine Arts Building on South Michigan Avenue, where he was subjected to the harsh tutelage of Grisha Borushek, a stout, gloomy refugee from Odessa who trained his pupils "by whipping them on the buttocks with his bow when he got sore at them." At the age of twelve, Solomon Bellow performed Bohm's "Moto Perpetuo" in a student recital at Kimball Hall.

When Léonide Massine's Ballet Russe de Monte Carlo or the San Carlo Opera came to perform at the Auditorium Theatre, Bellow worked as an usher to get in free. On Saturday afternoons, the New York Philharmonic's live radio broadcast boomed through the house. Even the Bellows' roomer, Ezra Davis, aspired to a career in music. "He sang for us in the kitchen," Bellow recalled: "He rose on his toes, his octagonal glasses sweated, and when he brought his hands together I wondered whether his calluses might not be causing pain. Talentless and fervent, he made his listeners smile. He had been an amateur boxer at the YMCA, his nose was flattened, and my private theory then was that a punch in the nose had ruined him as a dramatic tenor."

One promising local musician was the harpsichordist Rosalyn Tureck, who made her debut at Lyon and Healy Hall when she was nine. Bellow had a terrific crush on the proud and haughty Tureck girl; decades later, when she was a world-famous interpreter of Bach, he liked to remember her as the perky, flirtatious girl "who came up from gym sweating and fanning herself with her skirt so that the people in the class were inordinately excited."

The whole neighborhood seemed dedicated to the pursuit of culture. The Tolstoi Vegetarian Restaurant on Division displayed a photograph of its namesake in the window. By the front door of Walgreen's were barrels of used books and Modern Library editions—a twenty-five-cent bin, a nineteen-cent bin, and a twelve-cent bin. Finer, the tailor, subscribed to *The New Republic*. No one was more bookish than Bellow. He read "tremendously," said Ezra Davis, who would come in from work to find "Solly" hunched over *War and Peace* or *The Possessed* at the kitchen table. Bellow read even when he was supposed to be practicing the violin, spreading a book open on his music stand. He read the *Encyclopedia Americana*, Romain Rolland's *Jean Christophe*, the short stories of O. Henry and Maupassant, *The Decameron*, and L. Frank Baum's *The Wizard of Oz*. He read back issues of *Ballyhoo* (the *Mad* magazine of its day), Haldeman-Julius Blue Books that sold for a nickel, and a copy of the *Iliad* that he found on a closet shelf at his cousin Flora's.

One of Bellow's formative books was *The Decline of the West*, also a favorite of the local Polish barber and the insurance man. He was troubled by Spengler's theory that Jews were Magians, descendants of a disreputable human type that was hopelessly at odds with the Faustian spirit responsible for the great civilizations of the West. "When I read this I was deeply wounded. I envied the Faustians, and I cursed my luck because I had prepared myself to be part of a civilization, one of whose prominent interpreters told me that I was by heredity disqualified." (Herzog, too, recalls sitting at the kitchen table in Chicago on a freezing winter's night and poring over Spengler.)

Bellow's main source for books was the Budlong branch of the Chicago Public Library, in a storefront on North Avenue. (It was funded by the Budlong's Pickles family.) By the time he was nine, he liked to boast, he had gotten through all the books in the children's section and graduated to the adult section, where he began with Gogol's *Dead Souls*. Decades later, in a talk at the Chicago Public Library, he recalled the Budlong's atmosphere:

The North Avenue Branch, like a church or a school, offered a privileged environment. The books were bound in brown buckram. The pages were stained with soup, or cocoa or tomato ketchup or by tears or by nosebleeds, and they were also fiercely annotated by borrowers. Readers denounced writers or praised them, argued with other readers around the margins—self-made prophets, poets in their own right, patriots, subversives, philosophers, neighborhood historians arguing the Civil War or the Russian Revolution. One could learn a lot about the mental life of a democracy from these annotations. Strange forms of originality sometimes appeared, special kinds of intelligence, passion and madness.

This intense devotion to the life of the mind was enhanced by conditions special to Jewish immigration: the linguistic possibilities that an idiomatic English enriched by Yiddish, Hebrew, and Russian yielded; the adaptation of a scholarly rabbinical tradition to an essentially secular society; the confluence of Judaism, with its ancient devotion to the word, and a civilization that was still struggling to define itself. "A new life was forming in American society which belonged to nobody," Bellow recalled many years later. If the immigrant Jews weren't yet at home in this developing culture, neither was anyone else. "Everybody in America was a visitor, a tourist, a stranger, a foreigner. The language was there as everyone's resource." It was an ideal laboratory for a novelist.

Bellow's literary inclinations were largely invisible to his classmates. "He seldom spoke out," said Dave Schwab, an editor of the high-school newspaper. "I doubt whether anyone could have detected anything special about him." Bellow was the paper's sports editor but had few bylines; nor did his name appear among the Scholar Medallists cited each semester for superior grades. Still, many of his closest friends insist—perhaps retrospective prophecies—that Bellow was marked for distinction. "I sensed a genius in him," said his Tuley classmate (and girlfriend) Eleanor Fox, noting wryly that Bellow was glad to corroborate her intuition: "He thought he was a great writer when he was writing for the high-school newspaper."

"Saul read me his very first things, and I sat up," testified Fred Glotzer. "This was a person who could really write, who could handle the language, who had ideas, who could get beneath the surface of a character." Others were less impressed. "Saul wants to be a writer? What's he going to write about?" joked one of his classmates. "He hasn't got a thought in his head."

In 1930, when he graduated from Sabin Junior High School, his terse entry in the graduation issue of *The Sabinite* read: "Wit and humour abound in him." It made no prediction of a special destiny.

It is late afternoon, a spring day, and the Tuley Debating Club is meeting on the second floor of the old building, since destroyed by fire. The black street doors are open, the skate wheels are buzzing on the hollow concrete and the handballs strike the walls with a taut puncturing sound. Upstairs, I hold the gavel. Isaac rises and asks for the floor. He has a round face, somewhat pale, glasses, and his light hair is combed back with earnestness and maturity. He is wearing short pants. His subject is *The World as Will and Idea*, and he speaks with perfect authority. He is very serious. He has read Schopenhauer.

The boy with the gavel was Bellow, and Isaac was Isaac Rosenfeld, his classmate. They were the closest of friends and would live in each other's shadow for the next two decades. "Not only did he study Hume and Kant but he discovered dada and surrealism as his voice was changing," Bellow recalled in a touching but highly romanticized memoir of his friend. (There's no evidence that Rosenfeld was actually conversant with the categorical imperative.) They were comrades, but they were also rivals. Bellow struggled for years with a novel about Rosenfeld, in the end publishing—under the title "Zetland: By a Character Witness"—a fragment of his unfinished work.

Tuley was an intensely literary place. In addition to the Debating Club, where Bellow first spotted Rosenfeld, there was a Bibliophile Club and a Scribblers' Club, as well as the off-campus Russian Literary Society, which met at a hot-dog stand on Division; the school newspaper, *The Tuley Review*, gave considerable space in its pages to literary essays and reviews. Named after Judge Murray F. Tuley, a distinguished Chicago judge, the school enjoyed a certain local fame; when it opened in 1890, the *Humboldt Community News* praised the school as "one of the best and most modern in the city." The Latin motto over the door, *urbs in horto* (city in a garden), must have seemed fanciful if not incongruous to the sons and daughters of carpenters and cobblers, egg candlers and butchers who could barely speak English. There was an air of intellectual endeavor, even of refinement about the school. At lunch hour, students danced in the gym, accompanied by a pianist. "Tuley people enjoyed special status," a graduate of the rival Carl Schurz High School recalled enviously. "They were known around town as the intellectual crowd."*

In that crowd, it wasn't Sol Bellow who stood out. If Tuley had a literary star, it was "Ike" Rosenfeld, three years his junior. "Isaac was the more talented one," said Isadore Bernick—a verdict confirmed by his fellow Tuleyites, who invariably described Rosenfeld as "more dynamic" and "more alive" than Bellow. An eloquent expositor, Rosenfeld once stood up and gave a lucid account of conception to an embarrassed biology class. "Isaac was the outstanding kid," said his classmate William Karush. "He led Saul by the nose."

Even by Humboldt Park standards, Rosenfeld's family was obsessed with literature. His two maiden aunts read Russian novels and Yiddish poetry. He was a member of the Scribblers' Club, contributed to *The Tuley Review,* and played what Irving Letchinger, the faculty supervisor of the school band, character-ized as "a nice flute."

Pale and stout, with watery blue eyes and a yellowish complex-ion, Rosenfeld was noticeably fragile. "He seldom enjoyed good health," Bellow recalled. "He was haunted by an obscure sense of physical difficulty or deficiency, a biological torment, a disagree-ment with his own flesh." In the blazing heat of summer, he sat in his room with the shades drawn and a lamp burning. On his desk was an old office typewriter and a bust of Beethoven.

Bellow, meanwhile, read *How to Get Fit and Stay That Way,* a bodybuilding manual by the legendary football coach Walter Chauncey Camp. After his near-fatal bout of pneumonia, he had vowed to make himself strong, and he carried coal with the scuttle held at arm's length to strengthen his muscles. He played tennis

---

*Bellow's Tuleycentric view was manifest in the legend he scrawled on the inside cover of his copy of Thomas Carlyle's *Essay on Burns:* "Sol Bellow, Chicago, Ill., U.S.A., North American Continent, Western Hemisphere, The Globe, Space, Infinity (Tuley)."

and basketball and was a promising member of the Tuley track team. MANY TRACKSTERS ANSWER FINAL CALL, read an item in *The Tuley Review* on November 4, 1931, PROSPECTS GREAT. Among those singled out as promising "new material" were Ted Cieslakiewicz, Casimir Wrzecionkowski, Ray Frelk, and Sol Bellow.

Bellow was startlingly handsome in high school; *gorgeous* and *beautiful* were adjectives that women applied to him more than half a century later, remembering the boy they'd known. "He had a sensuous mouth, a gap between his teeth, and wide eyes that were like a doe's. He bounced on his toes as he walked." Rosenfeld, by contrast, had "a round, intellectual Jewish face, froggy lips, big goggles," according to Bellow's condescending description. But the two boys liked each other. They played recorder duets and read the same books—*The Return of the Native, The Brothers Karamazov*, Huxley's *Point Counter Point*. They dreamed of becoming great American writers. "On the public lagoon, rowing, we read Keats to each other while the weeds bound the oars," wrote Bellow. "They had a sense of mutual destiny," said their friend Edith Tarcov, whose husband, Oscar, had been the third member of the Tuley triumvirate. "They were going to accomplish great things."

Another frequent byline in *The Tuley Review* was that of Sydney Justin Harris. Harris was a regular columnist, warming up for the "Strictly Personal" column he was to publish in the *Chicago Daily News* for more than thirty years. Bellow considered Harris a kindred spirit. "I would walk Sydney home across Humboldt Park," he recalled:

> Then he would walk me back home. I would walk him back and so on until about two o'clock in the morning when we would stop and examine our pockets to see if there were enough pennies between us to buy a hot dog in a joint called MGM—it stood for Many Good Mouthfuls—where for 5 cents you got a hot dog plus potato chips, plus lettuce and tomatoes, plus all the pickle, relish, and mustard you could eat.

After school, the two fledgling authors often sat at the Harrises' dining-room table, composing poems and stories that they submitted to *Argosy* magazine.

The teachers at Tuley were just as book-obsessed as their students. They were big on memorization. Bellow could recite long passages of *Hamlet* and *Macbeth*, whole poems by Keats and Shelley. "You got a meager education, perhaps, but it was a sound one," he recalled. "You knew something of American history. And by the time you got out of high school, no one had to tell you who Socrates was." In "Starting Out in Chicago," he paid eloquent homage to his teachers, "old gents who boomed out Milton's *Lycidas* to kids from coal-heated flats." One such gent was Mr. Olson, the chemistry teacher and faculty sponsor of *The Tuley Review*, a baldish man with snow-white eyebrows who held court in the faculty toilet in the basement: "He'd sit on the can with his pants down around his knees and recite Shakespeare." Olson found Bellow's verse derivative; when Bellow used the phrase "dun gray pall," Olson pointed out that it echoed *Macbeth*'s "and pall thee in the dunnest smoke of hell."

In an early draft of *Herzog,* Bellow reminisced movingly about his bookish Humboldt Park cronies: "Weak boys, too undeveloped for whorehouses or gambling; sheltered by our fathers, we didn't have to worry about the Depression. Our only freedom was in thought." It was the parents of these high-school metaphysicians who had to worry. The impact of the stock-market crash had been virtually instantaneous. Despite President Hoover's bland reassurances—six months after Black Friday, he declared, "the Depression is over"—unemployment offices in the Loop were jammed. Within three years, nearly a third of the American workforce went on the dole.

Even Bellow's rich friend Sam Freifeld, a member of the Tuley literary crowd, fell on hard times. In the twenties, Sam's father, a wheelchair-bound lawyer famous in the neighborhood for his natty wardrobe and his nose for real estate, had amassed a considerable amount of property around Humboldt Park, including the forty-unit apartment house on Division Street where the Freifelds lived. Freifeld was hit hard by the crash and had to move his base of operations into the back of his pool hall on Division.

While everyone else was going down, the Bellows were going up. Prompted by Liza, Abram had left the Imperial Baking

Company in 1928 and gone into business on his own, peddling wood chips for bakers' ovens. Before long, the demand was so great that he was bringing in whole freight cars of the stuff from Michigan and Wisconsin. The Bellows could afford vacations. In the summers, Liza and the children stayed on a farm in Benton Harbor, Michigan; Abram joined them on the weekends.

In 1930, when Bellow was fifteen, the family moved a few houses down on their block to 2200 Cortez; and, a year later, to a spacious new apartment at 3340 LeMoyne, on the west side of Humboldt Park, where the Jews who had made it lived.

The Bellows were well-off, but they were hardly rich. Everyone in the family had to hustle. Maurice was making good money as a bagman, delivering bribes to a state congressman. Jane had a secretarial job in the Loop. Sam had taken premed courses at Crane Junior College and aspired to attend Northwestern Medical School, but there was a Jewish quota and no money for tuition anyway; instead, he became the family chauffeur, driving Abram to his business appointments. After school, Sol delivered arrangements for a florist on North Avenue. It was hard work, wrestling the big wreaths onto streetcars. The pay was fifty cents per afternoon.

On Saturdays, Bellow worked in the mail room of a shoe store on Chicago Avenue and in Goldblatt's department store. "I learned in the window-shade department how to tighten the spring of a shade by winding it with a table fork." He caddied for "puttering real estateniks" at the Sunset Ridge Country Club golf course, riding the Milwaukee Line out to Winnetka and hitchhiking the rest of the way, in his pocket a Modern Library volume of Flaubert or Swinburne or Wilde "with a streaking torchbearing Prometheus on the cover."

In summer, Bellow and his gang fled the parched Northwest Side on red streetcars with rattan seats. The Division Street line ended at Wells Street, seven blocks short of the lake, where the Gold Coast mansions sat. "There were twilight excursions, also by streetcar, to the municipal pier where the city offered free band concerts and fireworks were set off over the silken waters." Though he could be contemptuous of Chicago's crass materialism, Bellow was a lyric celebrant of its physical beauty. If he invested the city's drab streets with the magic of childhood, it was because those streets had given him the freedom to discover who he was.

What he left out of "The Chicago Book"—and perhaps the reason why he never published it—was the motif of unspoken trauma that was so much a part of those years. Bellow's freedom was double-edged; it was also an escape from the domestic storms of home life. In *Herzog*, his pivotal book, he vividly—and truthfully—evoked his own father's fits of brutal rage; the near-violent confrontation between Papa Herzog, then an old man, and his impetuous, troubled son Moses is an accurate rendering of the battles that raged between Bellow and his father. They were both under stress. The strangeness of America, the ripples of anti-Semitism, the viciousness of Irish and Polish immigrant gangs produced an atmosphere of menace for the sons, too. "We were always outsiders," said Dave Peltz. "You never felt American. In the Bible, when Abraham buys land to bury his wife Sarah, he's described as a 'resident alien,' and that's what we were. We felt like immigrant aliens."

Their one refuge was politics. The Bellows, like so many of their neighbors and friends, were familiar with the major historical events of that epoch; Bellow's grandfather had lived through the Revolution of 1917, and Jews were prominent in the Bolshevik party. In America, socialism found its way to Chicago—scene of the Haymarket riot and site of the national headquarters of the Industrial Workers of the World (the Wobblies) and the American Communist Party. "It was inevitable, given our experience of life under Tsarism, that our family and close friends would be politically radical, if not always socialist," noted Albert Glotzer, himself a speaker at the open-air forum on the corner of Division and Washtenaw and later one of Trotsky's bodyguards. "You could go into the main Jewish streets and see people who described themselves as the intelligentsia," Bellow recalled. "They dressed differently. They wore pince-nez. They smoked with curious gestures; they had a different vocabulary. They talked about capitalism and socialism. They talked about evolution; they talked about Trotsky."

Bellow was less interested in overthrowing the government than in the candidacy of Franklin Delano Roosevelt, nominated at the Democratic convention in Chicago in the summer of 1932. "I remember going to see a school friend, Joey Sugarman, on Division Street," he wrote sixty-four years later in the *Chicago Tribune*, on the occasion of the 1996 convention:

> From the convention hall the radio was broadcasting the traditional roll call of the states. Joey's father, a big, bearded Orthodox Jew, a shochet, or ritual slaughterer, was calling out the names of the states in alphabetical order, singing them out like a cantor, just ahead of the radio: "Maine, Maryland, Massachusetts." Very red in the face, very proud of his citizenship.

It was a key American moment.

The main organization for radical Tuleyites was the Young People's Socialist League (YPSL). Bellow wasn't much of a joiner, but he hung around their basement headquarters on California Avenue for the same reason that Augie March's brother Simon did: not just to attend "meetings, bull sessions, and forums, socials and rent parties," but to meet girls, "the big babes in leather jackets, low heels, berets, and chambray workshirts."

One coveted YPSL girl was Yetta Barshevsky, later the wife of Max Shachtman, a leader of the anti-Stalinist left. In high school, Bellow had a very public crush on her. On the steps of the Humboldt Park boathouse, she lectured him "on Leninism, on collectivization, on democratic centralism, on the sins of Stalin and his inferiority to Trotsky," while Bellow admired her "Jewish beauty."

Unfortunately, Barshevsky had a boyfriend, Nate Gould, whose powerful oratory electrified the graduating class of 1932. At the graduation ceremony, Barshevsky and Gould tossed away their faculty-approved commencement speeches and gave fiery lectures with quotations from Big Bill Haywood and Eugene Debs. "On the platform, this slight, high-voiced young woman was fearless and formidable," Bellow recalled. "Her manner was militant, urgent. From her you heard such words as 'penury' and 'mitigate.' " In a fit of vindictive jealousy after he learned about her relationship with Gould, he wrote a letter to Barshevsky predicting that she would be "fat and ugly" by the time she was thirty-five.

Bellow's actual girlfriend, Eleanor Fox, wrote the fashion column in *The Tuley Review*. Fox was a great beauty; Bellow portrayed her with reverence in *Humboldt's Gift* as Naomi Lutz,

Charlie Citrine's high-school sweetheart ("Your molecules were my molecules"), and in the story "Something to Remember Me By" as Stephanie, the narrator's girlfriend, who used to neck with him in Humboldt Park on cold winter nights. But, as was generally the case with Bellow's retrospective impressions of his youth, he romanticized their relationship, casting it as all sweetness and light. In reality, he was erratic in his constancy, greedy for attention, and fiercely jealous. On one memorable occasion, when he noticed that Fox was wearing the fraternity pin of a lanky basketball player who was popular with Tuley girls, Bellow grabbed it and tore it off, ripping her blouse. "I was afraid of the guy," she recalled. (This scene, too, found its way into *Humboldt's Gift*. "You were a violent kid," Citrine's high-school girlfriend Naomi Lutz recalls. "You almost choked me to death because I went to a dance with some basketball player.")

Her inconstant heart tormented him. For Christmas, Bellow gave her a leather-bound copy of *The Arabian Nights* with the churlish inscription:

> You will benefit more by reading the contents of the book than by reading this: Any poem I might plaster here to advertise my powers would not compare with the tales of Scheherazade. If it were the Harvard commemorative I would write an ode. The Ode would probably be boresom. This is all too trivial. Am I expected to compose masterpieces every time I give you something? No holiday spirit—nothing but reciprocity.

Bellow's relationship with Fox wasn't exclusive on his side either. Late at night, he would climb the porch to Zita Cogan's second-floor apartment on Kedzie Avenue. And Fred Glotzer, who had access to a "Polish basement"—a cheap first-floor rental apartment outfitted with Salvation Army furniture—used to lend Bellow the key for make-out sessions with various girlfriends.* It was a gesture that Glotzer must have regretted when he had to wait outside on freezing winter nights for Bellow to pull up the shade, indicating the coast was clear.

---

* "We didn't have sex in high school," testified Dave Peltz. "That all happened later. We talked about it, but we didn't do it."

"My first knowledge of the hidden work of uneventful days goes back to February 1933," Bellow wrote nearly sixty years later in "Something to Remember Me By." An elderly man recalls that, as a Chicago adolescent, he allowed himself to be seduced and humiliated by a prostitute on the day of his mother's death. "What I didn't tell you," the narrator confides to his son, "was that I knew she was dying and didn't allow myself to think about it." The hidden work was his mother's insidious illness; the "uneventful days" in fact concealed a loss that Bellow himself was to grapple with his entire adult life.

For two years, Liza Bellow had suffered from breast cancer. During his last year at Tuley, Bellow came home from his after-school jobs and sat by her bedside every afternoon. Bottles of pills stood in a clutter on the table beside her bed. She was heavily sedated. Bellow held her thin hand and listened to her rasping breath. His brothers and his sister were off at work. Solomon, her favorite son, the one she called *moi kresavitz*—my beauty—kept a solitary vigil.

On the last day of February 1933, at ten o'clock on a bitter Chicago night, Liza Bellow died at home. On her death certificate, the coroner estimated her age as "about 50."

"My life was never the same after my mother died," Bellow said, many years later. Even in his eighties, he groped for words to convey the vast and devastating import of this loss. "I was grieving," he stressed, as if these simple words could somehow express the immensity of the event. In his work, he rehearsed the death scene over and over, most wrenchingly in *Herzog*, in which young Moses thinks back to the "frightful January" when his mother lay dying, her eyes sunken, her beautiful long hair cropped: "He came into her room when she was dying, holding his school books, and began to say something to her. But she lifted up her hands and showed him her fingernails. They were blue. . . . Under the nails they seemed to him to be turning already into the blue loam of graves. She had begun to change into earth!"

It is significant that in the novel Moses is sixteen—as if Bellow, who was seventeen when his mother died, could draw only so close to the actual, unbearable fact. In his fiction—and sometimes in interviews—he altered his age by a year or two, suggesting that he had been fifteen when she died. In *Seize the Day*, Tommy Wilhelm and his father spar over the exact year of his mother's death, bracketing the real year by bickering about whether it was 1932 or 1934. Sixty years after the fact, in "Something to Remember Me By," the narrator finds himself unable to name the disease from which his mother died; the "hidden work" is hidden in every sense.

As he so often did in writing about the most painful episodes in his life, Bellow sought to mitigate loss through sentimentality. His work is studded with tender paeans to Mama: "When I lost a tooth she would throw it behind the stove and ask the little mouse to bring a better one," Charlie Citrine tells his daughter, remembering how his immigrant mother told fortunes with cards and sang "trembly Russian songs." When Charlie took a spill, she pressed the lump on his head with the blade of a knife to make the swelling go down. Moses Herzog recalls his mother pulling him on his sled when she was almost too sick to walk. But he also rose to the heights of eloquence. "Failed my mother!" cries Louie in "Something to Remember Me By," confessing to his young son the shabby sexual adventure that he engaged in as she lay on her deathbed: "That may mean, will mean, little or nothing to you, my only child, reading this document." To Bellow, it meant everything.

What made this death so hard for him? It was Liza who had kept the family together. "She was the backbone," attested Bellow's sister. But there was something more to his lifelong mourning: His mother's death made him—in the words of Herzog—"mother-bound." It was a bondage doomed to play itself out in five marriages and a string of failed relationships, as Bellow struggled to free himself from the intensity of his need by denying its primal hold over him. Of course, being bound had its pleasures, in the masochistic sense. Beating his breast over his failure to grieve was a way of remaining connected to his mother and to an Edenic childhood past in which his claim to a unique destiny in the world could thrive unchallenged.

"There was something lonely about Sol after his mother died," said Eleanor Fox—an impression confirmed by Fred Glotzer, who saw a lot of Bellow in those days and thought of him as "kind of a lonely guy who needed approval from his friends." Some nights, Bellow slept over at Sydney Harris's, on a couch in the living room. "I was turned loose—freed, in a sense: free, but also stunned," he recalled a lifetime later. "I didn't know anything."

3

It appears to be only when the gifted Jew escapes from the cultural environment created and fed by the particular genius of his own people, only when he falls into the alien lines of gentile inquiry and becomes a naturalized, though hyphenate, citizen in the gentile republic of learning, that he comes into his own as a creative leader in the world's intellectual enterprise.

—THORSTEIN VEBLEN,
Essays in Our Changing Order

BELLOW GRADUATED from Tuley in January 1933, just a month before his mother's death, and enrolled as a freshman at Crane Junior College on Oakley Boulevard. The tuition was five dollars a semester. There was no campus; across the street was the Grennan Cake Company, where damaged cakes sold for a nickel. "The students were children of immigrants from all parts, coming up from Hell's Kitchen, Little Sicily, the Black Belt, the mass of Polonia, the Jewish streets of Humboldt Park, put through the coarse sifters of curriculum, and also bringing wisdom of their own"—an academic melting pot. The Depression hit Crane hard. By the spring of 1933 it could no longer meet its payroll and was forced to close.

That fall, Bellow enrolled at the University of Chicago. It was a shocking transition. Founded in 1889 with a grant of $600,000 from John D. Rockefeller, the university had its origins in the strong Baptist community that established itself on the South Side during the middle of the nineteenth century; it was, however, an ecumenical institution and had received generous support from prosperous Chicago Jewish families such as the Rosenwalds and the Mandels (after whom the university's Mandel Hall is named). Even in its early days, when the Ivy League universities still maintained strict quotas, Jews in significant numbers entered the

University of Chicago—and not just the children of wealthy Jews. "Candidates for higher degrees, schoolteachers, casual listeners from the city, 'irregulars' of all kinds, immigrants and native born, Jew and gentile, rich and poor, orthodox believers and atheists, all walked the campus together," wrote Hugh Dalziel Duncan in *Culture and Democracy.*

The chief architect of this intellectual efflorescence was Robert M. Hutchins, the university's president, a determined proponent of general education. "An Aristotelian and a Thomist," as Bellow described him, "he saw to it that the huge fortunes amassed in slaughterhouses and steel mills were spent teaching generations of students the main achievements of Western culture." The centerpiece of Hutchins's curriculum was the Great Books—Chicago shorthand for the idea that the classics of Western civilization should form the basis of a liberal-arts education. (A joke around Hyde Park in those days: Chicago was a place where Jewish professors taught Roman Catholicism to Protestant students.) This stress on serious intellectual activity had produced a university unencumbered, as the Chicago sociologist Edward Shils put it, by "the inhibiting consequences of doctrines, schools of thought, and authoritative leaders." Independence was prized above all. "I think I was lucky to have grown up in the Middle West, where such influences are less strong," Bellow said many years later: "If I'd grown up in the East and attended an Ivy League university, I might have been damaged more badly. Puritan and Protestant America carries less weight in Illinois than in Massachusetts."

The ivy-covered buildings with turrets, Gothic arches, and leaded glass, designed to emulate the great citadels of learning, had a stirring effect on the sons and daughters of Jewish immigrants, who composed nearly a third of the entering class of 1933. For Bellow, eager to escape the tensions of home, the University of Chicago was to become a lifelong haven. From his itinerant-scholar days as a graduate student and struggling author in the 1930s and 1940s to the decades of his literary maturity and later fame, he made it his intellectual base, eventually serving as a tenured professor on the Committee on Social Thought.

The Tuley Trotskyites formed a significant part of the immigrant influx to Hyde Park, along with just about the entire mem-

bership of the Young Communist League. At Chicago, as everywhere else in those days, radical politics was bound up in the
power struggle between Trotsky and Stalin. The Stalinists dominated the American Student Union, while the Trotskyites formed
the Spartacus Youth League and met in a dingy rented hall on
North Wells to debate the issues of the day: Was Russia a genuine
workers' state? Was Trotsky justified in his criticism of the
Comintern? "Politics was everywhere," Isaac Rosenfeld wrote:

> One ate and drank it; and sleep gave no escape, for it furnished
> terror to our dreams: Hitler, Mussolini, the Moscow Trials, the
> Spanish Civil War, the plaguey bill of Stalinism, the stopgaps of
> NRA, WPA, and the New Deal, and the approach of inevitable
> war. We lived in the shadow of annihilation, drawing on the
> pattern of Guernica and Ethiopia to imagine what bombings
> would be like. Liaisons, marriages, and divorces, let alone
> friendships, were sometimes contracted on no other basis than
> these issues, and dominated, in a way that might seem incom-
> prehensible to the present generation, by events of the world
> order.

Bellow and Rosenfeld were both caught up in this passion for
politics; around campus, they were known as Zinoviev and
Kamenev, after the two disaffected Bolsheviks who had briefly
shared power with Stalin. They belonged to the Socialist Club and
helped edit its journal, *Soapbox*, which carried on the masthead a
quotation from William Randolph Hearst: "Red radicalism has
planted a soapbox in every educational institution in America."
One of Rosenfeld's liveliest pieces, "Liberty, Oh Liberty," was a
caustic satire in the form of a harangue against "Bolshevism, Communism, Anarchism, Atheism, Socialism, Stakhanovism," and
every other ism. In the last scene, a replica of the Statue of Liberty
turns her back on the florid speaker, bends over, and lifts her skirt.
   Politics was a perennial source of conflict between father and
son. Like so many immigrants who'd made it in America, Abram
was a New World patriot. What had Lenin done for the Jews?
Here, at least, they were free. "Don't you forget what happened to
Lyova," he cautioned, reminding Bellow of his Montreal Hebrew
teacher's son, who had gone back to Russia to join the revolution

in 1917 and vanished without a trace. "I haven't heard from my sisters in years," his father added. "I don't want any part of your Russia and your Lenin."

Bellow had a sophisticated grasp of the issues, but he was no ideologue. He read the classic Marxist texts as literature; for him, *The Communist Manifesto* was less a call to revolution than a classic. When he showed up at the Spartacus Youth League's socials, it was the social part that appealed to him. "He was our best performer," said Isadore Bernick. "He always had a new Polish joke." At one YPSL function, Bellow and Rosenfeld performed an improvised dialogue memorably titled, "A Dissertation on Beet Borscht." Their most celebrated routine was a Yiddish version of T. S. Eliot's "The Love Song of J. Alfred Prufrock"—a tour de force that friends could still recite verbatim after half a century.*

The "Chicago boys" (Bellow, Rosenfeld, Oscar Tarcov) were sophisticated about politics, but literature was their passion, Irving Kristol noted in "Memoirs of a Trotskyist," comparing them to the zealous ideologues he knew at City College in New York. At Chicago, where Kristol spent a few years as an "unofficial" student, "you didn't *have* to be political to lead a vigorous intellectual life and be a member of an authentic intellectual community."

Bellow and Rosenfeld were "infinitely ambitious," according to David Bazelon, who came to know them both. They were also highly competitive with each other. "I was peculiarly touchy, vulnerable, hard to deal with—at times, as I can see now, insufferable, and not always a constant friend," Bellow admitted. But Rosenfeld, too, could be treacherous. "His power to attract people might have made more difference to him than it did," Bellow complained—perhaps an oblique way of saying that Rosenfeld should have paid more attention to him.

In their emotional fragility, as in their reverence for books and music, Bellow and Rosenfeld were more alike than either of them acknowledged. They were both the sons of stern fathers and of mothers who had died when they were young (Rosenfeld never

---

*Among the more memorable lines: "*In tsimer vu di wayber zenen, / Redt men fun Karl Marx un Lenin*" ("In the room where the women go / They talk of Marx and Lenin") and "*Ikh ver alt, ikh ver alt, / un mayn pupik vert mir kalt*" ("I grow old, I grow old, / and my belly button grows cold").

knew his mother, who died when he was two); they were both talented and painfully unsure of themselves; and they both yearned to escape the narrow confines of Chicago, the Northwest Side, the conventional business lives imagined for them by their Jewish immigrant parents. Beyond their childish intoxication with "the big ideas" was a longing to transcend through art the ordinary circumstances of their lives—"a craving for expansion," in Bellow's evocative phrase.

In the spring of 1934, a year after the death of his first wife, Bellow's father married a neighborhood widow, Fannie Gebler, "one of those old-fashioned ladies with a terrific Galitzianer accent," as Bellow described her. Not long after their wedding, Abram and his new bride moved to a new apartment at 3434 Evergreen, a few blocks away. Bellow moved with them.

The Bellows were by this time a typical Jewish family of means. Abram had gotten out of the wood business and had bought the Carroll Coal Company on the West Side. It proved a shrewd move. All over the city, apartment buildings were converting from wood-burning stoves to coal-heated boilers. Meanwhile, Jane had married a dentist and moved to the North Side; Maurice and Sam had joined the family business. They weren't nostalgic for the old ways. As part of their Americanization—and to get some distance from their father—the brothers had added an *s* to their surname, modeling themselves after Charlie Bellows, a well-known Chicago criminal lawyer who had once been the Bellows' neighbor. (They pronounced it *Bellus*.)

A flashy dresser, large and stout, Maurice was an intimidating presence. He peeled off bills from a roll in his pocket and always seemed to have a girl on his arm. He knew the police lieutenants and captains, the gamblers and bookies, the men who ran the city. He was contemptuous of Sol's bookish proclivities. But there was an element of deliberate provocation in Maurice's philistinism; when he asked his literary younger brother who "Prowst" was, he was taunting him. In his own family, Bellow wasn't taken seriously.

There were still lean times, but—at least in the Bellows' case—not enough to cause real hardship. Bellow looked back on the

Depression as an idyllic period, the beginning of what he called his "mental life." The tenderhearted protagonists of his novels are invariably rhapsodic about this period in their lives, a time when they could idle away their days in the Crerar Library on Randolph Street, knowing there were no jobs. But the vanished Eden he conjured up in his books omitted what it felt like to be without prospects. On the one hand, his generation wasn't "tied to the wheel of a career," as Bellow's contemporary William Barrett observed in his memoir of that era, *The Truants;* on the other, they faced a potentially cheerless future as unemployable and irrelevant to society.

For Bellow, this condition of economic limbo was exacerbated by a growing estrangement from his family. He saw himself as the rejected one, the one who had been left behind, like the little boy in Ward H. While his brothers concentrated on making money, Bellow appointed himself the one to feel. (Moses Herzog names this powerful devotion to the family, or his idealized version of it, "potato love.") His father was stingy with affection, he complained to Oscar Tarcov, recounting a major confrontation at the coalyard in which the old man attacked his choice of friends, his work, and his politics before storming off, Bellow's shouted imprecations echoing after him in the warehouse gloom.* "I'm like my poor father, first testy then penitent," he confessed to a friend.

He could never be argued out of the conviction that being born last put him at a disadvantage—his older brothers and sister had gotten more of everything. "You have an enviable way of referring to your troubles," he once wrote to Robert Penn Warren. "I wish I had it. But as the youngest child I learned to make the most of mine." This satirical aside about his lowly place in the birth order concealed a truth: Bellow's self-dramatizing impulse, so crucial to his development as a writer, grew out of a need to make himself heard. To his siblings, he would always be the baby of the family. Sam thought of him as "a perverse child growing into manhood

---

*It's significant that this letter was virtually the only one Bellow declined to allow me to quote from, on the grounds that it was "boring." Revealing letters about the most personal matters, including his relationships with his own children, troubled him less than a letter that vividly described his unremitting battles with his father sixty-five years ago.

with no prospects or bourgeois ambitions, utterly unequipped to meet his world," Bellow wrote Tarcov. "He is wrong, am not unequipped but unwilling." *

In the early summer of 1934, when he had just turned nineteen, Bellow and his friend Herb Passin hit the road—a Depression rite of passage. It was the summer of the Dust Bowl; farms were going out of business, thousands of families were on the road. Passin, who had bummed around with Nelson Algren, already a veteran chronicler of the vagrant life, carried a knapsack; Bellow showed up with a heavy suitcase, as if he were going off to college. In their subsequent recollections of this episode, each sought to portray the other as a mama's boy, amply supplied with hidden funds in case of trouble. Passin claimed that Bellow had squirreled away some extra cash in case he wanted to bail out; Bellow suspected that Passin "had more."

They clambered aboard a freight train in the railroad yards of South Chicago and headed east. At South Bend, they passed the Studebaker plant and were cheered by a crowd of strikers on the roof. "We shouted and joked with them, rolling at about five miles an hour in summer warmth through the fresh June weeds, the Nickel Plate locomotive pulling us toward a horizon of white clouds," Bellow wrote with characteristic high spirits and selective memory. Bumming it was no lark. To gauge a train's speed while running along beside the tracks, grab a ladder, and swing aboard was a perilous enterprise—especially with a suitcase in your hand. The hoboes jammed in the boxcars were ragged and foul-smelling; the yards were patrolled by armed guards who fired their pistols into the sky as a scare tactic. "It was very dangerous, very rough," Passin recalled. In Detroit, the cops picked them up and held them overnight on a fabricated charge of stealing auto parts. Released the next morning, the boys made for Canada but were turned back at the border because they had no papers.

---

* "My resistance—and Augie's—to what I was 'born to be': a son of my family like my brothers," he wrote on the back cover of one of the spiral notebooks in which he composed *The Adventures of Augie March:* "When I appear to be doing nothing I am doing that, resisting."

After they got to Buffalo, Passin continued on to New York City, and Bellow went to Canada, slipping across the border at Niagara Falls. When he appeared at the back door of his aunt's house in Montreal, he looked so scruffy that she didn't recognize him. He stayed a few weeks, visiting his various Gameroff cousins, then wired Maurice, who sent him a bus ticket home.

It wasn't just an act of charity. Maurice had married a rich woman and, with money borrowed from her, had gone into business on his own, leasing a coalyard from the Bunge Coal Company. He needed a hand and recruited Bellow as a "weighmaster," to weigh the trucks before and after they'd been loaded up. He was also expected to help out with the bookkeeping, hustle up business, and make deposits at the bank. It was hard work, but the job exposed him to a side of the city's life that he'd never known before and provided material for his portrait of Augie March, who works in his brother Simon's coalyard and comes in contact with an assortment of hard-boiled characters rarely encountered in the scholarly precincts of Hyde Park. "I remember blasting away at [Marx's] *Value, Price, and Profit* while the police raided a brothel across the street—for non-payment of protection, probably—throwing beds, bedding, and chairs through the shattered windows," Bellow recalled in a late memoir, "Marx at My Table."

His sinecure didn't last long. Maurice lost patience with his brother's habit of reading on the job, and they parted after a bitter confrontation. That fall, Bellow moved out of his father's apartment on Evergreen and rented a room in a boardinghouse on Fifty-seventh and Kenwood, near the university, for three dollars a week—a lot of money then. It was sparsely furnished, with a shelf for his books, a single bed, prints from the Art Institute on the wall: a Velázquez Job, a Daumier Don Quixote. His brothers and his father doled out supplemental funds when he came up short. As an old man, Bellow liked to recite how much—or rather, how little—things used to cost: Breakfast at Stineway's Drugstore was fifteen cents; the blue-plate special—fried liver and onions, shoe-string potatoes, and cole slaw, with a bowl of Kosto pudding for dessert—was thirty-five cents. Being poor was cheap, Isaac Rosenfeld quipped. It was said of the dilapidated boardinghouse known as Coudich Castle that if the cockroaches were ever exterminated the whole building would collapse.

Living in Hyde Park on his own, Bellow steeled himself to act on the imperative that he sensed "in his very bones"—a belief, threatened by doubt but unshakable all the same, that he was destined for a significant life as a writer. "I felt that I was born to be a performing and interpretive creature, that I was meant to take part in a peculiar, exalted game." His friends, too, aspired to participate in this game; the literary flame burned bright among children of Chicago Jewish immigrants. But for Bellow, the game was in earnest: His innate talent and his fierce ambition conspired in his favor. He was disciplined; he worked at his craft. From adolescence on, he had acquired the habit of filling notebooks with stories, poems, essays. He was "always with the briefcase," in the words of his friend Zita Cogan, and he read aloud to any willing audience the stories he carried with him. But he was oddly diffident about his work. "At least half the members of the Socialist Club thought of themselves as future great writers and were fairly vociferous about it," said George Reedy, a member of the *Soapbox* editorial board (and in later life President Lyndon Johnson's press secretary). "Saul wasn't vociferous." To declare himself a writer was to invite judgment, and for that he wasn't ready. "I knew he was in training," said Dave Peltz, "but he could have been hurt if anyone knew what he was up to."

Bellow offered contradictory accounts of his time at the University of Chicago. When he was in an expansive mood, he extolled it as a citadel of higher learning, a haven for eager immigrants with a bent for literature; at other times, he belittled the education he'd gotten there. The professors were "caesura-hunters" devoted to pedantic exegesis. They had eyes only for "the glorious classical past." In this version of his undergraduate days, the University of Chicago was simply another obstacle to Sol Bellow's pursuit of his vocation. But he himself was partly to blame: By his own account, he was an erratic student. "If I signed up for Economics 201, I was sure to spend all my time reading Ibsen and Shaw," he wrote with jaunty insouciance in a foreword to Allan Bloom's *The Closing of the American Mind*. This dilatory attitude showed up in his freshman grades—all Bs and Cs.

He did manage to make an impression on a professor named Walter Blair, with whom he studied Shakespeare. Blair, a legend in his day—his classroom enactment of the rustics' scene in *A Mid-*

summer Night's Dream was famous—remembered Bellow as an outstanding student who didn't seem "a damn bit intimidated." (Yet Blair only gave him an S, for "satisfactory.") Norman Maclean, later acclaimed as the author of *A River Runs Through It*, had Bellow in his humanities survey course on English literature. Maclean liked to claim that the future Nobel laureate had given no indication of literary greatness—indeed, had been a "dud."

Bellow was discouraged by his teachers' failure to recognize his promise. "I suppose I wanted attention." Their neglect compounded his own fears about the futility of the enterprise on which he had embarked. It was hard at times not to wonder—if only to himself—whether his family might be right: Where did he get the idea that he could become a writer? But he might have stayed on at the university and graduated despite its indifference to his genius if fate hadn't intervened. In the winter of 1935, the driver of one of the Bellows' company trucks was killed in a loading accident just two days after their insurance lapsed; Sam had neglected to renew the policy. It would take years to pay off the lawsuit. Abram could no longer afford tuition—a hundred dollars per quarter. He pulled Sol out of school and put him to work on the scales in the Carroll Coal Company yard.

In the summer of 1935, Bellow scraped together enough money to enroll in the University of Wisconsin's summer session in Madison. He worked hard, carrying three English courses, and got two As and a B. That fall, he entered Northwestern University in Evanston, on the North Shore of Chicago. Its tuition was the same as the University of Chicago's, but Bellow saved money by living at home.

Founded by Methodists in 1851, Northwestern sat on a pastoral tract of land overlooking Lake Michigan and was devoted, in the words of one of its founders, to educating men and women "full of enterprise and hope and Christian zeal"—Christian in the literal sense. By the time Bellow arrived, Jewish students, many of them from poor immigrant neighborhoods in Chicago, made up roughly 5 percent of the class.

Evanston in those days was a lovely community of large Victorian homes on elm-lined streets; a thicket of steeples rose above the leafy trees. It was also deeply conservative. The Woman's Christian Temperance Union had its headquarters there. Negroes (as they were called) were banned at restaurants and on the campus beach. To Bellow, accustomed to the radical bohemianism of Hyde Park, Evanston was "a wax museum of bourgeois horrors."

Northwestern, nonetheless, had its own radical core. "There were plenty of renegades, intellectuals, and literati around," according to one member of the class of '37. "T. S. Eliot would have called them 'freethinking Jews.' " Bellow's contribution to the December 1936 issue of *Soapbox*, under the pseudonym John Paul—a misspelling of Jean Paul, the pen name of the nineteenth-century German satirical novelist Johann Paul Friedrich Richter—provided a lively polemical account of the Evanston zeitgeist. Entitled "This Is the Way We Go to School" and attributed to "a leading Northwestern student," the essay managed to attack Elizabeth Dilling, a prominent local resident and author of *Red Network*, an anticommunist diatribe; Northwestern president Walter Dill Scott and the university's board of trustees; the frat boys ("the inmates of the Greek houses, the cheerers, the swaggerlads"); and the town itself ("Evanston, the home of Northwestern, is not only intellectually flatchested, but holds it a virtue").

"This Is the Way We Go to School" was a spirited blend of H. L. Mencken's lip-curling prose and the fierce rhetoric of Jonathan Swift. Northwestern was an "educational Elysium created by culture-conscious tractor, wheat, newspaper, and power moguls," fumed the author: "The libraries, the laboratories, the cushy houses, the comforts produce only young men for bond houses, insurance companies, Dad's business, storm troops; and perhaps a few for the breadlines."

Going into Dad's business: What could be more contemptible than that?

For many years after he graduated, Bellow was too insecure to let on that he had gone to Northwestern. It was a good school, but it could hardly compete with the University of Chicago. As his own fame grew, he began to look more favorably upon the place and seemed almost defiant about his affiliation. It was less prestigious, he conceded, but his teachers there had shown greater appreciation of his talents.

Yet Northwestern was in many ways more elitist than Chicago. In the 1930s, the teaching of literature in universities was a career for gentlemen. English departments were dominated by New Critics and Southern Agrarians for whom all literature was English. "University English departments were still under the vigilant protection of something called the Anglo-Saxon tradition," wrote Diana Trilling in an account of the early career tribulations of her husband, Lionel. The professors' very names suggest the temper of English studies in those years: at Chicago, Walter Blair, Napier Wilt, and R. S. Crane; at Northwestern, Moody Prior, who taught Elizabethan drama, and Edward Hungerford, a Harvard Ph.D. and Shakespeare man. William Frank Bryan, chairman of the department, was a specialist in Old and Middle English. "An elegant, courtly Southern gentleman," as one of his colleagues described him, Bryan was an Episcopalian, a member of the University Club, and a dedicated golfer. There were no Jews on the English faculty.

In those days, a Jewish boy with large intellectual ambitions had a better shot at getting ahead in anthropology, which was relatively free from "genteel prejudice." Among its founders, Franz Boas, Emile Durkheim, Lucien Lévy-Bruhl, and Marcel Mauss were Jewish. Melville J. Herskovits at Northwestern was a spellbinding orator who filled the auditorium in Wieboldt Hall when he lectured on African art. Herskovits was a Catholic convert; otherwise he would have been one of the two Jewish professors on the Northwestern faculty. (The other was William Jaffe, a historian of economic thought.) Bellow resolved to study with Herskovits and elected a dual major in English and anthropology.

Herskovits was then at work on *The Myth of the Negro Past*, which was to achieve classic status in African-American studies—a field that didn't exist in 1933. Herskovits's thesis was that African culture had imported its own highly evolved traditions to the New World, where it survived in the culture of American Negroes. Bellow distilled his work into a limerick:

> *There was a guy named Melville J.*
> *Who does oodles of work every day*
> *To prove that Brer Rabbit*
> *And blues on the Sabbath*
> *Came from Old Dahomey.*

To a contemporary reader, Bellow's ditty sounds racist; and in light of his later widely publicized controversies over race—the portrait of the menacing black mugger in *Mr. Sammler's Planet;* remarks to reporters and inflammatory public statements about the cultural backwardness of blacks—perhaps it was. But it's also true—and Bellow often used this as a defense—that racial attitudes weren't closely scrutinized then. No one complained about the casually insulting references to Jews in the works of Ernest Hemingway and F. Scott Fitzgerald. From a later perspective, Bellow, himself a Jew struggling with real instances of social exclusion, had no business making fun of another (albeit former) Jew who took black culture seriously. From the vantage of that time, however, one could just as easily argue that he was indulging in good-natured satire.

In fact, Bellow admired Herskovits and worked hard at anthropology. He prefigured the example of his character Ijah Brodsky, the dilettante lawyer in the late story "Cousins," who spends his days poring over *The Jesup North Pacific Expedition,* Franz Boas's classic account of fieldwork among the Siberian Chukchee and Koryak tribes. "Anthropology students were the farthest out in the 1930s," Bellow recalled, looking back on his Northwestern days:

> They seemed to be preparing to criticize society from its roots. Radicalism was implicit in anthropology, especially sexual radicalism—the study of the sexual life of savages was gratifying to radicals. It indicated that human life was much broader than the present. And it gave young Jews a greater sense of freedom from the surrounding restrictions. They were seeking immunity from Anglo-Saxon custom: being accepted or rejected by a society of Christian gentlemen.

He also had a less solemn explanation for why he was drawn to anthropology: He was a savage himself, he joked; why not study his own kind? Anthropology, the study of foreign cultures, provided expression for Bellow's own sense of exclusion from American society—a condition that haunted him long after he had become an exemplary (and deeply assimilated) spokesman for the opportunities it offered. Like many Jewish intellectuals of his generation, Bellow never rid himself of the suspicion that he wasn't quite part of America.

Like Boas before him, he was fascinated by the Eskimos. For his senior thesis, he wrote on a tribe that reportedly had chosen to starve rather than to eat available food that was taboo. "How much, I asked myself, did people yield to culture or to their lifelong preoccupations, and at what point would the animal need to survive break through the restraints of custom and belief?" What had impressed Boas and Bellow was the Eskimos' willingness to obey a destructive prohibition out of allegiance to their god. It was a powerful lesson for an aspiring writer who considered himself the apprentice of a higher calling—the life of art—that seemed to have no place in philistine America. Bellow would rather starve than consign himself to a life toiling for the Carroll Coal Company.

For all his complaints, Bellow flourished at Northwestern. His grades improved, and his writing found an audience. In the spring of 1936, *The Daily Northwestern* ran a short piece under his by-line called "Pets of the North Shore," which offered some self-consciously whimsical speculation about the dogs owned by suburban women: "Who knows where they come from? It is as great a mystery, at least, as the Cretan alphabet. Nobody professes to know and nobody dares to guess. What is so strange about them is that they have no resemblance to the ordinary dog except a structural one. You wonder what has become of the primitive dignity that you associate with dogs." Women and their dogs were in conflict, Bellow noted; the dogs resisted their owners' leashes—from which he somehow managed to conclude that he was living in "an age of decadence."

He was also submitting short stories to the paper. Julian Behr-stock, the literary editor, rejected one of them with the laconic explanation that it was "not good enough." He had better luck when he entered the "Campus in Print" story contest; the judges, a panel of three English professors, awarded Bellow third prize, and the story was published in the paper's February 19, 1936, issue.*

---

*Forty years later, when Bellow won the Nobel Prize, the winners of first and second place, Constance Davis, a staff writer for the Elyria, Ohio, *Chronicle-Telegram*, and Mary Zimmer, an advertising copywriter from Dearborn, Michigan, had only the dimmest recollections of the third-place winner: "Neither of the women remembers being impressed with Mr. Bellow at the time," wrote a reporter from *The New York Times*.

The story, "The Hell It Can't," was a retort to Sinclair Lewis's novel *It Can't Happen Here*, which had appeared the year before. Its atmosphere is heavily Kafkaesque: A man is awakened in the middle of the night and led away by a faceless gang of nameless thugs, who march him off to a room and administer a brutal whipping. The Europe of those years is sharply drawn: Streets are filled with soldiers, and in the shop windows are posters that read DEFEND YOURSELF and FIGHT, DON'T BE AN ENEMY AT HOME. The saloons are full of men waiting to be called up. "It won't be long," the protagonist muses. "Everybody was in the swim."

"The Hell It Can't" has a static plot. Apart from the beating, not much happens; even the central event is never explained. The politics are straight out of Trotsky: capitalism as an anonymous, inhuman force that threatens individual freedom. The one thing we know about the protagonist, one Henry Howland, is that he's a thinking man; even as he's hustled away by the mob, he reflects on the inexorability of his fate: "He was silent and accepted the pain. 'Flick!' This is for men marching, for ships and bullets. 'Flick!' This is for taps at sundown, for patriot souls. Aaaah. This is for men speaking solemnly, for guns speaking, for men overseas marching. The whip howled over his head. The men beat him steadily, grimly, taking turns."

Like Joseph, the "dangling man" of Bellow's first published novel, Howland resists the social regimentation enforced by war and is made to suffer for it; and like so many of Bellow's later heroes, he suffers persecution with a bitter stoicism. But if the story's themes are consistent with later Bellow, its style reveals little. Nowhere in its bland and ponderous tone is there even a portent of the exuberant vitality that was to become a signature of Bellow's prose.

The author of "The Hell It Can't" had modified his name. Solomon Bellow was now Saul Bellow. "I wanted to break with everybody, even my own family, so I chose the other name, which was a legitimate name, and belonged to me," he explained, noting that he had been known as both Saul and Sol from the beginning. "I simply decided that Saul would be better than Solomon." As for his family, "they couldn't have cared less," Bellow maintained. "I didn't deny anything, didn't deny they were my family, didn't turn my back on them, didn't assume some fancy name like Courtney or Smithson. I didn't hide anything." But he didn't want a name that was too Jewish, either. If he was going to be an American writer, he would have to sound like one.

The official metamorphosis occurred a few months later. On his college transcript, Solon (a clerk's misspelled variant of Solomon) was crossed out and replaced with Saul. Below it was a registrar's scrawled note: "*Spelling changed 6.22.36*," almost two weeks after Bellow's twenty-first birthday.

During his first months at Northwestern, Bellow lived at home and made the long trip out to the North Shore on the El, working his way through the twelve-volume N. H. Dole translation of Tolstoy. In the spring of 1936, he capitulated to the "bourgeois horrors" of Evanston and rented a room in a boardinghouse on Gaffield Place, a quiet tree-lined street near the campus.

The decision to transfer had been a good one. Northwestern fostered Bellow's talent; the University of Chicago—or so Bellow claimed—had ignored him. Edward Hungerford of the English department realized when Bellow turned up in his creative-writing course that he had an exceptional student on his hands; John T. Frederick, a novelist and professor in the same department, invited the young writer to Cooley's Cupboard, a restaurant in downtown Evanston, and read his manuscripts over dinner.

Nor did Bellow's presence go unremarked by Northwestern coeds. "He was the new boy on campus," remembered Helen Jaffe, a student at the Medill School of Journalism. "He was shy and introverted but very handsome." His clothes—hand-me-downs from stocky Maurice—were too big for him, but at least they were high quality; Maurice shopped at Marshall Field. "He wore a navy blue suit with a white shirt when everyone else was wearing dirty corduroys and sweaters, and he was very distinguished," Jaffe recalled. "I chased him very, very assiduously and almost caught him, but not quite."

The competition was Anita Goshkin, who had transferred from the University of Illinois to the University of Chicago in 1935, the year that Bellow left. They had met that summer, on a street in

Hyde Park. The scene in *Herzog* in which Moses thinks back to his first wife, Daisy, faithfully reproduces that initial glimpse beneath the El: "Her dress was simple, thin-striped green-and-white seersucker, square at the neck. Beneath its laundered purity, she had small white shoes, bare legs, and her hair was held at the top by a barrette."

Goshkin's family history had much in common with Bellow's. The Goshkins had emigrated from Crimea following the pogroms that broke out in the wake of the Russian Revolution of 1905 and had settled in Lafayette, Indiana, where Goshkin's father had relatives. Dark-haired and "*menschlich* [warmhearted]," as the historian Gertrude Himmelfarb, then a graduate student at the University of Chicago, described her, Goshkin was strikingly attractive; another friend, Edith Tarcov, would later compare her to Simone Signoret. Herzog's description of Daisy is exact: "slant green eyes, large ones, kinky, golden but lusterless hair, a clear skin." She was also notoriously sharp-tongued. Herb Passin remembered her as "straightforward, big-bosomed, and very assertive"—a trait that in its masculine form would have been construed as "brilliant." A well-known campus radical, Goshkin was rumored to have once sold a hundred copies of *Soapbox* in an hour. By the spring of 1937, she and Bellow were engaged.

As graduation approached, the question of what he was going to do with his life acquired a certain urgency. In search of career advice, Bellow called upon the chairman of the English department, William Frank Bryan. "You've got a very good record," Bryan told him, "but I wouldn't recommend that you study English. You weren't born to it." No Jew could really grasp the tradition of English literature, the chairman explained. No Jew would ever have the right *feeling* for it.

Discouraged, Bellow applied for a fellowship in the Department of Sociology and Anthropology at the University of Wisconsin. Herskovits wrote an enthusiastic letter of recommendation praising his student's "tenaciousness of purpose": "In addition to being a person of great intellectual promise, his interests range over a variety of subjects in such a way as to make it reasonably certain that he will never be too restricted in his outlook. This does not mean that he does not have the capacity to concentrate his interests, for he has that capacity; it means that his is a rounded personality." Herskovits also noted: "He writes extraordinarily well."

On a glorious June day in 1937, Bellow received his bachelor of science degree, with honors. His fellowship came through, and in the fall, he was off to Wisconsin.

Literature was still Bellow's primary calling. In the spring of 1937, Sydney Harris had founded *The Beacon*, a monthly journal subsidized by a group of wealthy patrons; listed just beneath Harris on the masthead as an associate editor was S. G. Bellow. *The Beacon*, self-described as "Chicago's Liberal Magazine," had the somber, no-nonsense look of *The New Republic* and *The Nation* and featured earnest articles such as "Behind the Taxi Strike" and "Civil Liberties in Chicago." The magazine's advisory board was august: Robert Hutchins; the journalist Milton S. Mayer; Secretary of the Interior Harold Ickes. Harris produced a vitriolic attack on Hemingway, Faulkner, and John O'Hara, which he called "All the Tired Young Men," accusing them of cynicism and "spiritual debility." Other contributions, among them a profile of the journalist Westbrook Pegler and a feverish essay on Oscar Wilde, appeared under the name of "Herbert Sanders"—the title of an unpublished novel by Harris.

S. G. Bellow, as the author now identified himself—or sometimes the more magisterial Saul Gordon Bellow—was equally prolific. He wrote editorials, reviews, and political pieces, notably a pseudonymous fulmination by "John Paul," of *Soapbox* fame, against Northwestern's policy of forbidding navy students to participate in "communistic discussions"—i.e., antiwar forums—on campus; its melodramatic title was "Northwestern Is a Prison." When he was writing about politics, Bellow was shrill and humorless, his prose indistinguishable from that of an editorial in *The New Masses*. His book reviews were more lively. Defending *A World I Never Made*, James T. Farrell's novel about an Irish family on Chicago's South Side, Bellow acknowledged that Farrell was no literary craftsman but praised his "feel for the milieu of the *dramatis personae*, which no amount of stylistic care can supply." With a writer like Farrell, Bellow argued, style was beside the point. The prose mirrored the reality. "If a function of art is to give a true view of the world, and if the O'Neills and the O'Flahertys are a part of it, and if deceit and corruption and latrines are their sphere, it would be a parlous thing to steal lightly by them. By all means let us have them."

Bellow dismissed *Gone with the Wind* as "drugstore literature." The prose was "flatulent," the plot "a swamp of *clichés*." The novel was "an amazing amalgam of lavender, knee-pants, Hollywood historical recklessness, a hybrid sophistication pilfered from the smart magazines and Eugene O'Neill, imitation roguery and safe sexuality." The review was credited to Sydney Justin Harris—a "mistake," Harris apologized to Bellow, after the issue hit the stands.

Bellow got his own back in a letter to Farrell that depicted Harris as an editor of unscrupulous expediency, giving the Stalinist Young Communist League space to advertise its meetings while obstructing Bellow's efforts to radicalize the contents. Harris "thinks nothing of assassinating a scruple or knifing a principle if thereby he can profit," Bellow complained: "Editorially I can't push the magazine to the left because Harris is a shrewd, opportunistic bastard who won't permit it. However, if we load the magazine with Bolshevic writers of national reputation, we can have Harris hanging on a ledge before long." It didn't turn out that way. By autumn, S. G. Bellow was gone from the masthead.

In September 1937, Bellow moved into a boardinghouse on North Mills Street in Madison, near the campus. Isaac Rosenfeld had also been accepted there, as a Ph.D. candidate in philosophy. They shared a room and together attended an aesthetics seminar taught by Eliseo Vivas, who was impressed with the boys from Chicago—"the two best students in the class." In a letter to their mutual friend Oscar Tarcov, Rosenfeld provided a lively account of the temperamental roommates:

> We are together most of the time. We both have colds, and conversation flagging we talk of our colds and sniffle with common accord. Or we will argue, debate a debatable point, usually with reference to the abstract aspects of abstract art. He peppers me with anthropological references, and I counter with casuistries, nice logical buts and ifs and whereases. If neither of us is driven to the wall he will say—"All right—granted! So where is the argument?" By this time of admission the argument is usually forgotten. The trick always works.

Bellow's advisor was Alexander Goldenweiser, "a sort of Chekhovian character, more literary than anthropological," as Bellow
remembered him. Goldenweiser's uncle, A. B. Goldenweiser, had
been a famous pianist in Moscow and a member of Tolstoy's
coterie. Alexander Goldenweiser, who had been dismissed from
the Columbia faculty for various sexual misdemeanors and found
refuge at Wisconsin, wasn't a distinguished scholar; he preferred
to hang around the billiard table at the rathskeller. Bellow
attended his Russian parties, where Goldenweiser drank copious
amounts of vodka and wept over his own playing of Chopin. He
gave Bellow an A but assured him that he wasn't cut out for social
science; his papers had too much style. "It was a nice way of easing
me out of the field." Bellow was ready: He was discouraged by the
technical courses in archaeology, physical anthropology, and
linguistics, which were required of serious candidates in the field.
By the end of the first term, he had gotten nowhere with his dissertation, on the culture of French Canadians in Quebec. "Every time
I worked on my thesis, it turned out to be a story."

In an entry he wrote some twenty years later for *Twentieth
Century Authors*, Bellow gave a terse summary of his time at
Wisconsin. "Graduate school didn't suit me, and I behaved very
badly. During the Christmas vacation, I got married, and never
returned to the university."

It was a double wedding. Herb Passin, who was doing graduate
work in anthropology at the University of Chicago, and his girlfriend, Cora—a close friend of Anita from their University of Illinois days—had also decided to get married on the spur of the
moment. The trouble was that Illinois law required both partners
to submit to a blood test as a precaution against venereal disease,
a process that took days. Neither of the couples wanted to wait.
On the afternoon before New Year's Eve 1937, they all piled into
Cora's 1934 Ford and drove to Michigan City, Indiana, where they
found a justice of the peace who did the paperwork and hurriedly
pronounced them men and wives. They celebrated with a festive
postnuptial dinner at Wisteria, a Japanese restaurant on the Near
North Side. Bellow had no immediate plans. "In my innocence, I
had decided to become a writer."

4

*The greatest achievement in the world was to earn for yourself
the right to say—I AM AN ARTIST.*

—James T. Farrell,
My Days of Anger

THE HISTORY OF MODERNIST LITERATURE is in large measure a history of discipleship: Joyce saluting Ibsen; Beckett apprenticing himself to Joyce; Pound sitting at the feet of Yeats. But Chicago-area literary masters were in short supply in 1938. Apart from a few bookish friends, his Proustian "little band," Bellow was on his own. When it came to the lonely work of mastering his craft, he turned to the works of the writers he loved best: Dostoyevsky, Flaubert, Joyce, and his local hero, Theodore Dreiser.

Dreiser was "a revelation" for Bellow. "You saw what could be done with people like those you knew, people completely familiar—neighbors, relatives, working people, shopkeepers. You saw them, with astonishment, as characters." Carrie Meeber, the heroine of *Sister Carrie*, was engaged in a struggle against limitations; however primitive her education and morals, she had an inner life. That her story was set partly in Chicago excited Bellow's imagination. And he sympathized with the disappointments that Dreiser had endured in his career. Poverty, obscurity, and belated recognition had failed to crush the novelist's "allegiance to life," Bellow observed some years later, reviewing F. O. Matthiessen's influential study of Dreiser in *Commentary*. "His history is that of a man convinced by his experience of 'unpoetic reality' of the need to become an artist."

In Bellow's case, that need dominated all others. Perhaps as a defense against the aggressive contempt that his father and brothers directed at his literary ambitions, he entertained grandiose fantasies—fantasies that were eventually realized—of showing his family by achieving literary fame. As Edward Shils shrewdly noted, Bellow's vocation served as both "a form of self-enhancement and an expression of resentment against most of the rest of mankind for not appreciating his own intrinsic qualities—in addition to those entailed in being an artist."

This burden of being—or feeling himself to be—different from others was exacerbated by the complex ethnic and cultural identity Bellow brought to his craft. His dilemma as a writer was compounded by his dilemma as a Jew: In each case, he could see himself as at once "chosen" and reviled. It wasn't enough to immerse himself in the classics of English and American literature and then claim his place in the line of succession. The strains from which his work derives—Jewish immigrant, Canadian, midwesterner, heir to the Anglo-American novel—constituted a bewildering legacy. The question wasn't only what he should write but *how* he should write. In 1938, American novels written by Jews—as opposed to more ethnic Jewish-American novels such as Ludwig Lewisohn's *The Island Within* or Abraham Cahan's *The Rise of David Levinsky*—didn't exist.

Still, good books were being written, not far from where Bellow sat hunched over the card table at his mother-in-law's house in Ravenswood. Meyer Levin, a University of Chicago graduate, had just published *The Old Bunch*, a huge, sprawling novel about a group of Jewish teenagers growing up in Chicago, which earned laudatory reviews. *Judgment Day*, the last volume of James T. Farrell's *Studs Lonigan* trilogy about a family of Chicago Irish Catholics, had been published in 1935. Farrell is often dismissed as a one-book author—"He wrote *Studs Lonigan* first and he wrote *Studs Lonigan* last," in Bellow's brusque assessment—but the trilogy is a masterpiece of American realism. Studs Lonigan, like Augie March and Moses Herzog, was a fictional character who became an archetype.

Bellow was on friendly terms with Farrell, who had also studied at the University of Chicago. It was as if Farrell belonged to a different generation—he was born in 1904—and lived mostly in New York. Who, then, were Bellow's literary exemplars? And with whom did he talk shop? "The first writer I ever met," he disclosed in a 1967 lecture, "Skepticism and the Depth of Life," "was an elderly neighbor in Chicago, a tool-and-die maker who turned out pulp stories." He lived in a bungalow across the street and wrote pulp fiction for *Argosy* and *True Confession*. Bellow dreamed of writing for *Partisan Review*. But he and the old man typing across the street shared a common condition: They were the only able-bodied men in the neighborhood during the day. Everyone else was off at work.

Bellow's father was contemptuous of his son's literary aspirations. "You write, and then you erase," he said derisively. "You call that a profession? *Was meinst du* 'a writer'? [What does it mean, 'a writer'?]" And what good was all that education? "There was just no end," Bellow's sister, Jane, recalled. "He felt like it was one degree after another." (In fact, Bellow had only a B.S. from Northwestern.) In the eyes of his in-laws, too, he was "a crazy scribbler." He dressed "like a Canadian hick" and went around with a brief-case full of foreign books. And why was he always asking for money? Once, when Bellow came around looking for a handout, Abram—as histrionic as his son—threatened to shoot him.

What was Bellow writing? He later claimed that he couldn't remember, though "it must have been terrible." A strange notion: He prided himself on the acuteness of his memory and enjoyed dazzling his brothers with his vivid recollections of long-forgotten details from their Chicago childhood.* But when it came to his apprentice work, he didn't want to remember; it seemed to him, if not shameful, at the very least embarrassing. There are few early manuscripts in Bellow's archive. The literal evidence has been destroyed.†

---

* For example, he was able to recall Novinson, the shoe repairman on West Augusta Street, who "had trench souvenirs from 1917. He had brass shell casings and a helmet with holes in it. Over his bench was a colored cartoon made by his son Izzie of a customer squirted in the face and leaping into the air yelling, '*Hellp!*' The message was, '*Don't get soaked for shoe repairs.*' "

† Bellow, who was generally unconcerned—or at least a good sport—about granting permission to quote from his letters and unpublished work, refused to allow me to quote a high-school poem I'd unearthed on the grounds that "it wasn't any good."

By the fall of 1938, Bellow and Anita were back in Hyde Park. They had found an apartment on the second floor of a building on the corner of Harper Avenue and East Fifty-seventh Street, just a block from the Illinois Central tracks. It was small but comfortable, with a Pullman-sized kitchen and a dark bedroom in the back. There were four pieces of furniture in the living room: a couch, a desk, a huge bookcase, and a card table set between two windows overlooking the courtyard. Money was scarce. Anita, intimidated by the prospect of writing a dissertation, had given up on graduate school and gotten a job with the Chicago Relief Administration, delivering welfare checks. Her salary was twenty-five dollars a week. While she went off to work every day, Bellow audited classes and lived the dilatory life of an unofficial graduate student. That winter, he registered at the University of Chicago for Introduction to Linguistics but failed to complete the course. The following summer, he signed up for History 329—Economic History of the Middle Ages—and an anthropology course in Aztec and Mayan cultures. He got a C and an incomplete.

"Student life was entertaining," he wrote in a memoir of the period, "but when you had your degree and were a student no longer, and when your friends had gone to take up their professions, moving to New York, to California or North Africa, your life became difficult to justify." Alone for most of the day, assailed by the odor of cooking and the gurgle of the toilet down the hall, he would go out into the empty street on the pretext of an errand. He ate lunch at a coffee shop on Sixty-third Street, beneath the elevated tracks. The mail was the big event of the day. Like Joseph, the unemployed Hyde Park intellectual in *Dangling Man*, Bellow was in the business of waiting—"hungry for union and for largeness," he recalled in a memoir of this difficult period in his life, "convinced by the bowels, the heart, the sexual organs and, on certain occasions, by [the] clear thought that I had something of importance to declare, express, transmit." Just what that message was had yet to be revealed. Wandering the streets one day, he ran into Nathan Leites, an instructor in the political-science department. "And how is the *romancier*?" Leites asked. The *romancier*,

Bellow admitted, was "not so hot. I was angry, obstinate. The *romancier* was *dans la lune.*"

One solution was to get a job, but these were in short supply. Bellow put on a suit and went downtown for an interview with a Hearst executive by the name of Harry Romanoff, who had a nose "like a double Alaskan strawberry." Romanoff looked him over and told him he would never make a newspaperman; in fact, he might as well forget about writing altogether. He had no aptitude for it.

In the fall of 1938, Bellow finally managed to land a part-time post teaching anthropology and English composition at the Pestalozzi-Froebel Teachers College in the Fine Arts Building on South Michigan Avenue, across the street from the Art Institute, for three dollars an hour. (The "campus" was the same building where he used to go for violin lessons.) Most of his students were midwestern farm girls or second-generation Jewish immigrants who lived at home and traveled downtown on the El. On the first day, Bellow handed out a reading list: *Crime and Punishment; Madame Bovary; Portrait of the Artist as a Young Man; Sons and Lovers; Chrome Yellow; Winesburg, Ohio; Sister Carrie; Manhattan Transfer;* and *A Farewell to Arms.* The students were to turn in a book review each week. Bellow's practice was to read the best ones aloud, then deliver his appraisal—not of the review, but of the book.

Bellow was lucky to have a job. As the Depression wore on, the benches in Grant Park were fully occupied by the legions of unemployed. Even lawyers and doctors were out of work. Fortunately, one of President Roosevelt's most popular inspirations, the Works Progress Administration, which had been designed to ease unemployment by creating jobs in the public sector, was especially vigorous in Chicago—partly, it was said, as a posthumous payback to Mayor Anton Cermak, who had received an assassin's bullet intended for Roosevelt in Miami in 1933. By the mid-1930s, out-of-work bookkeepers and civil engineers all over the city were gratefully employed at often superfluous jobs. "I can remember an autumnal Chicago street very early one morning when I heard clinking and ringing noises," Bellow recalled in his memoir of the

Roosevelt era: "The source of these sounds was hidden in a cloud, and when I entered the sphere of fog just beginning to be lighted by the sun, I saw a crowd of men with hammers chipping mortar from old paving bricks—fifty or sixty of the unemployed pretending to do a job, 'picking them up and laying 'em down again,' as people then were saying."

Bellow himself became a beneficiary of federal largesse. Prodded by Anita, he went down to the WPA office and got himself certified for relief, a routine matter. All the applicant had to do was confirm that he was unemployed and had no prospects. On both counts, Bellow qualified—apparently his part-time teaching didn't count—and he was assigned to the Federal Writers' Project. Under the direction of John T. Frederick, one of his mentors at Northwestern, the Illinois branch of the Federal Writers' Project was a flourishing enterprise. Nelson Algren, who had already published a novel (*Somebody in Boots*, based on his experience of vagrant life), wrote a pamphlet on the rural town of Galena for the American Guide Series; Richard Wright, rescued from a job at the post office, spent most of his time on the job writing *Native Son;* Isaac Rosenfeld was assigned to research the history of pigeon racing in Chicago!

The Writers' Project operated out of a loft on Erie Street, north of the Loop. Employees were expected to show up from ten until two. The salary was twenty-four dollars a week. Bellow, described in a project brochure as "a beginning writer with promise," was put to work in the Newberry Library, compiling lists of Illinois newspapers and magazines. On his lunch hour, he loitered in Washington Square Park across the street—locally known as Bughouse Square—and listened to soapbox orators harangue bedraggled crowds under the dusty trees. Eventually, Frederick got wind that Bellow was bored and gave him a new assignment: writing biographical sketches of contemporary American authors.

Over the fall and winter of 1938–39, Bellow produced sketches of John Dos Passos, James T. Farrell, and Sherwood Anderson. The autobiographical component of *Studs Lonigan* wasn't lost on him: "Farrell's writing is founded on his life. Even in his short stories it is always himself who somehow is involved." It was an approach Bellow was to emulate. Sherwood Anderson, who had roots in Ohio but had made his name as a writer in Chicago after walking out on his job and marriage, also made a lasting impression. Bellow quoted with tacit approval from Anderson's memoir, *A Story Teller's Story*: "I was in my whole nature a taleteller. The taleteller cannot bother with buying and selling. To do so will destroy him." Anderson's decision to throw over a successful career in business for the sake of literature struck a chord with Bellow, like Anderson a self-proclaimed "nut" determined to resist his family's wishes and follow his vocation.

Bellow never quite fit in at the Writers' Project. He was ill at ease around the tough-talking Algren and his buddy Jack Conroy, a hard-drinking proletarian novelist and the editor of *The Anvil*, a militant left-wing journal. "I rather looked up to them, and they looked down on me." But he always spoke warmly of the project and its generous benefactors. Roosevelt and Harry Hopkins, head of the WPA, had "behaved decently and imaginatively for men without culture," he recalled, with a characteristic touch of condescension, "which is what politicians necessarily are."

Engagement in radical politics was an inescapable fact of life for intellectuals in the thirties. The rise of Nazism, civil war in Spain, and a worldwide depression offered compelling reasons to enlist in the Marxist cause. But for Bellow and his literary comrades, the real choice was still between Stalin and Trotsky, whose struggle for domination engendered in America a factional fight between the hard-liners of the Stalinist Young Communist League and the more moderate Trotskyites associated with *Partisan Review*. It was a struggle that the Trotsky side had lost by 1936, when Trotsky himself was exiled to Mexico. But the great revolutionary still played a significant role in the radical politics of Bellow's day. An intellectual and a Jew, the author of a book called *Literature and Revolution*, Trotsky was an eloquent (if unintentional) spokesman for the prevailing ideology of the New York intellectuals. "He instilled in his young followers the orthodoxy peculiar to the defeated and ousted," Bellow wrote almost sixty years later. The Trotskyites were "the Outs; the Stalinists were the Ins."*

---

*In *To the Finland Station*, an influential book of the period, Edmund Wilson characterized the revolution Trotsky hoped to bring about as a force "that blazes out from the shut-in man to illuminate this twilight of society." Wilson's book was published in 1940, but Bellow read excerpts from it in *The New Republic*

For Bellow, it was a congenial role: As an aspiring artist and intellectual, he already regarded himself as an Out. "My closest friends and I were not activists; we were writers." Still, he liked to demonstrate how knowledgeable he was about politics by quoting Trotsky's pamphlet on the German question. At first, Bellow embraced Trotsky's view of the impending war in Europe: that it would be an imperialist war, not a war to save democracy.

It wasn't until the end of 1939, when Trotsky wrote an article defending Stalin's annexation of Finland as a legitimate strategy to protect the Soviet Union from Hitler, that he began to have doubts. "The Trotsky line," as Bellow characterized it, was that invading Finland would advance the historical cause of socialism: "Its lands would be nationalized, cooperatives would be established, soviets or workers' councils set up and so on. Although Stalin had done his best to emasculate the revolution, it was still a revolution, and Trotsky told his followers they must not oppose this war because it was a war against the whitest of white regimes, a white guard, antirevolutionary regime." But ideological issues really mattered to Bellow only as another theater in which the issues of abusive authorities, intellectuals, and outsiders were enacted—his own struggles writ large: "I couldn't believe that liberal graduates of Harvard and Princeton were going to abduct Marxism from the Marxists and save the U.S.A. by taking charge of the dictatorship of the American proletariat. I secretly believed that America *would* in the end prove an exception. America and I, *both* exceptional, would together elude prediction and defy determinism."

If Bellow regarded himself as a socialist, he was a socialist indifferent to collectivism; it was the rights of the individual that mattered. Writing to his friend David Bazelon, who had gone to

---

and *Partisan Review* in 1939. On a boiling July day, Bellow spotted Wilson in a brown tweed suit, toiling up Fifty-seventh Street with a heavy gladstone bag, "hot and almost angry, shining with sweat and bristling at his ears and nostrils with red hairs." He had come from New York at the invitation of the University of Chicago English department to teach for the summer term. Bellow boldly introduced himself, and Wilson invited the young, unpublished writer to attend his Dickens seminar. "His voice was hoarse and his manner huffy," Bellow recalled. "He was the greatest literary man I had ever met." About Wilson's books he was less effusive, disparaging the showily erudite *Axel's Castle* as "a syllabus for world literature."

New York to make his way as a writer, he offered a nihilistic credo: "In general I would say, 'Be a revolutionist.' Nothing we have politically deserves to be saved. And I would include the U of C and the Great Books Project in nothing." Being a revolutionist, however, didn't mean fomenting revolution. Politics was only "one function of a person's humanity," Bellow insisted: "The forms outside do not assure the manhood of the man. We can ask of them that they should not impede it, as they do now, but we are not safe in assuming the assurance. The right political belief, in other words, in itself secures nothing. It is necessary to be a revolutionist. But I would deny that I was less one because I do not participate in a political movement."

For all his radical bravado and angry manifestos, politics fit poorly with Bellow's hunger to experience life's intellectual, aesthetic, and sensual pleasures—to follow his singular destiny. In reality, he was comfortable with—even comforted by—Roosevelt's benign paternalism. Loitering on the Midway at the edge of Hyde Park one summer evening, he realized that Roosevelt was delivering one of his fireside chats. It was after nine and still light. Drivers had pulled over to the curb beneath the elms to listen on their car radios. "You could follow without missing a word as you strolled by. You felt joined to these unknown drivers, men and women smoking their cigarettes in silence, not so much considering the President's words as affirming the rightness of his tone and taking assurance from it." It wasn't only Roosevelt's message that stirred him: "Just as memorable to me, perhaps, was to learn how long clover flowers could hold their color in the dusk."

In the summer of 1940, Bellow unexpectedly came into some money. Seven years after his mother's death, her insurance company made its payout: five hundred dollars. The policy was in Bellow's name; even from the grave, Liza Gordin favored her youngest son. Bellow decided to spend the money on a trip to Mexico. He was deeply immersed in the works of D. H. Lawrence and had been especially moved by *Mornings in Mexico*, with its celebration of the cleansing primitivism of Mexican culture, its instinctual, nihilistic sensuality.

Bellow and Anita quit their jobs and left Chicago in early June. They traveled by way of New York, arriving just as the Germans entered Paris. Images of Hitler's troops goose-stepping down the Champs-Elysées played over and over in the movie theaters of Times Square—"a devastating event," Bellow recalled. For seven years, Hitler had been consolidating his power; now he was laying siege to the citadels of civilization. For all of Roosevelt's efforts to keep the United States out of the war, the future was more uncertain than ever.

The Bellows visited Al Glotzer and other friends from Chicago for a few days, then boarded a Greyhound bus for the long journey south. Bellow had never been in the Deep South before and was stunned when the bus was held up briefly by a chain gang doing road repairs. "I sat in a window seat holding a copy of Stendhal's *The Red and the Black,*" he recalled. "Outside, a green landscape; the freshly turned soil was a deep red. The shackled convicts were black, the stripes they wore were black and yellow."

They stopped overnight in Augusta, Georgia, to visit Bellow's uncle Max, who had gone into the business of selling secondhand clothes to black sharecroppers. Over the next few days, they continued on to New Orleans and El Paso, then crossed the border to Mexico. In Mexico City, they checked into a small hotel at 25 Calle de Uruguay that came with a high recommendation: Lawrence himself had stayed there—omitting to mention that the hotel was "a house of assignation," as Bellow primly referred to it. He and Anita were the only guests and had the place to themselves during the day; at night, traffic was heavy up and down the halls. Herb and Cora Passin arrived a few days later. Passin had a grant from the University of Chicago to study the Tarahumara Indians and would be joining their tribe in the northern province of Chihuahua that fall.

In July, the two couples headed south to Cuernavaca, then on to Taxco, a picturesque mountain town with narrow cobbled streets and houses with red-tiled roofs. Dominating the main square were the rosy twin towers of a baroque church. Through a local real-estate agent, Bellow lucked into the perfect rental, a stunning villa owned by a Japanese painter on a hill overlooking the town. It was called Casa Kitagawa, and it came with a maid, who served breakfast on the terrace.

The town was full of expatriates, "escapists with their twisted sexuality and their hopeless freedom," according to Graham Greene, who had passed through two years earlier. Bellow adapted quickly, going about town in a sombrero and a serape. He picked up a fair amount of Spanish, and before long he and Anita were part of the crowd that made its headquarters at Paco's, the local cantina. Among the regulars were D'arcy Lyndon Champion (known as Jack), an Australian who wrote pulp fiction for *Black Mask* and *Dime Detective,* and Joseph Hilton Smyth, the publisher of *The Saturday Review of Literature,* and his companion, the black cabaret singer Hazel Scott.

During the mornings, Bellow wrote in a desultory way, but he was getting nowhere: "I was groping." In the afternoons, he went horseback riding in the mountains. Evenings were generally spent in the cantina. Bellow was never much of a drinker, but the tequila flowed easily. "We'd get so drunk we had to crawl up the hill," Herb Passin recalled.

Things were tense between Anita and Bellow. His lack of progress ate away at him. "The hero of art was unstable, stubborn, nervous, ignorant," to cite his own ironic portrait of himself at twenty-five. Anita was hot tempered and harsh. They fought in public—especially after Bellow went off for a week with another woman. When he got back, Anita informed him that she'd had an affair of her own in his absence. Not only that, she'd done it openly; Bellow was incensed that everyone in town knew about her infidelity. It was one thing for the man to sleep around; the woman was supposed to be faithful. After a big fight, Anita went to Acapulco alone. Not even three years into their marriage, the Bellows had established its pattern: infidelities (mostly on Bellow's part), recriminations, stormy periods apart followed by tense reconciliations—and then the cycle began again.

Bellow, meanwhile, headed for Mexico City to meet with Trotsky, who was living there in exile. The Chicago intellectuals had close ties with their revolutionary hero: When the portentous-sounding Commission of Inquiry into the Charges Against Leon Trotsky held its hearings in Mexico in 1937, James T. Farrell and Al Glotzer had been among those who attended. Glotzer, at one time Trotsky's bodyguard, had arranged for Bellow and Passin to visit Trotsky's heavily guarded fortress on August 21. That afternoon, they read in the newspaper that Trotsky had been murdered the day before, smashed over the head with an ice ax by Ramón Mercader, the mysterious agent known in Trotsky's circle as "Jacson."

Stunned, Bellow and Passin hurried to the morgue on Calle de Tecuba. Thousands of people were milling in the street. The police, assuming Bellow and Passin were American journalists, waved them through. They went up a flight of stairs, Passin recalled, "and there, by God, was Trotsky." The open coffin was surrounded by a crowd of photographers on ladders. "His cheeks, his nose, his beard, his throat, were streaked with blood and with dried iridescent trickles of iodine." Trotsky had often said that Stalin could murder him whenever he liked, "and now we understood what a far-reaching power could do with us," Bellow later wrote, "how easy it was for a despot to order a death; how little it took to kill us, how slight a hold we, with our historical philosophies, our ideas, programs, purposes, wills, had on the matter we were made of."

Bellow and Anita patched their marriage back together. Toward the end of August, he and the Passins joined her in Acapulco, in those days a tiny seaside village. They stayed at the Excelsior, a grand hotel up on the cliffs from which boys dove into the bay for coins. Down below, people slept in hammocks on the beach.

When the summer was over, Passin went to live among the Tarahumara. Bellow and Anita piled into Cora's Ford and headed back to Chicago.

"What sense did a writer make?" Bellow wondered, looking back many years later on that period in his life. He had returned to Chicago with no more prospects than he had had when he'd lit out for Mexico three months before. "Who was he, anyway? Did his name appear in *The Saturday Evening Post*, or *Colliers*, or *Cosmopolitan*? What *was* a real writer doing in Humboldt Park or Logan Square or Ravenswood, or even Hyde Park? Pale in an attic, typing strange pages, while others were at work, the streets maddeningly empty, his existence could not be explained to the neighbors." Only the fledgling writer's closest friends knew what he was up to. Walking with his Tuley friend Sam Freifeld in Jackson Park, Bellow would pull a manuscript out of the battered briefcase he carried with him everywhere and offer to read aloud from his work in progress. He was tireless in asserting that he was going to be a writer, but his boastful manner concealed tremendous insecurity. "There was a quality of great desperation about him," said Herb Passin. "He *had* to get something major published."

Bellow's desperation had a practical cause. The WPA had been disbanded in 1939, and Bellow's only source of income was the few dollars a week he earned teaching at the Pestalozzi-Froebel Teachers College. He had yet to sell a story.

Undeterred, he was hard at work on a manuscript called "Acatla"—the name alone would survive, as a fictional Mexican town in *The Adventures of Augie March*. Handwritten in a fluent script on pages torn from a yellow legal pad, it describes a group of Americans at a Mexican pension in a town very much like Taxco and their response to the presence of a mixed-race couple—perhaps based on Smyth and Scott—whom the proprietor is trying to eject. Inconclusive as it is, this partial manuscript clearly demonstrates Bellow's powers of observation. The prose is descriptive yet focused on the human drama:

> The sun lay around them on the smooth stones; the air was cloudless and soft; a pigeon coming down through the orange trees lighted on a dark branch, gripping with its red feet, intensely clear. There were watery reflections from the carp pond within the green awning. A waiter was slicing a melon for Mr. Hobart, who was gazing at the town while Mrs. Hobart drank her coffee in the flickering shade. She had the trained composure of a person who has mastered the secret of imperturbable privacy under the public stare.

Abandoned after a hundred pages, "Acatla," in its acerbity and self-assurance, contained the seeds of Bellow's mature style. It was vividly precise in its language; it revealed character through action; and it moved with ease from specific situations to general observations about human character and fate. It had both gravity and wit, playfulness and philosophical depth. What it lacked was an authentic voice; it was chiseled, Jamesian, writerly. But it wasn't original.

"Until I was twenty-five I had little success," Bellow wrote on his application for a Guggenheim Fellowship in 1943. For years, he had sent his stories out to magazines, only to have them returned. He had tried large-circulation journals such as *The Saturday Evening Post* and little magazines such as *Kenyon Review;* but the magazine that counted—the one that Bellow read faithfully every month—was *Partisan Review.* Its circulation hovered around three thousand, but its readers included just about everyone of importance in contemporary literature. Delmore Schwartz's youthful masterpiece, "In Dreams Begin Responsibilities," had led off the first issue. T. S. Eliot, Edmund Wilson, and Lionel Trilling were early contributors. John Dos Passos and James T. Farrell appeared alongside Arthur Koestler, André Gide, and Ignazio Silone.

Intent on a thorough renovation of American culture, the editors of *Partisan Review* were vigorous proponents of the idea— "perhaps the most powerful idea of the last half-century," claimed Irving Howe—that Europe was the creative citadel of modern literature. For Philip Rahv and William Phillips and the generation of young Jewish writers whose work they promoted, the great European literary masters represented both a spirit of political subversion and the triumph of art over mass culture—in Howe's words, "a mixture of rootless radicalism with a desanctified admiration for figures like Joyce, Eliot, Kafka." That the cultural heroes of the *Partisan Review* crowd were in many instances profoundly reactionary, even anti-Semitic, could be overlooked; they had turned literature into a new religion. The international sensibility manifest in the great modernists' work, which was willfully erudite and self-consciously intellectual, made American culture seem provincial by comparison.

Bellow was just as much of a culture snob as any of the contributors to *Partisan Review.* His novels are crammed with references to writers and philosophers whose gravity of thought he found intoxicating but with whom he had only a glancing familiarity—to Kant and Goethe, to Nietzsche and Max Weber and the duc de Saint-Simon. Referring to the best that has been thought and said was a literary tic. Yet he was suspicious of high culture for the same reason that he was suspicious of all efforts, real and imaginary, to impose on his freedom, whether in the form of brothers or wives or in the forms of institutions: They were all aspects of authority. One of the most striking features of Bellow's work is its refusal to be bound by the conventional definitions of what constitutes literary seriousness. Unlike so many Jewish writers of his generation—Leon Edel, Lionel Trilling, Harvard professor and critic Harry Levin—he was drawn to the gritty side of life. "He has a nose for bad odors to the point where he seldom smells anything else," as Edward Shils, Bellow's longtime colleague at the University of Chicago, put it. He worshiped European literature as much as these eminent professors did and was just as eager to demonstrate that he knew his way around it; but he disdained their habit of using their familiarity with the Great Books to put distance between themselves and their immigrant roots, invoking their preoccupation with Jane Austen or Henry James as evidence of their newly elevated class status. For all his assiduous reading—and pretense of reading—Bellow was impatient with the civilizing imperatives he'd encountered in the Great Books, eager to renounce what he called the "high-culture *gymnasium* route of Thomas Mann" and explore a subterranean realm. "Mortimer Adler had much to tell us about Aristotle's *Ethics*, but I had only to look at him to see that he had nothing useful to offer on the conduct of life."

His real education was formed by a different set of books. In the deserted second-floor library of the psychology building on Ellis Avenue, he was boning up on the works of Géza Róheim. A trained psychologist, Róheim was a pioneer of psychoanalytic anthropology. He was convinced that it was possible to discover within the rituals and customs of any human group the structure of its collective unconscious—a structure, Róheim hypothesized, that was invariably the same: The psyche of the most advanced European was identical to that of the most rudimentary tribesman.*

---

*In this, he was a precursor to the founder of structural anthropology, Claude Lévi-Strauss.

Róheim's work was a revelation. It supplemented the lessons about supposedly primitive cultures that Bellow had learned from his undergraduate work in anthropology (and from Dostoyevsky), positing the existence of a more spontaneous and robust human nature—what Lawrence in his book on Mexico called "the great origin-power of life." Bellow was a great believer in the quest for the essential self. In the fifties, he turned to the sexual-liberationist teachings of Wilhelm Reich, in the seventies to the mystical teachings of the anthroposophist Rudolf Steiner, who exhorted people to escape the prison of consciousness and experience the world the way it really is—to "burst the bonds that fetter the human spirit," as Bellow once proclaimed in a moment of rhetorical overheatedness. Lawrence was only one literary guru among many.

The May/June 1941 issue of *Partisan Review*—which offered one of T. S. Eliot's "Four Quartets," along with contributions from Clement Greenberg, Allen Tate, and Paul Goodman—included a story entitled "Two Morning Monologues." Its author was identified in a terse author's note at the back: "Saul Bellow is a young Chicago writer. This is his first published story."

The monologues were competent if undistinguished sketches. The first, entitled "9 A.M. Without Work," recounted the plight of a young unemployed man named Mandelbaum who is waiting to be called up by the draft board. His father hounds him to get a job and puts an advertisement in the newspaper on his son's behalf. Mandelbaum shares with his creator an aversion to his (very Jewish) name: "I can't remember a time in my life when I didn't swallow before saying it." He's also a deep thinker, preoccupied with the phenomenological texture of existence; he even finds significance in the sandwich that he carries in his pocket, "one of the closely curled leaves of my identity." Like Bellow's later heroes, Mandelbaum is a "noticer"—his mandate is to register, discern, observe. He is, in Henry James's famous description of himself, "the one on whom nothing is lost." Touchy, proud, assertive, Mandelbaum is a rudimentary version of the typical Bellow hero. His self-absorption is monumental—not even the sun can survive without him. He wanders the streets of Chicago and boards a streetcar for the Loop, glancing out the window to chart the sun's trajectory: "Just before we creep under the elevated lines it appears for a moment. Not much hope for it, I remark to myself. If it outlives me, it won't be for long."

One notable feature of "9 A.M. Without Work" is that Mandelbaum has no brothers: "I am the only son." Like Proust, who edited his brother out of *À la recherche du temps perdu*, Bellow wasn't ready to introduce the big brothers who were to figure so prominently in his later novels, brutish businessmen offering advice to a sensitive, impractical hero. One of Bellow's most urgent themes—the younger brother's struggle to define his own identity against his family—had yet to declare itself.

The other monologue, "11:30 A.M. The Gambler," featured an early version of Bellow's lowlife types, the con artists and touts he'd observed hanging around Freifeld's pool hall or in Brown and Koppel's restaurant on Division Street, where there was always a card game in progress upstairs. Bellow's gambler is an operator who knows every trick in the book. "You have to be on the spot when the kiss off comes, connect the pair, hit the straight, fill in when the right one snaps up." But he's also a sensitive soul— Mandelbaum without the books. Nostalgic for childhood, he sounds more like Joyce's Stephen Dedalus than a Chicago card shark with a cigar in his mouth. Bellow's shysters were never as authentic as his brooding, heartsore intellectuals.

Over the next year, he published two more stories, "The Mexican General" in *Partisan Review* and "Mr. Katz, Mr. Cohen, and Cosmology" in an obscure quarterly called *Retort*, edited out of Bearsville, New York. Set at a hotel in Patzcuaro where a high-ranking police official has just arrived with his retinue, "The Mexican General" recounts the story of Trotsky's murder through the eyes of the general's lieutenant, Citron. A direct witness to the death of the *viejo*, as Trotsky is called (he's never named directly), Citron describes the sequence of events to a compatriot named Paco: the assassin's attack; the chaotic scene at the Cruz Verde hospital, where the old man, his blood-streaked face "appearing between the cone of bandages and the sheet," lay dying; the frenzy at the morgue, where the corpse was displayed for photographers "like a slab of beef." But the story is really about the general himself, *el Jefe,* a pompous bureaucrat who muscles his way onto the stage of history, giving press conferences and getting his picture taken with the widow. Modeled on Colonel Leandro Salazar, chief of the Mexican secret police and later the author of a book about Trotsky's assassination called *Murder in Mexico,* Bellow's general is a decadent, rather vague character whose main interest is in the three "nieces" brought along to serve his needs. The intellectual, voluble Citron (an embryonic form of Citrine, the protagonist of *Humboldt's Gift?*) offers up Weberian interpretations of the events he's witnessed, using the high-minded language of a University of Chicago sociology professor. The general is "an important actor in history," Citron explains to Paco; he is a functionary who embodies "the role of the State," "a non-essential but typical category." The prose, stilted and faintly Hemingwayesque, sounds like a translation from the Spanish.

"Mr. Katz, Mr. Cohen, and Cosmology" was written in a more recognizable voice. Katz and Cohen are boarders in a Montreal rooming house. Katz is something of an intellectual; Cohen is a retired tailor, "stout and robust, with a rather Socratic head, a pink scalp under his few remaining white curls." Cohen is limited and thinks the world is flat; he's never heard of the Pacific Ocean. But the simpleton turns out to be profound. Katz fills his ear with a discourse on time, to which Cohen replies with his own cranky meditation on its swift passage: "To who is it a lot, a year? Sneeze and wipe your nose and it's a year already." The tailor's homespun musings are intended to show up the autodidact's theories.

The author of "Mr. Katz, Mr. Cohen, and Cosmology" would have been familiar to readers of *The Beacon.* It was S. G. Bellow. At the age of twenty-seven, he still hadn't settled on a name.

About his vocation he was less uncertain. While Anita went off every morning to her job as a social worker, Bellow set up shop at his card table in the sparsely furnished living room. Just beyond the wall, the El train rattled noisily by. In the closet were his brothers' hand-me-down suits, too large; on the shelves were his books: Coleridge's *Biographia Literaria, The Complete Works of Shakespeare, The Plays of Christopher Marlowe,* Gogol's *Dead Souls,*

Zola's *L'Assommoir*, Wyndham Lewis's *Tarr*, the major novels of Flaubert, Melville, D. H. Lawrence, Tolstoy, Dostoyevsky, Thomas Wolfe, Virginia Woolf, Sherwood Anderson, Joyce and Proust, Mann and Faulkner, Simon Dubnow's *History of the Jews in Russia and Poland*, and a book entitled *The Slaughter of Jews in the Ukraine in 1919*—a rehearsal for the slaughter then occurring in Europe. "All that appeared then," Bellow later recalled, "was a blind, obstinate impulse expressing itself in bursts of foolishness. I was extremely proud, ornery, and stupid."

In 1941, he was at work on a novel called "The Very Dark Trees." Written in the first person, it concerned an English professor named Jim, "an enlightened Southerner" who, on his way home from teaching at a midwestern university, is struck as if by a bolt of lightning and finds himself turned black. When he gets home, his wife doesn't recognize him at first, then locks him in the basement so he won't alarm the neighbors. "The Very Dark Trees" was both a fable about the tenuous nature of identity and "a caustic tale of a liberal Southerner confronted by the reality of prejudice," according to Bellow's Tuley friend Nathan Gould, who heard excerpts read aloud. It was also very funny, Gould remembered. Bellow's friends referred to the manuscript as "White No More." On the basis of the plot alone, it would have been no stretch to read it as a different kind of parable—one in which any personal transformation (say, from Russian-Jewish to American) was punished by estrangement from one's family, even by imprisonment. Nor was Jim the agent of his fate; it was something that was done *to* him by "a bolt of lightning." Thus did the premise of "White No More" conform to Bellow's passive construct of his life.

On the strength of his stories in *Partisan Review*, Bellow had managed to acquire a literary agent, Maxim Lieber, a card-carrying member of the Communist party. Among the writers Lieber represented at one time or another were Erskine Caldwell, Howard Fast, and Josephine Herbst. Lieber submitted "The Very Dark Trees" to the Vanguard Press, a logical choice. Established in the late 1920s as a left-wing charitable foundation, Vanguard had gotten its start publishing cheap editions of Engels, Marx, and Lenin. James Henle, a former newspaper reporter and editor at *McCall's*, had purchased the house a few years earlier and was determined to turn it into a genuine publishing imprint while preserving its radical flavor. In the thirties, the Vanguard list featured muckraking biographies of J. P. Morgan and Andrew Carnegie, books with titles such as *Graft in Business* and *The Public Pays*, an account of the Sacco-Vanzetti case, and fiction by Nelson Algren and James T. Farrell.

The readers' reports on what came to be known in the house as "that Negro manuscript" were mixed. "The Very Dark Trees" was "an extraordinary tour de force," wrote one editor. "In spite of the fantastic turn the plot takes, it seems to me the writer shows an original style and real ability." But this editor didn't see how Vanguard could market the book without testimonials from "big names"—and even then it would be a hard sell. Evelyn Shrifte, who eventually became the firm's president and publisher, found the novel "provocative" and "absorbing," but she also was worried that no one would buy it, "unless we could get it started by snob appeal—a strange, different kind of book." Another rather literal reader was puzzled by the protagonist's racial transmogrification: "Why didn't Jim have himself examined by a reliable physician?"

The editors at Vanguard weren't alone in their doubts about "The Very Dark Trees." James Laughlin, the enterprising founder of New Directions and publisher of Ezra Pound and Delmore Schwartz, read a few chapters and turned it down. Bellow offered Laughlin a suggestion: Now that he had inaugurated a poet-of-the-month series, publishing pamphlets by Schwartz, Malcolm Cowley, and others, why not a novelette of the month? Bellow himself happened to have several long stories on hand. "They are not *New Directions* in your sense of it. But then I think originality is a better criterion than bizarre form. Anything a young writer does is a New Direction if it is good." (Laughlin passed on the idea.)

"The Very Dark Trees" continued to make the rounds. Early in 1942, William Roth of the Colt Press wrote to Bellow after reading "Two Morning Monologues" in *Partisan Review* and asked if he was working on a novel. Roth, the scion of a wealthy San Francisco shipping family, published elegant gardening books and works of literary merit that hadn't found homes elsewhere. His small but distinguished list included Henry Miller's *The Colossus of Maroussi,* Edmund Wilson's *The Boys in the Back Room,* and Paul Goodman's early novel, *The Grand Piano.* Bellow submitted two hundred pages, cautioning Roth that it was a first draft but urging him, with a characteristic mixture of arrogance and humility, to "attend to it speedily (for better or for worse)," as the army was "hot on [his] heels." He was about to be drafted. As a Canadian citizen, Bellow was ineligible for the army, but as the war effort gained momentum and it became clear that his deferment was only temporary, he decided to put himself through the naturalization process.

Six weeks later, he got an answer: Roth wanted to publish "The Very Dark Trees." He offered an advance of $150, payable upon publication in November. "Your letter bowled me over," Bellow replied on April 3. "I am neither too shy nor too hardened to admit it freely, and I wish I could frame a very special kind of 'thank you'. The occasion certainly calls for it."

Excited by the prospect of publication, Bellow revised the whole book in a frenzy. The draft board had deferred him until the end of the term at Pestalozzi-Froebel Teachers College; he was to be inducted on June 15, 1942. When he reported for his physical, having stayed up half the night to put the finishing touches on his manuscript, he was deferred until mid-July. In the meantime, he had given up his teaching job, which meant "an incomeless month" unless Roth could advance him something. Roth answered with bad news: He himself had been drafted by the Office of War Information and was about to be shipped off to Alaska. All publishing activities of the Colt Press were suspended for the duration of the war. Enclosed was a check for fifty dollars.

Bellow was devastated. His book had finally found a publisher. He had even alerted the editors of *Partisan Review* to mention the novel's imminent publication in his contributor's note for "The Mexican General." But he was stoic about its fate. "I should like to explain that I feel I am miles and centuries away from The Very Dark Trees—whole developmental heights," he explained to Roth: "Oh, I still feel it deserves publication, in fact since I will never have time to finish any of the long things I have started I am determined it *must* be published, for it is to give me the right in the postwar period to continue as a writer. But in a sense it is business, not literature."

Whether or not "The Very Dark Trees" deserved publication will never be known, for soon afterward Bellow decided the book wasn't very good after all. Indeed, in his retrospective estimate, it was "very bad," "an overambitious piece of youthful writing." It may have shown evidence of talent, he wrote Roth, "but it certainly wasn't a book." To forestall posterity's judgment, he tossed the manuscript down an incinerator chute.

Even as his first novel was going up in flames, Bellow was beginning to acquire a reputation. Philip Rahv, one of the founding editors of *Partisan Review* and a shrewd appraiser of literary talent, had gone to Chicago with his wife in the spring of 1941 and scouted the local talent. "So far we've managed to meet quite a few people, and the best of them by far are the apprentice writers like Bellow and Harold Kaplan," he reported to F. W. Dupee. "I am quite enthusiastic about these youngsters—they are the Delmore Schwartz type: brilliant and yet at the same time methodical and responsible." (Kaplan had already published a long story, "The Mohammedans," in *Partisan Review*.) Rahv predicted Bellow would "come to something."

Dwight Macdonald, an editor of *Partisan Review* in its early days, also thought Bellow was promising, though this did not stop him from pointing out the young writer's faults. Macdonald, a self-proclaimed "Scotch argufier" who found criticism a highly stimulating activity, discerned in Bellow's earliest work one of his most persistent flaws. Returning a short story entitled "The Car," he objected to its "excess elaboration" and "centerless facility."

Bellow replied with a testy defense of his method:

> It is not because I write too easily that I sometimes fail. I would be more successful perhaps, if I did write with more careless dash. But what I find heartbreakingly difficult in these times is fathoming the reader's imagination. If he and I both were of a piece, it would not be so hard. But as it is I am ringed around with uncertainties and I often fail to pull myself together properly, banishing distraction and anxiety. And so I find myself

perpetually asking, "How far shall I take this character? Have I made such and such a point clear? Will the actions of X be understood? Shall I destroy a subtlety by hammering it?" Etcetera.

It was a measure of Bellow's vulnerability, his shaky sense of his own capacities, that he was willing to admit to another writer—and an intellectual authority figure at that—how little faith he had in his literary powers. But he was aware of this key weakness: his failure to empathize with others, be they wives or lovers, children or brothers, rivals or friends—the knowledge that he and they were not "of a piece." It was a disjunction that was to limit his achievement and bring him much personal misery.

To Macdonald, Bellow also defensively offered a practical excuse for the shortcomings of his work: It was hard to write when his future was so cloudy. He was still waiting to hear from the draft board, but as a 1-A he was disqualified from teaching: "It's impossible to make the best use of one's capacities at such a time, and it is nearly as crippling to know that one's talents are being kept hobbled." He offered to have his agent send a story entitled "Juif!" In the meantime, he was hard at work on a new novel: "Notes of a Dangling Man."

5

I had left home, as young men do, & had come to the largest city in the
world. Bless new life, bless novelty & difference oh ye lights while
I plunge underground, content now to roar home on the subway.

—ISAAC ROSENFELD
in his journal, 1941

R OSENFELD, MEANWHILE, had made his way in New
York. Awarded a one-year graduate fellowship from the
philosophy department of New York University, he had
arrived there in the fall of 1941 with his new bride, Vasiliki Sarantakis, a classmate from the University of Chicago. The daughter of
a Greek immigrant who owned a corner grocery on the North
Side, Vasiliki was "a touching, lovely, teasing young woman, a
pagan beauty with hibiscus in her teeth," as Bellow later described
a character based on her in one of his unpublished manuscripts.
(Edward Shils remembered her less kindly as "a noisy, frumpy sort
of girl.")

Installed in a brownstone on West Seventy-sixth Street, Rosenfeld quickly made a name for himself as a literary journalist. His
essays and reviews appeared in *Commentary,* his short stories in
Partisan Review, his poems in *The New Republic.* "He was our
golden boy, more so than Bellow," recalled Irving Howe in his
memoir *A Margin of Hope,* "for there was an air of Yeshiva purity
about Isaac that made one hope wildly for his future."

Back in Chicago, Bellow was reading with some alarm his best
friend's contributions to the journals they had passed around so
avidly as students. Hyde Park was dead; the campus seemed
empty. Albert Glotzer was in New York; Harold Kaplan was in

North Africa; Julian Behrstock was in London. "It looked, then, as if my wide-awake and energetic peers were going to take all the active roles in 'serious' life—in the professions, in business or research." In his fits of nostalgia, Bellow could look back on his youth and say—as does Joseph in *Dangling Man*—"Everything he ever wanted was there." But everything he wanted *wasn't* there. A "significant life"—that stirring phrase—was a life in which the distinctive qualities of S. Bellow were made known to the great world.

For intellectual sustenance, Bellow regularly made the long bus trip to New York. "New York was then a very Russian city," observes Charlie Citrine in *Humboldt's Gift*. "It was a case, as Lionel Abel said, of a metropolis that yearned to belong to another country. New York dreamed of leaving North America and merging with Soviet Russia." Bellow usually stayed in Isaac and Vasiliki's cramped apartment, where there was a bathtub in the kitchen and "cockroaches springing from the toaster with the slices of bread." Toward the end of 1943, the Rosenfelds moved to the big apartment at 85 Barrow Street that was to become a fixture of Greenwich Village cultural life in the forties.

New York in those days was crowded with brilliant exiles and émigrés. Bertolt Brecht and W. H. Auden had settled in New York; Hannah Arendt—later a colleague of Bellow at the University of Chicago—lived on Riverside Drive. In the 1940s, the city was the capital of international modernism—"the last outpost of Europe," in Delmore Schwartz's phrase. "It is not by its own genius alone that a capital of culture arises," wrote Harold Rosenberg in a celebrated essay, "On the Fall of Paris," which Bellow had read on a bench in Jackson Park in Chicago in the fall of 1940. "A whole epoch in the history of art had come into being without regard to national values." What Paris had been, New York was fast becoming. "The city had never looked so bright and frisky before," Alfred Kazin rhapsodized. The dingy Els were coming down, opening wide thoroughfares to light—symbols of New York's endless possibility. "The astonishing look of 'new' Third Avenue and the gleaming new structures of glass everywhere," "the frenzy of overwhelming buildings and crowds," provided a visual analogue to the sense of excitement that radiated outward from the centers of cultural power: the cluttered offices of *Partisan Review* on Astor Place; the New School for Social Research on West Twelfth Street, where Meyer Schapiro gave his electrifying lectures on modern art; the Minetta Tavern in Greenwich Village; the Cedar Bar on University Place, where painters congregated. Not the least of the city's intellectual attractions was Bellow himself. Even as an intermittent visitor, he was making his mark. Kazin, who met him through Rosenfeld (Vasiliki was Kazin's secretary at *The New Republic*), provides a spirited account of the young Chicago writer as he appeared in 1942:

> As I walked him across Brooklyn Bridge and around my favorite streets in Brooklyn Heights, he looked my city over with great detachment. He had the gift—without warning, it would follow a séance of brooding Jewish introspection—of making you see the most microscopic event in the street because *he* happened to be seeing it. In the course of some startling observations on the future of the war, the pain of Nazism, the neurotic effects of apartment-house living on his friends in New York (Chicago was different; it was a *good* thing to grow up in Chicago), he thought up some very funny jokes, puns, and double entendres. It was sometimes difficult to catch the punch line, he laughed so fast with hearty pleasure at things so well said. And they were well said, in a voice that already shaped its words with careful public clarity. He explained, as casually as if he were in a ball park faulting a pitcher, that Fitzgerald was weak, but Dreiser strong in the right places. He examined Hemingway's style like a surgeon pondering another surgeon's stitches. Then, familiarly calling on the D. H. Lawrence we all loved as our particular brother in arms, he pointed to the bilious and smoke-dirty sky over the Squibb factory on Columbia Heights. Like Lawrence, he wanted no "umbrella" between him and the essential mystery.

For all his apparent self-assurance, Bellow wasn't as confident as he seemed. The detachment Kazin remarked upon was a shield designed to protect his fragile identity—aloofness as a means of defense. "I didn't have an air of success," he said in response to Kazin's portrait. "I felt just as weak in the knees as everyone else. I didn't know what the hell I was doing." Kazin had published *On*

Native Grounds to considerable acclaim; Delmore Schwartz had published a collection of work, *In Dreams Begin Responsibilities,* that was praised by Allen Tate as "the first real innovation" in American poetry since Eliot and Pound. Bellow had published a few stories in little magazines.

Visiting Schwartz in his book-crammed lair in the Village, Bellow played the disciple. "The guy had it all," he declared of Von Humboldt Fleisher, the vivid, doomed poet in *Humboldt's Gift* who was based on Schwartz: "An avant-garde writer, the first of a new generation, he was handsome, fair, large, serious, witty, he was learned"—a *contrast gainer,* to borrow an epithet of Charles Citrine's—someone whose deficiencies paled next to those of people in even worse shape. In one early draft of the manuscript, when Humboldt was still "D." (Delmore), Bellow depicted himself, in the role of Schwartz's memoirist, as "overweight, with a straight nose and dark rings under the eyes, melancholy but somewhat haughty, dressed in an older brother's hand-me-downs, badly recut, the shirts a size too big, white on white, the initials not mine." Apart from the first adjective—Bellow remained slender all his life—it wasn't a bad self-portrait.

Rosenfeld didn't know how to dress either and favored ties "that you expected to glow in the dark," according to one of their friends. But the two "Chicago Dostoyevskians" made their presences felt. "It was the New York group that was parochial," said Gertrude Himmelfarb. "The Chicagoans were more cultivated: more literary, more musical, more philosophical." Alfred Kazin was struck by how Chicagoan, in another sense, Bellow and Rosenfeld were. "Chicago gave people the Midwestern openness, a sense of being at home in America," he observed in *New York Jew.* Bellow agreed. "For some reason neither Isaac nor I could think of ourselves as provincials in New York," he wrote to Kazin many years later, after reading an excerpt from his memoir in *The Atlantic Monthly:* "Possibly the pride of R. M. Hutchins shielded us. For him the U. of C. didn't have to compete with the Ivy League, it was obviously superior. It never entered our minds that we had lost anything in being deprived of Eastern advantages. So we came armored in self-confidence, and came to conquer. Ridiculous boys!"

If they didn't wear their learning lightly, it was because they had more to prove. While the editors of *Partisan Review* occupied themselves with politics, Rosenfeld and Bellow devoted themselves to their craft. "Notes of a Dangling Man," a chapter of the manuscript that would become Bellow's first published novel, appeared in the September/October 1943 issue of *Partisan Review*, and he was also at work on a novel about "a middle-class individual" named Victor Holben. The book's theme, he explained in an application for a Guggenheim Fellowship, was the meaning "of those capacities by which man at his best is distinguished: love, generosity and genius." Rosenfeld, who also applied for a Guggenheim, described a novel in progress about "the post-depression generation and man's resources against humiliation."

Not that either of them was oblivious to the grim import of world events. Robert Van Gelder, the editor of *The New York Times Book Review*, had given Bellow a shot at reviewing books, and one of his first assignments was Maurice Samuel's *The World of Sholom Aleichem*. Bellow closed his review with a pointed reference to the fate of that vanished world's heirs, "reduced to begging their existence of a civilization of which one-half is intent on wiping them out and of which the other half, for all its declarations and conferences at Evian and Bermuda, has thus far answered only with firm promises of nothing." For Rosenfeld, politics was a distraction from the more urgent matter at hand: how to live. "My patron saint is Dostoevsky's Underground Man," he confided in his journal. For Bellow, politics was a distraction from the life of art, especially his own.

When Bellow made the trip to New York, he generally went alone. Anita had gotten a job at Michael Reese Hospital, and to Bellow's friends she seemed the dutiful housewife, the childhood sweetheart. Sydney J. Harris referred to her as "the social worker." She cooked, cleaned house, and looked after the couple's modest finances. "She knows the price of oranges," Bellow liked to say, at once praising and disparaging her efficiency.

Their apartment was cozy, with Impressionist prints on the wall, a bust of Nefertiti on the mantel, and "bookcases and bookcases and bookcases." The Bellows were still in their twenties, but there was an air of premature domesticity about them. When Ruth Miller visited the newlyweds, Anita, in a dirndl and peasant blouse, served homemade strudel. The critic Lionel Abel had an explanation for their conventionality: "They had married in order to show their disapproval of the sexual promiscuity in the Communist party," he wrote in his engaging but unreliable memoir, *The Intellectual Follies,* claiming that Bellow had told him, "My marriage broker was the Fourth International."*

"You're so interested in the class war you've lost the sex war," Abel taunted the uxorious Trotskyites, adding, "They didn't stay monogamous, by the way." He was right on that score. "A compact with one woman puts beyond reach what others might give us to enjoy," thinks the philandering Joseph in *Dangling Man,* didactic even in his hedonism. "The soft blondes and the dark, aphrodisiacal women of our imaginations are set aside. Shall we leave life not knowing them? Must we?" For Bellow (even though he dedicated the book to Anita), the answer was clearly no. Even in the early years of his marriage, he made no pretext of fidelity. Nor did most of his friends. "The wives didn't know; they didn't want to know," said Mel Tumin, one of Bellow's closest friends. While Anita "stayed home and made fruit salad," as Tumin put it in his catty way, Bellow was off at "meetings"—the preferred alibi of Hyde Park Trotskyites.

Among Bellow's conquests in the forties was a woman named Bebe Schenk. "They really got it on," according to Mel Tumin. Bebe wore black leotards and ballet shoes and wanted to be a writer. Bellow gave her private tutorials. He was also carrying on a serious affair in New York with a woman named Marjorie Farber, whom everyone called Midge. Recently separated from her husband, the psychoanalyst and writer Leslie Farber, Midge had set herself up in a brownstone on West Sixty-eighth Street and talked her way into a job at *The New York Times Book Review.*

---

*Bellow found Abel's interpretation of his marriage "characteristically and amusingly cockeyed and foolish. To say that the Fourth International was my marriage broker is very funny. I wouldn't have had the wit—at that time—to say it. Lionel must have heard it from someone else, forgot the source, and conveniently attributed it to me."

"Handsome, sensuous, brilliant, devoid of self-doubt," as the artist Janet Richards described her, she later claimed that she was the model for the regal, horsey Thea Fenchel in *The Adventures of Augie March*. Farber and her purported fictional double were both pale, dark-haired, imperious, and notoriously undomestic; she was also said to be a passionate lover. ("With Thea," Augie confides, "it wasn't at all as it had been with other women, those who gave you their permission, so to speak, to undo one thing at a time and admire it.")

For his part, Bellow was intensely attractive to women—and knew it. Even decked out in his brother Morrie's ill-fitting business suits, he had what Alfred Kazin described as "the conscious good looks of the coming celebrity." Janet Richards's lively memoir, *Common Soldiers*, provides a glimpse of Bellow in those days: "Saul was irresistible, rather small and slight but strong, with curly black hair and large black eyes that missed nothing. They were ironic and sweet and not so much intellectual in expression as shrewd." Like the self-regarding heroes of his books, proud of their flat stomachs and their stamina on the paddleball courts, Bellow delighted in his physical appeal. ("You know you're a good-looking man," Ramona, one of Herzog's many women, chides him: "And you even take pride in being one. In Argentina they'd call you *macho*—masculine.") The narcissistic traits that a succession of psychiatrists diagnosed in him were no doubt fed by this gift from nature—as was his prose, which suffered at times from an excess of self-delight.

It didn't take Bellow long to embrace the progressive morals of New York bohemia circa 1943—to discover, as Alfred Kazin memorably put it, that "everything could fall apart at the sight of a young girl with very wide cheekbones standing at an overcrowded party in Greenwich Village." For Jewish intellectuals of that generation, sex was a revelation as charged as their first encounters with Marx and Freud. It opened up a whole new world. Their parents' marriages, constrained by provincialism and the pressures of adapting to the New World, seemed intolerably suffocating to their newly liberated children.

Bellow claimed not to feel guilty about his infidelities—indeed, he considered them his due. But the satisfactions of conquest outweighed the physical transaction; his sexual appetite was never voracious. ("It was his pride that must be satisfied," as Herzog acknowledges. "His flesh got what was left over.") "I miss Anita, but not carnally," he wrote to Sam Freifeld during one of his sojourns in New York. "Strangely enough I haven't had an erection in two weeks."

Bellow may have been a midwestern provincial, but he was a provincial with a plan. He compared himself to Stendhal's Julien Sorel, "the young man from nowhere"; there was an element of calculation in his innocence. Bellow was "wiser and more mature" than others in the *Partisan Review* crowd, observed Janet Richards. But he was deeply suspicious of people, intent upon fending off any entanglement that might interfere with the ambitious work he was preparing himself to undertake. Friends noted that Bellow was "touchy," unnervingly quick to take offense; on more than one occasion, Kazin watched him "nail with quiet ferocity someone who had astonished him by offering the mildest criticism."

His early fictional self-portraits captured this wariness and reserve. Joseph, the hero of *Dangling Man*, was also reflective, guarded, a diffident young intellectual with a straight nose, black hair, and large soulful eyes. "He does not have what people call an 'open' look, but is restrained—at times, despite his amiability, forbidding," Bellow wrote: "He is a person greatly concerned with keeping intact and free from encumbrance a sense of his own being, its importance. Yet he is not abnormally cold, nor is he egotistic. He keeps a tight hold because, as he himself explains, he is keenly intent on knowing what is happening to him. He wants to miss nothing." Keeping himself free from encumbrance was a strategy that was to govern Bellow's life. Whether it was wives, children, publishers, lawyers, friends, or even ideas, he maintained his distance as a way of preserving his fragile sense of self.

Yet he was naturally gregarious and thrived on conversation without trying to dominate it—not that any monologuist would have stood a chance among the crowd of aggressive talkers that climbed the steps to the Rosenfelds' convivial, chaotic fourth-floor walk-up. "Their Barrow Street apartment was open to janitors and mailmen and bartenders, who were treated with the same affable courtesy as Saul Bellow, Ralph Ellison, and Paul Goodman," recalled the novelist Wallace Markfield. The atmosphere was less bohemian than Old World European—"not second- but first-generation Jewish intellectual, Ye Olde East Side," as the writer Milton Klonsky defined it.

In 1943, Rosenfeld replaced Kazin as literary editor of *The New Republic* for a year—a steady job, but the salary of fifty dollars a week was barely enough to support a family, even in those days. To supplement his income, he wrote copy for trade journals—including one called the *Ice Cream Trade Journal.* Bellow managed to scrape together a living by writing for *The New York Times Book Review.* On his visits to New York, he called upon Robert Van Gelder, who let him carry off an armload of review copies. Bellow sold them at a third of their price to a book dealer on East Fifty-ninth Street.

In fact, things were looking up. "The air is thick with jobs," Bellow reported to Henle; he was being considered for an instructorship at the University of Chicago in a recently established graduate department known as the Committee on Social Thought. Founded in 1941 by the historian John U. Nef, the Committee was associated officially with the university's Division of the Social Sciences; but its mandate, according to Nef, was "to transcend specialties" and contribute "to the unification of all recent discoveries in the arts and sciences." He would miss his frequent trips to New York if it came through, Bellow wrote Henle. "Nothing less than this job could keep me in Chicago."

He was also hoping for a staff writing job at *Time,* where Henry Luce had assembled an impressive coterie of intellectuals. James Agee was the film critic; Weldon Kees, a midwestern poet, and Nigel Dennis, a clever, cynical Englishman, wrote book reviews. Agee had recommended Bellow for the job.

He was interviewed by Dana Tasker, the editor in charge of personnel, who seemed inclined to hire him on the spot. "It begins to appear that I will stay here, working on *Time,*" Bellow reported to Sam Freifeld on June 12, 1943: "It seems agreed that I will get a job. The question before the editors is whether I should write domestic or foreign stuff. I may do Art or Religion. (They like to put you in a field you know nothing about.) Or Education. I'm not sure. All novices start at 75 [a week] & after 3 months go to $100—formerly my average monthly earnings." Bellow was so sure he'd be offered the job that he invited Freifeld's wife, Rochelle, and their daughter Judy to come stay with him in New York—they could rent a house in Flatbush together while Sam finished his tour of duty: "I'll have more money than I ever had in my life & I won't know what to do with it." Whether Anita would also come along was never made clear.

There was just one hurdle—a formality, Tasker assured him. He would have to see Whittaker Chambers, who edited the back-of-the-book pages on books and the arts. The house highbrow at *Time*, Chambers prided himself on his grasp of Western culture and was rumored to keep a score of Beethoven's Ninth Symphony in his drawer. He was also a fanatical anticommunist. "In his own person he had experienced history," Bellow wrote of Chambers in one of his many unpublished manuscripts about these years, describing him as "a GPU agent turned Quaker" and a chain-smoking paranoid with rotten teeth. "Passing through hell, the suffering servant of God, he brooded from his high window in Rockefeller Center over downtown New York, stuffed with thoughts about the future of Christianity, the fate of the West, the spiritual struggle with satanic totalitarianism." Chambers had done more damage as an editor, Bellow joked, than as a spy.

At their interview—as Bellow often told the story, frequently altering the details—Chambers faced away from him, enthroned on a wing chair. Was Mr. Bellow familiar with Wordsworth? he asked. (Sometimes it was Blake.) Bellow protested that Wordsworth had nothing to do with writing journalism for *Time*, but Chambers adamantly pursued his English-lit line of questioning. Wordsworth was a Romantic poet, Bellow replied. And what was his greatest poem? Chambers persisted. "Ode: Intimations of Immortality," Bellow ventured.

He was sorry, Chambers announced curtly, there was no place for Bellow at *Time*. The only poem of Wordsworth's that counted was "The Excursion." Bellow had flunked. As he was leaving, a disgruntled employee shook his hand and assured him it was his "lucky day." (Years later, John Berryman told Bellow that he had suffered an identical humiliation at Chambers's hands.)

The interview wasn't a total loss. Like so many humiliations in Bellow's life, it showed up—turned on its head—in his fiction. In *The Victim*, published four years later, Asa Leventhal, a long-suffering job seeker, sits through a disastrous interview with Rudiger, the irascible editor of *Dill's*, a weekly newsmagazine, on the sixtieth floor of the Dill Building. Rudiger, "burning like a boiler," makes it clear from the outset that Leventhal is wasting his time: "This is a news magazine. If you have no news experience, you've got no business here." Instead of going quietly, Leventhal stands his ground. "There's nothing special about your magazine," he retorts. "Anybody who can write English can write for it." Rudiger, in a violent rage, orders the insolent young man out of his office. It is a powerful scene—and a fantasy. But grievance, in Bellow's hands, provided an imaginative spark. A major impetus to his novels was to set the record straight as he saw it or in ways that vindicated him. Ex-wives, ex-friends, journalists who had condescended to him, and New York intellectuals who had failed to recognize his genius were all liable to surface in one of his books, their biographies and physical traits portrayed minutely and recognizably. "You forgive people too easily," he once chastised a friend. "Jews don't forgive."

Dana Tasker, embarrassed by his failure to get Bellow the job, wrote on his behalf to Ik Shuman, an editor at *The New Yorker*. "Dear Ik," Tasker's letter began: "A young man by the name of Saul Bellow is presently weaving around New York in quest of a writing job. Although one of our editors knows and recommends him, we just haven't got a spot for him." *The New Yorker* didn't either.

Jobless, Bellow returned to Chicago. Throughout 1942 and 1943, his forays to New York had grown longer; there was little to keep him at home. Most of his friends were in the army, posted to Europe or the Aleutians. The war was at a turning point. The Battle of Stalingrad ended in February with the first major defeat of Germany on the eastern front; in the summer of 1943, the Allies invaded Sicily. It was clear to Bellow that he would eventually be conscripted, but he still had no word from the Selective Service. Meanwhile, his own domestic war with Anita was reaching a new stage of acrimony. At a party in Hyde Park, she drank too much and flirted openly with one of their friends, dancing close to annoy her husband. Why should infidelity be a male prerogative?

While he was waiting to be called up, he put the final touches on "Dangling Man." (He had dropped the Dostoyevskian "Notes" from the title.) Early that summer, he submitted it to James Henle at Vanguard, who had turned down "The Very Dark Trees" but continued to express interest in Bellow's work. On July 7, he received a telegram from Henle: AM DEEPLY IMPRESSED BY DANGLING MAN BUT WANT TO GET ANOTHER OPINION. Two weeks later, they had a deal. Henle offered a two-hundred-dollar advance—half to be paid upon signing.

Bellow had more good news: The post at the Committee on Social Thought had fallen through, but he had been offered "a whopper of a job" in the editorial department of the *Encyclopaedia Britannica,* working on the *Syntopicon,* a two-volume supplement to the *Great Books of the Western World.* Under the direction of Mortimer Adler, who together with Robert Hutchins had been instrumental in bringing the Great Books concept to the University of Chicago, Bellow was put to work with a team of fifty readers who had been assembled to compile an "index of ideas" that would summarize the writings in the full fifty-two-volume set. He was "a sort of strawboss" to whom the other readers reported: "I, in turn, am responsible to Hutchins and Hutchins to God and St. Thomas."

Working out of a damp, dusty basement in the Social Science Building—it soon became known as Index House—Bellow and his fellow indexers made their way through "the 443 works of 74 men, from Aristotle to Tolstoy and from Homer to Marx," as Herman Kogan described this herculean intellectual effort in *The Great EB,* his book about the making of the *Encyclopaedia Britannica.* Apart from his supervisory duties, Bellow was responsible for Plutarch and Tacitus, *The Republic* and the *Nicomachean Ethics,* Hobbes's *Leviathan,* Herodotus and Thucydides. Adler, "the Great Bookie"—Hutchins's affectionate but faintly condescending moniker for him—had determined that there were 101 great ideas, from "angel" to "world"; among the hundred in between were "citizen," "duty," "education," "family," "immortality," and "love." There was a fierce debate about the "angel" category; Bellow's psychoanalytically minded colleagues preferred the more up-to-date "ego," but in the end they were overruled.

For Bellow, a job was simply another form of authority—submitting to regular hours and bureaucratic responsibilities was being told what to do. When Joseph, in the closing lines of *Dangling Man*, declares his relief at having been drafted ("I am in other hands, relieved of self-determination, freedom canceled"), he's being ironic; his cry "Long live regimentation!" is the cry of a man for whom regimentation of any kind—whether in marriage, work, or the writing of fiction—was anathema.

As a declaration of independence, Bellow often did his *Syntopicon* research on a bench in Jackson Park. But the atmosphere of "high-pressure intellectualism" in the basement of Social Science was bracing, he admitted to Henle: "They're learning, gradually, that they've hired a philosophic Naturalist instead of a Thomist. Or rather that they can't win me from G. H. Mead and [John] Dewey." He liked to think of himself as a proponent of Mead's "Chicago pragmatism"—the belief that mental processes were determined by the environment as much as by the individual. The pay was two dollars an hour.

The question was where to live. Having given up their most recent lodgings on the assumption that they would be moving to New York, Bellow and Anita had taken up temporary residence in "a sort of students' den" at 1326 East Fifty-seventh Street, but they needed a more permanent domicile. Anita was pregnant.

Dangling Man was published on March 23, 1944, during the darkest days of the war. Hitler had just invaded Hungary; the gas chambers at Auschwitz were widely known; American fighter pilots were bombing Berlin. "There is no personal future any more," Bellow's defiantly isolated protagonist asserts.

Perhaps not, but the novel itself announced the arrival of a new and distinctive voice in American literature. From the first page, *Dangling Man* sounds a brashly declamatory note:

> Do you have feelings? There are correct and incorrect ways of indicating them. Do you have an inner life? It is nobody's busi-

ness but your own. Do you have emotions? Strangle them. To a degree, everyone obeys this code. And it does admit of a limited kind of candor, a closemouthed straightforwardness. But on the truest candor, it has an inhibitory effect. Most serious matters are closed to the hard-boiled. They are unpracticed in introspection, and therefore badly equipped to deal with opponents whom they cannot shoot like big game or outdo in daring.

If you have difficulties, grapple with them silently, goes one of their commandments. To hell with that! I intend to talk about mine, and if I had as many mouths as Siva has arms and kept them going all the time, I still could not do myself justice.

Written in the form of a journal, the novel chronicled four months in the life of a young intellectual named Joseph—more allegorical than Kafka's Joseph K, he lacks even an initial for a last name— from mid-December 1942 until April 1943. Out of work, having been laid off from his job at a travel bureau, Joseph awaits induction—a protracted business, as it turns out. A Canadian and thus a British subject, he is required to undergo an investigation of his background before he can be classified 1-A, ready for active service. In the fall of 1942, his induction is postponed because of a new regulation exempting married men. Thus, Joseph dangles.

Dangling Man bore the marks of an apprentice work: It was slight—less than two hundred pages—derivative of the existential, European, "literary" novel that was then in vogue, and nearly plotless. It is a novel about a man idling away his days in a fog of introspection, interrupted by minor encounters with friends, neighbors, and family. While his wife is off at work, Joseph wanders about the neighborhood, has lunch alone in restaurants, smokes, does errands, listens to the radio, reads the paper. Most of his friends have gone off to war. So uneventful is his life that he commemorates "the day I asked for a second cup of coffee" or "the day the waitress refused to take back the burned toast." He toys with the idea of going back to work, but doing nothing has become a moral test: "I am unwilling to admit that I do not know how to use my freedom and have to embrace the flunkydom of a job because I have no resources—in a word, no character."

What the story lacked in drama, it made up for in its power of perception. *Dangling Man* had the feel of actuality, of experience observed and recorded by a penetrating gaze. It conjured up the texture of life in Chicago during that bleak era: the lonely men in rooming houses; the unemployed, vaguely bookish drifters getting by on the largesse of friends and relatives; the Hyde Park intellectuals discussing "socialism, psychopathology, or the fate of European man." The jukeboxes in the taverns playing "White Christmas"; the rush-hour crowd on the El platform at Randolph and Wabash; the trains disappearing into darkness as the red lamps on the rear car vanish around a curve—not since Dreiser had a novelist so authoritatively captured Chicago's desolate beauty, its "unmitigated wintriness."

Bellow chronicled the way he and his friends lived—the long afternoons in cafeterias, the dispirited parties, the apartments decorated with prints by Chagall and "light furniture in the popular Swedish style"—with a sociologist's precision; Delmore Schwartz praised the novel as a catalog of "the typical objects of a generation's sensibility." But *Dangling Man* was more than a portrait of the manners and morals of Hyde Park intellectuals; it was a book about the struggle to sustain a sense of identity and worth amid the patriotic clamor of wartime. Joseph is contemptuous of society and oppressed by the tedium of his surroundings. Visiting his wife's parents on the Northwest Side, he gazes morosely out the window at a grim urban landscape of warehouses, billboards, electric signs, industrial gloom—the quintessential Chicago tableau: "It was my painful obligation to look and to submit to myself the invariable question: Where was there a particle of what, elsewhere, or in the past, had spoken in man's favor? There could be no doubt that these billboards, streets, tracks, houses, ugly and blind, were related to interior life." How could one conduct a meaningful existence in so harsh an environment? For Joseph, the grimy realm beneath the El tracks on Sixty-third Street threatens the very idea of human significance. Yet despite his inert self-involvement, Joseph retains a kind of intransigent optimism. "The giants of the last century had their Liverpools and Londons, their Lilles and Hamburgs to contend against, as we have our Chicagos and Detroits." Civilization can flourish—or at least survive—in a person as well as in a place. The novel is a brief on behalf of the individual, a plea for the recognition that each one of us is unique; yet—and this is what makes it, for all its outward modesty, such a commanding achievement—it is also an acknowledgment of the universal quest for meaning that defines our humanity. As Joseph observes, "We are all drawn toward the same craters of the spirit—to know what we are and what we are for, to know our purpose, to seek grace."

As a fictional hero, Joseph is not entirely sympathetic. Aware of his "inflationary, grandiose, tasteless attitudes," he claims to be tolerant of others—"a sworn upholder of *tout comprendre c'est tout pardonner*"—but judges his own friends harshly; he's impatient with their doctrinaire politics, their shallowness and lack of cultural sophistication. He longs for what he calls—to borrow a term from Isaac Rosenfeld—"a colony of the spirit," but he feels compelled to keep others at arm's length: "Goodness is achieved not in a vacuum, but in the company of other men, attended by love. I, in this room, separate, alienated, distrustful, find in my purpose not an open world, but a closed, hopeless jail. My perspectives end in the walls. Nothing of the future comes to me. Only the past, its shabbiness and innocence. Some men seem to know exactly where their opportunities lie; they break prisons and cross whole Siberias to pursue them. One room holds me." Clearly, the one room was representative of Bellow's imagination. He, too, yearned for a colony of the spirit, a life among others, but the isolation of the writing life and his own suspicious nature kept him apart. The room that held him was himself.

Joseph never claims to be a writer. "My talent, if I have one at all," he confides, "is for being a citizen, or what is today called, most apologetically, a good man." Still, like all of Bellow's novels, *Dangling Man* is highly autobiographical: Joseph's meditations on his Jewish ancestry, memories of his childhood in the slums of Montreal, references to his dead mother and to a disapproving father who wants him to get a job all resonate with Bellow's own life at the time. His habitual practice of closely basing his characters on real people was also in place: Iva, a "quiet girl" with "a way about her that discourages talk," bears a distinct resemblance to Anita; the cigar-smoking Alf Steidler, an amateur actor who goes around with a copy of *Variety* in his coat pocket, was clearly modeled on Studs Terkel.

Bellow's oblique reference to Ernest Hemingway—the chief literary representative of the "era of hardboiled-dom"—on the very first page of *Dangling Man* was meant to put the great man down. By the forties, Hemingway's flamboyant life had acquired a nearly mythic status. When he won the Nobel Prize in 1954, *Time* reported the honor under the rubric "Heroes" instead of "Books." Bellow approved of Hemingway's effort to achieve, in Joseph's words, "a strong and victorious identity," but he resented Hemingway's pose of manly stoicism. "The hard-boiled are compensated for their silence," Joseph complains. "They fly planes or fight bulls or catch tarpon, whereas I rarely leave my room." As far as Bellow was concerned, introspection demanded at least as much courage as big-game hunting.

Dangling Man was almost defiantly literary—again, a Bellow trademark. There were allusions to Shakespeare and Goethe, to the mystic Jakob Böhme and to Joyce, who had compared the artist to a god paring his fingernails. ("We are schooled in quietness," reflects Joseph, "and, if one of us takes his own measure occasionally, he does so coolly, as if he were examining his fingernails, not his soul, frowning at the imperfections he finds as one would at a chip or bit of dirt.") The dialogue that Joseph carries on with an inner voice called the Spirit of Alternatives—also known as "On the Other Hand" and "*Tu As Raison Aussi*"—is a variation on the self-interrogation that Dostoyevsky's Underground Man conducts in his wretched room. There is also an echo of the dialogue form employed in Diderot's *Le Neveu de Rameau:* One of Joseph's abandoned projects is an essay on Diderot, and the pontificating Alf Steidler reminds him of Rameau's nephew. It was as if Bellow needed to make the point that even a writer from Chicago read books.

But the novel's main influence was Rilke's *Notebooks of Malte Laurids Brigge.* (The translation that Bellow read bore the more descriptive title *Journal of My Other Self.*) Brigge, like Joseph, is in his late twenties, an intellectual dabbler with no visible means of support; the plot turns on the convolutions of his mind. In transposing the mental weather of Rilke's Paris to the South Side of Chicago, Bellow arrived at a style that encompassed both the American vernacular and the cerebral, inward-dwelling prose of the European writers he admired.

Bellow's ambition was huge. He had set out to become a great American writer. But at this vulnerable stage in his development, it would have been far too risky to admit what he was after, even to himself. The novel was an "ironic statement," he assured David Bazelon: "I don't encourage surrender. I'm speaking of wretchedness and saying that no man by his own effort finds his way out of it. To some extent the artist does. But the moral man, the citizen, doesn't. He can't." Total freedom is a myth. Binding ourselves to the common will is expedient; it releases us from the prison of solitude. But the inner life—the writer's exclusive domain—is the only one that matters.

Bellow was quietly apprehensive about the book's prospects, vacillating between bravado and anxiety. He was prepared, he wrote James Henle early in 1944, "to be ground by the critics" for insufficient patriotism: "Nowadays they want to see red, white and blue sepulchres." *Dangling Man* had given him "great wehtig," he confessed to Alfred Kazin, resorting to the Yiddish word for *pain:*

> Clearly, the book is not what it should be, not what I can write. A more resolute character would have refused to have it published. But, alas! I fancy that even now I can give a pretty fair estimate of it. The writing is sound, the idea—of the impossibility of working out one's own destiny freely in such a world—is a genuine one. The rest is a hash, a mishmash, for which I deserve to be mercilessly handled. But it's so hard now to find a way to use one's best powers. What can be done? Isaac labors with the same difficulty. He has not reached the level where he can thunder. Like myself he is still somewhere in the trees. In the trees one rustles. You know whence thunder comes.

It was a harsh self-assessment—harsher than the book deserved. It was natural for Bellow to feel that his first published novel had flaws and that he hadn't reached his potential. In his mature fiction, even dark novels such as *Mr. Sammler's Planet* and *The Dean's December,* a more expressive voice was to emerge, along with a less fatalistic attitude toward destiny. Looking back on his development, Bellow often referred to *Dangling Man* and his equally somber second novel, *The Victim,* as his M.A. and his Ph.D.—by which he meant to disparage them as dutiful and workmanlike. But his dismissive characterization of his apprentice work ignores its manifest virtues. For all its limitations, *Dangling Man* has about it an unmistakable air of authenticity; it grapples with deep themes, breaks narrative rules in pursuit of its idiosyncratic vision, and captures the temper of an era. It was more than a beginning; it was instrumental in bringing about what Philip Rahv identified as "the Europeanization of American literature," incorporating the tradition of the novel as practiced by Stendhal and Flaubert, by the great modernists Joyce and Mann, by the Russian masters, and imposing on that tradition a uniquely American idiom.

Writing to Kazin, Bellow resolved to "take [his] pannings manfully," but the pannings were far outweighed by praise. John Chamberlain, writing on March 25 in *The New York Times*, faulted the novel for being "rather haphazard in construction" but remarked on its psychological acuity; it had brought home the experience of suspended life that was characteristic of wartime "without ever getting close to the front lines." The poet Kenneth Fearing, writing in *The New York Times Book Review*, found *Dangling Man* "fresh and vivid," an "imaginative journal" that summoned up "what must seem to many others an uncannily accurate delineation of themselves." And Irving Kristol, applauding Bellow's "restraint, dignity and insight" in *Politics*, called *Dangling Man* "our best war novel."

There were some dissenters, notably *Time*, whose anonymous reviewer derided Joseph as a difficult, self-pitying character: "Whenever he grows too utterly unhappy, [he] goes out walking in the rain, getting his feet wet to spite everybody." *Dangling Man*, it said, was a well-written first novel, but it would have been a more sympathetic book if "Author Bellow" had recognized that Joseph was "a pharisaical stinker."

The review that mattered most was from Edmund Wilson. Writing in *The New Yorker*, Wilson grasped the book's central dilemma: Joseph's effort to preserve his independence in the face of nonnegotiable demands by the state, to "vindicate the value of the individual even in a crisis where the fate of Western culture seemed to hang on collective enterprise." Praising the novel as "well-written and never dull," Wilson pronounced it "one of the most honest pieces of testimony on the psychology of a whole generation who have grown up during the depression and the war."

6

There was a time when New York was everything to me:
my mother, my mistress, my Mecca. . . . I was young,
the war was just over, and I was free.

—HARVEY SWADOS,
"Nights in the Gardens of Brooklyn"

*D*ANGLING *MAN* had made Bellow a writer, but it hadn't changed his situation. The very week of publication, he learned that he had been turned down for a Guggenheim Fellowship; the early reviews, while for the most part favorable, hardly amounted to triumphs.

Among the criticisms, Diana Trilling's disparaging assessment in *The Nation*—"not the kind of novel I like"—hit him hardest. "Plainly she has such an antipathy to 'small sterile' books that if she thinks she has one before her she is incapable of giving it a dispassionate reading," he complained to his publisher:

> Yes, Dangling Man is bitter. I wonder if Diana thinks one could write "an affirmation of life" (damned phrase) upon such a theme. But the book is square and honest. It is probably not great, but it is not "small". It is too genuine for that. As for the accusation that my physical world lacks dimensions, that is just nonsense; she hasn't read the book if she says that. She's swept away by her initial antipathy. But if I thought I were merely talented and clever in a small way I would give up writing tomorrow and never write again, not so much as a letter.

What's most striking about this letter is the way it vacillates between extreme defensiveness and a serene belief in the scope of his abilities. Bellow knew—or at the very least suspected—that he was far more than "merely talented and clever." As Alfred Kazin recalled in *New York Jew,* "he carried around with him a sense of his destiny that excited everyone around him." But it was a fragile sense, based more on intuition than on hard evidence, and the need to protect it made him hypersensitive to criticism. Not long after Trilling's review appeared, Bellow, sitting in the dining hall at the University of Chicago with Mel Tumin, complained bitterly about the injustice she'd committed. When Tumin advised him to forget about it, Bellow flew into a rage and ordered him to leave the table. They didn't speak to each other for almost a year.

Bellow had begun to attract attention. An agent named Jacques Chambrun wrote offering his services, and another, Henry Volkening, who only a few weeks before had curtly dismissed a story by Bellow called "On the Platform," urged him to send new work if he could "forgive the wham we gave the short story."* And there was a note of praise from the sociologist C. Wright Mills.

He also got a call from Metro-Goldwyn-Mayer—but not, as expected, for an option on the novel's movie rights. A studio executive had seen his photograph in a newspaper and offered to make him a star. Bellow wasn't an Errol Flynn type or a George Raft type, the man from Hollywood explained—that is to say, he wasn't handsome or tough in the conventional sense. But he could have a great screen career in the sensitive role, the guy "who loses the girl to the George Raft type or the Errol Flynn type."

Bellow stuck with literature, but making a living at it wasn't easy. The job at *Encyclopaedia Britannica* interfered with his writing, and he was thinking of quitting if the book sold well—an outcome he tried to ensure by making the rounds of Chicago bookstores. He buttonholed William Targ in his shop on Dearborn Street and announced: "I've just published a book called *Dangling Man.* Would you put it in your window?"

Henle counseled prudence. *Dangling Man* had launched Bellow as a novelist, he acknowledged, but "as for living on what you

---

*Chambrun appears in Michael Korda's memoir of his publishing days, *Another Life,* as a colorful charlatan who had mysteriously acquired the title of comte and parlayed his representation of the works of Somerset Maugham into a somewhat shady but lucrative career as a literary agent.

earn as a writer, I have to warn you that there are very few human beings in this world who are able to do this IF THEY WANT TO PRODUCE HONEST WORK." Henle's advice was based on direct acquaintance with the ledger: The first edition of *Dangling Man* sold 1,506 copies.

In any event, it was hardly a propitious moment to be out on the street. On the morning of Sunday, April 16, 1944, Anita gave birth to a baby boy. It was a difficult labor and an emergency cesarean was required. The doctor hurried to the waiting room and told Bellow that he doubted he could save either mother or son, but he would try to pull Anita through. For two hours, Bellow waited alone before he learned that she would live. A day later, with the baby still in an oxygen tank, he wired Henle: DANGER PASSED EVERYONE SAFE.

It was a traumatic experience, and for weeks afterward Bellow rejoiced in his family's health. The baby—named Gregory, after Anita's grandfather—was doing fine, Bellow reported to Evelyn Shrifte on April 29: "He eats everything in sight at feeding time and then sleeps like a rock. His nose is straight and probably will be long, like mine, but all his other traits are his mother's, even to the Tartar eyes." He was regular in his eating habits, waking every night at two and then again at six. "So was Kant," asserted Bellow, always mindful of the Great Books. "People set their watches by his comings and goings."

His cheerful tone belied doubts about fatherhood that were to beset him the rest of his life. Like the father in his story "A Father-to-Be," written a decade later, he was troubled by the tyranny of biological reproduction. That a child's character, mental endowment, and appearance were in part genetically determined meant that these traits were beyond the parents' control—another threat to their freedom. In the story, Rogin, a thirty-one-year-old man (just three years older than Bellow was when Greg was born), is riding the subway when he notices a middle-aged passenger with "a straight and purely Roman nose" who reminds him of his fiancée, Joan. This outwardly minor coincidence prompts Rogin to a troubling meditation that echoes, in a darker tone, Bellow's report to Shrifte:

> Forty years hence, a son of hers, provided she had one, might be like this. A son of hers? Of such a son, he himself, Rogin, would

be the father. Lacking in dominant traits as compared with Joan, his heritage would not appear. Probably the children would resemble her. Yes, think forty years ahead, and a man like this, who sat by him knee to knee in the hurtling car among their fellow creatures, unconscious participants in a sort of great carnival of transit—such a man would carry forward what had been Rogin.

About this kind of legacy Bellow was decidedly ambivalent. Not only did it exclude him from the decision-making process, creating a child that was both his and not his, but it brought into stark relief the fact of his own mortality: " 'My son! My son!' he said to himself, and the pity of it almost made him burst into tears. The holy and frightful work of the masters of life and death brought this about. We were their instruments." It may have been in part to protest against the tyranny of these masters that Bellow abandoned each of his first three marriages after fathering sons.

In the summer of 1944, Bellow was at last called up for a physical, only to be diagnosed with an inguinal hernia. The medical examiner scheduled him for minor surgery; he was given a local anesthetic and chatted with the surgeon during the procedure. But recovery was slower than he'd anticipated, and he was in constant pain for weeks. Frustrated by the draft board's dilatory ways, he was angling to get a job with the Office of War Information; the future novelist Eleanor Clark, who worked for the OWI in Washington, tried to intervene on his behalf, but nothing came of it. In October, he was reclassified 2-A, even though he had made it clear that he wasn't requesting an exemption. "I don't want to dodge," Bellow explained to Henle. "But if they don't want me I'll go on writing. That's much more important, of course, but I didn't want to take it on myself to decide. Let *them* do that."

The tide of the war in Europe had turned: Paris had been liberated, Soviet troops had pushed back the Nazis, the Allied invasion of Europe was in full swing. But men Bellow's age were still being drafted; there was no sign that the fighting would end soon.

While Bellow awaited his fate, he was at work on a novel and stories, writing daily. "The new book is inching along," he wrote his publisher in October 1944: "I haven't had the courage to look back at what I've written; I might turn into a pillar of salt." He and Anita had found an apartment at 5400 Dorchester, a great improvement over their cramped quarters on East Fifty-seventh Street: "We have rooms and a wonder of a bath in which I can lie at full length." But he was finding it hard to concentrate with a new baby in the house. "A cubicle of my own would be ideal. A scientist could get himself endowed. But I—a minor priest of a minor cult, and self-appointed at that . . . Well!" This quest would become a major theme as Bellow struggled to protect his independence against the demands of domesticity. In every household he established, he maintained a room or an apartment off to the side—the literal expression of his character Joseph's need to keep "free from encumbrance."

Bellow was not a hoarder; he wrote copiously, throwing away what didn't work. Better to stop after a few chapters than be tied down by characters who weren't what he intended them to be— "unwanted and delinquent children," he called them. "My new book (no title as yet) has hit a fresh snag—no. 883," he wrote Henle in the winter of 1945. "But I think I can dislodge it by the usual method of going to the movies every night for a week." The book was called "The Adventurers," perhaps an early version of *The Victim*, perhaps the novel about "a middle-class individual, Victor Holben," that he had described to the Guggenheim Foundation. No trace of it remains.

Bellow's epistolary style veered between humility and condescension. To Jean Stafford, at that time a promising young novelist whom he had met on one of his trips to New York, he wrote a fan letter that revealed in the first sentence his anxiety about the status of his reputation—he had to remind her who he was—while at the same time making clear that he was sufficiently important to be "desperately busy":

Dear Miss Stafford:
    You remember me, I think; Bellow, the man who never called you back because he was desperately busy elsewhere. My purpose in coming forward now is to tell you how very happy I am to find you a fine writer. I haven't read the book [*Boston Adventure*], just the chapter in P.R. It is heartening to read such writing. I reserve the right to criticize on some heads, but the

writing, the writing I acknowledge with all my heart. I say it who should know by virtue of having slaved at it, if by no other. I've had no occasion to use Pepto-Bismol again, but I own a large bottle. It was all I had to remind me of you until the last P.R. arrived.

Stafford was at the time married to Robert Lowell. She was twenty-nine, Bellow's age, and they published their first novels the same year—*Boston Adventure,* a well-written but rather conventional tale about Beacon Hill society, became a bestseller while *Dangling Man* vanished from booksellers' shelves, not to reappear until Bellow was famous and Penguin began to keep all his books in print. But it was apparent from Bellow's oblique reference to past debauchery that Stafford was already embarked upon the hard-drinking ways that would eventually wreck her career.

On the evidence of Bellow's letters, domestic life agreed with him. He sent cheerful dispatches to his editors at Vanguard about Gregory's weight and feeding habits, his digestion, his new tooth. The doting father carried baby photos in his wallet. The only discordant note was a jocular reference to a novel he'd spotted in the Vanguard catalog about the perils of marriage. "Wives are prodigious creatures, aren't they?" Bellow observed to Henle in the spring of 1945. "Sometimes I feel I could understand a Bantu or a Papuan more easily—just so he knew Esperanto—than my wife." It was a joke that did the work jokes do, expressing an uncomfortable truth through humor. For Bellow, Anita—like all women, all wives—belonged to a foreign tribe.

In April 1945, fed up with the army's delays, Bellow volunteered for the merchant marine and boarded a train for the East. Serving there would give him more freedom, he reasoned, than being in an "army of occupation," and the recruiters had assured him that he would have plenty of time for writing once his training was over. Assigned to the Atlantic District Headquarters of the U.S. Maritime Service in Sheepshead Bay, Brooklyn, he was sent to Baltimore in June. The crew practiced abandon-ship drills (raising and lowering lifeboats), and rowed in Chesapeake Bay—three weeks of "boat drills, brine, heavy meals, sun, hell-raising." He was glad to get back to Sheepshead Bay.

A letter from Sam Freifeld awaited him; Sam's father had died. The reply Bellow wrote a few weeks later gave a clear account of his situation:

> Dearest Sam:
>   I was still in boot-camp when I heard of your father's death. It was bitter news. I thought how you would receive it, alone in some dingy English city. I lay on my sack in the barracks and thought about it. I couldn't write you. Any letter I wrote while at Sheepshead would not have lightened your burden. I simply took it for granted that you would know how I felt. We are so linked that neither of us ever faces a crisis without thinking of the other.

It was a characteristic letter: warm, vividly descriptive, at once a fervent expression of friendship and an exercise in self-exoneration. (It also managed to shift the subject from his friend's bereavement to himself.) Bellow had a sentimental attachment to his Chicago friends, substituting them for his hostile brothers. "The love I have for you is something literal brotherhood never gave me," he declared to Freifeld, long one of his most sycophantic followers. They were "blood-brothers." And blood brothers, unlike real brothers, were less judgmental, more easily impressed. Like many powerful figures, Bellow preferred the company of lesser lights who made few demands on him, didn't compete for attention, and enjoyed—or at least were satisfied with—reflected glory.

Bellow's job with the Maritime Commission was easy, and his barracks were convenient to Manhattan, where he had many friends. Isaac Rosenfeld was sitting out the war as the commander of a navy barge in New York Harbor. On weekend furloughs, Bellow often stayed with his friend David Bazelon, showing up at the door in a "sailor boy outfit," as Bazelon snidely described his whites.

On September 15, a month after the Japanese surrender, Bellow was released to inactive status. He wrote, hat in hand, to his Chicago literary mentor, James T. Farrell.

> Dear Jim:
>   I'm putting in for a Guggenheim (Jim Henle says my chances are better this time) and I'd appreciate it greatly if you would once more consent to sponsor me. I'm putting on one of my

annual drives to get out of Chicago. It grows more like Siberia all the time. I come in, petition the Czar to free me from banishment, he refuses and I get into the Pacemaker [the New York–Chicago train] with the other condemned and return. Seriously, Chicago oppresses me in a way only another Chicagoan can understand. It terrifies outsiders—Wilson, for instance in his piece on Jane Addams in "Travels in Two Democracies"—but it haunts the natives.

I don't know what you thought of my first book. I hesitated to ask you to back my Guggenheim application if you thought I was a ham. I asked Jim Henle about it and he said you thought I was a good writer. I didn't expect you to like Dangling Man but I would have been disturbed to learn that I was in your opinion a bum and ought to take up finger painting.

Bellow's eagerness to escape Chicago was a measure of his ambition. He was thirty years old, and his one book had gotten some good reviews; he could claim a modest renown within the circle of writers whose work he had read in *Partisan Review* back in his boardinghouse days. Yet he was still a Hyde Park intellectual with a closetful of ill-fitting suits, a wife and child to help support, and a postmark that read Stock Yards Station—in effect, nowhere.

At the end of September, Bellow packed up his family, stored their furniture in the Shoreland, a grand hotel on the Hyde Park lakefront that his brother Maurice now owned, and boarded the Pacemaker for New York. They sublet their apartment to Daniel Bell, then a young sociologist who had just been appointed to the University of Chicago faculty. "As a midwestern provincial, I had the obligation of going to the Big Town and taking it on," Bellow said many years later, invoking with retrospective bravado "the immemorial pattern of young hicks."

Only how to support himself? While Maurice and Samuel had continued to prosper, building vast real-estate empires, Bellow was still an indigent artist of the type that the big brothers in his books derided: impractical, dreamy, a philosopher-clown. What sustained him, he wrote many years later, looking back on this period in his life, was "my privilege, my painful freedom, to think and feel."

One of the few advantages of having no money—or one of the things that made it less humiliating—was that none of his friends had any money either. Living arrangements were casual, especially in the world of arts and letters. People lent one another apartments, offered one another spare rooms. There was nothing unusual about having a new address every three or four months or turning up unannounced in the hope of becoming a houseguest. In New York, the Bellows arrived on the doorstep of Arthur and Victoria Lidov. Lidov, another University of Chicago boy who had migrated to the East, earned a living as a commercial artist, doing illustrations for magazine advertisements and feature stories in *Life*. He had a studio on Pineapple Street in Brooklyn Heights, a few steps from Fulton Street and the Brooklyn Bridge. Lidov was a big, powerful man with an ample stomach and a full beard— "kind, large, oracular," as Alfred Kazin, a later tenant of Lidov, remembered him. "He went in for explanations in a deep, deep voice, a voice that seemed to rumble cosmic theories from the storm center of his belly." The walls of his fifth-floor walk-up were covered with his oil paintings of sensuous Jewish nudes and concentration-camp victims with baleful black eyes. The Lidovs were on their way to a farmhouse they had rented in Patterson, New York. On an impulse, they invited the Bellows to join them, rent free.

It was a happy arrangement—for a time. Lidov painted in the attic, and Bellow wrote in the living room. They imported their social life from the city. The Rosenfelds came up, and Alfred Kazin's sister Pearl, and David Bazelon. The Lidovs were so poor that whenever Arthur got paid by a magazine, Victoria drove the seventy miles to New York to pick up the check instead of waiting for it to arrive in the mail. Bellow contributed unsigned reviews to *The New York Times Book Review* and *The New Republic* and wrote readers' reports for Victor Weybright, who was starting up an American imprint of Penguin Books. He took the train in once a week, storing his manuscript in the freezer when Anita was away, in case the house burned down, and carried off a shopping bag full of books to evaluate. Weybright paid him five dollars for novels and ten dollars for nonfiction.

It wasn't long before the pleasures of communal living began to wear thin. What with the Lidovs' two cats and dog and the

Bellows' child—and one bathroom among them—the house felt crowded. In December, Bellow found another farmhouse in nearby Holmes. No sooner had they settled in than Anita and Gregory had to go back to Chicago; her brother was dying of cancer. "I'm holding down this eight-room house, a servitor to the pipes and heaters," Bellow reported to James Henle on January 12, 1946. "My nearest friends are ten miles away."

He was lonely for Anita, and eager for news of Gregory, addressing him as "Jemby" or "Hirsch," diminutive for Herschel, "a fine old Yiddish name." But domestic life wasn't Bellow's strong suit. Even when Anita was home, she had to chide him after he finished writing, "So it shouldn't be a total loss, why don't you take out the garbage?" As far as Bellow was concerned, he was keeping up a tradition. "There hasn't been an honest workingman on either side of the family as far back as can be known," he confessed to Henle. "Most of my forefathers were Talmudists. My maternal grandfather had twelve children and never worked a day in his life." Like the *talmid khokhem* of his distant shtetl past, wise men revered for their learning, he spent his days hunched over books.

In the New World as in the Old, learning conferred prestige, respect, and authority, but it didn't put supper on the table.* The only money coming in was from his occasional reviews, pronouncing on such ephemeral titles as *The Lonely Steeple* by Victor Wolfson and *The Journey Home* by Zelda Popkin, a stilted effort—in Bellow's crushing assessment—set on a train "rushing from Florida to New York through bright and dark, sun, mist and rain, the rhythm of wheels and rails sometimes matching the heartbeats of the passengers, but much more the ticking of Mrs. Popkin's Underwood."

He was also hoping for a Guggenheim, though he could scarcely be said to have exerted himself in preparing his application. Disdainful of any effort to get ahead in the literary world—a form of defensiveness—Bellow took literally the request for a "concise statement" of his project, describing it in its entirety as "a novel

---

*When the publisher John Lehmann made an offer on the British rights to *Dangling Man*, Bellow assumed rightly that the question of royalties would be "entirely an academic one." Not enough copies were sold to earn back the advance.

whose theme is guilt." Let the members of the Guggenheim Committee recognize his genius on their own; he wasn't going to help them out. Edmund Wilson submitted a mild endorsement, appending to a recommendation on behalf of the poet Randall Jarrell the scrawled afterthought that Bellow was also "a first-rate candidate," though "not so remarkable as Jarrell." Alfred Kazin gave more extensive testimony, calling Bellow "one of the most talented writers of our generation."

Once again, it wasn't to be. "I forgot to mention that I did not get the Guggenheim," Bellow informed Henle on April 12. "I must remain a struggling author for another year."

His sojourn in the country lasted too long. He was homesick for the Rosenfelds' fourth-floor apartment on Barrow Street—"a sort of Ellis Island" for Chicago intellectuals in the late 1940s, as Bellow described it in "Zetland," an unpublished novel based on the life of Isaac Rosenfeld that provides a vivid tableau of Greenwich Village literary life in those days. In New York, he wrote, they were "*naturalized.*" After the war was over, intellectuals put their Marxist era behind them and concentrated on their true passions: art, literature, what Philip Rahv liked to call the Big Ideas. "They were more concerned with Marx and Kierkegaard, with D. H. Lawrence and Baudelaire, than with Harry Truman and the Marshall Plan," Bellow noted of the fictional Elias Zetland and his cronies. Not that politics disappeared from the consciousness of the New York intellectuals; for the neoconservatives, their Marxism eventually gave way to anti-Marxism and a bitter struggle to discredit the ideology they had once embraced. But Bellow's association with this group was as tenuous as his association with the Hyde Park Trotskyites: He was essentially apolitical. It wasn't in his nature to join organizations. Like Ijah Brodsky, the quirky protagonist of his later story "Cousins," he did no marching.

Bellow would look back on the forties as an idyllic time, but the truth is that he never felt entirely comfortable with the Barrow Street crowd, whom he satirized remorselessly in his novel about Rosenfeld. The Hahn brothers, dissolute playboys who had inherited some real estate from their father and lived in picturesque squalor in a cold-water flat in the Village, were pitiless versions of two notorious local characters, William and Herbert Poster. A. Z. Crocker, "a very tough, hard-minded cripple" who had lost an arm playing in a railroad yard as a boy, was a distinctly recognizable—and devastating—portrait of the one-armed David Bazelon.

Bellow suspected—with some reason—that he was looked down on by this bunch. "He smarted from the notion that the Village hipsters thought he was square," said Bazelon—which he was; smoking "tea" and listening to bebop in a smoky jazz den weren't activities he found congenial. He had given up cigarettes in his twenties (though he liked to sit in the smoking car of trains, claiming the tobacco haze made him nostalgic); lately he had adopted a pipe instead, which he fancied made him look wise and mature.

He was more at home with the *Partisan Review* crowd that gathered at Philip Rahv's town house on West Tenth Street or William Phillips's apartment a block away. Rahv often summoned Bellow for private talks, holding forth on art and politics, Tolstoy and Trotsky, Kafka and Sartre in his rasping Ukrainian accent. In Bellow's unpublished novel, Rahv and Phillips appear as Ablove and Sharfer, coeditors of a left-wing literary journal very much like *Partisan Review.* Sharfer is timid, weak-willed, "overpsychoanalyzed"; Ablove is "ponderous, pale, Sam Johnson looking, radical-orthodox—as the Jews to God, so the proletarian to Marx, and as rabbis to small Russian synagogues, so Ablove to Village intellectuals."

Rahv *was* a dominating presence. Bearish and gravel voiced, with hooded Asiatic eyes—Delmore Schwartz called him Philip Slav behind his back—he was a penetrating critic, quick to crush a reputation if he thought it undeserved. Many a potential contributor to his magazine was dismissed with the terse verdict "He has no ideas." Mary McCarthy, who had created a scandal in the Village when she left Rahv for Edmund Wilson, later put him in her malicious novel, *The Oasis,* in the person of Will Taub, a Russian-born New York intellectual for whom the only reality was "the Movement, Bohemian women, the anti-movement, downtown bars, argument, discussion, subways, newsstands, the office." He regarded his contemporaries' efforts at fiction with lordly contempt. Bellow often told of being in the *Partisan Review* office on Astor Place one morning when the mail arrived. "Nothing came in," Rahv informed Phillips over the phone, "just fiction."

Whether one socialized *du côté de chez Rahv* or *du côté de chez Phillips,* as Schwartz used to say, an evening among these people carried an electric charge. One was likely to meet Clement Greenberg or Dwight Macdonald, who loved nothing more than a loud argument at a crowded party in a noisy, smoke-filled room. "They were not always friendly friends," Bellow recalled, "but they were always stimulating friends." Rosenfeld, a gentler soul than Bellow, found the contentious atmosphere hard to take. He said of an evening at Rahv's, "It was like throwing darts."

Bellow considered himself an inconspicuous member of this clan. Even after *Dangling Man* received highly respectful reviews, he remained deferential to his literary heroes, older men such as Rahv and Harold Rosenberg, Macdonald and Meyer Schapiro. To William Barrett, an editor of *Partisan Review* during the 1940s, Bellow was "the kid from Chicago, carrying a chip on his shoulder, and ready to show these Eastern slickers that he was just as street-smart (intellectually) as they were." He was invariably courteous and exerted a quietly civilizing influence on any gathering he attended, Barrett noted in his memoir, *The Truants*—a book whose subtitle, *Adventures Among the Intellectuals,* captures its ironic, rueful tone—"but the chip of self-confidence was there on his shoulder all the same." Bellow reminded Barrett of the Chicago welterweight Barney Ross, who had made his way to New York a few years earlier and beaten all the East Coast contenders.

First, though, he would have to deal with Isaac Rosenfeld. By the mid-forties, Rosenfeld had become a regular contributor to *Commentary, The New Republic,* and *The New Leader.* His novel, *Passage from Home,* about the troubled adolescence of a bookish Chicago boy, "sensitive as a burn," was published in 1946 and recognized instantly as an authentic and timely document; Daniel Bell praised it as "a parable of alienation."

Bellow had reservations about *Passage from Home;* he found it sentimental. But he was impressed by the way Rosenfeld had managed to make a name for himself in the New York literary world: "Isaac was the action." Bellow stood in Rosenfeld's shadow, like the narrator of his unpublished novel, "known in the Village only as a friend of the Zetlands."

Though they regarded themselves as literary brothers, in other ways the two Chicago Dostoyevskians were radically dissimilar. Bellow was fastidious, diffident, "reserved"—a word that crops up often in the recollections of people who knew him in those days. Rosenfeld was an incessant talker who found squalor and dirt invigorating; he once confided to Leslie Fiedler that he couldn't be attracted to a woman who didn't have a spot on her dress. Where Bellow hoarded his energies, concentrating with fierce attention on a task, Rosenfeld thrived on clamor. "Profligate with his being, his time, his thought," wrote Irving Howe in *A Margin of Hope*, "he lacked only that cunning economy that enables writers to sustain lengthy careers."

For all the tensions in their relationship, Bellow and Rosenfeld each depended on the other's opinion of his work. "I don't know how good it is until Isaac sees it," Bellow said. Rosenfeld read the drafts of his book reviews aloud to Bellow. But they were fiercely competitive. Bellow criticized his friend's "phony *gemütlichkeit*, the way he acted as if he was in a Dostoyevsky novel." Rosenfeld found Bellow similarly inauthentic. "Saul amazes me," he wrote in his journal:

> As a personality he is strong, sane, rational, spontaneous, lively, capable of fun, inventive, pliable. As a character he is weak, dependent, dull, blocked, incapable of fun or pleasure. It's a thorough split. The division occurs between ego-gratification, where he's thoroughly capable, and deeper gratifications, where he's lost.

By "deeper gratifications," Rosenfeld may well have been referring to Bellow's emotional distance from even his closest friends, his guardedness and resistance to intimacy. Or he might have been referring to sex. Rosenfeld regarded himself as something of a swinger, and boasted of his open marriage, while Bellow was secretive about his affairs; his rabbinical heritage was tenacious, surviving transatlantic migrations and generational change. Rosenfeld's journal entry offered a profound insight into Bellow's character: It perfectly captured his dual nature. The hedonistic (Joseph, in *Dangling Man*, confesses his "unwillingness to miss anything") and experience-hungry side of him was perpetually at war with his self-protective side, so bitter, distrustful, distant, and self-absorbed.

The spring of 1946 was another "gyre," as Bellow described his peregrinations, appropriating Yeats's term for the dialectic that spirals toward a transcendent sphere. In June, the Bellows, out of money again, returned to Chicago and moved back in with Anita's mother in Ravenswood—the neighborhood where, almost a decade before, the twenty-two-year-old Bellow had wandered beside the drainage canal after his morning's writing stint, fighting the impulse to howl like a dog. He was now "in a high state of excitement" about his work in progress, he wrote Henle, and had given it a new title: "The Victim."

By the end of the month, eager to see his friends and escape his stifling home life, he was back in New York. Leo Spiegel, a psychiatrist who was a friend of the Lidovs', lent the Bellows his apartment on West 113th Street for the summer. Weary of freelancing, Bellow was still looking for a job. Herbert McCloskey, an assistant professor of political science at the University of Minnesota who had met Bellow through Sam Freifeld, heard of Bellow's plight and managed to procure an invitation from the university's newly founded department of the humanities. The salary was $2,500—for Bellow, a considerable sum.

The University of Minnesota was a giant land-grant college with a rah-rah fraternity life and a flourishing agricultural school, but it also had a distinguished English department, a sort of northern outpost for gentlemen scholars—men such as Henry Nash Smith, Joseph Warren Beach, and Samuel Holt Monk, whose tripartite names certified their gentility. Beach, the chairman of the department, was a poet who had written books on Thomas Hardy and George Meredith; Smith, a Texan, specialized in Twain; Monk, Alabama born and Princeton educated, was the author of a book called *The Sublime*. Bellow was intimidated by these "well-bred WASPS," with their charming, acidic condescension, their moneyed airs, and their "Emersonian, gaunt New England" looks. They weren't above "unwitting" anti-Semitism, conceded Leonard Unger, a colleague of Bellow. Bellow and Unger, who grew up in a Yiddish-speaking home in Corona, New York, and described himself as a "Jewish Agrarian," became fast friends. In the corridors of the English department, the two young instructors unashamedly spoke Yiddish.

Bellow's main ally was Robert Penn Warren, who that fall was banging away at his typewriter on the top floor of the library, finishing up *All the King's Men*. He and Bellow often had lunch together at the Faculty Club, and Warren read "The Victim" in manuscript. A decade older than Bellow, Warren developed a protective attitude toward the younger writer and became a kind of father figure. When Bellow, driving the new DeSoto that Warren had purchased with his royalties, scraped the fender, Warren chided him gently. "It was a terrible crime, almost like original sin," Bellow recalled. "You don't do that to a brand-new car—put a long scratch on its shining fender. This thing attacked us right in the middle of our American Being."

Bellow set up shop on the top floor of Nicholson Hall, "where I have a desk in something that looks like the complaint department of Commonwealth Edison in Chicago," he reported to James Henle in October. He lived with Gregory and Anita in a Quonset hut on the ag-school campus, which wasn't much better. "We're in a kind of paper walled hutch that looks like something wasps make—I know that rabbits live in hutches, but this isn't a hive either. But hutch or hive, it has no running water and no dividing wall or partition." The only heat was from a kerosene stove. It was so cold Bellow was afraid he would develop arthritis. "I understand what Augustine meant when he said 'The devil has established his cities in the north,' " he complained to Warren.

That autumn, Bellow's father came up for a visit. The Bellows had no room for him in their Quonset hut, so he stayed with Herb and Mitzi McCloskey. Dignified in a suit and tie, Abram refused to eat in the McCloskeys' house because they didn't keep kosher, but he sat at the kitchen table drinking coffee and pouring out "a threnody of complaint." What was his son doing in Minneapolis? Why didn't he go into the family coal business, where he could make a good living? Why did he have to live this way? "He was heartbroken," Herb McCloskey recalled. "He really thought Saul was a failure."

Bellow was teaching advanced composition that term, which he likened to classes in manual training. But he was hard at work on his book and hoped to get it done by Christmas, if he could stay put: "This bounding from place to place, though it comes about through my own fault, exasperates me when I start to write. I feel like a man trying to sign his name in the last seat of a roller-coaster."

He had been brought to the University of Minnesota to teach courses in its humanities department that were modeled on the ambitious survey courses Robert Hutchins had instituted at the University of Chicago. Undergraduates were introduced to the touchstones of Western history and culture; they read *Candide, The Social Contract, War and Peace*—essentially, whatever their professors felt like reading. But grading freshman papers was a chore, and Bellow felt "enslaved" by teaching. One day, Joseph Warren Beach showed up in his classroom unannounced. Bellow was lecturing on *The Brothers Karamazov:* "I was terrified out of my wits, but I got through it somehow." Not long afterward, he was notified that he had been elevated to the rank of assistant professor, which came with a thousand-dollar raise.

By December, the Bellows had enough money saved to establish themselves in a comfortable gray-shingle house at 2225 Hillside Avenue in Saint Paul. There were parties at the Warrens' and Saturday-night get-togethers at the McCloskeys' in Dinkytown—a neighborhood of student hangouts, bookstores, and restaurants near the campus—where a diverse crowd gathered for popcorn and beer. Hubert Humphrey, who had been elected mayor of Minneapolis at the age of thirty-four, often showed up around midnight, after an evening of testimonial dinners and public appearances.

Bellow's legendary good looks had quickly attracted a following of young women on the Minnesota campus. When Anita was off with Gregory, visiting her family, girls would "climb the fire escape to get into his room," a friend recalled. "Saul went home at night, but Anita had him on a tight rope." Many of Bellow's friends discerned in the tense relationship between Joseph and Iva in *Dangling Man*, with its casual adultery, its flaring hostilities interspersed with moments of tenderness, a description of the Bellows' marriage. "I have had a great deal of trouble lately over Anita and several times in the last two months we have been on the verge of separating," Bellow confided to his old friend Oscar Tarcov:

> We have had quarrels which really originate not out of trivial things but out of the fact that in numerous ways we are thoroughly disagreeable to each other. And for another thing the principal reasons for marriage have no existence any longer. But I have been breaking myself in two to reconcile because I don't want another failure added to an already long list.

That winter, Bellow continued to put in five or six hours a day on "The Victim." He was a compulsive reviser, but with Bellow revision was less a matter of Flaubertian sentence polishing than one of rewriting the manuscript from start to finish—a process he went through on every book. On January 27, 1947, he sent Henle a "first draft"—which meant that he was just getting down to work.

Ten days later, he heard back from his publisher. It wasn't the enthusiastic response he'd expected. Among other things, Henle objected to two scenes involving a cafeteria kibitzer named Schlossberg, which struck him as "set-pieces." Bellow vigorously defended himself. Robert Penn Warren had read the manuscript and liked it, he stressed: "He predicts that it will sell widely." But he was clearly wounded by Henle's lack of enthusiasm. Responsibility for the novel's success rested in part with the publisher, he suggested. "And you have made no commitments or promises. Perhaps it is not businesslike for you to volunteer such things, but I have not guided myself by business standards in my relationship with you. You haven't mentioned that you have any particular plans for the book, and I wonder why that is."

Henle was more than a little annoyed. He scrawled in the margin of Bellow's letter, "This guy is just an author after all," and dashed off an irate reply. Vanguard had done all it could for *Dangling Man*, he maintained. No one had ever claimed that literature was a profitable enterprise. He was sorry Bellow had taken off his "philosopher's robe" and meddled in matters of commerce that he knew nothing about.

Bellow's response was conciliatory, but he was obviously aggrieved. "I've given a lot of thought to your letter," he replied on March 15:

> You say, "the better a book is, the less effect advertising has on its fortunes." It's of course true that some books can only be sold by plugging, like canned soup. But Dangling Man was well reviewed and didn't sell out its first edition. There must be a mean. I'll most respectfully hand over my robe when I write a book full of snares and bait, boudoirs and glitter. I'm not looking for the maximum. As I say, I may be upbraided for playing a double game and making my way smoother, or trying to, with assistant professorships, but it's not in order to be on the bestseller lists that I banish myself to Minnesota. And I've never asked for more than your assurance that you would do your damndest—as I do mine. But I have asked for that assurance and I think I was not unjustified.

He was still feverishly revising "The Victim" and "living on benzedrine tablets," Bellow confessed to Henle. He was convinced the novel was greatly improved but was "weary to the bone of it." Plans for the following year were up in the air, as usual. He wasn't sure if his contract at the University of Minnesota would be renewed, and his landlord had put their house on the market. "The Son of Man still hath no place for his head, and even the fox has lost his hole," Bellow wrote his publisher on May 13. Then, early in June, he was invited by the dean of the arts college to accompany a group of students to Spain. At least he had somewhere to go for the summer.

Accompanied by the McCloskeys and his charges from the university, Bellow sailed for Europe early in July. Anita and Gregory went off with her parents to a kosher resort in Wisconsin.

*My election to America and to Israel gives me my total identity,
the kind of identity which has never been permitted to survive
in all of Europe's history.*

—KARL SHAPIRO,
"The Jewish Writer and the English Literary Tradition"

T HE SHIP that Bellow and the McCloskeys boarded in New
York Harbor that summer of 1947 was no luxury liner but
a converted cargo ship named the *Marine Jumper* that had
seen hard use in the war. The passengers slept in narrow bunks,
twelve to a room, women and men separated. It was a slow and
stormy nine days across the Atlantic. Seasick a good deal of the
time, Bellow spent his days languishing queasily in a deck chair
reading the galleys of his novel. The task bored him so much that
he muttered about throwing them overboard.

Two years after the end of World War II, Europe was a ruin, its
cities bomb-ravaged, its citizens demoralized. The task of reconstruction had barely begun. But it was still the citadel of civilization. "The blasts of war had no sooner ended than thousands of
Americans packed their bags to go abroad," Bellow wrote many
years later, enumerating a Homeric catalog of the "poets, painters,
and philosophers" who thronged the European capitals, along
with "students of art history, cathedral lovers, refugees from the
South and the Midwest, ex-soldiers on the GI bill, sentimental
pilgrims . . . adventurers, black-marketeers, smugglers, would-be
bon vivants, bargain-hunters, bubbleheads—tens of thousands
crossed on old troop ships, seeking business opportunities or
sexual opportunities, or just for the hell of it." It was Bellow's first

trip overseas, and he invested it with powerful symbolism: Crossing the Atlantic by boat was a way of reliving the Belos' voyage to Halifax in 1913—"reversing his father's journey," as Mitzi McCloskey put it. In Bellow's mind, he was going home.

There were ten undergraduates—six men and four women—in the Student Project for Amity among Nations (SPAN), as Bellow's group was called officially. Most of the men had been in the war and were enrolled at Minnesota on the GI Bill. "They were hardly younger than I was," said Bellow. (The women in SPAN, he complained, were "dogs.") From Le Havre, they made their way to Paris, where the students were put up in a hotel on the Left Bank; Bellow stayed with Harold Kaplan ("Kappy"), a member of the old Hyde Park gang who had arrived in Paris just after the war to serve as an advisor to the newly founded UNESCO.

In mid-July, Bellow and his charges boarded a train for Madrid. It was a long journey, and they had to sit up for two nights in a filthy passenger car. One member of the group was left on the platform in Paris; two others lost their baggage. "He is having his troubles," Anita reported to Henle of Bellow on July 23. "He sounds rather lonely and depressed."

Madrid was decrepit, soiled, faintly ominous; the city was still visibly suffering from the effects of the Spanish civil war. Government buildings were pocked with bullet holes. "The trolleys were vintage 1900—Toonerville trolleys," Bellow recalled. On the boat from America, he had met Francisco García Lorca, a professor of Spanish literature at Columbia and the younger brother of the great Spanish poet Federico García Lorca, who had been murdered by the fascists; García Lorca introduced him to a circle of writers that gathered in a café near Bellow's pension in the Puerta del Sol; its members included the Basque novelist Pío Baroja y Nessi, the literary journalist Jimenez Caballero, and various members of the anti-Franco underground. Bellow was impressed by the high standard of living the Spanish intelligentsia enjoyed. "The poets own Fiats and eat ten courses at dinner," he wrote to Sam Freifeld. Another favorite hangout was Horchers, an elegant wood-paneled restaurant where the German community congregated. Among the regulars were Edouardo Fortsch, a journalist who had covered the civil war; the son of the Prussian chancellor Bernhard von Bülow; and a blond, buxom girl who had been the secretary of the head of the Spanish secret police. Bellow credited her with "keeping his acne down," a coy way of confessing that they were having an affair—evidently, he believed the schoolboy myth that masturbation was a primary cause of that adolescent affliction.

Bellow's responsibilities were light. His group met once a week in a café; otherwise, he was on his own. He was homesick for his family but exhilarated by the proximity of European intellectuals. The gilt-mirrored, high-ceilinged café where they held court was a world away from Isaac Rosenfeld's Barrow Street salon with its Salvation Army decor. To "a trivial instructor from Minnesota," as Bellow humbly characterized himself, Europe was every bit as exotic as he'd imagined it to be from his avid reading of nineteenth-century classics.

He adapted quickly to being in foreign countries. He was gifted at languages—his Yiddish was flawless, he could get by in French, and he had picked up Spanish during his summer in Mexico. Spain felt "ancestral" to him. "People had Tolstoyan-style households, with a feudal servant class. Even their gestures, the way they smoked, reminded me of my father. And the heavy white table linen was like the table linen my parents had brought over from Saint Petersburg."

A typical American intellectual of his generation, Bellow was familiar with the political map of Spain before he ever crossed its borders. The Spanish civil war had been a significant issue for the Left; the struggle against Franco embodied the general resistance to fascism, just as the internal struggle between the Communists and the Trotskyites in Spain during the early 1930s had foreshadowed many intellectuals' eventual disaffection with the movement. It was a war, moreover, that writers had witnessed firsthand: Dos Passos and Hemingway had gone to report on it; George Orwell had been on the front lines; Chicago boys whom Bellow knew had joined the Abraham Lincoln Brigade.

Now, a decade later, with Franco still in power, Spain was a virtual police state. In a "Spanish Letter" for *Partisan Review,* Bellow noted the ubiquitous presence of the Guardia Civil, "the gray-uniformed police with the red eagle on their sleeves and rifles hanging on their backs" and their "wooden-looking, shiny, circular hats." Passports were examined closely on the Irún–Madrid express; passengers had their luggage searched.

There were still pockets of Republican resistance. In August, Bellow accompanied an acquaintance from the American embassy to Alcalá de Henares, the birthplace of Cervantes, to attend a political trial. The defendants were ten tramway employees who had been arrested for distributing the communist newspaper *Mundo Obrero*. They were tried by a tribunal of army officers in a courtroom lined with soldiers from the national guard. The trial was a mockery of justice: Signed confessions were read out and confirmed perfunctorily by the accused, each of whom was then sentenced to between four and twelve years in jail. In his "Spanish Letter," Bellow gave a terse account of the proceedings:

> The trial is over and we file down under the guns with the silent relatives. I see the grieving face of a boy on the stairs and I talk to him. His father is one of those who received four years. Will he be allowed to see him? He does not know; since the arrest he had not seen him till this morning. He is now the eldest at home. There was an older brother, but he disappeared in the last days of the war. He has another brother of eight and two sisters. "How do you live?" I ask; he does not reply.

Late in July, leaving his students behind in Madrid, Bellow took a jaunt to Segovia, known for its Roman aqueduct and famous *alcázar* (royal castle). Like the American scholar Clarence Feiler in his story "The Gonzaga Manuscripts," Bellow was moved by "the ancient mountain slopes worn as if by the struggles of Jacob with the angel, the spires, the dry glistening of the atmosphere, the hermit places in green hideaways, the sheep-bells' clunk, the cistern water dropping, while beams came as straight as harp wires from the sun."

A few weeks later, he was on the road again, this time headed south. His companion was Robert Johnson, a genial Minnesota farm boy who had been in Bellow's humanities class. During the last part of their sojourn in Spain, Bellow and Johnson sublet an apartment together in Madrid, on the Plaza de Independencia.

Their train out of Madrid was a converted boxcar with holes cut in the sides for windows. The first stop was the ancient city of

Granada, where the Moorish kings had built their magnificent palaces. Arriving late, the two travelers went sight-seeing without delay, clambering over the locked gate of the Palacio del General-ife, the palace of the last Moorish dynasty in Spain. "It was eerie," Johnson recalled. "We were all alone in the light of a full moon. It looked exactly as it must have looked in 1492, untouched by the ravages of time."

Bellow felt comfortable with Johnson, a self-styled "pagan" who claimed the only commandment he'd never broken was the one that forbade worshiping a graven image. He was, to employ Bellow's own term, a "soul mate." Soul mates had to be men, but they didn't have to be Jewish; they just had to possess what he considered Jewish qualities: emotional intensity, a reverence for Russian literature, a love of high-minded gossip. Robert Johnson was "a goy with a *yiddische kopf* [a Jewish head]," as he described himself. "To the Sancho Panza of our Spanish summer," Bellow later inscribed a copy of his second novel that he gave to Johnson. In Johnson's recollection of that summer, "Saul tilted at windmills, and I came along."

While Bellow was in Spain, Anita, back from her sojourn in Wisconsin, sweated out a hot summer in Chicago with her family, proofreading more galleys of *The Victim* and attending to the details of publication. Greg missed his father, she wrote Henle, and she worried about Bellow's safety, especially after she read about a gas explosion that killed hundreds of people in Cadiz while he was on his way there: "I go on thinking he is all right as we are fortunate people and I am hoping our luck will hold out this time."

When Bellow returned to New York on September 23, Anita met him at the dock. She looked well and had lost weight, but it was a "troubled" reunion, according to Mitzi McCloskey. Anita was angry that Bellow had gone off and left her alone for three months with a small child. Bellow hinted that he was beginning to develop an ulcer. On the voyage home, he had voiced doubts about his marriage, complaining to the McCloskeys that he had never experienced true passion (though he did manage a shipboard romance with a nineteen-year-old undergraduate from the University of Wisconsin); he felt "deadened and burdened" by domestic life.

Anita was too practical, too controlling; she didn't give him room to breathe. Someday he would be "claimed" by a woman who appreciated him, Bellow vowed to Mitzi McCloskey, "and I will go." The passive construction was significant. For Bellow, choosing a lover meant allowing himself to be chosen. It was the same way that he "chose" jobs and domiciles and wives: He waited for someone else to make the first move. In his work, Bellow asserted himself with courage and tenacity, but when it came to domestic arrangements, others dictated the terms—until he chafed at them. *Saul does what he wants:* The phrase recurs among his friends and associates. Pretending to be at the mercy of others was a way of disguising his fiercely independent will. By denying responsibility for the choices he made in life, he could circumvent the powerful forces—father, brothers, society—ranged against his ambition. Passivity in Bellow's hands was an instrument of freedom.

At the end of September, the Bellows were back in Minneapolis, installed in a large old house at 58 Orlin Avenue in Prospect Park, a pleasant residential neighborhood near the campus. "They lived very comfortably," said Robert Hivnor, a young playwright who was teaching freshman English; but they were still short of cash. To make ends meet, they had two boarders, Bart Lieber and Ed McGehee, who taught at the university. It wasn't always a placid arrangement; Bellow resented McGehee for taking Anita's side when they fought.

The trip to Spain had taken a toll. Bellow was so exhausted—not from an ulcer, it turned out, but from a stubborn virus—that his doctor put him on "compulsory rest." He was allowed to teach his writing seminar but was otherwise out of commission. He had tried to put on weight in New York, treating himself to a week of "gluttony," but it was largely a patriotic gesture, he joked to Robert Penn Warren: "No doubt there was an ideological reason for eating so much—we may not be strong in Phoenician ruins but we *do* have steamed clams."

The Victim was due out on November 6, 1947. Bellow received his first copy that week. He thought it was "extraordinarily handsome," especially the jacket. "You've outdone yourselves with it," he wrote excitedly to Henle (though he felt the author's photograph had "a kind of 'sing sad songs' look" about it): "I only hope it's received as handsomely as it's presented. It should be; it's good, honest, solid work, but the world's so mad!"

Solid work it was. "I labored and tried to make *The Victim* letter-perfect," Bellow testified, claiming to have "accepted a Flaubertian standard." Like its predecessor, *The Victim* was a quiet book, though it had more of a plot: An ordinary New Yorker named Asa Leventhal, a subeditor on a trade journal, is bullied and harassed by Kirby Allbee, a man he barely knows who is obsessed by an imaginary grievance. In fact, the novel is less Flaubertian than Kafkaesque. The main characters are allegorical, indistinct; the novel's few events unfold with hallucinatory intensity. Allbee shows up uninvited at Leventhal's apartment; follows him to a crowded park, where he confronts him on a bench; doggedly rings his buzzer and hounds him at all hours of the night; and persuades Leventhal to put him up after he's evicted from his boardinghouse. The more Leventhal acquiesces, the more importunate Allbee becomes. Arriving home to find his door chained, Leventhal breaks it down and discovers Allbee in his bed with a woman. In a final, climactic outrage, the aggressive intruder puts his head in the oven in Leventhal's kitchen and turns on the gas.*

At the heart of the novel is a conflict between anti-Semite and Jew. Allbee claims to be an heir of Governor Winthrop and readily identifies Leventhal as a Jew from "Russia, Poland . . . I can see at

---

*The parallels between *The Victim* and Dostoyevsky's novella *The Eternal Husband* are inescapable. Bellow made no secret of the fact that he had been influenced by *The Eternal Husband* but denied that his borrowing of the plot was conscious—it was typical of him to both acknowledge and deny his sources, as if asserting that no deliberate agency had been involved somehow meant that he was not being derivative. In this case, however, the borrowing seemed overt. Alexey Velchaninov, like Leventhal, is haunted by a double, Trusotsky, who tries to corrupt him. Both books feature the appearance of a dreamlike figure who comes to the door on a hot summer night in the city. And there are other striking congruences: Trusotsky, like Allbee, is a widower still in mourning for his wife; in both novels, a young child dies; and both culminate in a violent struggle between the hero and his oppressor, followed by a reconciliation. Only when Leventhal and Velchaninov come to recognize their affinities with their doubles and experience their sufferings firsthand are they finally liberated from the shadows of the obtrusive others.

a glance." New York is "a very Jewish city," Allbee complains. "You know yourself how many Jewish dishes there are in the cafeterias, how much of the stage—how many Jewish comedians and jokes, and stores, and so on, and Jews in public life, and so on. You know that. It's no revelation." But Leventhal also feels imaginary persecution, fretting that his Italian mother-in-law resents him because "a Jew, a man of wrong blood, of bad blood, had given her daughter two children."

Bellow was troubled by his failure to address the Holocaust directly and often spoke of it as a significant omission in his work. "I couldn't tear myself away from my American life," he confessed. In *The Victim*, published just two years after the war had ended, the Holocaust is mentioned only once—when Leventhal, protesting Allbee's specious characterization of "the Jewish point of view," bursts out, "Millions of us have been killed. What about that?" Yet the novel is suffused with a consciousness of that unprecedented crime. In a dream, Leventhal sees himself in a crowded railroad station, with a loudspeaker blaring and guards pushing people into the trains—a nightmarish scenario that instantly summons up the Nazi transports of Jews to the death camps. And Allbee's halfhearted attempt to kill himself—and Leventhal—by turning on the gas in Leventhal's kitchen is a symbolic enactment (through suicide rather than murder) of the Final Solution.

Bellow had learned about this new dimension of evil in the way that many Americans had: by watching newsreel footage of the liberated concentration camps, showing American bulldozers pushing corpses toward a ditch. The experience filled him with "a deeply troubling sense of disgrace and human demotion," he noted later, compounded by a humiliating ambivalence, "as if by such afflictions the Jews had lost the respect of the rest of humankind and as if they might now be regarded as hopeless victims incapable of honorable self-defense, and arising from this probably the common instinctive revulsion or loathing of the extremities of suffering, a sense of personal contamination and aversion."

Indeed, one of the key motifs of *The Victim* is Leventhal's passivity. He permits Allbee to shadow him, to move in with him, even to appropriate his bed. "You keep your spirit under lock and key," Allbee chides him. There is something dutiful about Leventhal, a perplexity before the world confirmed in the book's final scene, in which he encounters Allbee in the lobby of a theater. Allbee is in the company of a well-known actress and has obviously pulled himself together; he confides to Leventhal that he's come to terms with "whoever runs things." As he heads back to his seat, Leventhal calls after him, "Wait a minute, what's your idea of who runs things?" But he never gets an answer. Whoever it is, Bellow means to suggest, it isn't the Leventhals of this world; it isn't the Jews. Written while Bellow was ensconced in a WASP English department, *The Victim* is troublingly ambivalent about its hero's Jewishness; Leventhal's acquiescent behavior in the face of Allbee's aggression suggests not defiance but self-hatred.

Implicit in the novel's portrait of Jewish passivity is the question of whether Jews collaborated in their own annihilation. In 1949, the editors of *Commentary* invited a number of Jewish writers, including Bellow, to respond to an essay by Leslie Fiedler, "What Can We Do about Fagin?" that had run in its May issue. It was an obvious choice of literary protagonist around which to organize a discussion of anti-Semitism—Fagin is the unscrupulous Jewish crook in Dickens's *Oliver Twist*, a figure, like Shylock, that represents Jews at their worst. The replies appeared in a two-part symposium entitled "The Jewish Writer and the English Literary Tradition." How could these writers reconcile their allegiances to "the Anglo-American literary tradition" with the presence in that tradition of "The Jew," a figure depicted with distaste and even malice in the works of Marlowe and Shakespeare, T. S. Eliot and Ezra Pound, Thomas Wolfe and Henry Adams? For Bellow, the Holocaust gave the lie to culture (a word he put in quotation marks) as a civilizing force: Many of its most admired ornaments had dishonored humanity by perpetuating the coexistence—even the collusion—of barbarism and high art. The tradition for which they stood was diminished by the enormity of the crime it had tacitly sanctioned. The Holocaust invalidated their authority.

Bellow later disparaged *The Victim* as a "victim" novel—a well-mannered, "repressive" book that reflected his upbringing as a child of Jewish immigrant parents. "I was still learning, establishing my credentials, proving that a young man from Chicago had a right to claim the world's attention," he explained, "so I was

restrained, controlled, demonstrating that I could write 'good' "—
which didn't mean writing Jewish. Bellow was adept at capturing
the subtle tonalities and cadences of Jewish speech, but he was
after something deeper. In a crucial passage, the Yiddish journalist
Schlossberg delivers himself of an eloquent soliloquy that goes to
the heart of the matter. To ignore the human condition, Schlossberg maintains, is to be less than human, while to think oneself
above it is to be inhuman in a different way: "If a human life is a
great thing to me, it *is* a great thing. Do you know better? I'm entitled as much as you. And why be measly. Do you have to be? Is
somebody holding you by the neck? Have dignity, you understand
me? Choose dignity. Nobody knows enough to turn it down."

For an earlier generation of Jewish-American writers, " 'Jewish'
equalled ghetto," as Alfred Kazin trenchantly put it. For Bellow, it
was both a limiting identity and a source of inspiration. "It is a
fact of your life," he once told an interviewer: "That's how I view
my own Jewishness. That's where the great power of it comes
from. It doesn't come from the fact that I studied the *Talmud*, or
anything of that sort. I never belonged to an orthodox congregation. It simply comes from the fact that at a most susceptible time
of my life I was wholly Jewish. That's a gift, a piece of good
fortune with which one doesn't quarrel." Yet once he had achieved
great fame and become the object of a flourishing academic industry, Bellow strenuously repudiated the notion that he was a
"Jewish" writer. He was "an American, a Jew, a writer by trade"—
a triadic identity that echoed (perhaps unconsciously, given its
author's views) Eliot's celebrated definition of himself as a royalist
in politics, an Anglo-Catholic in religion, and a traditionalist in
literature. (Many years later, when a reporter asked him if he had
won the Nobel Prize as a Jewish writer or as an American writer,
Bellow replied tartly, "I believe I won it as a writer.") In putting his
Jewishness second—he once gave a talk called "Americans Who
Are Also Jews"—Bellow laid claim to a larger, less provincial
public. It wasn't the Talmud he had read in the public library as a
boy, he often said: It was the classics of Western literature. His
mandate, as he defined it, was "to write about American life, and
to do with Chicago or Manhattan or Minneapolis what Arnold
Bennett had done with the Five Towns or H. G. Wells with
London." And to do it, he might have added, in the American

language—even if he had to make it up himself. *The Victim*, Martin Greenberg declared in a prescient review in *Commentary*, was "the first attempt in American literature to consider Jewishness not in its singularity, not as constitutive of a special world of experience, but as a quality that informs all of modern life, as the quality of modernity itself." It was through Bellow's efforts that Jewish literature was to become American.

Bellow was grateful for Vanguard's efforts to push the book, but he tried to be realistic about its prospects. "I'd like to make it clear to you that I understand perfectly well that the sale of a book depends on a great many imponderables and that I don't expect to make bales out of The Victim and as a matter of fact don't want to make bales," he assured Henle in mid-November, stating what he thought he had accomplished and where he had failed:

> I fully realize that many people will be alienated by the theme and will find the characters disagreeable. People who liked the Dangling Man because of its writing will be disappointed in The Victim. In writing it I deliberately renounced "style" and sought for transparency because I think the distinction between poetry and fiction has, from Flaubert to Virginia Woolf, been greatly weakened to the detriment of both and of fiction particularly. So I will have to write a few more books before people begin to see what I was after in The Victim.

It was a remarkably objective assessment of the book's strengths and weaknesses. If *The Victim* was overly somber and lacked stylistic verve, it possessed a strong authorial voice. Like *Dangling Man*, it managed to incorporate the techniques of modernist fiction—a near absence of plot, an introspective hero, a calculated disruption of narrative—without surrendering its originality. Working within the tradition of the European novel, it appropriated that tradition to the American vernacular and made something new.

The critics were beginning to register this fact. Robert Penn Warren, who had admired *The Victim* in manuscript, supplied Vanguard with a quote praising Bellow as "a vivid, compelling, and serious writer, destined to occupy an important position among the novelists of our time and place." Alfred Kazin found the book "amazing in its completely authentic and *personal* recreation of Dostoyevsky." *The Victim* was "one of the few really distinguished books published by an American of my generation," he wrote the Guggenheim Committee, to which Bellow had once again applied for a fellowship—his third try.

The reviews were mostly favorable. Diana Trilling, in her column for *The Nation*, reversed her low opinion of Bellow. *Dangling Man* had been too "small" for her, but *The Victim* she pronounced "hard to match, in recent fiction, for brilliance, skill and originality." Elizabeth Hardwick concurred, predicting in *Partisan Review* that "it would be hard to think of any young writer who has a better chance than Bellow to become the redeeming novelist of the period." Charles Poore, the daily reviewer for *The New York Times*, also seemed to like the book, though he managed to get to the end of his eight hundred words without once mentioning that Leventhal was Jewish; as far as Poore was concerned, *The Victim* was about "a lonely and complex man" who allows himself to be tormented by an annoying bully. The book's message? "You can never be finally rid of the Kirby Allbees of this world." The review in *Time* was equally obtuse, displaying the magazine's prep-school anti-Semitism in a lead that described the book as "a competent little story about a solemn and touchy Jew accused by a fantastic Gentile of having ruined him." (Two weeks later, *Time* praised the novel in its annual roundup as "the year's most intelligent study of the Jew in U.S. society.")

Bellow was disappointed but stoic. The reviews had been "singularly stupid," he complained to Henle. No one had understood the meaning of Allbee's reconciliation with Leventhal. "The last chapter was, I thought, obvious enough. Its entire meaning is contained in Allbee's 'I owe you something.' Allbee means that he was aware that Leventhal recognized his humanity at a time when no one else was willing to." But Bellow had his own doubts about the novel. *The Victim* was too harsh, he wrote Alfred Kazin, "the result of an incomplete assimilation of suffering and cruelty and an underdevelopment of the elements that make for harmony. I sense them but I don't see them as plainly as the others and haven't mastered them as elements of fiction." And to Henle he confessed that *The Victim* had fallen short. "I don't myself think that the execution of the novel is equal to the scale of its conception," he admitted. "I do however draw satisfaction from my first real success with character and feel I have completed one of the difficult stages of my apprenticeship." At the very least, he felt the book gave him the right, as he put it, to "hang out his shingle."

Bellow was vigilant about the progress of his book, urging his publisher to send out review copies and complaining that it hadn't been properly distributed in bookstores around the University of Chicago: "In '44 a lion in Hyde Park, in '47 a nonentity." Ever expedient in matters of literary politics, he regretted an outspoken essay he'd written for *The New Leader:* "I picked on Lionel Trilling, among others, and was a little abashed at my roughness when I saw that Mrs. T. had decided to take a milder line with me in the *Nation.*"

One thing was clear: *The Victim* wasn't about to alter his financial situation. He still needed regular employment. For the moment, his position at Minnesota was secure. He had taken over Robert Penn Warren's seminar in creative writing while Warren was on sabbatical, and he was also teaching the basic humanities course. But he didn't have his heart in it. As a teacher, Bellow was "a clock-watcher," according to Herb McCloskey. He wasn't one to nurture talent. "Just look on me as your friendly barber," he told one of his students. "I'll lather you, but you have to shave yourself."

In the end, his second book was a mild critical success and a commercial failure. Bellow vacillated between ironic acceptance of its fate—"I don't suppose the sales of *The Victim* will shoot up because *Commentary* reviewed it well," he observed wryly—and grandiosity: "Is there much of a chance for the Pulitzer Prize?" he inquired. "I'd feel foolish getting it when writers like Faulkner, Jim Farrell etc. have never made the grade." But he was brought down to earth again by the sales figures. *The Victim* sold 2,257 copies— only about 700 more than *Dangling Man.* "Dear Jim," he wrote to Henle on February 9, 1948:

> Surely you don't mean that the total sales of the book come to 2000! Why, you wrote last November that it had an advance-sale of 2300. Is the two thousand you speak of in addition to the advance-sale? That would be little enough for a novel that has been reviewed like mine. And if you mean that the *total* sale is

2000 I hardly know what to say after two years of wringing to pay bills and fighting for scraps of time in which to do my writing. Have I nothing to look forward to but two years of the same sort and a sale of barely two thousand for the next novel I write? And can it be worth your while to continue publishing books which sell only two thousand copies? I don't understand this at all; I feel black and bitter about it, simply.

Henle tried to placate his anguished author, but Bellow was inconsolable. "I never expected things to be easy," he replied, "but neither did I expect such a sharp disappointment." A week later, he wrote again, appending an epigraph from *The Duchess of Malfi*: "Miserable age, where the only reward / of doing well is the doing of it." The blame, as Bellow saw it, putting himself in the familiar "victim" role, lay with his publisher, who had failed to push the book. "Well, these are rough days," he signed off. "All I need now, and I shall probably get it, is a third rejection from the Guggenheim."

Henle was loyal to his authors and especially to Bellow. He had taken him on when no one else would; he had commended him to the Guggenheim Committee as "the most gifted, the most intelligent and the most sincere" young writer he had come across in years; in an internal memo circulated to his staff after the publication of *Dangling Man*, he had stressed that Vanguard "should do everything possible to keep Mr. Bellow happy—for he is a writer of distinction & we shd. feel proud to publish his books." But like many independent publishers who put up their own money, Henle was also tight. He had advanced Bellow five hundred dollars for *The Victim* and kept close accounts; when all the sales figures were in, he noted duly, Bellow owed him $170. It was Henle's fixed belief that there was no money in literature. Bellow's accountant agreed: Apprised of his client's debit on the novel, he recommended going into another line of work.

It was too late for that. "I never thought about doing anything else," he said later. "What else could I have done?" Writing had chosen him. He was already ten thousand words into a short novel about a diver, tentatively entitled "Who Breathes Overhead," an echo of Schiller's line, "Who breathes overhead in the rose-tinted light may be glad." He was also planning two other "novelettes."

The first, inspired by Luke 16:8—"The children of this world are in their generation wiser than the children of light"—was entitled "The Children of Darkness"; its subject was "the theology of this world." The second was based on the life of Croesus, not as a historical figure but as "an ex-man-of-property." A "devaluation of man" had occurred over the last two centuries, Bellow explained to the Guggenheim Committee in his proposal, writing at great length this time since brevity had failed him the last. The hero as a human category had become obsolete. Croesus was obsessed with greatness, "and I am interested in considering a condition of mind in which the idea of greatness is acceptable."

There was something almost touchingly naïve about Bellow's somber meditation on greatness; it was as if he had to prove to himself that the material wealth accumulated by Croesus (could he have been thinking of his rich brothers?) wasn't the only measure of achievement. On the other hand—just in case it was—mass society had made it all the more difficult for the artist, with his idiosyncratic and highly individual vision, to prevail. Bellow was never entirely sure of himself when he ventured into the realm of ideas; he tended to cloak his true concerns in a stilted, metaphorical language that put distance between his subject and himself. It was only in fiction and in the explicitly autobiographical prose he turned to increasingly in later years that he could get his experience onto the page, dramatizing the sense of marginality that haunted him rather than groping to give a ponderous historical explanation for it.

The most intriguing of the several projects Bellow described to the committee (under the heading "Plans for Work") was called "A Young Eccentric," the protagonist of which had two salient characteristics: "First, it is temperamentally necessary for him to create excitement and complications about himself. Secondly, he cannot bear to succeed but must always, after incredible stratagems, *almost* succeed." The fanciful plot contained an element that had been in short supply in Bellow's work: humor.

> The book begins with his returning, vaguely in disgrace, from a trip to Central America the reason for which is never made definite. . . . He gives what amounts to a lecture at a gathering on "Themes in History" and at the same time tries to promote a

scheme for buying coffee *fincas* in Guatemala. He borrows money to buy clothes he does not need, makes advances to other men's wives, proposes marriage to several girls at the same time and antagonizes the people whose support for his projects he has endlessly maneuvred to win. He "falls in love" with a young woman, becomes her invalid-mother's confidant and is soon managing all the affairs of the family. After courting the young woman for several months, he asks her younger sister to marry him and is rejected.

My conception of the protagonist of this comedy is that he resists definition; he cannot endure to be committed, to see an end to his possibilities, and in this he is thoroughly modern and thoroughly American.

"A Young Eccentric," like the two novelettes, was never written, but it prefigured the major themes of Bellow's work—and life. He, too, delivered high-minded lectures on the modern world and dabbled in improbable investments. He borrowed money from his brothers. He made advances to other men's girlfriends and on occasion to their wives; and he proposed marriage with unnatural frequency. He craved affection from those he antagonized. As for the young woman with whom the eccentric "falls in love," the quotation marks suggest Bellow's skeptical attitude toward that experience. For Bellow, falling in love was a make-believe event, not something that actually happened in the real world.

But it's not only the circumstantial similarities that are striking: The provocative formulation of a protagonist who "cannot endure to be committed" is a concise statement of Bellow's major theme, played out in book after book. The swagger of Augie ("First to knock, first admitted"), the cry of Henderson (*"I want, I want, I want!"*), the tempestuous confrontations of Charlie Citrine with lawyers, wives, and lovers, all offer variations on it. They point to a still deeper theme: Bellow's impulse to stir up trouble and create impediments—in short, his masochism, a trait he readily identified in himself. "A Young Eccentric" was Bellow's confession, a sketch for the autobiography he never wrote.

On April 1, 1948, Henry Allen Moe, the director of the Guggenheim Foundation, informed Bellow that he had been appointed to a fellowship. The stipend was $2,500. Two days later, Bellow acknowledged the award with a brief letter of thanks that contained a notable slip: He dated the letter April 3, 1943—the year he'd first applied.

Three weeks later, Henle learned from "an unimpeachable source" that Frank Taylor, an editor at Random House, was courting Bellow.

His source was accurate. Taylor *had* approached Bellow. So had Monroe Engel, an editor at Viking. Vanguard had an option on his next novel, but at the end of April Bellow asked Henle to release him from his contract. "It isn't easy to make this request," he wrote contritely. "I know I won't have another publisher I can like personally as much as you or one whose judgment I respect half as much as I respect yours. But I've come to the conclusion that I'm not the kind of writer that Vanguard can do much for." He was determined not to resume teaching when his Guggenheim expired, and he needed more money than Henle could offer.

In a follow-up letter, Bellow enumerated his grievances. To begin with, there was the letter in which Henle had reproved Bellow for seeking assurances that his publisher was committed to the book. Then there was the lack of aggressive marketing; in Chicago, Bellow's hometown, *The Victim* wasn't to be found in the stores. And finally, there was the matter of money: If Truman Capote could hit it big (*Other Voices, Other Rooms* had just come out), why couldn't he? "I know it is unpleasant to receive such letters," Bellow summed up his position, "but it's better for me to speak out than, like Job, to sin not with my lips when I am angry. You know, after four years, that I am not a prima donna and do not cast longing eyes upon the golden ladders and the big money. It's only that it galls me to go on teaching when I have as full a right as anyone in America to devote myself to writing." Demonstrating his Houdini-like ability to get out of any situation that demanded taking responsibility for his actions, Bellow managed to transform himself from the abandoner to the abandoned, preparing to forsake a publisher who had steadfastly supported him at the beginning of his career while depicting himself as the one cast out.

Henle was livid. "When you write that you are not the kind of writer that Vanguard can do much for, you imply that another publisher will be able to do more for you. That is quite possible; on the other hand, what is not possible but certain is that some publishers (and their handymen) will promise a great deal more than Vanguard. It will be interesting to see what they accomplish; much, of course, will depend upon the nature of your next book." Then he graciously released Bellow from his obligation.

Two months later, after visiting several publishers in New York, Bellow signed a contract with Viking for a new novel; its tentative title was "The Crab and the Butterfly." The advance this time was for three thousand dollars—a very substantial improvement over what he had gotten from Henle. To Frank Taylor at Random House, Bellow offered an explanation of his decision to go with Viking that was notable for its comically passive and convoluted syntax. He had "found things so working themselves out," he explained, "as to convince me that I had no other alternative. It was all like radar acting on my instructions." Viking had claimed him (in this instance with the help of radio waves), and he had gone.

"Henle and I have broken off as of last week," Bellow wrote Alfred Kazin on July 17: "He bungled both books awfully."

The Bellows decided to spend the Guggenheim year in Paris. "I'd still prefer a Jamaica-like place," Bellow wrote Frank Taylor, "but Anita has a severer travel-bug and won't be happy till she's crossed the Atlantic." Once again, he implied, someone else was calling the shots—in this case, his wife.

Bellow obtained a leave from the university and booked passage on the French Line's *deGrasse*. On September 15, 1948, the family set sail from New York.

8

But who could complain of this pert, pretty Paris when it revolved like
a merry-go-round—the gold bridge-horses, the Greek Tuileries heroes
and stone beauties, the overloaded Opéra, the racy show windows
and dapper colors, the maypole obelisk, the all-colors ice-cream,
the gaudy package of the world.

—SAUL BELLOW, *The Adventures of Augie March*

T HE PARIS to which Bellow brought his family in the fall of
1948 was frayed around the edges but, despite the ravages
of the Occupation, still a classically beautiful city—a
"great machine for stimulating the nerves and sharpening the
senses," as Malcolm Cowley had described it in *Exile's Return*, his
memoir of Paris literary life between the wars.

Bellow claimed to scorn the city's glamorous literary past. "I
was not going to sit at the feet of Gertrude Stein," he declared with
characteristic contempt for any legend not of his own making. "I
had no notions about the Ritz bar. I would not be boxing with
Ezra Pound, as Hemingway had done, nor writing in bistros while
waiters brought oysters and wine." To Bellow, Hemingway was
"the quintessential tourist," an American who had convinced himself that he was a European. The Jazz Age was a myth. The Paris
that Bellow admired was the Paris of its indigenous nineteenth-
century chroniclers, "of Zola's drunkards and prostitutes, of
Baudelaire's beggars and the children of the poor whose pets were
sewer rats." He had been moved by the Parisian settings of Rilke's
Notebooks of Malte Laurids Brigge, with their melancholy evocations of the streets around the Pantheon, the Pont-Neuf, and the
bookstalls on the Seine. Rilke, moreover, had written about Paris
as an outsider—Bellow's favorite vantage.

Postwar Paris was a cultural mecca—"the Holy Place of our time," in Harold Rosenberg's uncharacteristically worshipful phrase—for the thousands of American poets, painters, and free-lance intellectuals who repeated the pilgrimage that members of an earlier generation had made after the First World War. Many of them were eager to determine for themselves whether Paris remained the capital of modernism. "I was prepared to take part in the great revival when and if it began," Bellow wrote in "My Paris," a memoir of the city as he'd known it in those years.

He was disappointed. Paris in 1948 was "a sullen, grumbling, drizzling city." Bread was being rationed; coal was scarce. The weather was oppressive. "The city lay under perpetual fog and the smoke could not rise and flowed in the streets in brown and gray currents. An unnatural smell emanated from the Seine."

Bellow's letters home were almost defiantly antiromantic. "If it weren't for an occasional fusillade of French under the window or at the back of the house, I'd be able to imagine, without the least trouble, that I was in Minneapolis, except that Minneapolis houses are much better heated," he complained to Monroe Engel, his editor at Viking, on October 25. The writer's life was much the same no matter where he was: "I don't get out very often now and when I think of it resent this voluntary encapsulation and damn writing as an occupation."

The Bellows' apartment was in a "fussy" building at 24 rue Marbeuf in the elegant eighth arrondissement, far from the bohemian precincts of Saint-Germain-des-Prés. Crammed with heavy Chippendale- and Empire-style antiques, the dark, cur-tained rooms resembled the "mouldy though fancied-up" flat that Augie March sublets on the Right Bank, with its "cat-house pictures, alabaster owls with electric eyes, books of Ouida and Marie Corelli in leather binding." His friend Harold Kaplan was mortified when Bellow made inquiries about how to dispose of the garbage. "In Paris you don't ask about garbage," he admonished the greenhorn.

When Bellow was intimidated, he went on the offensive. "Old cultures are impermeable and exclusive; none is more so than the French," he later wrote in the foreword to a translation of Dostoyevsky's *Winter Notes on Summer Impressions*, an account of the Russian novelist's grim sojourn in Paris. Bellow had found a French translation of the book, *Le Bourgeois de Paris,* in one of the stalls along the Seine and read it hungrily, noting with approval Dostoyevsky's almost hysterical resentment of the French bourgeoisie: "I too was a foreigner and a barbarian from a vast and backward land." Bellow collected anecdotes that confirmed the chauvinism of the French: the Parisian shopkeeper who told him, on a boiling hot day, *"La chaleur est plus brutale chez vous"* ("It's hotter in America"); the time he wandered into his landlord's flat without knocking, only to be admonished, *"La France n'est pas un pays conquis, M'sieu"* ("France is not an occupied country").

Bellow's landlords, a retired British racing-car driver and his French wife, exemplified smug superiority, thrusting upon their cowed tenants an inventory of everything in the apartment, from the dining-room furniture to the tin spoons in the kitchen drawer. When they found one of their precious *objets* broken, they took Bellow to court. *"Sortez les mains de vos poches,"* the magistrate rebuked him: *"Ce n'est pas Amerique"* ("Take your hands out of your pockets; this isn't America"). Bellow was found guilty and ordered to pay damages, but the court ordered the landlady to refund his money after she failed to supply receipts.

Bellow's resistance to the city's charm was characteristic of his nonjoining mentality. "We're here and still not Frenchified," he notified Sam Freifeld on a postcard of Notre-Dame, boasting that he was "more stubbornly barbarian than ever." He regarded with skepticism the Paris-infatuation of friends such as Julian Behrstock, for whom the City of Light was "the answer to a dream nurtured from [his] boyhood in Chicago." Behrstock settled in Paris for life and had a long career with UNESCO, leaving the Northwest Side far behind.

Harold Kaplan had also become a virtual Parisian. An officer in the United States Information Agency and busy with the Marshall Plan—"Ka-Plan Marshall," his friends called it—Kappy spoke impeccable French, wore French gloves, drove a French car. The son of a successful immigrant carpenter who "built a very sizable section of Newark, New Jersey," he had been a graduate student of French literature at the University of Chicago and was a writer of some distinction, at least among the *Partisan Review* crowd;

indeed, many in their circle considered Kappy more promising than Bellow. He was at work on a novel about Americans in Paris called "The Plenipotentiaries." But Kappy had acquired a taste for the great world in his wartime travels; like the debonair, jaded American correspondent in his book, he had become "the most Parisian of foreigners, the prototype and founding father of the American-of-Paris," equally at home in the drawing rooms of the Faubourg Saint-Germain and the hashish parlors of the Arab quarter. He even spoke of "*mon Paris.*"

Bellow refused to make himself over in this way. "I was not at all a Francophile, not at all the unfinished American prepared to submit myself to the great city in the hope that it would round me out or complete me." Paris was a culture shrine, he noted derisively in his foreword to *Winter Notes on Summer Impressions.* Europe seemed to him less a citadel of art than a battleground, the site of a destructive war that had laid waste cities and cost millions of lives in a frenzy of nihilism. (His uncle Louis Dworkin, a refugee from the pogroms who would likely have perished at the hands of Hitler, referred to Europe as "a cemetery.") Bellow found Céline's *Les beaux draps*—a collection of harangues "seething with Jew-hatred"—as emblematic a text as Proust's *À la recherche du temps perdu.*

But if the glamour of Paris between the wars had faded, there was still a lively artistic scene. Parties in Paris were "serious," according to Lionel Abel, who was installed in a sublet on the Left Bank. People attended them "with the hope, and maybe even the expectation, of having a shattering experience of some sort." Kappy and his wife, Celia, entertained lavishly in their top-floor apartment on the boulevard Montparnasse, above Matisse's studio. With its fine furnishings, piano, and staff of white-gloved servants, Kappy's atelier was *the* salon in the years just after the war. The huge living room was "crammed with people and very, very open," remembered Nadine Raoul-Duval, an elegant young Parisian who was working for *Rapport,* a publication under Kappy's direction at the USIA. "There was always a powerful energy in the room."

Raoul-Duval herself contributed to this energy. "A beautiful blonde Frenchwoman with a fantastic body," as a contemporary remembered her, she was only in her early twenties but had already played a notable role in the romantic life of the city's intellectual elite; she later married the novelist Roger Nimier. Kaplan was also involved with Raoul-Duval; but Kappy was *très marié*, as she put it. Bellow was apparently less *marié*, for he and Raoul-Duval were soon lovers, to the considerable annoyance of Kappy; Bellow even suggested to Raoul-Duval that they run off to Africa together. "He was very insistent," Raoul-Duval recalled, "and so attractive that I was strongly tempted to go." He never mentioned Anita.

One of the chief pleasures of French intellectual life was its international crowd. Soirées chez Kappy included Georges Bataille, Maurice Merleau-Ponty, and Albert Camus; émigrés such as Arthur Koestler and Czeslaw Milosz; Americans such as Saul Steinberg and James Baldwin. Stanley Geist and his wife, Eileen—the Gerald and Sara Murphy of their day—also entertained frequently at their flat on the rue de Verneuil. Geist, supported by a traveling fellowship from Harvard, had come to Paris to try his hand at "the G.A.N."—the Great American Novel—an ambition so common in those precincts as to warrant an acronym. The Geists were comfortably off, at least by their friends' standards; "they had money and they spent money and they lived well," according to the novelist Herbert Gold, a frequent guest. Other members of their group included the poets Francis Ponge and Allen Tate and anyone on the masthead of *Partisan Review* who happened to be in town.

There was a natural confluence of the New York and Paris literary worlds. Jean-Paul Sartre and Simone de Beauvoir had come to New York just after the war and been entertained by the editors of *Partisan Review;* in the spring of 1946, the magazine put out a special French issue largely edited by Kappy. The subtitle of Lionel Abel's book *The Intellectual Follies* was *A Memoir of the Literary Venture in New York and Paris*—the two poles of intellectual current in the forties.

Bellow was often at the Kaplans' and at the Geists', but he was dubious about the Parisian intellectuals he encountered there and contemptuous of their naïvely pro-Communist, anti-American line. "Simone de Beauvoir knew, as any educated Marxist knew, that America was in the death throes of the class struggle and that Russia and the eastern Communist countries represented the forces and hopes of man's liberation," remarked William Phillips, offering a sardonic paraphrase of her views. Sartre and de Beauvoir had lately discovered American literature—or their peculiar version of it. They admired John Steinbeck and Upton Sinclair for having exposed the miserable lives of the American working class. Camus had discovered Faulkner: "I love the dust and the heat," he declared with a typical Gallic flourish. Bellow had little patience for this patronizing fascination with America's tough side: "People like Sartre understood less about left-wing politics than I had in high school."

Bellow liked to wander over to the basement bar of the Pont-Royal and observe Sartre from a distance, but for the most part his Paris circle was confined to Americans. He might as well have been in Hyde Park. He saw a good deal of Lionel Abel, Mary McCarthy, and Herbert Gold, who was putting the finishing touches on his first novel, *Birth of a Hero*. Chicagoans Richard Wright and James T. Farrell hung out at the Café Flore or the Café Roquet on boulevard Saint-Germain. (Farrell, disappointed by the familiarity of the clientele, was heard to mutter, "I don't see any geniuses here.") One night, the Bellows met Truman Capote at Wright's apartment—"very tiny, blond & effeminate," Anita reported to the Tarcovs.

William Phillips and his wife, Edna, were in Paris on a Rockefeller grant in the fall of 1949 and dined with the Bellows nearly every night. On gray, wintry afternoons, Bellow played cards with another of his Chicago cronies, the painter Jesse Reichek, in a café on the rue du Bac. "The American's inevitable fate abroad, from Henry James to Henry Miller, seems to be chiefly to bear witness to his own countrymen," Kappy remarked in a "Letter from Paris." Toward the end of his stay, Bellow complained to Daniel Bell that he'd been in Paris for two years and had yet to be invited into a French home.

Mostly, Bellow wrote. Every morning, he retreated to a tiny room at the Hôtel de l'Académie on the rue des Saints-Pères and wrestled with his work in progress, "The Crab and the Butterfly," a grim manuscript that revolved around two invalids who lie in adjoining beds in a Chicago hospital and talk—or, rather, one of them talks and the other one listens. (It was as if his Parisian exile prompted memories of his childhood isolation in the hospital in Montreal.) Weyl, the talker, is a moody young man in the mold of Joseph and Leventhal, the heroes of Bellow's first two novels; he has been to Europe and disdains his small-town relatives. He's an intellectual, but one "at loose ends," as the critic Daniel Fuchs described him.

In the one chapter of the novel that survives, Weyl reveals a didactic philosophical bent. "We're more and more in the open of our natures, nearer and nearer to the original personal quality in people," he explains to his bedridden neighbor, Scampi, as he broods on the state of contemporary ethics. "That's bringing the fight pretty close to the bull, it's full of risks; and if we're murdered it will be because the original nature is murderous; if not, because there's something redeeming in the original thing and a reason for all the old talk about nobility." Philosophy, then and later, was one of the unfortunate legacies of Bellow's immersion in the University of Chicago Great Books culture. His heroes shared a penchant for belaboring ideas. They were the products of a provincial Chicago boy's effort to show that he wasn't provincial, that he was at home with the whole of Western thought; unconsciously, perhaps, they expressed an impulse to distance himself from his true and more painful material—a flight into abstraction.

At its best, the habitual philosophizing of Bellow's characters was a marvelous satirical tool. Moses Herzog's elaborate disquisitions on Romanticism and phenomenology, Charlie Citrine's meditations on death and the immortality of the soul, were meant to be funny, Bellow plaintively reminded critics who took him too seriously (though these speculative flights also provided a showcase for his erudition). At its worst, his theoretical bent got in the way of his natural ebullience and prevented him from saying what he wanted to say. This problem was particularly acute in *Dangling Man* and *The Victim*, his "M.A." and "Ph.D." novels, but it continued to afflict him as he plodded on with "The Crab and the Butterfly." "I was terribly depressed," he recalled. "I think I came close to having a nervous breakdown."

While Bellow was struggling with this intractable material—he referred to it as his "hospital novel"—another book kept surfacing in his head; it was "bothering the life" out of him, he confessed to

Julian Behrstock. "I had a room in Paris where I was working, and one day as I was going there after breakfast, a bright spring morning, I saw the water trickling down the street and sparkling as it trickled." The free-flowing rivulet triggered an epiphany: It was the form that Bellow had been searching for, the way to write his "other" book. One of the hallmarks of Bellow's mature style is its exuberance; the long, prolix sentences, the profusion of adjectives, the seemingly effortless (but clearly worked) cascade of prose in his distinctive American idiom unfurl in the later novels with the controlled rhythm of a highly sophisticated jazz riff. In the water flowing down a Paris street he found a visual analogue for his style.

Over the years, Bellow developed a fondness for this epiphany, which eventually took its place in his well-worn "batch of poems" (to borrow Herzog's phrase). But he'd clearly struck some new, rich vein. He had been working diligently, he reported to Monroe Engel on October 24, 1949:

> But then I read over carefully what I'd done and saw that the book I'd been rather confident of was not what I thought it was. I'd opened something new and, I think, infinitely better in the last part of it; the first was simply not of the same order and had to be raised or scrapped. I didn't have it in me at this time to attempt this, so I've dived into something else I had started. On this, I've for some reason been able to work much faster than I've ever been able to work before. I do one fairly long chapter a week, and I expect to have the length of a book in first draft by Christmas. By the length of a book, I mean something like 100,000 words, not by any means the full length of what I plan. In any case, the first chapter is coming out in PR presently (November, they tell me), and if you'd like to see more I can send you carbons.

The chapter appeared as promised, in the November 1949 issue; its title was "From the Life of Augie March."

In the room below Bellow's at the Hôtel de l'Académie lived a Russian-born Italian writer by the name of Andrea Caffi. A classic *luftmensch* (a person with no visible means of support; literally, an "air man"), Caffí was the very embodiment of the European intellectual émigré in Paris: knowledgeable about politics, immensely bookish, devoted to conversation. He lay in bed all day, reading and drinking coffee, entertained his friends in the hotel dining room, and walked the streets imagining what it would have been like to drop in for a chat with Diderot. The eighteenth century of Goethe, Johnson, and Voltaire had been the last civilized epoch, in Caffí's opinion. Caffí himself was somewhat Johnsonian. "He had a large but frail body," as Bellow described him, "an immense head of hair, feeble but severe-looking eyes, a small nervous laugh but a serious and learned mind."

Bellow showed Caffí the first chapter of his new book, and Caffí was impressed. "He's a real writer," Caffí told Lionel Abel. One day, when a member of the American crowd noted archly that Bellow wasn't getting much out of Paris, Caffí defended him, saying that it was "only natural" for him to be thinking about America most of the time: That was his subject.

Sometimes Bellow called the book a "memoir," sometimes "a speculative biography"—a fictional narrative based on fact. Many of the characters in what became *The Adventures of Augie March* are composites; some are faithful portraits of people Bellow had known on the Northwest Side. "Your Papa and a few other relations are very lively daily preoccupations of mine," he confessed to Sam Freifeld, preparing him for the full-scale treatment of the Freifeld clan that was to show up in the novel: "Personages *like* them appear in *Augie March*. You don't, and needn't look for yourself (the way I have of scrambling things). Someone else is in your place. Most ways you'll be pleased by this monument; it's an honorable one; and you know your pa was too rich to be held by oblivion."

Living abroad turned out to be liberating for Bellow, as it was for so many American writers, from Hemingway and Fitzgerald to James Jones and Richard Wright. By putting distance between himself and his past, he could see it freshly. Chicago provided him with a strong identity, much in the way that Canada had. Bellow's status as a foreigner, a permanent outsider, enlivened his art, providing him with a vantage from which to survey the New World that was at once unique and universal. "I am a Canadian, too, you know," writes Herzog, the eponymous hero of Bellow's most popular—and most explicitly autobiographical—novel, adding still another register to his creator's versatile demotic voice. Exposure to Canada's European-based culture had an advantage, for it meant that he underwent a more gradual process of assimilation than Jews who debarked at Ellis Island and found themselves plunged into the bewildering New World. As one student of his novels put it, "he tested the cold waters of the St. Lawrence before entering the American mainstream." But it was his Americanness that was to define him, his openness to experience—the determination to "make the record in my own way," as Augie March says, echoing Saint Matthew ("to him that knocketh it shall be opened"): "First to knock, first admitted."

Exile was too strong a word for Bellow's condition, but it was something related. "I merely meant that, abroad, one wants to feel abroad *from* a place," he wrote in the memoir of his Paris years, "for Europeans do have such home places, and if their friends do not support them there are other things that do, so that one doesn't have to look into one's own consciousness or memory for proof that existence isn't accidental." What Europeans took for granted—a sense of national identity, of place—Americans had to conjure up out of their own imaginations. Where there was no tradition, the writer had to invent one. For Bellow, it was necessity that galvanized his imagination; instead of fawning over Europe the way so many intellectuals of his generation did, finding in its literary artifacts and monuments a refuge from the poverty of their own literary heritage, he regarded European culture as an oppressively dominating institution—another bullying authority to resist. A resource, yes, but also a geographic and historical version of his brothers. The fact that he was forced to struggle with a society that he felt excluded him proved tonic.

William Barrett, always a sympathetic observer of Bellow, spent a day with him in Paris and came away impressed by the novelist's ability to focus on the task he'd set himself:

> For all the time that Bellow is tenaciously sifting the European experience he still seems to have his feet firmly planted back in Chicago. With his big sensitive eyes he strikes me as half Hebrew dreamer, the other half being a solid Jewish business man, and yet the whole person is also the midwestern American who tells

me that every moment more he exists in Europe the more American he feels.

Writing the new book excited Bellow. "I had a wild time with the first half of *Augie*," he recalled. "I was stirred to the depths." At last he had found his own voice. Writing longhand in small, lined notebooks, he scribbled every morning for hours, rarely crossing out a word: "The book just came to me. All I had to do was be there with buckets to catch it." He was so confident of his progress that he consigned "The Crab and the Butterfly" to the fate that had earlier befallen "The Very Dark Trees": He destroyed it.

Outwardly, Bellow led the life of a "*bon bourgeois,*" as he described it; there was a full-time maid to care for Greg, and the Bellows even had a poodle named Malou. "We live like kings," Anita boasted to the Tarcovs. Bellow was repelled by the messy bohemianism that was supposedly a requirement of the writer's life. Once, walking down the boulevard Saint-Germain with Greg, he ran into Arthur Koestler, who radiated the world-weary cosmopolitanism of an eastern European intellectual; he was "all-knowing, slightly jaded, skeptical," in the recollection of William Phillips. "Is this *your* child?" Koestler asked Bellow in alarm. "You're married? And you've come to *Paris?*" Domestic life was thought to stifle the artist; it was middle-class. "To be modern," as Bellow glossed this encounter, "meant to be detached from tradition, traditional sentiments, from national politics and the family."

Yet while Bellow resented it when others prescribed an irregular life as one of the preconditions of creativity, domesticity did not come easily to him. He needed to keep a certain distance from his family. He was "used to having a room off to one side," he reminded Monroe Engel. His room at the Hôtel de l'Académie was distinctly off to the side—"the kind of room people get who are having problems in their marriage," as Herbert Gold bitchily described it. After his typewriter was stolen from the room, Bellow found lodgings at 33 rue Vaneau, a quiet street near the Invalides. His landlady, the French wife of a Swedish sea captain, had once owned a bookshop; she gave Bellow back issues of *Le Rire* to burn in the fireplace.

It was no secret to Anita that there were other women in Bellow's life, and the fact that his infidelities were public knowledge only made matters worse. At one point, after a big blowup, Bellow appeared on Herbert Gold's doorstep and announced that he was on his way to Spain. He was "totally frantic," Gold recalled, enraged and stifled by his wife; he had to get out of town, he claimed, and had commandeered Julian Behrstock's beat-up old car, a Deux Chevaux, for the purpose. Gold and his wife, Edith, agreed to go along for the ride. By the time they got to Banyuls-sur-Mer, a village near the Spanish border, "we were panting for breath, practically hyperventilating" from Bellow's pressured monologue about his disintegrating marriage and the pain Anita had inflicted on him. "We were totally worn-out." They found a hotel, and the Golds settled down at a table on the terrace to recover from their ordeal. A few minutes later, Bellow emerged, still damp from the shower, looking refreshed and ready for dinner. "He had an incredibly involving way of restoring himself by drawing you into his chaos, dragging you down, as if he was transferring the anxiety to someone else," said Gold. "There were times when he seemed almost suicidal. I'd stand with him at the window, feeling I had to hold him to prevent him from throwing himself out. Then all of a sudden he'd be fine."

Bellow gave a somewhat different account of their journey. In his version, recounted in a letter to Oscar Tarcov, it was Gold who talked incessantly:

> He went on for a thousand kilometers about his early days, his Papa, and his Mama and his favorite games and his school activities. He was much too young to reminisce at such length. As he was telling us how fond he was of graham crackers which had lain all night under the seat of the porch swing—just that overnight touch of mildew made them delectable—I stopped him. I told him he had tired me out so that I'd need two solid days of sleep—forty-eight hours of solid oblivion alone could heal me.

In Edith Gold's recollection, they *both* talked: "He was in great spirits. We had a lot of fun." Bellow made no reference to his argument with Anita, explaining obliquely that he "had to get away."

The *Rashomon*-like discrepancies in their recollections are humbling to a biographer.

One of the causes of the Bellows' marital unrest was the college student Bellow had taken up with on the boat home from Spain in the fall of 1947, a girl named Betty. She wrote to him care of American Express under an assumed name—M. Bacalao, Spanish for *codfish*. (Bellow had in mind a line of García Lorca's: "*Ya te veo, bacalao, dunque nienes disfragado*"—"Now I see you, codfish, under your disguise.") Their fling had turned into something more: Betty had made a clandestine visit to Bellow in Minneapolis, staying with the McCloskeys, and had seen him again in New York just before the Bellows sailed for France. Apparently, she expected more of a commitment than he could deliver. "I've had the feeling all along, and have it now, that though I've always kept clear of promises and commitments, that these appear in the air surrounding us," he wrote with his usual evasiveness (the promises and commitments appeared "in the air," as agentless as the radar-induced decision to change publishers):

> As they have a way of doing—a kind of chemistry in the soul where hopes are in the mixture. And I feel it isn't good enough to be "legally" fair but one must be fair where the most complex and subtle things happen. As for my writing now that is because I neither forgot you nor want to be forgotten—but remembered *en quelque sorte* [in a way]. If the memory has on your side changed its character so much the better for you.

It was a typical letter from a married man to a girlfriend, gently equivocating but with the clear signal that the relationship had no future. "We're not awfully good at thinking and had better put our trust more in feeling," the writer advised his mistress, taking the opportunity to remind her, in true *philosophe* fashion, that feeling "is a kind of thought too, and what we call reasoning doesn't take place without it."

Bellow was hoping to "slip over to London," he wrote his English publisher John Lehmann in the fall of 1949, "but *en ménage* it isn't easy to slip." Just before Christmas, he made a brief trip

across the Channel, *sans ménage*, in the company of William and
Edna Phillips; Cyril Connolly, the editor of *Horizon*, threw a party
in their honor. It was a lavish and crowded affair, with more than
one hundred members of the London literary establishment
present, among them Stephen Spender and the novelist Henry
Green; but Bellow felt "patronized," he complained to Lehmann,
insisting that Connolly had "cut" him. It was a doubtful scenario,
probably reflective of Bellow's brittleness and hypersensitivity,
traits easily aggravated by what he perceived as the haughtiness of
the English. On the other hand, William Phillips was equally
befuddled by the Brits: "I couldn't understand what they were
saying."

To Robert Hivnor, his colleague at the University of Minnesota,
Bellow gave an account of his first social encounter with the
English that shed more light on his own lack of social sophistica-
tion than on English manners:

> I wish I had stayed in a temperance hotel and with the temper-
> ate. Although I don't judge the inverted with harshness still it is
> rather difficult to go to London thinking of Dickens and Hardy
> to say nothing of Milton and Marx and land in the midst of
> fairies. My publisher is one; all the guests at his cocktail party
> were ones. All the Horizon people with the single exception of a
> man who suffered from satyriasis, likewise, at this cocktail
> party. This single exception was chasing Sonia Brownell, who
> didn't appear to have a husband on the point of death. [Her
> husband, George Orwell, died a few weeks later.] It was
> confounding.

Bellow was confused by and hostile to "inverts," as he referred
to homosexuals; they were "America's chief export to Europe," he
quipped maliciously. In England and France, they were an integral
part of the culture; back home, they were still regarded—by the
Partisan Review crowd, at any rate—as decadent and distasteful
curiosities. It was a stubborn prejudice—Truman Capote and
Gore Vidal were among Bellow's least favorite writers—but one
that he yielded up selectively: Half a century later, he would count
as his closest friend the homosexual Allan Bloom. As with other
of Bellow's prejudices, exception could always be made for the
particular case.

The nomadic Bellows had moved again, to 24 rue de Verneuil, in the heart of the Latin Quarter. It was a productive time for Bellow. He was excited about "Augie" and also turning out short stories. Working both ends of the literary market, he sold a story to John Lehmann's anthology, *Penguin New Writing,* and another, called "Dora," to *Harper's Bazaar,* which described it in "The Editor's Guest Book" as Bellow's "first short story to be presented to a wide audience." The story Lehmann bought, "The Thoughts of Sergeant George Flavin," was a brief monologue by a Chicago police officer in the tough-guy idiom of Ben Hecht and Nelson Algren. Subtitled "(On His Way to a Retreat for Catholic Men of the Chicago Police Force)," the story was aggressively knowing about ward politics, tavern payoffs, cops on the take, and sordid aldermanic scandals. But it had a strained feel to it, as if Bellow was working up material that didn't belong to him. Policeman or no, George Flavin was another intellectual, musing on the fragility of the social order and the isolation of the individual:

> There is something everybody knows: that just as you breathe, you breathe for yourself, and as your heart beats, good or bad, it beats for yourself; you never get around that. But we ain't that reliable, to let every man do how he figures, by fits and starts, he can, but have to be kept in line. And the ones with bad natures, no better than animals, kept from hurting the next guy.

"Dora," a long-winded monologue by a middle-aged dress-maker, suffered from the same inauthentic tone. Modeled after a baby-sitter who had once worked for Bellow's friends Leo and Nancy Spiegel, Dora chatters on about whatever comes into her head—her employers, her insomnia, the famous people she's worked for. (The baby-sitter had once been a dresser for Ethel Merman.) Her main obsession is the man next door, who has had a stroke: "When I heard the fall something told me it was out of the ordinary. He didn't just stumble and fall but dropped with his whole weight. My heart turned sick and it felt like a sponge." These excursions into the minds of such unlikely characters were significant, if only for what they revealed about Bellow's literary direction; he was clearly groping toward a voice capable of registering both his mental states and the intonations of his native speech—a voice of his own.

Two other stories, "Address by Gooley MacDowell to the Hasbeens Club of Chicago" and "A Sermon by Doctor Pep," date from this period. They were also monologues, but the speakers were more erudite—precursors of the brainy, garrulous protagonists whose meditations on existence would occupy prominent places in Bellow's later books. Gooley MacDowell and Doctor Pep derive from the orators Bellow had listened to at lunchtime in the park across the street from the Newberry Library during the Depression. A Chicago autodidact, Gooley MacDowell is an early incarnation of Herzog: He read the Haldeman-Julius Blue Books as a boy, put in long hours in the reading room of the Crerar Library on Randolph ("our homespun Bodleian"), boned up on Saint Augustine, Pascal, and Goethe. His manic, oddball rhetoric reads like Sir Thomas Browne: "Look at us, deafened, hampered, obstructed, impeded, impaired, and bowel-glutted with wise counsel and good precept." An agnostic who believes in the existence of the soul, he's cynical about humanity yet in love with "the life of thought."

Dr. Pep is another superfluous man who spends his days in Bughouse Square. Pale from a winter of arduous study in the Newberry Library, he's as ostentatiously allusive as Gooley MacDowell, invoking the Carthaginians and Canaanites, Acheron and Curtius, on behalf of his queer theories about mental and physical health. Like his imaginary mentor, Dr. Julius Widig, a self-proclaimed anarchist and the author of *Reefer Rosie, The Tragedy of a Girl Bum*, Pep is an optimist who believes in "embracing everything with infinite desire." He delivers his Whitmanian credo with a slangy verve that was new for Bellow:

> Yes, I feel the drum-bumps of the species in me. . . . I partake of everything in my own flesh; I strum on Venusberg and float in the swamp. I do a one-leg schottische along Clark Street and buff the friendly public with my belly. I stroll in the zoo with my colleagues and ponder the throat-digging nails of the lynx and the pillars of the elephant; I sit in the Newberry and compassionate with the tender girls who have never felt anything

warmer than a washcloth upon them. And I feel that I and all
these creatures and persons are images of spirit, icons, symbols,
versions and formations.

The prose was hectic, perhaps, and labored to achieve its strutting
effect, but it was copious and expressive, far from the "proper"
style of *Dangling Man* and *The Victim*. And it vividly displayed
the polar opposites contained in Bellow's own character: the cynical, "depressive" side, mired in abstraction, and the "peppy" side,
as exemplified by the succession of garrulous, high-spirited, life-
hungry protagonists who came to populate his books—Augie,
Henderson, Charlie Citrine, the belligerent but energetic Dean
Corde of *The Dean's December*. Dr. Pep also manifested another
trait that was soon to emerge in full cry: the monologue. The
brainy character who talks and talks and talks, brilliantly, digres-
sively, with a comic mix of high-flown erudition and vaudeville
brio—a character who is virtually always alone, entertaining
himself with the rhythm of his own thoughts—was to become one
of Bellow's trademarks. In these two stories can be heard the voice
that eventually came to be identified by the adjective *Bellovian*.

That winter, Bellow submitted the first few chapters of his work
in progress to Monroe Engel, who responded with temperate
enthusiasm. Bellow was clearly on to something, Engel assured
him, but could he sustain its "undifferentiated intensity" for the
duration of a book? "You almost had to read that chapter [in
Partisan Review] holding your breath." Bellow had similar
doubts. "I'm having such an enthusiastic labor with it that it
hadn't occurred to me—in my daily stump-bombings—how a
reader might feel about risking limbs in the clearing."
    He had also shown the book to the Guggenheim Committee,
applying for a renewal of his fellowship. But he wasn't optimistic
about his chances, and early in 1950 he confided to his agent,
Henry Volkening, that he was contemplating a return to America.
Paris was expensive; Anita had gotten a job with the Joint Distri-
bution Committee, a Jewish relocation agency that arranged for
the placement of children orphaned by the war, but they were still

struggling to make ends meet: "I'd have to go to work for Unesco or something like that if we wanted to stay."

In the meantime, he had resigned from the University of Minnesota—it was against the university's policy to grant a second year of leave—and he let his friends know that he was looking for another teaching job. What he really needed was "a shack wherein to finish the book," he wrote Alfred Kazin:

> After it's done, I'd as lief work in a factory as remain in what are called intellectual milieux—my heart's abhorrence, they're coming to be. Wherever there are people who still *desire* something, even if they are after false gods. Perhaps you know a kind industrialist who would give a writer still in fair physical condition a job in a cannery or mattress factory. I'm not joking.

It was a brave, idealistic statement, though in truth he hadn't fared well in menial jobs; his stints in his family's coal companies had ended disastrously. For all the contempt he bestowed on "intellectual milieux," they were to provide him shelter for the rest of his life.

It wasn't just a lack of money that made Bellow eager to head home: He was tired of Paris. "It's rather interesting that people don't believe Balzac, Flaubert and Stendhal when they write of French life and of Paris," he groused to Kazin on January 28, 1950:

> They prefer to trust Henry James, or Henry Miller or even Van Vechten and all that happy American throng that lived around the Montagne Ste. Genevieve. But if Stendhal were alive today, he might very conceivably choose to live in Washington DC—considering what has become of his beloved Milan. And of this I am sure: that he would do as I do with his copy of Les Temps Modernes, that is, scan the latest *sottises*, observe with brutal contempt the newest wrinkle in anguish and then feed Simone's articles on sex to the cat to cure her of her heat and give the remainder to little G. to cut dollies from; he can't read yet and lives happily in nature.

The main problem with Paris was the Parisians: They didn't seem to know who Saul Bellow was. At parties, Bellow talked about his book in a "heavy-handed" way, recalled a fellow expatriate, and vacillated between grandiosity and self-doubt. He was unaware that in Parisian literary circles to discuss one's work was considered gauche.

He had reason to be excited about his new book: It represented a significant breakthrough. It was his expectation that his friends share his excitement that caused trouble. When Harold Kaplan failed to show sufficient enthusiasm for a new chapter, Bellow accused him of not really liking it. "I was supposed to jump up and down and cry *Eureka!*" His touchiness was more pronounced than ever. "I don't think Mr. Moe [the director of the Guggenheim Foundation] cares much for me," he complained to Monroe Engel, offering no evidence for his suspicion. And to Kazin, who intimated that some members of their circle had been surprised by his disenchantment with Paris, Bellow retorted angrily, "A little list of disloyal people who are astonished at my wanting to come back to America will be just the thing, just the thing." *Disloyal:* It was a curiously regal adjective for a young, unemployed writer from Chicago whose first two books combined had sold fewer than four thousand copies.

"My prophetic heart has stolen all the bases," Bellow informed Engel on March 26: "I didn't get a Guggenheim, for reasons best understood somewhere else. I shall have to make do without, but energetically, and I suppose one can't expect to have first lick, always, at fortune's spoon." He was resigned to going back to New York and enlisted Engel to help him find an apartment, "large and cheap." He was even willing to live in Queens— "Isaac's neck of the woods." (The Rosenfelds, cramped on Barrow Street with two young children, had moved to a house in Saint Albans.) He couldn't pay more than eighty dollars a month, he instructed Engel, but he needed only four rooms. "I'd get myself a fifth in another part of town"—a room off to one side.

In the meantime, he was sending along one hundred thousand words of "Augie." He would await Engel's response, "a little uneasily," at Schloss Leopoldskron in Salzburg, where he and Anita were spending a month; he had agreed to give a series of lectures at the Salzburg Seminar in American Studies. His only stipulation was "a crow's nest somewhere, inaccessible, wherein to finish my *boulot*."

Schloss Leopoldskron was a baroque Alpine castle, with a grand marble staircase and cherub-painted ceilings, that had belonged to the theatrical producer Max Reinhardt before he was forced to flee the Nazis; it had originally been the home of Mozart's patron and chief tormentor, the archbishop of Salzburg, and later became well known as the castle where *The Sound of Music* was filmed. The rooms looked out upon a lake on which white swans floated. Beyond the castle rose the snowcapped peaks of Berchtesgaden.

Founded by a group of ambitious Harvard graduate students just after the war to foster amity between the United States and Europe, the Salzburg Seminar has often been described as an "intellectual Marshall Plan." Among the writers and scholars who visited were Kazin, F. O. Matthiessen, and Margaret Mead. In *New York Jew,* Kazin provided a vivid picture of Schloss Leopoldskron: "There was a hole in the roof from a misplaced American bomb, portraits of the detestable Archbishop, porcelain stoves in the bedrooms, three Australians, the great Italian scholar Mario Praz, an ex-Luftwaffe pilot, young Frenchmen from the Maquis, an Austrian Socialist who had fought Franco."

Bellow wasn't thrilled about lecturing, he wrote Ted Hoffman, the program's director. "I think discussions are more effective, and I've had considerable experience at Minnesota at whipping them up, even in large classes." He proposed a seminar with the title "American Fiction from Dreiser to the Present." His reading list included e. e. cummings's *The Enormous Room,* Dreiser's *Jennie Gerhardt,* Sherwood Anderson's *Winesburg, Ohio,* Faulkner's "The Bear," and "perhaps also Fitzgerald's *Babylon Revisited* and *The Last Tycoon.*" He was inclined to omit Hemingway "because he's discussed to tatters, but if pressed may bang away at *The Sun Also Rises.*"

Toward the end of his Salzburg sojourn, Bellow heard from Monroe Engel about "Augie March." "My first response is one of great excitement," Engel declared. "My God, Saul, the excitement moves across each line without a break, and what it must be for you to know that excitement that every serious writer knows in the act of writing." Bellow had found his own voice, in Engel's estimate—"it is always peculiarly yours, never derivative, unrealized, or merely literary." At the same time, Engel noted firmly but with editorial tact the book's defects: The abundant detail, he suggested, "operates to some extent against the novel, serving to bury it"; the book lacked "shape, centering, a sense of continuity through plot emphasis, not sensibility and intelligence alone."

Engel had put his finger on a fairly serious problem—one Bellow himself acknowledged. "In *Augie March* I discovered rhetoric, but I didn't have it under control," he conceded years later. "There was something delirious about the writing. It overran its borders." But the escape from formal restraints proved so exhilarating that he was reluctant to curb his newly effulgent muse. He was having too much fun.

He responded from Schloss Leopoldskron the same day.

I'm very pleased, very happy, about your response. While I didn't exactly take the Guggenheim rejection as literary criticism—how can such an organization *criticize*—I couldn't help, nevertheless, feeling uneasy . . . on the side where my judgments sometimes fail me, the helpless side. But then there's the stronger side, and there I knew that the course I'd been following for a long time was at last producing results, that I'd put my hand strongly to a good thing and was beginning to make it resound. Or, putting it another way, I believe I'm beginning to make some real excavations. I'm delighted that you agree. Ad n[auseam]. I've notified you that you were going to see the raw mass. You hear that far too often, I'm sure. And I must say that although I have some kind of instinctive sense of what the finished thing will be, I've never had such a mass to knead and shape either, and I don't know how I'll fare with it. The abundance gives me confidence, however, and wherever that and the life, the feeling of the book are connected there'll be no pruning. But I haven't read over what I've done, consecutively. When I do, I may very well share your objections. My own figure for the shape of the book is that of a widening spiral that begins in the parish, ghetto, slum, and spreads into the greater world, and there Augie comes to the fore because of the multiplication of people around him and the greater difficulty of experience. In childhood one naturally lives as an observer. And it may be that

Augie doesn't sufficiently come forward at first; but in my eyes, the general plan of the book, its length, justified this. . . .

Another two hundred pages, and the design will be almost entirely visible; and there will be *still* more, with sections on the war and the life of a black-marketer in Europe and a final, tragic one, on the life of the greatest Machiavellian of them all, Augie's brother Simon. Sometimes I'm not sure that Augie will bear so much traffic, and again think that he *must* bear it, be sent through the bitterest of contemporary experience if my purpose is to have its real test. In any case, publishing a first volume would give me a breather in which to mature the sequel.

Bellow's ability to shake off doubt, whether his own or others', showed both courage and obliviousness; he had a self-preserving impulse to accept in himself what he could not—or had no wish to—change. *Augie* may have been "too effusive and uncritical," as he later admitted; "but it [did] reflect one side of my character." For Bellow, the hunger for approval was outweighed by an even deeper hunger to express himself on his own unique and unnegotiable terms. Like Augie, he would go at things as he had taught himself, freestyle, making the record in his own way.

After brief stops in Venice and Florence, the Bellows continued on to Rome. Bellow's battered briefcase grew fatter with manuscript by the day. "Augie March" "increases & multiplies," he told friends with a biblical flourish. His morning routine was to claim a table at the Casino Valadier in the Borghese Gardens, overlooking the city from the Pincian Rock, light a cigar, and scribble for several hours in his notebook. (He was pleased to learn from a reference in Eckermann's *Conversations with Goethe* that the poet had also written in the Borghese Gardens.)

They stayed in Rome six weeks. Bellow was a "slow-saturationist," he explained to Robert Hivnor; he didn't feel he'd really been in a place until he'd absorbed it in his pores. (He had passed through once, but only for a few days.) He got to know Elsa Morante and Alberto Moravia and the "gentle, sad, and most silent" Ignazio Silone; he immersed himself in Italian culture. "This time I *saw* Rome," he declared, writing to Hivnor from the Pensione Vittoria in Positano, where the Bellows spent part of the summer. Rome was less intimidating than Paris; the crowded streets, the traffic, dirt, and noise reminded him of Chicago.

Positano, a gorgeous fishing village nestled in the cliffs of the Amalfi coast, was idyllic. Bellow worked each day from eight until noon, then went for a swim in the sparkling azure bay, followed by a "lethal lunch" of pasta and wine. He longed for "a more bracing life," he insisted to Hivnor. He was "beginning to think kindly of N.Y. where I can be gay with the Philosophy of History, fearing naught."

His plans for the fall were still up in the air, but he'd made up his mind: Europe wasn't for him. He enumerated his reasons to Sam Freifeld:

> Well, one doesn't form intimacies here, and I have a strong societal sense. The French are not the people to encourage intimacy. The Italians, yes; or, apparently, but you come to a place with them beyond which you cannot go, possibly because they don't for themselves go beyond it either. On the other hand, you may say, "Who wants your stinking intimacy anyhow?" and "stand off, you & your intimacy,"—with some justice. But then one is surrounded by signs of the great mutuality of this past, great *relation*, and wants to get off his egocycle & go home to see what he can do.

In part, his bellicose tone was a defensive response to the rejections, real and imagined, that he'd suffered at the hands of the Europeans with whom he'd come in contact during his two-year sojourn—combined with the envy that Americans can feel when they compare their own atomized, traditionless society with that of Europe, a civilization saturated with history. In part it was the expression of a wish to claim his independence by returning to a culture where, as he could now appreciate, he genuinely belonged.

Only the Bellows had nowhere to live. His best hope for a job was at New York University, where Ralph Ross, chairman of the humanities program, had recruited an impressive faculty that included Allen Tate and Isaac Rosenfeld. Henry Volkening had made it known to Ross that Bellow was looking for a position, and Ross was favorably disposed. The one obstacle was Rosenfeld. As Bellow's star rose, Rosenfeld's had begun to wane, not a good prognosis for friendship. Rosenfeld was having trouble with "The Enemy," a didactic, labored allegory that was turned down by publishers all over New York. When Rosenfeld admitted to Bellow that his book had been rejected, Bellow snapped, "I can see why."

As a courtesy, Bellow had written his old friend that spring about the possible opening at NYU, and Rosenfeld had replied with a frosty note. "Is Isaac's nose out of joint about NYU?" Bellow wrote Monroe Engel from Positano, his guilt about encroaching on Rosenfeld's turf making him defensive:

> Mine is a little. He makes me feel that I've undermined him there. I can still drop out if he's affected. How can I know whether he is? I have no way of telling what's at stake for him. For me there's nothing. I simply don't want to get in his way. Not from friendly feeling—there's not much lost between us now. He'd like to become strangers, and I'm not so opposed to that as I formerly was—but because I'd prefer, if I have to struggle with someone for survival, it be a person I never struggled with before.

In the end, the job came through.

9

You make every sacrifice to be free, you give up your child, your bed, your
comforts, and then you become a slave to misery. You aren't free at all.

—SAUL BELLOW, *"Golub"*

T HE BELLOWS' RETURN to America was a rude transition.
In the spring of 1950, they were living in a cozy apartment
on the rue Vaneau in Paris; by October, having retrieved
their furniture from storage in Chicago, they were settled in a four-
room apartment that Harold Guinzburg, the publisher of Viking
and possessor of extensive real-estate holdings, had found for
them in a drab redbrick building in Forest Hills in "the colossal
dingy borough of Queens," as the narrator of one of Bellow's
unpublished stories described it. Bellow also had one of his "rooms
off to the side" in Macdougal Alley, a cul-de-sac near Washington
Square in Greenwich Village.

"Saul Bellow is back from Paris, and now living in New York,"
Isaac Rosenfeld wrote to his maiden aunts Dora and Rae in
Chicago. "I see him quite often. It's not like in the old days—you
can't keep the old friends from drifting apart—but still, an old
friend." Rosenfeld and Bellow were now colleagues at NYU. To
Ralph Ross, who remembered them hanging around together in the
Department of General Studies office on Washington Square
North, perched side by side on a desk, whispering and laughing, the
two Chicago boys were "incredibly close." But to Oscar Tarcov,
Bellow confided, "Making every allowance possible, I still resent
his not too well hidden hope that I fall on my face." Rosenfeld,

meanwhile, thought Bellow was becoming full of himself. "The more I read his letters, the harder I find it to trust Saul," he noted in his journal: "There is a figure of speech in every sentence."

If Rosenfeld found Bellow altered, he, too, had undergone a drastic change. While Bellow had been in Europe discovering the voice of Augie March, Rosenfeld had been in the Village discovering Wilhelm Reich. "Village thought in the late Forties had a strong psychoanalytic tendency," Bellow noted in his "Zetland" manuscript. Reich's *The Function of the Orgasm* was as widely read in progressive circles as Trotsky's *Art and Revolution* had been a decade before. Paul Goodman, a reliable indicator of intellectual trends, was a Reichian, as were a number of former Barrow Street regulars, for whom Reich's emphasis on sexual gratification merely validated long-standing practice. Reich was an intellectual fashion of the day, and Bellow wasn't above embracing such fashions; a decade earlier, he had been just as enthusiastic about Trotsky. But the attraction of Reich went deeper; his method represented the psychoanalytic equivalent of what Bellow aspired to in his own work (and in his life): the freedom of unfettered self-expression.

Reichianism wasn't a philosophy, its founder insisted, but a science. Reich considered himself an heir of Freud and had developed an elaborate physiological explanation for his theories. It was his belief that cathartic total orgasm was the key to health, or what he called *full genitality;* but most human beings were prevented from achieving these convulsive orgasms by the presence of what Reich termed *character armor:* rigid defenses that stifle development and block the free flow of sexuality. Damming up the libido not only causes neurosis, he postulated, but represses psychic energy. For Reich, there was nothing hypothetical about the existence of this energy; it was organic, biological. He had even found a name for it: orgone energy, which was said to be a primordial cosmic power latent in all things. Thus was born the science of orgonomy.

By the time Bellow returned from Paris, Rosenfeld had already been in treatment for two years with a Reichian therapist named Richard G. Singer. (Vasiliki also saw Singer for a time.) Early in 1951, Bellow went to the Reichian Institute in Queens for a consultation and was recommended to Dr. Chester Raphael, a practicing Reichian with an office in Forest Hills, where Reich himself had established an Orgone Energy Laboratory during the war.

It was a strenuous form of therapy. Dr. Raphael was an orthodox interpreter of Reich: His vocabulary was full of phrases such as "orgonomic potential" and "breaking down biophysical and characterological armor." It wasn't enough to talk through this blockage; it had to be physically attacked. "You deal with the way they look at you, the way they talk, the way they breathe," Dr. Raphael explained. Lying naked on a couch, the patient was exhorted to purge the body of its defenses by acting out rage and sexual tension, shouting, gagging, grimacing, pounding the couch; the aim was to pierce the "armor segments" that sheathed neurosis. "The body revealed the diseases of the mind," Bellow wrote in "Zetland," which provided a sustained and richly comic account of a Reichian session. "This was no mental doctrine. Truth was tested by the nerves, blood and viscera." Under the authoritarian supervision of Dr. Sapir (an echo, perhaps, of Edward Sapir, the eminent anthropologist whose works Bellow had read in college), Zetland struggles to confront his own resistance. "You look to me like an overfed, jowly, snouty white pig," Dr. Sapir taunts him, offering a devastating appraisal of his patient's sex life. "You have erectile potency, but you are not a potent man. . . . I can tell by looking at you—the retracted pelvis, the stasis with accumulated fat, the shallowness of breathing. How can you have had real sexual experience?" ("He goes to Queens for fucking lessons," a cynical observer of the Village scene remarked of Rosenfeld's analysis.)

Both Rosenfeld and Bellow were skeptical of Reich at first. "The trouble with Paul Goodman, the anarcho-Reichians, the whole gang, is a failing of instinctive wisdom," argued Rosenfeld. "Sex repression is bad—so let's have freedom." For all their talk of personal liberation, the Reichians were a sect, obsessed with ideological purity; Bellow compared them to the Jacobins of the French Revolution. "The Freudians had their own Thermidor, and the Reichians were Sans-culottes. They were excommunicated."

Bellow's suspiciousness was characteristic; no system commanded his allegiance for long. To him, Reichianism was like

Trotskyism and every other ism: an effort to rein in his autonomy. But Rosenfeld, less sure of his direction, grew increasingly consumed by Reich. He interviewed people aggressively about their sex lives; talked of genital character, facial diagnostics, pelvic segments, and diaphragmatic blocks; and turned his literature class at NYU into a lecture course on Reich. Encountering the translator Raymond Rosenthal and his wife strolling in the Village with their infant daughter, he exclaimed: "What a wonderful baby! No armor at all."

One of Reich's more curious inventions was the Accumulator, a zinc-lined wooden box about the size of a telephone booth that was said to collect orgone energy; the patient sat naked inside the box, which was insulated with steel wool, and in this way could absorb a vitalizing dose. Rosenfeld had built his own; sitting inside his orgone box, he "looked lost," Alfred Kazin recalled, "as if he were waiting in his telephone booth for a call that was not coming through."

Bellow was also following a Reichian regimen. He, too, had installed an Accumulator in his Queens apartment and spent long hours in it, reading beneath a bare lightbulb strung from its ceiling. At odd moments, he stuffed a handkerchief in his mouth and screamed—one of the methods Reich had supposedly prescribed for achieving emotional release.

Monogamy played no part in Reich's scheme of things; marital fidelity was an obstacle to sexual fulfillment. "Even a healthy relationship can wear out," Dr. Sapir tells Zetland. "Marriages are not forever. Six years, eight years, and the sexual interest dies out." Both Rosenfeld and Bellow adhered to this view. Marriage was "a base of operations," Rosenfeld explained to Alfred Kazin. At one time or another, both Rosenfeld and Bellow holed up in the Casbah, a warren of shabby rooms on Hudson Street where writers and itinerant intellectuals sought refuge from their marriages. "You hardly knew who lived where or with whom," as Monroe Engel described the place. "There were women; there were always women," observed one of Bellow's friends. Anita knew about and apparently tolerated her wayward husband's amours, but the situation was hard on her. In his domestic life, as in everything else, he was accustomed to going his own way.

Bellow was a master of self-exculpation; he was never to blame for the breakups of his marriages or friendships, the books that found disfavor with the critics, the plans that went awry. He could always find an explanation—one that revolved around the notion of himself as victim. It was important for Bellow to see his life this way: He lacked the reserves of self-esteem needed to engage in rigorous self-criticism. "I never gave psychoanalysis so much as a two-year lease," he testified, depicting himself as a reluctant participant in Rosenfeld's Reichian experiments: "I enjoyed it as a game then being played." As far as he was concerned, his treatment with Dr. Raphael had been a gesture of solidarity with a friend. "I didn't want to lose Isaac when all that was happening. So I went through the analysis, too, just to stay close."

Dr. Raphael remembered Bellow's time on the couch rather differently: "That's a peculiar way to put it. He came because he had problems. He never expressed any of this to me." Nor could Dr. Raphael support the notion that Bellow's friendship with Rosenfeld was an important issue in his therapy: "He didn't talk about Rosenfeld, practically not at all."

Why did Bellow insist on presenting his experience of Reichian therapy in this way? Whether it helped him or not—Bellow maintained the whole experience was a "disaster" that destroyed his marriage—he saw Dr. Raphael as another person intent on interfering in his life, another threat to his independence. By minimizing the significance of his therapy, he could deny that he'd ever had problems acute enough to require treatment. It was as if the caution he exercised habitually was a way of protecting himself from the possibility of failure—a possibility that shadowed his early life, before it was at all clear that he would achieve the significant destiny on which he'd staked so much.

At the height of his Reichian phase, Bellow was at work on a one-act play called "The Wrecker." Its hero, intent upon resisting all efforts to force him out of the condemned building in which he lives, begins to smash up his apartment room by room with an ax. His wife, appalled at first by her husband's destructive fury, is soon persuaded to join him, and together they literally dismantle their past. "Where there's no demolition there's no advancement," the main character rails at his mother-in-law. "The old must go down."

Bellow's life in Queens was, outwardly at least, a good deal less bohemian than Rosenfeld's. The apartment on 102d Street, a few blocks from Queens Boulevard and heartbreakingly far from the towers of Manhattan visible in the distance, was "sad and awful and tractlike," as Herbert Gold remembered it. "The place was a real comedown from his elegant Parisian lodgings."

It was obvious to the Bellows' friends that the Bellows' marriage was in serious trouble. "It was a young marriage," noted Herb McCloskey, and other friends remarked on the couple's emotional immaturity. "The original attraction is gone," Isaac Rosenfeld wrote to Oscar Tarcov. "Nothing has taken its place, except an increased domesticity which he doesn't want. Anita acts sour and cranky at times." Out of marital loyalty, she had also begun treatment with Dr. Raphael and made occasional use of the orgone box in their apartment. "She didn't want me to be doing anything she wasn't doing," said Bellow churlishly. He also intimated to friends that Anita was unexciting in bed and told Dave Peltz that she was a lesbian—a dramatic way of blaming her for their sexual incompatibility. Anita in turn had to put up with Bellow's self-absorption, his infidelities, and the outbursts of bristling hostility that visitors observed.*

The precariousness of their financial situation didn't help matters. Anita had gotten a job at the South Shore branch of Planned Parenthood in Far Rockaway, running a birth-control center; Bellow was earning a modest salary as an assistant professor at NYU, supplemented by occasional book reviews for *Commentary* and *The New Leader*. But his prospects for the following year were grim. His job at NYU was part-time and on a

---

*In his fiction, Bellow portrayed their marriage as a stifling, joyless union. As Iva in *Dangling Man*, Anita was made to seem remote and sullen, asserting herself with a "brave, shaky new defiance." As Margaret in *Seize the Day*, she was a nag, badgering the hapless Tommy Wilhelm over the telephone about his obligations to the family ("He could picture her, her graying bangs cut with strict fixity above her pretty, decisive face"). In *Herzog*, as the hero's first wife, Daisy, she was a stern, repressive presence ("Stability, symmetry, order, containment were Daisy's strength").

year-to-year basis; there was no promise it would be renewed. In desperation, he borrowed five hundred dollars from Viking against his advance and applied again for a renewal of his Guggenheim, reporting to Henry Allen Moe that he had "very nearly finished" "The Crab and the Butterfly" and was at work on a novel that he now called "The Life of Augie March."

The new year brought a glimmer of hope. John Marshall, an associate director of the Rockefeller Foundation, was a fan of *The Victim*. Early in January 1951, he invited Bellow to his office for a talk. After giving a detailed account of his work in progress, Bellow came right out and asked Marshall if there was any chance of assistance from the Rockefeller Foundation. Marshall was equivocal but asked Bellow to write an essay on "the responsibility of the novelist in society." An honorarium of seventy-five dollars was allocated for the purpose.

Bellow composed a brief but searching essay. "The great issue in fiction is that of the stature of characters," he began, refining the argument put forth in the "Plans for Work" he'd submitted to the Guggenheim Committee. But the image of man had dwindled since the Renaissance, become undervalued in our "secular, doubting time." The revolutionaries and "great natures" of the eighteenth and early nineteenth century had given way to the antiheroes of Dostoyevsky: "As the external social fact grows larger, more powerful and tyrannical, man appears in the novel reduced in will, strength, freedom and scope." How ought the novelist to address this marginality? By facing it head-on:

> A point of view like mine is not conducive to popular success. I believe with Coleridge that some writers must gradually create their own audience. This is, in the short run, an unrewarding process. The commercial organization of society resists it and, let us face it, there is a widespread disgust, weariness, staleness, resistance, unwillingness to feel the sharp edge of life.

It was a thoughtful, earnest essay—a pitch for financial assistance, but a dignified one. John Marshall responded promptly with a letter of tepid enthusiasm: He had read Bellow's statement with "interest" but had to postpone any decision until he'd had a chance to meet with Edward "Chet" d'Arms, a fellow director at the foundation. On the office copy of his letter, Marshall—or someone—wrote: "I doubt this is worth the honorarium and therefore am withholding payment for the present. We might want to use it to get a further statement."

Two weeks later, Bellow was summoned to the foundation. Marshall was out sick, and Bellow met with d'Arms alone. It was a chilly conversation. D'Arms was annoyed by the memorandum; he didn't see how Bellow could reconcile the "narrow focus" of his own novels with the literary mandate he'd proposed—"extending the area of sensibility and producing a broader coverage of significant contemporary problems and phenomena," as d'Arms rather stiffly paraphrased it in a memo. Bellow responded testily that he was getting at broad, fundamental issues in "Augie March," a novel about "the Machiavellian dialectic in American society." D'Arms "was not greatly impressed at B's intellectual position nor encouraged by his slight but persistent truculence," he noted in the minutes of their meeting; but he acknowledged that Bellow's financial situation was "acute." The penurious novelist, "desperately anxious" for assistance, had "pressed tactfully but persistently" for a decision.

Six weeks later, on March 20, 1951, d'Arms wrote to Bellow. He had taken up the matter of a grant with his colleagues, but they had come to no firm conclusions about whether the Rockefeller Foundation should support young writers. John Marshall was in the Near East, and a final decision had to await his return in mid-April. The next day, Bellow received a form letter from the Guggenheim Foundation notifying him that his request for a renewal of his fellowship had been turned down.

Early in May, he finally heard from the Rockefeller Foundation. The board had come to the reluctant conclusion that it could not at present offer him any assistance: "This is one of those rather moral conclusions that I think involves a certain regret for all of us, but as I say, we found ourselves forced to it." (Marshall, like Bellow, favored ascribing painful decisions to some mysterious, unnamed cause.) He recommended that Bellow get in touch with the American Council of Learned Societies, which had established a fund for writers in need.

Chet d'Arms, meanwhile, had released the check for seventy-five dollars, "with our hearty thanks for this very interesting report."

Bellow vacillated wildly between excitement about "Augie" and doubts about how good it was. The book would be "consciousness-changing," he predicted to Herbert Gold, and would introduce the Jewish voice into American fiction in a new and definitive way. But his bravado masked a deep insecurity. When Mel Tumin dared to voice some reservations about the novel, Bellow raged, "You don't know what you're talking about. Red Warren says this is a work of genius." When David Bazelon, to whom he read parts of the manuscript, responded that Bellow "could change the course of the American novel," the novelist corrected him: "Not the American novel. The American language." Even by the standards of artistic touchiness, Bellow's fragile grandiosity stood out. He was capable of bearing a grudge for decades, but he was capable of forgiveness, too. At a party in Queens, Bellow felt that Dwight Macdonald displayed insufficient enthusiasm for the chapter of the book that had appeared in *Partisan Review*. The next day, Macdonald wrote Bellow a contrite letter, apologizing for his "bumptious polemical manner." Bellow was conciliatory. "I'm what the French call *très soupe au lait*," he replied, invoking the phrase he employed to describe his father: "I boil up and then subside."

Bellow also boiled up at his English publisher, John Lehmann; he was still rankled by the party that Lehmann had given for him in London. "This is the most ridiculous accusation I have ever heard," Lehmann responded.

> Perhaps in New York it's considered patronizing to try to arrange parties for an author from abroad when he suddenly turns up, and to do your best to introduce him to other authors who admire his work, but if so all I can say is that it's just another of those occasions when English and Americans don't seem to be talking the same language.

It was a trying time. Bellow was approaching forty, with a wife and child to support. He was dependent on freelance assignments and occasional handouts from his brothers, who looked down on him from the heights of material success: Cadillacs, furs for their wives, vacations in Florida. Their youngest brother, meanwhile, was still the threadbare artist, ill dressed and perpetually short of cash. He had a reputation among the *Partisan Review* crowd but was virtually unknown to the general public. Two books on the Chicago cultural scene that appeared that year, Albert Halper's collection *This Is Chicago* and A. J. Liebling's *Chicago: The Second City*, managed to ignore his existence altogether. Halper referred to the "Chicago School" of writers and listed, among the younger generation, Richard Wright, Meyer Levin, James T. Farrell, and Nelson Algren. Liebling, putting the emphasis on "second," remarked archly: "For a city where, I am credibly informed, you couldn't throw an egg in 1925 without braining a great poet, Chicago is hard up for writers."

Thanks to his friend Ted Hoffman, Bellow had been invited for a return visit to the Salzburg Seminar in American Studies. "Beyond that, don't see anything," he reported bleakly to Robert Penn Warren. He sailed from New York on December 17, stopping for the week between Christmas and New Year's with the Kaplans in Paris.

This time, Bellow was on his own at Schloss Leopoldskron; Anita and Greg had stayed behind in Forest Hills. Bellow arrived at Salzburg with two pieces of luggage, recalled John McCormick, a Harvard Ph.D. who had been appointed dean of the seminar: a suitcase and "the largest typewriter I'd ever seen in my life." "It was clear that he was betwixt and between," said McCormick. His description of Bellow's situation was apt, encompassing jobs, places to live, books, and—it was now becoming clear—wives.

At Salzburg, Bellow gave a series of public lectures on "The Novel from Hawthorne to the Present." As he explained to McCormick, "I am going to try to develop some notions about the artist in an industrial democracy, the relations of individual and crowd, the dwindling in the stature of heroes, the constant effort of writers to strike a reliable definition of human nature, *und so weiter.*" In his seminar, in addition to the standard American syllabus, Bellow assigned D. H. Lawrence's *Studies in Classic American Literature*, William Carlos Williams's *Life along the Passaic River*, and Henry James's essays on Flaubert, Zola, and Maupassant.

The students were generally of a high caliber. One, the English novelist William Sansom, had already published several books—a volume of stories and a Kafkaesque novel called *The Body*. Bellow's student evaluations were almost comically vague. In a display of what would now qualify as blatant sexism, he described Pia Jamar as "pretty at a distance; I say this because I never saw her close-up at any time." His sole comment on Izaak den Haan was: "a name from Henry Miller's mailing list."

The criticisms weren't unilateral; Bellow got mixed reviews as a teacher. He was "at his best when he was just talking with a few people," wrote one of his students; another observed that Bellow "didn't appear to want to lecture." There was a good deal of his lecturing style in Ralph Bernage, the protagonist of Bellow's unpublished manuscript "Don Juan: A Lover from America," about an itinerant intellectual who comes to Vienna to lecture on "The American Character": "His mind was profuse in ideas, though not strong in organization, and he could speak easily and with charm, especially after he had a few drinks. . . . It was always a struggle and an ordeal to give a speech, and he was always assailed by anxious fears when he approached the platform." Bellow had trouble engaging his students; they simply weren't real to him. He preferred—a remarkable act of chutzpah—to read from "The Life of Augie March." "It was obvious that he had work of more importance than writing lectures," as one of his auditors remarked magnanimously. One afternoon, Bellow read a passage about Augie's adventures in Mexico, laughing delightedly at what he considered the funny parts. "He was having a wonderful time," said John McCormick, "better than the rest of us." His self-delight was typical: Bellow always laughed at his own jokes and derived huge enjoyment from the recital of his work. He wasn't looking for criticism; he was looking for praise. By setting the tone himself, he had a better chance of getting the response he wanted—at least in the short run.

"Augie" was Bellow's obsession. Every morning at seven forty-five, one of the Austrian waitresses brought a bowl of porridge and a cup of coffee to his door; in the afternoon, he lectured or gave his seminar. His main distraction was the presence of beautiful women in his class. In his autobiography, *The Younger Son*, the poet Karl Shapiro, who was also in residence, claimed that two girls "were in love with the American novelist" and that one "might have spent a night with him." A puritanical drama professor with the Dickensian name of N. Bryllion Fagin reported this episode, according to Shapiro, and was promptly ostracized for his shabby deed.

By mid-February, after another brief sojourn in Paris, Bellow was back in New York. No job had materialized. A few weeks later, he was off again—still without his family—on a tour of the West, giving a series of lectures at the University of Oregon and the University of Washington to distract himself from his misery. An increase in his already frenetic pace of travel came to be a reliable portent of the dissolution of a marriage. Like Herzog, "heartsore" over his estrangement from his children ("It was painful to his instincts, his Jewish family feelings, that his children should be growing up without him"), Bellow suffered from the fraying of family ties, but not enough to mend them; the intensity of his own needs overrode all other considerations. A part of him longed for the stability of marriage; another part of him felt stifled by it—the theme of his 1954 play, "The Wrecker." Bellow and Anita had long been at war over this issue; only now, after fourteen years of marriage, did he begin to suspect that a truce would forever elude them. To friends, he confided that he was afraid of getting divorced; he couldn't live without Anita. Yet he couldn't bring himself to stay home, either. Let her decide.

In Seattle, he spent a few convivial evenings in the company of Theodore Roethke and Dylan Thomas. "I couldn't keep up with them," he recalled; he wasn't "a real drinking man." At Reed, Bellow had a brief fling with a promising young novelist by the name of Alice Adams, who later established herself as a major voice in the pages of *The New Yorker*. At the University of Oregon, he read from his forthcoming book to an audience that included Bernard Malamud, then a young instructor at the state agricultural college in Corvallis. Malamud was about to publish his first novel, *The Natural*.

Bellow's fortunes were finally looking up. In May, a dramatization of *The Victim* by Leonard Lesley had a brief Off-Broadway run at the President Theatre, and Brooks Atkinson of *The New*

York Times pronounced it "not uninteresting"—hardly a rave, but enough to buoy his spirits. Later that month, he received a grant of one thousand dollars from the American Academy of Arts and Letters; the judges were Van Wyck Brooks, W. H. Auden, Malcolm Cowley, John Hersey, and Mark Van Doren. And he finally secured a job for the fall—at Princeton.

In *Humboldt's Gift*, the novel he wrote to exorcise the ghost of Delmore Schwartz, Bellow offered a comically acidulous account of his Princeton days. The story of how the crazy poet Humboldt connives to get a job at Princeton, then commandeers Charles Citrine to serve as his assistant, is almost entirely based on fact. The Rockefeller Foundation—apparently having overcome its scruples about individual grants to writers in the year since turning away Bellow—had awarded R. P. Blackmur a traveling fellowship for the academic year 1952–53, and Blackmur was looking for someone to preside over his Princeton fiefdom, the creative-writing program, in his absence. "You might do worse," Schwartz suggested, than import "one of the children of Israel." Blackmur ended up importing two. Schwartz proposed Bellow as his assistant, and after a bibulous interview at Lahiere's, Blackmur offered Bellow the job. The salary was five thousand dollars. He was to start that fall. At once relieved and uneasy—to Bellow, Princeton was a WASP enclave, more inhospitable to Jews than even Northwestern—he packed up his Underwood and headed off to Yaddo, the writers' colony in Saratoga Springs, for the summer, determined to finish "Augie."

Yaddo's rule against spouses and children posed no inconvenience: Bellow's marriage was over. To Sam Freifeld, he offered a characteristic version of events, placing the blame squarely on Anita: "Her rigid unlovingness has driven me out—that and nothing else. I've done my best to stay and often I've felt that either going or staying threatened me with death. So I tried to choose the braver, at least the less ignominious death." For once, he acknowledged that it had been his choice. But in a sense—as Bellow saw it—divorce was never his choice. He fled his marriages (the divorce from Anita was the first of four) when they could no longer provide the emotional sustenance he required. That he refused to give up on the *idea* of marriage long after it should have been apparent to him that he was unsuited to the institution shows only how powerful its hold over him was. Bellow longed for a home and family, but he longed for them much as a child might: The need for constant attention and devotion alternated in him with a powerful need to go off and explore the world on his own at will. The contradiction seems never to have occurred to him. He was to pursue his fantasy of the perfect marriage and wife again and again, yet the marital bond was strongest with Anita. More than any of his subsequent wives, she belonged to Bellow's world—which helps to explain why his first marriage lasted as long as it did. Anita was part of him.

She never would have assented to the notion that he was "driven out." She was so devastated that her seventy-nine-year-old mother, Sonya, took the train from Chicago to New York and pleaded with Bellow on her behalf—to no avail. He would go his own way, unencumbered, whatever the cost.

Among Bellow's unpublished manuscripts is the draft of a story about a character named Golub, "a conscientious, well-bred, mild, brown-suited man, assistant art director in a television network," who has recently separated from his wife. Golub commutes to his job in New York from the dilapidated country house of a poet named Kilmer who lives in Frenchtown, New Jersey—the town where Delmore Schwartz was holed up in rural squalor. It was in an analogous situation that Bellow found himself in the fall of 1952.

Bachelorhood gave him the freedom he'd so long desired—and practiced—but it had its drawbacks. Separated from Anita and Gregory, Bellow stayed sometimes at Schwartz's, sometimes at the Casbah on Hudson Street (Rosenfeld, now divorced from Vasiliki, had a room there), or in Greenwich Village with various friends. On teaching days, he shared an apartment on the ground floor of 12 Princeton Avenue with Tom Riggs, an instructor in the English department whose wife had just left him; Bellow slept on a cot in the study. The cheerless, itinerant squalor of the divorced was a condition he was to become well acquainted with over the years.

Bellow was despondent about the breakup of his marriage. It was wrenching to have forsaken his wife and child, and he later claimed that he had never gotten over it. All the same, it didn't

take him long to find someone else. Her name was Sondra
Tschacbasov, and she was only twenty; she had graduated from
Bennington the previous June. She was working as a receptionist
at the *Partisan Review* office when Bellow rang up one day from
Princeton. Intrigued by her voice, he asked her name. The answer
inflamed Bellow's slavophilia: Anything Russian was evocative of
his own childhood and the world his parents had left behind. He
announced that he was coming right over—and he did.

Sondra's father, a Chicago businessman turned artist, was originally from Russia. Sondra's grandmother had the same maiden
name—Gordon—as Bellow's mother (though her family spelled it
in the conventional way), and her family had owned a bakery on
Chicago's West Side. Abram Bellow sold coal to the Gordons'
bakery. Sondra's father had undergone numerous name changes,
becoming Lichterman in America, then adopting the pseudonym
H. H. Richter before reverting to Tschacbasov; in the same way,
Sandra became Sondra and, to her close friends, Sasha. She also
went by the formal name of Alexandra. Richter/Tschacbasov had
a complicated past: When Sondra was a child, he'd abruptly pulled
up stakes and moved his family to Paris. Now he was a painter,
living a bohemian life in the Chelsea Hotel on West Twenty-third
Street and seducing his art students.

Sondra was by all accounts a great beauty—she was known
among friends as the Snow Maiden and the Russian Princess. "She
was stunning beyond words, with pale skin and china-blue eyes,"
recalled the poet Stanley Burnshaw, who first laid eyes on her
when she was a girl, at one of her father's noisy parties in the
Chelsea; she strode in, angelic in a white dress, and sat down to
play the piano. Sondra was the quintessential Bennington girl: She
danced; she wrote poetry; she hungered after the company of
artists and writers. ("I could have gone out with Philip Rahv or
Saul," she liked to say: "I chose Saul.") The biographer R. W. B.
Lewis, who taught at Bennington in the late 1940s, remembered
Sondra telling him she "wasn't interested in books, she was interested in experience." Still, she possessed enough literary acumen to
know a masterpiece when she saw—or, in this case, heard—one:
Laid up in bed after she twisted her ankle in the subway, she
listened to Bellow read aloud from "Augie" ("pretty much the
whole damn thing") and instantly recognized it as a literary event.

"The freshness, the exuberance. It was such a revelation. The poetic, flying feeling of the prose, the way he physically created characters with language. I was dazzled by it, and in a way, I really saw him for the first time."

Sondra was living in the Ansonia, an ornate, decrepit residential hotel on the Upper West Side (it would show up, barely disguised, as the hotel where Tommy Wilhelm and his father live in *Seize the Day*), but she spent most of her time at the lower Fifth Avenue apartment of her Bennington roommate, Anita Maximilian, a Polish refugee whose father had been a wealthy furrier in Warsaw; Maximilian Furs was in those days a famous New York institution. Maximilian was taking classes at the New School, and her place was "like *Partisan Review* headquarters," she recalled: "I'd come out of the shower and there would be Paolo Milano [an émigré Italian literary critic to whom Bellow dedicated *The Victim*] or John Berryman or Saul."

Maximilian found the men's interest in women just out of college a little peculiar. Bellow was already a minor legend around town; Berryman was a well-known poet. Why, as she put it, "would grown-ups be interested in girls?" She offered her own clear-eyed explanation: "Saul had always had trouble with women; maybe he thought he wouldn't have all these troubles with a girl." (There was also a practical motive: As Bellow crudely put it to R. W. B. Lewis, he "needed to get his ashes hauled.")

He was proud of his new "acquisition" and showed her off to guests like a merchant praising his wares: "Isn't she beautiful?" "She has breasts like green apples." Not that Bellow's obliviousness to the notion of women as independent, thinking creatures was so unusual in that pre–women's liberation era of the 1950s. It was customary for men to pursue younger women and praise their physical endowments at the expense of their intellects. If Bellow was extreme in this regard, he was still well within the normal range of male chauvinism for his day. The women in his life remained for him secondary figures who served his own fantasies of them as providers, entrappers, sexual predators: the Enemy.

Sondra was a frequent visitor to Princeton. But there was one impediment to Bellow's seduction scenario: She had converted to Catholicism (an effort, she later explained, to reverse the bohemian chaos of her childhood by imposing on her life a sense, however illusory, of order and tradition). Going to bed with a married man was a sin.

In keeping with her spiritual proclivities, Sondra had taken a job as the assistant to Fulton J. Sheen, a New York bishop. "I straightened his beanie before his television program." She faithfully studied the catechism, attended Mass, and edited a Catholic magazine. "She wore a big cross right between her boobs," recalled one of their friends. But like Madeleine, whose "Christian phase" Bellow satirized mercilessly in *Herzog*, Sondra embraced her new faith and her new lover with equal fervor. Bellow joked that he and the bishop were engaged in a struggle for Sondra's soul. ("She wanted Moses and the Monsignor to struggle over her," thinks Herzog. "It heightened the sexual excitement.")

Meanwhile, Anita was by no means going quietly. She and Bellow had fierce clashes over money and over Bellow's responsibilities to Greg. Bellow found visiting days a chore; the zoo, he said, was his Via Crucis. But if he was a less than dutiful father, he clearly pined for his son. In his "Golub" manuscript, he offered a poignant glimpse of his own loneliness. In Penn Station one rainy night just before Christmas, on the way back to his dolorous lodgings in the New Jersey sticks, the newly divorced Golub is suddenly shaken by an acute memory of his little girl climbing onto his lap to comb his hair while he sat reading the paper: "The heat coming from her skin, the narrowness of her bones, the odor of Castile soap given off by her round dark head. Go back! Go to her! His entire being told him. For the love of God, Golub, go back. This inner cry stopped him in the midst of the station."

Years later, Bellow began a story called "Out of Bounds," about a failed playwright from Queens named Robert Reimer. Reimer is fascinated by the parable of "a Chinaman who burned down his house to roast his pig."

Princeton was an unlikely berth for a Jewish Chicago boy. With its manicured campus, private eating clubs, and stately Victorian homes, it deserved the name by which its well-heeled residents knew it: The Best Old Place of All—if you belonged there, they didn't need to add. The Best Old Place was the epitome of WASP privilege, unsubtle snobbery, and inherited money. "Young wives in Princeton, when they went shopping, wore tennis clothes and riding clothes," wrote Russell Fraser in his biography of R. P. Blackmur. "Princeton men were ruddy-tanned and well set up like Tom Buchanan; they smoked pipes and wore tweeds, not always of the best."

The Princeton English department was dominated by Old Boys and prep-school classicists, men such as Willard Thorp, the Chaucerian Robert K. Root, and Carlos Baker, the Hemingway biographer—Irving Howe, who taught at Princeton in the 1950s, described them as "buckshoe humanists." Blackmur himself didn't qualify. Dour and drink-prone, he was given to anti-Semitic outbursts when in his cups. It was a casual anti-Semitism, his biographer asserts, and very much of the period. But he couldn't conceal his distaste for the New York intellectuals—his code word for them was "cosmopolite." Late in the evening, gesturing vigorously with a cigarette held between two of his middle fingers, Blackmur could become vicious. "After the first drink he was anti-black," said the critic Leslie Fiedler, "after the second anti-Jew; after the third, anti-woman; after the fourth, anti–the human race." Bellow, who when made socially insecure often settled the score in his fiction, was notably unkind to Blackmur in *Humboldt's Gift,* where the critic figures as Sewell, a thoroughly disagreeable snob, "with his depleted hair, his dry-cereal mustache, the drinker's face, the Prufrock subtleties, the would-be elegance of his clasped hands and crossed legs, with his involved literary mutterings."

Princeton was too *goyish* for Bellow. "We're a joke—Abie Kabibble and Company," the angry Humboldt complains to Citrine. "Unthinkable as members of the Princeton community." In case he'd forgotten, Citrine is "from nowhere." His ancestors were "village rabbis from Lithuania, herring-eating Hasidim." To R. W. B. Lewis, Bellow offered a blunt description of their status: He and Schwartz were Blackmur's "niggers."

In later life, Bellow took a more charitable view of Princeton, remembering it as "partly entertaining, partly touching, partly a scene of gloomy bravado." Thanks largely to the Gauss Seminars—

named after the beloved Princeton professor Christian Gauss and funded by the Rockefeller Foundation—the fifties were Princeton's golden literary years. Among the many writers who passed through were Theodore Roethke and Ralph Ellison; the poet and translator Robert Fitzgerald; John Berryman, who was at work on his book-length historical monologue, *Homage to Mistress Bradstreet;* and the dean of American letters, Edmund Wilson.

Parties were serious affairs at Princeton, where the consumption of alcohol ranked with writing as a literary pursuit. These parties were less festive than they sound. Signs of the dark, self-destructive strain that consumed the poets of the so-called Tragic Generation— Robert Lowell, Randall Jarrell, Berryman, and Schwartz—were already beginning to emerge. Berryman—demanding, high-strung, loyal in friendship to the point of suffocation (you liked him, Schwartz said, but you liked him to live in another city)—was a confirmed alcoholic. Schwartz, insomniac and pill-addicted, swilled gin straight from a jam jar as he wandered the dusty grounds of his decrepit New Jersey manor. "They were all Stradivarius violins," said Leslie Fiedler, "and at any moment a string could snap."

Bellow was a happier soul. Carlos Baker remembered him as "brilliant, lively, and effervescent, able to narrate sidesplitting Yiddish yarns by the hour, his bright, slightly exophthalmic eyes agleam not with tears but laughter." To Eileen Simpson, John Berryman's wife at the time, he was a "dish" whose "dark good looks had made the heart of more than one Princeton matron beat more rapidly." Berryman instantly sized up Bellow as a "pal"—to borrow a term of endearment from the *Dream Songs*. The night they met, at the home of Mel Tumin, now a professor of sociology at Princeton, Bellow played Purcell "very sweetly" on the recorder. Later that winter, the two writers went for a walk along Carnegie Lake. "I like Bellow more each time I see him," Berryman reported to his wife. "A lovely man. And a comedian. He threw a log he found at the edge of the lake into the water and, with a gesture of command, said, 'Go. Go be a hazard!' "

Bellow's equanimity stood out in that hard-drinking, hot-tempered crowd. Just before Christmas, he gave a party in the apartment he shared with Tom Riggs to celebrate the imminent appearance of a chapter from *The Adventures of Augie March* in *The New Yorker*. Bellow was in "a genial mood," according to Eileen Simpson, but no one else was: "The music we heard as we approached 12 Princeton Avenue was the growl of a saxophone. We entered a dimly lit, smoke-filled room where people were standing around with no-nonsense whiskey and gin drinks in their hands." The situation quickly deteriorated: Delmore Schwartz made a violent scene after he saw his wife, Elizabeth Pollet, reach into Ralph Ellison's pocket for a match while they were dancing; he suspected her of fondling him. Schwartz dragged Pollet off the dance floor, pushed her into their dusty Buick, and with a squeal of tires sped away. Bellow took off after them; Monroe Engel and Ted Hoffman—now teaching drama at Princeton—took off after Bellow. "We found Saul on Nassau Street at two o'clock in the morning," Hoffman remembered, "having coffee with Sondra."

At the end of December, Bellow came down with such a severe case of pneumonia that he had to be rushed to the hospital in an ambulance. ("There goes the last of the guests," commented the lady upstairs, referring to Riggs's raucous parties.) He was "utterly used up," Bellow reported to Robert Hivnor in the last days of 1952. Finishing *Augie* and fighting with Anita had taken it out of him: "To wind up the year I caught a disease that laid me in the hospital at Xmastide. They've just let me out, with orders to rest. So I'm trying to make like tranquil and not think of my family, of the last chapter of Augie which needs redoing, of various assignments, of money, of education or of love."

In 1952, *Partisan Review* published one of the symposia that were convened in the magazine's pages every few years to monitor the collective drift of intellectuals in the postwar era. Entitled "Our Country and Our Culture," it marked the magazine's first public acknowledgment that the radical disaffection of the thirties and forties was finally over. "To what extent have American intellectuals changed their attitude toward America and its institutions?" asked the editors in their introduction. It was clear from the way they framed the debate that "alienation" was no longer a necessary stance; Marxism, Trotskyism, and socialism were passions of the past. "Until little more than a decade ago, America was commonly thought to be hostile to art and culture," the editors stated. "Since then, however, the tide has begun to turn, and many writers now feel closer to their country and its culture. They now believe that their values, if they are to be realized at all, must be realized in America and in relation to the actuality of American life."

There was some basis for this spirit of accommodation. By 1952, the process of intellectual—or Jewish—assimilation was an accomplished fact. Critics once associated with a subversive leftist ideology had begun to reach "the larger public," noted Daniel Bell. Many of the Jewish intellectuals had obtained positions at universities: Irving Howe was teaching at Brandeis, and Philip Rahv soon followed; Lionel Trilling was a revered professor of English at Columbia. Harold Rosenberg, long a provocative commentator on the politics of art and culture, had entered the mainstream as a consultant to the Ad Council. "Intellect has associated itself with power as perhaps never before in history," wrote Trilling, "and is now conceded to be itself a kind of power."

By any measure, the New York intellectuals had achieved a great deal within the limited sphere of their influence. They had claimed American literature as their own, renovated its most important figures, and made criticism an instrument of moral purpose. *The Liberal Imagination*, Trilling's collection of essays on English and American literature, had appeared in 1950, supplementing Kazin's *On Native Grounds*. Irving Howe's studies of William Faulkner and Sherwood Anderson, Philip Rahv's revaluation of Henry James, and Delmore Schwartz's appraisal of Hemingway soon followed. To be sure, there was an element of self-consciousness and slavish immigrant devotion in all this literary activity—"*Our* forests, Alfred?" was a sarcastic rejoinder that made the rounds in the wake of Kazin's admiring essay on Francis Parkman's *Oregon Trail*. But there was no question that these critics had brought credit to themselves and to the writers they championed. They had made the giants of American literature, in the words of *Partisan Review*'s editors, "spokesmen for *their* dreams."

Still, the question remained: What had the New York intellectuals achieved that was likely to endure? Had any in their midst produced a major contribution to American literature? For the most part, they were commentators; however influential in the culture, they produced secondary texts. One candidate for canonization loomed: Enthusiasm for the as-yet-unpublished *Adventures of Augie March* was running high. The excerpt that appeared in *The New Yorker* during Christmas week of 1952 only heightened the sense that a literary event was in the offing. At a dinner at John Marshall's house, Lionel and Diana Trilling put forth the proposition that Bellow was the most talented novelist of his generation; Trilling predicted that he was "virtually certain" to produce four or five significant novels over the coming decade.

There was a lot riding on the book. If anyone could bring Jewish literature into the American mainstream, it was going to be Saul Bellow. He alone possessed the talent and ambition to transcend the narrow confines of the *Partisan Review* culture. "Bellow was not one of the family's own only because he was a Jewish intellectual," explained Norman Podhoretz in *Making It*, invoking by his Mafia-like term the closeness and insularity of the New York intellectuals—"He also spoke for and embodied the impulse to lay a serious claim to their identity as Americans and to the right to play a more than marginal role in the literary culture of the country." Bellow was the family's "White Hope," Podhoretz claimed: "There was a sense in which the validity of a whole phase of American experience was felt to hang on the question of whether or not he would turn out to be a great novelist."

10

*The achievement of American Jewish writers has, of course, a symptomatic,
a historical importance since they act as surrogates for the whole
Jewish-American community in its quest for an identity,
a symbolic significance on the American scene.*

—LESLIE FIEDLER,
"The Jew in the American Novel"

I N THE SUMMER OF 1952, *The New York Times Book Review* had carried a querulous article by Diana Trilling in its "Speaking of Books" column, lamenting the decline of fiction in America. New novels sold fewer copies than ever, she noted, and she found little worth reading in each season's crop. What was it about our "cultural situation," she asked, echoing the stiff critical diction of her husband, that made contemporary American fiction "the soggy thing it is"? The answer was that the novelists of Trilling's generation had succumbed to nihilism and become "childish" and self-absorbed. Instead of asserting "human possibility," they had embraced despair.

A week later, an ambitious young critic by the name of John Aldridge took up the same topic in "Speaking of Books." Aldridge confirmed Mrs. Trilling's dire estimate of the "situation," but he disputed her contention that it was the novelists themselves who were to blame. What had made the novel so robust a form in the nineteenth century had been the stratification of society; the manners and morals of the middle class had provided it with a significant theme. The reason why postwar American novelists— especially Southern novelists—dwelled on their childhoods was less a matter of "willful atavism" than a response to the breakdown of the old social order. Childhood provided a "code" as rigid as the drama of middle-class life had been for novelists a century before.

"You'd need no Swami powers, I'm sure, to divine the fact that I disagree most violently," Bellow wrote Lionel Trilling the day after Aldridge's piece appeared:

> Are most novels poor today? Undoubtedly. But that is like saying mutilation exists, a broken world exists. More mutilated and broken than before? That's perhaps the world's own secret. Really, things are now what they always were, and to be disappointed in them is extremely shallow. We may not be strong enough to live in the present. But to be *disappointed* in it! To identify oneself with a better past! No, no!

Bellow himself was given to decrying the barbarous epoch in which he lived, but when someone else disparaged the quality of its literary productions he was quick to take umbrage. It was like criticizing one's own family—fine except when someone who wasn't a member did it. Novelists had a license to criticize the novel; critics didn't. That America was mired in philistinism didn't mean it had no writers of the first rank. Reviewing *Invisible Man* in *Commentary* that month, Bellow held up Ralph Ellison's book as an example of "greatness." *Invisible Man* had all the ingredients that Trilling and Aldridge found lacking in current fiction: It was rich in character and incident; it grappled with politics; and it showed, according to Bellow, that "a truly heroic quality can exist among our contemporaries." Ellison's protagonist, however invisible to others, in the end achieves dignity through the assertion of his independence—for the reviewer, a familiar theme.

Bellow's piece in *Commentary* was more than a book review: It was a passionate vindication of the novel as a literary form. Revising the theme he had addressed in his letter to Trilling, he took issue with another of Aldridge's pronouncements, this one in *Partisan Review.* Aldridge had asserted that there were only two "cultural pockets" left in America: the Deep South and "that area of northeastern United States whose moral capital is Boston, Massachusetts. . . . In all other parts of the country people live in a kind of vastly standardized cultural prairie, a sort of infinite Middle West, and that means that they don't really live and they don't really do anything."

Apparently, Ellison's protagonist wasn't the only invisible man. With a stroke of the pen, Aldridge had disposed of a whole population—not the first time in recent history that such an impulse had been conceived of (and carried out). "Can we wonder at the cruelty of dictators when even a literary critic, without turning a hair, announces the death of a hundred million people?" Bellow rejoined. The "infinite Middle West" that Aldridge so airily condemned was about to produce a vigorous defender: Augie March, who declares at the outset of his long and virtuosic confession, "I am an American, Chicago born."

In his own quiet way, Bellow measured himself against the modern giants of the form: Dreiser and Sherwood Anderson and D. H. Lawrence. Though he didn't bluster about getting into the ring with Turgenev and Stendhal the way Hemingway did, he aspired to belong in their company; as Alfred Kazin had discerned, he was "going to take on more than the rest of us." Becoming a writer was a protean enterprise; Bellow's aim was always to develop and evolve. The task he'd set himself in these years of itinerant composition was to fight free of self-imposed constraints, "Flaubertian" standards, and discover his own voice: "A writer should be able to express himself easily, naturally, copiously in a form which frees his mind, his energies." With *Augie,* Bellow found his form.

The struggle to achieve a more natural idiom required innumerable false starts and discarded manuscripts.* One of Bellow's favorite jokes, repeated in numerous interviews and with numerous variations, was the old story about the American tenor at La Scala who sings his first aria to thunderous applause, returning a second and a third time while the crowd screams, "*Ancora, vita, vita!*" Puzzled after his fourth ovation and reprise about why he's

*In early drafts, Augie is affiliated with an outfit called The Committee for a Reconstituted Europe and goes off to postwar Spain, where he encounters a colorful assortment of characters (much of this material showed up later in Bellow's short story "The Gonzaga Manuscripts"); his ship is torpedoed off the New Jersey shore and he ends up in a Brooklyn hospital instead of in the Azores; and he goes to work for Trotsky, who makes only a cameo appearance in the final version of the book.

being called back still again, the proud but exhausted singer cries out, "How many more times must I sing this aria?" Upon which a voice in the audience shouts, "Until you get it right."

Once he got it right, *Augie* spilled forth with impressive fluency. It filled twenty-two notebooks, some eleven hundred pages in all, scribbled by hand in Positano and Rome, in Paris and London, in Forest Hills and Greenwich Village, at Yaddo and the Princeton library. "The last two paragraphs I completed on a Viking Press typewriter," Bellow recalled. "Not a single word of the book was composed in Chicago." In a brief account commissioned by *The New York Times Book Review,* "How I Wrote Augie March's Story," he quoted a remark of Robert Penn Warren's that he liked to write in a foreign country "where the language is not your own, and you are forced into yourself in a special way."

The book's ambition was evident from its sheer heft: 536 printed pages. Writing *Augie,* Bellow quipped, was "like giving birth to Gargantua." Crammed with allusions to Homer and Virgil, the Bible and Shakespeare, Burckhardt and Rousseau, the novel didn't wear its learning lightly. In its scope, its density of reference, its large cast of characters, *The Adventures of Augie March* consciously emulates the work of Bellow's literary masters—"the bedrock writers," he called them: Dickens, Balzac, Hardy, Melville, Hawthorne, "the Russians," Tolstoy and Dostoyevsky, and above all Joyce. "Joyce was a Flaubertian to begin with," noted Bellow, an early and assiduous reader of *Ulysses:* "He brought to pork kidneys and privies and Dublin funerals a Miltonic power of language mixing elegance with street talk, popular ditties, obscenities and advertising slogans with Homeric echoes, poetry and silliness, the high and low." Joyce's capacious style became the basis of Bellow's aesthetic credo.

Like Joyce, the Bellow of *Augie March* was rhapsodic about the sheer variety of human life:

> bigshots and operators, commissioners, grabbers, heelers, tip-
> sters, hoodlums, wolves, fixers, plaintiffs, flatfeet, men in West-
> ern hats and women in lizard shoes and fur coats, hot-house and
> arctic drafts mixed up, brute things and airs of sex, evidence of
> heavy feeding and systematic shaving, of calculations, grief, not-
> caring, and hopes of tremendous millions in concrete to be
> poured or whole Mississippis of bootleg whiskey and beer.

In Bellow's view, there was nothing ordinary about his characters. Whatever their limitations of class and personality, he imbued them with heroic stature. Grandma Lausch, the Marches' boarder, a fussy, conniving *baba*, "as wrinkled as an old paper bag," reminds the grandiloquent narrator of Pharaoh, Tamerlane, Jehovah, and the Praetorian Guard. Simon, Augie's burly older brother, is a virile specimen with "the arms of a cricketer," "Iroquois posture and eagle bearing," "the grace of Chevalier Bayard and the hand of Cincinnatus at the plough"—a Jewish immigrant boy endowed with "the universal eligibility to be noble."

No character in the book exemplified this nobility more than William Einhorn: At one time or another, Augie likens him to Francis Bacon, Hephaestus, Anchises, Sardanapalus, and Socrates. A voluble, wheelchair-bound autodidact, Einhorn presides over the thirteenth ward with princely authority, dispensing patronage and advice from his fiefdom, Einhorn's Billiards. A great reader of Shakespeare and the Bible, a collector of pamphlets on Fletcherism and Yoga, Rudolf Steiner and Henry George, Einhorn entertains "dynastic ideas" about his family, in whom the gospel of self-improvement has done its work, "the organizer coming after the conqueror, the poet and philosopher succeeding the organizer, and the whole development typically American, the work of intelligence and strength in an open field, a world of possibilities." In Bellow's hands, the American dream of self-improvement achieved mythic stature.

If Einhorn is a Chicago version of Trojan Brutus, Augie is, by his own account, "Achilles among the maidens." His days are busy with sexual conquest. As Thea Fenchel, one of Augie's lovers, says: "You want people to pour love on you, and you soak it up and swallow it. You can't get enough. And when another woman runs after you, you'll go with her. You're so happy when somebody begs you to oblige. You can't stand up under flattery." The autobiographical note is hard to ignore; Thea's critique of Augie was Bellow's pointed recognition of his own passivity, his suspension of judgment in the face of praise.

In other ways, too, Augie bears a distinct resemblance to his creator, not only in his adventures—the cross-country trip by boxcar, the job in his brother's coalyard, the years spent in rooming houses on the fringes of the university, the summer in Mexico, experiences in the merchant marine, and self-exile to Paris—but in his private struggle to figure out who he is. The heroes of *Dangling Man* and *The Victim* were also bookish, introspective types, but Augie was the first truly Bellovian character, the first to question his own nature and his place in the world. He possessed the incipient theoretical proclivities of Bellow's later deep thinkers—Henderson, Herzog, Sammler, Citrine, Corde—along with their resistance to convention. "You've got opposition in you," notes Einhorn approvingly.

Augie's occupation is hard to pin down. At one time or another he's a dog valet, a clothing salesman, a union organizer, a textbook thief. Bookish and brooding, purposefully engaged in a struggle to define his identity—to *become*—he's the prototypical sensitive young man of modern literature, a variant of Stendhal's Julien Sorel and Flaubert's Frédéric Moreau, Joyce's Stephen Dedalus and D. H. Lawrence's Paul Morel. *The Adventures of Augie March* is an American bildungsroman—a novel of education.

A terse note on the back of the manuscript illuminates its theme: "Doesn't want to be what others want to make of him. Stendhal exceptional champion of this." One of Bellow's favorite protagonists was Julien Sorel, who finds even prison no obstacle to his progress toward self-fulfillment. Augie was a case study of "inner-directedness," Bellow explained to Lionel Trilling, employing a term from David Riesman's *The Lonely Crowd*:

> It isn't that Augie resists every function [the word was Trilling's]—that would make him a tramp; and while I would not hesitate to write about tramps if I were called to it, Augie is something different. I was constantly thinking of some of the best young men I have known. Some of the very finest and best intentioned, best endowed, found nothing better to do with themselves than Augie. The majority, whether as chasers, parasites, bigamists, forgers and worse, lacked his fairly innocent singleness of purpose. They had reached the place where they fixedly doubted that Society had any use for their abilities.

That "singleness of purpose" distinguished Bellow from his contemporaries. Long before he had accomplished anything of value or had even shown any particular promise, he had acquired a belief in his own unique abilities. "I didn't know what to do," his stand-in Augie reflects in an early draft of the novel, "but yearned till I quaked for a summary, and to be bound into one. And not for myself, but to have a use, serve an end, give my powers satisfaction." It's still not clear at the end of the book what Augie does for a living or what he wants to do, but the narrative offers a hint. He has "written out these memoirs of mine," he confides, installed himself at a table at the Café Valadier in the Borghese Gardens and "declared that I was an American, Chicago born, and all these other events and notions." Augie had become a writer.

The Adventures of Augie March confirmed Bellow's claim that fiction was higher autobiography. The famous opening declaration altered two facts about his life in the space of six words: He was a Canadian, Montreal born. But it was a characteristic misrepresentation: The heroes of his novels aren't renderings of Bellow the man; they're idealized versions of himself. They are very often tall, like Artur Sammler in *Mr. Sammler's Planet* and Dean Corde in *The Dean's December* (Bellow is five foot seven); of distinguished lineage, like Eugene Henderson in *Henderson the Rain King;* or of indeterminate ethnic origin—even the characters who are obviously Jewish make little of the fact. And why should it be otherwise? Bellow was writing fiction, he impatiently reminded those who probed his work for clues about his life. What's remarkable about his inventions is the balancing act they negotiate between proximity to the truth and deviation from it: It was as if, by altering the details to suit him, Bellow could become, in his books, the person he wanted to be.

He acknowledged freely that Augie March was a composite of his next-door neighbors on West Augusta Street, Charlie and Morris August.* And in a literal sense he was: The circumstances of the March family described in the opening chapters of the

---

*It was typical of Bellow to appropriate and adapt real names for his fictional characters, in this instance inverting and Americanizing the original. In the same way, the name Einhorn may have been suggested by the Einhorn Prayer Book, an early Reform volume that had been written by a rabbi in South Carolina in the mid-nineteenth century.

book—the fatherless household, the dim-witted mother, the matri-
archal Grandma Lausch—closely paralleled those of the Augusts.
But as the story proceeds, the family sounds more and more like
Bellow's own. Simon was a dead ringer for Bellow's older brother
Maurice, a brawny, profane "bag man" who did the dirty work
for a Chicago alderman, married money, and prospered in the coal
business. Also like Simon, Maurice had an illegitimate son, the
existence of whom Bellow exposed. "It's all there for the world to
read," the son, Dean Borok, once told a reporter for a Canadian
newspaper. And so it was. In the novel, Simon keeps a mistress,
Renee, and has a child by her. (Speaking in the Jewish intonations
of Chicago, Maurice's daughter, Lynn, commented briskly on her
uncle's methods: "What kind of creative?" she said. "He just
wrote it down.") After the book came out, Bellow and his brother
didn't speak for five years.

As for the Einhorns, anyone who grew up in Humboldt Park
during the 1920s would have recognized them as Sam Freifeld's
family. William Einhorn was unmistakably modeled on Sam's
father, the real-estate king of Humboldt Park. "The personal identification is altogether warranted," Bellow admitted to Sam. "If
you didn't make it I'd feel that I had missed the mark." He
expected his sources to be identifiable. "Did you recognize the
man in the lifeboat?" he once demanded of Alfred Kazin. It was
Arthur Lidov, whose house in upstate New York the Bellows had
shared. Bellow had put him in the novel as Basteshaw, the mad
scientist from Chicago with whom Augie ends up marooned at sea
after his ship is torpedoed off the Canary Islands.

Of course, establishing the connections between life and art can
only take you so far. One of the most interesting things about
Augie—indeed, about all of Bellow's fiction—is the way in which
it *isn't* autobiographical. Bellow appropriated other people's experiences—even experiences he had heard about secondhand—as
readily as their physical characteristics. He never trained eagles in
Mexico, as Augie and Thea do; it was Daniel Mannix, a ruggedly
handsome outdoorsman from the Philadelphia-area Main Line,
who furnished the material for their Mexican odyssey. Mannix
had acquired something of a reputation in the forties, writing
wildlife articles for magazines. He and his wife, Jule, had gone

down to Mexico in 1940 with an American bald eagle they had trained to hunt iguanas, and Mannix published an account of their adventures in *The Saturday Evening Post.*
Bellow lifted the whole episode and put it in his book. The most dramatic scenes in the Mexico chapter—Augie's tense efforts to train the eagle, the sensation their entourage causes in the village squares of dusty Mexican towns, the lizard hunts in the desert—are a detailed rendering of the Mannixes' experience. *Too* detailed, according to Mannix. When Bellow's account appeared in *Harper's Bazaar* as a story entitled "The Eagle," Mannix threatened to sue; Bellow was forced to insert a passage obliquely crediting him. Thus the curious sentence in chapter 14 of the book explaining that Thea "had gotten the idea for this hunt from reading articles by Dan and Julie [*sic*] Mannix, who actually had gone to Taxco some years before with a trained bald eagle and used the bird to catch iguanas."

In fact, Bellow had visited their villa on the outskirts of town just once, in the company of Jack Champion. "I doubt if we talked together for more than a few minutes," said Mannix. That he borrowed liberally from their adventures is beyond dispute; Bellow never could have written these pages without Mannix's article. But he transformed them, turning magazine prose into literature. In his hands, the eagle, Caligula, became virtually a character in its own right: proud, beautiful, imbued with grace, a specimen of "wild nature" and "humanity mixed with it, such as there was in the beasts that embraced Odysseus and his men and wept on them in Circe's yard." What Bellow's borrowing showed was how genius assimilates and transforms whatever raw material comes to hand.

If the plot wasn't all his own, the style was. Augie's voice—"a mingling of high-flown intellectual bravado with racy-tough street Jewishness," as Irving Howe summarized it—sounded like no other in American fiction. His breezy confession incorporated the cadences and intonations of Bellow's foreign-born parents, Humboldt Park street talk, and a deep immersion in the classics of English literature; one of the authors Bellow kept going back to during the writing of *Augie* was Henry Fielding, whose picaresque *Joseph Andrews* furnished a model for the wanderings of Augie.

The Homeric inversions ("Hrapek, Drodz, Matuczynski these dealers were called") and odd hyphenated compounds ("catarrh-hampered mathematical genius," "old-world-imitated walls") gave the language a charged, mythic intensity; the profane dialogue brought it down to earth. The folksy idiom of Mark Twain ("by and by," "I lit out," "ornery," "I reckon") alternated with the feverish imagery ("a heaving Calcutta midnight," "a dark Westminster of a time") of Swift and Defoe.

To this compendious anthology of biblical stories, Jewish folktales, and European literature Bellow added his own distinctive linguistic upbringing. He never wished to be identified as a Jewish writer, yet he was Jewish to the core. One memorable afternoon in 1952—as Irving Howe records in *A Margin of Hope*—Bellow sat down at a typewriter in the apartment of Eliezer Greenberg, a Yiddish poet and translator who was collaborating with Howe on *A Treasury of Yiddish Stories,* and gave them a hand. Greenberg read out a story they'd chosen in Yiddish, and Howe watched "in a state of high enchantment" as Bellow transformed it over the space of a few hours into an English masterpiece. "It was a feat of virtuosity, and we drank a schnapps to celebrate." The story, with the translation credited to Bellow, appeared in *Partisan Review* and made its author famous: It was Isaac Bashevis Singer's "Gimpel the Fool."

Like Bellow, Augie played down his ethnic status, but it permeated everything he did. That he was a Jew among Jews would have been clear enough from the names—Klein and Weintraub and Feinberg—and eastern European origins of his characters. They have a taste for smoked fish and other ethnic delicacies; they speak in the convoluted syntax of Jewish immigrants ("I could not find myself in love without it should have some peculiarity"); they resort to Yiddish words such as *verpitzed* and *gedenk* and the all-purpose *oy*. In his description of a typical Friday night at Simon's house, Bellow beautifully captured the gathering of the clan, the "tumultuousness and family heat, melding yells at the pinochle table, the racing of the kids, pitchers of cocoa and tea and masses of coffee cake carried in, political booming and the sharper neighing of women and all this grand vital discord." If there is such a thing as Jewish atmosphere, this is it.

Yet *The Adventures of Augie March* wasn't a "Jewish" novel, Bellow insisted strenuously. It was a novel by an American writer who happened to be a Jew. To claim otherwise would have diminished its universality. From its earliest beginnings, Bellow's fiction is a synthesis of two vital cultural strains—a synthesis that, in true dialectical fashion, produced something original. "The American-Jewish novel," wrote Leslie Fiedler, one of the earliest chroniclers of this new genre, "is essentially an act of assimilation." Bellow's great achievement—his "breakthrough," as Fiedler described it— is that he managed this feat while keeping intact his Russian-Jewish roots. As a Canadian and as a Jew, he would always be an outsider, but that same ancestry enabled him to renovate the language, bringing to American literature the legacy of Babel and Chekhov, whose stories he remembered his father reading aloud— in Yiddish—at the dinner table. "It is the poetry of the Jew that makes his hero what he is," wrote Karl Shapiro, "in Chicago, in Mexico, wherever Augie happens to be."

In later years, Bellow came to regard *Augie* as flawed. "I felt undisciplined as I was writing the book," he said. "I was too high in excitement. It got out of hand." Indeed, its jazzy artifice is wearing, and Augie's voice is implausible at times, his run-on syntax hard to disentangle, his neologisms—the cars "fluddering," the guests "clobbering" downstairs—contrived. And there was something self-conscious about the willed largeness of the enterprise. As the British critic Philip Toynbee remarked shrewdly, Bellow "was aiming too early and too directly at the Great American Novel."

But the book also possessed a kind of exalted vigor. "A novel, like a letter, should be loose, cover much ground, run swiftly, take the risk of mortality and decay," Bellow wrote to Bernard Malamud, explaining what he'd tried to do: "I backed away from Flaubert, in the direction of Walter Scott, Balzac and Dickens." Like the American Transcendentalists of the nineteenth century, who had created a tradition of their own—the WASP novel, so to speak—out of their English predecessors, Bellow borrowed from the writers he'd grown up reading to produce a new literary style. Chicago as place leaped off the page, whether in its wintry aspect, "the blackened forms of five-story buildings rising up to a blind Northern dimness from the Christmas blaze of shops," or in the heat of summer, when "the shady yards gave up the smell of the damp soil, of underground, and the city-Pluto kingdom of sewers and drains, and the mortar and roaring tar pots of roofers, the geraniums, lilies-of-the-valley, climbing roses, and sometimes the fiery devastation of the stockyards stink when the wind was strong."

By 1953, the Jewish voice had yet to make itself heard in American literature, except as a localized ethnic phenomenon. The shelf of postwar American novels by Jews—Norman Mailer's *The Naked and the Dead*, Arthur Miller's *Focus*, Bernard Malamud's *The Natural*, Lionel Trilling's *The Middle of the Journey*, Isaac Rosenfeld's *Passage from Home*, and Delmore Schwartz's collection of stories, *The World Is a Wedding*—represented the beginnings of cultural assimilation for Jewish-American writers; but only Bellow had begun to produce an oeuvre. In his first book, he had described the experience of his generation; in his second, the experience of his people, Jews living in the shadow of the Holocaust. *The Adventures of Augie March* was his American book; it staked his claim as an heir to the country's native individualism. "Why, I am a sort of Columbus of those near-at-hand and believe you can come to them in this immediate *terra incognita* that spreads out in every gaze," says Augie in his famous closing peroration. For Bellow, the "near-at-hand" turned out to be fertile territory.

11

We are certainly cultivating a future cult of Bellow.

—*letter from Sam Freifeld to Bellow, November 19, 1953*

BELLOW WAS OPTIMISTIC about the reception of his new book. As early as the fall of 1952, months before publication, he was advising Sam Freifeld to set aside some time the following spring. "*Augie* is coming out then. I want you to be my guest in N.Y. and Princeton during the highjinks of publication week, to drink whisky and pinch the maidens and throw our weight around." It was the swaggering tone of a man who senses that he's about to become a success.

He was relieved to have the book done. "*Augie*'s finished, thank God," he reported to Robert Penn Warren in the first week of the new year. It had been a difficult birth. He'd thrown away the last two hundred pages and missed his deadline, postponing publication until the fall of 1953. "My slogan was, 'Easily or not at all,' but I forgot it. Too much of a temptation to speak the last word."

By spring, the novel was gaining significant momentum. In addition to his *New Yorker* debut, prepublication excerpts had appeared in *Partisan Review, The Hudson Review,* and *Harper's Bazaar.* It had been chosen by the Readers' Subscription, a high-toned book club presided over by the distinguished triumvirate of W. H. Auden, Jacques Barzun, and Lionel Trilling. The Book-of-the-Month Club made it an alternate selection, introducing the novel to its readers with a report from the unflappably middlebrow Clifton Fadiman, who claimed "there has been nothing like it since the debut of Thomas Wolfe." Trilling and Warren provided enthusiastic blurbs. *The Adventures of Augie March*, predicted William Phillips, would "put Saul over."

The prepublication excitement didn't solve the problem of how to earn a living. Bellow's one-year appointment at Princeton was not going to be renewed; Viking had advanced him another five hundred dollars; and there was a little money from Book-of-the-Month Club—hardly enough to support two households. But once again, fate intervened in the form of a teaching job. Its emissary was the itinerant Ted Hoffman, who had transferred from Princeton to Bard, a small liberal-arts college in Annandale-on-Hudson, two hours north of New York City. Hoffman had learned of a sudden vacancy in the literature division and had proposed Bellow's name to the poet Theodore Weiss, the division's chairman. Weiss offered Bellow a one-year appointment. The salary was $4,500. The job was to begin in September 1953.

"Despite a high tuition," wrote Mary McCarthy of Jocelyn College in her novel *The Groves of Academe*,

> despite a picturesque campus—a group of long, thick-walled, mansarded, white-shuttered stone dwellings arranged around a cupolaed chapel with a planting of hemlocks, the remains of a small, old German Reformed denominational college that had imparted to the secluded ridge a Calvinistic sweetness of worship and election—something, perhaps the coeducational factor, perhaps the once-advertised freedom, had worked to give the college a peculiarly plebeian and subversive tone, like that of a big-city high school.

Jocelyn was a thinly disguised portrait of Bard, where McCarthy herself was briefly on the faculty, along with a lively assortment of European émigrés, indigent novelists, and academic misfits who conspired to make the place a center of intellectual life during the 1940s and 1950s. Bellow's colleagues included the poet Anthony Hecht; Heinrich Bluecher, a European intellectual of the old school and the husband of Hannah Arendt; and the tweedy, genial Fred

Dupee, one of the founding editors of *Partisan Review*. (McCarthy depicted him as Howard Furness, a mildly cynical professor who frowns upon other people's ambitions.) "At Bard, Literature—with a capital *L*—was a religion," said one of Bellow's students.

Founded in 1860 as Saint Stephen's, an Episcopal men's college that emphasized the classics, the college had evolved over the years into a radical and innovative institution, a kind of rural New School for Social Research; in 1934, the name was changed to Bard in honor of its founders, a family of teachers. Its student body, said Bellow, consisted of "castaways from ships that had foundered en route to Harvard or characters who had fallen from grace at Yale, people still refining the airs they had acquired in the great Ivy League centers." Many of the students came from troubled families, and psychoanalysis was practically part of the curriculum; one of Bellow's advisees even complained to the administration that Bellow was inadequate as a supervisor because he hadn't been analyzed. The student body was defiantly bohemian; Sondra Tschacbasov referred to Bard as "Bennington with boys." (The Bennington student body at that point was all women.) As usual, Bellow found the teaching a chore. "My new job is also, to date, the roughest," he complained at the end of September to Simon Michael Bessie, an editor at Harper and Row whom he had gotten to know in Paris. "Progressive for the students, reactionary for the enslaved teachers."

Still, he enjoyed his new status as a country squire. For the first time in his itinerant life, Bellow ordered up stationery; it declared tersely:

> SAUL BELLOW
> BARRYTOWN, NEW YORK

Bellow's lodgings were the upstairs apartment of a carriage house on the grounds of Sylvania Farms, the estate of Chanler Chapman, one of the local upper-crust grandees known as "river people."

Chapman had more money than he let on, but he had come down in the world: He was a descendant of the Astors and the son of John Jay Chapman, author of such sturdy defenses of individualism as *Emerson and Other Essays* and *New Horizons in American Life*. Chanler lived in his father's considerable shadow, asserting his individuality by going about town in dirty overalls and by swimming nude in his pool. He called Sylvania Farms his "piggery." But his dirt-farmer persona belied his literary bent. He proudly showed off his father's vast library and published a monthly broadsheet, *The Barrytown Explorer* ("Dime a Copy, Buck a Year"), that featured his own irregular sonnets. He even had press license plates on his car. He was also proud of the fact that his first wife, Olivia, was a great-niece of Henry James. "There were three great James brothers," he would declare in his booming voice: "The philosopher, the writer, and the drunk—Olivia's related to the drunk." Chapman's own claim to literary posterity was to come to him through his tenant. Six years later, when *Henderson the Rain King* was published, no one in the Bard community failed to recognize the original of its protagonist. "Henderson *was* Chanler," said a Bard student, Elsa Heister.

Bellow's arrival on campus coincided with the arrival of his fame. *The Adventures of Augie March* came out the very week that he settled in at Sylvania Farms and the term at Bard began. The reviews were mixed but prominent. On the front page of *The New York Times Book Review*, the critic Robert Gorham Davis complained that Bellow was "too lavish with adventures" and that Augie didn't have much substance as a character; but he compared the novel to Dos Passos's *U.S.A.* and made it clear that he considered its publication a momentous literary event.

The cover of that week's *Saturday Review of Literature* featured a drawing of the author in a flannel shirt against a seedy neon background—the novelist of urban grit. The magazine's reviewer, Harvey Curtis Webster, began: "Reading 'The Adventures of Augie March' in 1953 must be a good deal like reading 'Ulysses' in 1922." Webster found the book's "total meaning elusive," but he was caught up in the story and in the vivid diversity of Bellow's characters. Webster closed with a "tentative" verdict: "Saul Bellow is perhaps a great novelist, 'The Adventures of Augie March' perhaps a great novel."

Most reviewers agreed. The novelist Harvey Swados, writing in *The New York Post*, pronounced *The Adventures of Augie March* "very possibly the most significant and remarkable novel to have been published in the United States in the past decade." Malcolm

Cowley, one of the most influential critics of his day, classified it—along with *Invisible Man*, William Styron's *Lie Down in Darkness*, and Nelson Algren's *The Man with the Golden Arm*—as an example of "the most hopeful tendency now to be found in American fiction."

Other reviews were more ambivalent. *Time* gave the book the same grudging treatment it had given Bellow's previous two books but praised his "self-generating power and authenticity." Granville Hicks, ranking the ten best American novels since 1945 for the Christmas issue of *The New Leader*, put *The Adventures of Augie March* ninth but with serious misgivings. "Would I recommend it? Certainly. Would I like to re-read it? Well, yes," Hicks equivocated, "had we but world enough and time." In other words, no.

The most wounding review came from Anthony West, the son of Rebecca West and H. G. Wells, in *The New Yorker*. West accused Bellow of hustling for "literary promotion" by trying to create an "All-America Everyman." Augie's New World brashness offended West: "Augie March is the twentieth-century equivalent of Henry James's Christopher Newman, who so tediously took his load of moral virtue along with him when he confronted the effete vulgarity and corruption of old Europe in 'The American.'"

Bellow was so incensed by West's review that he dashed off a letter to Katharine White, the fiction editor of *The New Yorker*. The review was "a disgrace," he complained, enraged by West's symbol-hunting efforts: "Out of his own turbulence, thoughtlessness and pedantry Mr. West has attributed to me things as remote from me as the moon. 'Simon' and 'simony', 'eagles' and 'virility', 'sex' and 'culture'—really, it is simply too much!" White tried to placate him. Editors at the magazine simply weren't allowed to interfere with a critic's judgment, she wrote in a long, explanatory letter, no matter how much they might disagree with it; and *The New Yorker* had no letters column in those days. In short, her hands were tied.

Two weeks later, a second letter from White arrived. She had just had a long talk with William Shawn, the editor of *The New Yorker*, who agreed that West had been "flatly wrong." Shawn had authorized her to say that if Bellow wrote a "judicious" letter eschewing "violent terms," *The New Yorker* would publish it under the coyly noncommittal heading it had devised for such correspondence: "Department of Correction." It was the first time in the history of the magazine, White noted solemnly, that such an invitation had been extended.

Bellow replied from Barrytown on October 27:

> There are some misunderstandings that simply weaken you when you contemplate their complexity. In some odd sense Mr. West's review is not a piece of criticism but a piece of fiction; it is a very bad short-story or something of that kind. For after all Mr. West invented what did not exist; he wrote what he thought to be my novel, and as he is a bad artist he produced a disfigured something. One cannot show the error of such a 'something.' I don't mean to try. What would be the good of it.

It was enough that Shawn had acknowledged the injustice. Bellow had written only for the sake of his "mental health." But he neither forgave nor forgot the offending review. When the historian Peter Gay brought up West's name at a dinner party, Bellow's face clouded over; after the guests had gone home, he turned to the hostess, Pearl Kazin, and said, "Don't you ever invite that man again."

West's attack could be dismissed as the fulmination of a British snob, but even within the *Partisan Review* "family" there was dissent, not least Norman Podhoretz's remorseless anatomy of the book in *Commentary*. The book's main defect was its style, Podhoretz argued: "The feeling conveyed by Mr. Bellow's exuberance is an overwhelming impulse to get in as many adjectives and details as possible, regardless of considerations of rhythm, modulation, or, for that matter, meaning." Nor was the hero a plausible character: "Augie reminds us of those animals in the cartoons who get burned to cinders, flattened out like pancakes, exploded, and generally made a mess of, yet who turn up intact after every catastrophe, as if nothing has happened." Bellow had produced "an impressive *tour de force*," Podhoretz concluded magnanimously; he had opened up the novel as a genre to new possibilities and given his audience a sense of "what a real American idiom might look like." It was "no disgrace to have failed in a pioneer attempt," Podhoretz allowed, but the damage was done.

Bellow was obsessed with Podhoretz's review. Lunching with William Phillips one day, he complained bitterly about Podhoretz, insisting that his review had been "a put-down" (which it was). "Nothing I could say," recalled Phillips, "could convince him that to say he, a young writer, was not yet as good as the classics was high praise." Bellow imagined—not without reason—a conspiracy. As Podhoretz reported it to friends, Trilling had "for some dark purpose" been insincere in his praise of the book and had—in collusion with the editors of *Commentary*—put up Podhoretz for the job. There might have been a shred of truth to this suspicion: "We told Podhoretz not to like it," the art critic Clement Greenberg, then an editor at *Commentary*, testified, displaying his gangsterish side; Podhoretz himself later acknowledged that he was "the designated hit man." But that Trilling had anything to do with the assignment is highly unlikely. For one thing, he had no official connection with the magazine; furthermore, conspiracy wasn't Trilling's style—he operated on a higher plane.

To Pascal Covici, who had taken over as Bellow's editor at Viking after Monroe Engel left, Trilling had delivered an encomium on May 27 that is remarkable for its apparently spontaneous enthusiasm:

> Dear Pat:
> I've just finished the galleys of Saul Bellow's novel and I'm delighted with it and enormously impressed. As you know, I went through the manuscript last summer in my search for a chapter for my issue of *Perspectives,** but I read the whole book through again with as much interest and excitement as the first time—indeed, even more. Forgive me if I am so dull as to say that I couldn't put it down and finished it at an ungodly hour in the morning: such is the fact. For some time now I've thought that Saul was the most interesting and promising of the young novelists and the new book quite confirms my earlier opinion. He really does a unique thing—he takes the naturalistic novel, the novel of commonplace, even sordid fact, and infuses it with poetry and intelligence without in the least betraying the factuality of the fact. I have—though perhaps you won't believe it of

---

*Perspectives USA was a journal funded by the Ford Foundation and edited by James Laughlin.

me—an addiction to the naturalistic novel, and actually read [James T.] Farrell with pleasure; but the after-feeling of most naturalistic novels is never for me very pleasant or interesting exactly because they don't have what Saul's book so preeminently does have—put it this way: that with all their presumed commitment to LIFE, they aren't very alive and they don't represent people who are really alive. But it's Saul's gift to see life everywhere. He really believes in the living will. There isn't an inert person in the book, just as there isn't an inert sentence—the prose is really wonderful in its vivacity and energy, in its fusion of the colloquial and the intellectual tradition; it would be remarkable as a *tour de force* if it weren't so much more than a *tour de force,* if it weren't, that is, a genuine style.

I know you think I don't know the first thing about publishing, but in spite of this rude and unwarranted opinion of yours, I'd like to give you a piece of advice. Saul's manifest talent and his exigent demands upon it mustn't mislead you into promoting the book as a highbrow effort. This will not pay the book the compliment it deserves. It's *not* a high-brow book, not what you publishers are believed to call a "prestige item"—it's a book for many people to enjoy, and if not everybody gets every nuance of it, that doesn't matter: they'll still enjoy it.

I need scarcely say how much good luck I wish you with it.

Coming from Trilling, a critic legendary for his reserve, such an excited testament to Bellow's powers as a novelist could hardly have been more unambiguous. But Trilling was "conflicted," he confessed to the poet Stanley Burnshaw; writing an enthusiastic description of *Augie* for the Readers' Subscription newsletter, *The Griffin,* had been a struggle. It showed. The essay, entitled "A Triumph of the Comic View," started off on a highly positive note, asserting that Bellow had created "a human reality at once massive and brilliant." Trilling proceeded to pile on grand comparisons, associating *Augie* with the masterworks of nineteenth-century English fiction; the great comic tradition of Cervantes, Fielding, Dickens, and Joyce; and, finally, the tradition of "American personalism" as exemplified by Melville, Emerson, Whitman, Thoreau, Mark Twain, E. E. Cummings, Sherwood Anderson, "even—Heaven help it!—by William Saroyan and Henry Miller." But having trotted out this Great Books syllabus and having declared that *The Adventures of Augie March* was a book with a "moral intention," an "idea"—"that whatever fixes life and specializes and limits a person to a function endangers the wholeness of the self"—Trilling found himself in the awkward position of nevertheless dissenting from the book's entire premise. He resisted Augie's belief that it was heroic to elude definition. "Without function"—that is to say, without a fixed identity—"it is very difficult to be a person and to have a fate." Trilling never did quite manage to conquer his reservations. Three years later, when he collected his essays in *A Gathering of Fugitives*, he omitted "A Triumph of the Comic View."[*]

Bellow chose to overlook Trilling's demurrals. "I know that you have contributed more than a little to the success of my book," he wrote him a few weeks after publication day:

> I'm in your debt also for mental support—for the intelligence of your reading of it. Though I'm not, perhaps, the most objective judge to be found, I thought your essay brilliant. The many criticisms of *Augie* I've seen since have made me appreciate yours all the more; I appreciate above all your sense of justice, for I know the book must have offended you in some ways.

It was a gracious gesture—and a shrewd one. In paying homage to Trilling's influence, Bellow acknowledged that the making of literary reputations was in part a collaborative venture. Months after publication, Bellow's friends were still beating the drums on behalf of *Augie*. In December, John Berryman weighed in with "A Note on *Augie*" in *The New York Times Book Review*, placing Bellow in the American naturalistic tradition of Dreiser and Crane. Delmore Schwartz, writing in *Partisan Review*, judged it "a new kind of book," superior to *Huckleberry Finn* and *U.S.A.*

"What is there to say except that the reviewers have been Augie Marchean reviewers?" Bellow wrote Alfred Kazin, making fun of the reviewers' solemn response to the novel:

> They have led me to coin a phrase, "low-seriousness." Comedy is illegal—it isn't even seen—it *isn't*. In low-seriousness no one

---

[*]A decade later, Trilling reversed himself again, allowing his essay to be reprinted as the introduction to the Modern Library edition of the novel in 1965.

laughs until the cue is given and then asks grandly, "Now, why was it appropriate to laugh?" Enter hereupon Bergson, Freud, Dante and Charlie Chaplin, each bearing a basket of rocks. The rocks are piled on our breast in a huge cairn—and so goes it.

That Bellow had intended his work to be taken seriously was never in doubt. But he also intended it to be read as an entertainment. "What makes people so sober?" he wondered in a letter to Leslie Fiedler. "We've sunk to a great depth if the funnyman also finds it necessary to be a prophet." For Bellow, humor was another manifestation of freedom, the writer thumbing his nose at the pretensions of high culture. A review of Joyce Cary's *Except the Lord* that he wrote early in 1954 for *The New Republic* defined his own art: "There is no reason why a novelist should be required to write always in his best vein. On the contrary, he should be encouraged to diversify his talents and deny himself no attitude or point of view, serious or comic."

Bellow's congenital suspiciousness found a convenient object in what he took to be the resistance of the WASP literary establishment to his fiction. In later life, when his reputation was secure, he continued to dwell upon the contempt he had been forced to endure from English departments at Northwestern, Minnesota, and Princeton and from the modernists championed in the pages of *Partisan Review,* whose ignorance of his work he turned into a deliberate slight. T. S. Eliot didn't notice him, Bellow observed with some resentment (as if Eliot, who had no interest in contemporary fiction, *should* notice him), "but I did feel that I would be consigned to a very low place by Eliot's historical consciousness, so I decided very early on not to be affected by his prestigious judgment." Eliot's overt hostility to Jews in *After Strange Gods* and elsewhere, like Henry James's notorious distaste for the immigrants of the Lower East Side in *The American Scene* and Pound's diatribes against usurious Jews in the *Cantos*, were literary chapters in a long history of discrimination. One of Bellow's favorite quotes was a passage from Goethe's *Wilhelm Meister's Apprenticeship:* "We do not tolerate any Jew among us, for how could we grant him a share in the highest culture the origin and tradition of which he denies?"

Direct experience of this exclusion was harder to document in the fifties than it had been in the thirties. The Holocaust had made anti-Semitism unacceptable—which didn't mean it no longer existed. Bellow pointed to Allen Tate, a self-proclaimed "Agrarian" from Tennessee who made no secret of his disdain for the predominantly Jewish *Partisan Review* crowd. "He thought we were an immigrant eruption into the literary life of the post-Confederate period," as Bellow wryly put it. It bothered him that Edmund Wilson never reviewed any of his books after *Dangling Man*—further evidence of "the whole WASP effort to suppress the Jewish novel."

Even Jewish critics collaborated in this act of literary suppression. "They have their own axes to grind," Bellow insisted in a talk he gave in old age, still rehearsing the injustices, both real and imaginary, that had impeded his early career:

> Descendants of those same people whose cackling and shrieking set Henry James's teeth on edge when he visited them on the East Side, they accuse themselves secretly of presumption when they write about Emerson, Walt Whitman, or Matthew Arnold. My own view is that since Henry James or Henry Adams didn't hesitate to express their own dislike of Jews, there's no reason why Jews, while respecting these masters, should not be free to write as they please about them. To let them, the hostile American WASPS, determine once and for all what the American psyche is, not to challenge their views, would be disloyal and cowardly.

Bellow's sensitivity to ethnic slights wasn't without basis: There *was* a strain of anti-Semitism in American literature and its spokesmen. Among critical keepers of the gate, Jews who wrote novels in those days were regarded with the same suspicion that, a generation later, black writers would face (often at the hands of Jewish critics). As for Edmund Wilson, he was no less guilty of casual anti-Semitism than his contemporaries Fitzgerald and Hemingway, for whom *Jew* was a term of physical identification as descriptive as *tall* or *thin*. Given the fact that T. S. Eliot was the literary standard-bearer of the day, Bellow's vigilance on this score could be excused. As his friend Delmore Schwartz liked to say, even paranoids have real enemies.

Augie was a modest triumph, though Bellow persisted in experiencing it as a trial by fire. "I am enjoying all the noise," he confessed that fall. "I've never been a bombshell before." For the first time, a book of his was making money; on December 11, Viking sent him a check for two thousand dollars. "Well, it's all very interesting," he admitted to Trilling, "and what fascinates me most is the book's sale. *That* I had never anticipated." (It eventually sold thirty thousand copies but never made the bestseller list.)

"From my family, not one word has come," Bellow reported to Sam Freifeld in September. His complaint was premature: A few weeks later, a communication arrived on the letterhead of the Carroll Coal Company in Chicago.

> Dear Saul
>   i am sending you a check for (250). You will send 15 copies of The Book the way Sam ask. y[ou]. and the Balance is in payment for the copy y. send to me. We are filling fine. I was in the hospital for observation. The X-rays come—and very good with the exception the find I had a slight heart attack. Still I hope to be good for the next ten years. The book made a hit all over America. I hope the next will be still better. Still from time to time send me few lines a letter.
>
> From time to time wright me a letter.
> Still I am the head of all of you.
>   Pa Bellow

Abram's postscript challenged in a few words Augie's novel-length assertion of independence, but his pride was evident. At last, the father had acknowledged that his dreamy son had accomplished something.

Isaac Rosenfeld paid ungrudging homage to Bellow's achievement. "I may not have been able to get along with you in recent years," he wrote from Minnesota, where he was teaching that year,

> but I got along famously with *Augie*. I loved it, immensely, most every bit of it, & even the parts I didn't like I liked. It's an ocean-full of everything you've been & not been & dreamt & wanted,

a tremendous spouting proclamation of someone struggling up from the depths. . . . It's a work of joy, & may you, too, now, be full of joy.

With every hope for happiness, Isaac

The Adventures of Augie March had made Bellow famous. His name seemed to turn up everywhere in the fall of 1953. Having "established his beachhead," as Harvey Breit, the editor of *The New York Times Book Review*, characterized the early stages of his career, he was at the age of thirty-eight "successfully fanning out into broader and brighter domains." Breit's interview with Bellow in the *Book Review* the week of publication gave the general public its first glimpse of the man. Breit was impressed with Bellow's modesty, the ease with which he abjured "the over-solemn, the too-pious manner, the inflated ego" and "made his momentous novel seem casual." Relaxed and bantering, Bellow refused every opportunity to pontificate. "I guess I'm getting on a professorial kick," he laughingly broke off one discourse on literature.

On the Bard campus, he was suddenly a figure of considerable renown. "Trailing clouds of glorious reviews, he was like the champion prizefighter who could not walk into a saloon without being challenged by local toughs," recalled Al Ellenberg, who had been in Bellow's class. Students crowded into Bellow's American literature seminar out of curiosity, "only to be put off by his mono-logic dissertations on Melville and Hawthorne." Elsa Heister also gave him low marks as a teacher—though when he talked about Dos Passos or Dreiser, "there wasn't any question that he knew all of it, and deeply."

Sexual *moeurs* at Bard were decidedly relaxed. There were plenty of compliant young women about, and Bellow was said to have "bedroom eyes." His physical charm was hard to resist. Michael Rubin, a Bard student, provided a vivid impression of Bellow in his novel *A Trip to Town*, about a womanizing professor by the name of Leon Kossoff who has just published a hugely successful novel, *The Fortunes of Shlomo O'Brien*. "His face," wrote Rubin, "despite the ill-considered addition of the writer's pipe, was as finely delineated as Michaelangelo's Apollo playing Jesus Christ in the Sistine Chapel. The arrogantly winged nose, the sensitive, fully sculptured mouth braced by a strong chin were compellingly handsome." But Bellow was generally careful about involvements with students. "He was sensitive and gentle, considering that young women with crushes were a dime a dozen," said Louise Gruner, an undergraduate who idolized the young literary star.* "He was kind—I think he sympathized with my history [she had survived Bergen-Belsen]—but he kept me at a sufficient distance so that I wouldn't get hurt."

Sondra Tschacbasov generally came up from New York on weekends. "Saul and Sondra entertained wonderfully," said Anthony Hecht, a frequent guest at Saturday-night dinner parties in Bellow's apartment above the tractors and boats in Chanler Chapman's carriage house. Bellow was "very genial, open, accessible, full of fun." For all Bellow's grumbling, "Greenwich Village-in-the-fields" (his sardonic name for the place) attracted its share of lively characters. It was at Bard that Bellow met Keith Botsford, a raffish novelist with a taste for sports cars and Bennington girls, who would become a lifelong friend. Botsford claimed to be a direct descendant of Machiavelli on his mother's side; his father, an American expatriate in London, had been a professional tennis player. (One New York editor described Botsford as "decaying gentility.") His preferred mode of dress was a cape, velvet pants, and a Three Musketeers–style hat. Bellow reproduced him in *Humboldt's Gift* as the grandiose literary entrepreneur Pierre Thaxter, "mad for 'Culture,'" conversant with the classics, an authority on Stravinsky and the Ballets Russes: "Sometimes he was a purple genius of the Baron Corvo type, sordidly broke in Venice, writing something queer and passionate, rare and distinguished."

Also on the faculty that year was Jack Ludwig, a Canadian who suffered from crippling gout in one leg and hobbled about campus in a thick-soled shoe, which he propped up on a footstool with Johnsonian pomp. "A robust vitalist with a deep, blasting voice," as a colleague characterized him, Ludwig considered himself a

---

*Bellow appropriated her name—though not her character—for Angela Gruner, the sensuous niece of Artur Sammler in *Mr. Sammler's Planet*.

great Joycean and an accomplished Yiddishist. He and Bellow met at a party in Bellow's apartment at the beginning of the term. "Saul was in the corner being browbeaten by this uncouth yokel from Winnipeg," in Botsford's recollection. Apparently Ludwig was trying out his Yiddish ("butcherboy Yiddish," according to Bellow). Ludwig admired Bellow with a fervor that verged on adoration. At a literary conference that fall, he stood up and addressed a question to the author of *The Adventures of Augie March*, "the greatest twentieth-century novel."

While Bellow reveled in the attention his book had brought him, Sondra often felt left out. "I didn't have a lot to do, and I wasn't happy there," she said. Like Hannah, Leon Kossoff's mistress in *A Trip to Town*, "she was the butt of committee-room jokes, an indignity to the administration and the prime object of teatime prattling of wives." Her youth—she was a good decade younger than most of Bellow's friends—and her intellectual insecurity put her at a disadvantage; it was hard to be the girlfriend of a Big Man on Campus, especially when the Big Man treated her like a little girl.

In the city, Sondra shared an apartment with Pearl Kazin on Riverside Drive. Having a place of her own served a pragmatic purpose: Bellow had filed for a divorce, but Anita was contesting the terms, and her lawyers weren't supposed to know that he was living with another woman.

Bellow came to New York often, to see friends and editors and, as winter approached, to escape the cold. Chapman, his landlord, was cheap to the point of eccentricity; he was known to serve vintage wines in Hellmann's mayonnaise jars. Bellow claimed that Chapman wouldn't provide wood for the furnace and was trying to freeze him out; Chapman maintained that writers got cold because they didn't move around as much as other people. As the novelist William Humphrey, another member of the Bard faculty, remarked, "Chanler could have a falling out with anybody over anything and so could Saul."

By December, the situation had grown untenable. "Am quitting unheated Barrytown," Bellow informed Fred Dupee two days before the end of the year. "Will be your neighbor soon at 333 Riverside Drive."

Bellow's new apartment had a temporary air about it. It was sparsely furnished, like most of his residences, but he was proud of the view: Inviting guests into the bathroom, he would direct them to climb up on the toilet—from which vantage, if they stood on their toes and peered out the window, they could catch a glimpse of the Hudson.

During the week, he camped out in a spare room at Ted Hoffman's house, a former rectory down the hill from the Bard campus. Ted's wife, Lynn, remembered it as a "damp and wormy place" with mouse dung smeared on the windows. Lynn worked three days a week at Viking Press in the city while the men fended for themselves. Things were "nice and quiet," Bellow reported cheerfully to Robert Penn Warren; he was writing and "in very good spirits." For once in his life, he had money; Pat Covici sent him a second royalty check for five thousand dollars, and Bellow gave his brother Sam ten thousand dollars to invest for him.

Early in the new year, Bellow learned that he had won the National Book Award for the most distinguished American novel of 1953. The judges were Mary McCarthy, Arthur Mizener, the social historian Gerald Sykes, the critic David Dempsey, and the biographer Leon Edel. Their deliberations were brief; Mary McCarthy was so convinced the prize should go to *Augie* that she declared there was no reason to meet at all. "Mary construed our procedural discussion as hostility to Saul's book," Edel recalled: "In the end, to clarify the matter, we passed a formal motion declaring our *unanimous* decision that Bellow deserved the award." But McCarthy, interpreting events in her own way, let it be known that Edel had argued against *Augie*. Word of Edel's "opposition" got back to Bellow—sufficient grounds for him to snub Edel when they next met.

The now-celebrated novelist wasn't one to rest on his laurels; he was as productive as ever that year. "The Gonzaga Manuscripts," his story about an American scholar's quest for the lost poems of a García Lorca–like genius in Spain, was included in the paperback anthology *Discovery;* he produced a theater chronicle, "Pleasures and Pains of Playgoing," for the May/June 1954 issue of *Partisan Review;* and he was collaborating with Delmore Schwartz on an anthology to be called "What the Great Novelists Say about Writing the Novel." (This promising project never materialized.)

In England, *Augie* received better reviews than it had in America. The chronically cynical Kingsley Amis, writing in *The Spectator*, was impressed with Bellow's "gaiety and good humor, his fizzing dialogue, his vitality." J. B. Priestley praised his "astounding zest" and claimed there had been nothing comparable in American fiction "since Thomas Wolfe first came roaring into it." The one sharp dissent came from V. S. Pritchett, who was put off by Bellow's "self-intoxicating style."

Bellow's good fortune was evident to his friends. Delmore Schwartz noted of a visit that winter: "Saul and Sandra [*sic*] arrived—very happy & looking very well—Saul looked much younger, not heavy & drawn." The poet Louis Simpson was also struck by Bellow's exuberance. Simpson was visiting friends in Greenwich Village one night when Bellow strode in with a briefcase, his overcoat sprinkled with snow. He had just given a lecture at the New School and was in a state of high excitement—not over his lecture, it turned out, but because of a showdown he'd just had with the critic John Thompson, who had followed him up the street afterward, trying to pick a fight. Goaded to the breaking point, Bellow had turned around and swung his briefcase at the obstreperous critic. "He was exhilarated," Simpson recalled. "There is nothing like opposition, driving a man against the wall, to make him believe in the reality of his ideas."

Bellow's high-spirited competitiveness charmed his friends. Even when he played his violin—he had kept up with the instrument, in an amateur way, since boyhood—he threw himself into the task with a kind of radiant verve. Listening to Bellow and Alfred Kazin race impulsively through Mozart's *Turkish Rondeau*, Kazin's wife, Ann Birstein, noted sardonically, "It was a question of who was going to win." Bellow had given up on Reich, but he still went off into the woods and howled "to express his animal ferocity at Bard." Not all his diversions were of the high cultural variety; afternoon walks with Ann Birstein in Riverside Park often ended up at a Ping-Pong parlor at Ninety-sixth and Broadway.

He was an inveterate joke collector and laughed the loudest at his own jokes. He had a gift for the devastating one-liner. Of a failed novel: "He never got his characters out of immigration." To an heiress who threatened to write her memoirs: "Will you use a typewriter or an adding machine?" One day, Pearl Kazin, a regular fiction reviewer for various quarterlies, read aloud the first sentence of Ralph de Toledano's *Day of Reckoning:* "The fingers of his mind were tired." Bellow replied, "From picking his mental nose."

Bellow's caustic wit spilled forth in his letters. He was an assiduous correspondent, producing over the course of half a century perhaps the last significant archive of literary letters. Postcards, scrawled missives on lined yellow sheets, and typewritten letters issued from Chicago, New York, Paris, Minneapolis, and Yaddo, crammed with jokes and maxims. Reporting on his trip to Canada, where he found that his quaint hometown had become Americanized, he wrote to Pat Covici: "Suppose you were to revisit the Black Sea and found that it had become Lake Erie? How would you feel?" To Leslie Fiedler, who had sought advice about his career, he recommended a by now familiar course: "Try to make no sense of life but throw yourself on God's mercy, I say."

He was ardently loyal to anyone who passed the rigorous test of friendship—for as long as they served his needs. On the deepest level, Bellow didn't attach to men any more than he did to women; Tuley friends such as Glotzer, Peltz, and Rosenfeld benefited from his attention because they were part of his life. "You realize that if you were to tell me to fly to Lima Peru tonight, I'd depart without a question," he wrote to Sam Freifeld in February 1954. And a few months later: "I am your old friend, who loves you. Whenever you need me, I'm ready to serve you. You can count on me absolutely." But he also depended on Freifeld, who had become a lawyer at forty after years in the insurance business, to look after his affairs—even to help him define his identity: "When I want to know *who* I am I must still turn to you." As far as Bellow was concerned, *The Adventures of Augie March* was a work of homage. "People *will* feel exposed, ridiculed, no matter how you deal with them. *Any* mention causes *them* shame. They can't think that perhaps it was my aim to love not shame them. If you wanted to think about, and find meaning in *my* existence I would thank you for it, not curse you."

Bellow maintained that his genius didn't belong to him alone. He was simply the medium. "I often feel, when I'm writing, that I'm a composite person," he confided to his old Chicago friend Louis Sidran. But this insistence upon his friends' collective share in his destiny contained an element of guilt. As Bellow's star rose, theirs had begun to fade. Dave Peltz, once an aspiring novelist, was in the construction business; Louis Sidran was an advertising copywriter. Some members of the old gang had made limited headway in their chosen vocations. Oscar Tarcov's slender, Kafkaesque novel, *Bravo, My Monster,* appeared in the same season as *Augie* and got respectful reviews; but his career as a playwright was stalled, and he had taken a job with the Anti-Defamation League. "Yours isn't a happy condition," Bellow acknowledged in the aftermath of a quarrel provoked by Tarcov's tepid (or insufficiently warm) response to *Augie:*

> I realized you were down on your luck and had no patience with me. But I was suffering too, and all I could do was withdraw from your harsh judgments. Had either of us been a little happier he would have done better by the other. But our miseries were anti-symbiotic, or something like that. I was in the strange condition of being envied while I lay at the bottom of hell.

Isaac Rosenfeld was also having problems. He got turned down for a Guggenheim in the spring of 1954, and his second novel had yet to find a publisher. Teaching at the University of Minnesota, he felt exiled from New York. "Living in Mpls doesn't help when the shit is upon me," he wrote Bellow in April, "but I keep going & it hasn't been too bad. If I could settle some of my sex & character problems I'd probably be a lot better off." He wasn't sure of his next move—whether to stay in Minneapolis, return to Chicago, or come back to New York: "I hope I'll have a clearer story to tell in the future."

It wasn't only the friends of Bellow's youth whose literary dreams were threatened. Some he had met on his way up were also floundering. Delmore Schwartz was embarked on a destructive regimen of alcohol and amphetamines. John Berryman was on his way to becoming a public drunk; at a Bard literary conference, he made a spectacle of himself grieving over Dylan Thomas, who had fallen off a bar stool at the White Horse Tavern and was in a coma at Saint Vincent's Hospital.

Bellow, meanwhile, was thriving. "I'm in pretty good shape," he wrote Sam Freifeld on April 25, 1954. He hadn't given up "investigating freedom"—his euphemism for philandering—but he had every intention of marrying Sondra as soon as he could get free from Anita. "I have to marry her," he told Mel Tumin, somewhat exaggerating the degree of Sondra's adherence to the precepts of her newfound Catholic faith (and the degree of her prudery): "I can't get into her pants if I don't." It was a remarkably adolescent way of looking at the challenge of seduction for a man of almost forty; even if he was joking—a generous interpretation—the crudeness of his language was significant. Sondra was (to put it less bluntly than Bellow did) a sexual object; as such, she didn't require fidelity. He sent Freifeld a postcard of Gloria Swanson curled up on a bed. On it, he wrote: "But to women I am highly susceptible."

The divorce from Anita was turning out to be a troublesome business. As Bellow saw it, he was being "sheared of his earnings" by a greedy wife. "Anita keeps me fairly strapped," he complained to Freifeld, managing once again to make himself out as the victim. "She always *took* more than she gave. I don't reproach her with anything. Her nature is its own reproach. I am genuinely sorry for her but I can feel more compassion as an ex-husband." Like the shrewish Margaret in *Seize the Day*, "She lived in order to punish him." But Bellow could be vindictive, too. When a cousin invited him to her son's bar mitzvah, and informed him that she had also invited Anita and Gregory, Bellow returned the RSVP card having checked "will not attend" and underlined the word *not* five times, followed by an exclamation point.

As usual in such situations, it was the child who suffered most. Bellow often had Gregory with him on weekends and in the summer for weeks at a stretch. Writing to Leslie Fiedler, who had invited him out to Montana, he explained his situation: "I couldn't arrange to have Gregory travel from his summer camp all by himself, and the time we spend together in summer is too important. It is the only time during which I live with the kid, and we both look forward to it."

Yet nothing could mitigate the fact that he was an absent father—even when he was present. Once, when Bellow and Freifeld went off to a baseball game, Bellow refused to take Greg along, giving the excuse that he was afraid it would rain. "I don't want to worry you, but I have the strange feeling that decisions like this are or can be used against you by Anita with Greg," Freifeld warned him. "Just take him to more ball games; he is a wonderful boy." It was good advice but hard for Bellow to follow. The emotional connection to Greg was there; the will to express it—or to make the sacrifices necessary to express it—was sadly lacking. Abram had provided a poor model of fatherhood. Like so many immigrants of his generation, he had been distracted from parenting by his own struggle to make his way in the New World. Compounded by Bellow's obsession with his work and by the social customs of a time when raising children was a task left largely to women, it wasn't a legacy that made for a nurturing father. Besides, Bellow wasn't a nurturing person—to students, children, wives, or parents. *He* wanted the nurturing.

For Bellow, like Rogin in his story "A Father-to-Be," children represented another encroachment on his "freedom," the life force "trampling on our individual humanity, using us for its own ends like mere dinosaurs or bees." Less grandly put, children—like wives and friends and lovers—were always in danger of making emotional demands, requiring attention, expecting to be loved. Bellow regarded the arrival of a second child as a happy event—"a sort of compensation for the death of Isaac," according to Pearl Kazin—but the transfer of attention from husband to child was more than he could tolerate. Raising children was still considered women's work: "The hand that rocks the cradle devastates all plans," he confided to Keith Botsford. And to what end? Small children didn't "need" a father, Bellow maintained. He liked to quote Groucho Marx's comment, upon being informed by Margaret Dumont that he had become the father of a large family: "Let's keep one of each kind and give the rest away."

The divorce was an ordeal for both parties. In an effort to put her life back together, Anita had enrolled in the School of Social

Work at Adelphi University, and she was back in therapy; but she was "shattered" by the breakup of her marriage. Bellow described his own feelings in a revealing letter to Fiedler:

> I suffered, and still do suffer, terrible pains after the separation. I found no alternative. I could not spend the rest of my life with her. Nor was it good for her to live with me. As for Gregory, I doubt that he will suffer as much from our divorce as I suffered from my parents' "good" family life. I love Gregory and I know how to make him feel my love. He is injured, but not really seriously injured and his position also has its advantages. At Princeton last year I nearly went down, and Anita's troubles were as terrible to me as my own. We are both infinitely better than we were.

His transparently self-serving explanations hardly obscured the basic fact that Bellow did what he wanted to do. It was a character trait so deeply ingrained that it constituted a virtual imperative. As Tommy Wilhelm in *Seize the Day* gropingly explains to his father, who harshly interrogates him about why he left his wife, "I had to—I had to."

Bellow resigned from Bard in June 1954. He had enough dough to get by for a while, he reported to Freifeld. And if things didn't work out, he had an invitation from the University of Minnesota to teach. He also mentioned that he had found a house he wanted to buy, a prospect that would make Greg happy. "I need a place of my own very, very badly," he confided: "I am nearly ready to *sit* and be Columbus's chronicler not one of his crew."

12

*There were many people who knew him, and each had a different idea
of the man. One saw him as a tough guy; another saw him
as* ein mensch, *sympathetic and full of wisdom.*

—LOUIS SIMPSON,
Views from a Window

THE HOUSE that Bellow coveted was in Sag Harbor, on the
eastern end of Long Island. But the owner was asking eight
thousand dollars, well beyond his means. A place of his
own would have to wait.

Continuing his itinerant ways, he was off to Cape Cod for the
month of July; he'd rented a cottage near Slough Pond in Wellfleet,
"in a setting of pines, ticks and sun." There was plenty of lively
company around: the Harvard professor Harry Levin; the historian Arthur Schlesinger, Jr.; Mary McCarthy and her third husband, Bowden Broadwater; Alfred Kazin and Ann Birstein. People
tended to work in the mornings and adjourn in the afternoons to
la plage des intellectuels, as the beach was sardonically known.

Social life in Wellfleet was intense. Almost nightly, according to
one of McCarthy's biographers, there were "huge outdoor parties
that could be heard and smelled by way of the alcohol fumes half
a mile away." McCarthy had encountered Bellow "with son and
dog," she reported to Hannah Arendt, noting that he was "not
very friendly."

The claim is probably true. Bellow never warmed to McCarthy,
this fierce intellectual who was almost violent in the formulation
of her opinions—a trait that (in a woman, anyway) he found unnerving. "Mary was unquestionably a witty writer," he conceded,
"but she had a taste for low sadism. She would brutally work over

people who weren't really worth attacking." Despite McCarthy's references in her correspondence to "Mrs. Bellow" (was this one more barb?), there was no such person in the summer of 1954. Sondra came up from New York only on weekends, and the frenetic Wellfleet scene yielded other romantic opportunities. "You could see the electricity starting up," Alfred Kazin observed of a developing flirtation between Bellow and a svelte German woman on the beach. But for the most part he was on his own, saddled with the not entirely welcome responsibilities of a single father. "I am completely worn out from acting as G[reg]'s tutor, governess, cook and baseball buddy and can't wait to get back to N.Y.," he confided to Robert Hivnor toward the end of July.

Bellow's onerous duties as a parent didn't slow him down on the literary front. "The tentative title of this book is 'Memoirs of a Bootlegger's Son,' " he explained to Henry Allen Moe when he applied for a second grant from the Guggenheim Foundation. "In it I give an account of the fortunes of an immigrant and his eldest son; I follow their lives for forty years, from Canada to the States, and describe the efforts of the father to make a fortune and those of the son to remain a son. In the end, is it the old father, perhaps, who has become the American?" By the end of 1954, he had typed nearly two hundred pages.

Written in the first person, from the point of view of a sensitive, observant boy named Joshua, "Memoirs of a Bootlegger's Son" is a scarcely veiled portrait of the Bellow family circa 1920, newly arrived from Russia and struggling to "make good"—that universal immigrant aspiration—in the slums of Montreal. A pithy title—"Jews"—graced the cover of early notebook drafts. The book was even more overtly autobiographical than Bellow's three previous books. The redbrick rowhouse on Saint Dominique Street; the three brothers and their dutiful piano-playing sister Zelda (her actual name); the drunken boarder Daitch (also his real name); the Hebrew lessons in the basement cheder: All this was fact and was to find its way, a decade later, into the fictional background of Moses Herzog. In another way, too, "Memoirs" was autobiographical: Joshua, the youthful narrator, is already a ladies' man. Chasing after a girl, he bumps into a pole and bloodies his nose. "I was reckless about girls," he confesses. "I flung myself after them, lost my head, stuffed snow down their backs." But, he explains with typical Bellovian passivity, "they had to provoke me first."

"Memoirs of a Bootlegger's Son" replays Bellow's past with soulful zest. The lore he'd absorbed as a child at the dinner table is recounted artfully, along with events that Bellow had witnessed firsthand: The matzohs mailed back to his grandfather in the Old Country; the letter describing his uncle's death from typhus that his mother read in tears beside the washtub; the arguments over money between his father and his aunt. The book ends with Pa planning to leave Canada and go work for his cousin, who owns a bakery in Minneapolis.

"Memoirs of a Bootlegger's Son" hinted at the sibling rivalries in Bellow's family, but it never got to the heart of them. The feelings resolved so neatly in his book were still unresolved in life. Bellow's brothers were as intensely competitive and dismissive as ever. "It's true that my name won't go down in the *Encyclopaedia Britannica*," Maurice Bellows said in reference to his newly famous brother, "but I have money, and he doesn't." Sam, now a partner in the family coal business, also spoke disparagingly of his kid brother, whose name "you could look up in the library" but who still turned to his big brothers for handouts. Bellow could never shake off their put-downs. It didn't matter what the critics said: He longed to make good in their eyes.

He also depended on his father, the third member of what he perceived to be a disapproving triumvirate. "His whole life was a struggle against these brothers and his father, none of whom ever thought he would amount to anything," said Mel Tumin. Yet in "Memoirs of a Bootlegger's Son" Pa is seen through a haze of gemütlichkeit—congeniality and warmth. He beats his son (as did Abram Bellow), but never mind: "When he touched me and said I was pretty good, I wanted to take his hand and kiss it, and say how well I understood what was happening, and how much I loved him." And when Pa comes home beaten bloody by rival bootleggers, the boy laments: "My father! Why he was like a king to me, and the image of everything noble and great."

Bellow himself thought the manuscript was too sentimental. The real story was contained in its opening sentences: "I never

could do much to please my father. He was a severe critic of me."
But then he backed off from telling the rest of that tale. However
true in the biographical details, "Memoirs of a Bootlegger's Son"
was untrue to its author's deepest feelings. Not long after Abram
Bellow's death, "The Son of the Oedipus Complex," as Bellow
jokingly referred to the manuscript, joined his archive of unpublished works, though it was spared the fate of "The Very Dark
Trees" and "The Crab and the Butterfly." If it wasn't good enough
to publish, it was good enough to keep.

As pleased as he was with Bellow's literary accomplishments,
Abram remained skeptical; how successful could his son be if he
was always short of funds? In 1955, nearing forty, Bellow was still
accepting money from his father. "I am mailing a check for you,"
Abram wrote that winter.

Living in modest but comfortable retirement in a brick bungalow on Rockwell Street on the North Side, an elderly Jewish
burgher active in local affairs, Abram fretted over his son's non-
bourgeois ways. Why couldn't he settle down with one woman?
For his part, Bellow complained that his father, an Old World
patriarch not given to displays of affection, was withholding: "He
belonged to the Jewish school who never praised children." When
Maurice complained that he'd never been a "pal" to his sons,
Abram exploded: Where was it written he should be a pal? He was
a father.

Bellow's friends were witnesses to tense family scenes. Ruth
Miller, his former student and future biographer, once sat in the
dim parlor on North Rockwell Street as Abram interrogated her
about her father. Where in Lithuania was he from? What did he do
for a living? When did he come over and on what ship? Bellow was
embarrassed. "All the way on our ride back, he fumed and
groused about his father," Miller recalled. "Abram was nosy. He
was impolite. He had submitted me to an inquisition. He did not
respect his son's friends but grilled them."

Things became so acrimonious at one point that Sam Freifeld
was called in to mediate. "I don't know what anyone can do about
my father except to change his character and that lies within the

power of no one," Bellow wrote Freifeld not long after the publication of *Augie*, his anger thinly veiled by a pretense of generosity:

> I see no reason why I should not be faithful to whatever was, in the past, venerable in my father and I do my best to make allowances for the rest. I wouldn't be uneasy about this at all if I were you. It's just like my father to begin to be generous long after the rest of the world has begun. He's impressed by my new fame and even more by the sales of the book and so now he feels uneasy and wants, too late, to go on record as a good parent. I try to make him feel there is plenty of time.

There wasn't. On February 7, 1955, Abram Bellow wrote his son from the Waverly Hotel in Hot Springs, Arkansas:

> Dear son Saul,
> I hope everything is fine by y[ou]. also Hershel [their name for Gregory] is filling good. We are alone. Two weeks we improved a little. Stil we no so well. We are not anymore young—I am 75. Also aunte [Abram's wife] is not more a spring chicken. So to late philosophical. According the age we are very fine. I hear from Chicago from Jane and Sam. The[y] are fine. We are figuring to stay over the Jewish Easter if it no to much. Send my Sam journals with your articles. We'd be proud to read.
> Be god.
>
> Bellow

Whether his slip was simply an immigrant's misspelling or the ultimate in a Jewish father's unrealistic expectations, it was Abram Bellow's last written injunction to his son. He died of an aneurysm three months later.

The *Chicago Sun-Times* ran the obituary on May 2, below the headline: ABRAM BELLOWS, 74, DIES.* The notice read: "Abram Bellows died Monday in his home at 6135 N. Rockwell. Mr. Bellows was President of the Carroll Coal Company at 1800 W. Carroll. Surviving are the widow, Fannie, sons Maurice and Samuel, a daughter, Mrs. Jane Kauffman, and several grandchil-

---

*The added *s* may have been the result of Abram's other sons getting their names in the paper so frequently, with the pluralized spelling they had adopted; Bellow himself was often identified in Chicago newspapers as Saul Bellows long after he'd achieved world fame.

dren." There was no mention of the youngest brother. A later edition corrected this oversight, noting that the deceased was NOVELIST'S FATHER and identifying Bellow as "the author of 'The Adventures of Augie March.'"

Bellow was devastated by his father's death. "When my father died I was for a long time *sunk*," he wrote years later to the novelist—and Bellow biographer—Mark Harris, consoling Harris on the death of his own father. Arriving at 333 Riverside Drive to pay a condolence call, Ruth Miller heard the doleful strains of Mozart's *Requiem* floating through the corridors. "When Saul opened the door, he was weeping." He told her he'd been playing it for two days. "Since my father's death last month I've been slow at everything," Bellow wrote Leslie Fiedler a few weeks later, apologizing for his tardy reply to a letter. It was an excruciating loss. All his life, Bellow had labored to become someone his father could admire; their conflict had provided an impetus to create. Though he now had a child of his own, he defined himself more as a son than as a father. His father's death had thus deprived him of a major component of his identity. Even in extreme old age, he would long to see Abram "on the other side."

Bellow and Anita were still squabbling over the terms of their divorce, and Sondra was pressing him to get married. But the Guggenheim had come through with a second grant, and Bellow hoped to go somewhere exotic—*not* Paris, he stressed to Leslie Fiedler; perhaps to Spain or Italy. "How do I know where that old spirit in my feet is going to lead me?"

Uncertainty held no fear. Bellow was rarely calmer than at those junctures in his life when he had no idea where he would live or how he would support himself. Matters would "straighten themselves out," he assured Alfred Kazin, employing the impersonal syntax he favored. There was nothing contrived about this cheerful fatality. Waiting for life to sort itself out, like being claimed by women and trusting in God, was Bellow's way of reposing his faith in the vindicating power of his own talent.

That August, after completing a feature story on the small towns of rural Illinois for *Holiday* ("Write your impressions," as Bellow summarized his assignment), he packed up his old Chevy and headed west. He would be spending his Guggenheim year in

Reno, Nevada, one of the few states where it was possible to obtain an uncontested divorce in those days. A six-week stay was required. Bellow's voluminous correspondence in the fall of 1955 bore the unlikely return address of Sutcliffe Star Route, Reno, Nevada.

"After several weeks at a place for dudes, I took a cabin in the desert," he reported to Ruth Miller on November 5. He was "absolutely, unconditionally and almost astrally alone" but not unhappy:

> I found that I had acquired such a charge during the last few years in New York that it gave me a case of the bends to change pressure. I've been here now for almost six weeks and have almost fulfilled the minimum residence requirement. Of course, unless Anita is converted I shall have to be here a good while longer; and if she is on some Road to Damascus it's odd she hasn't reached it yet, for she's been around the earth several times, in miles. I don't expect her to stop persecuting me. All the same, she's in for a bit of a shock herself. Sometimes it strikes me funny, and when I laugh no one hears. I can whoop my head off out here; it startles only the coyotes.

The cabin, at the edge of a Paiute Indian reservation forty miles outside of Reno, overlooked Pyramid Lake and was surrounded by mountains. Electricity came from a generator: a Model A Ford engine. The only means of communication was a lone telephone booth out on the highway. For company, Bellow relied on his land-lady, Peggy Marsh, a hard-drinking divorcée from Saint Louis who was to figure as Hattie in his story "Leaving the Yellow House." "You will be astonished not to hear complaints from me, but I haven't any," he declared to Freifeld:

> Oh yes, now and then it's gone a little hard with me, but nothing mortal has happened. And now the first six weeks are almost out, and I find myself almost regretting that they've gone so quickly. This sort of life suits me more than I would have thought possible. I fish and ride, and walk and read and write; at moments I even think. On Columbus Day I lit a little candle, for isn't this what America was supposed to have been? Wasn't one supposed to think a bit here?

If Freifeld heard no complaints, Pat Covici at Viking heard plenty. Covici was a venerable figure in the publishing world. Among his authors were Malcolm Cowley, John Steinbeck, and Arthur Miller. A large, voluble Romanian with a shock of white hair, Covici carried out his editorial responsibilities with an old-fashioned European grace, entertaining his writers at wine-drenched lunches and writing them long, hortatory letters. He was less an editor than a village elder—"some part psychiatrist, some part lawyer, some part priest," according to Harold Guinzburg, the publisher of Viking.

Bellow's letters to Covici—he sometimes addressed him face-tiously as "Father Covici"—had the same bristling, affectionate tone that had characterized his letters a decade earlier to James Henle, another "surrogate father." From Reno, he poured forth a litany of complaints: He had to speak at a function sponsored by the *San Francisco Examiner*; the article he'd written for *Holiday* had been rejected ("it turns out that I wasn't pious enough about Carl Sandburg and Marshall Field or somebody"); he had to sit out in Nevada until his settlement with Anita was complete. "None of these things do I want to do," he noted, apologizing for the "hornet's tone" of his letters: "Hence the temper. Please forgive me."

His primary grievance concerned money. "You millionaires are all alike," began one typically irascible letter responding to the news that Viking had bought the rights to *The Victim* from Vanguard:

> In your surfeit with money you imagine there is no lower class.
> It is very good of you to reprint my book and I thank you for it
> heartily (thank you heartily), but is there anything in it for me
> other than the honor? You forgot to mention. If I were as
> cautious with words as you are with sums we'd never get
> through first grade on our combined minds.

Bellow was also unhappy about the advance Covici had offered for a collection of stories, and he made it known that he was "in no mood to be trifled with. . . . In fact, I'm damned sore about everything, and down on everyone—no exceptions. I've been idiotically timid and meek, and I begin to feel it's time I made a fight."

Covici was hard to provoke, but even his equanimity was challenged by this outburst. He was "perturbed" by Bellow's "fantastic accusations," he confessed on October 19, deploring his star author's latest "mouthful of poison and sand."

The phrase proved ill-advised. Bellow replied the same day, pointedly leaving off the "Dear" in his salutation:

> Pat:
>
> Sand and poison, eh?
>
> Look, Pat, let's not make baby talk. I am not one of your money mad writers, and whatever you and Henry [Volkening] decide upon will be acceptable to me. You know perfectly well why I was sore. But I'll spell it out for you, so that you can't possibly avoid my meaning.
>
> I am not Andrea del Bellow the faultless writer; I am a sinner like the rest. I can't expect to please everyone, I know, least of all some of your editorial colleagues. They, I realize, are indispensable to you, whereas I am not. But you are my editor, aren't you? Now when they grumble about me, I hear the echo from you, and should I deny my own hearing? And should I be pleased about it when complaints about my unpleasantness come down to me? And should I be happy when it is necessary to submit my stories, like any lousy beginner, before a contract can be drawn? The stories should have come to me for reworking, and when I was satisfied with them it is my opinion that Viking should have received them and published them without a single damn syllable of protest.
>
> If you don't want these stories, you needn't take them. I won't get my sand and poison up and bolt Viking. I love you too much and don't want my books to be published by a canning concern. But stand by me honorably, and don't give me any Madison Ave. double-talk, but consider my pride as a workman. I am not unqualifiedly enthusiastic about everything I write. When I have read through them, I myself may not want to publish these things. But that should rest with me.
>
> As for the advance, I am not one of your 4-star generals weighed to the balls with medals and prestige; nonetheless you haven't lost much money on me yet.
>
> You old bat, if I didn't love you like a parent I'd never get so worked up.
>
> Yours, Saul

Like a parent: The phrase is key. Covici belonged to the long line of powerful and disapproving businessmen on whom Bellow focused his need for approval and the anger that insatiable need engendered. But Covici was determined to hold on to his author. "I am proud to be your editor, your mentor, your conscience," he replied a week later, listing every role short of (holy) father.

Demanding of his authority figures, Bellow was generous toward his peers. Like a newly rich immigrant spreading the bounty among poor relatives, he lobbied indefatigably on behalf of the less gifted and less fortunate. In his "Theatre Chronicle" for *Partisan Review,* he praised the work of Ted Hoffman, Lionel Abel, and Robert Hivnor. He offered to send an essay by Ruth Miller to Delmore Schwartz at *Partisan Review;* recommended Jack Ludwig to Henry Volkening; submitted a poem by his Salzburg student Pearse Hutchinson to Karl Shapiro at *Poetry.* He even tried to get *The Saturday Review of Literature* to let him review Oscar Tarcov's novel.

When Bellow offered criticism of his friends' work, it tended to be of the constructive variety, though women generally received theirs with a dose of condescension. Ruth Miller was "a good woman" with "talent to burn," he declared, while praising her "beautiful face." When he had to express reservations, he used the occasion to expound his own aesthetic credo: Go further, do more. "For a long time I allowed myself to be pushed into these small spaces, too," he wrote Alice Adams from Reno: "I am only urging you to utter the magic syllable 'Whoosh' in the face of psychological oppression. The nineteenth century drove writers into attics. The twentieth shuts them in nutshells. The only remedy is to declare yourself king, or queen, of infinite space."

To oppose this "psychological oppression" was Bellow's self-appointed task. The effort to break free of constraints, both personal and literary, to elude categories of every kind, had become by the mid-fifties an increasingly persistent theme—in a way, *the* theme. In his letters, in book reviews, in the essays and articles he was called upon to write more frequently now that he had achieved a certain eminence, Bellow issued proclamations asserting his newfound literary freedom from critics, Englishmen, professors, and "the tyranny of the Oxford style." Writing to Berryman about his long poem, *Homage to Mistress Bradstreet,* in the summer of 1956, Bellow pronounced it "a triumph," but he also noted the limitations imposed by its stringent form: "All the formal properties have to be cracked and the simplicities released—like, 'Torture me Father lest I be not thine.'" It was a striking image: He wants the father, by torturing him, to make him the father's—to suffer the ordeal required to be a son.

Yet in another sense, Bellow's mandate was to "be not thine"—or anyone else's, for that matter. "You must learn to govern yourself, you must learn autonomy, you must manage your freedom or drown in it," he wrote in "The University as Villain," published a year later in *The Nation:* "Don't tie yourself down—and you will turn out fine." It was as if he needed some obstacle, some impediment, to define himself against. Any attachment, even a geographical one, he experienced as oppressive and demanding. If his path of willed rootlessness made Bellow feel free, it also indicated an effort to inoculate himself against the perilous isolation of the writer's life—"drowning in freedom"—by embracing that life on his own.

The university was another potential oppressor, like fathers and brothers and wives. By the time he was forty, Bellow had taught at Minnesota, Princeton, Bard, New York University, and the New School for Social Research, but the only job he'd held for more than a year had been at Minnesota, where he lasted for two. Novelists and college English departments have a long history of ambivalent relations; that literature is their shared focus makes it only a more hotly contested domain. In "The University as Villain," Bellow conceded that the practice of hiring writers to teach wasn't wholly pernicious; there was good conversation to be had in the faculty lounge, and a bucolic campus wasn't necessarily any more unreal than Greenwich Village: "You may find illumination anywhere—in the gutter, in the college, in the corporation, in a submarine, in the library." All the same, too many professors were "discouraged people who stand dully upon a brilliant plane, in charge of masterpieces but not themselves inspired, people who are to literature what Samuel Butler's clergymen were to religion."

For Bellow, the prime specimen of this type was Lionel Trilling. Trilling had undergone his own discouragements at the hands of the WASP academic establishment, securing a professorship at Columbia only after his book on Matthew Arnold irrefutably proved his credentials; but that was no impediment to Bellow's fixation. "I tell you, you'd better keep these things away from the English Dept.," he warned Louis Simpson about his poems: "L. Trilling would be the first to bring you up on charges." And to Granville Hicks, who had approached him about contributing to an anthology of essays on contemporary fiction, Bellow replied testily:

> Of course we are continually aware, while working, that we are under attack, and so perhaps it is wiser not to pretend that we are a species without enemies. I am familiar with Lionel Trilling's attitude, of course. It is one of the historical blessings of Jewish birth that one is used to flourish in the face of hostile opinion.

And what was Trilling's "attitude"? What pronouncement had issued "from the summit of Morningside Heights," as Bellow slyly identified his new nemesis in "Distractions of a Fiction Writer," the essay he wrote for Hicks's anthology? In all likelihood, the spark for his annoyance was an essay in which Trilling had remarked upon the apparent cultural poverty of American life, its lack of traditional institutions ("no Oxford, nor Eton, nor Harrow; no literature, no novels, no museums, no pictures, no political society, no sporting class"). From this chronicle of deficiencies and from Trilling's arch Anglophilic declaration that America offered "no opportunity for the novelist to do his job of searching out reality," Bellow construed a challenge to his very existence. That Trilling had been one of his earliest and most ardent supporters was forgotten; like the critic John Aldridge (and like Trilling's wife, Diana), Trilling seemed to be questioning the centrality of fiction, its claim to attention in a culture that worshiped virile action and material gain. Writing novels, Bellow complained in "Distractions of a Fiction Writer," was a marginal activity. It was "the businessman, the administrator, the political leader, the military man" who held the cards in our society: "These have the power; they are the representative men; in them manhood is mirrored." A novelist could never be—in Chicago parlance—one of the big boys. But it was different when Trilling said it.

Bellow hadn't chosen his vocation, he claimed; like wives and lovers and jobs, it had chosen him: "It occurs to a man that he is a writer." He discovers that imagination is the medium through which he experiences the world; his job is the cultivation of his own sensibility. Consciousness is his line of work, as Herzog puts it. How to reconcile that occupation with the business of money-making that Americans—including Bellow's family—considered the only legitimate form of work? "The whole world is in motion, blazing," he wrote in his essay. "And what are you doing? You're doing nothing commensurate. Only sitting here alone, oddly faithful to things you learned as a boy . . . practicing a peculiar and, some say, an obsolete art. You may have an inherited Jewish taste for such things." It was a familiar refrain. Two decades earlier, Bellow had sat at the bridge table in a back bedroom of his mother-in-law's apartment in Ravenswood, writing short stories while his brothers toiled at the Carroll Coal Company; now he was a writer, officially recognized as such. His adolescent fantasies of literary fame had become triumphantly real. Yet writing seemed as doubtful an occupation as ever. "My interest in literature is beginning to revive," he wrote, only half facetiously, to Ralph Ellison from Nevada: "I hate it less now than I did last year. God knows how my back ever came to be under *this* cross. To do something once in a while is a thrill, if you don't have the money spectre waiting on the throne for you to perform and grovel like a damn clown. It hasn't become easier; it's that I care less."

In mid-November, Bellow drove to Malibu to visit Sondra, who had been staying there with friends. A week later, they headed up the coast to see Bellow's old friends Herb and Mitzi McCloskey in Palo Alto. Bellow was "horribly excited," he wrote Ruth Miller on the eve of his departure, and could hardly sleep.

Glad as he was to be reunited with his fiancée—as he now identified Sondra—Bellow still mourned the dissolution of his marriage. At a New Year's Eve party in Palo Alto, McCloskey asked Bellow why he was looking so glum. "Tonight is the eighteenth anniversary of my marriage to Anita," he answered sadly.

For the wives who got left behind, it was even harder. After years of a lonely existence raising her only son in Queens, Anita moved to California and eventually remarried. But the trauma of a broken home, the legal and emotional acrimony of divorce, the ordeal of raising a child alone in reduced circumstances, dependent on irregular alimony checks, would recur twice more. The gallery of grasping ex-wives featured in Bellow's novels told one side of the story; the wives themselves remained mute.

Early in 1956, Bellow's friends received in the mail a formal wedding announcement, elegantly printed on a white card:

> Married
> Miss Alexandra Tschacbasov
> and
> Mr. Saul Bellow
> the first of February
> Nineteen hundred and fifty-six
> Reno, Nevada

It was "the dead of winter," Sondra recalled; the only guests present were the Covicis and the Ludwigs. The service was performed in a synagogue by an English rabbi who was more interested in discussing the latest issue of *Commentary* than in overseeing their vows. The newlyweds spent their wedding night in Bellow's cabin in the desert, with the groom reading aloud to the assorted company from a new novel he called his "African book."

A week later, Bellow reported to Sam Freifeld: "In all my life I have never stood so level. The bubble is in the middle of me. Perhaps an uneven landscape like these mountains makes your head sit straight on your shoulders." About the fact that he had just gotten married he had oddly little to say.

He was writing with feverish intensity—"working like a miner," as he put it to Covici. By February "the Africa whatever-it-is" was in its sixth chapter "and going strong." He had also finished a short novel, called "Here and Now"—or, as it appeared in the summer 1956 number of *Partisan Review*, taking up nearly the whole issue, *Seize the Day.**

---

*Other titles Bellow considered were "Hail and Farewell," "One of Those Days," and "Carpe Diem."

Bellow had submitted the novella first to *The New Yorker*, where it was turned down on the grounds that it was too long. The editors were apologetic and admiring, but Bellow found the experience so painful that he couldn't risk repeating it. From then on, he resorted to the stratagem of "showing" a new story to his editor at the magazine, Rachel MacKenzie, on the pretext of soliciting her opinion; MacKenzie then took it to William Shawn. If Shawn liked the story enough to make an offer, MacKenzie would explain to Bellow that she "hadn't been able to resist showing it to Mr. Shawn."

Partisan Review gratefully accepted *Seize the Day* in its entirety, but Bellow was insecure to the point of paranoia and turned upon Pat Covici with unprovoked fury, having gotten it into his head that his editor didn't like the new book:

> I am sure some of your colleagues find it depressing, and perhaps you have caught a contagion of opinion. Well, maybe it is depressing, but this is a term that people throw whenever they feel pressed to come into focus. Nobody likes that of course. However, I wouldn't dream of asking you to publish something of which you did not approve. On that score I want to make myself absolutely clear. If you and Harold [Guinzburg] and Marshall [Best, the editorial director of Viking] don't like these stories of mine then *don't* print them.

Covici was stunned. "Your aberrations are not simple to explain and I shan't try," he replied heatedly on May 11: "I thought I made myself clear over the telephone when I told you what a brilliant job of revision you did with 'Seize the Day.' Please tell me why should Viking want to publish it if we do not approve of it?"

In his next letter, Bellow adopted a more conciliatory tone. He *was* "a little nutty," he admitted, and joked that he'd had "the insane wisdom at least to pick a profession in which it would profit me." But Covici's assurances didn't entirely placate him. "I did have to phone and extract a statement about Seize the Day from you," he reminded his editor, "and it naturally grieved me." No amount of praise was enough. The void could never be filled. In the words of Bellow's Bard colleague Theodore Weiss, "He was a hungry man."

After months of wrangling between their lawyers, Anita and Bellow finally agreed upon a settlement—a costly one for him. He was to pay $150 monthly for Greg's support and another $100 in alimony until Anita remarried. He also had to pay all the lawyers' fees for both sides and retroactive installments back to October. "The settlement is made," he wrote Ruth Miller: "I have won and lost. So fair and foul a day we have not seen." In his mind, the emphasis remained on "lost" and "foul." Bellow was the one who had walked out of the marriage, yet he'd managed to retain his status as the aggrieved party. "At money, I can't win with Anita," he complained to Sam Freifeld. "I prefer to attend to my work, and to make love. I am doing very well in both endeavors, and that's enough for me."

Six weeks later, Bellow, still settled in Reno, had a letter from the playwright Arthur Miller, to whom he had been introduced by Pat Covici. The playwright was also going through a divorce and was on his way to Reno. He had a problem "of slightly unusual proportions," he explained:

> From time to time there will be a visitor who is very dear to me, but who is unfortunately recognizable by approximately a hundred million people, give or take three or four. She has all sorts of wigs, can affect a limp, sunglasses, bulky coats, etc., but if it is possible I want to find a place, perhaps a bungalow or something like, where there are not likely to be crowds looking in through the windows. Do you know of any such place?

The "visitor" was Marilyn Monroe. They were just waiting for his divorce to come through.

Miller arrived early in April and moved into a cottage behind the Bellows'. (Monroe was back east, shooting *Bus Stop*.) Once a week, the two writers drove into Reno to buy groceries and do their laundry. Several times a day, an Indian messenger trotted up to Miller's door and notified him that he had a call at the pay phone at the trading post from "Mrs. Leslie"—Monroe's code name. Once, a camera crew showed up to interview Miller about his impending marriage. Bellow, meanwhile, was often up in the hills, "emptying his lungs roaring at the stillness," Miller recalled. His Reichian exercise was "the day's biggest event."

By the end of May, having served his mandatory six weeks in Nevada, Miller was back in New York for a highly public reunion with his bride-to-be. Bellow and Sondra were also getting ready to face civilization—Bellow reluctantly. "New York is deadly," he wrote Louis Simpson, declaring that he had "just reached the point of peace, casting off the last and deepest strains." His excitement at finding acceptance among the New York intellectuals had given way to contempt, his sense of inadequacy vanquished by grandiosity. He no longer needed their approbation, and the more his reputation grew in the literary world, the more distasteful he found that world. The very notion of "a *Partisan Review* crowd" was anathema to Bellow. When Leslie Fiedler, writing in *The New Republic*, included him among writers associated with the magazine, the mere suggestion of an affinity elicited a harsh rebuke: "I'm grateful for the kind mention you gave me in the N.R. piece, although I don't consider myself part of the Partisan group. Not those dying beasts." New York was another adversary—"Too rough. Too choking," as Bellow put it to Ralph Ellison. "It won by a decision over me. No knockout but I'll never be the same." It was a curious response to a city that had been the stage of such unequivocal literary triumph: Bellow required an enemy—even one that adulated him.

Once again, the future was uncertain. Bellow had some funds left from his Guggenheim and a three-thousand-dollar advance from Viking for a collection of stories that was to include *Seize the Day;* they could live where they chose. In the end, he and Sondra decided to settle in the Hudson Valley.

In June, the newlyweds set off on a meandering cross-country honeymoon, stopping to see friends in Chicago and Minneapolis, where they stayed with John Berryman, who was teaching at the University of Minnesota. By the end of the month, they were back home—such as it was. Their address that summer was c/o Ludwig, Bard College, Annandale-on-Hudson, New York.

13

Is it time now? They will lay him out, washed, anointed, shrouded.
They will fold his arms across his chest, with the palms turned in,
completing the figure. Now his own hands will lie pressed to his breast,
and he will sleep with his fathers.

—ISAAC ROSENFELD,
"King Solomon"

IN CHICAGO THAT JUNE, Bellow had seen his old friend Isaac
Rosenfeld and found him "in bad shape." His marriage to
Vasiliki was over, and he was back in Hyde Park, holed up in
"a hideous cellar room"—the same room he had lived in as a
student. "The sympathetic glamour of the thirties was entirely
gone; there was only a squalid stink of toilets and coal bins here."

The two friends' paths had diverged sharply. Well into the
fifties, Rosenfeld continued to swear by Reich. He found "the
poisonous orgone bracing," he wrote Bellow in the summer of
1955, reporting that he had "improvised an orgone blanket" that
seemed to work: "I'll send you the recipe, if you're interested. It
can be put together in two or three hours for a total cost of say
$5." But Bellow had given up on Reichianism, despite his fondness
for roaring. Never a very orthodox adherent, he was put off by
Reich's authoritarian prescriptions for sexual health; if he wanted
to "investigate freedom" he would do it on his own. And he had
come to regard with suspicion the brutal candor at the heart of the
Reichian regimen. Rosenfeld's "peculiar adaptation of W. Reich
was bringing up material from the psychic drainage system," as
Bellow described it. "Isaac felt he owed it to *truth* to bring it to the
surface and let it spin and be purified." Bellow was convinced the
process had done neither of them any good; it had only made them
both "nastier."

For Rosenfeld, abjuring academic affiliations had become a point of honor. His role model was Kafka's hunger artist, fasting in his cage. When Bellow tried to get him a job at Bard, Rosenfeld was ungracious. They should pay "carfare," he replied; he was broke. That summer, he gave up the gritty environs of Hyde Park for a furnished room on the North Side—"the kind of place," a friend recalled, "where you expected to see Raskolnikov sharpening his axe." He had always been sickly; in the late photograph on the back of *An Age of Enormity,* his posthumous volume of essays, Rosenfeld's pasty face is enshrouded in cigarette smoke. He looks a decade older than he was.

On July 14, 1956, Rosenfeld died of a heart attack in his room on West Walton Street. The last entry in his journal read:

> This is what I have forgotten about the creative process, & am only now beginning to remember—that time spent is time fixed. One creates a work to outlive one—only art does this—& the source of creativity is the desire to reach over one's own death. Maybe now, if I want to create again, I want once more to live; and before I wanted, I suppose, to die.

The funeral was well attended, with large contingents from New York and Minneapolis. Bellow was conspicuously absent. "Where's Saul?" asked the mourners. Sam Rosenfeld, Isaac's father, was furious that he hadn't come. Others suggested that Bellow's absence was typical. "Saul doesn't go to funerals" was Vasiliki's rationalization.

Still, this funeral was not like others. A man of thirty-eight, his closest friend, was dead, forcing Bellow at a young age to confront his own mortality. "I've never known anyone so afraid of death," said Sam Freifeld. But Bellow may also have stayed away for another reason: To fully grieve would have been to recognize his dependence on Rosenfeld. Mourning isn't only a tribute to the dead; it's an acknowledgment of their power over the living—a form of commitment. Failing to attend his closest and oldest friend's funeral was a dramatic instance of a lifelong pattern: the tendency to deny and run away from pain. He had been "thrown millions of light years" by Rosenfeld's death, he wrote to Delmore Schwartz's first wife, Gertrude Buckman, but he would deal with it in his own way, declaring his independence even from death.

In private, he atoned for his dereliction. He helped organize a fund for Rosenfeld's two children; published a touching eulogy in *Partisan Review;* and began work on the novel that was to metamorphose into *Humboldt's Gift.* The story of Humboldt the mad poet had its inception in the story of Zetland, a Chicago boy with a passion for Tolstoy and Dostoyevsky. "He combined all the reticence of and shyness of a small sickly Jewish boy from Chicago with heroic ideas about destiny," Bellow wrote two decades later, looking back on Isaac Rosenfeld's legacy. "And after all, history would not have been history without these apparently timid and inconspicuous Jewish children."

Earlier that summer, Bellow had been readying for publication a less explicit but equally compelling testimony to "his dead," as Herzog possessively refers to the departed members of his family. Awaiting him in Chicago as he made his way east were the proofs of *Seize the Day,* the novella that was to occupy pride of place in the summer issue of *Partisan Review.*

Seize the Day harked back to a type of fiction he had written "a great deal of at one time," he explained, referring to the morally earnest works of his apprenticeship, *Dangling Man* and *The Victim*—"victim literature," he called it now. The main character, Tommy Wilhelm, is a failure in business, unemployed, and separated from his wife and two children. He lives in an Upper West Side residential hotel occupied largely by old people, including Wilhelm's father, a retired doctor. The book's action is confined to a single day, in the course of which Wilhelm is brutally rejected by his father, mercilessly harangued by his wife, and lectured by the wily Dr. Tamkin, a charlatan who offers him financial and spiritual advice. In the end, he loses his last seven hundred dollars on ill-considered speculations in the stock market.

As a fictional protagonist, Tommy Wilhelm was an anomaly in the Bellow canon. His physical model was Delmore Schwartz. Both Schwartz and Wilhelm were large, shambling insomniacs who popped pills, swilled Coke, and dropped cigarette butts into their coat pockets. Tommy's small teeth and wavy blond hair clearly belong to Schwartz in his mid-forties; by the time of *Seize the Day,* he was well on his way to becoming the human ruin Bellow was to depict so remorselessly in *Humboldt's Gift.* But there is little of the poet about Tommy Wilhelm. He is an ordinary man. Like Arthur Miller's Willy Loman, he's a failed salesman who can barely articulate his thwartedness. His life has been a chronicle of disappointments: He dropped out of college, got nowhere in Hollywood as an actor, and wound up selling children's furniture. At forty-six, he's a man with "no position."

Yet in another sense, Wilhelm, too, is an autobiographical creation. The parallels are overt: A Hollywood talent agent tells the hapless Wilhelm—as Bellow himself was once told—that he'd be ideally suited for the role of "the guy that loses the girl to the George Raft type or the William Powell type." The fact that he changed his name from Wilhelm Adler to Tommy Wilhelm to assert his independence rehearses Bellow's youthful shedding of the name Solomon. And the portrait of Wilhelm's wife, Margaret, as a harridan who hectors him about child support was inspired directly by Bellow's fights with Anita.*

Their troubled relationship was depicted more clearly in early drafts of the book. For Wilhelm, the breakup of his marriage was catastrophic. "I thought it was all up with me—my life was finished!" In addition to the loss of his wife, he fears estrangement from his sons. He's also a womanizer—a detail remarked upon only glancingly in the final version:

> Then he started to think whether his two boys believed that he cared for them. The doubt hurt him greatly. Margaret would have turned them against him. They were old enough to reflect on sex and they would talk about all the women in his life. . . .
> In almost every town he had someone to go out with. How could he stand this life otherwise? There was nothing worse than to have to spend the night alone.

One can only surmise why Bellow omitted this passage from the book. Perhaps Wilhelm's infidelities would have made him seem

---

*Anita bitterly resented Bellow's fictional depictions of her. Once, when she was complaining to the McCloskeys about *Seize the Day,* Mitzi McCloskey asked, "How do you know it's you?" Anita replied firmly, "I know."

less sympathetic as a character; or perhaps it was simply too explicitly autobiographical even for Bellow, himself the father of a boy.

Bellow's father, however, was no longer alive; Bellow felt he could write about him more openly now. As the book deepened in complexity over numerous drafts, Wilhelm's struggle with his father emerged as the main theme. "In that short book I examined a man who *insisted* on having a father, who demanded that his father *be* a father to him," Bellow said. The father's neglect has infantilized the son, made him hunger for what he never had. Wilhelm's wife, Margaret, "nurses" him; he's moved by a line of Keats: "Like an own babe I nurse thee on my breast!" And when the charlatan/guru Tamkin asks him if he loves the old man, Wilhelm replies:

> "My father. My mother—" As he said this there was a great pull at the very center of his soul. When a fish strikes the line you feel the live force in your hand. A mysterious being beneath the water, driven by hunger, has taken the hook and rushes away and fights, writhing. Wilhelm never identified what struck within him. It did not reveal itself. It got away.

"You have lots of guilt in you," Tamkin says to Wilhelm—the guilt that comes from his rage at his rejecting father. Bellow often referred to himself as "a melancholic," a depressive temperament. But he was also high-spirited and energetic. Stressing the tortured side of his nature may have been Bellow's way of accounting for the deep sense of rejection he carried within him—and of which Tommy Wilhelm, for all his physical differences from Bellow, is the very embodiment. To punish his father, he must punish himself. His misery serves as a silent accusation—a testimony to his victimization by his father.

Wilhelm's other father figure, Dr. Tamkin, from whom he solicits the disastrous financial advice that wipes him out, bears a striking resemblance to Yellow Kid Weill, a Bughouse Square autodidact whom Bellow had interviewed for *The Saturday Review of Literature* that year. Like Weill, with his genius for self-mythology, Tamkin is full of dubious lore. His incessant talk of the "here and now" is a parody of Gestalt psychology; in early drafts, he's openly a Reichian, going on about character armor and "congestion."* But he's a shrewd student of human motive; he grasps the human drive "to be Something."

In the book's climactic scene, having lost his last dollar on the commodities market, Wilhelm descends into a hotel steam room and confronts his father as he's being worked over by a masseur. Brushing aside Wilhelm's request for a loan, the doctor lectures him about his fecklessness. "You want to make yourself into my cross," the old man thunders from his massage table: "But I am not going to pick up a cross. I'll see you dead, Wilky, by Christ, before I let you do that to me."

Stunned by this outburst, Wilhelm rushes to a phone booth to answer a message from his wife, and forces a confrontation. He beats the walls in frustration, tries to tear out the phone, and runs into the street, stumbling into the midst of a funeral procession. Carried along by the mourners, he finds himself in the chapel, staring down into a stranger's coffin and weeping uncontrollably:

> The flowers and lights fused ecstatically in Wilhelm's blind, wet eyes; the heavy sea-like music came up to his ears. It poured into him where he had hidden himself in the center of a crowd by the great and happy oblivion of tears. He heard it and sank deeper than sorrow, through torn sobs and cries toward the consummation of his heart's ultimate need.

This catharsis expresses a profound depth of mourning. It is hard not to read it as an elegy to Bellow's father, dead only a year before. Daniel Bell and Pearl Kazin, who saw a good deal of Bellow during this period, conjectured that the closing pages of *Seize the Day* were partly inspired by the loss of Rosenfeld—a plausible thesis, since he was still revising the galleys in the days just after Rosenfeld's untimely death.†

---

*Wilhelm also possesses Reichian traits. It's significant that his last name is Reich's first.

†The book's closing pages also clearly owed a debt to the scene in Dreiser's *Jennie Gerhardt* in which Gerhardt slips into the back pew of a church during the funeral of her lover, Lester Kane: "She was as a house filled with mournful melody and the presence of death. She cried and cried." Bellow claimed that he didn't read Dreiser's novel until after he'd written *Seize the Day*, but it had been required reading in his American literature course at Salzburg in 1950. Bellow often acknowledged his debt to Dreiser, but in general terms. Dependence, even upon dead writers, was still dependence; the true connection had to be denied.

Elsewhere in Bellow's work, it's primarily the mother whose death is mourned. In the beginning, *Seize the Day* was also intended to rehearse this crucial event. An early draft opens with Wilhelm dwelling on the death of his mother—"a personal disaster from which he has never recovered." In the published version, the mother has all but disappeared, though Wilhelm recalls a visit to his mother's grave, and there is the significant exchange between Wilhelm and his father in which they skirmish over the year she died. But here it is the father, living still but dead to his son's needs, who dominates the story. "One parent or another is always missing in Bellow's human chronicles; or in effect they both are," the critic Maxwell Geismar observed.

Where *The Adventures of Augie March* was a loose, baggy monster (in Henry James's famous phrase), *Seize the Day* was a slender and tightly composed work of art. The culture of New York's Upper West Side, so rich in elderly Jewish immigrants, was rendered beautifully. Bellow was on intimate terms with the relics of the Old World: the Gameroffs in Lachine; his father and his friends' fathers in Humboldt Park; the immigrant bohemia of the Tschacbasovs. Yet for all its vivid particularity, *Seize the Day* was less "ethnic" a novel than *The Adventures of Augie March.* Tommy Wilhelm recites kaddish at his mother's grave, but imperfectly. He thinks of himself as a Jew (even though, in his father's eyes, he's "the wrong kind of Jew"), but he's not observant. He's Jewish, but not *too* Jewish. With *Seize the Day*, argued Leslie Fiedler, it was no longer necessary to label Bellow a Jewish novelist, "for he emerges at the moment when the Jews for the first time move into the center of American culture, and he must be seen in the larger context." Just as Jews had secured advancement in other areas of American life—in business and government and the entertainment industry—so Bellow had "worked himself up," wrote Fiedler, employing a phrase from their fathers' generation.

That summer, at Bard, Bellow showed the manuscript to Louis Simpson. "When I came to the end," Simpson recalled, "I had a feeling I have had only two or three times in my life—that I was witnessing at first hand the creation of a masterpiece." When Simpson delivered his verdict, Bellow "smiled and had a cunning look in his eyes. As with all first-rate writers at the height of their power, he knew very well what he had done."

In the summer of 1956, after a brief stay with the Ludwigs, who had "given [him] asylum"—a phrase that dramatized Bellow's constant sense of being harried by hostile forces—the newlyweds could finally afford a home of their own, "bought in a dream of happiness" with a small inheritance from Bellow's father.* Hundreds of letters dispatched over the next few years bore its estatelike address: Tivoli, New York.

Perched on a hill not far from the Hudson, the Bellows' new home was a decrepit three-story Italianate pile—"an old Faulkner mansion that had drifted north." The fourteen-room house had a Charles Addams look about it. The grounds were overgrown, the wraparound porch on the verge of collapse. On the first floor was a grand ballroom with white-tiled walls and ornately corniced floor-to-ceiling windows. The Dutch kitchen was hotel sized, the staircase "lordly"; the large bedrooms were high ceilinged, with sooty fireplaces. Known around town as the White Elephant, it was an impractical purchase for a novelist with no job and no fixed income. "I'm not sure I'll have enough money to keep things going," Bellow wrote to Ralph Ellison in September 1956: "Plaster, paint, carpentry, taxes, fuel. But I'm not supposed to worry about these problems here. I came to work on my book." Also, it was time to settle down: Sondra was five months pregnant. "We're going to have a child," she had reminded Bellow, "and we have no place to live." They got the house cheap: six thousand dollars in cash and a six-thousand-dollar mortgage.

"I poured my life's blood into that place," Bellow recalled, "hammering and sawing, scraping and painting, digging and planting and weeding until I felt like a caretaker in my own cemetery. So that as I mowed the grass I would think, here I will be buried by the fall." In August, the well gave out. "We may have to

---

*Bellow's father had bequeathed him around eight thousand dollars, along with stock in the Carroll Coal Company. A year after Abram's death, Bellow's brother Sam, the estate's administrator, agreed to buy out his shares, which increased the amount to twenty thousand dollars. "Last summer Sam told me he was not going to share in the remainder of my father's money," Bellow reported to Sam Freifeld. "He seems to have changed his mind, the privilege of women, businessmen and brothers."

drill a new one—another $1,000 down the hole, literally," Bellow lamented. "Oh, well, Pa didn't *really* think I could hold on to his legacy."

"It was not a good idea to buy that house," Sondra admitted. "It was my fault: I had a nesting instinct." A self-proclaimed city girl, she bridled at the rigors of country homemaking: "I'm accustomed to a janitor." Like Madeleine in *Herzog,* she had social aspirations. "Her parents are Russian Jews, but she preferred to say that she was Russian," Bellow noted unkindly in a passage later deleted from *Herzog.* "It wasn't till I met them that I realized they were also Jews." But the finer the distinction, the more crucial it becomes. Sondra considered the Tschacbasovs a cut above the Bellows, whom she regarded as an archaic immigrant clan. She was scathing about Bellow's brother Maurice, "a big fat pig of a vulgar man," whose apartment on Goethe Street (Maurice gave it the Chicago pronunciation, "Go-ee-thee") had a mural of an Italian scene on the wall. "I said to Saul, 'Lose my number: I don't need these people.'" A child of bohemia, she had grown to resent her father's Greenwich Village crowd—poets and painters who hung around his studio in the Chelsea Hotel. "My wife had *had* it with artists," said Bellow. At a gallery opening, Sondra announced glumly, "I hate painters." She yearned for bourgeois domesticity, only to end up in the middle of nowhere, married to a writer whose financial fortunes (and emotional stability) were as precarious as her father's.

Bellow was in rebellion, too, but he was running in the opposite direction. He liked to describe himself as a "fundamentalist," and he did have a rabbinical quality about him, despite his indifference to the biblical injunction against adultery. He was both unnerved and fascinated by the notion of sexual freedom—especially when it turned up in his own family. "This Svengali circle was fun—in a hateful way," he said of old Tschacbasov and his crowd. "But my young wife and I should have agreed to jettison all 'formative experiences' and, to the extent possible, make a new start, shelve our respective fathers." What he really wanted was a conventional wife, someone who would put meals on the table and entertain his friends. "He tried to make a *balabosta* [housewife] out of her," said Sondra's friend Anita Maximilian.

Bellow's maternal grandfather.

Bellow's father, Abram (far right), in the Old Country.

The Bellow siblings in 1918:
two-and-a-half-year-old Solly, with a Buster Brown haircut,
is seated beside Samuel, age six; behind them are Jane,
age eleven, and Morris, age nine.

The Bellows in Montreal, ca. 1920. Left to right: Sol, Liza, Jane, Abram ("sulking because he didn't want his picture taken"), Morris, and Samuel.

The Bellows, ca. 1919. Left to right: Sol, Liza, Morris, Samuel, and Jane.

*Bellow (right), just out of the hospital
and still in short pants,
with Samuel, ca. 1924.*

Bellow's first home in Chicago, on West Augusta.

The Chicago boy at the age of fourteen, summer 1929.

Double-breasted Bellow in Chicago, late 1930s.

Bellow in Chicago, late 1930s.

*Bellow's pal
Oscar Tarcov,
age sixteen,
September
1935.*

*Tuley High crony
Sam Freifeld.*

A trio of Tuley alums in the fall of 1938: Isaac Rosenfeld,
Sam Freifeld, and Fred Glotzer.

*Bellow's other half,
Isaac Rosenfeld,
playing the clarinet.*

*Isaac Rosenfeld and his
wife, the "pagan beauty"
Vasiliki, in New York,
early 1940s.*

*Dwight Macdonald (1906–1982), American author and editor
at* The New Yorker *and* Partisan Review.

Ralph Ellison, Bellow's friend and Tivoli housemate.

*Marjorie Farber, a literary journalist and one of Bellow's
New York girlfriends, in the mid-1940s.*

Bellow in Granada,
summer of 1947,
on his first trip to
Europe.

The novelist ca. 1947,
when he was finishing
The Victim.

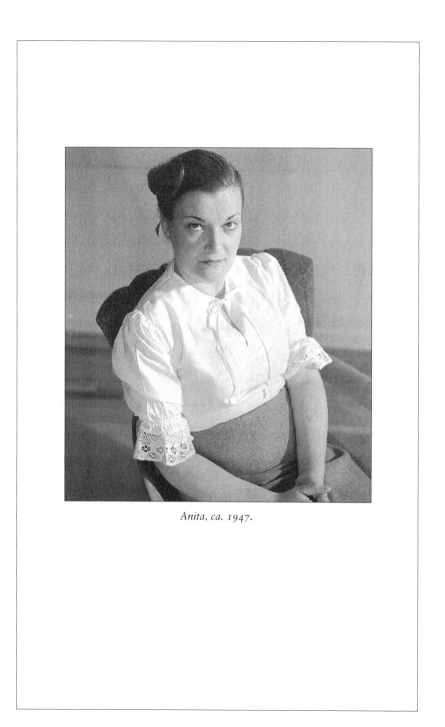

Anita, ca. 1947.

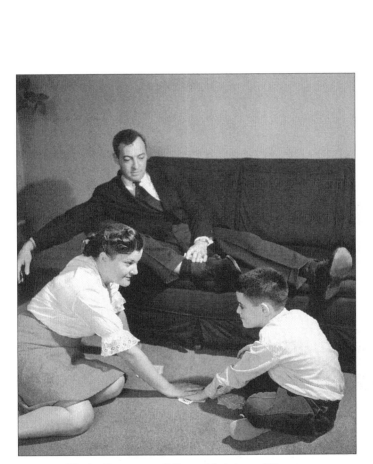

The family romance: Bellow with Anita and Gregory.

The impending arrival of a baby exacerbated these tensions, as did the household chaos. Bellow's twelve-year-old son, Greg, was in residence for most of that summer, with dog, as were Vasiliki Rosenfeld and flocks of summer refugees from New York. Guests were encouraged to bring their own sleeping bags. To add to Bellow's burdens, Sondra was unwell—she suffered for years from unspecifiable ailments—and he was "none too hot, either, since Isaac's death."

All that summer, Bellow grieved. "I had never seen Saul so affected by anything," remembered Pearl Kazin. "He was utterly broken up." To John Berryman, who had sent him a commemorative poem about Rosenfeld, he confessed:

> I think and think about Isaac, and my recollections are endless— twenty-six years of which I've forgotten very little. Isaac himself began to have doubts about thinking, and he passed them on to me. Now I feel more than ever what a strange activity thinking is. Anyway, since his going my life has been far less my own, and there are days when I care less. I have to recover my negative capability.

Like Milton's young poet friend, "dead ere his prime," Rosenfeld endured in Bellow's prose testaments. If having the field to himself meant freedom, it also meant responsibility. As he told the McCloskeys, "I have to write for both of us now."

In the summer of 1956, he seemed to be doing just that. While carpenters hammered in the ballroom, Bellow sat in the study out behind the house, producing steadily. In addition to finishing *Seize the Day*, he was turning out a fair amount of literary journalism to meet the mounting expenses and was also hard at work on his "African" novel—now referred to as "Henderson." "I don't do very much," he wrote to Berryman in August, deprecating his labors:

> Every once in a while I put Henderson on me like a plumber's level. The bubble is usually in the wrong place, so I sigh and knock off for the day. But Sondra is a beautiful mother-to-be, and Greg gave me much pleasure last month, so my life is far from barren. Too many awful distractions, however, big gloomy houses, money, alimony problems, friends low in spirits, and ghosts, large numbers of highly individual ghosts.

Omitted from his list was that other perennial distraction of a fiction writer: teaching. Toward the end of August, he was preparing for a fall class at the New School, an ordeal that he saw as a hunt, with himself as the prey. "So, we'll meet in NY when the New School season on me opens," he reported to Ruth Miller. "The sharpshooters are oiling their guns."

Three weeks later, he wrote her again—from Yaddo. "Had to take refuge here for a while. Too much noise in Tivoli, N.Y."

14

*There were moments during his public lecture—this was at Chicago,
my last year there—when Abravanel had to pause at the lectern,
seemingly to suppress saying something off the cuff that would
have been just too charming for his audience to bear. And he was right.
We might have charged the stage to eat him up alive if he had
been any more sly and engaging and wise.*

—Philip Roth,
The Ghost Writer

FOUNDED IN 1926 by a philanthropic family from upstate
New York, Yaddo, the famous writers' colony in Saratoga
Springs, was an ideal temporary residence for a novelist in
search of peace and quiet. Guests lived in the main house, a huge
gray stone Victorian mansion, or in houses and studios scattered
about the wooded estate. Dinner was communal. "This has been
my hideout for awhile," Bellow wrote the novelist Richard Stern:
"You should come, it's a first class refuge and one of the most tran-
quilizing establishments I know. The greatest characters hereabout
are the trees."

At Yaddo, Bellow got to know John Cheever, who had been
going there since the Depression and was a member of the Yaddo
Corporation. Bellow and Cheever had met at Eleanor Clark's
apartment in New York shortly after World War II and admired
each other's work. Cheever claimed to have written "first-person
slang" long before Bellow published *The Adventures of Augie
March,* but he had been impressed by the "French and Russian"
qualities of *Dangling Man,* "the cockroach and the peeling wall-
paper described with precision and loathing." Cheever's journal
affords a vivid glimpse of Bellow at Yaddo in the 1950s:

> At dinner I am conscious of being in the same room with Saul.
> We speak after dinner and I am delighted by his presence. He is

about my size, I guess, his hair quite gray, and I think I feel here that sometime tragic fineness of his skin, that tragic vitality. His nose is a little long, his eyes have (I think) the cheerful glint of lewdness, and I notice his hands and that his voice is light. It has no deep notes.

Over the years, the two novelists developed a warm if formal friendship. "We share not only a love of women but a fondness for rain," as Cheever put it in his lyrical way. That Cheever was so determined to be a proper WASP might have been off-putting to Bellow, who never felt entirely comfortable with those he identified as goyim—especially goyim with social pretensions; but Cheever also possessed a touching and genuine humility. Just as Bellow felt most comfortable around Humboldt Park Jews, Cheever was drawn to working people such as Nellie Shannon, the cook at Yaddo, and the regulars at the Highland Diner in Ossining. Cheever put "human essences in the first place," Bellow observed: "first the persons—himself, myself—and after that the other stuff, class origins, social history." The two writers' democratic instincts overcame their mutual wariness and made them lifelong allies. When Cheever was elected to the American Academy of Arts and Letters in 1957, one of his first acts was to nominate Bellow, drafting a citation that declared him "the most original writer in America."

Bellow had high hopes for his new novella. "It delivers a good swift kick in the guts of the reader," he boasted to Philip Rahv. He was convinced that the book had commercial potential. "All the divorced men in America will buy it."

Seize the Day appeared in book form in November 1956 to mostly glowing reviews. It had its detractors, notably *The New Yorker*'s Brendan Gill, who pretended not to understand the ending, meanly observing that Wilhelm was "sobbing his heart out over his plight and yet feeling rather better than usual." Some reviewers detected—not all of them approvingly—a reversion to the formal style of *Dangling Man* and *The Victim*, but others saw the book as an advance. Alfred Kazin rated it "the most moving single piece of fiction that this young author has as yet written." Bellow was now "not merely a writer with whom it is possible to come to terms," Leslie Fiedler maintained, "but one with whom it is *necessary* to come to terms." His work was "a part of our lives."

As usual, it was the negative reviews that registered with him. "That New Yorker outfit is a strange one," Bellow complained to Granville Hicks. The editors had assigned his book to Gill "knowing full well (Wm. Maxwell was present) that Gill and I have had a hassle." The "hassle," according to Gill, barely even qualified as a dispute: At a literary conference at Smith College two years earlier, Bellow had made a disparaging comment about *The New Yorker*, and Gill had risen to its defense. "Bellow replied in a way calculated to give further offense," as William Maxwell remembered the episode. In the ensuing debate, neither one "ever hesitated for a second before replying, and they had to an equal degree the talent for giving expression to anger, contempt, deliberate insolence, and personal dislike." The flare-up ended in a draw, according to Maxwell; as far as Bellow was concerned, the WASP literary establishment was up to its old tricks.

Bellow detected the establishment's malevolent hand everywhere. When Cleanth Brooks, a Yale professor and leading member of the New Critics, gave a negative review to Kazin's volume of essays *Contemporaries*, Bellow was outraged. "Eastern white-collar?" he protested in a letter to Kazin, echoing a phrase from Brooks's review:

> Why, he might as well have come out flatly with "Jew." What vileness! How I detest these "rooted" southerners among us poor deracinated Hebes of the north. I notice that they teach at Yale, though, or Minnesota. If they are not missionaries from southern culture they are liars and cowards. Christly heavens, what chutzpah!

For Bellow, the issue of Jewishness—*his* Jewishness—was no less urgent now that he had begun to find acceptance as an American writer. Even though "Jewish" was an epithet that he abjured with vigor, insisting on his right to be judged by his art—if a qualifying adjective was required, let it be his nationality—he never relaxed his vigilance toward anti-Semitism, to the point of detecting it where it didn't exist. He was "very possessive about Jewishness without having any feeling for the religious essence or faith of Judaism," said Anthony Hecht. Being a Jew, like being a novelist, confirmed Bellow's status as an outsider, a member of still another beleaguered minority, whose interests he felt called upon to defend.

His combativeness found a vivid opportunity for expression that fall. Summoned by an urgent telegram from Harvey Breit, editor of *The New York Times Book Review*, he came to New York to attend a meeting of the writers' committee of People to People, a public-relations effort dreamed up by the Eisenhower administration to combat Soviet propaganda and promote the message of American freedom overseas. The committee's chairman was William Faulkner. They met in Breit's Manhattan living room a few days after Thanksgiving 1956: the novelist Edna Ferber, the publisher Donald Klopfer, the poet Donald Hall, and Bellow. There was much talk of the plight of Hungarian refugees. "Saul got really mad that night," Hall recalled. Under the unsteady chairmanship of Faulkner, who'd had "a hell of a lot of bourbon," the meeting soon degenerated into a free-for-all. "Faulkner suggested we should bring ordinary folks over here [from behind the Iron Curtain], give them a used car and a job, and show them how America really worked." Bellow pointed out that these "ordinary folks" would be put in jail or executed when they got back home, but Faulkner paid him no attention. Eventually, Bellow lost patience and stormed off—thus missing out on a fierce argument about whether Ezra Pound should be released from Saint Elizabeth's Hospital in Washington, D.C., where he had been incarcerated on charges of treason for his seditious radio broadcasts during World War II.

Pound's deeds persistently stirred up controversy among intellectuals. In 1949, Pound had been awarded the prestigious Bollingen Prize, sparking a heated public debate, with Delmore Schwartz and Irving Howe passionately denouncing the verdict. Now it was Bellow's turn. In a letter to the chairman of the writers' committee of People to People, he addressed the matter at hand.

Dear Mr. Faulkner:

. . . I am writing this letter in order to give you my views on your suggestion, made, I assume, after I left the meeting, that we ask for the release of Ezra Pound. "While the Chairman of this Committee," you say, "was awarded a prize by the Swedish

Government and was given a decoration by the French Government, the American Government locks up one of its best poets." This is a truly astonishing piece of reasoning. You, Mr. Faulkner, were deservedly honored by these governments. But you did not, to my knowledge, try to overthrow or undermine either of them. Besides, Pound is not in prison but in an insane asylum. If sane he should be tried again as a traitor; if insane he ought not to be released merely because he is a poet. Pound advocated in his poems and in his broadcasts enmity to the Jews and preached hatred and murder. Do you mean to ask me to join you in honoring a man who called for the destruction of my kinsmen? I can take no part in such a thing even if it makes effective propaganda abroad, which I doubt. Europeans will take it instead as a symptom of reaction. In France Pound would have been shot. Free him because he is a poet? Why, better poets than he were exterminated perhaps. Shall we say nothing in their behalf?

America has dealt mercifully with Pound in recognizing his insanity and sparing his life. To release him is a foolish and feeble idea. It would identify this program in the eyes of the world with Hitler and Himmler and Mussolini and genocide. But I am not so much concerned with the practical side of the matter here. What staggers me is that you and Mr. Steinbeck who have dealt for so many years in words should fail to understand the import of Ezra Pound's plain and brutal statements about the "kikes" leading the "goy" to slaughter. Is this—from the Pisan Cantos—the stuff of poetry? It is a call to murder. If it were spoken by a farmer or a shoemaker we would call him mad. The whole world conspires to ignore what has happened, the giant wars, the colossal hatreds, the unimaginable murders, the destruction of the very image of man. And we—"a representative group of American writers"—is this what we come out for, too? A fine mess!

That the world sought to distract the writer from his task didn't mean the writer could afford to maintain a Flaubertian distance from it.

L ife at Tivoli was straight out of a Russian novel. Bellow's new habit of addressing his friends with patronymics ("Dear Yevgeny

Pavlovitch") contributed to the dachalike feel of the place, as did Sondra's long-standing nickname: Sasha. Bellow even bemoaned his "Russian lack of organization." Like all writers, he needed a certain amount of solitude in order to write; yet he was gregarious by nature. "I've never known anyone who found it so hard to be alone," said his friend Dave Peltz. For a person who campaigned tirelessly against distraction, he deliberately sought it out. He thrived on stimulation, writing lectures on the train in from Rhinebeck ("Motion stirs my sometimes sluggish imagination"); teaching at the New School; and entertaining at his "manorial" estate. At odd hours, he retreated to his desk and wrote. "That g-d book," "Henderson," was "going strong."

In the afternoons, he did chores: feeding Rufus, the rusty, bush-tailed cat; doing push-ups to keep in shape; driving to the hardware store in town. At dusk, he liked to grab one of his rakish hats from the shed and go for a walk in the fields that surrounded the house—"a beardless Tolstoy," as a visitor described him, "the temporary gentleman-gardener, uneasy landlord of Tivoli, digging his city heels into the ripe earth."

This country-squire existence was marred by a shortage of cash. The Guggenheim stipend was just about gone by the end of 1956; most of Bellow's inheritance had been put toward the purchase of the house. That fall, he and Sondra subsisted largely on freelance income and advances from Viking. The situation was so desperate by September that Sondra called Pat Covici herself and asked for the balance of the five thousand dollars that Viking had agreed to pay for Bellow's work in progress. The author remained serene. "Don't worry about money," he counseled his publisher—a curious role reversal: "Money never yet saved a good man or improved a bad one."

In his copious correspondence, Bellow provided comic daily dispatches, addressing John Berryman in pidgin French ("vous avez peigne ze human situation more better than J. P. Sartre avec une seule strook") and distributing his latest *mot* ("Now there are no more frontiers, only borderline cases"). To Alfred Kazin he submitted a poem deriding J. Donald Adams, whose column in *The New York Times Book Review* was notorious for its belligerent philistinism:

Hurrah, hurray, hurray!
For Adams, Donald J.
He stands for the best of everything
In his column on Sunday.

Ah, Fielding & Tolstoy
He loves like an artless boy.
But give a boost to Joyce and Proust
And he straightway cries out "Oy!"

"Give me a yarn to read.
I ask for nothing subtle.
The best is what I understand—
the rest you can damn well scuttle."

In February 1957, a card went out from Tivoli—engraved announcements were one form of bourgeois regimentation Bellow condoned—informing friends of the birth on January 19 of Adam Abraham Bellow.

Bellow didn't stick around for long. "Bon! J'y suis," the peripatetic novelist announced from Minneapolis to Keith Botsford a month later. Short of cash, he had accepted a temporary appointment at his old haunt, the University of Minnesota. He arrived in February, just days after the birth of his second son; Sondra followed with Adam a month later. Ralph Ross, Bellow's academic patron at New York University, had come to the rescue again. Ross had since become chairman of the humanities department at Minnesota and took Bellow in after the English department, hostile—in conformance with English departments everywhere—to "creative" writers, spurned him.*

Bellow felt at home in Minneapolis. For another writer, the frigid northern campus might have seemed like exile from New

---

*It had also spurned Isaac Rosenfeld, John Berryman, and Robert Penn Warren. At various times, Ross found places for them all in his department, which was under the administrative jurisdiction of the English department but had a certain amount of latitude in hiring its own staff.

York. ("You think it was cold at Washtenaw & Division?" he joked to Dave Peltz.) For Bellow, it was a comfortable haven where life was simple and he was held in high regard, a big fish in a little pond—and where the noise of Manhattan literary politics was a distant whisper. "The Midwest agrees with me," he wrote Ralph Ellison in the spring of 1957: "Here I recognize things. And I'm near *Chicago*, which is not unimportant." At heart, he told Ralph Ross, he was a midwestern boy.

Bellow and John Berryman, who had joined the faculty the year before, shared an office in a wooden hut called Temporary North of Mines. (It was near the School of Mines.) "From the window we saw a gully, a parking lot, and many disheartening cars," Bellow wrote in a foreword to Berryman's novel *Recovery*:

> Scorched theology books from a fire sale lined one of the walls. These Barths and Brunners looked as if they had gone through hell. We had no particular interest in them but they helped to furnish forth a mental life in the city of Minneapolis. Minneapolis was the home of Honeywell, of heart surgery, of Pillsbury, of the Multi Phasic test, but it was not celebrated as the home of poems and novels.

As far as Bellow was concerned, this absence of culture was no disadvantage. It gave perspective to the marginality of the literary enterprise. Besides, he was more comfortable as the odd man out—the role he'd been assigned in his own family—than among dominating types who threatened his sense of specialness.

His new job didn't solve his financial problems. Even with a regular salary, he was "having a nasty time about money," he complained to Pat Covici. Was *Seize the Day* selling? Could he expect royalties? Covici didn't have good news. The book had "stubbornly" refused to show up on the bestseller list, despite Viking's best efforts and excellent reviews. In fact, it wasn't anywhere near the bestseller list.

Bellow was stunned. After a National Book Award and serious critical acclaim for two books, he was financially and geographically back where he'd started a decade earlier. "I am—I have to reach for a word—astonished at the sales of *S. the Day*," he replied: "No more than 5000 copies."

One afternoon early in May 1957, Bellow, visiting from Minneapolis, sat in on a creative-writing class at the University of Chicago taught by Richard Stern, a young novelist on the faculty who had obtained a modest stipend to bring writers to the campus. The story under discussion that day was by a friend of Stern's, a part-time Ph.D. candidate and teaching fellow at the university who submitted it anonymously. It was called "The Conversion of the Jews," and the author "wanted to see how it would go over," Stern recalled. The author's name was Philip Roth.

"I was twenty-three, writing and publishing my first short stories, and like many a *Bildungsroman* hero before me, already contemplating my own massive *Bildungsroman*," as Roth described a similar moment in the literary career of Nathan Zuckerman, the hero of his novella *The Ghost Writer.* Zuckerman is elated when Felix Abravanel, a Bellovian older novelist with "Bombay black eyes" and a gorgeous young wife, approves of his story; and so it was in life. Roth, Bellow pronounced, was "the real thing."

"The Conversion of the Jews," about a Jewish boy with a Talmudic bent who teaches his whole neighborhood a lesson in theology by threatening to leap from the roof of his synagogue after an altercation with the rabbi, showed unmistakable talent; it wasn't just precocious, it was a minor classic. Roth had already learned a great deal from Bellow, as he acknowledged in the dedication of his 1975 collection of essays *Reading Myself and Others:* "To Saul Bellow, the 'other' I have read from the beginning with the deepest pleasure and admiration."

Roth represented a later stage in the drama of Jewish assimilation. Where Bellow's resolutely American-born characters still bore traces of their immigrant parentage—they spoke Yiddish, were city bred, struggled to decipher a new world—Roth's grew up in the suburbs. But they came out of the same world: Ozzie Freedman, the disputatious Hebrew-school student in "The Conversion of the Jews," is a 1950s version of young Herzog laboring over the Talmud in a basement *cheder* in Montreal. "It was Dostoyevsky who said 'We all come out from under Gogol's overcoat,'" Roth has observed. Roth came out from under Bellow's.

After class, Bellow, Stern, and Roth adjourned to a coffee shop. Bellow was "very handsome," Roth recalled. "He seemed sharp, alert, tremendously confident, charming, witty in the extreme— and in my case, very generous." Two years later, when *Goodbye, Columbus* appeared, Bellow gave it a highly favorable review in *Commentary,* praising Roth's debut as the work of a "skillful, witty, and energetic" writer, "not the book of a beginner."

In the fall of 1957, Roth attended a lecture by Bellow at Hillel House on the University of Chicago campus. Roth brought a date: a stunning blond student named Susan Glassman, who was working toward a M.A. in English at Radcliffe. After the lecture, Glassman headed for the podium. She had met Bellow at Bard, she explained to her date; she would just go say hello.

"And that," said Roth, "was the beginning of Saul's *tsuris.*"

15

Yours from square old Evanston.

—*Bellow to Pat Covici*

B ELLOW GOT TO A POINT in every book, he confided to one of his girlfriends, at which he had to "tear up his life." The opposite of Flaubert, he cultivated chaos at home. "I have everything I need here, but it's getting to be too safe," he said of his Tivoli haven, acknowledging that he "thrived on adversity." As the manuscript that was to become *Henderson the Rain King* gathered steam, so did the disarray he seemed to find ideal for composition. While he holed up in his sunny workroom in Tivoli during the summer of 1957, charting the imaginary adventures of Henderson in Africa, the drama that was to fuel *Herzog* was unfolding a good deal closer to home.

He was "having a time of it with all these changes," he wrote to Alfred Kazin ("house, child, book, money, relatives, trains"), but, outwardly at least, he seemed happy. Sondra was "ravishing," Pat Covici remarked. "She looks ten years younger since you married her," he wrote his author, "all a-bubble with love and enthusiasm and praise of you." Bellow agreed. "I am perfectly satisfied with Sondra and marriage, with the house we live in and the work I am doing," he reported to Sam Freifeld. He was *glücklich*, he liked to say—lucky.

If so, it was in the material his naïveté—or blindness—would provide to feed his art. Sondra and Jack Ludwig, Bellow's "pal," were having an affair. The trouble had started the year before, when Ludwig was living near the Bellows' Tivoli manse with his wife, Leah, and their first child. The two couples were inseparable: Hudson Valley versions of D. H. and Frieda Lawrence and Katherine Mansfield and John Middleton Murry, the tempestuous literary quartet whose complex friendship formed the basis for *Women in Love*. Leah was "a sweet, mouselike person," a friend of the Ludwigs recalled. "She was the housewife, he was the literary lion."

Sondra was also married to a literary lion, but she herself cut a considerable figure. With her bold blue eyes, black hair piled regally on her head, and bracelets jangling on her wrists, Sondra could be formidable, even intimidating. "There was a kind of Artemis quality about Sasha, a rigidity and purity," said Ted Hoffman, who described her as both "challenging" and "seraphic."

And—he might have added—extravagant. She filled the kitchen shelves with fancy goods from S. S. Pierce and put in all-new appliances.* She had little patience with Bellow's literary friends; when she was bored at a dinner party, she amused herself by mentally composing obituaries of the guests. And she disparaged Bellow's sexual prowess, letting it be known among their friends that he was a selfish lover, deficient in technique. ("The ejaculatio praecox!" thinks Herzog, when his aunt, a confidante of Madeleine, accuses him of failing to perform in bed.) But she was also vulnerable in ways that were invisible to her husband. Bellow was a figure of considerable stature by this time and tended to dominate the scene. The household revolved around *his* needs. "I was just a nice Jewish girl who got in over my head," Sondra later claimed: "I was absolutely invisible." She, too, harbored intellectual ambitions and worked fitfully at a doctoral thesis on church history in the Byzantine era. "Sasha is pounding out med. history on the

---

*Writing to Ralph Ellison, who had been installed in the Tivoli house while the Bellows were in Minnesota, Sondra enumerated a list of things she needed sent: "The iron, some yellow and blue bath towels (not the martex ones but those that are already worn a little thin—about four)—the small black and white Chinesy print, two double bedsheets, my Gourmet cook book (all maroon and gold), the Bach B minor mass, my portable typewriter, the short silver candlesticks, the Handel concerti grossi."

typewriter," Bellow reported proudly to Ralph Ellison that winter. But his work took pride of place. Wives were there to type their husbands' manuscripts and answer their mail. At the bottom of a letter to Keith Botsford, Bellow noted that it had been *"dictée"*—to Sondra, no doubt.

Bellow taught at the New School on Thursdays, leaving Sasha alone in the big, empty house with Adam. The general impression was that he had "girlfriends stashed everywhere," in Herbert Gold's phrase.

But the deepest bond was between Ludwig and Bellow. "Jack worshiped Saul," said Pearl Kazin. "They were disciple and guru." Since their Bard days, they had developed one of those intimate, stormy male friendships for which Bellow had a particular affinity. They had much in common: literary ambition, nostalgia for their Jewish-immigrant roots, a fondness for company. More important, Ludwig possessed the key element for a close friendship with Bellow: an admiration that verged on sycophancy. "Saul was always a sucker for flattery, and Jack would lay it on with a trowel," remarked Anthony Hecht. When Bellow went out to the woods to perform his Reichian exercises, Ludwig often went along. "He would take Jack with him and they would both roar," Hecht recalled.

An aspiring novelist himself, Ludwig was painfully short of talent as a writer. He had published here and there, but he really hadn't made his mark. His only book so far was an anthology called *Stories, British and American*, which he had coedited with the critic Richard Poirier. Bellow was eight years older and well on his way to fame. "There was something very lacking in Jack," said Elsa Heister, who had studied with him at Bard: "He wanted to *be* Saul Bellow." There was "an enormous amount of jealousy there."

Ludwig's prose bore the unmistakable imprint of Bellow's. His work was full of picaresque urban characters with names such as Boyczuk and Mottyeh, Bibul and Wilkoh Joe; autodidacts with a propensity for quoting Coleridge and T. S. Eliot, "Kierky and Nietsch"; and streetwise types who gloated over "classy broads." ("I got one picked out, a blondie with a pair of tits you can tee your head on.") His epistolary persona was indefatigably bluff: "What gives?" "Twang here and there a heart string." "Joy find!" He even talked like Bellow, coining enigmatic aphorisms: "There are no concessions in God's circus." At parties, he sang with willed gusto—a *tummler*, as one of his colleagues described him, meaning someone who stirred things up, a noisemaker.

Idolatry, however, poses its own dangers. Bellow depended on Ludwig—there was even talk of Ludwig becoming his literary executor—but he was conflicted about his friend. When Ludwig lectured Bellow during their long country walks, dispensing "avuncular" homilies about how to operate in the conjugal bed, Bellow was grateful for the sexual pointers but put off by Ludwig's Yiddish malapropisms.

Ludwig made no secret of his affair—he even dined out on it. "There was something very malevolent about Jack," said Anthony Hecht. "He took an Iago-like pleasure in double-crossing someone who didn't know he was being double-crossed." "Jack was offering amorous advice on how to please a woman," noted a mutual friend. "Meanwhile he was sleeping with Sondra." At a literary dinner party in New York, one of the guests came up to Ludwig and said, "I understand you know Saul Bellow."

"Know him?" Ludwig replied. "Hell, I'm fucking his wife."

So much for the myth of the fifties as a decade of boring domesticity. In that prefeminist era, men—especially literary men—saw women as booty, to be shared around. Ludwig and Bellow were rivals over "some other chick in the chickenyard," remembered Ralph Ellison. But there was something different about this particular exchange. The main object of Ludwig's affections wasn't Sondra at all, claimed some observers. His affair with Sondra was "a gesture of love"—for Bellow. Theodore Weiss summed up Ludwig's motive best: "If he couldn't go to bed with Saul, he'd go to bed with his wife."

This may not have been an entirely fanciful interpretation of events. In an early draft of *Herzog*, the relationship between Herzog and the character then called Valentine Grenzbach borders on the homoerotic. In one scene, Grenzbach enters the bathroom while Herzog is in the tub: "I was soaping myself," recounts Herzog, "and then I realized that he was staring at my genitalia."

And perhaps I showed off a little, for lathering makes it semi-tumescent." (This episode was omitted from the book, and the manuscript in the archives of the University of Chicago library was eventually put off-limits to scholars.) Nor was Bellow's friendship with Ludwig the only one with sexual overtones. Sam Freifeld and Bellow shared "a boyhood closeness that was almost like a teenager's homosexuality," said Freifeld's second wife, Marilyn Mann. "There was something funny about it." Aaron Asher, his editor for many years, also remarked on the unnatural intensity of Bellow's friendships with men: "People noticed."

The Bellows' growing discord was out in the open now. One particularly acrimonious scene ended with dinner flung on the floor. Another time, Bellow claimed that Sondra had tried to run him over in the driveway. In the fall of 1957, having returned to Chicago, the Bellows gave a party in the suburb of Skokie for friends and relatives; it was a crowded scene, one guest recalled, "with people from too many chapters in their lives." Sondra came up to Bellow "with fury in her eyes" and complained that he wasn't pulling his weight; "We were embarrassed."

That winter, the Bellows were back in Chicago. The Northwestern English department had invited him to teach for a term. Bellow and Sondra and Adam, now a year old, rented a room in the Evanshire, a small residential hotel in Evanston where widows sat all day in the lobby. Lake Michigan was a few blocks to the east; a block to the west, the El train rumbled by. In the mornings, Sondra drove around with the baby and visited relatives while Bellow wrote.

His discipline was prodigious. Whatever else was happening, he usually managed to put in a morning's work. "For months now I have been lost in the remotest bush of Africa with Henderson," he reported to Berryman on February 19, 1958. He had torn up the manuscript and started over, writing five hundred pages in long-hand since Labor Day: "The last fantasy is taking place in the neighborhood of Newfoundland. Crash fire—crash ice. I need to cool things off. Anyway E.H.H. [Eugene Henderson, the book's hero] will give you a run for your money. And I believe he comes out sane, though he goes in mad. And that's news."

Bellow was excited by "Henderson." Since *Dangling Man* and *The Victim*, his style had become more daring and expressive. Even so, the new book seemed to come out of nowhere. Like Tommy Wilhelm, the brash and well-born Henderson bore no outward resemblance to his creator; the setting was a continent where Bellow had never been. "If I can't touch the heart of the great mystery (this time) I may as well spin a yarn," he wrote Ralph Ellison. The novel's originality turned out to be its greatest strength. He had never written a book with such a forceful, authoritative voice. One day in Tivoli, while Herbert Gold was "hanging up his wet clothes from having been pissed on by Ralph Ellison's big black dog," Bellow said to him, "Pretty soon I'll be unassailable, and I can write philosophy like Tolstoy."

A Tolstoyan note could already be heard in his critical prose. In "The Sealed Treasure," an essay for *The Times Literary Supplement*, he returned to a familiar theme: the philistinism of American life. Its love of commerce, its indifference to culture, its will to obliterate the past—all this was anathema to the novelist's task, which was to exhume the "human qualities" buried within each heart. "A modern mass society has no open place for such qualities, no vocabulary for them and no ceremony (except in the churches) which makes them public," he wrote. It was the job of literature to supply this vocabulary, to express humanity's inchoate needs.

"The Sealed Treasure" begins with an account of Bellow's trip to southern Illinois a few years earlier, when he had been on assignment for *Holiday*. His mission had mystified the locals. When he explained that he was writing an article about Illinois, people told him there was nothing to write about. "The streets were boringly empty, and at night even the main street was almost deserted," he wrote. Yet even in this barren landscape, Bellow found something of value: a hidden life of the mind. Librarians told him that people in central Illinois read Plato, Tocqueville, Proust, and Robert Frost. Most of the repositories of this inner life were women. "The intelligence or cultivation of a woman in Moline, Illinois," Bellow wrote, "would necessarily be her secret, almost her private vice."

Bellow was not a complex thinker. He had laboriously worked his way through the classics when "boning up" on the 101 Great

Ideas for Mortimer Adler's *Syntopicon;* he was conversant, in a literary way, with Plato and Aristotle, Kierkegaard and Nietzsche. They were part of his "intellectual" credentials—his passport from the book-adoring culture of the Jewish ghetto to the New World. But there was nothing abstract about Bellow's theme: The cataclysmic events of the century—the two world wars, the Holocaust, the rise of mass society—had made art superfluous. The modern world had conspired to drown out the novelist's—*his*—distinctive voice:

> The enormous increases in population seem to have dwarfed the individual. So have modern physics and astronomy. But we may be somewhere between a false greatness and a false insignificance. At least we can stop misrepresenting ourselves to ourselves and realize that the only thing we can be in this world is human. We are temporarily miracle-sodden and feeling faint.

In mid-career, in the middle of his life, Bellow was still wrestling with the primal issue of where he stood in the great world, still taking his own measure. Where in the span between greatness and insignificance should he locate himself? However large his public reputation, he still felt like the youngest child in the family.

Viking was eager to get its hands on "Henderson the Rain King." All through the early months of 1958, Pat Covici dispatched imploring letters and telegrams to the Evanshire. "My tongue is literally hanging out for the last chapter of your book," he wrote just after the start of the year. An artist was already sketching the jacket. "Hurry, hurry, hurry! The show must begin." By mid-March, the book was done. Bellow sent off the manuscript to New York, and a week later Covici replied: "The ending is as natural as rain. And strange as this may sound to you, I was saddened when I read the word 'End' in the middle of the last page. I guess I didn't want to part from Henderson."

16

If I am out of my mind, it's all right with me.

—SAUL BELLOW, *Herzog*

AN OBSESSIVE REVISER, Bellow didn't like to relinquish his books, writing them over even on the galleys. The handwritten notebooks and manuscripts that presaged *Henderson the Rain King* amounted to more than four thousand pages. In the spring of 1958, he was dispatching new chapters to Covici on a weekly, sometimes a daily basis ("Ditch those pages of ch. 18"). "I'm bushed," he admitted. "Between Evanston and Henderson, I've worn myself out, but I recover quickly and I should be fit to start the final campaign after a couple of weeks of sleep in Tivoli." Finally, Covici installed a secretary in the house, and Bellow dictated the manuscript, composing in his head as Henry James had—"eight, ten, twelve and fourteen hours a day for six weeks," he wrote to the novelist Josephine Herbst, who had become a friend during a season she had spent in Chicago on a research fellowship at the Newberry Library. "By mid-August I was near suicide."

It was a long summer. In June, after a "blowup," Sondra went off to New York City with Adam, leaving Bellow to deal with Greg, who had just arrived for a visit; in August, she smashed up the car. And there was tragic news about one of Bellow's nephews. "Toward the end of the month," he confided to Josephine Herbst, "in his Army barracks in San Francisco, being in great trouble and seeing no way out, he killed himself." Bellow drove all the way to Chicago from Tivoli for the funeral. But domestic crises, far from slowing him down, had an oddly stimulating effect on his imagination. "The worse my personal disasters became," he recalled of that time, "the funnier *Henderson* seemed to get."

By the fall of 1958, chronically short of funds, he was back in Minneapolis, teaching at the university, thanks again to Ralph Ross. (Bellow and Sondra had "patched things up.") There was only one catch: Bellow made it a condition of the appointment that his "pal" Jack Ludwig had to be offered a position, too. "I had to understand one very peculiar complication," Ross recounted: "Ludwig was so close a friend that they had made a pact; neither one of them could go anyplace unless both of them could go." This was a convenient stipulation for Ludwig, since Bard had no intention of keeping him on, and it also enabled him to be in close proximity to his mistress. "Bellow was conned into this arrangement because Ludwig wanted to be where Sondra was," suggested Ross. While Bellow was in Tivoli, revising "Henderson the Rain King," Sondra and Ludwig were in Minneapolis looking at real estate.

Amazingly enough, it still hadn't dawned on Bellow that Ludwig and Sondra were having an affair. ("Both knowing and not knowing," muses Artur Sammler in a later book—"one of the more frequent human arrangements.") Still, he couldn't ignore the fact that his marriage was in deep trouble. Sondra was in such a constant rage that her doctor ordered tests to see if she had a neurological condition. More likely, it was the constant subordination of her own needs and wishes to those of her husband—the suppression of her identity, the demand that she conform to the domestic role assigned her—that provoked Sondra's temper. Bellow had other notions, offering a clinical diagnosis—"a small lesion of the temporal lobe," he explained to Pat Covici. This mystifying analysis seemed to comfort him: His wife's problem was physiological; no human agent was involved. "She may have to take drugs to control it. Meanwhile she's having treatment from my doctor. He says it's not a dangerous illness but needs to be understood and watched."

Bellow's doctor was Paul Meehl, a clinical psychologist at the University of Minnesota. "Partly it was situational," said Meehl, as vague as his patient, in interpreting Bellow's decision to submit to therapy, a process he'd come to regard with considerable suspicion:

"His marriage was not in good shape." In *Herzog,* Madeleine insists that Herzog go into therapy—a stipulation that Sondra imposed on Bellow. "The book is a description of reality," attested Meehl. (Herzog speculates that Madeleine and Gersbach had a practical reason for contriving his analysis: "Four afternoons a week they knew where I was, on the couch, and so were safe in bed.")

Meehl was an eclectic therapist. A "calm Protestant Nordic Anglo-Celtic," as Bellow described him in the person of Dr. Edvig (a portrait his model admitted was "not bad"), he had a pronounced theoretical bent that found an ideal object in Bellow. "He was what we call in the profession a YAVIS," said Meehl: "young, attractive, verbal, intelligent, successful." Also somewhat grievance prone. "Between man and wife the rules are rules of war," Bellow wrote to Sam Freifeld when Freifeld's marriage fell apart: "The good rules of war, chivalrous rules—but it is still war." In the battle that his own second marriage had become, Sondra, as Bellow saw it, was the aggressor. He was again the victim, a docile, mild-mannered writer at the mercy of his wife's unpredictable and increasingly violent moods.

It wasn't long before Sondra, too, was in therapy with Meehl—a highly unorthodox practice. (Anita had also been in therapy with Bellow's Reichian analyst; Bellow didn't like to be alone, even on the couch.) Jack Ludwig was a focal point for both of them—Sondra confiding her divided affections to Meehl while Bellow tried to find out what the doctor knew. She thought they were making progress. "We are both in the midst of analysis at the moment," she reported enthusiastically to Ralph Ellison,

> and it is such a relief to me not to have to lie down & *breathe* Reichian-style but to be permitted speech—our wild and insane summer has left its marks but we are trying to recover from all the blows & at least a measure of peace is possible—not always, but more often than before. Saul's analyst confesses that he finds him "baffling" & I figure there's some justice in my bewilderment if the good doctor whose business it is to make the opaque transparent is puzzled.

It wasn't an arrangement that made for effective therapy. Bellow lent Meehl the galleys of *Henderson* and entertained him with displays of masterly invective. "I found him a fascinating patient," Meehl admitted. Fascinating and elusive: "To put it quite frankly, I never quite figured this man out." Not that it mattered to Bellow. He made no secret of his contempt for therapists and therapy, even when he was in treatment. To lack self-knowledge was almost a point of honor. Like many artists, Bellow had a kind of talismanic belief in his powers of creativity, and he was reluctant to tamper with the source of his inspiration, believing it to be, if not divine, then beyond the reach of prying analysts.

"I am to suffering what Gary [Indiana] is to smoke," says Henderson: "One of the world's biggest operations." Herzog, too, dwells intensively on his "peculiar suffering," and so does Tommy Wilhelm, who tearfully discovers that his "real business" in life is "to carry his peculiar burden, to feel shame and impotence, to taste these quelled tears." In a chapter of *Herzog* that appeared in *Esquire,* Edvig offered what was essentially a paraphrase of Meehl's diagnosis: "You are fairly normal. Complicated, yes. Depressive, yes. But reactive-depressive. Not the worst of the depressives, by any means." (This passage was dropped from the book, perhaps because it was too explicit.)

"Reactive-depressive" was in those days a prevalent term, later retired from the therapeutic vocabulary, that described an essentially healthy patient's responses to setbacks, as opposed to a persistent underlying condition. Bellow ascribed to himself a more romantic, "literary" affliction, preferring to diagnose himself as being "melancholic," possessed of "a depressive temperament," which he considered different from being a depressive. Even in the midst of domestic travails, Meehl noted, Bellow manifested a jaunty vigor: "I could never make up my mind how unhappy he was."

Herzog, in a letter to a rival scholar named Mermelstein, offers the thesis that "people of powerful imagination, given to dreaming deeply and to raising up marvelous and self-sufficient fictions, turn to suffering sometimes to cut into their bliss, as people pinch themselves to feel awake." For Herzog, as for Bellow, suffering was redemptive, "a more extended form of life, a striving for true wakefulness and an antidote to illusion"—and perhaps, less exaltedly, a form of masochism. If the masochist's job is to see himself as a victim, to control his pain by bringing it upon himself, an adulterous drama such as the one being played out in Minneapolis would be an ideal vehicle. Bellow could look upon his personal travails with detachment, experience them as theater. Meehl couldn't tell if his patient was really suffering because in a sense he wasn't; he was merely observing himself suffer.

For Bellow, if not for Sondra—who was to pay in a variety of ways for her sins—there was something comical about the whole affair; he later likened it to a "Goldoni comedy." During its Minneapolis run, he played his part beautifully. In his supporting role—according to one story that made the rounds—he'd gone off with another woman after a party, leaving Sondra with Ludwig. ("And of course, from what you tell me," says Edvig to Herzog, "you haven't been guiltless.") The literary possibilities were endless. Herbert Gold half-facetiously suggested that Bellow "set it up so that he could write his book"—a theory corroborated by Dr. A. Boyd Thomes, the physician to the Minneapolis literary community. "Bellow has a tendency to set up situations and study them," said Thomes. "He sets them up and knocks them down again—like a pinsetter."

That Bellow, whether consciously or not, abetted Sondra's treachery is entirely plausible. How else explain his failure to unmask it? In itself, campus adultery was hardly news. The offices at Temporary North of Mines were "drenched in extramarital affairs," according to Philip Siegelman, a graduate student who taught in the humanities department: "Seminal fluid practically dripped out of the paving stones." Even by these standards, Ludwig's conduct was flagrant.

Around the campus, though, people were slow to get the drift. For a long time, said Ralph Ross, "nobody had the faintest idea" that there was anything between Ludwig and Sondra. Philip Siegelman and his wife found out first: The Bellows and the Ludwigs, distracted by their own needs, delegated the Siegelmans to look after their children, a chore that required the official care-takers "to calculate who was with whom, and where." Ralph Ross also began to get "a funny feeling about Jack and Sondra" at a big party when Bellow was away lecturing; Ross greeted Sondra by kissing her shoulder, and he saw Ludwig's face redden: "I thought,

'What's it to him?'" Not long afterward, Ross and a friend went to a bar on the outskirts of town; there, in a dark corner, were Ludwig and Sondra.

Bellow, meanwhile, still ignorant of where matters stood, was busy advancing his pal's cause. As a teacher, Ludwig got mostly negative reviews. (According to the critic Peter Shaw, a student of his at Bard, Ludwig was "a great name-dropper" but could be an inspiring teacher, "even if a lot of it was fakery.") Word of his uneven performance in the classroom had gotten back to the English department, and his position was far from secure. Sondra persuaded Bellow to pay a call on John Clarke, the department chairman, and threaten to resign if Ludwig wasn't reappointed. He also furthered Ludwig's career in other ways, proposing to Pat Covici that the two of them coedit "an altogether new sort of text—D. H. Lawrence for use in college courses."

Covici poured cold water on the Lawrence scheme, but the two literary entrepreneurs had better luck with another idea: a magazine of fine writing. Aaron Asher traced its inception back to 1956, when *The New Yorker* turned down *Seize the Day*. If he couldn't get general-circulation magazines to publish his work, Bellow would publish it himself. By the fall of 1958, he had persuaded Asher, who was then working for Meridian, to support the magazine. During Christmas week, Bellow met with Asher and Arthur A. Cohen, the publisher of Meridian. They were "wildly enthusiastic," he reported to Covici, and had offered to underwrite a semiannual paperback with a first printing of twenty-five thousand copies. He had already lined up Wright Morris, Herbert Gold, John Berryman, and Josephine Herbst, among other literary cronies; Ralph Ellison was "finishing a novelette" for the first issue. Bellow amused himself by floating titles: "New Orbit," "Now," "The Pinwheel," "Chanticleer." Covici worried that the new project would distract his prize author from his own work, but Bellow maintained that it would energize him: "The more I do, the more connection I feel with people, causes, the more fluently I write."

Things had improved on the marital front. "Sasha and I stand much better now than we did before," Bellow reported to Keith Botsford, who was teaching at the University of Puerto Rico in San Juan, on February 4, 1959:

She's erratic, to put it modestly, and I'm a little nuts myself, and the house in Tivoli was just the priceless ingredient, the catalyst to our explosive mixture. So we had an explosion and it blew everything to bits except the essentials. Despite the shock of it it was rather profitable than no. We carry on our relations now in a propositional fashion—that is, each saying exactly what he thinks. No more dragging of the frills in the soup. It works very handsomely, ⁹⁄₁₀ths of the conceptual interference having been trimmed away.

Covici, entertaining the Bellows in New York, confirmed this optimistic account. "You looked and felt wonderful," he wrote his author after he had returned to Minnesota. "You were your old self again. Sandra [*sic*] is your best medicine, and I hope you are doing the same for her."

The main problem, as always, was money. Bellow hoped, as he did with each book, that *Henderson* would make it big; but Viking had advanced him fifteen thousand dollars over the last three years, and he realized there was little chance of the novel earning it back. "It turns out I don't earn enough annually to ship a goat to Guatemala from next door in Honduras," he complained to Covici, scrawling at the bottom of the letter: "No check for Jan.?"

His one hope was the possibility of a grant from the Ford Foundation, which had inaugurated a program to fund established but struggling writers. "During the last ten years I have lived mainly on advances from my publisher which I have supplemented by teaching and magazine work," Bellow explained in a letter to McNeil Lowry, the Ford Foundation's president. His debt to Viking had "grown steadily and my anxieties with it." As part of his application, he submitted a financial form. Bellow's income for 1956 came to just over $8,000; in 1957, he'd made $10,650 from lecturing at the New School, teaching, and royalties; in 1958, he made $13,775 from the University of Minnesota alone. In other years, he reported, he'd made as little as $6,000. As one anonymous Ford official noted dryly: "He's not getting rich on writing, that's evident."

His plans for the next year were up in the air. Sondra refused to consider going back to the rural banishment of Tivoli; it made her "stir-crazy." She was studying sixteen hours a day; she had hired a sitter to look after Adam. "Foolishly," Bellow had signed up to teach only two quarters at Minnesota, he confided to Botsford—which meant that he'd have to make up the difference "lecturing and writing reviews and bits of things to eke out the sum we need." Was there any prospect of a job down in Puerto Rico? "Lecturing? Window washing?"

Bellow professed—indeed, considered it a matter of honor—not to know what his own books were about. When Josephine Herbst praised *Seize the Day,* he was grateful: "It's hard for me to know, because so much of the time I'm deaf, dumb and blind, the slave of unknown masters." He was just as in the dark about *Henderson.* "I can tell you what I wished it to be, but I can't say what it *is,*" he wrote to Richard Stern in Chicago: "Every ability was brought to bear except one—the talent for self-candor which so far I have been able to invest only in the *language* of what I've written. I should be able to do better than that. People are waiting. My own soul is waiting." It was a revealing observation, at once insightful and blind; how could he express self-candor in his writing without knowing what he'd expressed? It was as if he was aware of a crucial deficiency in his work—the inability to plumb his own depths—but unable to fix it.

While he wasn't sure he understood his own work, he was sure the critics understood it even less. On February 15, 1959, less than a week before the official publication date of *Henderson the Rain King,* he issued a manifesto on the front page of *The New York Times Book Review.* It was called "Deep Readers of the World, Beware!"

His title was taken from a playful remark E. M. Forster had made on the occasion of a visit to Harvard, reputed to harbor so many deep readers of his books. The criticism of literature had become a symbol-hunting game, Bellow complained. To a Marxist, the *Pequod* in *Moby-Dick* was a factory; to a religious critic, it was a "floating cathedral"; to a Freudian, Ahab was afflicted with an Oedipus complex—the whale was his mother.

Ideology had taken all the fun out of the enterprise, in Bellow's view. Contemporary readers had lost their sense of intuition, their literary innocence. Is it necessary to grasp the structure of *Ulysses* in order to appreciate it? "The beauty of the book cannot escape you if you are any sort of reader," Bellow insisted, "and it is better to approach it from the side of naivete than from that of culture-idolatry, sophistication, and snobbery." Meanings are "a dime a dozen." What human beings hunger for is the particular; they look to literature in order to find their own experience reflected in it. "What, *again* about the feelings?" he scolded himself in his essay, adopting the Yiddish inflection of a mother chastising her bookish son for his excessive sensitivity. But it was the feelings that fiction was supposed to explore.

The timing of the appearance of "Deep Readers of the World, Beware!" was no coincidence. If there was any book in the growing Bellow canon that cried out for deep reading, it was this comic allegorical novel, which staked out new territory in the most literal sense. By chapter five, its hero was in the African bush, wandering among the Arnewi and Wariri tribes in the remotest outposts of civilization.

Eugene Henderson, like the great American novelist whose initials he bears, is a brawny, bullying adventurer. He fought in World War II; is a prodigious drinker; carries a .375 H and H Magnum. At six foot four, Henderson looms even larger than Bellow's other "large" and "tall" protagonists. His physical stature is matched by a wild, anarchic energy. He rages against his wife and children, brawls in country taverns, smashes up the furniture in a resort hotel. Henderson's recurrent cry—"*I want, I want!*"—expresses his insatiable character.

Most of Bellow's lead characters, however outsized, bear a distinct resemblance to their creator. Henderson, apart from a weakness for women and a devotion to the violin, could hardly be more different. His biography and his physical characteristics belong unmistakably to Bellow's landlord at Bard College, Chanler Chapman.* Like Chapman, Henderson goes about in soiled over-

---

*Bellow freely acknowledged his model. "Chanler was so phenomenal a phenomenon that no one could really 'have' him," he wrote a later occupant of the carriage house on Chanler's estate after the book came out. "I made an amusing try."

alls and takes up as a pig farmer. Like Chapman, he has an illustrious father—"the famous scholar Willard Henderson who wrote that book on the Albigensians, a friend of William James and Henry Adams." And like Chapman, he's inherited money.

Yet Henderson, despite his bluff rural manner and patrician ancestry, turns out to be quintessentially Bellovian. His sense of grievance, his immense ambition, his eager quest to "burst the spirit's sleep" (the phrase is from Shelley) put him squarely in the tradition of Bellow's more high-minded personae. Unlike the all-purpose intellectuals who more often stand in for Bellow, Henderson has no literary aspirations; at fifty-five, he wants to go to medical school. But for all his belligerent philistinism, he shares with Bellow's other characters an autodidactic strain. He refers to Jung, Freud, Sartre, Wordsworth, and Whitman, is a fan of William James, quotes Tennyson and Blake. Even the refrain "*I want, I want!*" is appropriated, perhaps unconsciously, from Blake; it's the caption for one of the plates in *The Gates of Paradise.**

On the surface, *Henderson the Rain King* is a departure from the Great Books ambience of Bellow's earlier novels. The jungle setting, the outlandish plot, the cast of naked concubines and primitive tribesmen who accompany Henderson on his journey . . . clearly, we are no longer in Chicago. *Henderson* displayed more conclusively than anything else he'd written Bellow's ability to conjure up worlds he'd never known. His Africa possessed an eerie authority—an ethnographer's field notes in the hands of a master novelist. Yet in another way, it's his most "literary" novel. The biblical motifs are hard to miss: Henderson longs to go about in sackcloth and ashes like an Old Testament prophet; to wander in the desert like John the Baptist and subsist on locusts; he sets a bush on fire, Moses-like, with his cigarette lighter; like Daniel, he frequents a lion's den. Henderson's journey toward self-understanding ("I am really on a kind of quest") is also a parody

---

*Bellow carried around a copy of *The Portable Blake* for years and told Richard Stern that when he was writing *Henderson* the lion imagery of "Little Girl Lost" in *Songs of Innocence and Experience* had "sunk deeply" into his unconscious.

of the Grail legend. The novel is a deliberate commentary on literary tradition, a "composite parody"; it satirizes the very allusiveness that Bellow warned against in "Deep Readers of the World, Beware!"

Some of his sources are more recondite. An account of the Wariri ceremonies and customs drew heavily on a book by Melville J. Herskovits, Bellow's anthropology professor at Northwestern. "Joxi," the tribe's method of "trample massage," was described in Richard Burton's *First Footsteps in East Africa*. The rituals of the cattle-worshiping Arnewi tribe were derived from the works of John Roscoe, a nineteenth-century missionary; the resplendent King Dahfu was a composite of King Gelele, encountered by Burton, and King Gezo, described at length in Frederick E. Forbes's two-volume *Dahomey and the Dahomans*. Bellow insisted he hadn't cracked an anthropology book since his undergraduate days, but all those long afternoons in the ethnology stacks had clearly paid off.

Whatever he borrowed, he transmuted; *Henderson the Rain King*, as one of Bellow's critics remarked, was "an astonishing feat of creative synthesis." King Dahfu, for example, was an African version of Wilhelm Reich. In one episode, King Dahfu introduces Henderson to the lioness Atti: "Contemplate her. How does she stride, how does she breathe? I stress the respiratory part." Indeed, Dahfu sounds just like Dr. Chester Raphael, who had put Bellow through his Reichian paces in Queens nearly a decade before.

Bellow openly acknowledged the Reichian connection: "All the while I was writing Dahfu I had the ghost of Rosenfeld near at hand, my initiator into the Reichian mysteries." A more explicit source, referred to in the manuscript by Dahfu, was Dr. Paul Schilder's *The Image and Appearance of the Human Body*, a work that had some currency in psychoanalytic circles during the 1950s. Like Reich, Schilder believed that psychic energy that is suppressed has somatic effects. Schilder's stress on free will and on the coherence of the self was key. The unconscious wasn't only an agent of repression, he argued, but a vital source of images—"symbolizations and condensations"—that shape and change our identities. "It was from Schilder that I got the notion that one's physical self really does represent an inner picture, and that we are perhaps responsible for the way we come out," Bellow explained. "This carries one step forward the doctrine that a man's fate is made by his character."

Henderson's most distinctive trait is his vitality. "Moody, rough, tyrannical, and probably mad," as he presents himself, he's stifled by the confining bonds of domestic life; he berates his children, fights with his wife, storms about his pig farm like some rural Lear. It's after his spinster housekeeper drops dead in the midst of one of his rages that he lights out for Africa.

Only Henderson's Africa isn't so dark; he ventures abroad more in the spirit of William Boot, the journalist in Evelyn Waugh's *Scoop*, than of Conrad's brooding Marlow. Read from today's vantage, informed by multiculturalism, *Henderson the Rain King* is racist in the extreme. "Except for King Dahfu," the critic Carlos Baker scolded Bellow, "all the natives talk like a combination of Uncle Remus and the Emperor Jones." The African women are notable mainly for their big behinds, and their speech is right out of *Amos 'n' Andy* ("Wo, dem be trouble"). The men are "wild savages." Henderson is equally antiquated, a grandiose American boor trampling obtusely on the manners and morals of foreigners he doesn't understand. But he doesn't come away empty-handed. He's learned, in one of the book's great comic scenes, the principle of grun-tu-molani: "Man want to live." In Henderson's colloquial paraphrase: "God does not shoot dice with our souls." Life has a purpose; the individual matters.

Henderson broods over his impending mortality and plays the violin to commune with his dead father. (Bellow also resorted to this method of mourning his father.) That there should be nothing after death, that his unique existence will be swept away, is unbearable to him, as it is to Augie March and Moses Herzog and Charlie Citrine. What Henderson was looking for, according to Bellow, was "a remedy to the anxiety over death." But of course there is no remedy, and under the tutelage of the masterful King Dahfu, Henderson comes to some kind of acceptance of his place in the world. Employing the existentialist terminology of Sartre and Heidegger, he confesses to Dahfu that he's still in a state of "Becoming," while Dahfu is a "Be-er," fulfilling his nature. As Bellow glossed the book's message in a letter to Richard Stern:

If we have only to say "humanity stinks in our nostrils" then silence is better, because we have heard *that* news. Our own bones have broadcast it. If we have more than this to say we may try but never require ourselves to *prove*—oh, no, that is not shit but the musk of the civet, it smells bad because it's so concentrated. Diluted it's the base of beautiful perfumes. No amount of assertion will make an ounce of art.

The novel's most glaring fault was a weakness for burlesque plot developments. Bellow has a tendency in his novels to push his plots so far that they verge on farce: Augie March ending up in a lifeboat at sea with a fellow Chicagoan after his warship is torpedoed; the indigent poet Humboldt bequeathing Charlie Citrine a movie script that becomes a commercial hit. *Henderson* is full of grotesque slapstick: his brother's freakish death in a shooting accident; the death of his spinster housekeeper; a scene at one of the Wariri festivals in which an old woman wrestles with a dwarf. The most egregious instance is the book's final scene, in which Henderson, who is bringing a lion cub back to America, encounters an orphan from Persia on the flight home. With the boy asleep in his lap, he thinks back to a summer job he once had, riding a roller coaster with a bear named Smolak—"outcasts together, two humorists before the crowd, but brothers in our souls." The one character with whom Henderson achieves genuine intimacy isn't even a human being but a fetid old brown bear, and not a figure from his present but from his past.

Henderson, Bellow's least autobiographical creation, was the one he identified with the most. Years later, when an interviewer asked him which of his characters most resembled him, he replied: "Henderson—the absurd seeker of high qualities." It's not hard to see why. The pleasure afforded by King Dahfu's harem of sixty-seven nubile wives is also the source of his doom. Among the Wariri, a king's failure to satisfy his wives is punishable by death; rather than face this challenge to perform in the role of successor after King Dahfu dies, Henderson decides to scram. As Bellow wrote his jungle book, he too faced periodic sentences of banishment from the marital bed—a fate short of capital punishment, to be sure, but painful nonetheless.

A more subliminal and primal conflict was enacted in the powerful scene in which Henderson lifts the wooden idol that will earn him glory—a scene that mimed Bellow's efforts to come to terms with the central loss of his life, the death of his mother. Henderson raises up the heavy wooden statue and is crowned the Rain King. The statue's name is Mummah. No wonder it was so heavy.

On February 19, 1959, the week that *Henderson* appeared, Bellow wrote to Covici. The grant from the Ford Foundation had come through: sixteen thousand dollars, payable over a two-year period. He could stay put for a while:

> Naturally, we'll be in Minnesota for part of the next year so that the psychiatry and the neurology can go on. They tell me I'm making good speed, and Sondra too is much better. All's well in the sack, unusually well, and we're beginning to feel much affection for each other. So it'd be ridiculous to depart for long from this base.

Like many writers, Bellow claimed unconvincingly that he didn't read his reviews; and like all writers, he kept his ear to the ground as publication day approached. "Any news about Henderson?" he wheedled. "If it isn't very very good, please spare me."

He had reason to worry. Orville Prescott, the dour reviewer for *The New York Times*, found Henderson a bore, "the apotheosis of fatuous egotism." Charles Rolo, writing in *The Atlantic Monthly*, was "left with the impression of an attempted tour de force which has failed to come off—an impression of labored cleverness and stretches of pseudo-portentous mumbo jumbo." Elizabeth Hardwick, a dangerous critic when aroused against a book, was devastating. *Henderson*'s Africa was a "joke" Africa, she objected in *Partisan Review;* Henderson was a boozy blowhard, a Village hipster: "He might be an action painter or he might, wearing a little goatee, be Dizzy Gillespie."*

---

*The English critics demonstrated a greater appreciation of the novel than did their American counterparts. V. S. Pritchett, reversing his earlier judgment, declared Bellow the heir of Faulkner. Malcolm Bradbury considered *Henderson* a novel of the highest order, a romance that managed at once to entertain and to grapple with "the great spiritual problems of man." And Margaret Drabble expressed devout admiration for the book's "passionately exhilarating fervour."

The novel had its allies—mostly Bellow's friends. Richard Stern, in *Kenyon Review*, called it "a stylistic masterpiece." Harvey Swados, in *The New Leader*, pronounced Bellow "the most significantly exciting novelist now at work in the United States." "What a writer! It made me dance," Henry Miller—not a friend—effused in a letter to Pat Covici: "I feel I've made a great discovery. It's how I'd like to write myself."

Bellow felt predictably vexed by the book's reception. "It beats me that I should be accused of cunningly willing the whole thing into being," he grumbled to Covici. "Do these people who are called (but why?) critics suppose that anyone would want to feel as I did! I can't imagine what the hell they're up to. *They* are the mystery." His growing fame hadn't diminished his sensitivity to criticism; reviewers were "jokers," "rats." But being misread, he shrugged, was the price he paid for being a cultural Rorschach: "I'm practically a diagnostic technique all by myself. One book by me & the whole ugly picture is illuminated."

The critics' ambivalent response to *Henderson the Rain King* didn't help its sales. Briefly on the bestseller list, it dropped off after three weeks. Bellow revised his expectations downward, from fifty thousand to forty thousand, then thirty thousand. By May, he was pleading with Covici to "tell me that Henderson has now sold 20,000 copies." In the end, it just about did—respectable sales but hardly a commercial triumph.

While *Henderson* hadn't made him rich, it had increased his fame. Lecture invitations poured in. Could he speak at Texas Technological College? A book club in Darien? The First Methodist Church in Evanston? In March, he gave a talk in Champaign ("no bubbles here"); in April, he spoke in Chicago and Pittsburgh, as well as at Purdue, "earning $700 en route." In May, he was in New York, staying at Covici's. A postcard to Dave Peltz summed up his situation: "The winds of heaven stream under my fanny."

In Chicago, he had dinner with Marilyn Monroe, in town for the premiere of *Some Like It Hot*. Bellow arrived at the Ambassador East Hotel to find the star surrounded by an entourage that included a manicurist and a bodyguard, who left the door open when he went to the bathroom. "He's not supposed to let me out of his sight," Monroe explained. After dinner at the Pump Room, she signed the guest book, "Proud to be the guest of the Chicago writer Saul Bellow." In a starstruck letter to Covici the next day, Bellow reported: "Marilyn seemed genuinely glad to see a familiar face, I have yet to see anything in Marilyn that isn't genuine. Surrounded by thousands she conducts herself like a philosopher."

He had a less congenial encounter with Nelson Algren, who after Bellow was the best-known novelist in Chicago. Algren was the antithesis of Bellow: a self-styled tough guy in a leather jacket (though he had grown up Jewish in Chicago just like Bellow; his given name was Nelson Algren Abraham). *The Man with the Golden Arm,* his portrait of junkies and whores in the dives around Rush Street, had been turned into a movie starring Frank Sinatra. Bellow prided himself on his streetwise grasp of the city, but Algren still lived in its midst, inhabiting a bona fide dump on Wabansia Avenue. Whatever his limitations as a writer—his characters tended to be two-dimensional, and he had even more trouble portraying women than Bellow did—Algren belonged to the tradition of Dreiser and Richard Wright and James T. Farrell. The authenticity of his down-and-out characters made Augie March seem bourgeois.

They met in a Polish saloon on the Northwest Side, "a place so sordid even Algren didn't usually go there," recalled Dave Peltz, who was also a friend of Algren and who had arranged the meeting. Christmas lights were strung over the bar. Algren was waiting in a booth when they arrived, wearing army fatigues—"to let Bellow know 'You weren't in the army like I was.'" They quickly got into an argument, and Bellow left. The town wasn't big enough for both of them.

Writers who posed a threat to Bellow's hegemony got the cold shoulder; writers who occupied a place safely below his own on the literary ladder were seen as comrades in the "travail business," as Bellow liked to refer to his profession. Toward these needy souls he gladly extended a helping hand. "We lost a lot of our humanity, struggling," he wrote Josephine Herbst in the spring of 1959. "The challenge is not to lose, rather to regain, to refine. What, if not that, are we for?" When Herbst was going through a difficult time, holed up in a stone farmhouse in Bucks County, Pennsylvania, writing her memoirs, Bellow lent her "cat-food money." "So much the mainstay of her literary existence did Bellow become," wrote Elinor Langer in her biography of Herbst, "that without his contribution it is not certain that any of her memoirs would ever have appeared."* And to John Berryman, who was in the process of getting divorced from Eileen Simpson, he offered moral support and an invitation to Tivoli: "There is coal in the grate, whiskey on the shelf, feather in the beds."

He also tried to help Delmore Schwartz in the poet's long and sad decline. After Schwartz threatened the life of Hilton Kramer and ended up in Bellevue Hospital like Von Humboldt Fleisher ("rushed off dingdong in a paddy wagon like a mad dog, arriving foul, and locked up raging"), Bellow organized a fund to pay for treatment at the Payne-Whitney Clinic. He was the only one of Schwartz's friends with "the guts" to visit him at Bellevue, according to Herbst.†

By June 1959, Bellow was back in Tivoli, consumed by a new play: When a work in progress was going well, he wrote with fiendish energy. But he also found time for more Whitmanesque pursuits: "loafing, inviting my soul and looking out for the interests of the *Noble Savage.*"

The magazine he'd long been plotting to launch now had a name. In a letter to Keith Botsford, the third coeditor alongside Bellow and Jack Ludwig, Bellow furnished a bracing manifesto: "It was to be contemporary . . . it was to make a stir . . . it was to be *new*"—and it wasn't to be "too literary." The whole idea was to "get writers into the world again," he explained to Harvey Swados, exhorting him to go out and cover the Floyd

---

*Herbst died a year later, leaving her memoir uncompleted. On the strength of the two chapters Bellow published in *The Noble Savage* and a later chapter that appeared in *New American Review,* the book would have vindicated his enthusiasm.

†His intervention was to no avail. Schwartz pocketed the money, signed himself out, and began calling Bellow in the middle of the night, "using techniques the GPU might have envied."

Patterson–Ingemar Johannson boxing match. (Swados's excellent reporting on the match appeared in the first issue.) *The Noble Savage* was "a move against the cold, companionless boredom of the writer's life," an effort to reconstitute the literary vigor of an earlier time:

> I want to make it possible to let off some steam, to write in the good old ranging way that was natural to novelists in the 20s—in the spirit of The Dial and the Mercury, The Enormous Room or of The American Jitters (while [Edmund] Wilson yet lived, and before he became the great blimp of The New Yorker).

Some of the contributions to the first issue of *Noble Savage*—in particular Harold Rosenberg's "Notes from the Ground Up," a critique of received ideas, and Herbert Gold's "How to Tell the Beatniks from the Hipsters"—were sneeringly polemical; but for the most part, the magazine did publish—in the words of Bellow's manifesto—"brilliant things." Among the many memorable pieces that appeared in its brief but distinguished five-issue run were stories and excerpts from longer works by Ralph Ellison, Thomas Pynchon, and Edward Hoagland; a selection of John Berryman's early "Dream Songs"; and the memoirs of Josephine Herbst. The contents page reflected Bellow's editorial dominance; the bylines of friends and girlfriends past, present, and future (Isaac Rosenfeld, Richard Stern, Ruth Miller, Marjorie Farber) appeared in disproportionate number, and the editors gave liberal space to their own work. But the magazine also published writers such as Dan Wakefield, Jules Feiffer, and Seymour Krim, who evoked the bohemian Village scene of the fifties. *The Noble Savage* was both hip and highbrow.

Bellow confined his contributions to squibs and diatribes called Arias, which were unsigned but unmistakably his own. In a characteristic Aria, he took issue with "one of our commissars of culture," a figure of "mountainous solemnity" (Philip Rahv?) who had dismissed *The Noble Savage* as "junk, junk, and more junk." At least the magazine had passion, Bellow remonstrated; it invited writers to "look at the world clearly and comment on it." What more could one ask? Quoting Shakespeare—"The time is out of joint. O cursed spite, / That ever I was born to set it right!"—he ended with a sarcastic aside: "Lucky Hamlet. He had only *one* uncle to kill."

As with all such enterprises, there was a good deal of squabbling among the editors. Botsford complained that Ludwig and Bellow were a "faction"; Ludwig complained that Botsford was acting high-handedly and threatened in bad Yiddish to "kasher him *oop a bissel* [to "kosher" him a little] with salt and a red-hot stone." The two men devoted as much energy to keeping each other out of the magazine as to getting new talent into it. Forced to mediate between his jealous colleagues, Bellow was—in Botsford's phrase, borrowed from Confucius—"the unwobbling pivot."

When it came to his collaborators' work, Bellow erred on the generous side. He pronounced Ludwig's clownish marital farce, "Confusions: Thoreau in California," an "extraordinary" piece of work and was full of praise for Botsford's "Memoirs of a Russophile." But he was annoyed by his colleagues' indecisiveness. "I am sure that I could learn more of your real opinion by watching you load your pipe," Bellow upbraided Botsford about a story under consideration at the magazine:

> You condemn the thing almost totally and yet conclude that we ought to publish it. Until I understand better (perhaps I should say in some small degree) what this is all about I shall not be able to proceed with the work of the magazine. What is at issue is not the story itself—I have a better opinion of it than you—but a question of honor among the three of us.

It didn't take much to provoke a touchy outburst. "Frankly, you are too ready to be suspicious of the motives of others," Botsford admonished Bellow, not unfairly.

"Of course *Fresh Air* attracted large numbers of kooks, fanatics, plausible lunatics and counterfeiters," Bellow wrote of Charlie Citrine's magazine in a draft of *Humboldt's Gift*. While Bellow made a point of soliciting manuscripts from famous friends, he also opened the magazine's pages to the rather large pool of literary oddballs he'd collected over the years. An erratic correspondent, capable of ignoring the most urgent letters, he nonetheless found the time to answer crank mail, often at great length. His tolerance of eccentricity served him well as an editor. Louis Gallo, a proof-reader who lived in Queens with his mother, was startled to receive a warm reply to a story he'd submitted—it was about a proof-reader who lives in Queens with his mother—from "Saul Bellow, friend and admirer." Gallo's story, "Oedipus-Schmoedipus," appeared in the fourth issue of *The Noble Savage.*

Another unfamiliar byline in the magazine was that of Hyman Slate. Bellow had known Slate since his University of Chicago days, when Slate had been a locally celebrated polymath. An able mathematician and a gifted chess player, Slate made his living as a social worker, but his favorite pastime was metaphysics. He contributed an Aria to the third issue refuting ontological argu-ments for the existence of God. If there was any proof for God's existence, Slate argued, it was his divine sense of humor, which had made the world such an improbable place. "Before the creation of the planets, before the Milky Way, in the hot primor-dial gas—potential—floated one of Manny's Specials—a hot dog, amply doused with mustard and piccadilli." The piece was quin-tessential *Noble Savage* ("No-*bel*," as Slate pronounced it, antici-pating its editor's future glory): caustic, irreverent, at once erudite and deflating of pretension. "You have a good voice or tone, and a lot of knowledge and ability," Bellow wrote to Slate, soliciting further contributions. "I'm not printing Slate's Proof for old times' sake."

Mark Harris, a young novelist with a Boswellian proclivity for cultivating famous writers, also showed up in the magazine's pages. He had written an unctuous letter to Bellow praising *Henderson the Rain King* that had elicited friendly encourage-ment: "It's silly not to know each other, isn't it? We've crossed the same ground any number of times and besides I have a sympa-thetic impression of you." Harris followed up with a complaint about the treatment one of his novels had received at the hands of Carlos Baker (who had also treated *Henderson* roughly). "I wish I'd read the book before that dreary Midas had touched it," Bellow replied, inviting Harris to submit work. A short story, "The Self-Made Brain Surgeon," graced the inaugural number.

There was something indiscriminate about Bellow's letter writ-ing; it denoted a kind of literary profligacy. That he wrote so openly to so many correspondents reflected his egalitarian spirit, his willingness—as he put it to Hyman Slate—to "accept the wider range of other people's facts." But it also reflected his loneliness, his eagerness for company, any company. There was a certain impersonality in his boisterous epistolary style; no matter whom Bellow was writing to, his letters have a single tone. It was as if he was writing to just one person: himself.

In the fall of 1959, the migratory Bellows rented a house at 3139 East Calhoun in Minneapolis. Sondra arrived first; her graduate-school classes began in September. Bellow followed at the end of the month, after a stop-off at Martha's Vineyard, where he showed his play in progress to Lillian Hellman. "She says I've written a lot of interesting soliloquies but there's no play in sight," Bellow reported to Keith Botsford: "no *play* play for Broadway."

No sooner had Bellow arrived in Minnesota than he and Sondra were fighting. "I'm having an ugly time—suffering no end," Bellow confided to Richard Stern on November 3. "Sondra and I are both in despair over the course things have taken and I *don't* expect a happy ending." He was indefinite—and perhaps not entirely forthright—about the cause of their problems. "There are no frigidities, impotencies, adulteries, only miseries." There *were* adulteries, of course, on both sides—Bellow had at least one fling with a student, and Sondra, still unknown to Bellow, was carrying on with Ludwig. In any event, Bellow saw things the way he always did: It wasn't his fault. The passive grammar again revealed the nature of his thinking on the matter. "Poor little Adam doesn't know he's about to be sentenced. I can't help him because it has nothing at all to do with me. I love Sash & respect her. But she has drawn the sword, and is just meshugah enough to swing it. And perish by it, maybe."

In fact, she had already swung. A few days after Bellow returned to Minneapolis, Sondra strode into the living room and declared "with icy control," as Bellow remembered it, that she wanted a divorce. "Sondra and I are finished," Bellow wrote dramatically to Covici:

Sondra doesn't have enough feeling for me to continue. *I* have it, and I don't know what to do with it, either. I'm beginning to

think of such things as antiques. They belong to older times or
to childhood. It seems crazy for a man of 44 to have such *feeling*
for his wife. Especially since she, being younger and more up-to-
date, doesn't even know what it is.

The blame was all on Sondra's side: She had rejected him. "It all
comes down to this: She doesn't love me, never did, never could."
He was moving out.

Bellow's letters to Covici chronicling the breakup were oddly
lighthearted, almost cheerful. He was "keeping his head" and
"acting sensibly." After Covici compared him to Moses, searching
for the Promised Land, he answered wryly, "So far I've seen
nothing but the desert. But perhaps God will choose me for His
servant. I know he has nothing comfortable in mind for me."

Banished by Sondra, Bellow sought refuge at the home of a
Minneapolis lawyer, Jonas Schwartz, a tiny man with "a deformed
body and a huge head," as a fellow lawyer described him. Schwartz
appears as Sandor Himmelstein in *Herzog*, a reliable guide to this
episode in Bellow's life, according to Ralph Ross, who delivered
Bellow to Schwartz's door.

Schwartz, like Himmelstein, was a volatile, high-strung character who hectored his client about the treachery of women, judges,
juries—what Herzog calls a "reality instructor." ("They'll put a
meter on your nose, and charge you for breathing," the hunchback
lawyer screams at Herzog.) Like Paul Meehl, Schwartz worked
both sides of the street: He was Sondra's lawyer, too. It wasn't just
greed that made Schwartz long for a piece of the action; it was
vanity. In the fall of 1959, the Bellows' marital crisis was the best
show in town. "Everyone wanted to get into the act," said John
Goetz, the lawyer whose services Bellow retained after it became
clear that Schwartz couldn't represent both man and wife. Even
the cuckolding Jack Ludwig played a supporting role, presiding
over meetings between the two attorneys.

In his letters to Covici, Bellow alternated between equanimity
and rage. That he had lost "almost everything" left him "sorrow-
ful but undestroyed." His address was now his office: Temporary
North of Mines.

"She may not have loved me at all," he wrote Pat Covici on
November 1, submitting the first of many postmortems:

She certainly doesn't love me now, and perhaps even hates me. When I was weaker there was more satisfaction for her in being the strong one. But when I recovered confidence and loved her more than before, even sexually, she couldn't bear it. So last summer when things seemed at their best they were really, for her, at their worst. Because now she was the sick one. I don't know why she waited until we were in Minnesota, holding a lease, etc. I guess she leaned on her psychiatrist. With his support, she was able to tell me she didn't and couldn't love me, and perhaps had never loved anyone except the child. The psychiatrist doesn't approve of what she's doing, but he's bound to help her and so she's able to make use of him.

A week later, he was more bitter. "You know what a thorough sufferer I can be. I not only hit bottom, I walk for miles and miles on it." He was trying to hate Sondra, he reported, but he wasn't very good at it: "She has a Tschacbasov heart—an insect heart. But really I love her too much and understand her too well to feel the murderous hatred that would help me (therapeutically)."

He still didn't know about Ludwig.

For Bellow, the end of his marriage was another causeless event— "home blew up under me," as he put it to Mark Harris some months later, the metonymy canceling out any human agent. But he must have known something was up: The previous summer, he had accepted an invitation from the State Department to travel abroad for three months as a lecturer in its "Experts and Specialists" program. Beginning January 1, 1960, he was to be off on a tour of Poland and Yugoslavia, accompanied by Mary McCarthy.

On November 26, he flew to London. While he was on tour, Bellow joked after the dust had settled, Sondra stayed in Minneapolis and spent his Ford Foundation grant.

17

You've probably heard that Juliana and I are no longer together.
When we were married, I was forty. I had the idea that at last
I was settling down for good. Suddenly everything has to be done
all over again. I don't know how many times I've been at the
starting-line. Every few years it all begins again as if for the first time.
A new beginning. Will I ever get beyond first base? I wonder.

—SAUL BELLOW, *early draft of Herzog*

THE STATE DEPARTMENT TOUR, under the auspices of the
United States Information Agency, was heavily scheduled.
In Zagreb, Bellow gave four lectures in two days, in addition to radio and press interviews, a meeting with the Writers'
Union, and various social functions. "He lectured in freezing
amphitheatres," Bellow wrote of Herzog in an early draft of the
novel, poking fun at the inquisitions he endured. " 'Sair, what is
thee opinion of Zhack London?' '*Burning Daylight* is a stirring
book.' But this hall is colder than Alaska. "

Anxious about developments in Minneapolis, he was discon-
solate to find no mail awaiting him in Skopje, Macedonia. The
only letter he'd gotten so far was from Jack Ludwig. "Adam is
terrific, tanning, a sand and water boychik evidently," Ludwig
wrote, shamelessly imitating Bellow's signature compound adjectives. "He's also losing a certain amount of pudge and getting
that growing-up long-headed look." The message did little to
allay Bellow's fears; he made a transatlantic call to Dr. Meehl,
who had now added Adam to his clientele, to find out how the
boy was faring. "This was Macedonia's first call to Mpls.," he
reported to Ralph Ellison, installed in the Tivoli house for the
winter: "Adam's all right. He'll win out—he's built for it. "

The new year found Bellow in a hotel room in Kraków. "The

synagogues, the ritual baths, the gloomy yards, the muddy streets, the yellow pages of prayer books"—it could have been the Jewish ghetto of Montreal. But the familiarity of the scene only made him feel more alone. "There's a black rain dropping on 500 churches, and under the glass of this table-top there's a two-foot doily of lace," he wrote to Covici on January 3: "And if you think I know what I'm doing here, think again. I couldn't swear I've got all my marbles. I could easily testify to the contrary. Just now I gave myself a scare. I couldn't remember some phrases I coined this morning. Still can't. My mind's gone thick with age. Or too many women, perhaps."

One of the many was a Polish sculptress who spoke no English and only rudimentary French—and happened to be married. None of these impediments mattered to Bellow. "I thought also she had given me the clap, and I was very proud but the doctor in Warsaw said it was only a trifling infection," he confided to Covici. "The clap *can* be arranged, I suppose, if a man has a serious ambition to get it. I'm just a dilettante, however."

A dilettante with a deep knowledge of his subject, if the imploring letters from Ariana, Daniela, Maryi, Iline, Jara, and others are any indication. ("I am in Paris, come." "I am in Dubrovnik, come.") Like Ralph Bernage, the itinerant scholar whose European adventures Bellow chronicled in an aborted novel called "Don Juan: A Lover from America," Bellow had countless brief affairs. Leafing through the love letters crammed in his briefcase, Bernage feels moved by one from a heartbroken woman who declares their relationship over: "Bernage was sorry, too, forgetting in that moment the innumerable girls, young women, older women, single women, married women, divorcees and widows about whom he had always been sorry. He did not like to realize how high the number of these had risen." Or maybe he did.

Notably absent from the list was Mary McCarthy, Bellow's companion on the tour. They were together a good deal, and Bellow was aware of her reputation for sexual availability. (She divulged in her memoirs that she once slept with three men in a single day.) By 1960, she was already on her third marriage, to Bowden Broadwater, and poised to leap to her fourth, to the diplomat James West, whom she was to meet on this trip. Given

Bellow's proclivities, a liaison between the two writers wouldn't have been surprising, and Bellow did claim to detect a "sexual motive" in their long, intimate conversations. But he was put off by McCarthy's intellectual and sexual intensity. She was "a *devoradora des hombres*," he told one of her biographers. "I was a little timid for that sort of thing." That McCarthy was a powerful figure and a writer of great distinction no doubt also counted against her—Bellow needed more subservient women in order to serve his own shaky self-image. It was hard enough for him to deal with men who were his intellectual equals; women who challenged his dominance were profoundly threatening.

To Hannah Arendt, McCarthy offered a casually incisive account of her Belgrade days with Bellow:

> Saul and I parted good friends, though he is too wary and raw-nerved to be friends, really, even with people he decides to like. He is in better shape than he was in Poland, yet I felt very sorry for him when I saw him go off yesterday, all alone, on his way to Italy, like Augie with a cocky sad smile disappearing into the distance.

It was a characteristically shrewd portrait, one that captured Bellow's brittleness and bristling distrust—the very qualities, as McCarthy noted (not without a certain touching sympathy; for all her toughness, she could be softhearted when the mood struck her), that condemned Bellow to end up so often alone.

As sorry as McCarthy felt for her compatriot, it wasn't as sorry as he felt for himself. "My condition is utterly lousy," he wrote Harvey Swados from Rome: "I'd never have consented to be a world-tour-bum or culture functionary without this need to wear myself out so that I could bear the misery of the divorce. It's pure American insanity—American female ideological madness." This weird allocation of blame seems to imply—if one can even parse it—that in leaving him, Sondra was acting out of political motives based on the rights of women. Well before the rise of feminism, Bellow saw its hand everywhere. The news wasn't all bad: He was sleeping through the night again, without sleeping pills, and "pecking" at a three-act play, "The Last Analysis." He was also writing a story about Sondra "that might turn into a novel."

After a two-week "dash" through Italy, he sailed from Naples to Haifa, returning to Rome early in March. Then it was on to Paris, Edinburgh, Manchester, and London, where his new British publisher, Lord Weidenfeld, gave a reception in his honor, attended by Louis MacNeice, Karl Miller, Anthony Powell, Stephen Spender, and J. B. Priestley, among numerous eminent others. It was a far cry from the reception sponsored by John Lehmann a decade earlier that Bellow remembered as so disastrous; the London literary world turned out in force, eager to meet the author of *Seize the Day* and *Henderson the Rain King*.

It had been a productive trip. "Dear Boss," he wrote Pat Covici from the Accadia Gran Hotel in Tel Aviv:

> Stranger pilgrimages have been made, but few so fatiguing. I'm down about 20 lbs & ready to go back to my business, which is to be [a] father & to write books. I've had too much of sights & flights, & girls. Still I wanted to wear myself out, & I'm well satisfied with the results I've gotten.
>
> There's hardly anything I do as well as I know I can, and that includes travelling. I'm still waiting for my life to begin. However, I'm nearer to a beginning than I've ever been.

It was a striking admission. At forty-five, Bellow was still living the way he'd lived when half his age: itinerant, unattached, provisional in his living arrangements, without a real job. His nomadic existence reflected his unwillingness—or inability—to make commitments, whether to a person or a place. In a sense, it was the main theme of his life: finding a place in the world. Yet even this painful, floating condition failed to dampen Bellow's natural exuberance: In his own eyes, being lost in middle age represented less a crisis than a "beginning."

By the end of March, he was back in the States. His temporary address in Minneapolis was, once again, c/o Jack Ludwig.

In the midst of his European tour, Bellow received a letter from Marshall Best, the editorial director of Viking, passing on the information that a Ford Foundation executive had expressed "distress" about Bellow running around Europe when he was supposed to be writing. Bellow responded with a sharp defense. He was writing while he traveled, he stressed: "I always manage to keep at it." Besides, if he hadn't gone off to Europe he might have ended up in "the loony bin." He had "almost cracked" when Sondra asked for a divorce: "You know that I'm not reckless and irresponsible and that I wouldn't go off on a toot abandoning all work and responsibility. An emergency arose and I met it as well as I could." If he had stayed in Minneapolis, he added, he might have written a thousand pages and thrown them all away.

But he was clearly troubled by Best's allegation. A day later, he wrote again: He could now "see the whole thing clear." Best had recommended Bellow for the Ford grant, and his author's "gay lark" had put him in a tough spot. "But suppose it hasn't been a gay lark? Suppose I have been dutifully suffering my way from country to country thinking about Fate and Death? Will that do as an explanation?" In Poland, he had visited the death camps, and what he saw there had "made a change" in him. Though merely a tourist, he felt like a victim. At Auschwitz, examining the sofas made of human hair and the lamp shades made of human skin, Bellow was seized with "a feeling of terror." The Holocaust was a glimpse into human nature. Auschwitz was "the history of mankind as it really is, a museum of human history." The Jews were at once exceptional and transitory, marked out for distinction only to be eradicated; and it was to this people, this terrible destiny, that Bellow allied himself. "I can't tell you what an impression Poland makes on me," he wrote Covici. "It's too deep. As deep as death, and more familiar than I can admit at the top of my mind. It's family history."

On previous trips abroad, he had experienced this history as a nostalgic tremor, detecting in the Old World quaintness of Spain traces of his "ancestral homeland" and in Salzburg vestiges of the late war. Over the bombed-out towns there had hung the shadow of deportations and mass murder. In Paris, he had met survivors. But—at least in his own mind—it was only now that he had really begun to confront his origins. "For the first time I am trying to ascertain what my Jewish parentage & upbringing really signify," he had written to Keith Botsford a few months before his trip. On the one hand, he longed desperately for assimilation—to be, unambiguously, an American; on the other, he found in his ethnic past an anchor, a story, a mental homeland. To be labeled was to be tied down; yet to deny or play down his origins was to forfeit a rich potential for belonging.

The most onerous consequence of being identified as a Jewish writer was that it denied a claim to universality. "In much the same way one might be called a Samoan astronomer or an Eskimo cellist or a Zulu Gainsborough expert," Bellow objected. But critics need categories, and by the end of the 1950s he was being identified as "a pivotal figure on the Jewish-American scene," to cite a phrase from an essay by Theodore Solotaroff entitled "A Vocal Group: The Jewish Part in American Letters" that appeared in *The Times Literary Supplement* toward the end of 1959. Jewish-American literature was now an official category.

It wasn't an affiliation that Bellow sought. "We had no sooner arrived and begun publishing books—first Malamud and I, later on Roth—than we were tagged as Jewish writers; no one wants to be tagged in that way. We thought of ourselves as belonging to the mainstream. We were Americans of Jewish origin." The three writers, he noted bitterly, were becoming the Hart, Schaffner, and Marx of the literary trade—as commodified as the men's clothing industry. There was an element of snobbery in Bellow's reluctance to affiliate himself with Jewish writers. Just as his parents had prided themselves on their Russian refinement and considered themselves "above" the shtetl Jews of Maxwell Street, Bellow instinctively kept his distance from Jews who were "too ethnic," noted Dave Peltz—in other words, too Jewish.

He was clear, however, about what being Jewish *didn't* signify. A review by Leslie Fiedler of Karl Shapiro's *Poems of a Jew* in the April 1960 issue of *Poetry* so infuriated him that he dashed off an irate letter. Jewish prose writers had discovered their Jewishness to be "an eminently marketable commodity," Fiedler contended; their "much vaunted alienation" had in fact turned out to be "their passport into the heart of Gentile culture." Augie March was the heir of Tom Sawyer and Huck Finn, adventurous young boys discovering their American identities.

Bellow was enraged. "I've just read your Shapiro piece in Poetry," he wrote from Tivoli that June, and I really think you're way out. How you got there I don't know, but it's time to come back. I'm in earnest. You have a set of facts entirely your own, and you interpret people's motives most peculiarly. What is this "marketable" Jewishness you talk about? And who are these strange companions on the bandwagon that plays Hatikvah.* It's amusing. It's utterly wrong. It's (I don't like the jargon, but it can't be avoided here) Projection. What you think you see so clearly is not to be seen. It isn't there. No big situation, no connivances, no Jewish scheme produced by Jewish minds. Nothing. What an incredible tzimmes [a commotion; literally, a stew] you make of nothing! You have your own realities, no one checks you and you go on and on. You had better think matters over again, Leslie. I'm dead serious.

Saul

Bellow's annoyance with Fiedler was understandable, but the fact remained that, however secular, American, and universal, his work was profoundly rooted in his identity as a Jew. His characters, so robustly American in their actions and appearance, were unmistakably Jewish in their sensibilities and the intonations of their speech. The moral complexity of his style, its introspective heroes, and its vernacular language belong to a storytelling tradition that goes back to the Haggadah.† Visiting the Hebrew writer S. Y. Agnon in Jerusalem, Bellow had found himself in the presence of a living emblem of that tradition. "This spare old man, whose face has a remarkable youthful color, received me in his house, not far from the barbed wire entanglements that divide the city," Bellow recalled in his introduction to *Great Jewish Short*

---

*Fiedler had accused Shapiro of trying to "ride beside Wouk and Salinger, Bellow and Malamud, Philip Roth and Uris—the bandwagon which travels our streets, its calliope playing *Hatikvah*," the national anthem of Israel.

†The correspondence he carried on with Bernard G. Richards, whose *Discourses of Keidansky* had evoked the character of Jewish immigrant life in the New York ghetto at the turn of the century, revealed a deep familiarity with this tradition. "From earliest youth I've been an admirer of Keidansky and used to denounce people all over Chicago for being unfamiliar with it," he wrote the author, liberally tossing in Yiddish phrases and inviting him to revive his literary persona in the pages of *The Noble Savage*: "Probably some of my notions about Jewish life in America come to me from your book." (Richards recalled with pleasure Bellow's "racy Yiddish which came over the wire from Tivoli, New York.")

Stories, "and while we were drinking tea he asked me if any of my books had been translated into Hebrew." If not, Agnon advised, Bellow ought to see to it immediately; they would survive only in the Holy Tongue. When Bellow noted that Heinrich Heine, a Jewish poet, had done well in German, Agnon countered that his work had also been translated beautifully into Hebrew—Heine was "safe." Bellow told this story with gentle irony, but his point—that Jews had long been writing in languages other than Hebrew and in doing so had flourished—wasn't to be taken lightly: If Heine could write in German, Bellow could write in English. "One's language is a spiritual location—it houses your soul," he declared in a talk entitled "The American Writer."

Great Jewish Short Stories, an anthology of texts from the Bible and the Haggadah to Bernard Malamud and Philip Roth, may well have been a direct legacy of the "change" Bellow had described to Marshall Best. Bellow's masterly introduction got at the heart of his own enterprise: "We do not make up history and culture. We simply appear, not by our own choice. We make what we can of our condition with the means available. We must accept the mixture as we find it—the impurity of it, the tragedy of it, the hope of it."

Bellow's art, Richard Poirier has noted, represents the fusion "of the Jew as poor immigrant, the outsider whose native resources save him from the bitterness of alienation, and of the Jew as successful *arriviste* in American society, enriched and burdened all at once by traditions of high culture." Bellow was never comfortable with this balancing act; to accept America on its own terms, to *belong,* would have violated a deeper need to feel singled out, recognized as special. He would always be at home in his parents' adopted land, yet he was eternally suspicious of the acceptance that he'd found and homesick for the simpler, more familiar world of his Humboldt Park youth—"a kind of insider looking out," in Poirier's words. It was this insider, "Chicago" status that enabled Bellow to explain America to itself.

Bellow's return to Minneapolis to visit Adam quickly turned into an ordeal. Sondra refused to see him and threatened to call the police if he came to the house. She allowed Adam to visit him only at the hotel where he'd moved after a few days at the Ludwigs'. She had "socked" him for four hundred dollars charged to Dayton's department store; she was demanding to keep the car and most of their furniture, in addition to having Bellow pay her rent. In his absence, she had started divorce proceedings; he protested that he was being "sacked"—as if marriage were a job. "There's been a great lack of reality on both sides—on all sides, for the Ludwigs must be counted in this conflict," Bellow reported to Botsford:

> Towards me Jack behaved *appropriately* in Mpls. This is an observation rather than a complaint. He did for the most part what a friend should have done, but his compassion is spoken rather than shown. Once he has made up his mind about the issues, he tends to be the King & to speak from a throne. What I needed was good sense, not authority.

What *appropriately* meant in this context is difficult to judge, unless it meant behaving like a friend while sympathizing with his wife. But that was Ludwig's way.

Toward the end of April 1960, Bellow fled Minneapolis for the friendlier precincts of Chicago, where the Friends of Literature, an Evanston book group, awarded him its best-book-by-a-local-author prize. In a whirl—his usual response to domestic crises—he then flew to Washington for a debriefing on his State Department tour. In May, he was back in Tivoli, "inundated by a towering wave of unsorted papers." But the old house restored his calm. "I'll be all right here," he assured Botsford. "I am feeling rather more optimistic about bailing out than I did a month ago. The road back is open before me."

Banging out long letters on his Smith-Corona, he badgered his friends for contributions and Arias for *The Noble Savage;* negotiated the business side with Aaron Asher and Arthur A. Cohen at Meridian; and wrangled endlessly with his coeditors. Ludwig's editorial laissez-faire infuriated him. "I can't persuade him to do a thing," Bellow railed to Botsford. "I have to write apologetic notes to the authors."

Botsford was more hands-on, but interfering with Bellow's vision also had its perils. Annoyed by an Aria Botsford submitted that he judged "substandard," Bellow threw down the editorial gauntlet. The stuff Botsford was submitting was "fitter for a college magazine"; Bellow had done most of the work; his name was "better known" than Botsford's, so he should have the final word in editorial decisions; and so on for a page and a half of single-spaced bellicosity, ending with the admonition, "Let us do the thing properly, sensibly and fairly or knock it off." Botsford responded with a long, cringing, defensive letter. "I beg you to resist the temptation to squash, annihilate, rupture and destroy people, Saul. Why look for quarrels with those who have the most affection and respect for you?"

Bellow's own explanation for his suspiciousness in those years was that he was easily intimidated and parried with arrogance. "My lack of humility was aggravated by the rejections I met or expected to meet." For all his faith in his literary gifts, he saw himself as the child of immigrants and ill equipped to make his way in the sophisticated East. Like other intellectuals of his generation, Bellow was eager to assimilate; but unlike them, he also longed to preserve the imaginary innocence of his past. He clung to his origins the way he clung to his neuroses; to leave them behind would have been to alter his fundamental nature. "I must sit tight & work hard & re-assess," he wrote to Botsford. "The objective must be to know rather than to change myself. I've gone at it the wrong way these many years."

The trouble was that knowing himself wasn't a process for which Bellow showed much talent or enthusiasm. "As I creep near the deepest secrets of my life I drop off like a lotus-eater," he confided to John Berryman. He had been "helped" by his therapy with Dr. Meehl in Minneapolis, he admitted to Oscar Tarcov, but he continued to disparage—or at least distrust—the therapeutic process. "The Last Analysis," the play he was writing in these years, was a satire of Freudian therapy. Yet he was also a devoted student of Freud. Like Herzog, who is impressively conversant with Freud's *Collected Papers*—an early draft includes a long eloquent "Dear Dr. Freud" letter taking issue with Freud's famous essay "Mourning and Melancholia"—he had clearly done his homework. For a period in the sixties, Freud was Bellow's "nightly bed-time reading," according to Daniel Fuchs.

Freud himself had approached the interpretation of works of art with uncharacteristic humility, declaring in "Dostoyevsky and Parricide" that psychoanalysis must "lay down its arms" before the problem of the creative artist. Bellow, despite his appreciation of "that tart old man," as Herzog calls him, wasn't entirely reassured by this show of humility. In his view, Freud posed a threat to the artist's independence; he was one of "these great geniuses who create systems which then take the mind captive." Psychoanalysts belonged in the camp of parents and brothers and wives and literary critics—all parties trying to tell him what to do.

Nevertheless, in the spring of 1960, he was once again on the couch, this time under the care of the sexologist Dr. Albert Ellis. ("That wasn't psychology," Bellow said of the Reichian Dr. Raphael, "that was zoology.") A famous figure in his day, Ellis shared with Bellow a Jewish-immigrant background and a reputation as a ladies' man. He'd already been through several wives and bragged openly about his conquests; Bellow diagnosed him as a "phallic-narcissistic type" (the same diagnosis Ellis applied to Bellow). Flamboyantly eccentric, Ellis, a tall, hawk-nosed figure with a long, sallow face, munched on sandwiches during sessions, explaining that he was a diabetic and required a special diet. Apparently, it didn't agree with him: Bellow later remembered Ellis's "high-smelling farts."

Ellis's libertine views found a sympathetic ear in Bellow. Speaking to packed halls around the country, Ellis anticipated the "free love" movement of the late sixties, espousing the credo that puritanical views about sex "create untold havoc in our love, marriage, and family relations," as he put it in one of his popular manuals. The goal of therapy, Ellis proclaimed, was sexual pleasure, pure and simple. Freud "didn't know a fucking thing about sex." Part of Ellis's persona included talking like a drill sergeant: Reich was "full of horse-shit"; the human race was "out of its fucking mind." For Ellis, therapy was a matter of common sense: "I talk people out of their bullshit." His method was to get his patients to act on their wishes and *not* feel bad. No one was perfect: Even Hitler, he said, was just "a fallible, fucked-up human being." (There Bellow drew the line: He and Ellis had a heated argument over Hitler.)

Bellow entered treatment to cope with his rage at Sondra. "My goal was to get him unangry," Ellis recalled, "which wasn't easy with a person like that because he was a novelist, and novelists think that all emotions are good." Bellow minimized the therapy, as he always did. He went into therapy when he was desperate and left as soon as he could tolerate the level of pain. "It was poolroom grad work: what to do, how to lay a girl, getting rid of character problems that are an obstacle to pleasure." He broke off treatment after a few months.

Ellis, like Meehl, never reached a formal diagnosis—not that Bellow would have accepted one. In the end, he was convinced that psychoanalysis could no more "explain" him than any other dogma could. "What a man thinks he is doing counts for nothing," he wrote in a draft of *Herzog*. "All his work in the world is done by impulses he will never understand." As with marriage, Bellow went through the therapeutic process but never engaged with it—instead he found material for satire. For Bellow, it wasn't the psychiatrist's couch that promised insight but the writer's yellow legal pads. "The depressive character is narcissistic," writes Bellow's protagonist Herzog. "It fears the disappearance of the beloved. Above all terrors it places the terror of abandonment and naked solitude. So with secret hate it cuts off the deserters." Divorces, estrangements from friends, abrupt departures from jobs, nonattendance at funerals—the defensive mechanism was the same: Leave before you're left.

Bellow's legendary accumulation of women reached a new level after his second marriage fell apart. "He thrashed about wildly from bed to bed," as Ruth Miller put it in her bald way, quoting a sample of the hopeful letters from women in Bellow's archive: "Remember, we were an 'item' at Yaddo?" "I want to join your class: I am 44, divorced, with 4 children, but I have a lot of Jewish stories." Another girlfriend, Bobby Markels, also fancied herself a writer. She and Bellow had an affair during the sixties, when she was living in Evanston. (Years later, she moved to Mendocino,

California, and wrote a regular column for the local paper, "Babbling with Bubula.")

As a lover, Bellow received indifferent marks. He was "the put-it-in-and-take-it-out type," noted the poet Sandra Hochman, a self-proclaimed "art tart" who took up with Bellow not long after *Henderson the Rain King* came out: "He didn't know a clitoris from a kneecap." Another lover, who found him "passionate and virile," remarked on his lack of interest in "experimentation." Like Herzog, he was "a Quaker in his lovemaking" who "couldn't abandon himself sexually." "The compulsive seducer invariably turns out to be the most insecure man," observed Helen Garrie, an actress who had a brief affair with Bellow in the sixties. She also remarked on Bellow's "sexual dos and don'ts."

Sex was never the driving impulse behind his conquests. "He doesn't seem to have chosen women merely out of lustful desire, and I had no reports which described him as a stud," said Ted Hoffman, who knew a number of Bellow's women. "I think he sought some kind of uncommitted temporary intimacy, perhaps even affection, rather than sexual possession." The truth was, he found women "overly demanding sexually." Their sexual aggressiveness was just another effort to impose upon his freedom—another demand.

Bellow, however, persisted in viewing himself as an old-fashioned romantic spurned by unfeeling women. "If I were miserably weak, she would pity and protect me," he explained to Keith Botsford, ruminating on the failure of his marriage to Sondra:

> It's what I am that's unbearable to her. The essence of me. So there's no hope. For if my wife doesn't want *that*, what am I to do? Sasha is an absolutist. I think I've loved even *that*, in her. I believe I learned to love a woman, and I can't see when or how my heartsickness will end.
>
> Perhaps I could name other subtler failures—I failed to master my own freedom or to interpret the world to the satisfaction of her mind. But for such inadequacies a husband might reasonably expect compassion from his wife. *If* she loved him. But she doesn't love me.

Bellow's interpretations of his own conduct were elliptical at best. When he spoke of "subtler" failures, was he referring to his infidelities? Was failing to "master his freedom" a euphemism for philandering? When he felt cornered, Bellow sought refuge in abstraction and elusive phrases—failing to "interpret the world to the satisfaction of her mind" was an elaborate way of saying that he and Sondra were incompatible. However one glossed this strange letter, its message was familiar: Bellow was once again the victim.

"Why would one marry a Fabergé?" Botsford once asked him, overestimating Sondra's pedigree. "Because of the attraction of art," Bellow replied, invoking E. T. A. Hoffmann's story "The Sand-Man," which features a mad professor who constructs a woman out of "springs, pillows and wires"; a student falls in love with the inventor's contraption and commits suicide when he discovers that the object of his passion isn't real. Bellow interpreted the story as a parable of Sondra's deficiencies, implying that she, too, was a "'constructed' personality." But the story could be read another way: Bellow had no idea who Sondra really was and never bothered to find out. "He met these women and he made them up," a friend said of Bellow's wives. "Sondra" was one of his inventions.

Another was Rosette Lamont, later the model for Ramona Donsell in *Herzog*. Rosette was the daughter of Russian immigrants—White Russians, she stressed—who had fled Hitler. A professor of comparative literature at Queens College and the City University of New York, Lamont was vain about her Jewish-aristocratic roots and liked to say she was "well-born," not from the shtetl; her mother was a pianist, her father "a bank president and an educated man."* About her beauty, Bellow was dead-on; she was a stunning brunette with a frankly sexual allure and eyes that were "intensely black."

Lamont was as taken with Bellow as he was with her. They met at the home of Aaron Asher in the spring of 1960. A lively crowd, including the novelist Grace Paley, Mike Nichols, and Jules Feiffer,

---

*There was some speculation among Bellow's friends that "Lamont" had originally been "Solomon," the new name derived from the last two syllables of the old; but Rosette insisted that her Europeanized surname had been in the family for at least a generation.

had come to hear Bellow read from "The Last Analysis." Lamont had arrived on the arm of Bellow's friend Paolo Milano. "The bell rang, and there was a ripple of laughter in the foyer," she recalled in a vivid portrait of Bellow:

> The man who entered the room had a shock of white hair, but the unlined, sun-tanned face was younger than the one I had seen in the newspapers, or on book jackets. As he stood there, a manuscript under his arm like a tightly rolled up towel, ready to take the plunge, he looked delighted at the sight of close friends, and a little off-guard, like a boy brought to a surprise party. Later, I discovered the reason for this slight demurral: Bellow had brought with him that untried part of himself, an unborn work.

He had also brought a date: Susan Glassman, who had approached him after his lecture at the University of Chicago three years before. The daughter of a prominent Chicago orthopedic surgeon, Glassman was, by all accounts, a head turner. "She was a very beautiful girl, very intelligent," in the estimate of Philip Roth, who had dated her briefly when he was teaching at Chicago: "Literature student, nice Chicago family, rich—she had everything. When you're forty-four, twenty-four looks good." Even the art critic Hilton Kramer, as harsh in his appraisals of women as of art, grudgingly admired Glassman's looks: "She wasn't as beautiful as she thought she was, but she was very beautiful."

"So many of these ladies who hungered after Saul wanted to be touched by the magic of his artistry and they would willingly give themselves to Saul—to be touched by his magic wand, so to speak," said Dave Peltz. From the first, Susan Glassman had her cap set on Bellow, but he was still in the midst of a divorce—and in pursuit of other women. Despite Glassman's presence at the Ashers' that night, he asked Lamont for her phone number. A few days later, he called and invited her up to Tivoli.

Bellow might have been "le prince d'Aquitaine à la tour abolie," Lamont noted with dry wit, "had he not emerged from Nervalian self-pity to undertake instead a Candide-like struggle with the garden he was determined to cultivate." Unlike so many of the New York Jewish intellectuals, who panicked at the thought of leaving Manhattan (Philip Rahv, taking a leaf from Flaubert, grumbled about "rural idiocy"), Bellow genuinely enjoyed the country. He had a green thumb and landscaped the grounds with mock oranges and tulips and peonies. In later years, he ascribed his love of Vermont to a nostalgia for childhood summers in Valleyfield, Quebec.

His favorite outpost was the hammock, to which he retired to read Blake or Donne. "Cooking was also a form of creation," Lamont recalled. "In his country kitchen he whipped up a wonderful dinner of spaghetti and fresh tomato sauce made from his garden's crop." The tomatoes were "the size of dinosaur's balls," he boasted. He prided himself on his handyman's skills—climbing a ladder to wash the tall windows, taking down a hornet's nest, weeding the garden. Then there was the mail—an increasingly heavy volume of letters from friends and fans, lawyers, and his colleagues at *The Noble Savage*. "The most arduous task was that of dealing with the trail of women left throughout European capitals," according to Lamont: "'Chère Amie' would be amended to 'Amie,' leaving some hope of future bliss."

Only Sondra and Anita intruded on his rural ease. Dunning letters from Minneapolis arrived almost daily, and he was having an epistolary scrap with Greg over his failure to pay Anita's alimony in full. "Don't make me ashamed to admit I'm your son," Greg wrote him, to which Bellow replied defensively that Anita had a job while he was broke and thousands of dollars in debt to Viking: Why should he pay her alimony? "Is it rightfully Anita's? By what right? Because I injured her? But I've never billed her for the pain she caused me. Or is it a one-way street?"

With Sondra, the main bone of contention was Adam. Bellow saw him only once in the summer of 1960, and he was enraged at Sondra's apparent willingness to use the boy as a pawn in their negotiations. He was convinced that his affection for his second son was sufficiently strong to compensate for his absence. "I love that boy and I have a hunch that, in the end, that love is going to count for more in his life than the 'protection' of lawyers." About "the dough" he was adamant; as he put it to John Berryman, he wasn't going to allow his "veins [to be] used to string Sondra's harp." Bellow never ceased to think of himself as an innocent abroad, surrounded by conniving lawyers, wives, and publishers, like a country boy fallen among wily thieves. (*The Adventures of Augie March* was originally titled "Life among the Machiavellians.")

On June 1, their divorce was final. Bellow inveighed against the terms of the settlement—no alimony, and $150 a month in child support—but he was relieved to have it over. "The world *is* sound somewhere," he wrote his lawyer.

Bellow was "a happier man" since the divorce, he maintained—an assessment his friends confirmed. "Our best times with Saul were in the late fifties and early sixties, usually when he was between marriages," remembered Fred W. Dupee: "Good companionable times." They went rabbit hunting with Ralph Ellison and sailed on the Hudson with Rosette Lamont in the Dupees' dinghy: "It was rough, Saul was scared, and Rosette made fun of him. Nonetheless we liked her."

Ellison and Bellow became inseparable. Ellison had established a more or less permanent study on the first floor of Bellow's house, where he installed his collection of bonsai. Later on, he took over Jack Ludwig's job at Bard. One day, around the time that Leslie Fiedler published his widely read essay about Mark Twain, "Come Back to the Raft, Huck Honey," making the case that Huck Finn and Nigger Jim were homosexual lovers, Herb Gold remarked that he'd heard Ellison was living in the Tivoli house. "Don't tell Leslie," Bellow joked.

"Ralph and the nobs loved one another," Bellow claimed. The nobs remembered otherwise: Fred Dupee liked to make jokes about Ellison's African violets. "It's funny," he remarked when Ellison arrived at the house and set off the Dupees' dog, "he only barks at the garbage man and you." Gore Vidal, who maintained a grand house in the neighborhood, wasn't too hospitable either. According to a perhaps apocryphal story, he once asked Ellison, "What's a jungle bunny like you doing in these parts?"

Bellow wasn't just imagining the chill that emanated from the big old houses along the Hudson where the river people, the local gentry, entertained. One night, the Dupees had the Ludwigs and

Bellow over for dinner, recalled Dupee's wife, Andy: "All the Jews sat on one side of the room and the WASPS sat on the other; we sort of shouted back and forth all night." Another time, when a "river lady" by the name of Mrs. Hoit showed up at the Dupees', Bellow took off his shoes and propped his feet up on the porch rail—protesting her hoity-toity attitude, he said.

He was more at ease with the Bard academic crowd. He loved to play the recorder at parties, "particularly under the influence of drink, which improved his playing," recalled Andrews Wanning, who taught in the English department. His range was wide; he could play Bach and pop, Cole Porter and Gershwin, Mozart sonatas and "Sheep May Safely Graze," even Beethoven symphonies. "He looked like the little god Pan," said Rosette Lamont.

Literary fame could still leave an empty bank account, as Bellow (like generations of writers before and after him) was beginning to discover. Not only had *Henderson* not made him rich, it hadn't even made him solvent. In the fall of 1960, he was once again wondering how he'd make a living. He was working at his play "for the *money* in it," he stressed to Keith Botsford. "Sash & Anita have busted me."

John Clarke, the chairman of the Minnesota English department, had equivocated about having Bellow back "because I am *scandalous*," as Bellow put it to Ralph Ross. "It seems a shame this poor sonofabitch should be merely head of the English department," he said of Clarke: "In the great Republic of the immortals he would be doing the laundry service for a chain of brothels."

In desperate need of a berth, Bellow accepted a job offer from the University of Puerto Rico, where Botsford was teaching in the English department. Shortly before Christmas, he packed up his blue Chevrolet and drove down with Greg to his brother Maurice's winter house in Miami. At the beginning of the new year, he loaded the Chevy onto a freighter bound for San Juan.

"They'll never carve 1960 on my tombstone," he wrote Ralph Ross in an end-of-the-year valedictory.

18

I've never known what it is to lead an accepted life.

— Bellow to Louis Gallo

THE UNIVERSITY OF PUERTO RICO was a far cry from Princeton or Bard, but the island didn't lack for intellectual stimulation. "Everyone came through here," recalled William Kennedy, who was then working as a reporter for *The Puerto Rico World Journal* and writing his first novel. "Hunter Thompson, Joseph Heller. Lawrence Ferlinghetti showed up in the newsroom one night. I interviewed Jack Kennedy at the airport. Eisenhower came to play golf." Bellow claimed he was there "to study skin-diving."

He got a place on the outskirts of Río Piedras, a basement apartment in the home of Jack Delano, an old leftie who had been a photographer for the Farm Security Administration. Delano was now the general manager of the government-owned television station and lived with his wife and two children in a simple concrete house surrounded by tropical vegetation.

Puerto Rico was "excellent," Bellow reported to Josephine Herbst: "Of course it's barbarous, noisy, undisciplined etc. And dirty, too, with a great many rats. But there are even more lizards than rats, and more flowers than lizards (I love both) and more perfumes than stinks. And somehow the relation between beauty and garbage strikes me as being right." For Bellow, poetry resided in the least likely places. "The island is beautiful," he wrote his

Tivoli tenant, Ralph Ellison: "The crowds are aimless, cheerful, curious and gaudy. Drivers read at the wheel, they sing, they eat and they screw while driving."

His teaching load was light: a course called "Character in the Novel" and a writing seminar. The books he taught were the books he had always taught: Stendhal's *The Red and the Black*, Flaubert, Dreiser, Tolstoy, and Dostoyevsky. "He'd stand in front of the classroom, kind of shy, folding his arms over each other, look at the ceiling, and start to talk," recalled Bernard Lockwood, a fellow instructor in the department. "If someone had taped those lectures, they could have been published as is, without changing a comma or semicolon."

His writing class was run along the same informal lines; student conferences were held in the faculty lounge or on his patio. Sometimes he gave useful advice. "Don't be afraid to write a lot," he advised William Kennedy. "Be prodigal. Think of all those sperm: Only one is needed to create life."

Bellow was glad to be temporarily beyond the reach of Sondra and her lawyer. "They carry on like poltergeists, by letter wire and telephone, but I got a large shot of their stuff and it's given me a fine immunity," he wrote jauntily to Ralph Ross. "I feel very little pain"—pain that he was aware of, in any case.

Ludwig, meanwhile, kept up his charade, dashing off a cheery, willfully oblivious letter full of circumstantial lies. He'd heard from the writer Angus Cameron that Bellow had been looking for him in New York, he began, admitting that he had "sneaked into town" to deliver his novel to his publisher—"and though I should have called you I, shmok," he apologized (displaying his faulty command of Yiddish), all he had done "other than MS" was "squire Sondra around new haunts a couple of times." Anyway, he thought Bellow was in Tivoli. He was sorry it had worked out "lousy." Bellow forwarded the letter to Keith Botsford with a scrawled note at the bottom: "Keith—this won't do. I spoke to Cameron several days before Jack left. Also Jack was in town about December 20th, on good evidence. This is all phony, and I won't go along."

By then, going along was no longer an option. Somehow, in arranging social plans between the Ludwigs and the Bellows—"it had something to do with the kids," their Minnesota colleague Philip Siegelman recalled—Sondra's affair with Jack had gotten discovered. Visiting Ralph Ross's house that night, Bellow announced in great agitation, "I'm going to catch that son-of-a-bitch Ludwig and beat him to a pulp." Ross had to physically restrain him. At the Quadrangle Club in Chicago a few days later, Bellow talked wildly of getting a gun.

Instead, he resorted now to what was—for him—a far more effective weapon, drafting a reply to Ludwig's "phenomenal" letter that was, even by Bellow's standards, a masterpiece of comic invective. (Bellow must have thought so; a copy, undated and unsigned, is among his papers.) After warming up with a long and detailed catalog of Ludwig's derelictions as an editor of *The Noble Savage*—his "inept and scarcely readable" Arias, the ludicrous memos he dispatched from "Ludwig Disneyland"—he got to the heart of the matter:

> I don't think you are a fit editor of the magazine. You have, in some departments, good judgment. I trusted your taste and thought you might be reliable as an editor, but you are too woolly, self-absorbed, rambling, ill-organized, slovenly, heedless and insensitive to get on with. And you must be in a grotesque mess, to have lost your sense of reality to the last shred. I think you never had much to start with, and your letter reveals that that's gone, too.
>
> In fact it's a fantastic document and I'm thinking of framing it for my museum. You thought I'd be at the boat to greet Keith? Which boat? I've heard of no boat. You took Sondra's word for it that I was in Tivoli? Well, for several days with Adam I was there. But I was in New York a good deal of the time, and so were you, before Sondra arrived. And besides, why take Sondra's word for it? She and I exchanged no personal information. How would she know where I was? Did I write her that I would be at Tivoli? Without consulting me, you phoned John Goetz in Mpls to find out whether I was giving you an accurate account of the legal situation last Spring, but without a second thought you simply accept what Sondra tells you of my whereabouts. There seems to me to be a small imbalance here. Espe-

cially since we're not only colleagues but "friends," and haven't seen each other in nearly a year. Pretty odd, isn't it. And if you had phoned (and I believe you'd have had the strength to resist my invitation to Tivoli) wouldn't I have come to New York to see you? In all this there is some ugliness, something I don't want explained, though I'm sure that as a disciple of the Hasidim and believer in Dialogue and an enthusiast for Heschel, and a man of honor from whom I have heard and endured many lectures and reproaches and whose correction I have accepted you have a clear and truthful explanation. All the worse for you if you are not hypocritical. The amount of internal garbage you haven't taken cognizance of must be, since you never do things on a small scale, colossal.

It wouldn't do much good to see matters clearly. With the sharpest eye in the world I'd see nothing but the stinking fog of falsehood. And I haven't got the sharpest eyes in the world; I'm not a superman but superidiot. Only a giant among idiots would marry Sondra and offer you friendship. God knows I am not stainless faultless Bellow. I leave infinities on every side to be desired. But love her as my wife? Love you as my friend? I might as well have gone to work for Ringling Brothers and been shot out of the cannon twice a day. At least they would have let me wear a costume.

Coventry, pal, is not the place.

One of the most notable features of this remarkable document is that it never confronts Ludwig about his perfidy; indeed, it makes it clear that Bellow didn't *want* to know and had tried as hard as he could to remain ignorant of it. He was too busy with the search for "a meaningful life" to notice what was going on around him.

The tone of the letter is puzzling: angry but also self-delighting in its satirical high-spiritedness. Whatever betrayal Bellow felt he masked with antic, clownlike imagery that focused the blame more on his own gullibility than on the gross transgressions of his friend. If, as he claimed, Ludwig had lost all "sense of reality," so had Bellow—in his case, knowingly.

"Saul wanted women to go after him and to make up his mind for him," said Rosette Lamont, who had parted ways with Bellow on the eve of his departure for Puerto Rico. The letters she wrote him from Israel, where she'd gone on sabbatical, had a who-needs-you tone. John Dos Passos had read an article of hers on *Dr. Zhivago*, she reported, and pronounced her "a genius." She had met Marcel Duchamp and Elie Wiesel; she had interviewed Eugène Ionesco. When Bellow sent Lamont a copy of *Esquire* with an excerpt from his work in progress and the inscription "For Rosette from her tough friend Saul," she responded curtly: "You are not *my* tough friend, only little provincial Susie Glassman's tough friend."

Lamont wasn't far from the mark. In Puerto Rico, letters were arriving almost daily from Susan Glassman, addressed to "Dolly, Dolly," with "love, love, love, love." She also reported that she might be pregnant. (She wasn't.) "I hear Susan was down in P.R.," Richard Stern wrote Bellow in April, sounding a Gallic note of caution. "SAUL: ATTENDS. Nice as she is, fuckable as she is, let this friend say quickly ATTENDS. You know the epigraph for EUROPE: 'Every man of character has a typical experience which recurs over and over again.'"*

Bellow's typical experience was marriage. One of the mysteries of his life was his attraction to an institution for which he clearly was ill suited and which he held in low regard. He seemed as baffled as anyone by his marriages. "What did I know?" he once told the McCloskeys, airily explaining away his third—or was it his fourth?—marriage. "I was in the middle of a book." He was so unsure of his judgment in marital matters that he canvassed his friends before taking the plunge. What did they think of this or that prospective bride? Was she lively? Beautiful? A potential wife, or only appropriate for a fling? The idea of marriage appealed to Bellow; it meant stability, companionship, a normal family life. The obstacle was intimacy, the fact that it involved sharing his life with another person. It was this aspect of marriage—its essence— that posed the biggest challenge. When things didn't work out, Bellow tended to blame his friends for their bad advice. After his marriage to Sondra broke up, he berated R. W. B. Lewis (on whose Princeton couch he'd courted her), "Why didn't you warn me?"

Europe was a novel by Stern. Bellow defended his new love interest: "I think by now I know her quite well. I can tell you more about her than most others can tell me. I shrink from marriage still, but not from Susan."

For someone as cynical as he was about the virtues of marriage, Bellow was notably casual about proposing it. Sandra Hochman, who had met Bellow on the pretext of interviewing him for a magazine, claimed that he talked about marriage on their second date—a story that would seem unlikely had other women not reported similar discussions at premature phases of an affair. Bellow made much of the fact that Hochman was his "physical type," the woman he'd been looking for all his life. But after he took up with Glassman, Hochman realized she "was just someone he wanted to fuck."

Helen Garrie, whom Bellow invited to join him in Puerto Rico, also sensed that a proposal was in the works. She recalled resisting: "If I got involved in his grinder, it would be bad news." Bellow made light of these refusals. "Don't you think the Bennington alumnae association owes us both wound-stripes?" he joked to John Berryman, whose second marriage, to Ann Levine, a roommate of Sondra at Bennington, had rapidly fallen apart. Bellow called himself "the Nathan Hale of sex": He would sacrifice his life to it. The only time he liked being married, he quipped, was at dinnertime.

Bellow's insouciance about his irregular marital history masked his deep confusion about it. On the one hand, he missed his boys. "Twelve years in one marriage, seven in another, two sons whose lives are withdrawn from me," he summed up his situation to Keith Botsford, sounding a rare note of regret (while getting the dates wrong; his marriage to Anita lasted fifteen years, to Sondra four). "I measure my complaints. I try to come to clarity with grief." But he never made a concerted effort to grapple with the issues that underlay his propensity for serial marriage, preferring to attribute it to women's supposedly predatory natures. ("What do women want?" Herzog says plaintively, supplying a histrionic answer to Freud's question: "They eat green salad and drink human blood.")

Still, Glassman's aggressive pursuit paid off. "She felt that she had caught her lion," said Keith Botsford. Elizabeth Hardwick, a lively (if sometimes fanciful) raconteur, remembered "Susie" Glassman introducing herself at a party with the perky announcement, "I'm Saul Bellow's girlfriend." Not that she had the field to herself. Mark Harris, once in Tivoli for an overnight visit, was fleetingly aware, "in some room or other," of "a woman of extraordinary beauty"—a woman who wasn't Glassman. A few days later, Harris had dinner in Manhattan with Bellow and the theater critic Herbert Blau, "passing from there with Bellow to a lady's apartment. I hoped it would be the lady I had pondered in the night in Tivoli, but it was not, though it was another as fine." There was a cultural component to Bellow's misogyny: This was how men talked and thought in the early sixties. For all the distinctions they made among ladies and girlfriends and mistresses, Harris and Bellow might as well have been horse traders.

At the end of May 1961, Bellow returned to the States and a hectic round of engagements. He delivered the Hopwood Lecture at the University of Michigan and stopped in Chicago to see Adam, who was now four; Sondra and the boy had moved to Skokie. Back in Tivoli, he faced a "himalaya" of submissions to *The Noble Savage*.

The journal was teetering on the brink of crisis. Meridian was losing money, and its parent company, World Books, wasn't happy; no matter how illustrious the journal's contents, its economics didn't work. They needed to sell thirty thousand copies to break even—a lot for a literary magazine. Aaron Asher was an unflagging booster and prepared to back it for as long as he could persuade Meridian to foot the bills. But editing a literary magazine was hardly the road to wealth—the editors were each paid fifteen hundred dollars per issue. Nor did Bellow have a teaching job lined up. John Clarke continued to equivocate about inviting him back to Minnesota, despite a gratifying collective letter from Bellow's graduate students urging his return. They were impatient with "the elaborate systems of literary criticism" promoted at Minnesota, they wrote, and hungry for the "stimulation" Bellow had provided. This letter is an important document, challenging the oft-heard criticisms of Bellow's teaching. That he was uneven as a teacher few would dispute. His heart wasn't in it, and if he hadn't been required to teach in order to make a living, he probably wouldn't have bothered at all; it wasn't until late in life, when he was a world-famous figure at the University of Chicago, that he came to view teaching as a diversion from the solitude of the writer's life. But he loved literature in a way that few professors did, and he conveyed that love in class. "We are active Bellowites all," his students concluded: "We read your books and follow your articles and have put you at the center of our intellectual life. We sincerely hope that you will be with us again at Minnesota." Their petition was to no avail: Bellow didn't get invited back.

He displayed his usual genial fatalism. Something would come up, he assured Botsford: "It always does." In the meantime, he retreated to his Tivoli study and set up shop. "I have no money coming in and I must hack," he groused, "and since I'm not too good at it I hack for a long time at some trifle and spend weeks brooding unhappily over assignments then push them over in a single morning, usually a Sunday when I have a headache and a nightmare beforehand to stir me up."

His main hackwork was reviewing novels for *The New York Times Book Review* and *The Saturday Review of Literature*, though he also found time to complete what must have been, even by literary standards, a low-paying assignment: an essay on Shakespeare's sonnets for *The Griffin*. He was also feverishly revising "The Last Analysis," otherwise known, after its hero, as "Bummidge." "It seems as if the play will be produced, and I'll be rich as a pig," he boasted to William Phillips.

No sooner had he established himself in Tivoli than he was off to Wagner College on Staten Island for a two-week writers' conference. Bellow claimed that he had been promised "leisurely days and idle nights," but it didn't turn out that way. "The temperature throughout was at an average of 106 degrees, like a stokehold," he reported to Botsford; he'd been "sweating over papers and talking 12 hours a day til my mouth was like an ashpit." The younger writers' hunger for approbation from their famous teacher was intense to the point of "hysteria." Susan Dworkin, a young writer at the conference, put the matter bluntly: "That summer, no one in the world mattered more than Saul Bellow."

Never mind that he was brutal about their work. A story by "Buzz" Farber, who was to attain mild notoriety as an actor in some of Norman Mailer's films, annoyed him because it appeared to romanticize poverty: "I've lived in dirt, and when you've lived in dirt, there's nothing interesting about it." Donald Barthelme brought in a story, "The Big Broadcast of 1938," about an obsessive radio announcer and his unconsummated affair with a fan, that was to become widely anthologized; Bellow's only comment was "Do you really believe it's that hard for people to talk to each other?" Bette Howland, who would go on to publish several books, submitted a story involving an abortion that elicited a misogynistic remark about "women writers who wear their ovaries on their sleeves."

Another young writer, Arno Karlen, submitted a chapter from a novel about eastern European immigrant Jews—"Augie March territory," he acknowledged. Bellow pointedly ignored him: "I reminded him too much of himself." Karlen also conjectured that Bellow may have been attracted to his beautiful young wife. Even so, he gave the novelist high marks. "He was an absolutely brilliant reader of people's fiction, utterly apposite and penetrating—a brilliant teacher." After the conference, Karlen wrote Bellow what he later described as a "Herzog" letter, complaining about the way he'd been treated. Bellow's poignant reply lends credence to Karlen's suspicions:

> That I should have failed you was inevitable, since no one ever gives up the belief that there is a "mana," as the Polynesians call it, which must be transferrable. I myself have often been indignant with older writers, and I know how you must have felt. But I believe you may have missed something Jewish that passed between us. Whom the Lord loveth he chasteneth, goes the old saying. . . . I saw my own pale tense face twenty years ago, and I spoke and no doubt I said the wrong thing.

If he was tough on those with whom he felt competitive (especially the men), Bellow was also capable of tact. "You'll be a good writer," he told Susan Dworkin. It was a self-protective move; his students' "ego-stricken needs" unnerved him. Listening to a student read her work in class, "he sat with his thumb pressed to his temple, like a man rehearsing suicide," Dworkin wrote in a memoir of that summer. "Sometimes he gazed into space—and when he was forced to look at us, it was with *fear*."

Fame had increased Bellow's legendary magnetism. His Minneapolis ordeal had aged him—by his forties, his hair was white—but he was still strikingly handsome. He kept a safe distance from his female students at Wagner, according to Eleanor Bergstein, who later wrote the screenplay for *Dirty Dancing*. He was especially drawn to Bergstein's type—long hair, guitar, Jewish intensity—but he gave the excuse that he was leaving his old ways behind and didn't try to seduce her.

"I have a very sweet girl, Susan," he reported to Ralph Ross, "and one of these days—when I stop trembling at the word—I may get married again."

As Bellow's reputation increased, so did his self-assurance as a literary commentator. His Hopwood Lecture, "Where Do We Go from Here? The Future of Fiction," offered a pointed message: The twentieth century was not a good time for "narrative art." The kind of "unitary" character depicted in the works of Shakespeare, Cervantes, Fielding, and Balzac had broken down beneath the forces of social fragmentation; the notion of community was "old-fashioned," a thing of the past. "The real self, unknown, is hidden, a sunken power in us; the true identity lies deep—very deep."

Bellow's versatility as an essayist was nowhere more evident than in the "Literature" entry he wrote for a revised edition of the *Encyclopaedia Britannica*, a project on which he labored for months, producing in the end some twenty thousand words. More than a literary survey, it traced the development of the modern concept of the individual, a regression in which the unique Self proclaimed by Rousseau dwindled to the marginal, sickly protagonists of modern literature. "An industrialized mass society cannot accommodate any sizable population of Prometheans and geniuses," Bellow insisted. Even the greatest contemporary novels—Solzhenitsyn's *One Day in the Life of Ivan Denisovich*, James Jones's *The Thin Red Line*—were about "the submergence of the individual." As for other Americans—Roth, Updike, Salinger—their fascination with adolescence mirrored a general malaise. He quoted from one of his touchstone texts, Erich Auerbach's *Mimesis:* "There is no common world of men, because it could only come into existence if many should find their way to their own proper reality, the reality which is given to the individual—which then would be also the true common reality."

Bellow touched upon this same theme in "Facts That Put Fancy to Flight," a front-page essay in *The New York Times Book Review,* deriding "the obstacles of the literal" that interfered with the artist's vision. Research departments at magazines bedevil authors with questions about irrelevant details: How many stories does the Ansonia really have? Is it really possible to see its television antennae from the corner of West End Avenue and Seventy-second Street? (Bellow had been asked these very questions by the copy editor of *Seize the Day.*) But fact wasn't the same thing as truth. And truth—as he liked to put it—was his particular line of work.

He wasn't oblivious to the political realities of his time—the Bay of Pigs, the intensification of the Cold War. But he viewed politics as a distraction from the real business of life. It wasn't *l'art pour l'art* that Bellow espoused; the Romantic notion of the artist as somehow not of this world held no appeal for him. His unwillingness to be drawn into the vortex of world events was another version of his demand for autonomy, an unwillingness to allow events to dictate his subject matter: "One has the choice now of coming before the world as a writer or actually being one."

When he did address himself to current events, Bellow did it in his own idiosyncratic way. In his "Literary Notes on Khrushchev," published in *Esquire* in 1961, it was the human details that caught his eye—the Soviet leader pounding his fists on a desk at the UN, banging his shoe, raising his coattails in a parody of the cancan—not Khrushchev as a statesman but Khrushchev as a literary character, like the shrewd peasants and provincial officials of Gogol's *Dead Souls.* Khrushchev's posturing, Bellow observed, was "an entirely new mode of historical interpretation by the world leader of Marxist thought who bodily, by the use of his own person, delivers a critique of Western civilization."

"I'm well into a book which makes Henderson look like the Scout-masters Handbook," Bellow reported to Ralph Ross with typical braggadocio in the summer of 1961. The opening pages appeared in the July issue of *Esquire* under the title "Herzog."

Bellow's life and work were so intimately intertwined that it was sometimes hard to say which came first—*Herzog* or the events that precipitated it. Even before he learned of Sondra's affair with Jack Ludwig, he had been contemplating a novel about a duplicitous marriage; its tentative title was "Cassandra." Once he knew the whole story, the plot fell into place. Now he had *two* villains. Relating the sordid denouement of his second marriage, Bellow announced gleefully to his former Bard student Al Ellenberg that he would "fix" Ludwig: "I'm going to stick him into my new novel. By the time I'm through with him, he'll be laughed right out of the literature business."

In the beginning, at least, revenge fueled his narrative. "I have finally found it in my heart to write about wicked people," he told Ralph Ross, giving a theological cast to the mythology of his own life. It had been a painful episode, but who could deny that it was good material? When a letter arrived from the grant committee of the American Academy of Arts and Letters listing Ludwig among possible candidates, Bellow circled his old friend's name and forwarded the letter to Ross, scrawling on the back: "Con man and psychopath?! And he never runs out of marks." Ludwig had so many irons in the fire, Bellow joked, that he didn't know which one to burn himself with.

But the main object of satire was himself. "I thought in *Herzog* I was having a certain amount of fun at my own expense; or if not at my own expense, I was making fun of my own type. I was really taking Herzog at a moment of crisis and putting on and removing the masks he had used throughout his life: the scholar, the Jew, the husband, the father, the lover, the romantic avenger, the intellectual, all the rest of that." Bellow had never been shy about plundering his experience for his books; in *Herzog* he had the audacity to put the most intimate details of his own life at the center of his art.

He was never at a loss for material. While Bellow labored away at his new novel, he was unwittingly gathering material for the final work in his trilogy of H novels, *Humboldt's Gift*. ("Three H's," he wrote Richard Stern, "as if I'm finally getting my breath.") A brief item in the *Chicago Tribune* on December 1,

1961, made public his wedding to wife number three. "Dr. and Mrs. Frank Glassman of Lake Shore Drive were in New York recently for the marriage of their daughter, Miss Susan Alexandra Glassman, to Saul Bellow of Tivoli, N.Y. The new Mr. and Mrs. Bellow will make their home in New York City."

They did keep a small apartment in Manhattan—Susan was teaching at the Dalton School—but Bellow preferred his rural dacha, where he could write and garden undisturbed. He was living in "high style," he reported to Herbert Gold. "Nothing seems to get finished, but I *work* very hard, and that's a comforting mode of life to a child of Duty. How I labor—sheer slavery. I turn livid every day, at about 2 P.M. and look for a merciful way to pass out."

Bellow didn't exaggerate his iron discipline; he was always working. He rose early and headed for his desk, where he proceeded to type away on his Smith-Corona or fill notebooks with his boyish scrawl. He made of his burden a comedy; for Bellow, there was nothing solemn about the enterprise of literature. He didn't ritualize work as some writers did, insisting upon a priest-like silence and regular hours of work. He thrived on distractions, interruptions, household errands, and rarely turned off the phone.

As for making a living, God would provide, but Bellow played an aggressive part in the negotiations. His agent, Henry Volkening, was genial and easygoing, a prodigious drinker who liked nothing more than a prolonged "drunch" at the Century Association, a venerable literary dining club on West Forty-third Street; any negotiations conducted in the afternoon were at his own—and his author's—peril.* It was the author, not the agent, who proposed serializing *Herzog* in *Esquire* after he'd written a mere twenty-three pages; the author who demanded to know what Cheever and Nabokov were getting. When it came to protecting his interests, Bellow could be as hardheaded as his brothers.

Once again, however, teaching presented itself as the only steady source of income. For the winter term of 1961–62, he had

---

*On one occasion, Volkening confessed that he couldn't remember whether George Weidenfeld's six-hundred-pound advance for British rights to *Henderson the Rain King* was "half on signature and half on—now hell, what *did* he say?—either submission or publication."

a temporary appointment at the University of Chicago, as what the university's public-relations department called "Celebrity in Residence." But the English department there was no more enlightened than English departments anywhere about the value of having writers on the faculty and resisted hiring Bellow on a more permanent basis. Ralph Ellison had preceded him in the job for a term in 1960 and also been passed over. Besides, there was already one writer in the department: Richard Stern. "I think they felt one was enough," said Stern.

In the end, the sociologist Edward Shils found Bellow a permanent position. They had known each other since the late 1930s, when Shils was a young instructor at the university. Shils had since achieved distinction as a member of the university's Committee on Social Thought; his idea was to find Bellow a home on the committee.

Early in 1962, Shils approached Edward Levi, the university provost. Levi considered the trend toward appointing writers to academic posts a "pernicious movement," but he agreed reluctantly to meet Shils and Bellow for lunch. "I changed my mind completely," Levi recalled. "It was quite clear that I was talking to a learned person who was serious about his learning and serious about teaching." That summer, Bellow was offered a five-year appointment as a professor at the Committee on Social Thought.

The committee's mandate was to encourage a small number of highly qualified graduate students to range among disciplines, working closely with professors, on the model of the Oxford tutorial system. (One alumnus described the department as "a secular monastery.") Since its founding in 1941, the committee had assembled an eminent and diverse faculty. Current members included Mircea Eliade, the prolific Romanian professor of comparative religion; Marshall Hodgson, then at work on a definitive history of Islamic civilization; the literary critic Ralph J. Mills; the economist Friedrich von Hayek, who was to win a Nobel Prize in 1974; and the classicist David Grene, an Irishman who rode horses on weekends and sported Victorian muttonchops. Despite having edited a widely praised edition of Hobbes's *Thucydides* and the works of Sophocles, the defiantly eclectic Grene had been spurned by the classics department on the grounds that he was "too difficult to work with." The Committee on Social Thought had provided Grene with intellectual shelter; it would be home to Bellow for more than thirty years.

In May 1962, Bellow received an invitation from the Kennedy White House to attend a dinner for André Malraux. It was "a big cultural blowout," as Edmund Wilson, also a guest, described the affair.* Seated beneath crystal chandeliers in the two grand reception rooms were Robert Lowell and Elizabeth Hardwick, Robert Penn Warren and Eleanor Clark, Allen Tate and Caroline Gordon, joined by Arthur Miller, Tennessee Williams, Mark Rothko, Leonard Bernstein, and George Balanchine. "This is becoming a sort of eating place for artists," President Kennedy joked. He had "a sleek look," Bellow noted, "despite the cortisone puffiness. He looked like a man fed by the power of his position." Kennedy and Susan had a long conversation: "She was sizing him up as an influence for the good; he was sizing her up as a lay."

The *Partisan Review* crowd, accustomed to thinking of itself as a marginal constituency, was excited by all the attention intellectuals were suddenly getting. "Intellect was in touch with power," as Alfred Kazin rather grandly put it. Bellow pretended to be unimpressed. "The next day I realized the president had spent the whole evening talking to David Rockefeller about fiscal matters. I didn't get to find out the presidential views on the future of the novel." Describing the event afterward in a *Noble Savage* Aria, he compared his fellow guests in their black-tie splendor to the apes, dogs, and horses in H. G. Wells's *Island of Dr. Moreau*, "changed by the mad surgeon into approximately human forms." The way to behave in the company of the president, he maintained, was to emulate the courtly dignity of Dr. Johnson when he was summoned by King George III. "I should have bowed and stammered through the whole of it," Oliver Goldsmith had said admiringly of Johnson's performance. Bowing and stammering weren't in Bellow's nature, no matter who was the host.

---

*In his journals, Wilson disdainfully noted the presence of Bellow and his wife, whom he mystifyingly identified as "a Frenchwoman who taught at Smith, I don't know why she was there." How tireless writers are in putting each other down!

19

*I came back to settle in Chicago with the secret motive
of writing a great book.*

—Charlie Citrine
in Humboldt's Gift

*Soon I will be in Chicago, melancholy euphoria following paranoid
hypochondria. Alert the clinicians and stand by.*

—Bellow to Richard Stern

C HICAGO IS BELLOW'S great theme: "When people ask
whether I have roots here I say that tangled wires would be
more like it." Those wires bind together his oeuvre. From
his first published story, "Two Morning Monologues," in 1941,
with its geographic specificity ("I wait for the Cottage Grove car")
to the elegiac "Something to Remember Me By," published half a
century later and studded with references to the landmarks of his
early youth, Bellow's work is a virtual reconstruction of the city,
neighborhood by neighborhood and street by street. "It was the
setting of my deepest emotions," he once explained to a French
journalist who had asked him about his passion for his hometown:

> It was the place in which my human attachments were strongest,
> for most of my life, to families, school friends, lovers; it was the
> locus of all these things. How can you not put some of your own
> feeling into it? Even its barbarism had a certain appeal and its
> rawness, even its wicked history, is something that Chicagoans
> are pleased by when they look back. People tend to set a certain
> value upon experience even when the experience is not so good.
> Just as veterans of the wars take their families back to show
> them where they suffered.

For Bellow, New York—a city much on his mind as he labored
over "Herzog," with its Manhattan-based hero—represented

everything he despised about "the art life." It was "the center of
the culture business," he argued in a lecture delivered the year
after he moved back to Chicago, the place where literature is
"prepared, processed, and distributed." New York was the center:
"But the center of what?" Not long after he moved back to
Chicago, Bellow vowed to Arthur Schlesinger, Jr., that he "would
never set foot in New York again."

At first glance, his resentment seems curious. After all, in
complaining so bitterly about what he snobbishly referred to as
"the West Side Kibbutz," Bellow was lashing out at the very
people who had made his reputation. At the age of forty-seven, he
was, by common consensus, America's leading novelist. In a
symposium that appeared in *The New York Times Book Review*
that autumn, "Who's to Take the Place of Hemingway and
Faulkner?" his was the name mentioned most often.* Bellow
achieved primacy, in some small measure, by default—"taking the
place" implied that someone had to be first, and who else was
there? But he had earned it book by book, from the succès d'estime
of *Dangling Man* and *The Victim* to the exuberant breakthroughs
of *Augie* and *Henderson,* paced by his compact masterpiece *Seize
the Day.* It was a career built by accretion, by stamina, as well as
by genius.

He was returning to what he liked to call "provincial Chicago"
in triumph, not in defeat. But such a scenario failed to account for
Bellow's need to create obstacles and enemies. It was more satisfying to convince himself that the New York intellectuals, however
much they respected his work—even saw in it a vindication of
their own cultural moment—still regarded its author as an inter-
loper, a Chicagoan, not one of them. ("You like to picture yourself
as an outsider, positively a greener," Matilda Layamon [Lay-a-
man?] hectors her egghead husband in *More Die of Heartbreak,*
making fun of his "strange steerage mentality.") Besides, there
were too many big fish in New York—not as big as Bellow was
now, perhaps, but still competitors for attention. And New York
had an additional disadvantage: It was too socially and ethnically

*When John Steinbeck won the Nobel Prize in 1962, he inscribed a copy of his
Stockholm lecture to Bellow, "You're next."

various. The city's inhabitants inevitably bump up against a diversity of human types, not all of whom are quick to recognize one's uniqueness. Bellow preferred to be among the people he'd grown up with, childhood friends and family whose love and approval seemed less conditional. He was never more at ease than in the streets of Hyde Park, the Riviera Club, the Italian Village in the Loop—the haunts of the Chicago born, or raised. "I feel I have unfinished business here," he told a reporter from a local newspaper who came to see him a few weeks after he arrived. "I don't know what it is, but I'm trying to find out."

After a few weeks at Susan's parents' on Lake Shore Drive, Bellow and his new bride moved into an apartment at 1755 East Fifty-fifth Street, just off the park that ran along the lakefront in Hyde Park.

The city had changed in the two decades he'd been away. Urban redevelopers had razed the jazz clubs and student dives on Fifty-fifth Street in an effort to halt the spread of the slums that now surrounded the university, threatening to fulfill the prediction made by Robert Maynard Hutchins as early as the 1930s that the university would become "an island in the midst of the black race." Crime, once virtually unheard-of in Hyde Park, was on the rise. "Hyde Park is now an enclave in Black Chicago where gangs roam the streets beating old school-teachers & bricklayers to death—I don't exaggerate," Bellow wrote dolefully to Ruth Miller. "One ghetto more. Maybe that's among the attractions that drew me back."

For a time, there had been talk of moving the university out of the city altogether. But a vast urban-renewal project had saved Hyde Park from the destruction visited upon other Chicago neighborhoods—at the expense of pushing the black community farther from its center.* The area from Forty-seventh Street to the Midway on Fifty-ninth Street—the former site of the World Colum-

---

*It is an irony, often noted by writers on the city, that the term *ghetto* is applied to the vast neighborhoods on three sides of the university, where millions of black citizens live, instead of the besieged encampment of (primarily white) academics.

bian Exposition of 1893, now a patchy strip of grass separating the university from the ghetto to the south—was an urban oasis of sorts, a pleasant, integrated community dominated by the university's Gothic quad; by Frederick Law Olmsted's Jackson Park; by stately old apartment buildings and Frank Lloyd Wright's Robie House; and, to the north, by the stately mansions of Kenwood. It was a neighborhood, as Bellow noted in *Herzog,* of "spacious, comfortable, dowdy apartments where liberal, benevolent people live." (Even the local telephone exchange—MU, for *museum*—gave off a cultural emanation.)

Susan resented Bellow's attachment to the city of their youths and referred to him, with more contempt than irony, as her "ghetto lover." She hungered for the sophistication of New York. "Susan did not like his connection with the old Division Street culture," confirmed Dave Peltz. "She was an upper-middle-class Jewish lady whose father came from the West Side of Chicago and fought his way into becoming one of the more distinguished bone surgeons in Chicago." Like Bellow's mother, Susan had married down. She had little patience for Bellow's family attachments. On one occasion in Tivoli, now their summer home, a carful of Bellow's Montreal relatives showed up for supper—a less than joyful occasion for Susan. She had been offended to see the antique refectory table littered with bottles of Pepsi cola. (She would have preferred to serve wine.) When the relatives began singing Yiddish songs, it was the last straw. Another time, Bellow brought out pictures from the family album, one of his favorite pastimes; Susan impatiently waved them away.

She missed her own friends in the East. "Life here in this gray, gloomy city is somewhat less than amusing," she complained in a letter to Margaret Shafer, the wife of the Bard chaplain and a close friend in Tivoli. As far as Susan was concerned, the porpoises in the aquarium were more interesting than Bellow's academic colleagues. "All in all, Chicago seems to be a place in which one has to work very hard to find a little cheer." Two months after their arrival, they were still sitting on orange crates, waiting for their new furniture to be delivered.

Susan wasn't impressed with Bellow's fame—or liked to pretend she wasn't—and complained to anyone who would listen about how hard it was to be the wife of a writer. "Susie was angry from day one of the marriage," according to a friend. People were interested only in her husband. "I'm just Mrs. Bellow," she said. Yet the letters she wrote to various friends in her role as "the wife" were vivid and literate, full of cheerful domestic chatter and news about the books she was reading—Yukio Mishima, Isak Dinesen, Dostoyevsky's *The Eternal Husband*. She was an aspiring writer herself; she had a drawerful of unpublished stories.

For Bellow, Chicago represented stability—a rare thing in his life. Despite his "God will provide" attitude, he was glad to have what looked like a steady job at last. "I love the professorial bit," he admitted to Herbert Gold. "What a marvelous racket." And to Ralph Ross, he praised the Committee on Social Thought as "the most beautiful of all my employers." As always, in the early phase, he found married life congenial. "Susie and I are settling slowly," he reported to John Berryman on November 13. "Susie is a perfectionist and must have plenty of time. She's an adorable woman."

He was already hard at work—the one constant in his life. He did less book reviewing now and had taken up reviewing movies for *Horizon*, which paid better. Like other *Partisan Review* intellectuals who did their share of slumming as film critics—Delmore Schwartz, for one—Bellow adopted an arch and condescending tone when it came to movies. ("*Let* Jack Palance show his white teeth in sadistic glee à la Richard Widmark as he rides down poor clods in his chariot. *Let* the Italian extras fall down, gushing tomato paste.") He didn't take the medium seriously and never aspired to the status of James Agee, Dwight Macdonald, or Manny Farber, for whom film—the term *movies* didn't do justice to the importance of the genre—deserved the same high-minded scrutiny as literature did. Bellow saw movie reviewing as an excuse to revisit his familiar themes. Luis Buñuel's message, he asserted in a review of *Viridiana*, was that modern life had diminished the self: Man must go in quest of "new and higher forms of individuality."

He had also returned to his play. The discarded titles of "The Last Analysis" (also known as "Bummidge") give a sense of its many transmutations. Among the rejects were "Do It Yourself," "The Upper Depths," "Know Thyself," "Crash Program," and

"In a Beautiful World (or Off the Couch by Christmas)." Several acts appeared under yet another title, "Scenes from Humanitis—A Farce," in the summer 1962 issue of *Partisan Review*. But its length and Bellow's ignorance of the conventions of dramatic writing created obstacles. It was "a novel of a play," said Lillian Hellman, who had been advising him on the script. Hellman observed sarcastically that it would run eight hours "without Wagnerian orchestration."

"The Last Analysis" did suffer from garrulity. It had virtually no dramatic action, no plausible characters, no plot. It wasn't really a play at all—more a hybrid of Yiddish theater and a Lenny Bruce nightclub shtick. Its hero, Philip Bummidge, a Hollywood celebrity whose star has long since waned, is Bellow's least literary character; one of his models was the clarinetist—and much-married autodidact—Artie Shaw. (Another was the intensively psychoanalyzed Sid Caesar.) Raucous, vulgar, "a clown driven to thought," Bummidge was Bellow's rebellion against the demands of art, a holiday—as he'd once said of *Augie*—from high seriousness. "I had in mind an old-time farce—just a series of vaudeville scenes with an excuse for a play in between them. Now I look at the play and think someone else wrote it. I recognize only certain passages as mine—the blood ranting!"

The action—such as it is—takes place in a loft on the Upper West Side, where Bummidge is preparing to demonstrate his method of "*Existenz*-Action Self-Analysis" on closed-circuit television before an audience of psychiatrists, artists, and fellow comedians at the Waldorf-Astoria. Gathered around Bummidge is a crowd of Bellovian types: his cousin Winkleman, a lawyer with "the Harvard Club manner" who's got his hand in a lot of unsavory deals, including an "old-People's-home racket" (interesting in light of Sam Bellows's later involvement in what became known as the Chicago nursing-home scandal); his embittered mistress Pamela; and his ex-wife, Bella, described in Bellow's notes as "an aggressive, hammering woman, large and masculine," decked out in spike-heeled shoes and "a whopping patent-leather purse." Together with Bummidge's family—his importunate son, Max; his rich older sister, Madge; an ill-tempered aunt by the name of Velma—they constitute a kind of hectoring chorus, intent upon airing old grievances and making demands. Limbering up for his performance with some "couch work," Bummidge regresses before his tormentors' eyes, performing slapstick reenactments of early primal scenes—ransacking his sister's bureau; fondling her underthings—and rehearsing his sexual history: "Seduced on the counter of a dairy restaurant by a certain Mrs. Friedmacher . . ." He broods on the deaths of his parents, guilty about his own wish to live: "Down goes the coffin. Down. The hole fills with clay. But Bummidge is still spilling gravy at life's banquet." By the play's close, he's worked his way back to his most primal scene, the moment of his own conception: "Oh, no Mama, no! Pa! Ma! Wait! Hold it! Consider!"*

"The Last Analysis" is a satire on the patient-analyst transaction, and, like any effective satire, it demonstrates a serious knowledge of its subject. "I had such bad experiences with my psychiatrists I finally decided to do it myself," Bummidge says in an early version, noting that he's been to "Freudians, Jungians, Adlerians, Horneyites, Sullivans, Rogerses." Why, then, is he still "sick"? According to his clinical self-diagnosis, Bummidge is "masochistic, narcissistic, paranoid and depressed, exhibitionistic, compulsive, fixated and perverse." But what he's really suffering from is a more general condition: "Humanitis," Bummidge calls it, the "Pagliacci gangrene," a disease caused, "as all gangrene is, by a failure of circulation. Cut off by self-pity. Passivity. Fear. Masochistic rage." It's often the lesser works of art that afford a glimpse into the artist's true condition, before the labor of artifice and concealment takes over. In "The Last Analysis," Bellow gave vent to his self-loathing without having to disguise it. The play is a therapy session in the open air.

What animates Bummidge is what animates all of Bellow's heroes: pure rage. "I'm hampered, hindered, held back, obstructed, impeded, impaired," he frets, a variant of Macbeth's "cabin'd, cribb'd, confin'd, bound in." By the end of the play, his

---

*The scene is a comic version of Delmore Schwartz's most famous story, "In Dreams Begin Responsibilities," in which the narrator, watching his parents' doomed courtship on a newsreel, stands up in the theater and cries, "Don't do it. . . . Nothing good will come of it, only remorse, hatred, scandal, and two children whose characters are monstrous."

self-analysis show proves a great hit with his audience. But for Bummidge, success is just another form of bondage, and he goes off to found the Bummidge Institute of Nonsense. "I must reach everyone," he proclaims. "Everything. Heart, reason, comic spirit. I have something tremendous to say." In Bummidge, Bellow had found an ideal vehicle to simultaneously pursue and ridicule his periodic attempts at self-analysis: "The self-absorption of people who never tire of exploring their depths is the source of our comedy." Humor was his defense.

Bellow's third marriage was a mystery to his friends. For one thing, he hadn't yet extricated himself from his second. Visitation rights with Adam were proving to be a complicated issue. On Labor Day, Bellow came to pick up the boy, but Sondra wouldn't let him go. Bellow alleged that she tore his clothes and "bruised" him. "He beat me up," Sondra countered, claiming she was "bedridden for a week. Did I give him a slap? I did. But he retaliated violently—more than once." At one point, she claimed, she had to get a restraining order. On September 30, 1962, Bellow fired off a letter demanding that a "fixed pattern" for his visits with Adam be established. He was particularly incensed over Sondra's habit of refusing to let him come to the house; he wasn't going to wait for his son in a restaurant "like a wrongdoer."

Given such a problematic marital history, why marry again? To friends, Bellow offered an ironic explanation: "I'm a slow learner." An early version of *Herzog* provides deeper insight into his marriage to Susie, if not into his marriages in general: "The reason for the marriage to Juliana was to arrange for the continuation of his blindness and cowardice. Because he knew she did not love him and he took no chance of fulfillment by being married to her. Thus he could continue to be a slave of the world, and within its system of necessity." Marriage, according to this explanation, was another evasive tactic; to admit that his wives loved him would have been to acknowledge his own role in the dissolution of his marriages. Better to see his marital martyrdom as voluntary: Choosing to be a slave meant exerting a measure of control over his destiny.

With Susan, things were good for a while. "Susie & I could be happy on an ice floe," Bellow crowed to Oscar Tarcov. Susie concurred. On Christmas Day 1963, she wrote to their friend Margaret Shafer: "We are simply splendid. I've never felt better, or looked better if I am to believe my uxorious husband." For all her grousing about Hyde Park, she found it stimulating. Mary McCarthy had been through town; Leslie Fiedler was arriving for the Modern Language Association conference. Bellow was thirty pages from the end of his novel, "and it's going marvelously. I can't imagine what life without Herzog will be like."

There was also about to be another new arrival. The holiday greetings to Margaret Shafer were "from the 2⅔ of us"—Susan was pregnant.

Bellow, the father of two sons, often expressed the wish to have a daughter. (Was it only to change the facts that he made one of Herzog's children a girl?) "How I envy you your daughter!" he had written John Berryman early in 1963, congratulating him on the birth of his second child: "If I thought I'd get a similar result I'd start now to persuade Susan, renew the covenant, show our trust in the species (what have I done for it lately?!)" A girl was somehow less threatening than a boy, less a replica of himself. In his story "A Father-to-Be," the child that the reluctant parent Rogin imagines having is a son; it never occurs to him that he might have a daughter. Would Bellow have been a more responsive father to a girl? It's hard to know. Children played a role in his life similar to that of wives: He liked the idea more than the reality. Like Herzog, he was "a bad but loving father." He felt tenderly toward his children and enjoyed having them around. It was the raising of children—the daily, often tedious grind—that he found intolerable.

Still, the imminent arrival of a new child comforted him, for it coincided with a new bereavement. Oscar Tarcov, his dear friend from Tuley days, had been carried off by a heart attack at the age of forty-eight. They had been in frequent communication during the previous months, writing back and forth about a play that Tarcov had in the works. (Bellow pronounced it "thorough, subtle and complete.") Aware of his health problems, feeling time was short, Tarcov had quit his job at the Anti-Defamation League and plunged into writing full-time. "I feel I'd rather die myself than endure these deaths, one after another, of all my dearest friends," Bellow wrote to Berryman a few days after Tarcov's death. "It wears out your heart." First Isaac, now Oscar. The inevitable thinning of contemporaries was off to an early start.

Once again, Bellow skipped the funeral, though he did show up a few days later at the home of Tarcov's widow, Edith. "He was distraught—spooked," said the critic Ted Solotaroff, who had gotten to know the Tarcovs. "There was this triumvirate [Tarcov, Bellow, and Rosenfeld], and now he was alone." Bellow was "very tender" that day, Solotaroff recalled. Tarcov may not have had a successful life as a writer, Bellow admitted, but he'd had a successful life as a man.

Birth followed death. Just as, seven years earlier, the arrival of Adam had followed fast upon the loss of Isaac, the arrival of Daniel followed the loss of Tarcov by a year. "I'm praying now for a daughter to guide my last steps to Colonus," Bellow, ever the Oedipal son, wrote to Ruth Miller on March 5, 1964. But it was not to be. Two weeks later, another engraved announcement went out:

Saul and Susan Bellow
announce the arrival of a son
Daniel Oscar
17 March 1964
at 6 lbs

The spring of 1964 was a chaotic time. Susan was up at night with the new baby; Bellow was up at night with his own twins: the novel and the play. "I don't recall that I ever worked harder," he wrote Dave Peltz. He revised "The Last Analysis" three times that spring, adding seventy new pages of dialogue; it was beginning to look like a play. And, amazingly enough, it was headed for Broadway. The cultural impresario Roger L. Stevens, tipped off by Gore Vidal, had agreed to produce it; the director was Joseph Anthony, who had brought *The Rainmaker* to Broadway, where it had become a long-running hit. "Immortal? And rich, too?" Bellow exclaimed to Dave Peltz. "Gadzooks!"

The two projects fueled each other. In one month, Bellow wrote forty thousand words. His colleague Wayne Booth ran into him on a Hyde Park street and found him in a state of high excitement: He was revising at high speed for four hours every morning, "going through the manuscript and weeding out parts of myself that I don't like." It was a remark that revealed how closely he identified with his main character.

"I seem to have expanded my capacity for cares and complications to the limit, to see how much pressure I can withstand without a diving-suit," he wrote to Ruth Miller on June 13:

> Since November, things have gone something like this: Finished *Herzog*, rewrote my silly play. Taught school; re-wrote *Herzog*, did another version of the play; prepared the novel for the printer, went to NYC to see Adam and cast the play; came home and found galleys, rewrote the book again on the galleys. A batch of 50 of these galleys were taken in a holdup of the Hyde Park post-office. The thieves were caught and the money recovered, but my work had been torn to bits (first critical reception?).

The gunmen, driving a yellow Cadillac, had scattered bags of mail in vacant lots all over the West Side, and it was a few days before the tattered proofs of *Herzog* were recovered. "We are in a state of nature here in Chicago," Bellow told a reporter from the *Sun-Times*. Late one night, his phone rang. The caller, in a gangster's voice, said he knew where the proofs were and offered to meet Bellow beneath the Illinois Central tracks at midnight. Then he let out a loud cackling laugh. It was his brother Maurice.

The Bellows had rented a house on Martha's Vineyard for July and August. "We've seen a bit of island society," Bellow reported to Alfred Kazin, enjoying his new social circle while pretending to make fun of it: "Styron is our leader here, in little Fitzgeraldville. Then there is Lillian Hellman, in whom I produce symptoms of *shyness*. And Phil Rahv who keeps alive the traditions of Karl

Marx. I'm very fond of Philip—he's *mishpocha* [family]—and he gives us a kind of private Chataqua [*sic*] course in hackpolitick from which I get great pleasure." But he quickly wearied of Vineyard social life. It was too insular, too snobbish, too frenetic—too much like New York. He preferred his "sandy bed" on Menemsha Pond, where few writers came and lobster boats bobbed placidly at the docks.

In the mornings, Bellow applied the finishing touches to "Herzog" while Pat Covici, who had been panting after the novel for two years, tried to wrestle it out of his hands. Bellow revised up to the last minute, first filling the margins of the manuscript, then pinning new pages to the galleys, then scribbling on the final proofs, and "practically following it to the bindery." At Viking, the feeling was that he had at last written his Big Book—a feeling that was beginning to reverberate outward. "In some quarters there is talk that Bellow is now the greatest living American writer," claimed *The Saturday Review of Literature* in a prepublication interview. Alfred Kazin, from whom Covici had solicited a blurb—not that Bellow needed one at this stage in his career—replied excitedly that the book had left him "in a daze of newfound comprehension. It seems to me that Saul Bellow has written his best book, and incidentally the book of his generation and mine."

The gathering drumbeat of acclaim reached a crescendo on September 20, 1964, with a front-page review in *The New York Times Book Review* by the novelist and critic Julian Moynahan, who pronounced *Herzog* "a masterpiece." To V. S. Pritchett, writing in *The New York Review of Books*, Bellow was now "the most rewarding of living American novelists," a writer whose genius for the details of daily life far surpassed Hemingway's "stylized naturalism." To Philip Rahv, *Herzog* signaled Bellow's emergence as "the finest stylist at present writing fiction in America." Even Brendan Gill, Bellow's *goyisher* nemesis at *The New Yorker,* liked it.

There were a few dissents. *Time* derided the brainy protagonist's unworldliness and passivity. ("They seem to think of me as a Bad Guy Jew, and Bernard Malamud as a Good Guy Jew," Bellow remarked acidly.) John Aldridge, who rarely had a kind word for Bellow, resented the commotion, suggesting that *Herzog* had been promoted out of some communal need "to produce a novel we could all accept in good conscience as major." The most hostile review was from Richard Poirier, in *Partisan Review*. Poirier, a defender of Norman Mailer (and a crony of Ludwig), acknowledged the novel's "brilliance," but he was annoyed by its satirical attitude toward ideas; Herzog's bouts of theory were "tiresome" and "pseudo-philosophical," Poirier complained, more "a glib presumption to Thought" than thought itself. (Apparently Herzog's mimicry of the high-flown intellectual style came a little too close for comfort.)*

The demurrals were mild and, in the end, inconsequential. *Herzog* had captured the public imagination—something no other book by Bellow had ever done. Within a week of publication, it had gone back for a second printing, then a third; it was the main selection of the Literary Guild. By October, it was on the bestseller list. And on October 19, Bellow received a telegram from his editors at Viking: HERZOG NUMBER ONE REPEAT ONE SUNDAY.

The fall of 1964 in New York was a "Bellow festival," trumpeted a reporter for one of the tabloids in a full-page feature headlined ABOUT BOOKS, BROADWAY, SCANDAL AND SUCCESS. "On publishers' row, Bellow is receiving the equivalent of an astronaut's ride up Fifth Ave. Grateful reviews are falling about his shoulders like confetti. In its very first week, 'Herzog' stole past 'The Spy Who Came in from the Cold' to become No. 1 on New York best-seller lists, and in almost every book store in town it has the coveted 'Fanny Hill' place alongside the cash register." Pete Hamill began a profile for the *Herald Tribune*, "Last week a writer named Saul Bellow woke up one morning to find himself a star." *Vogue* gushed over him in its "People Are Talking About . . ." column, alongside a full-page Arthur Penn photograph of the author, head cupped in hand: "In one Nureyev leap, Saul Bellow suddenly, after twenty years and five novels, has become with his sixth, *Herzog*, the big American novelist. . . . His talk is delightful,

---

*A few months later, after the Christmas holidays, there was a sour parody in *The New Yorker* by Thomas Meehan that took off from the book's opening line and tried (without a great deal of success) to capture its self-consciously neurotic tone: "If I am entirely imaginary, then who is the overweight *misnagid* in all of the Coca-Cola ads, wondered Santa E. Claus."

colloquial, forthright. His eyes, ringed like those of an eagle, are older than his handsome face—and his mind is far older than both, overflowing with a marvelous ranging erudition. Bellow, after twenty years, has at last caught up with his own brilliance."

The Broadway part of this heartwarming success story wasn't going quite as well. Holed up in "furnished squalor" at the Hotel Alden on Central Park West, Bellow was engaged in feverish bouts of revision. "Here I am, having heart-attacks in New York while the play rehearses, the book publishes etc.," he reported to Dave Peltz in mid-September.

Secretly, he harbored fantasies of a huge success for the play; to friends, however, he predicted its "bloody sacrifice on Broadway's smoking altars." The early signs were ominous. At one point in the rehearsals, Bellow and his theatrical agent, Toby Cole, met with Roger Stevens and actually urged him not to open the production.

One problem was the casting. "The play was written for a great personality," noted Stevens. "And without that personality—the *right* personality—you're in trouble." The director, Joe Anthony, had big plans for "The Last Analysis." He was determined to get Zero Mostel for the lead, and if not Mostel then Jackie Gleason or Milton Berle. In the end, Berle was intimidated by the role, and Mostel "elected to entertain the Hadassah ladies in *Fiddler on the Roof,*" as Robert Brustein unkindly put it. Sam Levene, who finally got the job, was out of his depth. A popular actor who had enjoyed celebrated roles in such Broadway hits as *Guys and Dolls* and *Dinner at Eight,* he was clearly intimidated both by the role and by the author, whom he addressed as "the Scholar." The long, convoluted soliloquies persistently eluded Levene. "Sam Levene is a dear man," Bellow acknowledged in a postmortem published in *The New York Times,* "but he found it hard to speak a sentence with a subordinate clause." In the end, Bellow's assessment of his leading actor's performance was more devastating than the critics': "If any fiddler attacked a concerto as Levene did his role he'd be stoned from the stage."

Bellow put in long days in the darkened Belasco Theatre, "looking for all the world as wilted and dapper as that actor-philosopher Moses Herzog," according to one newspaper report. At first, he was enthusiastic about the communal nature of the stage; he had discovered "the happiness of collaboration." Like many writers, Bellow was naturally gregarious; theater liberated him from the self-imposed prison of the novelist—"a bitter and painful privation." Its only drawback was the colossal vanity of the players. "At times I feel about people's neuroses (my own included) as I do about Victorian furniture—Oh, how very quaint!" he complained in a comical diatribe to Toby Cole: "Everyone's ego must be appeased. The elephants must be fed. Here, I lay down my last peanut. 'Eat.' Jesus gave the multitude gefilte fish, but I have no supernatural aid." After rehearsal he adjourned on occasion to the Algonquin Hotel to be interviewed by a procession of reporters who came to pay court. "At a time when his career seems to be moving towards a stunning climax, Bellow appears remarkably calm, modest, yet quietly self-assured," wrote the interviewer for *The Saturday Review of Literature*. "Like Herzog, he has the brooding air of a man who has been through a lot."

His mood changed once it became evident that the play was headed for disaster. "An air of despair pervaded the rehearsals," recalled Edward Hoagland, who had taken to hanging around the Belasco in the hope of cultivating Bellow's friendship. "On the spider-webby stage set, the desperate actors launched their lines as if still trying to understand them. Bellow's Reynard face had lost its shape and grown irregular in coloring. In his posture he resembled a man awaiting an announced punishment."

As opening night approached, Bellow's geniality vanished entirely. Joe Anthony felt the impact of his wrath: "It was when Saul sensed that we had made wrong judgments that the conflict occurred. There's a bad side to Saul's nature, and once he sensed that the production wasn't going to work, he was quite capable of ruthless indifference to human values—to the point where I had to prevent him from working with us in the theater."

The Last Analysis opened on October 1, and the reviews were savage. *Time* derided the play as "claptrap." *Newsweek* said it had "committed suicide before its assassination." Walter Kerr, the powerful critic of the *Herald Tribune*, attributed the play's failure to Bellow's "almost frightening naivete as a dramatist." The trouble with *The Last Analysis*, as Kerr saw it, was that the playwright had no idea what he was trying to achieve. Was Bummidge a comedian? A philosopher? A fraud? "Bellow sayeth not. Levene sayeth not. Director Joseph Anthony sayeth not."

There was some faint praise amid all the damnation. Howard Taubman, the *New York Times* reviewer, responded warmly to the play's vitality and wit, "the work of a true writer." The *New York Post* credited its "hearty hilarity." The most temperate review came from Robert Brustein, Bellow's recent neighbor on the Vineyard, who saw the failure of *The Last Analysis* as less Bellow's failure than Broadway's. "There is an awful lot of noise issuing from the stage of the Belasco these days," he wrote in *The New Republic,* "but the loudest explosion of all can be heard only with the inner ear: it comes from the head-on collision of a gifted writer, Saul Bellow, with the crassness and incompetence of the whole commercial theater system." Brustein also faulted the critics: "The next time these men begin asking 'Where are the playwrights?' let them look at the corpses they have buried under their own reviews."

In his preface to the Viking edition of the play, Bellow good-naturedly acknowledged the "cluttered and inconsequent plot, which puzzled the audience (and even the playwright)," but he claimed to have learned from the experience: "The rehearsals, the previews, the cold and peevish first-night audience, the judgments of the critics, were of the greatest value to me." This equanimity emerged in retrospect; at the time, he was deeply wounded by "the quantity of spittle." His play was in part a victim of revenge; the huge success of *Herzog* had provoked the critics to cut him down to size. "There was something like a riot," he claimed, on the night when Sam Levene stepped out on stage at the Belasco and announced the play's demise. "People started to pass the hat." Levene even offered to forgo his salary. It was no use. *The Last Analysis* closed after only twenty-eight performances. Like the messenger whom Bummidge implores to strangle him ("Choke me!"), the critics who panned *The Last Analysis* were provoked to spoil the triumph of *Herzog.* In the midst of his most unequivocal success, Bellow had contrived to fail.

20

One of the ironies of literary history most likely to be discussed in the future will be the fact that a book so private as to constitute a parallel to Rousseau's Confessions should have become a record breaking best-seller.

—ROSETTE LAMONT,
"The Confessions of Moses Herzog"

I T WAS SURPRISING ENOUGH that after two decades of struggling from book to book, Bellow hit the bestseller list with his most cerebral, "difficult" novel. What he found even more astonishing—apart from its sheer volume—was the intensely personal nature of the correspondence forwarded to him in bundles by his publisher. "I received two or three thousand letters from people pouring out their souls to me, saying 'This is my life, this is what it's been like for me.' And then I understood that for some reason these themes were visited upon me, that I didn't always pick them, they picked me."

Female readers, perhaps excited by the photographs of the handsome, silver-haired author, were especially assiduous, "writing to ask me how they should behave with intellectuals, for recipes of dishes mentioned in the book," Bellow confided to Robert Cromie, the host of a Chicago TV show called *Book Beat*. "They make me feel like an editor of *Vogue*." But it was more than Ramona's recipe for shrimp Arnaud that they were after. *Herzog* was a book that reflected the temper of its time.

The novel's premise—a beleaguered academic on the verge of a nervous breakdown embarks on a program of writing polemical letters "to everyone under the sun"—had great comic potential. Moses Herzog, feeling a need "to have it out, to justify, to put in perspective, to clarify, to make amends," writes "endlessly, fantastically, to the newspapers, to people in public life, to friends and relatives and at last to the dead," indulging in a mixture of "clairvoyance and spleen, *esprit d'escalier,* noble inspiration, poetry and nonsense, ideas, hyperaesthesia." Narrative was never Bellow's strong suit; in writing a novel with strong epistolary elements, he could make digression part of the story.*

Once Bellow had stumbled upon this conceit, Herzog's letters spilled forth in profusion: to Jung; to the Maryland police; to the makers of Quaker Oats ("Dear Sirs: It disturbs me from time to time that you should advertise your puffed wheat as Shot from Guns, under the brand name of Quaker"). At some point, as version after version piled up, Bellow incorporated "Memoirs of a Bootlegger's Son," the manuscript about his Montreal childhood that he'd abandoned in the fifties. The title also went through many drafts, from "Hertzog" to "Some Bones to Pick" to "Alas and Hurray." (He also thought of calling it "The Fornicator.") One thing never changed: the opening sentence. "If I am out of my mind, it's all right with me, thought Moses Herzog."

Herzog essentially related the story of Bellow's cuckolding by Jack Ludwig. In the early drafts, Bellow's rage toward Juliana and Grenzbach (as the characters Madeleine and Gersbach were called in early drafts) is out of control; in one scene, Herzog imagines Grenzbach "leaping on my wife and smearing himself with the saliva of her open mouth and in her juices." The sex scenes were notably explicit—"Antaeus, but covered with schmutz," as Bellow described the book to Richard Stern, managing in a single phrase to invoke both his classical and Yiddish roots.

He omitted even the pretext of transitions from scene to scene ("Herzog abandoned this theme with characteristic abruptness"; "Abruptly he broke off"). Yet it is his most *written* book: His always keen eye missed nothing—the lights in Grand Central Station, "like drops of fat in yellow broth"; the industrial wasteland of New Jersey glimpsed from a train window, "volcanic

---

*The name Moses Herzog appears on the first page of the "Cyclops" episode of *Ulysses;* when the Joyce scholar William York Tindall wrote to Bellow, pointing out this coincidence, Bellow replied that "it must have happened subliminally."

shapes of slag, rushes, dumps, refineries, ghostly torches"; the harbor at Woods Hole, its "stony bottom webbed with golden lines." Chicago, that "clumsy, stinking, tender" city, had never been rendered more compellingly. Driving with his daughter, Junie, Herzog catalogs the city, "familiar ground to him for more than thirty years," with a deep, almost instinctual sense of place:

> And out of its elements, by this peculiar art of his own organs, he created his version of it. Where the thick walls and buckled slabs of pavement in the Negro slums exhaled their bad smells. Farther West, the industries; the sluggish South Branch dense with sewage and glittering with a crust of golden slime; the Stockyards, deserted; the tall red slaughterhouses in lonely decay; and then a faintly buzzing dullness of bungalows and scrawny parks; and vast shopping centers; and the cemeteries after these—Waldheim, with its graves for Herzogs past and present; the Forest Preserves for riding parties, Croatian picnics, lovers' lanes, horrible murders; airports; quarries; and, last of all, cornfields. And with this, infinite forms of activity—Reality.

For all its hero's defiant secularity, *Herzog* is also an anthropological record of American Jewish life—particularly of Chicago Jewish life. The vulgar, tart-tongued lawyers in their wood-paneled clubs; the Yiddish-speaking old aunts in their Northwest Side bungalows and suburban homes equipped with new Westinghouses and French provincial furniture—Bellow recorded the characteristics of this distinctive social type with the same zeal that Melville Herskovits had once applied to the Arnewi of East Africa.

In life, the Bellows were a contentious bunch, always quarreling over money or slights to pride, both real and imagined. But when Bellow wrote about his family, it was with an emotional hunger that verged on sentimentality. "Potato love," Herzog's name for the "amorphous, swelling, hungry, indiscriminate" affection for brothers and relatives, suffuses his portrait of his Russian-Jewish clan. It is perhaps a weakness of the book that Herzog sees himself exclusively as a sensitive, warmhearted soul. "By God, Will, I'm about to cry!" he exclaims to his younger brother. "How did that happen? I won't do it. It's only love. Or something that bears down like love." Likewise, he lavishes love on his children but rarely sees them. Herzog, like so many of Bellow's heroes, is the sensitive one. Never questioning his own probity—philandering and breaking up his first marriage apparently don't count—he's a tireless moralist. His ambition, he tells his friend Luke Asphalter, is "to force Madeleine and Gersbach to have a *Conscience*." *Herzog* is a sustained exercise in self-vindication. As Bellow's niece Lynn Rotblatt put it, offering a succinct critique of the book: "Enough already." Yet Rotblatt marveled at his description of her grandfather's house on the North Side: "The crescent moon in the doorbell, the chimes that play 'Merrily We Roll Along,' his stepmother's shuffling footsteps in her slippers—I'm reading this and the tears are rolling down my face. He was writing my life. That's when I knew he was a genius."

The genius and the self-regard are of a piece. The solicitude Bellow displayed toward his male characters didn't extend to his women characters, except the elderly ones. Madeleine, Herzog's adulterous wife, is a magnificently imperious character, but she's *too* masterful, too much the spoiled bitch, running up a charge account at Marshall Field, throwing tantrums, disparaging her timid husband's prowess in bed. (Bellow later admitted that he was "blind with rage" when he wrote those passages.) The other women in his life exist only to serve Herzog's needs. Their primary function is to kindle Herzog's sexual reflex, "the old quack-quack at the fragrance of perfumed, feminine skin." *

As usual, Bellow made no effort to disguise the models of his characters—and they weren't pleased. "I'm not just a flower girl," complained Rosette Lamont, the basis of Herzog's hot-blooded mistress, Ramona. Jonas Schwartz, the Minneapolis lawyer who had represented Sondra in the divorce, was furious to find himself represented as the hectoring, dwarfish Sandor Himmelstein. "Have you read *Herzog*?" he ranted to Bellow's lawyer, John Goetz, grabbing him by the lapels in an elevator: "He makes me into a son of a bitch." Only Ludwig was reported to be happy with

---

*In later years, Bellow came under angry attack from feminists—most notably Vivian Gornick in *The Village Voice*—who were offended, justifiably, by the way he depicted women in his novels. There is a sameness to the wives and girlfriends who populate his books, harassing his women-baffled heroes. From the bitter Iva of *Dangling Man* to the brutal, emasculating Madeleine of *Herzog*, the wives in Bellow's novels come off as harpies, while the mistresses—the buxom, lingerie-sporting Ramona in *Herzog*, the hot number Renata Flonzaley in *Humboldt's Gift*—exhibit an intimidating sexual rapacity.

his likeness. "I'm Valentine Gersbach," he boasted to his students, predicting that someday he would show up "in a lot of books."

Bellow made no secret of the fact that his work drew heavily upon his life. "When a writer runs out of other people to write about there's no reason why he can't use himself," he said. But it annoyed him when people asked if *Herzog* was autobiographical. "It's very hard for any person to give a real account of his or her life," he told a classroom at Franklin and Marshall College. "You try it sometime. You'll find out how hard it is." And when he heard that his friend Ben Nelson, a medieval historian, was going around claiming to be Herzog, he snapped, "Maybe he is." (It was a rather baffling claim; Nelson was instantly recognizable to friends as Shapiro, the gluttonous pedant.)*

In the end, as the critic Stanley Edgar Hyman argued, Herzog was "a self-caricature, not a self-portrait." Yet the novel captures the emotional truth of Bellow's life: the discovery that, like Herzog, he was a man both "mother-bound" and "his father's son," condemned to reenact the pattern of betrayal and rejection passed from one generation to the next. The power of *Herzog*, its purity of style, derives in large measure from its self-knowledge, its awareness of the person its author had become. Hyman, whose achievements as a critic have been insufficiently appreciated, saw this clearly: "Bellow has developed one aspect of himself—his guilt and desperation—into a character and a story."

Bellow had had no great expectations for *Herzog*, predicting it would sell maybe eight thousand copies. He'd been disappointed

---

*Like much great fiction, *Herzog* was a transmutation of its author's life into something with a life of its own. Bellow used himself as material, but details were changed when doing so suited his artistic purpose. He had grown up on Saint Dominique Street in Montreal, but he put the Herzogs a block over, on Napoleon—"a name," noted Theodore Solotaroff, "that evokes not only one of the archetypal figures of Romantic individualism but also the Code that enabled the Jews to leave their ghettoes and enter the mainstream of Western culture and history on which Herzog feels himself being swept along." Bellow also appropriated from other sources, most notably a key passage in which Herzog recalls the time his dying mother rubbed her hands together, producing a thin film of dirt to show him what man is made of: It was lifted practically verbatim from Freud's *Interpretation of Dreams*.

too many times, and how many people would want to read a book about an obscure academic who writes letters to the dead? No one was more stunned than he was by its success. *Herzog* spent forty-two weeks on the bestseller list and sold 142,000 copies in hardcover. Its popularity increased the demand for Bellow's earlier works. In October, New American Library paid $77,000 for the paperback rights to his first two books; two weeks later, Fawcett bought the paperback rights to *Herzog* and *The Adventures of Augie March* for the then-stupefying sum of $371,350. Suddenly, at the late age of forty-nine and after a lifetime of financial struggle, Bellow was a wealthy man. "The kid finally did it," commented his brother Maurice. Between his royalties and his salary, he was making so much money that his accountants frantically tried to hide it, "averaging" his income. In December, Bellow returned a five-thousand-dollar award from *Kenyon Review* with a gracious note acknowledging his year of "unprecedented prosperity." In need of tax deductions, he donated the manuscripts of *Augie* and *Henderson* to the University of Chicago library. The house in Tivoli he gave to Bard, furniture and all.*

Herzog wasn't Bellow's triumph alone; Pat Covici savored it just as keenly. He and Viking had supported Bellow for a decade with advances that had never come close to earning out; before the new book's rise to the top of the bestseller list, Bellow was ten thousand dollars in debt to his publisher. Covici had never given up. "You are both my joy and despair," he had written his tempestuous author in the winter of 1961. "Joy because I find exhilaration and excitement in you, despair because life runs too fast and I am in constant fear that I might not see your next." *Herzog* was dedicated to Covici, "a great editor and, better yet, a generous friend."

Early in October 1964, Covici dropped dead of a heart attack. He had lived long enough to witness his author's triumph but not the full extent of his success. "I loathe funerals and wasn't planning to attend," Bellow wrote the novelist Norman Rosten, "but I did love the old man dearly and at the last minute I found I was

---

*Reamer Kline, the president of Bard, wrote Bellow an ecstatic letter of gratitude, pointing out that "its service as part of the background for Herzog gives promise of its becoming one of the 'famous houses' of American literature."

unable to sit it out in Chicago." His moving eulogy described a loyal friend and editor who "twice every day, morning and evening, went down into the streets with his briefcase full of papers. Disregarding lights and horns, he strode among the cars and buses, the fine white hair floating from his head as he whistled on his fingers for a taxi." The loss was a tremendous blow; Covici had been a father figure, a sympathetic older man who gave Bellow the encouragement his own father never had.

In December, while *Herzog* was still riding high on the bestseller list, the Modern Language Association held its annual convention in New York. Among the many panels was one chaired by Irving Howe entitled "Topics in Modern Literature." Scheduled for a small conference room, the panel was moved to the main ballroom when word got out that it was to feature a talk entitled "Bellow, Mailer, and Ellison" by a professor from the State University of New York at Stony Brook: Jack Ludwig. "Preliminary rumors hinted that this one would set off fireworks, and almost 1,000 members turned out to watch them," reported Lewis Nichols in *The New York Times Book Review.* "Alas, it did not."

Two months later, his chutzpah undiminished, Ludwig reviewed the book in *Holiday,* comparing it with *Ulysses* in the scope of its achievement. Then, as if to clear his own name, he went on to rebut the suspicion that *Herzog* was autobiographical, "as if an artist of Bellow's enormous gifts were simply playing at second-guessing reality, settling scores and justifying the ways not only of Moses to Saul, but of Saul to Moses." *Herzog,* Ludwig grandly asserted, was above all "a novel."

"It's a masterpiece in its own way," Bellow wrote Alfred Kazin of Ludwig's review, "a great virtuoso performance on the high-wire of self-justification, ingenious, shrewd, supersubtle, shamanistic, Rasputin-like. I'm really rather proud of the man. His cast-iron effrontery is admirable, somehow. If I ever commission a private Mt. Rushmore I'll stipulate that his head be given plenty of space. Anyway, don't miss this performance."

On March 17, 1965, Bellow was in New York again to collect his second National Book Award. In his acceptance speech, he sounded a Herzogian note, calling upon writers to reject the pretentious modernist credo that relegated them to the margins of society: "Without the common world the novelist is nothing but a curiosity and will find himself in a glass case along some dull museum corridor of the future." Having achieved a height of success beyond anything he'd ever dreamed, he still found it difficult to give up the role of *gegner*—againstnik. The public commotion over *Herzog* was "far beyond anything I ever projected or wanted," Bellow told Jack Mabley, a columnist for the *Chicago Sun-Times*. Success had a destabilizing effect on him; after so many years of struggling to become a writer, he was more comfortable with opposition. Now there was nothing to resist.

Perplexed to find himself "part of the 'literary establishment,'" Bellow worried that all the attention would go to his head. He wasn't ready to become an institution and lose his anonymity, as Arthur Miller had done; writers were by nature solitaries, eccentrics. In January, he turned down an invitation to Lyndon B. Johnson's inauguration, not wanting to be seen as a "cultural ornament." And when the Midland Authors' Society bestowed upon him a five-hundred-dollar award for *Herzog* at a city hall ceremony, he was delighted by Mayor Richard Daley's response to a reporter who asked him if he'd read it. "I've looked into it," said Daley, a master of evasion. "Art is not the Mayor's dish," Bellow told a reporter. "But why should it be? I much prefer his neglect to the sort of interest Stalin took in poetry, phoning Pasternak to chat with him about Mandelstam and, shortly afterwards, sending Mandelstam to die."

Not that Bellow kept a low profile in Chicago. He appeared on *Kup's Show*, a popular local TV program hosted by the columnist and man-about-town Irv Kupcinet, and was frequently mentioned in the gossip columns of the *Sun-Times* and the *Tribune* (sometimes as "Saul Bellows"). He was what Chicagoans call a "notable." He managed to convince himself and others that he was a diffident, reclusive artist even as he sat for journalists and television commentators; nearly every interview with Bellow—and there were many over the years—began by claiming that he granted few interviews. Many years later, in a malicious story entitled "Another Rare Visit with Noah Danzig," Joseph Epstein described a long interview with a fictionalized Bellow, noting that "over the years there would be no fewer than 235 such 'rare visits' in print." Epstein scarcely exaggerated. Bellow ignored most letters requesting interviews, claiming not to have received them, but he was gregarious and loved to discourse on his favorite subjects to just about anyone who would listen. In the sixties, he gave sixteen interviews; in the seventies, he gave even more.

In the spring of 1965, *Glamour* sent Gloria Steinem to Chicago to spend a day with "the publicity-shy novelist." Steinem's profile was respectful to the point of reverence, but it captured aspects of Bellow's character that seldom came through in newspaper interviews, where he tended to rely on the same few anecdotes and axioms. His spontaneous, bantering, frequently hostile wit was much in evidence. Noting that Nelson Algren had made a speech against capital punishment, Bellow, "looking kindly," observed that he thought Algren was the biggest argument *for* capital punishment he knew. And when the talk turned to Richard Poirier's cranky review of *Herzog*, Bellow patiently explained, "I'm fair game now. I'm on top and must be cut down." Steinem asked where Poirier taught. "Harvard, of course," Bellow answered in a scornful tone of voice.*

Steinem made much of Bellow's sartorial elegance. He looked "natty and not at all provincial in a dark brown suit, sunglasses and a narrow-brimmed hat," she noted approvingly: "Mr. Bellow makes it clear by his careful dress that he is vain of his looks. But by exaggerating that care just a little (he must surely be one of the few native-born Americans who can effect a walking stick—not a cane, but an elegant stick too thin for anything but gesturing), he seems to be making his vanity a small joke and inviting onlookers to share it." By the time of *Herzog*, Bellow had adopted the mode of dress that came to be identified with him in the decades to follow—it could almost be called Chicagowear. His wardrobe verged on the outlandish: green-checked sports jackets, tasseled socks, blue suede shoes, a battered Borsalino. "He dressed like a

---

*Like Harry Levin, the distinguished professor whom Bellow insisted on referring to as "a Harvard kike," Poirier was anathema to Bellow on account of his affiliation with the Ivy League.

tout," said one of his students—"a tout who's just lost six races in a row." Like his wisecracking, it was a style designed to forestall criticism by anticipating it—irony as a form of self-defense. But it was also an expression of Bellow's cultural innocence, mistaking extravagance for sophistication.

"As he nears fifty he looks considerably more benign than he used to," Alfred Kazin wrote in *The Atlantic Monthly* in January 1965, reminiscing about their early days in New York:

> Yet the elegant aptness of his most informal observations, though more brilliant than ever, still yields easily to that tragi-comic sense of buffoonery that urged some Yiddish genius to write: "If God lived on earth, His windows would always be broken." That wit is Bellow's habitat, and the terms of the joke are natural to him. The proud, moody, and handsome young writer who, like Joseph in the Bible, airily confided his dreams of greatness to his brothers has always been a man who suffers, as he would say, "in style"—with an air. In Bellow, anguish and wit have always been natural companions.

Success hadn't changed his old friend, Kazin noted. He was still the fresh and independent mind he had always been, "a scholar in the formidable University of Chicago style, full of the Great Books and jokes from the Greek plays"—in other words, a Chicago boy.

"I enjoyed seeing myself through your eyes in The Atlantic," Bellow wrote to Kazin that spring:

> Because I'm accustomed to run the portrait gallery myself, I was taken aback for a moment; then I grew accustomed to the novelty and thoroughly enjoyed it. You may have been a little too generous. I remember being a very arbitrary, overly assertive type. Maybe there was no other way, in the democratic-immigrant's-son situation, to obtain the required authority of tone. To me, now, the whole thing is a phenomenon; the *personal* element no longer counts for much. You were absolutely right about the Chicago side of things.

A public figure is invited to make public pronouncements, and Bellow's name now began to show up on lists of prominent intellectuals supporting one liberal cause or another. Like most writers of his generation, especially the old *Partisan Review* gang, he had put his radical days behind him. He was a strong supporter of SANE—the Committee for a Sane Nuclear Policy—and of civil rights. At the invitation of CORE, the Congress of Racial Equality, he drafted a preface to a book about the three Mississippi Freedom Summer volunteers who were brutally murdered in the summer of 1964, attesting to their courage and affirming his belief in the cause for which they died. (It was never published; a copy reposes among Bellow's papers at the University of Chicago library.) But he could no more be classified as a liberal than, a quarter of a century earlier, he could have been classified as a doctrinaire socialist. As always, he resisted the party line. In a letter to the *Chicago Sun-Times*, he objected to the unruly demonstrations that had marred a SANE rally in Washington, putting on record his opposition to civil disobedience "and to all the unreasonable forms of rebelliousness we have recently witnessed." At the same time, he defended the teach-ins and rallies that had broken out around the country in the spring of 1965 as legitimate expressions of dissent. "It would be very curious and very sad if all discussion of the political and moral meaning of the Vietnamese war were suppressed in the interests of solidarity with the Administration."

That June, Bellow accepted an invitation to a festival of the arts at the White House. The occasion had distinctly political overtones; Eric Goldman, a Princeton history professor and cultural advisor to President Johnson who organized the event, conceded that it was "a tool to quiet opposition to the war." Assembling the nation's top cultural emissaries at the White House would send a tacit signal of support for Lyndon Johnson's embattled administration. Goldman drew up a distinguished guest list that included Mark Van Doren, John Hersey, Edmund Wilson, Robert Lowell, and Bellow.

There was trouble from the start. Wilson, who enjoyed displaying his indifference to the blandishments of power, refused the White House's invitation, Goldman recalled, "with a brusqueness that I have never experienced before or after in the case of an invitation in the name of the President and First Lady." Lowell at first agreed to attend, then abruptly changed his mind and wrote a letter to the beleaguered president (copied to *The New York*

Times), protesting in high-flown rhetoric the direction of LBJ's foreign policy. Meanwhile, the poet Stanley Kunitz and Robert Silvers, the coeditor of *The New York Review of Books,* circulated a petition endorsing Lowell's stand. The *Times* made note of it on the front page, beneath the headline TWENTY WRITERS AND ARTISTS ENDORSE POET'S REBUFF OF PRESIDENT.

At this point, Bellow's nonjoining instincts were fully aroused. Once it was clear what he was expected to do, he reacted the way he generally did: against. Resentful of pressure from "the New York crowd," members of which were barraging him with telegrams and phone calls in an effort to dissuade him from attending, he dug in his heels. Bellow stressed that he thought the recent invasion of the Dominican Republic "wicked and harmful" and that he was against the war in Vietnam; but the White House festival was not "a political occasion." The president was "an institution" as well as a political figure, and President Johnson was seeking "in his own way to encourage American artists," Bellow told *The New York Times.* "I accept in order to show my respect for his intentions and to honor his high office. I am sure that he does not expect me to accept every policy and action of his Administration together with the invitation." It was an honorably high-principled position, even if it ignored the fact that the festival *was* "a political occasion."

But by the time he got to Washington on June 13, Bellow was "in a decidedly unsettled mood," recalled Goldman. He was stung by a sharp letter from Harvey Swados, castigating him for accepting the invitation. "Going to the White House in June 1965 is not an innocent amusement [but] an act of solidarity with those who will be bombing and shelling even as you read from your works to the assembled culture bureaucrats."

Bellow had long admired Swados's work and had published him in *The Noble Savage.* The rebuke smarted. "These quarrels are hateful," he replied from the Jefferson Hotel:

> I dislike the slap in the face formula and the implied responsibility for death in Vietnam. Let me at least make it clear that the glamor of power means little to me. More, I don't like what J. is doing in Vietnam and S. Domingo, though you and I might not agree in our criticisms. But I don't see that holding these posi-

tions requires me to treat Johnson like a Hitler. He's not that. He may be a brute in some ways (by no means all) but he is the President, and I haven't yet decided to go in for civil disobedience. Have you? You sound ready to stop paying taxes.

But—no quarrels. My attending a ceremony at the White House doesn't make a fink or criminal of me. Intellectuals, and esp. former Marxists, will really have to decide in the end what they think a government *is*.*

The festival was held on Monday, June 14, a fine summer day. The White House lawn was impressively adorned with abstract sculptures by Alexander Calder and David Smith. Bellow read from *Herzog*, Catherine Drinker Bowen read from her biography of Oliver Wendell Holmes, Jr., John Hersey read from *Hiroshima*. (The festival organizers had tried to persuade him to substitute a less charged work but to no avail.) Johnson, who was livid over the whole affair, put in a pointedly brief appearance. "They insult me by comin', they insult me by stayin' away," he railed.

One of Johnson's most vociferous opponents was Dwight Macdonald, who found himself in the awkward position of having signed the telegram protesting the festival the day before his invitation arrived in the mail. After much hand-wringing, Macdonald decided to attend but to use the event—in the words of his biographer—"to propagandize against Johnson's war." He drew up a petition of his own and circulated it during the event. Bellow remembered him, "tall, satyr-bearded, walking into the Rose Garden in sneakers, the great bohemian himself going around with a resolution endorsing Lowell's boycott."

Saul Maloff, a noisy ex-radical who edited the books column at *Newsweek* and had been sent to cover the event, was intent on a confrontation with Bellow. Maloff cornered his prey near the stairs to the East Room. "How could you stand there and read after what that man has done in Vietnam?" he upbraided Bellow. Bellow firmly reiterated his argument: He would air his views on foreign policy elsewhere. Maloff would not relent. "We made you, and we can break you," he muttered ominously.

---

*Looking back on this episode years later, Bellow softened his stand, attributing his intransigent behavior to "a weakness for stupid loftiness."

For Bellow, the episode confirmed his persistent suspicion that he was surrounded by resentment. Weeks later, he was still obsessed with the affair, recalled Robert Hatch, the editor of *The New Republic*. "He can't keep off the subject of Lowell or the New York intellectuals whom he sees as enemies," Hatch wrote to Macdonald from Martha's Vineyard. But Bellow was more exercised about income-tax law than about Johnson's escalation of the Vietnam War, according to Hatch: He had just written out a check to the Internal Revenue Service for forty thousand dollars—its share of his royalties for *Herzog*. He sounded ready to stop paying taxes himself.

On the Vineyard, there was a steady stream of visitors to the modest A-frame on Menemsha Pond that the Bellows had rented again that summer: the director Herbert Berghof and his wife, Uta Hagen, who were to play supporting roles in Bellow's theatrical career; the publisher Helen Wolff and the drama critic Robert Brustein. Lillian Hellman recruited the Bellows for her circle. "She was a horror," recalled Barbara Hanson, a recent Radcliffe graduate and the Bellows' au pair that summer. "She had a bourbon voice and a barrel body and long fingernails. She came over all the time. She wanted to be in Bellow's orbit."

Bellow wasn't interested in celebrity, according to Hanson; Susan was. "She just sort of swanned around; she *loved* being Mrs. Saul Bellow. It was her career. Susan wanted to go out to dinner all the time and play tennis with all the swells." Bellow wanted to work; he wrote every day from nine until one and made it clear that he wasn't to be disturbed. In her journal, Hanson noted: "Mr. Bellow is constantly reading." Outwardly, life appeared serene. Bellow was "cheerful." He was playful with Adam, who came to stay for a few weeks; Bellow pretended Adam was a flute, then a fiddle, then a guitar, and beat out the tune to "America the Beautiful" on his son's stomach.

Barbara Hanson was struck by Bellow's affection for Adam, the child of another marriage, whom he hadn't seen since Christmas. "I could sense Mr. Bellow's intense feeling of aloneness," she wrote in her journal:

It's all very sad—divorces and all. Mr. Bellow is one who loves his family, and as far as I can see it, his family now consists of himself and his sons. Granted, I'm sure he loves Mrs. Bellow, but there is *more* to his family than merely exists in this *particular* family consisting of Susan and Daniel. There's Gregory and Adam, too, but there again, it's oddly enough still not a whole family. He is the only connecting link between his three sons, and his family life will always be a bit incomplete.

There were other subtle signs of discord. Bellow was mired in "a Gobi desert of papers," he complained to his lawyer, Marshall Holleb, early in the summer. Susan, writing to Margaret Shafer, alluded lightly to "the usual storm of our domestic life." But she tried not to dwell on the arguments that broke out with increasing frequency; they were part of marriage. "People fight," she told Hanson. "It's a fact of life."

By the time Holleb and his wife, Doris, arrived for a visit in early August, it was apparent that things were deteriorating. Susan met them at the ferry in curlers, clearly out of sorts. Back at the house, Bellow let her know he felt embarrassed by her appearance. "It was one of the more unpleasant times," said Holleb. The visit was "a disaster." The Hollebs left after ten days, convinced the Bellows' marriage was over.

Flush with royalties from *Herzog*, the Bellows had purchased a co-op in a grand building at 5490 South Shore Drive, just a block from their old apartment and overlooking Jackson Park. (Their neighbors, Bellow reported to Ruth Miller, were all psychiatrists and "clap doctor magnates.") Susan aspired to have a salon and fitted out the apartment with furnishings she thought appropriate to a great writer. She spent money "like a drunken sailor," said her lawyer, George Feiwell: "It was decorate, decorate, decorate. She wanted the lifestyle she'd enjoyed as a child; he thought she was trying to spend him into the grave."

"When you walked into the living room," recalled another one of their lawyers—Bellow's life was sufficiently complicated now that he required several—"you felt like you were drowning in two feet of carpet." The furniture was plump and white. The hallway seemed to have more mirrors than Versailles. Bellow found this plush new environment stifling. Later on, he said he knew the marriage was doomed when he saw the study his wife had designed for him; it was done up like a nineteenth-century boudoir.

Bellow wanted desperately to have a home. Yet he found domestic life, especially Susan's bourgeois version of it, oppressive. "He couldn't breathe in that relationship," said Dave Peltz. When Peltz visited Bellow, they sat on a park bench across the street and Bellow was "nearly hyperventilating," Peltz recalled. "Sometimes it took him five minutes to recover."

One of the main drawbacks of marriage, as far as Bellow was concerned, was monogamy. As early as November 1962, less than a year into his third marriage, he was writing in a jocular tone to Jack Leggett at Harper and Row: "My wife wanted to know *whom* you had seen me with in Central Park. I don't take girls to Central Park. At my age one needs steam heated love." Pete Hamill, having interviewed Bellow at the Hotel Alden, referred obliquely in the *Herald Tribune* to his "companion." There was also the matter of a mysterious bill from the Hotel Allerton on North Michigan Avenue in Chicago, at a time when Bellow and Susan were still living in Hyde Park.

None of this constitutes evidence of infidelity, but Bellow made minimal effort to hide his affairs. Anthony Hecht once stayed with the couple in Chicago and shared a flight back to Newark with Bellow, who confided that he "had to get in his quota of adultery." They boarded a bus into the city, and when they got to the Port Authority terminal, Hecht had to wait for his bags to be unloaded; Bellow, meanwhile, had "cagily sneaked his bag into the overhead rack so he could beat it with the gorgeous blonde who had come to meet him. It was a scene out of a Bellow novel."

The gorgeous blonde was Maggie Staats—in the fictional scorecard of Bellow's women, Demmie Vonghel in *Humboldt's Gift*. They had met in New York at the home of Harold Taylor, the former president of Sarah Lawrence, early in 1966. Brendan Gill, Bellow's nemesis at *The New Yorker*, had escorted her to the party; she left with Bellow, accompanying her new catch to his room at the Plaza.

Bellow's portrait of Vonghel as a wild girl, descended from old American stock, was true to Staats's life, though it made her out to be less educated than Staats actually was.* After a brief stint in graduate school at Northwestern, where she had studied with the biographer Richard Ellmann, Staats had transferred to Yale, then gotten a job in the *New Yorker* typing pool. She was twenty-four when Bellow met her. Staats's WASP looks set her apart from Bellow's other women. "She is not beautiful," Mark Harris noted in his journal, "but she has an upturned nose, short straight hair, fitting the stereotype in face of a saucy barmaid." Bellow admired her self-reliance. "I was a pioneer, I was American," she said. "He was the Old Testament." Staats eventually moved into a studio apartment on the East Side, and Bellow flew in often from Chicago for the weekend.

Of all Bellow's lovers, Staats was the one he felt consistently most passionate about. His letters to her over the years are touchingly conventional love letters—vulnerable, tenderhearted, needy. He addressed her with endearments—"my lovelorn soul," "Maggie-o," "Y.D." [Your Darling]—and pined for her in the traditional language of the lovelorn: "I miss you so much, it's like sickness or hunger"; "Not to see you makes me suffer"; "With you I have a feeling I've never had before, that of being infinitely satisfied with another." He was bewildered by the intensity of his own feelings, surprised to find himself so unarmored against the disorienting power of love. "I didn't expect that my whole soul would go out like this to anyone," he wrote her during one of their separations: "That I would lie down and wake up by love instead of clocks." He was troubled by the gap in their ages: twenty-seven years. "My age, my situation! It is absurdity." He was insomniac, taking sleeping pills. But he was funny, too, excited by the novelty of his emotional state. "A cold coming we had of it," he wrote her once from midwinter Chicago, quoting Eliot's "Journey of the Magi"—then added, "Well, it's all cold and no coming."

---

*Bellow tended to subtly demote the women in his life when he put them in his books. His Tuley girlfriend Eleanor Fox, later on a junior high–school principal, became a crossing guard in *Humboldt's Gift*, and the shrewish Susan depicted in so many unflattering incarnations had a highly developed literary side.

It wasn't long before he began to think about marriage. "If we feel and mean what we say we had better be ready to do what's necessary." Staats wasn't ready—and never would be. Over the years, despite their marriages to other people, they talked about getting married. At one point, Bellow actually proposed to Staats and bought a ring from a jeweler in the Loop. But it wasn't to be, though she remained one of Bellow's closest friends through four marriages of her own. Bellow killed off Demmie Vonghel "in a plane crash in South America." Maggie Staats he resurrected fourteen years later as the stylish, high-powered executive Clara Velde in his novella *A Theft*.

Bellow's traumatic experience with *The Last Analysis* hadn't dimmed his enthusiasm for the genre. "I begin to think that the theater and I will never hit it off, and in all likelihood I shan't be bothering much more with it," he had written Toby Cole a few months after his play closed on Broadway. But he continued to bother with it a great deal. He negotiated (unsuccessfully) with the Guthrie Theatre in Minneapolis about a production of *The Last Analysis* and labored away on a stage version of *Seize the Day*; it was performed at the Theatre of Ideas, an avant-garde workshop, with Herbert Berghof directing and Mike Nichols in the role of Tommy Wilhelm. Another director, Nancy Walker, flew to Chicago early in 1965 to consult with Bellow about putting on his work Off-Broadway. "Not only did her approach seem right to me," Bellow reported to his agent, "but in conversation she stirred my imagination so that on the spot I dreamed up two one-acters, which I promised to deliver next month."

He was true to his word, writing two plays, "Orange Soufflé" and "Out from Under," and also finishing revisions on a third, "The Wen," which appeared in *Esquire* in January 1965. A fourth play from this prolific period, "A Work of Art," survives in draft; it was never produced. "I enjoy writing these trifles," Bellow admitted to Toby Cole. They were "a holiday from responsibility and earnestness." (On the title page of the manuscript of "A Work of Art," he described it as "Silliness in one act.")

Despite their insubstantiality, Bellow's new plays achieved a kind of intermittent life over the years, being produced as a trilogy both in England and in America, and—some years later—at the Spoleto Festival in Italy, under the direction of Gian Carlo Menotti. Bellow himself had no great opinion of them. He was enthusiastic when his agent proposed signing up Shelley Winters for the lead, but he had scaled down his theatrical aspirations since he'd held out for Zero Mostel in *The Last Analysis:* "Aren't we low on the scale for the likes of her?"

Winters had appeared in Stanley Kubrick's movie version of *Lolita*. Bellow defensively dismissed Nabokov's novel: "Suppose we admit it's not too horrible for middle-aged men to copulate with small girls, do we then have to make a philosophy of it? I could write a better book from Lolita's point of view."* In a way, his plays were an effort to do just that—or at least to concede that she might have one (a remarkable admission for Bellow). They were all, in some form, about the complex moral negotiations between men and women, and none of them showed the men in particularly favorable light. "Orange Soufflé" revolves around the stinginess of a rich codger toward the prostitute who's been servicing him for years. "Out from Under" is about a timid man who on his wedding eve performs the first rebellious act of his life by letting the air out of the tires of a car that's clogging his street—a tart commentary on the way some grooms drag their heels on the way to the altar; they'll do anything to get out of it. (The fiancée's name is Flora Molar, undoubtedly meant to suggest that women land prospective husbands by getting their teeth into them.) In "A Wen," Solomon Ithimar, an eminent physicist, tracks down a childhood girlfriend, Marcella Vankuchen, in a "third-class" Miami Beach hotel, intent on verifying his memory of a birthmark in a once-forbidden zone that transfixed him in their youth. Ithimar, now "a Stockholm laureate," is a compulsive, more neurotic version of Bellow; for all his worldly fame, he's still Little Iggy, "the kid who put our neighborhood on the map." There's something at once touching and self-involved about his obsession with

---

*Bellow's hostility to Nabokov was vehemently reciprocated. "Saul Bellow, a miserable mediocrity, should never have appeared on the jacket of a book about me," he protested to his publisher apropos a blurb Bellow had given to Carl Proffer's *Keys to Lolita*. "Is it too late to eliminate that exhaust puff?"

his high-school sweetheart, now the fat wife of a chiropodist: It's not sex that Ithimar is after so much as the recovery of his own past.

Presented at the Fortune Theatre in London during the summer of 1966 with a new title, *Under the Weather,* the trilogy received mildly favorable reviews. "Occasionally delectable, sometimes irritating, but always worth seeing," concluded *The Evening Standard,* summing up the general view. They fared less well in New York, where they opened at the Cort Theatre on October 27 with Shelley Winters and Harry Towb. Bellow, accompanied by Maggie Staats, sat in the back row, right behind the critics. "Fifteen minutes into the play it was clear this was a dog," recalled Marshall Holleb, who had invested money in the production. "I could hear the critics muttering."

Afterward, the playwright adjourned to Sardi's with a large party to await the critics' verdict. The reviews were punishing. "The atmosphere was casual, trivial, a trace condescending, as though Mr. Bellow hadn't really had much time to devote to the intricacies of a secondhand and not particularly distinguished form," wrote *The New York Times*'s Walter Kerr. *The New Yorker*'s theater critic, Edith Oliver, voiced the same complaint: "Apparently, Mr. Bellow believes that it is a good idea to earn while you learn, and although his first full-length exercise, 'The Last Analysis,' was a full-blown disaster when exhibited on Broadway in 1964, he has gamely come on once again to show us how he is progressing in his studies."

Whatever he may have learned from the experience, Bellow earned nothing; in fact, he took a substantial loss, forfeiting the five thousand dollars he'd put up, along with the investments of his partners, Holleb and Dave Peltz. The show closed in less than two weeks.

In contrast to his plays, Bellow's prose—essays, reviews, and lectures—had acquired an almost vatic solemnity. "I dislike making statements about a literary development that depends on the imagination and will have no real existence until imagination has brought it forth," he wrote Harold Rosenberg. "*Herzog* may change the picture, my arguments in *Encounter*, never." In other words, art spoke louder than criticism. All the same, he was skilled in polemic. Like Wyndham Lewis, whose work he cited often, Bellow was an able interpreter of his own practice—"the outstanding 'theoretician' among the major novelists of our period," according to the critic Nathan Scott—even if he made it clear that the business of the writer was to write, not to theorize.

In a short-lived journal of the arts called *Location*, edited by Rosenberg and Thomas Hess, Bellow offered a forceful refutation of the "hollow-man version of things" put forward by Eliot, Pound, Joyce, Yeats, and company: "The 'doom of the West' is the Established Church in modern literature." The revulsion toward modern civilization had become a literary convention, Bellow claimed. "Common commodities, chainstores, cheap hotels, empty city lots, subway cars, graveyards for automobiles, Main Street, Coney Island: they are recognized as soon as they are mentioned because Realism has given them a color which is not easily changed." It was the artist's job to oppose such reductive associations, not to foreclose judgment on the capacities of humanity. Art wasn't "diagnostic"; its purpose was to represent experience on the artist's terms. All the rest was artificial speculation, "culture-history." Bellow had been refining these ideas since the days when the Russian Literary Society met at a Division Street hot-dog stand. Their later development owed a great deal to Rosenberg, a first-rate polemicist whose column on contemporary art in *The New Yorker* during the fifties and sixties must be counted one of the intellectual achievements of the age. Rosenberg was so impressed with Bellow's mastery of ideas that he urged him to give up fiction and concentrate on critical prose.

The practitioners of "culture-history" increasingly became the objects of Bellow's wrath, especially the ones who practiced this specious discipline within the confines of the academy. In "Skepticism and the Depth of Life," a lecture he gave at colleges around the country during the sixties, Bellow argued that "universities had no such thing as a unified intellectual life." Professors were "manufacturers of intellectual opinion," "agents, managers or impresarios of Henry James or the French Symbolists," he complained, sounding a note first heard a decade earlier in "The

University as Villain." They constituted a new professional elite—what Bellow, appropriating a term of Stendhal's, derisively called "the happy few of culture." Greenwich Village, once a haven for writers, had been relocated to the perimeter of the university: Berkeley, Harvard Square, Hyde Park. The university was to the writer, declared Bellow, what the reservation was to the Indian. Creative-writing courses were "psychiatric case work." That Bellow himself made a living as a professor seemed not to have occurred to him—if it did, he exempted himself on unspecified and unstated grounds.

But it wasn't only the university that posed a threat to the creative artist, in his view. Editors and journalists—"culture-bureaucrats," he called them—were just as exploitative. If criticism had been taken over by tenured professors, the freelance intellectual of an earlier generation was now in journalism or the mass media. New York was no longer the center of culture, Bellow charged in "Skepticism and the Depth of Life"; it was the center of "the publicity industry." The literary intellectual was obsolete. Writers in turn had become commodities, "a privileged class, a breed of holy men. Artists are more envied than millionaires. They are beyond authority; for them the rules are waived."

He could be startlingly blunt. Delivering the keynote address at the PEN Congress in New York in June 1966, he told a large audience at New York University's Loeb Student Center: "We have at present a large literary community and something we can call, faute de mieux, a literary culture, in my opinion a very bad one." Yet there was something curious about Bellow's animus toward the very cultural institutions that had showered praise on him. (Morris Dickstein, commenting in *Partisan Review* on Bellow's PEN speech, went so far as to call it "paranoid.") Early in his career, Bellow had been angry that he wasn't recognized; now that he was recognized, he was angry that he was misunderstood. It was a challenge to remain embattled when so many were ready to embrace.

Bellow regarded Chicago as a refuge from the glare of publicity, but it was harder now to hold the world at bay. In the spring of

1966, he was presented with the James L. Dow Award at the Sheraton-Chicago Hotel and awarded the ten-thousand-dollar Prix Internationale de Littérature (also known as the Formentor Prize) in a ceremony at the offices of Grove Press in New York. A poll taken by the *Chicago Sun-Times Book Week* found that Bellow, by a wide margin, had written "the most distinguished fiction of the 1945–1965 period."* In the same poll, three of his six books (*Herzog, Seize the Day,* and *Henderson the Rain King*) were voted among the "best" novels of the postwar years.

Bellow proclaimed himself wary of this tendency to lionize. In 1965 he "sat for" his *Paris Review* interview—one of the rituals in a significant literary career. When the interviewer asked if the fairly recent deaths of Hemingway and Faulkner had created a "vacuum" in American literature that Bellow would be required to fill—a recurrent theme by now—he answered graciously:

> Well, I don't know whether I would say a vacuum. Perhaps a pigeonhole. I agree that there is a need to keep the pigeonholes filled and that people are uneasy when there are vacancies. Also the mass media demand material—grist—and literary journalists have to create a major-league atmosphere in literature. The writers don't offer to fill the pigeonholes. It's the critics who want figures in the Pantheon. But there are many people who assume that every writer must be bucking for the niche. Why should writers wish to be rated—seeded—like tennis players? Handicapped like racehorses? What an epitaph for a novelist: "He won all the polls"!

Unlike so many of his tragic predecessors, for whom success itself became a hazard—F. Scott Fitzgerald, wrecked by hackwork and drink; Faulkner, squandering his genius in Hollywood; Hemingway, destroyed by his own myth—Bellow adapted easily to fame. "*Herzog* hasn't changed my life so much," he told Gloria Steinem. Apart from the new suits in his closet and his new co-op and a new car—"a modest, American-made sedan"—he showed

---

*The survey offered a revealing portrait of American fiction in the postwar era. Just below Bellow were Nabokov, Faulkner, Malamud, Salinger, Ellison, Mailer, and Hemingway. Of the "20 Best Books," *Herzog* ranked fourth, after *Invisible Man, Lolita,* and *The Catcher in the Rye.*

few signs of outward alteration. Successful writers, he noted in a lecture called "The Arts and the Public," which he delivered around this time, are transformed into major literary figures and for the rest of their lives do little more than give solemn interviews to prestigious journals or serve on White House committees or fly to the Bermudas to participate in international panel discussions on the crisis in the arts. The writer is eclipsed by the celebrity.

Bellow was adept at managing both. If he was comfortable in his new role, it was because, on some level, it fit his self-image, ratifying his conviction that he had been destined for greatness: Fame was only the world's belated confirmation of S. Bellow's genius. As far as he was concerned, nothing had changed. "The writer will have to believe that what he writes will evoke a public, that it will be summoned up by the force of his truth," he concluded in his 1966 PEN Congress address. "The forms he invents will create a new public."

On the day he was to be awarded the Formentor Prize, Bellow decided to buy a pair of new shoes for the occasion. But he couldn't very well show up at such a solemn event with a pair of old shoes in his briefcase. As he stood in front of the New York Public Library with Rosette Lamont and his friend Paolo Milano, waiting for a bus down to Grove's office in the Village, he decided to put the old shoes on the library steps and see if anyone claimed them. They watched for a few minutes, but none of the bums hanging around paid any attention to Bellow's offering. As the trio boarded the bus, Milano said, "I guess there isn't anyone ready to step into Saul Bellow's shoes."

21

My life is a mess like everyone else's.

—*Bellow to a reporter*

MARRIAGE, BELLOW MAINTAINED, was a state of war. And in the chronology of his life, 1966 marked the outbreak of new hostilities. The precipitating event, according to subsequent family lore, was Susan's discovery that an unfamiliar phone number was showing up with suspicious frequency on the Bellows' monthly bill. It belonged to Maggie Staats. "I don't want to talk about it," Bellow said when Susan confronted him.

At the same time, he was fending off Sondra, who kept furnishing his lawyer with itemized lists of Adam's expenses, from "juice" to "bowling" to "Adam's cat." When could she expect reimbursement for the cello she'd bought? What about the boy's music lessons? What about the dentist's bills? "I should like Mr. Bellow to send me $150 in addition to the $250 for JUNE so that I might get Adam his summer and camp clothes immediately," began one of her astringent communications to his lawyer, Marshall Holleb: "If he should prefer to do this himself, I will send Adam with the three pairs of shorts he now owns and a camp list, and he and Mrs. Bellow can sew on nametapes, shorten clothes and pack his trunk." Once Sondra called Holleb from a pay phone to hector him about unpaid bills; another time, he recalled, she showed up at his office looking like "a latter-day Ophelia." "I'm not as bad as you think," she said plaintively. "I've had a bad press."

Bellow's response to these marital and postmarital crises was to flee. To further complicate his life, he had taken on an assignment from *Life* to write a profile of Robert F. Kennedy. For a week in June, the novelist tagged after the politician, notebook in hand. It was a frustrating experience. "Every other sentence was off-the-record," Bellow recalled. "He would say all kinds of things about Johnson, then say 'Don't quote me.'" Kennedy made use of him as an intellectual tutor. "He had a lot of catching up to do: 'Tell me about Veblen, Walter Lippmann, H. L. Mencken.'"

Bellow also interviewed Kennedy's former sister-in-law, Jackie Kennedy. She had read his most recent book. "I feel sorry for the author of *Herzog*," she told him condescendingly. Mrs. Kennedy made it clear that she thought Bellow was out of his depth writing about the Kennedys. He would never be able to understand a man like Joe Kennedy, she said—"meaning," Bellow recalled, "'What do you Chicago Jew boys know about an Irish Catholic who would buy the Presidency for his son?'" In the end, Bellow abandoned the profile; he liked Kennedy too much to write about him.

After a month in East Hampton at a cinder-block house on Louse Point Road—"a very agreeable place notwithstanding the name"—he was off to London, where he gave a lecture at the American embassy, "scurrying out at the end before the audience could leave their seats," according to a reporter from *The Observer* who provided a trenchant sketch of the novelist: "He affects a rather folksy American look, wearing black boots, a rumpled suit, and undoing his collar before speaking. He smiles a lot, particularly at his own jokes, speaks quietly, and doesn't give much of himself away."

It was a triumphant visit. *Herzog* was "the rage of London." The reviews were "solemn to the point of stupidity," Bellow wrote self-deprecatingly to Toby Cole, but he was quietly gratified to have such estimable reviewers as George Steiner and V. S. Pritchett celebrating his achievement. After a brief stop in the Netherlands—"Holland Mich[igan] was never like this," he gloated on a postcard to Sam Freifeld—he continued on to Poland, where he had research to do for his work in progress, a novel that turned in part on the experiences of a Polish Jew during World War II.

By the time he got back to Chicago, it was clear that his marriage was over. It had lasted four years—roughly the length of his previous marriage. The end was undramatic, Susan recalled. Bellow simply "moved out." His grounds were that she nagged him, made unreasonable demands, and was "cold." A few weeks before Christmas 1966, he moved in temporarily with Edward Shils, then sublet a garden apartment in the Windermere, an elegant old building near the university.

At least outwardly, the breakup with Susan caused Bellow a minimum of anguish. His third marriage, like those before and after, had supplied a wealth of new material for future books. "You've been a real Klondike," he brutally told Susan. She seemed just as relieved as he was. "Well, we haven't even received all the furniture we ordered when we moved in here, but it's a lot more pleasant with him gone," she confided to a friend.

By this time it was apparent, to Bellow's friends if not to him, that he wasn't cut out for family life. Susan complained bitterly that he neglected Daniel, who seemed baffled when his father, impervious to the child's plaintive cry of "dinner, dinner," went off to meet friends at Morton's Steak House. How could he leave a three-year-old child behind? Mark Harris asked Susan when he learned that Bellow had fled the nest. "After the first one it's easy," she replied.* The arrival of a child meant that Bellow himself was no longer the child; he had been displaced by his own son. This was always the moment he chose to leave.

As a supplement to Maggie Staats, Bellow had acquired Bette Howland, a young divorced mother of two who was studying for a master's degree in creative writing at the University of Iowa. They had met a few years earlier, at the writers' conference at Wagner College, and Bellow had subsequently published one of her early stories in *The Noble Savage*. A stocky woman with a pockmarked face, Howland was herself a Chicagoan; her family was from the tough Uptown neighborhood on the North Side—

---

*After encountering Bellow with his oldest son, Greg, in a Hyde Park restaurant, Harris remarked to Susan that Greg seemed like a well-adjusted young man; Bellow must have "worked that relationship through." "No, Saul hasn't changed," she noted. "*Gregory* has worked it through."

the landscape of her novel, *Blue in Chicago*. (Edward Shils snobbishly referred to her as Bellow's "working-class queen.")

Bellow's sexual conduct was a paradox: He regarded with increasing dismay the so-called sexual revolution, inveighing against the unregulated sex of the permissive sixties while passing up no opportunity to indulge in it himself. His courtly manners—the elaborate propriety with which he referred to his women by their last names ("Mrs. Howland," "Miss Staats")—were consistent with his disapproving public pronouncements on contemporary *moeurs*. "In an age as defective as our own, Eros, too, is inevitably kinky," he lamented, deploring free love, feminism, and gay rights. It was as if he hoped his persistent moralizing could somehow neutralize his own libertine impulses—the ineffectual superego chastising the guilty id.

"He had a biblical Old World morality, but his fly was entirely unzipped at all times," said Arlette Landes, a young painter who met Bellow in the elevator of the Windermere that year. Landes was twenty-six and had recently come to Chicago from Stanford with her first husband, an assistant professor in the economics department. Their marriage had just broken up, and it was her apartment that Bellow had sublet. "'You're living in my apartment,' I said to him, and he said, 'Would you like to see what it looks like now?'" The apartment tour marked the beginning of their affair. "It was the sixties," explained Landes.

Bellow's "quota of adultery"—as he had described his needs to Anthony Hecht—wasn't satisfied by extramarital affairs; he cheated on his girlfriends, too. "I don't know when he was first unfaithful, but he certainly was," said Maggie Staats. "Once the chase was over and he had me, he began to wander." On one occasion, when Staats was staying with Bellow at the Windermere, Landes stormed in and confronted them in a jealous rage. "Don't you want to marry me?" she demanded. Bellow hesitated, then answered firmly, "No."

An oil painting that Landes did toward the end of their affair captured its essence. The picture shows a nude Bellow with his arms spread wide in a Chagall-like dance, his thick penis exposed; Landes, also nude, stands in a marching pose on his left. On the right are two children, Adam Bellow and Landes's daughter,

Bonnie.* As Landes interpreted the picture, "He did his own thing, and people danced around him." When Bellow was shown the painting, he inspected the ample penis and pronounced it "not bad."

After his third divorce, Bellow was featured in a magazine called *Single: For the Married, Divorced, Widowed, and Unattached*. The article, entitled "Superior Singles," consisted of interviews with eight celebrated Americans who were unmarried, among them Arthur Ashe and the equestrian Chrystine Jones. Bellow admitted that he missed "sharing the excitement" after a bout of composition. "When I get up from my table, I sometimes feel odd and unconnected, and I greatly dislike coming home to an empty place. But I've learned the pleasures of being alone, too. And when I think of hellish times I've had, these solitary evenings are heavenly."

The idea, if not the reality, of marriage still appealed to him. He visited a jewelry store with Landes, just as he had with Staats, and offered to buy her a ring; she later maintained that he would have married her if she had pressed him to. When the interviewer from *Single* asked him if he would like to marry again, Bellow answered, "Ideally, yes. But it's a question like, 'Would you like to live in Utopia?' or 'Would you like to go to heaven?'"

Bellow never kept a journal, confining his private commentaries to occasional brief notations scrawled randomly among his papers. But around 1966, apparently under intense emotional pressure, he jotted down a few terse notes that offer vivid insight into his struggle to master his conflicts—to explain himself to himself:

> Unwillingness, reluctance to recognize the reality of the present moment because of attachment to something in childhood.
> Therefore a brother rather than a father to the children.
> And the great fatigue of a struggle of 50 years. Feel it in my arms, in my very *fists*.
> Locate the Old System with passion—not so other things.
> Maggie is part of this. Has the purity of earliest connections. Miraculous to have accomplished so much in the world while in such bondage.

*Originally, there had been a third figure in the painting, Landes revealed: "I painted out Maggie; she got in the way."

> But they heard my childish voice—and their own childhood
> in it.
> Nadine [Nimier] said *T'es un bébé.*

At fifty, Bellow still experienced himself as the son—a fact that may help account for his inability to sustain relationships with women. "He felt he had unfinished business," as one of his sons put it; Bellow himself often spoke of "a failure to properly mourn" his mother's death. This, in essence, was his "bondage," and in the absence of any psychological resolution it had to be played out over and over again. It's significant that he recognized the ways in which the life he led as a middle-aged man kindled emotions associated with a much earlier phase of existence: *T'es un bébé.* The most authentic and deeply felt passages in his fiction are the memories of his early life. "He can't form permanent attachments," Marvin Gameroff said of his uncle. "His fidelity is to his past." Out of that fidelity, more enduring than any he felt toward the living, Bellow fashioned his art.

The "Old System" mentioned in his notes refers to a story Bellow wrote around this time, about a successful businessman whose sister, convinced she had been cut out of a real-estate deal that would have made her rich, forces him to pay her twenty thousand dollars in cash as the price of a deathbed reconciliation. The story was based closely on an episode in the Gameroffs' lives, but the main character, as in all of Bellow's work, was its omniscient, introspective, deep-thinking narrator—in this instance Dr. Braun, an eminent scientist with a penchant for dwelling on the bonds that yoke together even the most discordant families. "It was said of him, occasionally, that he did not love anyone," wrote Bellow of his scientifically minded persona, who prefigures another doctor in his oeuvre, Artur Sammler. "This was not true. He did not love anyone steadily. But unsteadily he loved, he guessed, at an average rate."

In his work, Bellow could evoke the sometimes claustrophobic intensity of Jewish family life as no American writer (except perhaps Philip Roth) ever had. His great themes were the rapid evolution of Old World Russian Jews into modern-day Americans (Cousin Braun keeps a leather-bound copy of the Psalms in the glove compartment of his Cadillac) and their souls' constancy amid this transformation. What he described in his jottings as "the purity of earliest connections" lent gravity to his chronicle. But these connections, in the end, were random, notes the clear-eyed Dr. Braun; our most urgent feelings were no more than "molecular processes—the only true heraldry of being." Despite the beauty of the language, it was a cold, unsentimental insight: The brute, ineradicable fact of our mortality, Bellow was saying, makes a mockery of all human attachments, reduces them to mere biological phenomena. Love is a force of nature, and death nullifies even that.

Despite his pleas for privacy, Bellow nevertheless managed to let himself get ensnared by fans; apparently, his need for solitude was easily vanquished by his need for adulation. In the wake of *Herzog*, scholars and potential biographers appeared at his door, supplicants for special attention. Bellow's response to them was equivocal: He rarely turned them away outright, preferring to make himself elusive rather than slam the door. Mark Harris pointedly identified this style in *Saul Bellow, Drumlin Wood-chuck*, an eccentric and entertaining account of his decade-long effort to write Bellow's biography. The reference in Harris's title is to a poem by Robert Frost celebrating the evasive strategies of that calculating creature, "so instinctively thorough / About [its] crevice and burrow," who "shrewdly pretends / That he and the world are friends" while diving for cover at the slightest alarm.

Bellow approved of the metaphor as long as it was applied to someone else. "Very much liked your Sandburg-Frost article," he wrote Harris in 1962, congratulating him on a literary profile he'd written for *Life*. "How neatly you let Sandburg portray himself. One or two strokes of the dollar sign and the thing was done. Frost is a different kettle of woodchuck altogether. Woodchuck I say because he has more exits to his burrow than any man can count." It was a typical Bellow letter: amiable, gracious, ingratiating. In his generous, democratic way, Bellow treated the struggling novelist as an equal. "I know very well—all too well—what you mean when you say that you've overtaken yourself," he replied to Harris's lament that he felt stalled in his career:

But then it's not so much yourself you're repeating as it is a way, a system, a procedure, a method which originated with certain old gentlemen in France, England, Russia. So let's say you've overtaken Turgenieff (for example). I don't know your work well enough to say this. Let's assume I'm speaking of myself. Without an influx of new life the situation becomes depressing in the extreme, as it was in the end for Turgenieff himself. Once more a woman who loves, in the same old way; once more a lazy nobleman. The benefits of a literary education soon come to an end. Is this what you're talking about? Or is it only what I am making of it?

Needy, gregarious, ever a disciple in search of a master, Harris had found a willing mentor. Bellow praised his novels, published him in *The Noble Savage,* invited him up to Tivoli—unaware, perhaps, that in the course of his research Harris seemed to be making a Ludwig-like play for Susan, inviting himself over to her apartment late at night, inviting her over to *his* room, bombarding her with suggestive letters. It was only when Harris began to make noises about writing his biography that Bellow glanced around in woodchuck fashion for the exit.

It began, innocently enough, with a request to profile Bellow for *Life.* Bellow demurred. "Thank you for your offer, it's a very good one," he replied on October 18, 1965, still recovering from the commotion over *Herzog.* "But the fact of the matter is that I've had about all the public attention I can safely absorb. Anyone who held a geiger counter on me now would hear a terrible rattling. . . . What I want to do now is to lie low and gather a little shadow."

Undaunted, Harris renewed his overtures, finally working up the nerve to introduce "a bad subject," as he put it. "Great biography may be creative, too," he assured his quarry in a letter declaring his intent.

Bellow didn't respond.

Not taking no for an answer, Harris arrived in Chicago the following spring and put the matter directly. "He won't say No," predicted Richard Stern, who served as a kind of unofficial press agent for Bellow. Stern was right: *No* would have been too direct. (Stern also noted that he wouldn't say yes.) Confronted in his apartment as he and Stern were on their way out to dinner, Bellow denied he'd ever received a letter from Harris regarding any prospective biography. About the biography itself he remained silent.

Bellow's impassivity in the face of this newest hazard of fame was understandable. Why should he make his life available to a biographer while he was in the midst of living it? He was still "groping," he explained to Harris; he was not yet "*fini.*" That a biography would violate his privacy was the least of his concerns. When Harris suggested that he might be nervous about revelations of "sexual scandal," Bellow retorted sharply, "Who could reveal more than I already have about *that*?" Anxiously seeking formal permission—the one thing Bellow would never grant—Harris came away with a promise of nonintervention: "You can write any thing you want about me." Bellow knew he would be written about eventually, that he was now part of the public record; he often said, half jokingly, that Stern ought to have a piece ready to go if he went down in a plane. He didn't relish the prospect of writers delving into his life. "The less I read about myself the better," he told Harris. In private, he dismissed the importunate biographer as a nuisance, another member of that constituency of lawyers, wives, critics, and friends who wanted something from the beleaguered novelist. "There are enough people with their thumbprint on my windpipe," he complained. But he was as reluc-tant to discourage the biographer as he was to encourage him— attention was attention.

In his "Chicago circle," as Harris called it, Bellow found the companionship that had eluded him in New York. There were his academic colleagues in Hyde Park, notably the classicist David Grene and the Falstaffian Harold Rosenberg, who liked nothing more than to stay up talking far into the night, a drink in one hand, a Pall Mall in the other. "He was disappointed when Saul went off with one of his girls to bed," said Rosenberg's girlfriend, Joan Schwartz—they were depriving him of company.

Women were essential, but they were no substitutes for male friends. Bellow's mainstay was the loyal Richard Stern. Stern and Bellow often lunched together at the Quadrangle Club or drove around town on errands, stopping off at the grocery store, the post office, the Maxwell Street flea market. When he was home writing, Bellow rang up Stern four or five times a day. "Life's just a series of long afternoons," he complained.

Sam Freifeld continued to serve as Bellow's general factotum. Sam took care of Bellow's driver's license and automobile insurance, negotiated with Bellow's editors at Viking over the film rights to his books, and even fixed him up with women. Together, they hung around the same places they'd hung around as high-school boys forty years before: the Art Institute, as grand as ever in its green bower on the lake, the famous lions still guarding the doors; the sooty-facaded Civic Opera House on Wacker Drive, where Bellow had once been an usher; the oak-paneled Berghoff, a noisy German restaurant in the Loop that had been around since the nineteenth century. However dramatically it had been transformed since their youth, the old cast-iron buildings of the Loop now overshadowed by skyscrapers, Chicago was still Chicago: home.

Perhaps the best thing about the city was that it wasn't competitive, writer-crowded New York. The essayist Joseph Epstein liked to say that writing about the city's literary life reminded him of the Finnish ornithologist who, when it came time to write his chapter on the owls of Finland, produced a single sentence: "There are no owls in Finland." The guest of honor at one literary dinner Bellow attended was Benjamin Gingiss, whose name in Chicago was synonymous with a chain of stores that sold men's formal wear; Gingiss had written his autobiography. On another occasion, Bellow shared the podium at a local luncheon with Winifred Wolfe, the author of a novel called *Never Step on a Rainbow*.

Bellow's older brother Maurice got his own share of local news coverage. Maurice—or Morrie, as he was known—had several brushes with the law in those years. He was a rich man by now, a Gold Coast millionaire who tooled around town in a big black Cadillac. But his life was as turbulent as ever. In the sixties, he got caught in a shady deal involving the sublease of a sanitary-landfill site owned by the government, testified in the trial of "an alleged crime syndicate figure" who had been charged with tax evasion, and was sued by stockholders opposed to his efforts to buy the Illinois Central Railroad. Still another item in the *Sun-Times* recounted the details of Morrie's divorce: His ex-wife charged that he "struck her on numerous occasions," once beating her so badly that she ended up in the hospital. (He was rumored to have taken a shot at her in the basement of their Lake Shore Drive high-rise.) His daughter, Lynn, had a name for her father and his ruthless cronies: The Animals.

Bellow was also becoming familiar with Chicago courtrooms. Dour dispatches arrived periodically from Marshall Holleb: "It seems that Susan is exploding the bomb"; "Another meteorite fell from the sky." She wasn't about to go quietly. In court briefs, she claimed (as Anita had done before her) that she had been instrumental in Bellow's literary career, forcing him to revise *Herzog*, and was thus entitled to share in the considerable proceeds. Her claim is vindicated at least partially by a letter written by Pat Covici to Bellow when the book was in production: "Tell Susie, alas, I took the idea of her being paid for the work she's doing on the galleys up the line, but got nowhere." Bellow himself admitted that his wife had been a help, but that didn't mean he felt she was entitled to any money. He had given Susan the apartment and all its furnishings as part of their settlement, but he, too, gained from the divorce; he wrote about it. "I'll get you," he threatened at the height of one of their quarrels. "I'll grind you to powder. Your name will be mud." And he did: Susan is the central marital adversary in *Humboldt's Gift*, unflatteringly depicted as the "curt and tough," "warlike and shrill" Denise.

Sam Freifeld played a Cassandra-like role in the proceedings. Freifeld adored Bellow and loved to wheel and deal on his behalf. But in the landmark case of *Bellow v. Bellow*, he was a sideline kibbitzer; Holleb, who didn't handle divorces, had turned his client over to another lawyer, Stanton Ehrlich. (Freifeld was later portrayed cruelly in *Humboldt's Gift* as Alec Szathmar, a chiseling lawyer with a "broad can, Roman nose, and mutton-chop whiskers.") At issue was how best to shelter Bellow's assets from his wife—in short, whether he should hide income.

There was plenty to hide. On his 1966 tax return, he reported income of $140,000, the aftermath of *Herzog* (about $800,000 in today's terms); a year later, he reported nearly the same amount—

$137,834.69, to be precise. In 1967, he was still making $10,000 and sometimes $15,000 a month from various sources—royalties, advances, the sales of foreign rights. Yet his lawyers calculated that his income in subsequent years would amount to no more than $30,000, "subject to fluctuation," an amount derived from Bellow's University of Chicago salary—$20,000—and from lecture fees, investments, and "a dribble of royalties." In court, Bellow maintained that the figure represented "an attempt to average out into the future as I had averaged back into the past"—a strategy arrived at in consultation with his lawyer. "Mr. Ehrlich seemed to feel that the lower the figure the better," he told the judge, passing the blame. As Freifeld later summed up the matter: "It was a dumb thing to do."

However vehemently he maintained that he was an American writer who happened to be a Jew, Bellow identified strongly and publicly with the fate of his people. In the spring of 1967, he signed a letter to *The New York Times* demanding that the Soviet Union be more responsive to "Jewish cultural institutions," and he made known his support of Israel. "It would be very strange and unnatural for a Jew not to want to know what is happening in Israel," he explained to a reporter, offering a typically noncommittal justification for the frequent trips he made there starting in the sixties. But the fact was that Israel evoked in him profound feelings of identification. What could be called the Jewish sensibility—nomadic, Yiddish speaking, steeped in irony and a consciousness of history—was second nature to him. In that sense, Bellow, despite his protestations, was a Jew who happened to be an American writer.

"On Saturday it struck me that I should go to Israel to report the crisis for *Life*, *Look*, or *The New Yorker*," he wrote to Ruth Miller on the last day of May 1967, a few days before the Six-Day War had broken out. "I have made myself available, there is some interest, and I may be gone in a day or two."

A week later, he was at the Grande Bretagne Hotel in Athens, on his way to the war—but for a more modest publication. "I could not explain why," he recalled. "I have never been a Zionist. I never

had strong feelings on the subject. But something about that
particular occasion—the fact that for the second time in a quarter
of a century the Jews were having a gun pressed to their heads—
led me to ask *Newsday,* a Long Island newspaper, to send me as a
correspondent."

From the Grande Bretagne, he wrote a moving letter to Maggie
Staats that conveyed both his excitement and his apprehension
about heading off to a war: "It puts one in touch with reality.
Otherwise one's decades begin to feel empty. Like an old amusement park, no longer patronized and oneself the caretaker remembering childhood, boyhood, youth as side shows (the fire-eater, the
strong man, the tunnel-of-love etc.) Though I do love you, and my
little children and a few other people—but this is all movie-talk!"
He would be home soon, he promised her, and safe.

Bellow's first report, datelined Tel Aviv, was reminiscent of
Hemingway's terse dispatches from the front in the midst of the
Spanish civil war. "Day and night the armored columns came
down the main street of Tiberias, turned left at the Lake of Galilee
and continued northward past the Mount of the Beatitudes, where
Jesus preached," it began: "From the mountains on the Syrian
side, the road was occasionally shelled at night. One could see the
fields blazing, set afire by artillery, and hear the deep growling of
bombs. Tiberias was blacked out. People sat by the water and
listened to the news, exchanging rumors and predictions." Bellow
didn't just hang around the porch of the King David Hotel, observing the fighting from afar; he wandered the streets of Old
Jerusalem, where casualties were heavy, and ventured out to the
battlefield in Sinai, recording with a sympathetic but dispassionate
eye the stench of the dead, the bloated corpses "black and stinking
in the desert sun." There was very little first-person commentary;
the self-regarding *I* was kept to a minimum.

Bellow's dispatches from the Six-Day War were both beautifully
written and politically shrewd. His final report, dated June 16,
1967, was remarkably prescient. Visiting a Palestinian settlement
in Nablus, he saw that "if the old system is followed the UN will
be supporting more dozens of rotting slums in which demoralized,
idle young men can concentrate on 'politics.'" He didn't pretend
to be objective, and he was openly hostile to the superpowers who

had abandoned Israel to its fate. As for the Arabs, their zealous national pride could spawn only more destruction. "What good are these traditional dignities?" he concluded. "Not good at all if they lead to the Sinai roads with their blasted Russian tanks, the black faces of the dead dissolving and the survivors fighting for a sip of brackish ditchwater." That the modern strife he had witnessed evoked biblical enmities hardly needed to be articulated; it was implicit in his prose.

In the summer of 1967, Bellow returned to Louse Point Road in East Hampton, this time to a shingled two-story house near the bay. Having had a taste of war, he found the Hamptons disorientingly superficial. The social scene, more frenetic even than on the Vineyard, wasn't to his taste. "People here go out at five and come home at one o'clock in the morning and think they've done a day's work," he complained. But Harold Rosenberg and Saul Steinberg provided stimulating conversation, Maggie Staats provided female companionship, and Adam provided family. "It was such a perfect time," Staats recalled, despite periodic outbreaks in Bellow's latest divorce war. "We lived very much the way we wanted to live."

22

Sometimes I think I have bought myself a white outfit for running in the Olympics. Five hundred times I've gotten the outfit and pranced around in it but never yet got to the starting-line.

—Bellow to Marshall Holleb

Bellow had been writing stories for as long as he had been writing. Like most novelists, he regarded short stories as welcome interludes, "'scale models' for bigger jobs," as he once explained to Mark Harris. By the mid-sixties, he had enough stories for a collection and signed a contract with Viking for ten thousand dollars; but it wasn't until he'd written the last story in the volume that he settled on a name for it: *Mosby's Memoirs*. The title story was published in *The New Yorker* in the summer of 1968, the book a few months later. It was a stringent selection, six stories in all. "Two or three of the stories may meet a good standard, one does not, and another is only a toy," Bellow confided to Robert Penn Warren.

But there was nothing slight about *Mosby's Memoirs*. If it wasn't major Bellow, at the very least it affirmed his stature as a practitioner of fiction whose moral depth and commanding vision were unequaled by any of his contemporaries—a writer who, in the words of Ivan Gold, "seem[ed] to know more than any American novelist now writing." The characteristic Bellow voice was much in evidence, a voice so distinctive that it had become as much a cultural as a literary force. Theodore Solotaroff, one of the first critics to recognize the extent of Bellow's achievement, began his review with a reverie on the human prospect as glimpsed from the window of a

Long Island Rail Road train returning to the city through Queens. What did the "counsels of the heart"—Solotaroff's theme in a talk he'd just given to an audience of "suburban Jewish ladies"—have to do with the desolate scene before him? How could the novelist's sensibility matter? In *Mosby's Memoirs*, Solotaroff declared, Bellow provided clear evidence that it did. His work spoke to those, like Solotaroff, who were "hot for uplift."*

However diverse in subject matter and style, the stories expressed a single theme: the desire to find meaning in the random, scattered facts of our existence. The hero of "Looking for Mr. Green," George Grebe, is a classics scholar who has fallen on hard times during the Depression and gotten a temporary job as a social worker. His first assignment is to deliver a relief check to a client somewhere in the vast South Side ghetto, but Mr. Green, a shadowy phantom, is hard to locate: "Nobody will tell him anything." Grebe is a typically sentient Bellow protagonist. Contemplating the urban ruins all around him, he thinks, "It wasn't desolation that this made you feel, but rather a faltering of organization that set free a huge energy, an escaped, unattached, unregulated power from the giant raw place." Mr. Green, a modernist convention out of Kafka, is never found.

"Looking for Mr. Green" was really a story about the difficulty of establishing connections. In its form and style, it belonged to an earlier phase of Bellow's career; it sounded the somber, formal note of *Dangling Man*, registering the atmospherics of sprawling, mammoth, dingy Chicago with a keen eye. But its theme echoed through Bellow's work from decade to decade. Why were we put on earth? What is our purpose? Do the menial tasks that give order to our lives redeem us from the universal sentence of annihilation? "Rebuilt after the Great Fire, this part of the city was, not fifty years later, in ruins again," Grebe reflects as he goes about his fruitless quest, "factories boarded up, buildings deserted or fallen, gaps of prairie between." It is out of this landscape—an omen of human futility—that mankind must labor to create significance.

---

*Stanley Edgar Hyman later made a similar point in his fiction column for *The New Leader*, impatiently reviewing *Mr. Sammler's Planet* on the basis of excerpts in *The Atlantic Monthly* because Bellow was the only novelist around writing about "the actual world in which we live."

"It was kind of you to write," Bellow had replied to Mark Harris on January 25, 1968, answering his fawning letter in praise of "The Old System," another story in *Mosby's Memoirs*. (It had appeared that month in *Playboy*.) "A few people responded to it as you did. Most, I suppose, don't know what to make of it. Afraid it may not be the THING? Afraid of being Square? Worried that Susan Sontag might not like it? To this we seem to have come."

That spring, Bellow had his first direct encounter with the New Left, when he gave a talk at San Francisco State College. The Bay Area was the crucible of the student movement; it was where the social revolution that would come to be identified with the sixties had begun. Bellow made no secret of his contempt for student radicals, and the way the event had been organized—or disorganized—virtually guaranteed a confrontation: The sponsors had failed to book a large enough auditorium, and hundreds of disappointed students were left milling around outside the doors. Bellow's talk, introduced by Wright Morris, was called "What Are Writers Doing in the Universities?" His tone was moderate and engaging. "He was an exciting speaker," recalled a member of the audience, "witty, entertaining and definitely cynical." It was an uneventful performance until Bellow opened the floor to questions—perhaps unwisely; San Francisco State was on the verge of a student strike. "Bellow's talk was, in this context, provocative," acknowledged the novelist Leo Litwak, who was on the faculty.

The first question was civil enough: What did Bellow think of the black playwright LeRoi Jones's insistence upon the distinction between black art and white art? Bellow gave a measured reply, noting that the twentieth century had seen numerous instances in which "the line was laid down" by one party or another "that the artist should be at the disposal of history and the working class, and that he should make sure that victories of working classes and of social progress triumphed—and we have seen how useful that was. Why worry about this sort of thing?"

Just as Bellow was warming to his theme, invoking "the doom of the white day" as D. H. Lawrence saw the future in *Studies in Classic American Literature*, a disturbance erupted at the back of the room. An instructor in the creative-writing department by the name of Floyd Salas—"a feisty little ex-boxer and writer," as Leo Litwak described him—burst through the door and shouted: "Are you saying the university should offer writers a haven from the vulgarities of the contemporary world? Is this what you said in your speech?" The audience laughed.

"Since you came in late, I have the right to refuse to answer your question," Bellow answered coldly. "I mean, I'm sorry you couldn't get in, but at least other people have notes and you can find out what I said."

"I want to challenge you if that's the case," Salas persisted.

"But you don't know what you're challenging."

"I've read your books."

By this time the audience was tittering nervously. People who hadn't been able to get a seat were pushing in and crowding the aisles. "My books are my business," retorted Bellow, prompting a string of expletives from Salas, who accused him of "trying to make the university a genteel old maid's school."

"It would have been better if you had heard my speech," Bellow said patiently. "I mean, I'm an old soap-box speaker. I used to be a Trotskyite in my youth, and I'm well accustomed to handling this sort of thing, but I don't really like to do it."

"Because it's *vulgar*?" Salas shot back.

Trying another tack, Bellow pointed to someone else who had raised a hand. But this questioner, too, was looking for a fight. "Why did you use 'Herzog' instead of 'Bellow' as the last name in the novel? Isn't *Herzog* your own real biography?"

The place was in an uproar by now. "If it were, it would be none of your business," Bellow replied, trying to give a serious answer. "And if you knew more about literature, you'd realize that it's very hard to write an autobiography, and once you begin to write, even if it's about yourself, you've invented a fiction and you have to be consistent."

At this point, Salas "went berserk," in the words of one witness, and began ranting: "You're a fucking square. You're full of shit. You're an old man, Bellow. You haven't got any balls."

"I think this meeting is pretty well broken up now," Bellow announced to general laughter. "I don't mind answering questions,

but it's not hospitable to insult your speakers, so let's call it off."
He gathered up his papers and left the podium.

Kay House, a professor in the English department, hustled
Bellow out of the auditorium and drove him to her house in
Sausalito "and after three drinks in the sun on the deck over there,
Saul and Wright finally started to come out of shock." House was
less surprised; she had already seen, when the historian Richard
Hofstadter had tried to engage students in a debate on Black
Power, "how much sheer hate and rage could build up in a crowd
on our campus." Yet Bellow, too, had been provocative. "Somehow I felt he invited this by reacting very sharply to questioners,"
she noted. "He lacked graciousness, courtesy or an attitude of
sympathetic understanding."*

"The thing at S.F. State was very bad," Bellow reported to Mark
Harris:

> I'm not too easy to offend, at my age, and I don't think I was
> personally affronted—that's not my style. The thing was offen-
> sive though. Being denounced by Salas as an old shit to an
> assembly which seemed to find the whole thing deliciously
> thrilling. Being told furthermore that "this is an effete old
> man—he can't *come!*" My impulse was to say, "Let's choose a
> young lady from the audience for a trial heat and see about
> this." But the young lady wouldn't have known the difference
> between one man and another. One glance at the audience told
> me this. So I left the platform in defeat. Undefended by the
> bullied elders of the faculty. While your suck-up-to-the-young
> colleagues swallowed their joyful saliva. No, it was very poor
> stuff, I assure you. You don't found universities in order to
> destroy culture. For that you want a Nazi party.

A year later, Bellow made this episode a central event in *Mr.
Sammler's Planet*. For Bellow, as for Sammler, it was an education
in reality: "He was not sorry to have met the facts, however
saddening, regrettable the facts."

---

*A hostile article in the next day's *San Francisco Chronicle* also put most of the
blame on Bellow, describing him as "prematurely old and cranky" and "an alienated super-intellectual afflicted with defensiveness and hostility." The reporter
seemed vague about just who Bellow was, identifying him as the author of a play
"that bombed so badly on Broadway that no one can remember the title."

But of course, they were only the facts as Bellow saw them, from the vantage of an aging conservative who had himself been, in his student days, a self-styled "revolutionist." The radicals of the sixties weren't known for their politeness, and there was a strain of bullying philistinism in the student movement that was particularly virulent in the Bay Area, the headquarters of sixties' radicalism. Bellow, who, it seemed, was always looking for a fight, had walked into a polarized setting where emotions ran high. That he presented the conflict to Mark Harris in the macho terms of a virility contest—even if he wasn't the one who initially framed it this way—showed how out of touch he was.*

That summer, Bellow was back in East Hampton with Maggie Staats. He was "getting in some good travail," he wrote cheerfully to Richard Stern, confessing that he continued to *poursuivre des femmes.* From the Hamptons whirl, he remained aloof: "All the artist roses are preening, even the ailing and the possibly dying are drinking their gin in the sun and talking welfare reform or revolution, anarchy, guerilla warfare, action—building stately mansions on foundations of personal wretchedness." The only person he could talk to was Adam, who was spending part of the summer with him—"in excellent condition," apart from "a spot of mother-induced neurosis here and there." At eleven, the boy was "*surtout raisonnable.*" Not all was serene, however. Bellow's New York lawyer, Sam Goldberg, was ill; John Steinbeck was in the Southampton Hospital, and Jean Stafford had just gotten out. "The Angel of Death is floating over the house."

In August, it arrived on his doorstep. His Tuley friend Lou Sidran was dying of cancer. Sidran, who had driven east with his

---

*Compared with some other campuses, the University of Chicago got off lightly, but "it was hardly a place remote from the upheavals of the time," according to the anthropologist Clifford Geertz, who was on the faculty in those years: "There were teach-ins, marches, strikes; the administration building was occupied, professors were physically attacked. Off-campus, the Black Panthers were shot up, the Chicago Seven were tried, the yippies attempted to levitate the Merchandise Mart, and the Democratic convention exploded. . . . If in fact the whole world was watching, it was a very good place to look."

younger son, Ezra, for a tour of Civil War monuments, came to see Bellow for the last time. Sidran was another member of the Old Bunch whose life had failed to measure up, at least in his own mind. He had worked for *Esquire* when the magazine's offices were in Chicago, then as an advertising copywriter for Leo Burnett; but what he'd really wanted to be was a writer. Like Isaac Rosenfeld, Oscar Tarcov, and Zita Cogan's husband, Herman—"Cogey," a businessman whose library boasted complete sets of *transition* and *Scrutiny* and who died at forty-nine—Lou Sidran would be another friend gone in middle age. He arrived with his son the week of the Democratic Party's convention in Chicago, where a massive contingent of Yippies and members of SDS—Students for a Democratic Society—were gearing up for a confrontation with Mayor Daley and the Chicago police. The Chicagoans watched the ensuing chaos on TV in the company of Gore Vidal, appalled by the civil disorder on the streets of their hometown.

It was a good visit. His old friend "never looked better in his life," Bellow told Sidran's wife, Shirley, over the phone. A month later, Sidran was dead. Not long afterward, Bellow met Sidran's older son, Ben, for a drink in Chicago "and cried through the whole thing"—especially when Ben told him that his father had been trying to grow a beard in the month before he died: "That really broke him up." That Sidran had resorted to such a transient and superficial means of reinventing himself in the last moments of his life struck Bellow as acutely sad. The deaths of contemporaries bring home the fact of one's own mortality—in Bellow's case, the process of mourning was intensified by his habit of experiencing his dead friends as aspects of himself.

As the Tuley crowd declined, Bellow flourished. Awards continued to accrue: On January 15, 1968, he had been made a *chevalier des arts et lettres* by the president of France at a reception at the French embassy in New York ("Shoveleer!" crazy Humboldt writes Citrine, "Thy name is lesion"); a week later, in Philadelphia, he had received the Jewish Heritage Award for Excellence in Literature from B'nai B'rith. His income from his writing that year was at least $150,000, in addition to other revenues—enough that Marshall Holleb was looking into tax-sheltered real-estate ventures in Chicago. Instead of borrowing money from his brothers, Bellow was handing over substantial sums for them to invest. Once, after dinner at the home of Meyer Schapiro, Schapiro's wife, Lillian, offered Bellow a jar of her canned peaches to take home. "You forget, Lillian," Bellow declared grandly, "I'm a rich man now."

He certainly lived like one. When he traveled to Europe—which he did sometimes twice a year—he checked into the ritzy Westbury in London, the Plaza in Madrid. That September, he flew to Italy for a stay at the Rockefeller Foundation's luxurious retreat on Lake Como. But his life was as chaotic as ever. A letter to Dave Peltz vividly summed up his situation:

Villa Serbelloni
Bellagio
Sept. 20, 68

Dear Dave:

It's been mighty fine, in some ways, and in others one of my famous exercises in suffering. For one thing, I had only been here a few days when Maggie found she had to have breast surgery, and then there was a spell of waiting for news— fortunately good. After the good news, came hysterics. All kinds of transatlantic telephone oddities. Time out for sobbing. I thought the whales and the winds were talking to me. The Lord sent relief in the form of a wet dream or two. I've had no other. All my ladies seem furious. Not one of them has written, not even Bette. She must have done research in my apartment and found sinful evidence. I feel neglected, old and a bit sick. I don't think this is hypochrondria. I feel the hook down my gullet, and I hear that old reel spinning. I think I'd better come back to dreadful Chicago and find out what, if anything, is the matter. In spite of everything I have, as usual, done a certain amount of work. It may turn out all right, but I'm not at my best these days. Maggie's line with me now is that I must mark time while she tries to develop other interests, especially, she says, since she does this out of rejection and therefore I owe her perfect fidelity. Seeing her twice a month is perfectly adequate. I have no more real needs. At my time of life they must be imaginary and delusive. She blushes for me, thinking of the Arlettes. Sondra, also, has sent me some record-breaking words. Those I've saved for you, together with my reply, for to try to describe this exchange would be like trying to paint Hell with Daniel's fingerpaints. She claims I made use of her, and of the divorce, to make a fortune which I now must share with her. For as things are I treat myself to European trips etc while she and Adam have to scrape along on pennies. If Barnum were alive, he and I could make a really great show of this. The great men are gone, though, we have nothing but punks.

I'll see you quite soon—early in October. I've missed you badly. Flee some, lose others, and that's the story.

Love
Saul

He was being suffocated by Staats's demands; he needed "an armistice, a moratorium," "a breather." Commitment made him claustrophobic. "Why should people like me, who have won so much freedom, or had it handed to them, feel themselves in jail?" It was a question so central to his life that it cried out for an answer: Was it because freedom, despite his protestations, was not what he was really after? Freedom carried with it an implication of neglect. What Bellow required was confinement, complication, harassing demands from all sides—a situation that released him from responsibility while providing the conditions for resistance in which he thrived. Feeling himself to be in jail was oppressive, but it was also oddly comforting.

He led a "monk's life" at Villa Serbelloni, he reported to Richard Stern, omitting one temptation: the poet Louise Glück, who was also in residence. "Yesterday Saul Bellow arrived just in time for lunch," another guest, Leslie Garis, reported in her journal: "Before post-lunch coffee was served he approached Louise and asked her to show him the grounds. On which walk he kissed her. Fast work. They'd never met."

Glück, who was only twenty-five, already had a reputation as a poet, but Bellow wasn't interested in her work. "His attentions were based on the fact that I was nubile rather than intelligent," Glück recalled. At first, she was intimidated by the great man. "There was something imperial in his manner." One night, the guests were sitting around in the library after dinner, listening to a record. When it ended, Bellow nervously cleared his throat and announced, "Well! If no one is going to play the piano I guess I'll go and see about another record." The records were next door, in the same room as Glück. Bellow failed to return. Later that night, Garis passed her on the stairs: "Her hair was down and her face flushed."

According to Glück, Bellow's wooing was more literary than physical: He read to her from the manuscript of his new novel, and she read him a poem. Like Stendhal's Fabrizio del Dongo in *The Charterhouse of Parma*, whose sermons caused maidens to swoon, Bellow preferred to seduce with words.

It had been "a disorderly season," he reported to Mark Harris a month later. There were continued skirmishes with Susan over the divorce settlement, and he had to contend with Sondra. She and Adam were living in Great Neck, only a few miles from Jack Ludwig, who was still teaching at the State University of New York at Stony Brook and had an apartment in Oyster Bay. She had written Bellow with a litany of grievances. She thanked him for having sent money to cover her moving expenses, but what about the money she'd spent on a rug and new linoleum, on drapes and window shades? He lived well, bought clothes, flew off to Europe. He could afford to be generous. At the very end, she introduced a conciliatory note: "I forgive you *Herzog*, as I assumed you forgave me Jack."

It wasn't a propitious moment to mention Ludwig's name: He had just published a novel that rehearsed the central episode of *Herzog* from the paramour's point of view. Entitled *Above Ground*, it was an astonishing performance. Like *Herzog*, the book was strewn with letters, and the cast of characters would have been identifiable to any reader of Bellow's novel. There was the hearty, cuckolding Josh; the Madeleine-like Mavra, "a nymphomaniac, an egomaniac, a jealous, predatory woman, a mess of tears, saliva, and stale effluvia," in Ruth Miller's apt characterization; and, finally, there was "small, bug-eyed" Louie, "a great guy for shooting letters out to his buddies and old girl friends all over the place." Ludwig's novel reads like a clumsy, unwittingly grotesque caricature of Bellow's. During a violent fight with Madeleine, Herzog notices "an odd white grime in the corners of her mouth." In *Above Ground,* when Josh interrupts an argument between Louie and Mavra, Louie says, "Look at the froth on her mouth and tell me who is sane?"*

Bellow's reply to Sondra's letter was restrained, considering the circumstances. "I shrink from letter-tournaments," he began, calling for "a permanent hatchet-burial." But he made it clear that he didn't want to hear any more about money. His trips were no business of hers; her window shades meant nothing to him. "I will do everything I can for Adam, whom I love. There will be certain fringe benefits for you. But don't push things." As for Ludwig's novel,

> I've put that behind me, but I haven't forgotten the smallest detail. Nothing. I assure you. I made something of the abuses I suffered at your hands. As for the "humiliations" you speak of, I can match you easily. There is another book, isn't there. It is the product of two minds and two spirits, not one. Kind acquaintances and friends have made sure that I would read it. The letters of the heroine are conspicuously superior in style, but the book is garbage. It is monstrous to be touched by anything so horribly written. The worst thing about it, to a man who has been faithful to his art for thirty years, is the criminal vulgarity of the thing. I don't worry too much about my reputation, the "image" (I don't think you pay much attention to that, either) but I loathe being involved even peripherally with such shit. Now I've gotten a foot in the cesspool. Enough of that. But suppose the book had been good, successful. Can you see me demanding damages? I don't think you can. So now, let the thing stop there.

Sondra, perhaps now regretting her infidelity, answered in a chastened tone. She, too, was revolted by Ludwig's book, she confessed; it seemed like an act of murder. Why had Ludwig done

---

*Bellow wasn't the only writer Ludwig emulated; the novel also included a stream-of-consciousness meditation right out of Molly Bloom's soliloquy in *Ulysses:* "loingyre lovefunnel whirlwind headballsthroattongue whirled turning breastcunttongue spaceflopping darkswirl lightswath love a love this way found."

it? Out of jealousy, she speculated: She had made the mistake of telling him that Bellow was "a far more sensitive and elegant man" than he was, "much finer-drawn and with a keener intellectual edge." Sondra had another humiliating admission to make. She had never even suspected that when Ludwig left her each night he wasn't going off to his rented room in Oyster Bay to write, as he had told her. He was going home to his family in Great Neck.

Having pushed Arlette Landes out of the picture on the grounds that "the boys were used to Maggie," Bellow found himself companionless after one of his periodic breakups with Staats. When his British publisher, George Weidenfeld, invited him to London, he restored Landes to favor and asked her to come along. They flew over in early December and stayed at the Ritz, but eventually moved to a small guest house next door to Lord Weidenfeld's grand establishment in Chester Square.

Bellow crabbed endlessly in letters home. Weidenfeld neglected him; literary London neglected him. It was a characteristic refrain but odd given the circumstances: There were luncheon parties with Stephen Spender, drinks with Orwell's widow, Sonia Brownell, and a cocktail party at 11 Downing Street, the home of the chancellor of the exchequer. "Saul was treated like a great artist," Landes recalled. The attention failed to register—only the fancied slights. "Mordantly witty when he wanted to be, he could also be self-pitying and irascible, particularly towards those who hurt his vanity," observed Weidenfeld, who found Bellow at once "manifestly charming" and "self-absorbed." He was a "difficult" author: "He sometimes behaved outrageously, thinking his distress excused everything."

For all his complaints, Bellow was at home in London. He bought smoked salmon at Harrods and "own-make" shirts from Turnbull & Asser ("Asser & Kisser," he liked to call it); his photograph appeared in *The Listener*, showing him in a pullover with a scarf draped rakishly around his neck. His literary stock was high among the English; once, the Ritz's elevator opened to reveal none other than Graham Greene. Bellow introduced himself, shyly reminding Greene that they had met at the offices of Viking—also

Greene's publisher—in New York. "You could see that he respected Saul immensely," Landes recalled.

Landes was only a temporary measure in Bellow's efforts to ensure that he never slept alone. In the midst of their London trip, he invited Landes to spend the summer with him in Spain. She refused. By the end of January, he and Maggie Staats were reconciled. But in the spring of that year he made a new conquest: Fran Gendlin, a Hyde Park faculty wife who edited *The Bulletin of the Atomic Scientists*. Gendlin was young, but not too young—she was thirty-two the year they met. She had gotten married at seventeen, while an undergraduate at the University of Chicago. "I was this nice Jewish housewife," as she described herself—apparently just what Bellow was looking for. "My *yideneh* is here," he would announce if one of his friends called up while she was visiting. It wasn't a complimentary term. In *The Joys of Yiddish*, Leo Rosten defines a *yideneh* as a "gossipy, interfering, stupid" woman.

Bellow's reputation as a philanderer had become something of a legend in Hyde Park by now. That spring he moved to the Cloisters, a grand apartment building in Hyde Park that was home to many University of Chicago faculty. One day as he stepped off the elevator, he encountered a neighbor and former professor of his, Walter Blair. "We heard that you'd moved in," said Blair. "When will the orgies begin?"

The life of juggling many women wasn't without its emotional stresses; in the spring of 1969 Bellow again found himself on the couch. His fourth—and last—analytic foray was with the distinguished psychoanalyst Heinz Kohut, who also happened to be his neighbor in the Cloisters. Bellow himself later minimized the extent of his treatment with Kohut, insisting that he had gone to see him only a few times during "a period of turmoil" in his life. Ever the reluctant analysand, Bellow characterized their relationship as more literary than professional: "He liked my work."

Whatever the extent of their therapeutic engagement, Kohut, unlike Bellow's other therapists, was intent upon honoring his patients' right to privacy; before his death in 1981, he shredded all confidential documents. But even in the abstract, his work is instructive. Kohut was one of the preeminent figures of modern psychoanalysis, founder of an influential school of thought to which he gave the name "self-psychology." He was not a strict Freudian and slighted the importance of early infancy on the development of character. For Kohut, in the words of one of his acolytes, "the real environment and the role of culture" were far more determining.

Kohut made every effort to disguise the identities of the patients he wrote about, but his account of "a forty-year-old university professor" is revealing of his method. Like Bellow, this patient had been in a previous analysis ten years earlier; like Bellow, the patient had a "joyless, guilt-producing mother" who was unsympathetic to his intellectual aspirations (Liza Bellow had wanted her son to be a fiddler or a rabbi) and a "self-absorbed, attention-demanding father [who] had actively belittled and ridiculed him."

How many patients have such parents? A great many, no doubt.* What was interesting about Kohut's patient, identified as "Mr. I.," was the way in which he coped with the damage suffered at his parents' hands: He developed a "*Don Juan* syndrome," "the attempt to provide an insecurely established self with a continuous flow of self-esteem." His patient's avidity for women, according to Kohut, was "motivated not by libidinal but by narcissistic needs." For Mr. I., erotic stimulation was a relief from loneliness.

Bellow preferred to blame his infidelities on the zeitgeist: In his view, his promiscuity was "political." The sexual revolution had been "a thirty-year disaster," he contended years later, looking back on the long era of "investigating his freedom" that he traced to his Reichian experiments in the fifties. "It was terribly destructive to me; I took it as entitlement, the path to being a free man." That his philandering didn't begin then, or in the sixties—it began early in his marriage to Anita—somewhat weakens his case, though he would have derived a certain comfort from Kohut's elevation of creative people to special status. "The artist stands in proxy for his generation," Kohut argued: "He anticipates the dominant psychological problem of his era." For Kohut, "the under-stimulated child, the insufficiently responded-to child, the son deprived of an idealizable father" had become a "paradigmatic"

---

*One suspicious detail was a reference to the patient investing in property at a Colorado resort: It was around this time that Bellow bought property in Aspen.

figure; and it was this figure, "the crumbling, decomposing, fragmenting, enfeebled self of this child and, later, the fragile, vulnerable, empty self of the adult" that the great artists of the late twentieth century sought to describe. In his public role as a lecturer and essayist, Bellow decried this nihilistic, empty self, with its litany of personal grievances—"alienation, anomie, privation of instinctual needs." In his life, he suffered its ravages.

In the spring of 1969, Bellow once again proceeded to tear up his life to feed his art. As Fran Gendlin put it: "Maggie went at a particular point in *Sammler.*"

Bellow was never one to let experience marinate; his work tended to reflect his circumstances at the moment of composition. To read his books in consecutive order is to follow the contours of his biography. From the wartime Chicago gloom of *Dangling Man* to the postwar New York of *The Victim,* the suffocating fifties of *Seize the Day,* and the sexually liberated sixties chronicled in *Herzog,* Bellow's novels closely mime those decades in his life. (Only *The Adventures of Augie March* goes back to an antecedent period; yet that book, too, ends up in Paris, where Bellow wrote it.) None was as explicit a response to its own historical moment as *Mr. Sammler's Planet,* begun in the late sixties—in Alfred Kazin's words, "so openly Bellow's mind now."

A novel in the form of a polemic, *Sammler* registered in no uncertain terms Bellow's displeasure with the escalating protest movement. "The children were setting fire to the libraries," broods Dr. Sammler, expressing sharp contempt for that "narcotized, beflowered" generation. Bellow was manifestly intolerant of the demonstrators. When Michael Denneny, a graduate student in the Committee on Social Thought, tried to negotiate a truce between students occupying a campus building and the administration, Bellow, in league with Edward Shils and David Grene, threatened to take away his fellowship. And when Candace Falk, a graduate student in his Joyce seminar, swept into class in the midst of the national student strike with a list of "non-negotiable" demands, Bellow shouted, "You women's liberationists! All you're going to have to show for your movement ten years from now are *sagging breasts!*"

For Bellow, there was nothing innocent about these protests. Like Irving Kristol, he considered the New Left political naïfs whose radicalism had taken the form "of a secession from the life of the mind." When Amiri Baraka—formerly LeRoi Jones—arrived at the university to lobby for a black-studies department, Bellow saw it as "one of those 'Benito Cereno' moments in American history. The question was whether Captain Delano"—who in Melville's tale saves Captain Cereno from a black mob—"was going to bend his neck, and in some other universities, Delano bent pretty good." Not to bend was an imperative for Bellow: In the women's movement, the Black Power movement, the student uprisings on campuses across the country, he saw an insurrection against all the things he valued. His whole identity as an intellectual, a representative of the high culture that had celebrated his own work—indeed, had made him one of its chief spokesmen—was suddenly under violent attack.

It was against this backdrop of turmoil that *Mr. Sammler's Planet* unfolded—a book calculated, as the critic Joseph Epstein noted, "to offend whole categories of the reading public as well as most of the people who write about books." Sammler, a "Polish-Oxonian" survivor of the Holocaust who lives a marginal émigré existence on the Upper West Side of New York City, had been a journalist in London between the wars, where he was personally acquainted with the Bloomsbury intellectuals Lytton Strachey and John Maynard Keynes. With his Old World manners and European education, Sammler was something of an anachronism in New York. A fierce critic of the social pathology of the sixties, he saw the sexual revolution as emblematic of decline: "A sexual madness was overwhelming the Western world." He deplores the provocative tights worn by his sluttish niece Angela, noting with distaste her "fucked-out eyes." In an early draft excerpted in *The Atlantic Monthly,* her fallen state was rendered even more explicitly: "He could not look at her eyes without thinking that she had had too much sex, and a worse fancy had the white of semen on her mouth."

It was significant that Bellow chose a woman to represent sexual excess, thus avoiding any conflict with his own Don Juanism. When the culture at large indulged in promiscuous behavior, that was a whole other matter; for one thing, it made his own conduct less singular. There was no distinction in doing what everyone else was doing. But there was something about the new liberation movements that infuriated him; it was as if he felt his time had passed. He'd gone from being a pioneer to being obsolete. In *Mr. Sammler's Planet*, Bellow gave vent to an outburst of puritanical intolerance that signaled a new phase—the transformation of a Herzogian character resisting the complacent political atmosphere of the late fifties and early sixties into a full-blown reactionary, shrilly defending the very institutions he had once satirized and slyly undermined.

Nowhere is this new attitude more explicit than in the early scene in which Sammler witnesses a black pickpocket at work on a crowded Broadway bus. The thief, aware of having been noticed, follows Sammler back to his lobby and exposes his penis, "a large tan-and-purple uncircumcised thing—a tube, a snake." To Sammler, the "great black beast" is the embodiment of a new barbarism, an embrace of the polymorphous perverse, "sexual niggerhood for everyone." A more overtly racist cluster of images is hard to imagine.

The episode was based on a story Bellow had once heard from Oscar Tarcov about a thief Tarcov had observed working an Upper West Side bus. But there also exist in Bellow's archive fragments of a manuscript set in Chicago that opens with a Mr. Pawlyk being assaulted by "two young Negroes" beneath the Sixty-third Street El in the Black Belt: "Elderly, foreign (anyone could tell that), heavy, Pawlyk with a bleeding eye was picking himself up when the squad car came, a blue cyclops, and the police took charge." Pawlyk had trouble describing his assailants; his English was "academic." In short, Pawlyk is another victim.

In the end, it was the story of Pawlyk—later Sammler—that seized Bellow's imagination. He had been struggling with the Holocaust for more than two decades, yet had addressed it only obliquely in his fiction, most notably in *The Victim*, where it hovered like a kind of spectral presence. Herzog, too, brooded on the Holocaust, "the black cloud of faces, souls" that flowed out from the extermination chimneys, but for him it was only one catastrophe among many—the threat of nuclear war, the totalitarian reign of Stalin—that distinguished the twentieth century by its horror. It wasn't until Bellow had traveled to Poland and Israel—

and gone back to Israel during the Six-Day War—that he felt prepared to "take it on."

Mr. Sammler's Planet is a meditation on that unspeakable event in the guise of a novel. Its most vivid and disturbing scenes are those in which Sammler recounts his ordeal at the hands of the Nazis—when, hidden in a mausoleum, his wife dead, eastern European Jewry being viciously killed off, he waits out the end of the war, subsisting on crusts of bread supplied by a sympathetic groundskeeper. In one momentous flashback, Sammler himself kills a German soldier. ("Sammler then pulled the trigger. The body then lay in the snow. A second shot went through the head and shattered it. Bone burst. Matter flew out.") For this part of the story, Bellow drew upon Holocaust memoirs. He was particularly moved by Alexander Donat's *The Holocaust Kingdom*, published in 1965, a harrowing personal account of the death camps by a Polish Jew who had miraculously survived.

Donat's book had been touted by its publisher as a work that disproved Hannah Arendt's controversial thesis, expounded two years earlier in *Eichmann in Jerusalem*, that the Jews had gone passively to their deaths. Bellow also took issue with Arendt, a fellow member of the Committee on Social Thought. He and Arendt never got along; she wasn't his type. Bullying, humorless, authoritarian—"a Nazi of the intellect," as one of her students described her—she was a Central European version of Mary McCarthy. "No, that is not correct," she would say crisply in her German accent, ending debate. Bellow found her—against all evidence—unsexual. "Saul resented women who didn't act like women," said his student and girlfriend Judy Shavrein—or the way he thought women should act.

When Arendt's book came out in 1963, Bellow stayed on the sidelines, noting that it was "difficult to mention it without arousing one faction or another to fierce denunciation." By the end of the sixties, he'd changed his mind. "The idea of making the century's great crime look dull is not banal," Sammler thunders at his niece, Margotte (a recognizable portrait of Oscar Tarcov's widow, Edith):

Intellectuals do not understand. They get their notions about matters like this from literature. They expect a wicked hero like

Richard III. But do you think the Nazis didn't know what murder was? Everybody (except certain bluestockings) knows what murder is. That is very old human knowledge. The best and purest human beings, from the beginning of time, have understood that life is sacred. To defy that old understanding is not banality. There was a conspiracy against the sacredness of life.

Sammler, "a man of seventy-plus," was one of Bellow's most fully realized characters. Dignified, erudite, unobtrusively courageous, he may have owed something to Marek Edelman, a leader of the Warsaw ghetto uprising whom Bellow had met on a trip to Poland when he was in the midst of writing *Sammler*. Bellow himself identified his model as "an old half-Russian, half-Italian" he'd encountered in Paris during his Guggenheim sojourn— probably Andrea Caffí, who had lived below him at the Hôtel de l'Académie. But he also drew upon the testimony of survivors introduced to him by Edith Tarcov; Bellow listened carefully to their accounts of escaping the Lódz ghetto.

Another plausible model was Edward Shils. Shils was a formidable intellectual presence around the university, renowned for his scholarly contributions to sociology and the editor of a distinguished academic journal called *Minerva*. He was also acerbic to the point of rudeness; he habitually referred to colleagues and students as "foolish," "mediocre," "ignorant." (Sammler condemns the then-popular left-wing theorists T. W. Adorno, Herbert Marcuse, and Norman O. Brown as "worthless fellows"—one of Shils's favorite terms of opprobrium.) To Bellow, Shils became an intellectual mentor, like Harold Rosenberg (and later Allan Bloom, a younger man whom Bellow nonetheless converted into an elder) a figure of immense intellectual authority. Walking together on campus, Bellow and Shils were "God the Father and God the son," in the words of Fran Gendlin.

Shils's influence on *Sammler* was more than conjectural. Bellow gave him a copy of the typescript, and Shils annotated it so extensively that the novel became—according to Daniel Fuchs—"something of a collaborative effort." He disentangled syntax, corrected details of Bloomsbury geography, emended "Lord Keynes" to "John Keynes." (Keynes didn't become a baron until 1942, and

Sammler was said to have known him before the war.) There were "too many ideas," Shils wrote in the margin beside one of Bellow's abstruse ruminations—"and ideas not consistent with the character of Sammler." It was Shils who suggested toning down the sexual passages. "I had no suspicion that old Sammler had phantasy for such things." But he also praised, exclaiming in the margins, "Good!!" and "Very good!"

Bellow heeded most of Shils's suggestions concerning facts; the more general criticism he ignored at his peril. *Mr. Sammler's Planet* is a novel of ideas, to describe it in its kindest light; it consists largely of Sammler's musings on history, religion, human character, the origin and future of the species, delivered in page-long paragraphs. "Once you begin talking, once the mind takes to this way of turning, it keeps turning, and it dips through all events," Sammler says to Dr. Govinda Lal, a Hindu scientist whose manuscript on the feasibility of relocating humanity to the moon is stolen by Sammler's daughter. This, in essence, is the novel's method, culminating in a dialogue between Sammler and Lal that goes on for almost ten thousand words before being "rather mercifully interrupted" (in the words of an otherwise sympathetic reviewer) by one of the book's few actual events: the flooding of the Westchester home that belongs to Sammler's nephew and patron Elya Gruner. Virtually the only scenes are a confrontation at Columbia between Sammler and a radical who insults him in precisely the language of the student who disrupted Bellow's talk at San Francisco State; the self-exposure of the thief; and the loss and eventual recovery of Lal's manuscript—and even that, wrote *Time* (in the first respectful review it had ever given Bellow) was little more than "mechanically produced piffle intended merely to give the reader a respite between Sammler's soliloquys."

There was something eighteenth century about Bellow's Diderot-like discourses ("Please do say something about love," Margotte prompts him); and also something a touch self-congratulatory about "Mr. Minutely-Observant Artur Sammler," a precursor of Dean Corde, with his gift for "noticing." Sammler's meditations on the work of H. G. Wells, on Kant and Marx, and on the philosophy of history veer between the profound and the ponderous. The other characters scarcely exist—apart, perhaps, for Elya Gruner, whose death provides the occasion for a touching meditation on family feeling and the human contract, the terms of which Sammler forcefully reiterates in the book's famous last line: "For that is the truth of it—that we all know, God, that we know, that we know, we know, we know." As Alfred Kazin summed it up: "One can admire the man's intellectual austerity and yet be amazed that Bellow's hero should be so intelligent about everything except his relation with other human beings."

Bellow was aware of the book's failings. It was "out of control," he admitted later, and had no dramatic center. "Sammler isn't even a novel," he confessed to Daniel Fuchs. "It's a dramatic essay of some sort, wrung from me by the crazy Sixties." Bellow's vantage on the decade was that of an old man—a "*past* person," as Sammler says of himself. It was a vantage that made Bellow seem crotchety; *Mr. Sammler's Planet*, several critics remarked, was the first book in which Bellow aligned himself with the fathers. His earlier heroes—Joseph, Augie, Wilhelm—were defiant, rebellious sons; even Herzog, in his mid-forties, was neurotically wrapped up with his father. In *Mr. Sammler's Planet*, the hero is an authority figure. "*Sammler*," wrote Mark Shechner, "is the superego's book."

It was also prescient. Like Lal, for whom the moon promised a refuge from the travails of life on earth (the book was originally entitled "The Future of the Moon"), Bellow now possessed a certain detachment from life. His characters—Sammler, Braun in "The Old System," Mosby in "Mosby's Memoirs"—were older, more reflective versions of their creator: portraits of the artist as an old man. If this book was any indication (and his books generally were), Bellow had achieved a new state—not resignation, but what Sammler, in a memorable phrase, called "earth-departure objectivity." Not yet old, Bellow was already beginning to take his leave.

The final version of *Mr. Sammler's Planet* emerged over a few hectic months in 1969. Meanwhile, Bellow was as peripatetic as ever—in Italy by himself in June, then with Adam in London, then with Maggie Staats to Spain, "polishing off the Sammler-saga" on the Mediterranean coast. Life was anything but placid; there were "grandes difficuldados in England and in the south" with Staats, he reported to Richard Stern, "but I finished just the same. I am obstinate. I make my own obstacles but jump 'em meself."

By August, he was back in the States, "dealing with little boys, ex-wives, publishers, lawyers, fishhooks in the fingers, sunburn, car rentals" on Nantucket. His old flame Rosette Lamont had arranged for him to rent an apartment on Sunset Hill, not far from her own cottage on North Liberty Street. He was glad to be back in America, watching pheasants forage for blackberries in the backyard. The "siege-guns of Chicago" seemed a world away.

Every morning, he walked up the narrow, mint-perfumed path to Lamont's house and read her a few pages of his work in progress. His life, he assured his new love, Fran Gendlin, was "celibate and austere." Bellow seldom relinquished old girlfriends. When Lamont remarried, he was best man at her wedding. On the wall of her Nantucket home was a photograph of her former lover, inscribed *à ma chère cousine.*

The novel was published on February 1, 1970, and instantly elicited a dissonant chorus of praise and blame. To some reviewers, it was "an enduring testament," "appealingly elegiac," "a culmination." The dissenters were equally emphatic. John Bayley, a judicious English critic, found the book tiresome and familiar; Alison Lurie wearied of Bellow's gallery of "Dickensian grotesques." Alfred Kazin, after paying tribute to Bellow's "formidable" intellect, scolded him for the "punitive moral outrage" that Sammler directs at every character in the book.

Still, if the verdict on *Mr. Sammler's Planet* was mixed, the general consensus was clear. By 1970, approaching the age of fifty-five, Bellow was a writer destined to last. An essay the following year by Joseph Epstein in *The New York Times Book Review* summed up his situation:

> Saul Bellow is the premier American novelist: the best writer we have in the literary form that has been dominant in the literature of the past hundred years. He has come to his eminence not through the mechanics of publicity, self-advertisement or sensationalism, but through slowly building up a body of work, an *oeuvre,* that with each new novel has displayed greater range, solidity, penetration and brilliance.

In his work perhaps alone among that of living American novelists it is possible to trace a clear line of development, to find a steadily increasing confluence of intellectual power with the more sheerly joyous aspects of narrative art. From the skeletal "Dangling Man" (1944) to the more artistically rounded "The Victim" (1947) through the spirited breakthrough of "The Adventures of Augie March" (1953) on to the urban intensities of "Seize the Day" (1956), to the exuberance of "Henderson the Rain King" (1959), to the rich comic complexity of "Herzog" (1964), to the masterwork that is "Mr. Sammler's Planet" (1970), Bellow has advanced from being a promising writer to an interesting writer to an exciting writer to a major writer, which is where he is today.

23

—It takes me so long to read the paper,
said to me one day a novelist hot as a firecracker,
because I have to identify myself with everyone in it,
including the corpses, pal.

—JOHN BERRYMAN,
"Dream Song #53"

Saul wasn't made for happiness.

—EDWARD SHILS

HENDERSON'S AFRICA had been conjured up out of dusty anthropology monographs. But now Bellow, too, could say he'd been there. He went in February 1970 with Dave Peltz, who had made the journey twice before; Peltz was in correspondence with "an ex–Mau Mau terrorist in Nairobi" who was hoping to persuade him to invest in a beryllium mine in Kenya. Bellow claimed that he could obtain a letter of introduction to the naturalist George Schaller, who was studying lions in the Serengeti. "He said 'Let's go, Dave,'" Peltz recalled. "'We'll live in a tent and get a look at the lions. I'll pay your way.' True to form, he never did."

Hardly the Conradian heart of darkness, Africa proved a comically small world: On a crowded street in downtown Nairobi, the two Tuleyites encountered the artist Saul Steinberg, Bellow's neighbor on Long Island. "The streets were filled with men in tunics or togas or droopy drawers, women in turbans and flowered dresses," Bellow recalled. Bellow and Steinberg were both wearing many-pocketed bush jackets, "but what identified us positively as Americans was the long-billed baseball cap each of us wore." Steinberg was, by his own account, "an old Africa hand." Together, they flew to Kampala and hired a van with a driver, then set off in their safari suits for Murchison Falls. The mining deal had failed to materialize; it was "pure con," Bellow reported to Fran Gendlin on East African Airways stationery: "Peltz's man w'd not appear. Evidently it was an intercontinental swindle. Hugely funny."

On the launch that took them down the river, Bellow was more interested in a Danish woman on board than in the wildlife. (He later claimed it was Steinberg who tried to make time with "the pretty Scandinavian.") In any event, he missed the primal episode in which a pair of water buffalo, drinking by the water's edge, witnessed the disappearance of their calf in the jaws of a crocodile, but picked up enough details to use it later in his fiction. In "A Silver Dish," a masterly portrait of Peltz, Bellow has Woody Selbst, a bluff, congenial contractor from south Chicago, recall the scene:

> There were giraffes along the tropical river, and hippopota-muses, and baboons, and flamingos and other brilliant birds crossing the bright air in the heat of the morning, when the calf, stepping into the river to drink, was grabbed by the hoof and dragged down. The parent buffaloes couldn't figure it out. Under the water the calf still threshed, fought, churned the mud. Woody, the robust traveler, took this in as he sailed by, and to him it looked as if the parent cattle were asking each other dumbly what had happened. He chose to assume that there was pain in this, he read brute grief into it.

It was a characteristic appropriation. "Saul has used my life and my stories and never given me a by-line," Peltz complained (while graciously acknowledging the brilliant literary use Bellow made of his material).

They had a close call when a crocodile tried to climb into their boat. "What went through my mind was the comical obituaries," Steinberg recalled, imagining the headline: CROCODILE EATS TWO SAULS. Bellow had the same thought: "This is it! Killed in Africa by a crocodile!" Then one of the boatmen pushed against the sand-bank, and the beast slid back into the water. "Steinberg helped the Danish lady to her feet, but there was nothing he could do to please her," as Bellow remembered the scene three decades later, speaking at Steinberg's memorial service (and still seeking to depict his late friend rather than himself as the one who had been spurned).

The trip put Bellow in a jaunty mood. He was "feeling great," he wrote to Gendlin; and, a week later, on the back of a postcard of a pair of lions at play: "This, the Upper Nile, is simply astonishing. If the tstetse fly doesn't bite me I shall never forget it. If it does, give away my Mercedes and burn my bills."

What made Bellow more nervous than crocodiles or tsetse flies was Peltz's purchase of some marijuana joints from their driver. "I lit one and in one puff was stoned," Peltz said. "It was incredibly powerful stuff." Then Steinberg came to their hotel room, and he and Peltz both got stoned: "Steinberg was neighing and prancing around." While his companions dissolved in hysterics, Bellow lay on the bed "like a patient," working up the resolve to join them. Finally, he took one puff and decided he couldn't go further. "I was deeply depressed by the stuff."

On the way home, Bellow and Steinberg made a whirlwind tour of Addis Ababa ("On the boulevards there were no cars, no buses or taxis—no shops, no people"), then flew to Rome by way of Khartoum, Cairo, and Athens, "12 hours that left me somewhat vacant and pill-bilious," he wrote Gendlin from the Hotel Raphael. When he met up with Peltz at the Rome airport, he was still fretting about his friend's stash. "What are you going to do with all that pot?" he asked suspiciously as they prepared to board the plane for home. Afraid of getting arrested, he refused to stand in line with Peltz, who smuggled the marijuana through customs in the pocket of his raincoat. ("Risk was a wonderful stimulus," Bellow wrote of Woody Selbst.) But the trip had served a purpose. "I am better, more settled in mind and am willing—no, longing—to come back," he wrote Gendlin on the eve of his return.

The reception of *Mr. Sammler's Planet*, mixed though it was, had elevated Bellow's reputation beyond the realm of literature. He was by now "a cultural frame of reference," noted the critic Peter Prescott in the spring of 1970. *Esquire* that year included him in its feature "The 100 Most Important People in the World Today."

But the gravity of his reputation had the effect—as fame often does—of distancing him from contemporary events. More and more, he viewed the political and social turmoil of the period from an Olympian height. His deepening estrangement from the

younger generation was revealed starkly in a profile by Jane
Howard that appeared in *Life* in the spring of 1970. Howard
opened her piece with an account of a dispiriting evening at Yale,
at which Robert Penn Warren had invited Bellow to address a
small group of English students. "There he sat captive, donnishly
tweedy . . . and there they sat, long-haired, languid and oddly
unresponsive." Bellow made no effort to be accommodating. "The
trouble with the destroyers is that they're just as phony as what
they've come to destroy," he replied to a question about campus
revolutionaries: "Maybe civilization *is* dying, but it still exists, and
meanwhile we have our choice: we can either rain more blows on
it, or try to redeem it." By nine o'clock, the students' questions had
died out. Making the excuse that he had a train to catch, Bellow
shrugged on his sheepskin coat and left.

In April 1970 he spoke at Purdue. Wary after the confrontation
at San Francisco State, Bellow contemplated the prospect with
distaste. "I shouldn't be put into a shock box," he objected when
Mark Harris, who had organized the event, told him that a scheduled morning seminar had burgeoned into a formal dinner for six
hundred. "I'm not being *punished* for something. I shouldn't be
put on display like Eichmann in Jerusalem. I shouldn't be a clay
pipe in a shooting gallery." Bellow as Adolf Eichmann, the
murderer of a million Jews: This was taking victimization—or was
it guilt?—to a new level. Instead of respectful pilgrims, the large
audience that came to hear Bellow was in his mind a gallery of
prosecutors.

But it was the guest of honor, not his auditors, who came out
swinging. Bellow's talk, delivered from the podium of a crowded
banquet hall in the Purdue Memorial Union, was a masterpiece of
sustained invective; its very title—"Culture Now: Some Animadversions, Some Laughs"—portended trouble. Literature had been
drowned out by "the power of great public questions," Bellow
maintained. It was no match for the noise generated by politics, by
the momentous mass events of the twentieth century: war, revolution, slaughter on a staggering scale. How could intellectuals hope
to be heard? In their hunger to capture the public's attention, they
had thrown in their lot with the very mass culture they had once
scorned. The avant-garde was putting itself out of business.
Describing a few "miserable" afternoons spent in the library

perusing literary magazines, Bellow quoted at length from an essay by William Phillips on the work of Susan Sontag, for whom—in Phillips's lame paraphrase—"the idea of silence is actually used as a metaphor for the opposite of talkiness in art." Reading Phillips, according to Bellow, was "much like trying to go scuba diving at Coney Island in urinous brine and scraps of old paper, orange rinds and soaked hot dog buns."*

Phillips's gloss on Sontag *was* a fairly egregious piece of work, slavish about fashionable ideas of which he had a poor grasp. But Bellow's polemic was immoderate in its vehemence. For nearly a decade now, he had been attacking the very constituency most devoted to his work, the New York intellectuals. How account for the tone of resentment, of personal bitterness behind his animus? ("They want to cook their meals over Pater's hard gemlike flame and light their cigarettes at it.") Bellow turned on them— especially the Jewish ones—the way he turned on his friends and his wives. It wasn't that they didn't love him; they didn't love him enough.

Bellow's audience at Purdue was baffled by his rage. Enervated by the heat in the auditorium and the heavy banquet food, many found Bellow's seventy-minute talk "tedious, inscrutable, mysterious, difficult, and finally affronting," Mark Harris recalled. They were in no mood for an ill-tempered lecture. But it was a characteristic performance. Bellow never tailored his message to suit his audience. "He'd do his thing, as the saying was, not *ours*," Harris aptly summed up: "He had not offered himself nor even really wanted to come, neither for the money nor the friendship. But when he did come it was his person who came, it was who he was, not some genial man."

Two months later, Bellow flew to New York to collect an honorary degree from New York University. He had accepted the award "out of sheer decency, and because universities have taken such punishment for the sins of society as a whole," he wrote in a satirical account of the proceedings.

*Phillips had joined Bellow's lengthening enemies' list after he published Richard Poirier's attack on *Herzog* in *Partisan Review.*

The NYU commencement was a strange event, charged with the political contentiousness of the time. Bellow was accompanied to the ceremony by Mrs. Vincent Astor, a trustee of the university and "one of the historic names in Society," he noted, citing her family's involvement in "fur trading, the Revolutionary War, Manhattan real-estate, the great house in Newport." He got on famously with Mrs. Astor, admiring the way she "carried her billions with admirable lightness." After the commencement speaker, George Wald, a longhaired Harvard Nobel laureate in physiology who fancied himself a radical, delivered a sixties-style diatribe, a wave of protest arose from the audience of proud parents and relatives. "There's going to be a riot," Astor whispered excitedly as a procession of muscle-bound marshals—actually police in disguise—trooped in through the back of the hall. "Isn't it exciting! This is simply marvelous!" As another speaker, in a gesture of pragmatic patriotism, launched into a loud recitation of the Pledge of Allegiance to calm the crowd, Astor and Bellow slipped away through a side door.

Bellow's version of events was funny but cruel and even racist in the objects of its satire, notably one "Mrs. Nattash," the pseudonym of "a black lady from the U.N." with a substantial bosom—"It was her country that was underdeveloped, not herself." In Bellow's self-serving and sanctimonious account, he was the only one to keep his dignity: "A reader of Plutarch, he began to appreciate the fact that Scipio Africanus had retired into solitude."

In the summer of 1970, Bellow was on his way to Israel again, this time at the invitation of the Hebrew University English department. He had a crowded schedule. On the last Sunday in June, he was the featured guest at a symposium sponsored by the U.S. Cultural Center in Tel Aviv, where he answered questions from six Israeli literary figures, among them the poet Yehuda Amichai and the novelist A. B. Yehoshua.

Bellow's topic was America and the cataclysmic changes that were occurring there. What had happened to the American dream? Speaking to an Israeli audience, Bellow dwelled on the experiences of his generation of American Jews, caught between the "terrible nightmare" of their own childhoods and the unregulated freedom they had bequeathed to their children, with alarming consequences. Bellow's generation had grown up in a claustrophobic atmosphere, oppressed by their parents' struggles to adapt themselves to the New World. Their children "were going to be free and were going to enjoy every privilege of life." Instead, they had raised a generation indifferent to its own legacy. America was "in a state of siege," Bellow maintained. The New Left was a haunting incarnation of the Old Left, whose vision of a classless society had culminated in the terror of Stalin. As Bellow framed the issue before a large, attentive audience: "The real question is whether the United States can survive the role that it is playing today as a great world power, and also whether two hundred million people can live in a capitalist democracy without losing their liberties and without poisoning themselves out of existence."

The turmoil of the last decade, both public and personal, had aged Bellow. He had the face of "a very sad wise man," observed the Israeli journalist Shlomo Grodzensky, who had first met Bellow in 1960. Ten years later, Grodzensky marked the changes: "His face is still wonderfully youthful, but cast in an almost aged wisdom." In his mid-fifties, Bellow already referred to himself, somewhat prematurely, as "elderly"; he identified more with his venerated Jewish predecessors—Isaac Babel, I. L. Peretz, and S. Y. Agnon—than with writers of his own generation. What he described as "the strong Jewish element" in his character was becoming more pronounced than ever. At the same time, he remained proud of his Americanness—especially in Israel, where writers and intellectuals were so eager to claim him as their own. For Bellow, the tragic history of the Jews was inscribed in his soul, but so was an American habit of skepticism and independence.

That summer's trip coincided with the twenty-fifth anniversary of the liberation of Bergen-Belsen, and Bellow had been invited to a banquet in Jerusalem. The main speaker was the novelist Elie Wiesel, a survivor of Auschwitz who had devoted his life to consecrating that experience. Alfred Kazin, who was also present, described Wiesel's speech as "a survivor's soliloquy, a litany, a hymn, a *Kaddish*," but also "rhetorical, hysterical, a writer's public performance without irony." Bellow looked bored. He was more responsive to the feisty message delivered by the chain-smoking Israeli prime minister, Golda Meir, who stood up, surrounded by Mossad agents and soldiers armed with Uzis—the memory of the Six-Day War still lingered—and declared in Yiddish, "No matter what they do to us, we'll beat them." "There wasn't a dry eye in the house," recalled Fran Gendlin, Bellow's companion on the trip.

Gendlin's passionate affair with Bellow lasted five years—on the long roster of Bellow's women, she qualified as one of the "serious" ones. In his memoir, *New York Jew*, Kazin described Bellow "laughingly translating the Prime Minister's Yiddish into the left ear of the girl accompanying him." In Gendlin's recollection, Bellow wasn't translating the prime minister's remarks; he was whispering, "Has Kazin made a pass at you?"

For all his globe-trotting—"Without O'Hare, / Sheer despair," his character Charlie Citrine liked to say—Bellow was rooted in Chicago. He loved reminiscing about his Chicago youth. His capacity to summon up the minutest details about Humboldt Park in the 1920s amazed and delighted his friends. Answering a letter from Nate Gould, an eloquent Tuley radical, he wrote: "The other day I recalled talking to you after a lecture by Maxim Olay at the Anarchist Forum (opp. Humboldt Park). We agreed with him that private property was a wicked thing." With Al Glotzer, another Tuleyite, Bellow traded recollections about Nestor Johnson skates, Hammersmark's bookstore, and the old high-top boots that came with a penknife in a sheath. What was it about the city in those days that exerted such a powerful sway over their emotions? "I suppose we had instinctively understood that it filled our need for poetry," Bellow wrote Glotzer: "Besides, maturity meant work, and work was something dark and blind to which we were sentenced when boyhood ended. It seems to me that we made excellent use of the liberty we enjoyed as schoolboys."

This attachment to his past endeared Bellow to his friends: It made their own lives somehow more vivid. That he had found meaning in their experience, had imposed on the gritty landscape of Chicago the order and significance of art, gave him a special place among them. It was his fiction, and his example as a writer, that had enabled his friends to "put their identities together," in the words of Mel Tumin. In a tribute delivered at one of the many award ceremonies Bellow attended in his later years, Tumin recalled that Bellow had loaned him two dollars to buy a marriage license and a necktie to wear to his own wedding and had gotten him a job working on Mortimer Adler's *Syntopicon.* "We learned from him—surely I did—the importance of applying to the world the force of one's own being; and of harnessing one's powers, and pressing down with them on the refractory material of experience and imposing on that experience a shape and a vision that one could call one's own."

However proud he was of "knowing" Chicago, Bellow relied on his friends to take him behind the scenes—their lives formed the basis of his research. Three contentious divorces had given him plenty of exposure to lawyers and courtrooms, but he also depended on sources like his old Tuley classmate Julius "Lucky" Echeles—who referred to him as "Bellows"—to supply him with low-life lore. The cigar-smoking, fast-talking Echeles was often in the news; "local legal legend," the *Chicago Tribune* called him. Echeles defended—in Chicago parlance—"B-girls" and "juice loan racketeers"; in the fifties, he was debarred and nearly sent to jail for conspiring to sell post-office jobs—a typical Chicago activity. Bellow tagged around the State Street courthouse with Echeles, collecting data.

Bellow was as vivid a presence in Chicago as Henry James had been in London or Beckett was in Paris. Chicagoans regularly glimpsed him lunching at the elegant Whitehall Club on the Near North Side or rummaging through used books at Staver's bookshop on Fifty-seventh Street. Joseph Epstein, writing in *The New York Times Book Review,* remarked on the novelist's "singular" appearance: Gap-toothed, white-haired, with a nose "Gogol would have approved," he radiated a quietly charismatic presence. His eyes were his most notable feature: "They are dark brown and go deep and seem extraordinarily young. All the more young for the fact that the rest of his face looks to have taken its full 55-year share of the ravages of weather, work and general human tribulation." Bellow was beginning to look "Sammleresque," Epstein

remarked, adding, "Can it be that novelists come to resemble their
literary creations the way some people do their pets?"

Unlike Sammler, however, Bellow was far from reclusive and far
from old: He thought nothing of setting out for a long peripatetic
evening that could involve several stops—a reception in Hyde
Park, dinner at Morton's Steak House, followed by a party on the
Near North Side, a twenty-mile trip along Lake Shore Drive. He
still played a vigorous game of squash at the Riviera Club.
(Epstein, a quarter century his junior, was a regular partner and
could barely outlast him on the court.) He was lithe and trim and
as proud of his figure as Herzog, who boasts of his thirty-four-inch
waistline to a sales clerk in a menswear store; he could have worn
the same suits he'd worn as a young man if it hadn't been for his
highly developed taste in bespoke tailors.

In his own family, Bellow's status was less exalted than in the
collective consciousness of Chicago; he remained, and would
always remain, the youngest son. The literary "business," even for
a writer who showed up regularly on the bestseller list, was less
lucrative than the businesses his brothers were in: real estate, nursing homes, utilities. Maurice's empire was far-flung: He owned, in
addition to Bunge Coal, two hotels and extensive property in
Florida. He lived in a sleek high-rise at 20 East Cedar—"a real
swanky building," according to Bellow.

Sam, too, was by now a wealthy man, though the memory of
passing the windows of a Montreal bakery on the way to cheder
with empty pockets was so ineradicable that he still kept a freezer
filled with napoleons and éclairs in his office. More conventional
than his brothers, Sam maintained an Orthodox household; on
Passover, Bellow was invited to a lavish seder at Sam's South Side
home. A prominent member of the Jewish community, Sam had
been cited by the Academy Associates, a local organization of
businessmen, as a "distinguished personality." Clearly, the three
brothers had made it. "There's a main thread that held them
together," said Maurice's daughter, Lynn: "The striving for success,
the materialism, the achieving. Success was money—money and
power."

In his fiction, Bellow was eloquent on the intensity of family
ties, the "immigrant loving" that infused his feelings toward his

older brothers, but he felt his difference from them as keenly as his affinity. Sitting on a park bench in Washington with Walter Pozen, a young lawyer who became a close friend in the early seventies, Bellow complained gloomily that he was still condescended to because he didn't make tons of money: "A lot of people in my family just think I'm some schmuck with a pen."

In the world beyond the Bellow clan, Bellow's stock continued to rise. The chairmanship of the Committee on Social Thought rotated among its members, and from 1970 to 1975 the position fell to Bellow. He regarded with pride his new "eminence" as a department chairman, but the position entailed hard work. A few months into the job, he complained about the lack of funds: "This rich university has been caught in the squeeze. Deans now nag you about secretarial pennies and send out memos about the urgent need to increase enrollment. A sort of Bowery twilight has dropped over us."

Classes in the committee were intimate; Bellow's English-novel seminar, taught with David Grene, had only five students one year. Bellow didn't need a large audience to inspire him; he was "inventive, eloquent and discursive," recalled Semon Strobos, a graduate student during the mid-seventies; like Dr. Johnson, he was "able to speak more or less as he wrote." Straying from the text at hand, he offered autobiographical digressions about his Canadian childhood, his student days at the University of Chicago, writers he had known. "He talked about his own life as an artist—he figured that was what people came to hear—and he was enchanting when he did," said Arlette Landes. He called his courses "episodes in the history of the soul in modern times."

He taught what he liked: the novel from Defoe to Joyce; Tolstoy's shorter works. He devoted almost a whole semester to *Madame Bovary,* a book that "excited" him, according to Carol Brightman, the future biographer of Mary McCarthy, because of the way Flaubert had entered into the lives of ordinary people. If he wasn't sufficiently engaged, he called it quits; one year, he folded up a seminar on *Ulysses* two thirds of the way through. He had a high opinion of his own powers; once, when a student came in late, Bellow reprimanded him, "Would you walk into an opera in the middle of an act?"

He was impatient with the fashion of psychologically overinterpreting literary works, but Bellow himself was a close reader, shrewdly attentive to what made for good prose. Picking out sentences at random from *Gulliver's Travels,* he showed how the energy of Swift's prose came from the weight placed on verbs. He also relied heavily on Erich Auerbach's *Mimesis,* a weighty compendium of essays on the classics, sometimes reading aloud pages at a time. As a teacher, he was somewhat aloof, but he compiled a respectable record for his Ph.D. candidates in a department notable for its students' dilatory ways. "Though he had a reputation for being difficult and was resented, or usually envied, for teaching so little, I never saw him anything but unfailingly courteous and gentle in an old-world manner," observed Semon Strobos.

Bellow also co-taught a Flaubert seminar with Edith Hartnett, a specialist in French literature. Hartnett came to occupy a controversial place in the lore of the Committee on Social Thought. Bellow had known her since the forties, when she was married to Herbert Gold. In the seventies, she became one of Bellow's many "girls"—as friends of a certain age referred to the women in his life. Hartnett was the committee's secretary, but she had a Ph.D. in comparative literature from the University of Michigan and was "not a trivial person," according to James Redfield, who taught classics in the committee. Hartnett was regarded as Bellow's "protégée." In those days, the chairman could appoint one assistant professor during his term; Bellow chose Hartnett, then tried to promote her to a tenured position. Shils, a formidable opponent in academic politics, blocked the appointment on the grounds that Hartnett wasn't "a real scholar." Bellow was filling the department with his "whores," Shils spluttered.

The epithet was grossly defamatory, but the plural was not entirely unmerited. Bellow also tried to forward the academic career of another girlfriend, Bette Howland. Bellow denied that he was *shtupping* Howland—to use Shils's word—but their affair was common knowledge, and it was Shils's firm belief that, as far as academic positions were concerned, "you shouldn't push a screwee."

James Redfield, Bellow's predecessor as chairman, got in a wrangle with Bellow over the status of another secretary, Herman Sinaiko. Sinaiko had a modest reputation as a scholar and hadn't published a great deal; some members of the committee, notably Bellow and Shils and Grene, felt that he "didn't contribute to their prestige," as Redfield put it. After Redfield went on sabbatical, the trio decided to drop Sinaiko from the committee, and Grene wrote to Redfield informing him of the decision; Bellow was reluctant to write the letter himself. The episode dampened their friendship. "Saul has this way of making you feel everything's your fault," Redfield said.

For Bellow, the Committee on Social Thought provided structure and diverted his energy from more self-destructive pursuits. "I write from about eight o'clock in the morning until one," he once told a reporter: "Then I go out and make my mistakes." As a professor and administrator, he had less opportunity for private misdemeanors—a blessing.

D̲espite his vow not to become a "cultural functionary," Bellow was now a public intellectual, required to make the rounds of weighty symposia and serve on committees. In December 1970, he attended a Conference on Soviet Jewry in Washington, along with Alfred Kazin, Arthur Miller, and Norman Podhoretz; he put his name to a petition drawn up by an organization called the Ad Hoc Committee for Intellectual Freedom to protest the Soviet persecution of Alexander Solzhenitsyn. The following summer, he attended a lofty forum at the Aspen Institute for the Humanities.

He was also busy with a new project: a journal in the mold of *The Noble Savage*. Keith Botsford had landed a job as head of the National Translation Center at the University of Texas in Austin, and Bellow flew down often to confer about their new venture. By the spring of 1970, they had a handful of manuscripts and a working title: "The Ark." "With three sons, I qualify as a Noah," he wrote to Richard Stern.

In a statement of purpose drafted for potential benefactors, Bellow invoked *The Dial, transition, Criterion, Hound and Horn,* and *Horizon*. "How stirring these magazines were!" he declared in his manifesto:

Behind these old pages stood an international cultural community which respected art, reason, and knew the value of order. It was also hostile towards these excellent things, sometimes saw them in dissolution or decline, but did not seriously consider living without them. It said goodbye, but so, so lingeringly. It comes to something like this: between 1919 and 1929, after the first world crisis, civilization took a long breath. It was a melancholy period. It seems to us now enviably tranquil, the golden age of the modern masters. The Depression, Fascism and Communism put an end to this, not so much by the weight of crisis as by shifting the interest of mankind to the contemporaneous. The fascinating questions were those of the moment—unemployment, war, money, labor, capitalism, revolution. The dramatic powers of these proved irresistible.

Where was this international cultural community now? Did such an entity still exist? Yes, answered Bellow, but it was much more "diverse, disorderly, and turbulent." It was the job of "The Ark" to give it voice.

By press time, "The Ark" had become *Anon*. No editors were listed; the issue had been put together, according to an editorial statement, with the "anonymous collaboration" of Bellow, Mark Harris, and Roger Shattuck, a professor of French literature at the University of Texas. Paid for out of Bellow's own pocket, it was a lively debut. There were poems by Edwin Honig and Cesare Pavese, among others; a memoir by the Indian writer G. V. Desani; an interview with André Malraux; and the usual contributions from Bellow's writer friends: Robert Hivnor, Rosette Lamont, Richard Stern. But a good part of *Anon* consisted of Arias, that curious genre pioneered in *The Noble Savage*—anonymous squibs, screeds, diatribes, and fulminations that struck an unmistakably Bellovian note. "Mr. Wollix Gets an Honorary Degree," about the commotion surrounding Bellow's degree from NYU, is demonstrably by Bellow's own hand; a touching obituary of Heinrich Bluecher, Bellow's colleague at Bard (and the husband of Hannah Arendt), is conjecturally his. The first issue appeared with the date December 31, 1970, and carried an announcement that future issues would appear "every six weeks or eight times a year." None ever did.

Early in March 1971, Bellow learned that he had won a third National Book Award for *Mr. Sammler's Planet*. The ceremony was held on March 4 at Alice Tully Hall in New York before a capacity audience of over a thousand.

Fame hadn't mellowed him. The acrimonious political climate of the Vietnam era and the racial tensions around the university, surrounded on three sides by a vast black slum, exacerbated Bellow's chronic feelings of embattlement and persecution. He was still dealing with the book's aftermath, a residue of ill feeling among the easily recognized targets of Sammler's wrath. When a reporter for a Chicago paper mentioned that a black friend of his had been offended by Sammler's reference to "the barbarous world of color erupting from underneath," Bellow "paled" with anger and quoted one of his favorite Yiddish proverbs: "A fool throws a stone in a pool, and ten wise men cannot find it." Why should blacks—or Negroes, as he still called them—be treated differently than any other minority that had made its way in America? Bellow asked. "I have learned there is more truth in my imagination than there is in the public relations habits of minorities."

This querulous, defensive tone echoed through his correspondence. He accused Ruth Miller of saying "damaging things" about his books behind his back. When Mark Harris made the mistake of referring to an article by Nelson Algren, Bellow sniped: "What puzzles me and intrigues me too is that editors go on stealing these cadavers from the literary medical school and rig them with wires to make life-like jerks."

He also had an epistolary dustup with Alfred Kazin, himself a prickly character. Kazin had published a negative review of *Mr. Sammler's Planet* in *The New York Review of Books*, objecting to Sammler's arrogance and contempt for ordinary people, his need "to be right all the time." Bellow was particularly incensed by the condescending note on which the review ended. "God lives," Kazin had written, suggesting that Sammler had appointed himself the supreme moral arbiter. "About my books you may say what you like," Bellow wrote him. "For that matter, you may also say

what you please about my character, too. You haven't much gift
for satire and 'God lives!' didn't hurt much. What offended me
was that you were not reviewing my novel, you were saying that
its author was a wickedly deluded lunatic."

Why go after Kazin? It *was* a tough review, unsparing in its
enumeration of the novel's failings. And it struck awfully close to
home: Sammler's character as Kazin described it—"profoundly
moralistic and world-weary," blinded by a "total identity with his
own thought"—bore a disquieting resemblance to its author's.
Bellow had reason to be hurt. Still, there was something immoderate about his vehemence. Kazin was one of his most ardent
supporters. He had praised each book in succession, privately and
publicly, and had paid homage to Bellow's charisma in a memoir
honoring the author of *Herzog*. But he had—once—dared to criticize his literary hero.*

"I know my sins well enough," Bellow concluded his letter to
Kazin. "They distress me, and I struggle with them. You may not
believe this but I can, oddly enough, bear to be corrected." Those
who did it, however, paid a price. From then on, Kazin was an
enemy.

Fending off interviewers, symposium organizers, literary-
awards committees, aspiring writers, anthologists, magazine editors, and academic specialists in his work, Bellow contrived to feel
neglected. When Susan Cheever asked him to support her application for a Guggenheim, he agreed to write a letter but warned her
that the selection committee routinely disregarded his recommen-
dations. (Cheever got her Guggenheim.) "No one gives me the
time of day anymore except yourself, and John Cheever and I
forget who else," he wrote self-pityingly to Mark Harris.

He could always count on attention from Susan's lawyers.
"Some things are bugging me. Legal and judicial things," Bellow
confided to Harris. He promised to read Harris's new novel, *The
Goy* (Bellow deplored the title), after women stopped suing him

---

*Where Bellow's work was concerned, Kazin remained loyal to the end. In
1973, writing in his study of American fiction, *Bright Book of Life*, he gave an
impassioned account of Bellow's career, and he continued to review Bellow's
books respectfully until the year of his death.

"on improbable charges." "I read almost nothing these days except legal briefs and complicated proposals from the CPA."

Susan, building what Rosette Lamont described as "Pharaonic pyramids of litigation," had filed a petition to vacate the property-settlement portion of the Bellows' divorce agreement on the grounds that Bellow had deliberately underestimated his income—in the language of the court, a "material misrepresentation." The Long Divorce, as it came to be known among their friends, endured longer than any of Bellow's marriages. "He didn't want to resolve it; he wanted to go on fighting," said one of Susan's lawyers. But Susan, too, was in no mood to settle. "It was her profession," noted Bellow's old friends the McCloskeys. "She wanted to divorce Saul and punish him and still stay married to him."

There was merit to Susan's charge that Bellow was hiding income. While claiming he was "a broken-down college professor," he was earning substantial sums: $163,622 in 1969; $169,165 in 1970. He was also on thin ice in claiming that the apartment on South Shore had belonged exclusively to him. "I paid for it and assumed that it was mine," Bellow told the court, unaware—or pretending to be unaware—that it was held in a joint tenancy.

When Susan sued for payment of her legal fees, it was the last straw. "Now I have Susan's suit to keep me company in my insomniac hours," Bellow griped to Sam Freifeld. "The thought of paying her legal fees, even, incenses me. At a time like this I think very fondly of death. I think death may be good for some people. I may even be one of them myself." Susan had "cleaned him out," he complained to his old friend Julian Behrstock. "If this keeps up, I'm going to have to go back to where I started—on the WPA."

But divorce court, like all of Bellow's self-created tribulations, provided material—whole chapters of *Humboldt's Gift* are set there—and occasioned some of his most celebrated mots ("Her fig leaf turned out to be a price tag"). It was also therapeutic. When Herbert Gold complained that Edith Hartnett had put him through a bruising divorce, Bellow said: "It's good that you hate her: it cauterizes the wound."

Bellow adopted a comic attitude toward his procession of wives. "Talking to me about marriage is like talking to the man who runs the zoo about rabbits," he said to Philip Roth—it wasn't his field. Yet he continued to dwell on his marital prospects with several women; he needed someone to "take care of his life," he admitted. Among the active candidates during the seventies were two Frenchwomen: Nadine Nimier, Bellow's old flame from his Guggenheim sojourn in Paris, and Monique Gonthier, a journalist. The daughter of Russian-Polish Jews who had fled to Paris in 1930 after Stalin came to power, and survived the war in hiding, Gonthier was a tough, independent-minded young woman who was also something of a literary groupie. (She counted William Styron among her conquests.) She and Bellow had met at the home of James Jones, whose luxurious apartment on the Ile Saint-Louis was a salon for visiting American writers in those years.

Almost from the start of their affair, Bellow talked about the possibility of marriage—but "in a tortuous way." He complained that Gonthier's English wasn't good enough and objected to her liberal politics; they once had a huge fight about Angela Davis and the black liberation movement. There were also sexual conflicts; Gonthier intimated that Bellow was unexciting in bed. But if she had pushed matters, she said, she might have ended up his wife.

If not Gonthier, why not Nimier? Would she come live with him in Chicago? he proposed on one of his trips to Paris. Nimier was *sceptique:* For Bellow, she felt, women were *"un rêve, un fantasme, pas une réalité."* And there were other women in his life, she knew—lots of other women. "I wasn't number one, or even number two. If he proposed marriage and you rejected him, he wasn't hurt; it scarcely even registered. He would say, 'I'll come back and write my next book *chez vous.'*"

Age hadn't diminished Bellow's ardor. Joining the English biographer Claire Tomalin on the podium at a literary conference, he complimented her "nice legs." Sitting beside Sandy Broyard, the wife of the *New York Times* book critic Anatole Broyard, at a New York dinner party, Bellow was so flirtatious that she half expected to feel his hand on her knee. In this (as in every other detail), Joseph Epstein's 1990 portrait of Noah Danzig is drawn directly from life:

> He was sexually prideful. He once told me that a young lesbian
> approached him to propose that he father the child she and her

lover wanted to raise, the two having decided they admired his genetic endowment. Another time he mentioned that his physician told him his prostate was in remarkably good repair for a man of fifty-seven. Fame, especially artistic fame, can be a splendid aphrodisiac, and Noah seemed to want to take advantage of his resources in this line whenever possible.

Bellow was attracted to strong, accomplished women (as long as they weren't *too* strong and accomplished), but his interest in their work was perfunctory at best. "Leave the writing to me," he advised Rosette Lamont when she tried to share her authority on modern French literature; it was the function of women to listen, not to be heard. "He liked me as his audience," said his student Judy Shavrein. When Fran Gendlin came over to his apartment in the Cloisters for lunch, Bellow would read aloud his morning's work. Once, when Gendlin showed him a review of a biography of Einstein that she'd written for *The Bulletin of the Atomic Scientists,* he reached inside her blouse, cupped his hand on her breast, and said: "Aren't you glad you do other things so well?" To Helen Garrie, yet another one of his marital prospects, Bellow summed up his view of relations between the sexes: "Women are the rails on which men run."

It wasn't only women who experienced the vicissitudes of his allegiance. Lawyers and accountants came and went; literary executors were appointed and dismissed. Richard Stern was to be "removed entirely" from his will, Bellow instructed his attorneys in the wake of some blowup with his old and loyal friend. After Bette Howland was appointed his literary executor (a temporary appointment; she was soon succeeded by Maggie Staats), one of Bellow's lawyers noted wearily—and oxymoronically—on his client's file: "His life is always in flux and therefore there is no even temporary permanence about his selections."

His one mainstay was his agent at Russell and Volkening, Harriet Wasserman, an energetic if abrasive woman who had started out at the switchboard of the venerable firm and had taken over the management of Bellow after Volkening retired. "Saul was the ass on which Harriet rode into Jerusalem," as one of their friends unkindly described her triumph. Stocky and yentalike ("a museum piece trapped inside a middle-class liberal Jewish girl, living in a ghost town of virtue" was the way Bellow described her), Wasserman was a bundle of energy—negative energy, according to publishers who had to deal with her. "To say that she was attentive to Saul is an absurd underestimate of her attitude; she was completely absorbed and obsessed," said Ed Burlingame, one of Bellow's many editors at Harper and Row. "The more crises and dramas there were, the more she had to do for him. She needed to be seen as a key defender against the hordes of darkness." In a way, they were made for each other: They each had a dramatic sense of victimization and fantasies of valiant self-defense. What mattered to Bellow was the attention she paid him. She negotiated his contracts with a fierce eye, fended off journalists, answered his mail, and even did his shopping for him. When he needed Wilkinson Bonded Razor Blades in Spain, Wasserman sent them.

They had one sexual encounter, a disastrous episode early in their relationship when Bellow came over to Wasserman's apartment for dinner and the flustered agent dressed for the occasion in what she described as "a black Lastex body suit" under a caftan. As they headed for the bedroom and the caftan came off, her new client exclaimed, "You're not coming to bed in that diving suit!" "That night was never mentioned again," Wasserman recalled. "There was no flirting anymore. It was strictly business—and a growing friendship," she added piously.

In the spring of 1971, Bellow's revision of *The Last Analysis* was ready for a new Off-Broadway production at Circle in the Square. He had worked on it extensively since its Broadway run, preserving "some of the timbers of that shipwreck," as he put it in a preface to the published script. "Regrettably, the Broadway version neglected the *mental* comedy of Bummidge and his family, and I have tried to restore it." The new version opened on June 23, 1971, under the direction of Theodore Mann.

It was no use. The revival turned out to be "as misconceived a production as the original," according to theater historian Marilyn Stasio. Joseph Wiseman in the part of Bummidge was just as ineffectual as Sam Levene had been. In his efforts to simplify the play, Bellow had "dehumanized" it, complained Toby Cole, one of the few members of Bellow's professional retinue who was willing to speak her mind about his work: "Bummidge has become a bag of wind."

For the most part, the critics agreed. *The New York Times's* Walter Kerr pronounced the play "toneless and boneless" and "excruciating" to sit through: "Mr. Bellow seems to have no feel for the way the stage functions." "I'm still carrying around Walter Kerr's stuffed kleenexes in my pocket," Bellow wrote in disgust to Irving Kristol.

The Last Analysis closed on August 1.

In the fall of 1971, Bellow flew to London to serve as one of the judges of the Booker Prize, the prestigious English literary award given to the year's best novel. (The other judges were John Fowles, Antonia Fraser, and Philip Toynbee.) He was very fussy about his room at the Ritz and demanded a view of the Thames. "They paid my expenses," he explained to Edward Shils.

From London he dropped down to Lisbon, then proceeded to Turin to take in an Italian production of *The Last Analysis*. There was also a sojourn in Ireland ("as green as advertised") with Adam. "Evidently I come back to life when I voyage," he wrote to Nadine Nimier from his brother's house in Florida, chronicling his itinerary for 1972—Japan in April, Aspen in July, Europe in August: "I feel sometimes like a novel written by the ghost of Jules Verne and raised by Tutankhamen and Wm. Faulkner—about a Prince of Egypt reincarnated in the 20th Century, fond of southern whiskey and doomed to jet about the earth."

A letter to Fran Gendlin from Japan vividly summed up that trip (as well as their relationship):

> There are many reasons why I didn't write. For one thing, the jet lag was awful. It took more than ten days to recover. For another, I turned out to be a real or perhaps imaginary celebrity, and immediately began to do seminars, lectures, interviews, radio programs and Japanese semi–state dinners, sitting on the floor, using chopsticks and eating raw fish, or trying to eat it. I drank a good deal of sake to help myself to sleep, but I kept waking at four AM, utterly wretched most of the time. . . . Kyoto

I thoroughly enjoyed, staying in a Japanese inn, old style, sleeping on the straw mat and lying on the floors half the day, admiring the little moss garden. Being on the floor was childhood again, and childhood is still the most pleasant part of life. A confession of adult failure. Well, I'd better own up. I haven't done too hot, as the old Chicago phrase runs. For three weeks I didn't hear from you at all, and I was quite put out about it. If you wrote a letter you didn't send, I did, too. And then I was disheartened—appalled, is probably a more accurate word—to find that I had crab-lice. I felt peculiarly shaky and stupid to make that discovery. I'd had nothing at all to do with women here, except to smile at them over the raw fish held in chopsticks. Going to the doctor was awful. Thinking about it all was awful. Cured, now, I feel lousy still. Anti-self, anti-others, but above all the old fool. The world seems to expect that I will do all kinds of good things, and I spite it by doing all kinds of bad ones. They're not terribly bad, either. Striking sins are out of reach, too. I try to break into the next sector, or find the next development, but nothing comes of this except unhappiness for myself and others. The unhappiness to myself I don't much mind. The effect on others is a curse to me night and day. It's true I haven't taken a shot at [George] Wallace, but there isn't much else I can take credit for. At the end of all this, I can say that I think of you a great deal and lovingly. I'm flying to San Francisco on the 26th. I suppose I'll be there before the letter arrives and back in Chicago about the first of June.

This notably candid letter afforded a glimpse of the guilt and sense of failure, of being stuck, trapped in his limited repertoire of sexual conquests, that Bellow suffered. Nearing sixty, he could still employ the language of a child, seeing himself as alternately "good" and "bad"—but not *too* bad. When he did "bad things," he did them to "spite" the world. Yet he craved to be forgiven; he wasn't "terribly bad." Indeed, he was virtuous—"perfectly straight, and non-adulterous," he assured Gendlin a week later: "There's no inclination, no temptation, and I seem to have lost touch with the seducer's mentality." It was a disingenuous statement, intended to reinforce his sense of himself as a reformed sinner, too preoccupied with his work to be concerned with sex. Meanwhile, he was on the prowl for geishas.

John Nathan, a young American scholar, served as Bellow's official guide in Japan. Nathan was, by his own account, "a great master of the Tokyo night"—a kind of Augie March of Tokyo, at home with gangsters and hoodlums, a haunter of low bars: "Bellow told me I was the best 'squaw man' he had ever met." Years before, William Faulkner had been over on a similar mission and apparently spent most of his time closeted in his room with a Japanese woman he'd managed to pick up, a feat Bellow was determined to emulate.* "This was the burning focus of Bellow's stay in Japan: to outdo Faulkner in his amorous accomplishments," Nathan recalled. "The man was obsessed with getting laid."

One potential conquest was a "dark, literary creature" who had been assigned to show Bellow around, but he got nowhere with her, and his lack of progress made him surly. He gave a lecture on Joyce, reading faster and faster—"I heard him rip through this thing," said Nathan, who thought there was "something passive/aggressive, hostile" about Bellow's brisk presentation. Mornings, Bellow holed up in International House, a squat modern building in the embassy district, and wrote. "I do this to keep sane," he told Nathan.

His sense of humor was still intact. To Dave Peltz, he sent a postcard of sumo wrestlers, with the message: "A few of these guys at the Riviera Club would set a higher standard." Bellow's scrawled missives from faraway places were generally on the light-hearted side, but they also showed his resilience. "I still don't like my life, but as a good Kantian, must I?" he wrote to Richard Stern that summer. "There are higher things. I'm looking, ain't I?"

In the spring of 1973, Bellow was back in England for an extended stay. The historian Asa Briggs had invited him to give a lecture at the University of Sussex and arranged for him to live at Monk's House, Rodmell, famous as the home of Leonard and Virginia Woolf. Dating from the sixteenth century, with an orchard and a walled garden, it was a house rich in history. The Woolfs had

---

*According to Joseph Blotner's massive and decorous two-volume biography of Faulkner, the writer spent all his time in Japan discussing literature with earnest Japanese scholars and translators.

lived there from 1919 until Virginia's suicide in 1941; it remained in Leonard's possession until his death in 1969.

Bellow found his digs both "beautiful and spooky," he wrote to Gendlin on April 22, 1973. "The gardens are grand, the house cold, everything creaks but I was not haunted by the ghost of Virginia." He had no phone and virtually no social life; except for a trip to London to attend a dinner in honor of Heinrich Böll and a brief visit with Edward Shils in Cambridge, he had seen no one except the maid and "some drunks at the pub."

Stuck alone deep in the Sussex countryside, he dispatched almost daily letters to Hyde Park, urging Gendlin to join him. He complained bitterly about not hearing from her ("I wonder why it is that you are too busy to send me a note"), brooded about the time she had told him to "bugger off," wondered if she was seeing other men. Admitting a tendency to wallow in self-pity when he was alone, he compared himself to Robinson Crusoe. By early May, he had prevailed; Gendlin would come.

She didn't have an easy time of it at Rodmell. "The house was cold, the doors were low; we kept hitting our heads," she recalled. The floors were uneven, and the bathtub was tilted: "It was like flying over the English Channel." Bellow didn't like the big bed in the master bedroom because Leonard was rumored to have died in it. Instead, he slept in the room where T. S. Eliot used to stay. Literary pilgrims frequently showed up at the door. Bellow passed himself off as the caretaker until a tourist from North Carolina declared, "I know who you are." Bellow introduced Gendlin as his typist.

He was "grinding it out," he wrote his friend Walter Pozen from Monk's House, deep into a new novel. But he also found time for other activities—attending a literary conference in Edinburgh; picking up honorary degrees from Harvard and Yale; overseeing his business and literary affairs. Leon Kirchner was writing an opera based on *Henderson the Rain King*. Bellow's theatrical agent, Toby Cole, was wrangling with movie producers who wanted to buy up rights; all the later novels were optioned by the movies, some of them several times. "Bercovici and Polonsky—

and Bellak—were only three of the tens of phonies who came to me looking for rights whose foul breaths I spared you," reported Cole, adopting the idiom of Augie March. Bellow kept on top of the details, annotating Cole's letters in the margins.

He also found time for nonfiction, most notably a long, ambitious essay entitled "Literature in the Age of Technology." Originally delivered as a lecture at the Smithsonian Institution in November 1972, it was an impressive performance, once again demonstrating Bellow's range as a social critic, his wide knowledge of Western culture, and, above all, his willingness to passionately defend his art. For Bellow, the vision of dehumanizing mechanization put forth by popular middlebrow visionaries such as Theodore Roszak was a "platitude," as was the vision of a utopian new age made radiant by the miracles of technological progress—a world in which art would become obsolete. For Bellow, there was a third possibility: "that man is an artist, and that art is a name for something always done by human beings." The novelist had lost ground—to psychoanalysis, to the universities, to intellectuals and sociologists who had no real interest in literature; in Bellow's view, "the authority of the imagination ha[d] declined." Where the public once listened "deferentially" to Dickens, Tolstoy, or Victor Hugo, it now listened to reporters and journalists, to writers of fact.*

In support of this pessimistic diagnosis, Bellow invoked an essay by Lionel Trilling that he had come across in *Commentary*, "Authenticity and the Modern Unconscious"—a chapter from *Sincerity and Authenticity*, Trilling's last major work. Trilling referred to an essay on Nikolai Leskov by the German Marxist critic Walter Benjamin in which Benjamin lamented that the art of storytelling had fallen on hard times. Ignoring the fact that he himself had often made the same argument, Bellow launched into an intemperate diatribe against "this Benjamin" ("Why does it matter what *he* said?"), somehow making both Trilling and Benjamin, profoundly bookish men (one of whom had been dead

---

*Within a year, Tom Wolfe would publish his famous anthology, *The New Journalism*, with its incendiary preface proclaiming the death of the novel. ("The Huns are at the gate, Saul!")

for thirty years), responsible for the philistinism of "modern literary culture." Benjamin, despite his Marxist jargon, was decidedly old-fashioned, a quirky, inward-dwelling critic who had never been comfortable with the modern world. And Trilling was no radical; the whole of *Sincerity and Authenticity*—the whole of Trilling's life—was a dignified and melancholy dirge for the end of literature as he had known it.

Yet for Bellow, Trilling had inexplicably become the enemy, even as he aspired, Bellow wrote sarcastically, to become "one of Aristotle's great-souled men." There was a distinctly aggrieved note in this attack on Trilling, a note of personal animus—as Bellow must have sensed. On July 7, 1974, he wrote a nervous letter to Trilling, disclosing that he was about to publish his lecture in *Harper's* and had begun to have "second thoughts" about it; Trilling would think him "silly." He had based his remarks on the *Commentary* essay, he hastened to explain, and should have read the whole book before "sounding off":

> I feel guilty—no, that won't do—I feel remorseful about it. You do, however, appear to agree with the views of Eliot and Walter Benjamin, and you do say that the narrative past has lost its authenticating power, and perhaps you are too ready to take for permanent what I see to be a mood. What is permanent in this age of upheavals is hard to make out, but I am reluctant to grant moods their second papers. For writers the most important question is simply, What is interesting? I try, inadequately and frivolously, to say something in my article about what it is that intellectuals do or do not find interesting. I've thrown no light on this, and perhaps I've even thickened the darkness a little, but the matter was worth mentioning. I take it we agree, as square old liberals, that without individuals human life ends in a cold glutinous porridge—despite our different opinions as to what makes an "identity." Freudian theory is, to me, another story, albeit a fascinating one. I take the Unconscious to be what we don't know, and don't see that it advances us much to take this unknown psychologically. Why not metaphysically? However, I prefer to remain an amateur in these matters. What I wish to say here is that it was idiotic of me to fix on one chapter of your book. I shall get a copy of it when I come back from Spain later in the month and read it attentively.

The letter was signed "Yours apologetically," but it was too little too late. For all its surface geniality, Bellow's effort at self-exculpation was feeble; he had willfully misread Trilling and struck at the heart of his enterprise. His "second thoughts" were so halfhearted as to seem more provocative than contrite.

Trilling's reply two weeks later was vintage Trilling—judicious, eloquent, magisterial. "I have now read your *Harper's* piece and my doing so has not, as you suggest it might, led me to think of you as 'silly,'" he began. "The adverse words which occur to me are, I am sorry to have to say, rather graver than that." He then proceeded to offer a closely argued refutation of what he called, with a reserve so exaggerated it was almost comical, Bellow's "strange transaction with [his] ideas." Bellow had "inverted" his meaning, Trilling patiently showed, and had contrived to ignore the elder critic's clear expression of "regret" over the diminished authority of fiction. Trilling justifiably wondered how "a reader could conclude that I regard the phenomenon with satisfaction." He also objected to the "vulgarity" of Bellow's innuendo that his reference to Benjamin was a pretentious display of erudition.

"But of course the crucial point is how are your violations of fact and truth to be accounted for?" asked Trilling. A good question. Given Bellow's proven abilities as a reader of literary texts, he couldn't have simply gotten it wrong: "On the other hand, it is scarcely to be conceived, let alone believed, that you would consciously and deliberately pervert the meaning of what I had written." Yet Bellow had done precisely that—had violated, Trilling observed in a characteristic turn of phrase, the "disposition of [his] mind." Surely Lionel Trilling would be the last person to gloat over the end of art. Therefore, the misreading must have been deliberate: "a conscious and deliberate intention *not* to comprehend or present truthfully what I have said."

And so it was. Bellow, nursing old and largely imaginary wounds, was still convinced that Trilling didn't endorse his work with sufficient enthusiasm. And he had always resented Trilling's patina of civility, the apparent ease with which his intellectual nemesis had adopted the habits and customs of that formerly WASP enclave, the Columbia English department. But Bellow's essay bristled with a more generalized defiance, as if he was once again looking for an occasion to assert the right of the artist against those who tried to oppose him—or those he imagined were trying to oppose him. It was almost as if he needed to provoke a fight. Privately, Bellow acknowledged his error, writing to Edith Tarcov that he'd been an "idiot" and had "a shamed face as big as the new harvest moon. I think I dislike T's way of writing so much that it inflames my brain." Publicly, he bore Trilling's reproach in silence.

Bellow's relationship with Fran Gendlin was also on the rocks. When they returned to Chicago from a trip to San Francisco in the spring of 1974, Gendlin remembered, Bellow was acting strangely remote and didn't want to plug in the phone. She theorized (rightly, as it turned out) that he was expecting a call from another woman. A few weeks later, after a brief visit to England, he called her up and announced that the affair was over. He had taken up with a beautiful raven-haired mathematician from Romania, Alexandra Ionescu Tulcea, a professor at Northwestern; the mysterious phone call he'd been waiting for was from her. Born in 1934, Tulcea was nineteen years younger than Bellow and recently divorced. They had met at the home of her compatriot Mircea Eliade.

Bellow seemed "utterly enraptured" with Alexandra, according to Dave Peltz. She had a European grace, a refinement and sophistication absent from his trio of wives. Her father had been minister of health in Romania after the war; when he died, after a painful struggle with the regime, her mother, a child psychiatrist, had been appointed to the post. They were members of the intelligentsia and had raised their daughter well. Bellow was charmed by Tulcea's Old World manners. "Most of the girls he brought over to the house were bimbos," said Marshall Holleb, who regularly entertained Bellow in his Lake Shore Drive apartment. "Alexandra was different." The day after she came to the Hollebs' for dinner, she sent flowers.

Holleb's favorable impression of Bellow's new love was shared by all their friends. She was "a wonderful person for him," attested Ruth Miller—"beautiful, warm-hearted, caring, I thought, enjoying him and his wit and his stories." Alexandra Tulcea was also distinguished in her own right: She had an international reputation in the rarefied world of higher mathematics.* In *The Dean's December,* Bellow depicted her as Dean Albert Corde's elegant wife, a world-renowned professor of astronomy who "sat in her corner hours on end with a pad and pencil, writing symbols, her face turned downward, the upper lip lengthened, the chin compressed and dented." Tulcea professed to know nothing about literature; where Bellow's work was concerned, she was admiring but uncomprehending.

Bellow raised the question of marriage at the outset. Tulcea had doubts. After dinner with Dave Peltz and Bellow one night, she walked Peltz to the elevator and asked him, while Bellow stood in the doorway listening, "Should I marry him?"

Bellow offered a different version of their courtship. Tulcea was pressuring him to marry her, he complained to Joseph Epstein; but why be tied down? "Sex is hanging like salamis in the deli windows."

Once again, hope triumphed over experience. They were married in November 1974. The general consensus was that Bellow had chosen wisely. His fourth marriage, his friends were convinced, would endure. Bellow thought so. As he put it tersely to Dave Peltz: "This is it."

---

*She was an authority on Banach spaces, named after the Polish mathematician Stefan Banach, a pioneer in the field of topological vector spaces. Among her contributions to the field were two dauntingly titled papers: "An Application of Number Theory to Ergodic Theory and the Construction of Uniquely Ergodic Models" and "Probability on Banach Spaces."

24

O N JANUARY 7, 1972, John Berryman jumped off a bridge
in Minneapolis, plunging to his death. An intractable
alcoholic, Berryman had suffered from severe depression
for many years; his own father, too, had committed suicide. Outwardly, he had much to live for. He was on his third marriage, to
a young Irishwoman, and had a new infant daughter; he was an
esteemed professor with an endowed chair at the University of
Minnesota. As an American poet, he was rivaled only by Robert
Lowell. "Let's join forces, large and small, as in the winter beginning of 1953 in Princeton, with the Bradstreet blazing and Augie
fleeing away," he had written to Bellow in the summer of 1971.
"We're promising."

Their enthusiasm for each other's work had sustained them
both in the two decades since that golden era at Princeton. Berryman was inspired by Bellow's progressive liberation, in novel after
novel, from the constraints of the form. "Nobody has ever sat
down & wallowed to this extent in his own life, *with* full art—I
mean, novelists," he had exulted upon reading *Herzog*. "I don't
know of anything to compare it to, except you. . . . Go to heaven."
Bellow responded in kind, claiming that Berryman's "The Hell
Poem" and "Death Ballad," two harrowing late works, had
changed his life. For years, Bellow had served Berryman as a spir-

itual mentor, fielding drunken late-night phone calls and visiting
him at deceptively named drying-out facilities. "It's always Pleasant St. Golden Valley Lotus Island," he remarked wryly.
In January 1971, Berryman had come to Chicago to deliver a
lecture. "He looked decayed," Bellow recalled in a foreword he
wrote to Berryman's posthumous novel, *Recovery:*

> He had been drinking and the reading was a disaster. His Prince-
> ton mutter, once an affectation, had become a vice. People
> couldn't hear a word. . . . We left a disappointed, bewildered,
> angry audience. Dignified, he entered a waiting car, sat down,
> and vomited. He passed out in his room at the Quadrangle Club
> and slept through the faculty party given in his honor. But in the
> morning he was full of innocent cheer. He was chirping. It had
> been a great evening. He recalled an immense success. His cab
> came, we hugged each other, and he was off for the airport un-
> der a frozen sun.

They never saw each other again.
Two weeks after Berryman's death, Bellow answered a condolence letter from Robert Hivnor: "I often wondered whether he
would; I guessed that he wouldn't. I seldom guess right." He could
now add another name to the melancholy and ever-lengthening list
of his dead. "Not so many old friends left—a dwindling breed," he
mourned in a letter to Ruth Miller (perking up at the end to add a
flirtatious postscript: "What's more, you have a first-class face &
I miss it").
The following summer, in Aspen, a letter from Ralph Ross
prompted Bellow to rueful reflections on the loss and on where he
had come to in his own life.

> The subject was painful but your letter was very pleasant. I don't
> know what we survivors *should* do with this slaughter legacy
> our old friends have made for us (I think of Isaac, of Delmore
> Schwartz). Maybe my little foreword made things too easy. It
> had the conventional charm for which John himself had a weak-
> ness or talent. I was sincere enough, but there were terrible
> things to say, and I didn't say them. You touched on some of
> those in your letter. John telling you that he'd never drink again,
> that he wanted more love affairs. At the same time he knew he
> was a goner. One moment the post-tomb lazarus, the next Don

Juan, and much of the time someone who merely looked like John, as you put it. I knew that feeling.

Having written a few lines about John I now have "privilege" of observing the attitudes of people towards the poet and his career. There's something culturally gratifying, apparently, about such heroic self-destruction. It's Good-old-Berryman-he-knew-how-to-wrap-it-up. It's a combination of America, Murderer of Poets, and of This Is the Real Spiritual Condition of Our Times. Perhaps you've seen Boyd Thomes' review of *Recovery*. Maris [Thomes was Berryman's doctor; Maris was his wife] sent me a copy. It may not have reached you, so I'll quote a few sentences.

> "This combination of erudition and progressively more suicidal chaos became his subject matter, and it was his artistic triumph to create a style sufficiently flexible and powerful to express it . . . John did more to elevate the potential of paranoia than anybody of our generation."

Then he speaks of John as a "poetry-making machine" and so forth. Boyd's all right, one of the Minnesota pals, and all of that, but there's something amiss with John's disaster as confirmation of the views on life and society of a sophisticated medical gentleman—"elevating the potential of paranoia." It rather scares me to see how very satisfactory John's life and death can be from a certain point of view.

On this green and sunlit Colorado afternoon, that'll be enough of that . . .

But it wasn't enough; Bellow still had more to say on the subject of what America did to its poets. He was several hundred pages into *Humboldt's Gift*.

Bellow wrote *Humboldt's Gift* "in my usual way," he told an interviewer not long after the book came out in the fall of 1975: "Lots of beginnings, three years on the middle and then the last third in six weeks flat out."

Beginnings always gave him trouble. As early as the spring of 1972, he had mentioned the difficulties he was having with his work in progress to an audience at Loyola University in Chicago.

The novel wasn't "working out," he confided. "It's all in bits and pieces now. Besides, there's an old proverb which warns that you shouldn't show half-finished work to fools." (One wonders how the respectful crowd that had gathered to hear Bellow read felt about his ungracious characterization.) In the years that followed, draft upon draft joined the fossils of discarded novels strewn among his papers. Bellow routinely threw out work that was better than what most novelists published.

Rising promptly at six o'clock in the morning, he would fortify himself with two cups of strong coffee heated in a pan and get down to work. From his window, he looked out at a university playing field and, in the distance, the spires of Rockefeller Chapel. Often still in his ragged striped bathrobe when the typist arrived, he would sit down in a chair beside her and dictate from the notes he'd accumulated the night before—up to twenty pages a day. Like Dickens, who wrote his books with company in the living room, Bellow thrived on chaos. In the midst of composition, he fielded phone calls from editors and travel agents, friends and students; stood on his head to restore concentration; bantered with his son Daniel when he was staying at the house. He generally broke off at noon, did thirty push-ups, and had a simple lunch of tuna salad or smoked whitefish, accompanied—if the work had gone well—by a glass of wine or a shot of gin. As he neared the end of his long labor, he grew increasingly excitable. "I can go on forever," he told his typist, Karyl Roosevelt, but his nerves were clearly raw. When he finished a morning of dictation, he now slumped in his chair, exhausted.

Humboldt's Gift was really two novels that were never quite reconciled: the story of Von Humboldt Fleisher, the goofy genius poet, a "hero of wretchedness" whose tragic downfall exemplified the predicament of the artist in America; and "an easy, funny book," as Bellow described it, based loosely on the low-life adventures of Dave Peltz. The narrator of this second story—whose own adventures eventually took center stage—was Charlie Citrine, a worldly, wealthy Chicago "notable," the author of a successful Broadway play, *Von Trenck,* about a Humboldt-like character, as well as a biography of Harry Hopkins and a book on Woodrow Wilson that won the Pulitzer Prize. Ensconced in a Chicago high-

rise loaded with fine art and Persian rugs, Citrine is now at work
on the second volume of his magnum opus, a social history entitled *Some Americans: The Sense of Being in the USA.*

In early drafts, the narrator was a somewhat down-at-the-heels
figure named Orlansky who had left the East in defeat and made a
comeback in, "of all places, provincial Chicago, as a biographer
and national television figure." (The novel might have been more
moving if he'd remained one.) Orlansky was "a connoisseur of
lives"—a memoirist, social historian, and editor of a series of
volumes entitled the Biographia America: "Orlansky would decide
how many pages [Humboldt's] career was worth in the Biographia."

By the final version and with a new name, he had become a
character unmistakably contemporaneous with his creator. Charlie Citrine is a big success. On assignment for *Life,* he flies in a helicopter over Manhattan with senators Javits and Kennedy; he
knows his way around Europe; he stays at the Plaza. He drives a
Mercedes 280SL and wears Sea Island cotton underwear. A health
nut, he stands on his head, plays paddleball, and ingests massive
quantities of vitamin E—very much like his health-conscious original. As the Bellow scholar Daniel Fuchs notes tartly, "We are a
long way from the early hack."

The most painful excision Bellow made was the long "Zetland"
section (in its earliest versions a separate novel). For years, Bellow
had struggled to write about his dear friend Isaac Rosenfeld, under
the name of Elias Zetland. A Chicago intellectual whose childhood
precocity makes him a legend among his friends, "Zet" arrives in
New York with his young wife, Lottie, a vividly true-to-life rendering of Rosenfeld's wife, Vasiliki, and establishes himself as a
Greenwich Village sage: "The real business of his life was with
comprehensive visions." But Zetland, like Humboldt, comes to no
good end. His writing career stalls; his household—the children,
the pets, the noisy Village parties—is no longer picturesque. "Life
as we've made it isn't worth living," he confides to the narrator:
"I'm sorry for these children Lottie and I brought here. Posterity is
a mistake." In the end, Bellow published only a fifteen-page fragment, "Zetland: By a Character Witness." It was too harsh, too
unremitting a catalog of failure. "He loved Isaac too much to write

that book," suggested Herb McCloskey. Gradually, Zetland/ Rosenfeld faded from the manuscript, and Humboldt/Schwartz came to dominate.

Daniel Fuchs offers a thematic explanation for the disappearance of Zetland: "The visible sky can hold only one comet at a time." But there may have been another, deeper reason why Bellow could never bring himself to finish this book. To write about a friend who had failed as a writer was to exploit Rosenfeld's memory, advancing the survivor's reputation at the expense of the victim. (Bellow sometimes referred to the discarded "Zetland" manuscript as a "victim" novel in the tradition of his early work.) But it may also have been his habitual avoidance of the deepest and most painful subjects that kept him from persisting with the novel. Apart from the few passages in *Herzog* where he focuses so powerfully on his mother's death, Bellow had tended to deal with loss at one remove: He hadn't been as emotionally involved with Delmore Schwartz as with Rosenfeld; it was easier to write his story.

Not that Schwartz didn't provide plenty of conflict. Literary rivalry and guilt about success—a main theme of the novel—had also figured in Schwartz's troubled relationship with Bellow. Like Berryman, Schwartz had initially been a great Bellow enthusiast; the two poets had both written praising reviews of *The Adventures of Augie March*. But as Schwartz descended into madness, he had tormented Bellow, making fun of his awards and honors, depicting him as an Establishment stiff, mocking the wealth that *Herzog* had brought. ("Now he's got a million bucks," Humboldt rants about Citrine. "What kind of writer or intellectual makes that kind of dough?") Where Rosenfeld was a true victim, Schwartz was a former antagonist, equally doomed but somehow less vulnerable— a fairer target of satire.

He was also a more dramatic character than Rosenfeld, more flamboyantly self-destructive, a *poète maudit* whose tragic death in a fleabag hotel could serve as a convenient vehicle for Bellow's high-flown meditations on art and success in America. The narrative of Schwartz's last years—the chronic insomnia, the abuse of pills and alcohol, the intensifying psychosis that culminated in him being carted off to Bellevue—evoked the sad squalor of his decline.

As Dwight Macdonald shrewdly noted, Bellow "transformed, literally, the key episodes in S[chwartz]'s life and yet kept the feeling, the truth of them, that marshy, fertile ground where the creative imagination raises its crops." To Schwartz's friends, there was no ambiguity about it: Humboldt *was* Schwartz.*

Bellow generally responded to imputations that his novels were romans à clef with a shrug. Let people say what they would—there was nothing he could do about it. But he was particularly resistant to efforts to identify Schwartz as the original of the poet Humboldt. As word of the novel got around and excerpts began to appear in *Esquire* and *Playboy,* the connection was often evoked and just as often denied. When James Laughlin identified Schwartz as the model for Humboldt, Bellow replied with elegiac candor: "I am writing of a composite poet, inevitably. Sometimes I feel there wasn't a whole man in the lot, and I include myself as a fragment. Life, ourselves assisting, broke everyone up."

Yet despite Bellow's denials, it was hard to miss the resemblances between the characters in his book and their real-life sources. Friends, enemies, former lovers, even his doorman at the Cloisters, could easily identify themselves in the pages of *Humboldt's Gift.* No old member of the Tuley crowd could fail to recognize Sam Freifeld in the character of Alec Szathmar, the shrewd, literary-minded lawyer who "tried to cover his broad can with double-vented jackets." (In high school, Sam was known as "*Arse Poetica.*") Keith Botsford was equally recognizable as Pierre Thaxter, the polymathic luftmensch with a shadowy past and an ostentatious reverence for European culture. So was Dave Peltz, represented by the contractor George Swiebel, a warmhearted

---

*In early manuscripts, this connection is explicit. As early as the summer of 1966, Bellow had embarked upon a manuscript that began: "My friend the poet Delmore Schwartz died last week in New York, presumably of heart failure, in a derelict's hotel in the Broadway area." By that fall, the work that he described, in a letter to Richard Stern, as "a memoir of D. Schwartz" had metamorphosed into the "D. S. novel." In the decade that followed it would evolve into many novels, as Bellow wrestled with his dead friend's emotional legacy, discarding draft after draft. The final portrait is unmistakably Schwartz, but a Schwartz whose tragedy incorporates the lives of Berryman, Rosenfeld, and Bellow's other thwarted friends who died too soon. He was a novelist, not a biographer, he stressed.

health nut whose rude appetites appeal to the Chicagoan side of Citrine's nature.

For all his resistance to speculation about his real-life models, Bellow was aware of how they might feel upon encountering themselves in his books—and not insensitive to the consequences. To Joan Schwartz, who had asserted—with some reason—that she was a character in one of Bellow's stories, he cited a letter from Alexander Pope to "a lady named Arabella Fermor" who had detected a resemblance to herself in the character of Belinda in *The Rape of the Lock:* "The character of Belinda resembles you in nothing but beauty," Pope had asserted. When the resemblance was unmistakable, he sometimes called his friends and lovers to let them know that he'd made fictional use of them. Some were flattered: Freifeld went around telling everyone that he was Szathmar. So was Keith Botsford: "A tiny part of me had been transformed magically, into a character in a novel, enlarged upon, recreated."

Others were more ambivalent about Bellow borrowing from their lives. Coming across an excerpt from *Humboldt's Gift* in *Playboy*—the scene in which Citrine is threatened by the gangster Rinaldo Cantabile for stiffing him in a poker game—Dave Peltz was stunned: The whole episode was based on an incident in which Peltz and Nelson Algren had reneged on a loss incurred in a game with a small-time gambler and Peltz had been forced to undergo a humiliating ordeal of atonement. The meeting at the Russian baths; being threatened with a baseball bat: It was all there. Bellow had "given his word" that he wouldn't use the story, "and there you had it in Playboy," Peltz wrote him in protest, "even down to the baseball bat." Whether or not his own work ever got published, it was Peltz's "life fabric." He was saving this material for his old age.

On July 14, 1974, Bellow replied from Europe, where he was on vacation:

Dear David

I'm sorry you feel hurt. I'm baffled as well. Three years ago Bette [Howland] told you that I was writing about you. You were angry and forbid it. It wasn't *you* who were the subject. People have written about me. Their me is not me. It couldn't matter less. What matters is that good things be written. Dear

God how we need them! But when you banned this book, which was affectionate and (I think) charming, I put it aside. I promised not to write Your Life. But this was all I *could* promise. We've known each other forty five years and told each other thousands and thousands of anecdotes. And now, on two bars suggested by one of your anecdotes, I blew a riff. Riffs are irrepressible. Furthermore no one should repress them. I created two characters and added the toilets and the Playboy Club and the fence and the skyscraper. What harm is there in that? Your facts are unharmed by my version. Writers, artists, friends, are not the Chicago Title and Trust Company or the Material Supply Corp. These aren't questions of property, are they? It might even make you happy that in this world writers still *exist*. And I should think it would touch you that I was moved to put a hand on your shoulder and wanted to remember you as I took off for the moon. For what you think is so major is really quite minor, a small feel taken by your goofy friend to reassure him as he got going. Your facts, three or four of them, got me off the ground. You can't grudge me that and still be Dave Peltz.

Now David, the nice old man who wants his collection of memory-toys to play with in old age is not you! You harm yourself with such fantasies. For the name of the game is not Social Security. What an error! Social Security is an entirely different game. The name of the game is Give All. You are welcome to all my facts. You know them, I give them to you. If you have the strength to pick them up, take them with my blessing. Touch them with your imagination and I will kiss your hands. What, trunk-loads and hoards of raw material? What you fear as the *risk* of friendship, namely, that I may take from the wonderful hoard is really the *risk* of friendship because I have the power to lift a tuft of wool from a bush and make something of it. I learned, I paid my tuition most painfully. So I know how to transform common matter. And when I give that transformation has that no value for you? How many people in Gary, Chicago, the USA, can you look to for that, David? As for me I long for others to do it. I thirst for it. So should you.

I'll be back from Spain in about ten days. When we talk I will make a particular effort to understand your feelings. When you think about me, remember that we've known each other since about 1929 and make an effort for my sake to understand the inevitability of your appearing among the words I write. And if you think that your friend Bellow, who loves you, is on the whole a good thing, not a bad one, let be. Let be, let be, for God's sake. Let me give what I can, as I can.

Love,
Saul

Bellow's letter is a remarkable testament to the artist's sense of self-sovereignty—the needs of art trump all other needs. It also offers a glimpse of the soaring valuation he placed upon his own work ("as I took off for the moon") and his belief in the rejuvenating spiritual value of literature. For Bellow, borrowing was in effect an act of generosity: "The name of the game is Give All." He wasn't taking from a friend; he was paying tribute. The ever-tolerant Peltz, in an affectionate letter of forgiveness, agreed to let be.

Susan Glassman—depicted in the novel as the nagging bitch Denise—wrote a highly intelligent essay, never published ("Mugging the Muse"), in which she questioned the morality of depicting real people in fiction. At what point, she asked, does the artist's impulse to draw from life intrude on the privacy of those whose lives are drawn? Quoting judiciously from Matthew Arnold, Robert Lowell, and the letters of Vincent van Gogh, among others, she made the persuasive case that art as autobiography had gone too far: "It is ironic that in a time when the artist has attributed to him the magical properties of the priest, he has ceased to be both the guardian of the temple and the temple itself."

For Bellow, there were lessons to be learned from Humboldt's doom. He was an emblematic figure, enacting "The Agony of the American Artist"—a role with a long history. "Edgar Allan Poe, picked out of the Baltimore gutter," as he enumerated the victims in *Humboldt's Gift*, "And Hart Crane over the side of a ship. And poor John Berryman jumping from a bridge. For some reason this awfulness is peculiarly appreciated by business and technological America. The country is proud of its dead poets. It takes terrific satisfaction in the poets' testimony that the USA is too tough, too big, too much, too rugged, that American reality is overpowering." It was a familiar theme: The artist had no place in American life. But there was an autobiographical motif as well: In writing about the sacrificial figure of Delmore Schwartz, destroyed in part by America's indifference to poetry, Bellow was again dramatizing his tenacious conflict with his businessmen brothers, for whom he was still the "scribbler," his book-lined Chicago apartment a "Fort Dearborn deep in Indian (Materialistic) Territory."

What Bellow's fictional portrait of Schwartz missed was the deep sadness of his life—the talent wasted, the bright youthful ambition turned to ash. There was something vindictive about Bellow's emphasis on Schwartz's manic pranks and tiresome volubility. *Humboldt* was an act of revenge against the poet who had once taunted him so mercilessly in the guise of a tribute. "I thought about Humboldt with more seriousness and sorrow than may be apparent in this account," Citrine insists. But the dominant note is one of self-satisfaction. The hero is a ladies' man—"They come in Volkswagens and Cadillacs, on bikes and motorcycles, in taxis and walkin'," marvels Roland, the servile black doorman in Citrine's building—a connoisseur of the good life, a man important enough to have in tow an army of lawyers and accountants.

Despite its poignant themes, the prose reflects Bellow's glow of well-being. When he was in the throes of composition, he once told an interviewer, he alternated between "the feeling of pleasure and enthusiasm" and "painful agitation." *Mr. Sammler's Planet* was a "painful agitation" book; *Humboldt* was a "pleasure and enthusiasm" book, written with *Così fan tutte* blasting in the background. "I HEARD the words as I wrote Humboldt," Bellow explained to one of his many correspondents, a reader who had sent him a classified ad from a California newspaper placed by a blind man looking for someone to read *Humboldt's Gift* aloud. "And towards the end I DICTATED it from beginning to end—a typist took it all down. What couldn't be spoken was dropped from the text."

It reads that way. Like *The Adventures of Augie March*, *Humboldt's Gift* marked a change in Bellow's style. The first-person narrative voice—digressive, idiomatic, rich in Chicago turns of phrase—represented an effort to break away from the chiseled perfection of *Herzog* and the formality of *Sammler*. The jazzy cadences of Citrine's nearly five-hundred-page monologue, the unpunctuated series ("black bread raw onion bourbon whisky herring sausage cards billiards race horses and women"), the bantering self-mockery ("C. Citrine, Pulitzer Prize, Legion of Honor, father of Lish and Mary, husband of A, lover of B, a serious person, and a card"): It's the inauguration of Bellow's late style, the style of *The Dean's December* and *More Die of Heartbreak*, exuberant and freewheeling. At times, perhaps, *too* freewheeling: Writing in *The New Yorker*, John Updike damningly compared the opening passage of *Humboldt* to the "more electric and cadenced" opening passage of *Augie*, noting that the lax, overly colloquial style felt "fallen away from a former angelic height." Gone was the somber moralizing tone that had given Bellow's work authority; gone also was the rigor of his early books, replaced by the jaunty tone of the garrulous, well-read, and self-important elder statesmen of Chicago who would come to dominate his books. "*Humboldt* is a *Henderson* for the Jews," said Bellow, who considered it his funniest book.

The plot is as untidy as the prose. Full of improbable characters and events, it ventures into an Algrenesque world of crooks and gangsters that Bellow didn't really know firsthand. The hoodlum Rinaldo Cantabile, who bashes in Citrine's Mercedes and punishes him for the unpaid poker debt, never quite achieves plausibility. A hectoring, streetwise bully, Cantabile sounds like just another one of the many "reality instructors"—another marvelous Bellow coinage—who besiege Citrine with advice. (It didn't help that Cantabile's wife was a Ph.D. candidate in English from Radcliffe, doing her thesis on the poetry of Von Humboldt Fleisher.)

If the story line is weak, the novel's great strength is its evocation of Chicago, a "home-world" that stirs Citrine to rhapsodic reminiscences of the Humboldt Park he knew: the old Chicago of ice wagons and planters made out of boilers on the Poles' front lawns; the pool halls and funeral parlors and Hungarian restaurants; the nickel-plated kitchen ranges and giant stoves with "a dome like a little church." This was Bellow's great theme—"rise fall and rise"—the efflorescence and swift destruction of human habitats, a phenomenon so strikingly visible in Chicago, where entire civilizations sprang up and disappeared in a single generation. His impulse to commemorate the richness of Chicago Jewish life—the psychiatrists in their Kenwood mansions, the real-estate moguls sweating in the whirlpool bath at the Standard Club, "chatting about Acapulco and numbered bank accounts in the Cayman Islands"—gave his prose a tremendous vitality. The courtroom scenes were "as devastating as anything in *Bleak House*," Updike noted in his review; Bellow was still "the best portraitist writing American fiction."

Toward the end of his labor on the novel, Bellow had discovered the work of Rudolf Steiner, the Austrian-born philosopher and founder of anthroposophy.* In 1973, he had begun attending meetings of the Anthroposophical Society at the home of Peter LeMay, a local Steinerian. "It was kind of a Socratic dialogue," recalled the poet William Hunt. There were perhaps a dozen people in the group, and the meetings were informal. The leader and his disciples would have dinner and then head to LeMay's room at the Christian Community Seminary on North Dearborn Street for a session on astral bodies and the Science of the Invisible (as anthroposophy was known). Thus it was that Charlie Citrine came to be poring over a copy of Steiner's *Knowledge of the Higher Worlds and Its Attainment* in his Madrid hotel room.

At the heart of Steiner's doctrine—as expounded by Bellow in a foreword to *The Boundaries of Natural Science*, a collection of Steiner's lectures—was the belief that a gulf existed between the private, inward-dwelling experience of human consciousness and the primacy of science in the modern world. It was Steiner's ambition to bridge this gulf, to transcend the limits of empirical human knowledge and attain another, higher form of consciousness, a higher "spiritual reality."

Bellow was no mystic. Like Citrine, he was skeptical of Steiner's more outlandish notions—"the lotus flower organs of spiritual perception or the strange mingling of Abraham with Zarathustra,

*From the Greek, meaning "wisdom of man." Anthroposophy is a variant of theosophy, a doctrine that stresses meditation as a means of acquiring knowledge about God through the attainment of a Consciousness Soul, a "soul within a soul" that unites "man's existence with an eternal existence."

or the coming together of Jesus and Buddha. It was all too much for me." But he was nonetheless an earnest disciple; he kept a photograph of Steiner on his desk and practiced the meditation exercises. When in New York, he made pilgrimages to the Anthroposophical Society on Madison Avenue, lugging away shopping bags full of the master's works. He liked the fact that Steiner, who edited a volume of Goethe's writings on science, "had credentials." And he was excited by Steiner's Shelleyan exhortation to awake from the spirit's slumber, to *see:* "It puts back into life a kind of magic we've been persuaded to drop. . . . When Steiner tells me I have a soul and a spirit, I say, yes, I always knew that."

Bellow made no secret of his religious impulses, but the appeal of Steiner wasn't only spiritual; it was the challenge Steiner issued to modern technology, which had (in Bellow's view) come to dominate the consciousness of twentieth-century man. Science—a term Steiner used in an all-encompassing sense—was in a class with business, politics, the mass media.

In the end, Citrine's spiritual quest rang hollow. It felt more like a "search for a higher selfishness" than a search for God, as Roger Shattuck remarked. The "Chicago states" he experienced, the "fits of noticing," were intensely vivid responses to this world, not the next: "About Higher Things, I was just an imposter." His genius—like his creator's—was for translating the texture of places and states of mind into words, observing without judgment the folly of our human struggles.

On January 30, 1975, Bellow attended a dinner at the White House given by President Ford for the British prime minister, Harold Wilson. Bellow, by now a veteran of such occasions—he had been to the White House twice before—took a dim view of the proceedings. "On these great evenings the East Room fills with celebrities who become ecstatic at the sight of other celebrities," he wrote in a "Self-interview" for the London-based *New Review* soon after the event. "Secretary Kissinger and Danny Kaye fall into each other's arms. Cary Grant is surrounded by Senators' wives who find him wonderfully preserved, as handsome in the flesh as on film." In such a high-voltage atmosphere, the mere writer of novels is anonymous, able "to pass half disembodied and unmolested by small talk from room to room, looking and listening." His encounter with Senator Fulbright of Arkansas may have contributed to his bad mood. "You write essays, don't you?" said Fulbright, who was slow to recognize his name. "I think I can remember one of them." The Bellows left early, searching for a cab on Pennsylvania Avenue in the rain.

Bellow worked hard at not being cowed by "the big boys," as he referred to brothers and politicians alike. Describing a lunch with Henry Kissinger, he portrayed his evasive interlocutor as "a man with a full face and a remarkable head of hair, the tight curls mounting in dense waves, a most American sort of foreigner, speaking the language of Harvard and Washington." Kissinger was a "master manipulator" who measured out each word and wouldn't allow himself to be quoted. Bellow wondered if a tape recorder was spinning underneath the table in the secretary of state's private dining room. But he was proud of his ability to navigate the corridors of power. "Finally, I found I could more than hold my own against the Kissingers and the Abba Ebans and the Moshe Dayans," he boasted to one of his students. "I had made it."

In June, he turned in the final proofs of *Humboldt's Gift* and flew off to London with Alexandra. *The Times* of London had assigned David Pryce-Jones to write a full-length profile, and Bellow spent a long day "volatilising"—in Pryce-Jones's description—on the literary life: Auden was "a victim of adult education"; Mary McCarthy's *The Group* had "too many pessaries." He turned sixty that week, an occasion that prompted him to complain of "bone fatigue."

One of the main reasons for his trip was to meet the philosopher Owen Barfield. Barfield, an English barrister who described himself as a "historian of consciousness," had produced a shelf of abstruse texts. His key work, *Saving the Appearances*, was an erudite defense of Rudolf Steiner by way of philosophy, anthropology, medieval theology, Romantic poetry, and whatever other disciplines could be marshaled to shore up his assault on "the brute acceptance of phenomena." Though skeptical of art's capacity to produce a faithful representation of nature, Barfield provided the scholarship to vindicate Bellow's belief that humanity had lost touch with its inner nature—had undergone, in Barfield's words, "a contraction from the cosmos of wisdom to something like a purely brain activity."

Over the next few years, a copious correspondence between these two unlikely Steinerians ensued, as Bellow, sounding more like a dutiful, insecure undergraduate than a world-famous author, tried to grasp the essentials of Barfield's thought. "It wasn't until I read your book on Romanticism that I began to understand something about the defeat of imaginative knowledge in modern times," he wrote later that summer, asking for "a few hours more" of the sage's time:

> I don't want to labor a point which you yourself have brought to my attention; I only want to communicate something in my own experience that will explain the importance of your books to me. My experience was that the kind of life that is represented in the books I read (and perhaps some that I wrote) had been exhausted. But how could existence itself become uninteresting. I concluded that the ideas and modes by which it was represented were exhausted, that individuality had been overwhelmed by power or "sociality," by technology and politics. Images or representations *this* side of the mirror have indeed tired us out. All that science did was to make the phenomena technically (mathematically) inaccessible, leaving us with nothing but ignorance and despair. Yes, psychoanalysis directed us to go into the unconscious. From the dark forest of its unconscious—a sort of presence of things unknown—painters and poets, like good dogs were to bring back truffles.

It was a fair exposition of Barfield's ideas; Bellow was a good pupil. But he was painfully unsure of himself. "I was a totally unknown quantity and felt that I had failed to show why I should be taken seriously," he wrote a few weeks later. "That you should come down to London to answer the ignorant questions of a stranger greatly impressed me." Barfield, who confessed to Bellow that he couldn't get through *Humboldt's Gift*, found himself wondering "what exactly you had *got* from Anthroposophy."

Alexandra regarded Bellow's mystical proclivities with bemused tolerance; as far as she was concerned, anthroposophy was just another of his "amiable eccentricities." "Don't let him convert you," she warned Pryce-Jones. She was a formidable scholar and her own discipline was antithetical to Steiner's antiscientific musings on the Soul-Spirit. Bellow accompanied her to a series of professional meetings—in London, Alexandra attended a lecture at the Royal Society, followed by a mathematical conference in the Black Forest, where she had been invited to read a paper on measure theory. "And he will listen," noted Pryce-Jones, depicting Bellow as the subservient husband. Bellow liked to portray himself as second fiddle to Alexandra. When asked what he would be doing in Germany, he said, "Carrying my wife's papers."

There was a barbed note to Bellow's ironic description of himself as an academic water boy. Anthroposophy offered him a way to assert, against the claims of Alexandra's mathematical preoccupations, that it was the artist who mattered. Early on in their marriage, he enlisted her in the legion of bullies whose determination to push him around had to be resisted at all costs. As he wrote of a character modeled closely on his fourth wife: "Vela had a stiff upper lip. I have always been inclined to give a special diagnostic importance to the upper lip. If there is a despotic tendency it will reveal itself there." Without making the connection explicit, he mentioned in the same paragraph the mustaches of Stalin and Hitler, noting cruelly that Vela had a bristling upper lip that "apparently had to be shaved." Alexandra, like Vela, was a tyrant.

For the moment, the soon-to-be-warring couple had arrived at an uneasy détente. By the end of June, they had settled in at Bellow's favorite retreat—his London publisher Barley Alison's vacation home on the Costa del Sol, Casa Alison. Alison was a distinctive figure in London literary life and, for more than twenty years, an important friend to Bellow. A former diplomat and journalist who had been recruited to publishing by Lord Weidenfeld, she was famously social. Her gloomy but elegant flat in Chelsea was the scene of many a boisterous book "launch." But she was also a hard worker and a zealous servant of her authors. She was an ideal editor for Bellow, who didn't require editorial advice so much as attention to details. Like Catherine Carver before her, who wrote long and elaborate memos about the minutiae of editing—repetitions, chronology, inconsistent details—Alison was a devoted reader of Bellow's work. When she left Weidenfeld and Nicolson in the late sixties to start her own imprint at Secker and Warburg, there was no question that he would follow her.

Fragile and diminutive, Alison could nonetheless be physically commanding. "She had a deep smoker's voice, and a very intense cobra-like gaze," as her niece Rosie Alison described her. "There was an aspect of her physique and face which was not unlike Edith Piaf or the rather ravaged look of Judy Garland in the 1960s." Did she and Bellow have an affair? More likely, she was one of the many women who fell in love with him and found their love requited in the form of friendship. "Barley specialised in being a martyr in her relationships, and she enjoyed being the slave to powerful men," according to her niece. The incessant letters she wrote to Bellow over the years reveal a fervent, unwavering adoration—but also, at times, a weary sense of what a full-time job it was "stroking and buttering up" her most prized author, "that difficult genius, Saul."

"The place is beautiful," Bellow wrote Dave Peltz from Casa Alison that summer, offering "a short report" on himself:

> I'm not. I arrived in an exhausted state and have been sleeping, swimming, eating, reading, and little else. Let's see if I can get myself flushed out. Life lays a heavy material weight on us in the states—things, cares, money. But I think that the reason why I feel it so much is that I let myself go, here, and let myself feel six decades of trying hard, and of fatigue. My character is like a taste in my mouth. I've tasted better tastes. But it'll pass, and one of these days I'll be able to see that the ocean is beautiful. And the mountains, and the plants, and the birds. Life isn't kind to people who took it on themselves to do something about life. Uh-unh!

On a happier note, Adam "smiles at his peevish pa and goes on reading science fiction and thrillers." Alexandra—Bellow referred to her as "the queen"—was "in her parlor eating mathematical bread and honey." About *Humboldt's Gift* he had mixed feelings: "It's like the end of something. I'm like a fat Sonja Henie—no more fancy figures on the ice. Overweight. That's the end of that. I'm hanging up my skates, retiring. If I ever do it again it'll be in my own back yard for God's amusement."

By all indications, the book was going to be big. It was a Book-of-the-Month Club main selection. Back in London at the end of July, Bellow submitted to a long interview with Walter Clemons for *Newsweek,* in preparation for a cover story. "I can't get any famouser," he groused good-naturedly to the photographer. "I'm already too famous." *People* magazine had commissioned a profile by Karyl Roosevelt, Bellow's typist. "In his 60th year, with another book completed, with friends, success and a new wife, Saul Bellow's life seems fine indeed," she wrote. "Yet in repose Bellow's gentle face has a look of sorrow; darker questions drift behind his eyes."

Among the perils of celebrity was the renewed pursuit of journalists, biographers, and literary hangers-on of every stripe. The most dogged was Mark Harris, who was hard at work on his questbook about Bellow. Nervous that his subject might preempt him, Harris brought up a rumor he'd heard: that Bellow was writing his autobiography. "I wouldn't dream of writing my own autobiography," Bellow reassured him. "There would be nothing much to say except that I have been unbearably busy ever since I was circumcised."

Harris was a model of reticence compared with Barnett Singer, a young historian who developed a fixation on Bellow, bombarding him for nearly a decade with intimate sexual confessions, diatribes, and long-winded exercises in free association. "I had become something of a nut," Singer admitted later, recalling his passion of the seventies. "An idolizer? A hero worshiper? I plead guilty." Bellow was fond of quoting Oscar Wilde's admonition about the writer who had been ruined by answering his mail, but if a correspondent struck a sympathetic chord, he answered— sometimes at considerable length. He could identify with Singer, a Canadian and the son of "a big deal-maker," as Singer described his businessman father. His crazy letters were themselves Bellovian, or perhaps Herzogian. Like Louis Gallo, whose largely oneway correspondence had filled Bellow's mailbox in the fifties, Singer had a deep, idiosyncratic knowledge of the Bellow canon and could quote entire passages by heart. "I devoured *Herzog* once, twice, four times, ten times, lovingly boning its already wellfilleted meat and locating the many kinds of subtlety there," he wrote in "Looking for Mr. Bellow," a strange, vivid account of his "addiction." It was an addiction the two men shared: They were both obsessed with Bellow.

Throughout the seventies, Bellow and Singer continued to exchange letters in staggeringly lopsided proportion; Singer sometimes wrote a few hundred before he received a reply. But Bellow clearly valued his opinion. Writing from Aspen in the late summer of 1974, he responded to Singer's mild suggestion that *Mr. Sammler's Planet* had been too prudent, too restrained, with a candid assessment of his strengths and limitations—and a generous acknowledgment of his correspondent's literary acumen:

> Dear Barney Singer:
> I've kept your letter of July 4 all summer. I see your point. I think you're probably right. More *should* be left on the page. I don't think I've "censored" myself with *dullness;* but I've been wrong before. It took me a very long time to learn to write English. Perhaps I did my lessons publicly? That too is possible. You seem to be saying that you want more *book*, less performance. If that is what you mean you are entirely correct.
> I don't recall that you ever sent me any "crummy" letters. You've sent me a truthful and useful criticism, and I'm much obliged to you.
>
> Saul Bellow

The following spring, Singer, on his way to a professional meeting in Madison, Wisconsin, wrote asking for an audience with the great man. His account of their afternoon together, like Boswell's momentous first encounter with Dr. Johnson in Mr. Davies's bookshop, had all the literary elements of a classic biographical quest: the young writer, after much calculation, finally getting to meet the author whose work has meant so much to him. If no commensurate *Life* emerged, Singer's memoir is still valuable, for it provides one of the most detailed portraits we have of Bellow at the apogee of his career.

Singer showed up at Bellow's office on the fifth floor of the Social Science Building on a cold April day. "Suddenly at twenty of two it happened—l'arrivée de M. Saul Bellow, écrivain!" Bellow looked radiant that day, Singer noted with approval—"tanned, relaxed, wearing a nice outfit complete with silk vest, and giving his secretary a wide smile."

They adjourned to Bellow's tiny room, with a window looking out on the Midway. Singer asked Bellow what he thought of Balzac. Bellow mentioned Balzac's gruesome death, purple faced from caffeine poisoning, "as described by Hugo in *Choses vues.*" Had Singer read it? "No, I had not. And me—a French historian! Beaten in my own trade . . . scooped." Did Bellow's students realize what they'd got? Singer asked. "'They realize,'" Bellow murmured. "In other words, *you're* no special interpreter. He was too gentlemanly or busy to expand on this. Greatness is Humble? The lesson was only starting to dawn on me that dark day." But not so humble that it didn't require constant affirmation. Amazingly, Bellow invited his eager disciple to come back and chat after class. Singer took in the plush sofa, the glass coffee table, the Persian rug, the photograph of Bellow's mother on the wall. It was she who had given him the confidence to become a writer, he told Singer.

When it was time to go, Bellow put on his leather coat and fedora, grabbed his Javanese walking stick, and drove his guest back to the Hilton in his rattly Mercedes Benz. For admirers, the busy novelist had plenty of time.

Humboldt's Gift was published in August 1975 and received a by-now customary front-page review in *The New York Times Book Review.* But the reviewer, Richard Gilman, was equivocal, applauding the portrait of Delmore Schwartz while objecting to the novel's rabbinical didacticism: "Its large themes pull and tug like an insecurely moored balloon, crossing each other's paths, and its 'solutions' to the dilemmas it poses are arbitrary, lacking in weight and vigor."

Most of the other important reviews were equally tough. Jack Richardson, writing in *Commentary*—his review was ominously titled "A Burnt-Out Case"—deplored Bellow's efforts "to bully and bustle the reader into a point of view about the artist and society that is a mixture of antic exaggeration and simplistic *parti pris.*" Anatole Broyard, *The New York Times*'s daily critic, felt the book didn't do justice to his old friend Delmore. The one unequivocally favorable review came from John Aldridge, who had sniped at Bellow over the years; here at last, he asserted, was a novel suffused with "a Jamesean sense" of "felt life."

Aldridge's enthusiasm came too late to redeem him in Bellow's eyes. He was jumping on the bandwagon to ingratiate himself, "a corkhead who bobs to the convenient surface," Bellow complained. He was also highly annoyed with Broyard, "a low-grade moron," and with the whole reviewing business—"gossip, annihilating reputations, backstabbing," as he bitterly described it to Carlin Romano, a Princeton undergraduate (later a critic himself) who interviewed the novelist for his college literary magazine. Didn't the critics see that *Humboldt's Gift* was *funny*?

25

*Our very vices, our mutilations, show how rich we are in thought
and culture. How much we know. How much we can feel.*

—SAUL BELLOW,
the Nobel Lecture

IN OCTOBER, Bellow began a three-month sabbatical in
Israel. Alexandra had been invited to give a series of lectures
on probability theory at the Hebrew University in Jerusalem.
They stayed at Mishkenot Sha'ananim, the artists' colony on the
outskirts of Jerusalem. Its Hebrew name—"the dwellings of seren-
ity"—evoked its character: Their comfortable, simply furnished
apartment with a garden looking out at Mount Zion and the
Judaean desert was a refuge from the intensity of Israeli life. "Here
in Jerusalem, when you shut your apartment door behind you you
fall into a gale of conversation," Bellow noted in *To Jerusalem and
Back:* "exposition, argument, harangue, analysis, theory, expostu-
lation, threat, and prophecy." Israel was a nation under siege.
Violence was a daily thing: Buses were blown up by Arab terrorists, bombs exploded in cafés. Bellow, for whom Hitler's extermination of the Jews was the central, if still unfathomable fact of our
time, found it scarcely credible that "a people that was nearly
annihilated 30 years ago is threatened again."

He had a deep personal connection with Israel. He had family
there: One cousin, Liza Gordon, owned a tiny grocery store in
Jerusalem; another, Nota Gordon, was a sweater manufacturer in
Tel Aviv; cousin Bella was a cashier in a department store.
(Bellow's brother Sam also maintained an apartment in Jerusalem

and showed up one morning at Bellow's door.) Bellow was moved by these relatives from Riga, so reminiscent of his own original "home world," and struck by how much he resembled them: "We are obviously from the same genetic pool." But in other ways, their experience of life had been profoundly different from his. A captain in the Russian army during World War II, Nota had seen fierce combat; he was "war-hardened," unlike his "amiable, good-natured, attractive perhaps, but undeveloped, helpless American cousin," as Bellow described himself—a contrast-loser. Nota was an Israeli version of those bullying reality instructors—judges, lawyers, brothers—who were always disparaging Bellow's grasp of the practical world.*

His new friend John Auerbach had also been through hard times. His family had perished in the Warsaw ghetto; he alone had escaped, managing to survive as a sailor on German freighters for the duration of the war. Now he lived on a kibbutz with his second wife, Nola Chilton, an American theatrical director. He was also a writer, and a fine one.† Bellow was drawn to Auerbach by a natural affinity of temperament. "I had been warned that as I grew older the difficulty of forming new friendships would be great," he wrote in *To Jerusalem and Back,* which contains an affectionate portrait of Auerbach. But he was less guarded now—or so he claimed—especially with those who had endured life's sorrows.

Bellow hadn't planned to write a book when he went to Israel. "My intention was to wander about the Old City and sit contemplatively in gardens and churches," he explained to his guru, Owen Barfield—whom he addressed as "Mr. Barfield," still at sixty the deferential student: "But it is impossible in Jerusalem to detach oneself from the frightful political problems of Israel. I found myself 'doing something.' I read a great many books, talked with scores of people, and before the first month was out I was

---

*Even nation-states played out this dichotomy: Israel was tough, worldly, shrewd, to Bellow's way of looking at things, while America was naïve—a paradigm of his relationship with his brothers. Once again, the old themes materialized, this time in a geographic metaphor.

†Some of Auerbach's harrowing stories about life at sea appeared in the literary magazine *Bostonia,* under the editorship of Keith Botsford.

writing a small book about the endless crisis and immersed in politics. It excites me, it distresses me to be so immersed."

The embattled state of Israel stimulated him; it was like being
back in Humboldt Park half a century before, listening to soapbox
debates on Trotsky and the Fourth International. He flung himself
into the task, boning up on the history of the Middle East, reading
policy papers, interviewing politicians. He had lunch with Prime
Minister Yitzhak Rabin and visited the former foreign minister
Abba Eban at the Knesset. He interviewed scholars and political
scientists, diplomats and editors, and toured Jerusalem with the
mayor, Teddy Kollek, who bombarded the Bellows with invitations to concerts, dinners, teas. "I'm like a piece of confetti in a
wind tunnel," the happily beleaguered novelist told a reporter
from the *New York Post*. "So I started whirling around."

The state of Israel matched Bellow's inner state: a rapid alterna-
tion between hunger for argument, debate, activity and an equally
avid hunger for spiritual enlightenment, which satisfied "a very
different part of the mind." With its biblical history, its population
of Holocaust survivors and refugees from eastern Europe, its civilized Old World customs—the fruit in the bowls, the flowers on
the table, the high-minded talk of books and music and art—the
country appealed to his sense of "Jewish transcendentalism." The
light of Jerusalem, he wrote movingly, had "purifying powers and
filters the blood and the thoughts; I don't forbid myself the reflec-
tion that light may be the outer garment of God." In his sun-filled
apartment, he practiced the "I Am It Thinks" meditation exercise
outlined in one of Rudolf Steiner's pamphlets.

On the eve of his departure for Israel, Bellow had submitted
to an interview with Alden Whitman of *The New York Times*
in which he propounded the distinction between "great-public"
and "small-public" writers. The distinction was borrowed from
Wyndham Lewis, who noted in his book *Rude Assignment* that
nineteenth-century novelists had written for a broad public; the
modernists—Eliot, Pound, Joyce, and Proust—were "small-
public" writers. Bellow cited Theodore Dreiser, Sherwood Anderson, and Upton Sinclair, along with Dickens and Zola in Europe,
as writers who "addressed grand issues of social justice and political concern." *Humboldt's Gift* had been "intended to hold up a

mirror to our urban society and to show its noise, its uncertitudes, its sense of crisis and despair, its standardization of pleasures." In that sense, it was a "great-public" novel.

Writing from Jerusalem, Bellow complained to his Minnesota lawyer John Goetz that Whitman had "garbled" the distinction: "Whitman misunderstood everything. He may even have misunderstood his own questions. I didn't speak of myself as 'a large-public writer,' and I didn't speak of Proust and U. Sinclair in the same breath, although I'm not an idolator and see no reason why doves and artists should not share a man's breath. When you publish a book you learn what journalism is—a dreadful thing." He wanted to be read "on his own terms," as he put it later, "to be, in my books, as odd, difficult, idiosyncratic as I need to be in order to get said what I feel needs to be said." And if that meant being a "small-public" writer, so be it. At the same time, he yearned to be—and tended to think of himself as—a "great-public" writer, whose reach extended far beyond the modernists he admired for their high seriousness but disdained for the "difficulty" that estranged them from a wider audience. Bellow wanted it both ways: to be special, a member of an esoteric cultural elite, and popular, a writer in the great tradition of the nineteenth-century European novel. Maybe Whitman hadn't gotten it wrong after all in lumping him with the "great-public" writers; Bellow just didn't want to foreclose his options.

But journalists were high on Bellow's list of those he considered had been put on earth to harry him, and Whitman's supposed misreading wasn't the only instance of malfeasance in the *Times*. To Ruth Miller, he poured out his heart about "a long series of detractor viruses eating at [his] nerves"—chief among them Louis Simpson's article in *The New York Times Magazine*, "The Ghost of Delmore Schwartz," which called attention in a very public way to the parallels between Humboldt and Schwartz.

It wasn't a generous performance on Simpson's part. "Bellow has trouble imagining a character who is not like himself," he charged, and he unfairly held Bellow accountable for Charlie Citrine's negative judgments about Humboldt as a poet, as if the character was purely a biographical figure. He also oversimplified to the point of parody Bellow's diatribe against American society, which had made life difficult for poets: "In his view poets have to compete with Boeing and Sperry Rand, and if they don't survive it is because they are weak." As far as Bellow was concerned, poets were doomed for the same reason that novelists were neglected: In America, art didn't matter enough.

Simpson's article was "cheap, mean, it did me dirt," Bellow fumed to Miller:

> I had no idea that he was in such a rage. But age does do some things for us (nothing comparable to what it takes away) and I have learned to endure such fits. I don't ask myself why the Times prints such miserable stuff, why I must be called an ingrate, a mental tyrant, a thief, a philistine enemy of poetry, a narcissist incapable of feeling for others, a failed artist. Nor why this must be done in the Sunday Magazine for many millions of readers. Nor what crime I committed in writing a book. Nor anything. Such things are not written about industrialists, or spies, or bankers, or trade-union leaders, or Idi Amin, or Palestinian terrorists, only about the author of a novel who wanted principally to be truthful and to give delight. It doesn't stab me to the heart, however. I know what newspapers are and what writers are and know that they can occasionally try to destroy one another. I've never done it myself, but I've seen it done, often enough. As I've been in Jerusalem for ten weeks I know too what it is to have enemies dedicated to your extinction. Louie's hatred and my discomfort are minor matters, comparatively. He can't *kill* me. He's only doing dirt on my heart (by intention—he didn't actually succeed). And I don't compare myself to the Israelis. I'm only talking about the destructive will.

He was especially offended by a quote from Miller herself in the piece, suggesting that Bellow was an "artist manqué" who failed to create independent characters:

> I wondered why *you* should find it necessary to testify against me and say that I was an artist *manque*. After many years in the trade, I'm well aware that the papers twist peoples' words and that at times their views are reversed for them by reporters and editors. But you *were* angry with me, and Stonybrook *isn't* exactly filled with my friends and admirers. Nor do I, from *my* side, think of Stonybrook as a great center of literary power in

which a renaissance is about to begin, led by Kazin and Jack Ludwig and Louie. (Not that I've written reviews and articles about *them*). So I didn't expect you to say kind things about me. But I didn't expect unkind things in print, and I was shocked by the opinion attributed to you that Humboldt was my confession of utter failure. Louie I could dismiss. A writer who doesn't know quality when he sees it doesn't have to be taken seriously. A reader who doesn't see that the book is a very funny one can also be disregarded. One can only wonder why the deaf should attend concerts. But you I don't dismiss. And I thought "I've steered Ruth wrong. What has this girl from Albany Park gained by ending up in Stonybrook? Is it *possible* that she should have become one of those killers?"

Never mind, Bellow concluded in one of his sudden mood reversals: He was still Miller's "old loving friend." A few weeks later, he sounded a more conciliatory note. "It is absurd for you and me to work up these Old System Jewish family quarrels," he confessed, invoking his short story about a vindictive, unforgiving sister. "In spite of a massive effort to remain adolescent, I am approaching my 61st year—I've always loved you. And there are no more decades to burn. We ought to try again to have a conversation. I promise to be sensible."

Bellow's outburst was characteristic. He vacillated between sentimentality and spite. His good deeds were legion: He arranged for his old friend Edith Tarcov to edit the Viking *Portable Bellow*; he visited Hofstra at the behest of Schwartz's widow, Elizabeth Pollet, who taught in the creative-writing program there. And so were his unpredictable displays of wrath: After Sam Freifeld warned him about the potential consequences of misrepresenting his income in his court battle with Susan, their relationship was never the same. "Saul Bellow is a great artist but a lousy friend," Freifeld announced to the world in the pages of *Newsweek*.

The Bellows returned to America early in 1976, but Bellow was still "whirling around." In January, he flew to Miami Beach to accept the S. Y. Agnon Gold Medal for Literary Achievement from the American Friends of the Hebrew University. A week later, he was off to Stanford University, where Alexandra was being considered for an appointment by the mathematics department. He "looked regal," recalled Dana Gioia, a graduate student at the Stanford Business School who later made a name for himself as a poet:

> Entering a room, he appeared intimidatingly confident. At sixty he was still trim and handsome. His well-tanned skin was unwrinkled. His thin grey hair brushed into deceptive thickness. And a king's haberdashery would not have surpassed his wardrobe. His tight, expensively-tailored suits and handsewn shirts stood aloof from the crowds of crumpled tweed and corduroy around him.

John Cheever was also on the Stanford campus that week, visiting his son Frederico. Cheever and Bellow had maintained a sturdy friendship since their Yaddo days in the 1950s. Once, when Cheever was visiting Chicago, Bellow had taken him to the Russian baths on Division. "Wreathed in vapor he [Bellow] looked more immortal than I but I think he was trying," Cheever reported to his brother, Fred, noting that Bellow had openly studied his guest's private parts.

Bellow had won so many prizes that he used to joke "there weren't any more to win." One prize, however, had eluded the three-time National Book Award winner: the Pulitzer, "the pullet surprise," as Charlie Citrine, a surrogate winner, called it in *Humboldt's Gift*, dismissing the prize as "a dummy newspaper publicity award given by crooks and illiterates—for the birds." In May 1976, the Pulitzer committee, known for its often perplexing choices, bestowed the prize on the very novel in which it had been burlesqued. Ducking a press conference, Bellow taped a simple message to the door of his office: "I am delighted with the award."

That summer, *To Jerusalem and Back* was excerpted at length in *The New Yorker*, taking up a considerable part of the magazine's July 12 and July 19 issues. For Bellow, to have a long, reported piece appear there was "major, major, major, major," said Elisabeth Sifton, who had become his editor at Viking. If ever there was a citadel of WASPdom, it was *The New Yorker*, whose genteel anti-Semitism was embodied by its remote and enigmatic editor, William Shawn (himself a reluctant Jew), and his magisterial aide,

Katharine White. According to Bellow, Isaac Bashevis Singer was "their kind of Jew"—foreign, ethnic, "Jewy."*

Bellow's literary triumphs had no mitigating effect on his legal troubles. The week that *The New Yorker* appeared on the stands, Susan dragged him back to court. On July 14, the First District Court of Chicago upheld the finding that there had been, in the language of the judge's ruling, "an intention by the defendant to mislead the plaintiff with respect to the income projection." The defendant was ordered to pay Susan's legal costs—a whopping two hundred thousand dollars.†

Eager to put distance between himself and the knot of judges and lawyers deciding his fate in the Cook County courthouse, Bellow made off with Alexandra at the end of July to Cortina d'Ampezzo, in the Italian Alps. In August, they retreated to Block Island. "I do nothing here but lie about," he reported to Richard Stern. "Luckily A. has her mathematics and doesn't much mind my silence and mental nullity."

Meanwhile, rumors of the Big One—the Nobel—continued to circulate. "If I win I'll buy you a mink coat if you promise to make love to me in it," Bellow had told Fran Gendlin in 1974. But the prize that year went to the Swedish writers Eyvind Johnson and Harry Martinson, and in 1975 Bellow was passed over again in favor of the Italian poet Eugenio Montale. "I'm not disappointed," he told a reporter. "There's plenty of time to win it yet."

---

* "Singer is like a Chinese stage Manager, supplied with props from the *shtetl*," Bellow wrote scathingly to the critic Milton Hindus: "In its final form, it is *Fiddler on the Roof*, and Zero Mostel makes a third with Singer and Chagall." In other words, Singer was too ethnic. But if so, how could he have been *The New Yorker*'s "kind of Jew"? The Jewish writers who thrived at the magazine—S. J. Perelman, A. J. Liebling, E. J. Kahn, Edith Oliver—"seemed as assimilated as it was possible to be," according to *About Town*, Ben Yagoda's history of *The New Yorker*. Yagoda quotes Alfred Kazin: "There was an unspoken attitude that it wouldn't do to be too 'Jewish.'" This was Bellow's own attitude; *The New Yorker* provided a screen for his thinly veiled class snobbery.

† Sam Bellows was also in trouble with the law that summer, charged with receiving kickbacks from pharmacies that had prescriptions filled at the nursing homes he owned. After a lengthy trial, he was fined two hundred thousand dollars and sentenced to sixty days in the Metropolitan Correctional Center.

The deliberations of the Nobel committee have always been cloaked behind a veil of secrecy, but there were rumors that some of the Swedish delegates were troubled by the narrowness of Bellow's concerns, his unwillingness to strut on the world stage. There was talk of dividing the prize between Bellow and Isaac Bashevis Singer—a solution that no doubt would have annoyed both parties. The achievement of *Humboldt's Gift* had improved Bellow's chances of winning the prize on his own; *To Jerusalem and Back*, a book that grappled manfully with global politics, may well have clinched it.

"It is sure to enrage hundreds of people," Bellow had predicted of the Jerusalem book, reflexively (and perhaps hopefully) imagining himself beset by enemies. In fact, when it was released in the fall of 1976, his first book-length foray into nonfiction earned some of the best reviews of his career. Irving Howe, who had not always endorsed Bellow's work, was enthusiastic. "The best living American novelist is also a man of brains," he noted with approval. Unlike those "intuitive artists, redskin magicians of literature," who prided themselves on being unlettered, Bellow was a serious writer who was also an intellectual.*

Written in brief, journal-like vignettes, *To Jerusalem and Back* was not a systematic book—Howe, for one, was troubled by its loose form. But it was a work of great depth and subtlety. Through his extensive interviews, Bellow had assembled a highly sophisticated portrait of the political situation in the Middle East. Like the earnest University of Chicago boy that he was, he included footnotes from *The Middle East Review, Foreign Affairs,* and an obscure journal called *Dispersion and Unity.* He invoked Mozart, Elias Canetti, Stendhal, the metaphysical poet George Herbert. "Why are you quoting so much?" Rachel MacKenzie, his editor at *The New Yorker,* had asked: "*You're* the original thinker. You're the one people want to hear."

---

*Howe was alluding to Philip Rahv's famous distinction between two types in American literature, the paleface and the redskin. Redskins (Whitman, Twain, James Fenimore Cooper) "gloried" in their American identity; to palefaces (Hawthorne, James, T. S. Eliot), it was a source of "endless ambiguities." Bellow, Howe meant to suggest, was a paleface.

But if his display of learning was a little ostentatious, it was also grounded in a lifetime of reading and thinking about history. Bellow's knowledge of the past—of Weimar Germany and the Spanish civil war, of England in the imperial age and Russia during the revolution—gave weight to his observations. He brought to bear on the current crisis a mind and sensibility formed by the habit of analogy; what was happening now could be understood from the perspective of what had gone before. No Zionist, Bellow was a moderate who believed firmly "in the right of Israel to exist." He was offended by the anti-Semitism of French intellectuals, the pro-Arab sympathies of *Le Monde,* and the fashionable Marxist theorizing of Jean-Paul Sartre: "A great deal of intelligence can be invested in ignorance when the need for illusion is deep." The fairest political solution, in Bellow's view, was to create a Palestinian state on the West Bank, "a state that recognizes the interdependence of the contemporary world." Only by negotiation could Israel secure its own continuance.

But *To Jerusalem and Back* isn't a political treatise. Bellow's mandate was to give reality to "human feelings, human experience, the human form and face." He captured his subjects' physical presences in a few deft strokes: the old barber in the King David Hotel, with his "senile strength and cheer"; the Arab newspaper editor Mahmud Abu Zuluf, "stout and large—a very large, unmenacing, and even dreamy round-faced man"; the poet Dennis Silk, with hair "in long and random tufts," a nose "nobly hooked, and slender." One of the most poignant episodes in the book is the account of an afternoon spent drinking with Silk and another poet friend, Harold Schimmel. Bellow reminisced about Theodore Roethke at Yaddo and read Berryman's "Dream Songs" in the poet's voice: "Drink and poetry and feeling for a dead friend, and the short December afternoon deepening by the moment from a steady blue to a darker, more trembling blue—when I stop I feel that I have caught a chill."

Irving Howe's front-page review in *The New York Times Book Review* on October 17, 1976, was the portent of a momentous week. For days, word about the Nobel Prize had again been circulating. "I've heard lots of rumors, but nothing official," Bellow told Edward Shils early in the week. A day later, the well-connected Walter Pozen called from Washington to say that a source at *The Washington Post* had confirmed it, and in midweek the news was actually leaked to the Swedish press—an unprecedented event in the annals of the Nobel. Stuart Brent, a former Tuleyite who owned a bookstore on North Michigan Avenue, ran into an excited Bellow on the street; in his exaltation, Bellow spoke to Brent in Yiddish.

On Wednesday, October 20, a representative from the Swedish embassy called and asked Bellow if he would accept the prize if it were offered. (Sartre had refused it years earlier.) That night, Bellow went out for dinner with Alexandra and a reporter from *Newsweek,* who had arrived in anticipation of the announcement. The next morning, Harriet Wasserman called at six-thirty to let him know that an announcement was imminent. "I'm under the covers with Jane Austen, and I'm going to stay with Jane Austen until it's all over," Bellow said. A half hour later, a reporter from Reuters called and read him the press release from the Swedish Academy. The decision had been unanimous.

By midmorning, "things already were chaotic" at the Bellows' apartment, according to a reporter for the *Sun-Times* who was on the scene. Bellow and Alexandra had happened to choose that day to move to the other side of the city, in order to be closer to Alexandra's job at Northwestern. By the time Richard Stern arrived to congratulate him, Bellow had already driven to the new apartment, on Sheridan Road, to open it for the movers.

It was "an uninspired day, neither hot nor cold, bright nor murky, a gray, medium October day, the thunder god's day (but who regards old Norse fiction in Chicago?)," wrote Stern in a lively account of that day's events for *The New York Times Magazine.* A long, white moving van was parked out front, and a reporter from Swedish television was setting up his equipment. On the sidewalk stood Bellow's broccoli-green sofa and armchairs, chiffoniers, and his antique desk. Bellow was dressed in a green turtleneck and slacks: "He's tired; the face, which can alter more and more quickly than any other I've ever seen, is now drawn, and if not quartered, grooved, pallid, a bit puffy at eyes and throat." Stern had brought a bottle of champagne, and he and Bellow drank from a pair of highball glasses.

The phone rang off the hook. "Now you know why I was after you to be quiet thirty years ago," Bellow told his oldest son, Greg, who called from San Francisco. His sister, Jane, called and wept over the memory of their father's angry resistance to Bellow becoming a writer: "Long after everybody was dead I won the fight," he said regretfully. Maurice called from Georgia, where he had just moved to a horse farm. There had also been calls, Bellow reported to Stern, from "a few old profs of mine who are pleased with my progress." At least he didn't have to worry anymore about recognition. He wasn't "a total loss. *Spurlos, versenkt*"— "Sunk, without a trace." But he wasn't cocky, either. "Maybe now, I can write something really good for a change," he said.

Later that morning, the president of the university, John T. Wilson, drove him over to the Social Science Building for a press conference. He had violated his usual custom of writing every morning, Bellow told the reporters gathered in the auditorium, his green turtleneck now supplemented by a dark green suit. There were tears in his eyes. "I haven't had the time today to be happy or miserable."

How did he feel about the prize? asked a reporter. Mostly he felt "confused," Bellow replied. On the one hand, it seemed premature: "I have scarcely begun to master my trade." On the other, he had paid his dues: "Nobody who wants to write a book likes to be ignored and neglected. There's a primitive part of me that is gratified by it. The child in me is delighted; the adult in me is skeptical."

The adult's point of view was much in evidence at the press conference. Americans had swept the Nobels that year, winning in five categories; Bellow's University of Chicago colleague Milton Friedman had gotten the prize in economics. Informed that President Ford had declared the results evidence of the country's intellectual primacy, Bellow said: "Somebody must have told President Ford that because I don't think he would have discerned it for himself." As for the money—$160,000, tax free—he had no plans: "At this rate, my heirs will get it in a day or two" (more likely Susan). He spoke fondly of his fellow Nobelist John Steinbeck, who had predicted many years before that Bellow would be the next winner of the prize: "I think it made him feel quite wretched.

I hope it isn't going to make me wretched. But then I'm a more cynical character." Others were equally deserving, he noted, mentioning Henry Miller, André Maurois, Ignazio Silone, and Christina Stead. "I'm glad to get it," he said matter-of-factly: "I could live without it." Then he put on his black leather jacket and his battered fedora and headed out into the cold afternoon.

The next day, on the front page of *The New York Times*, John Leonard, the paper's resident literary man, offered an appraisal that managed to rob Bellow of his achievement while purporting to celebrate it. "If Saul Bellow didn't exist," Leonard began, "someone exactly like him would have had to have been invented, just after the Second World War, by New York intellectuals, in a backroom at Partisan Review." He was the "highbrow with muscles" who could "tell the story of the Jewish romance with America"—as if the role came before the man. Leonard also managed to turn Bellow into a Sammy Glick character who had "made it."

Letters and telegrams of congratulation poured in from old friends: John Cheever, Robert Penn Warren, Wright Morris, Philip Roth; from the "notables" Mayor Richard J. Daley and President Ford; from Tuley classmates and neighbors from Humboldt Park days.

Around town, Chicagoans took the announcement in stride. At the Riviera Club, a well-known Chicago gangster clapped Bellow on the shoulder and crowed, "Hey, Solly, I hear you won the big one!" Not everyone rejoiced. Edward Shils, encountering Bellow in the quad, remarked acidly: "So you join the august company of Halldór Laxness and Carl Spitteler"—two previous Nobel laureates who had since lapsed into obscurity.*

The most touching tribute came from a Tuley classmate. In his column for the *Daily News*, "Strictly Personal," Sydney J. Harris exulted: "When I woke up one morning and heard the news, it seemed as fantastic as landing on Mars." He recalled the days when he and his "boyhood chum" had sat around the dining-room table dreaming of their future literary fame. "In those days,

---

*Bellow was aware of the many writers of the first rank who hadn't gotten the prize, among them Tolstoy, Conrad, Lawrence, Joyce, and Proust.

deep in the Depression, we saw no plays, heard little music, trea-sured our thumb-worn 'Modern Library' softback books, and walked incessantly, across the park and back, all the while talking about the abysmal state of writing in this still-barbarous country of ours." Harris had failed to measure up to their early dreams, he confessed. "But I am delighted that one of us was able to trans-mute those adolescent fancies into a supreme reality. There is no reflected glory, but a reflected pleasure—that these two steeds did actually come out of the same stable, even though one of them is Pegasus and the other Dobbin."

Bellow, too, was mindful of those who had fallen by the wayside—especially dear, dead Isaac Rosenfeld. Back in 1948, when the young Truman Capote had been featured in the pages of *Life* magazine as a rising star, Rosenfeld had comforted a jealous Bellow. "Don't worry," he'd said: "One of us is going to win the Nobel Prize." Now, when Dave Peltz called to offer congratula-tions, Bellow said, "It should have been Isaac."

Perhaps to ward off excess grandiosity, Bellow spoke of the prize in the darkest terms. It was "like an inoculation against some dread disease," he said. He was overwhelmed by "the Niagara of publicity"; his private life had been "wiped out." Instead of being a writer, he was a spokesman: "Suddenly you become a cultural functionary of society without wanting to be, the great finger has reached out and touched you. It really has nothing to do with your own design of life."

But he wore his new laurels with grace. *The New York Times*'s cultural correspondent, Herbert Mitgang, who caught up with Bellow at an Anti-Defamation League luncheon in New York, remarked on Bellow's equanimity in the face of the media onslaught: "Wearing an air of dignity beneath his silver hair with penetrating, now skeptical eyes, Mr. Bellow seems to be carrying the burdens of laureateship lightly." At a formal dinner held for him by his University of Chicago colleagues, he rose in white tie and tails to offer a few remarks. "After years of the most arduous mental labor," he began, "I stand before you in the costume of a headwaiter."

A week later, he flew to Southern Methodist University near Dallas at the invitation of Pascal Covici, Jr., the son of his revered editor and himself the chairman of the SMU English department. For Bellow's public reading, 1,600 people showed up at the McFarlin Auditorium on campus and gave him a standing ovation. "I feel like Jimmy Carter, ready to enter into a dialogue with all of you," Bellow joked.

Being thrust into the limelight took an inevitable toll on his family. His son Adam was besieged by the press. A photographer showed up at his Princeton dorm early one morning while he was in his underwear. Asked by a reporter what it was like to be Saul Bellow's son, he answered that it was "like stepping on a rake. It comes up and smashes you in the teeth once in awhile."

The Bellows set off for Sweden in the first week of December, accompanied by a large contingent. Among the party were Bellow and Alexandra; the three boys; Alexandra's mother; Bellow's brother Sam and his wife, Nina; his sister, Jane (who complained about having to fly from Florida to Chicago to get her mink coat out of storage); his niece Leisha, along with her husband and their children; his publishers, Tom Rosenthal of Secker and Warburg and Thomas Guinzburg (son of Harold) of Viking; and Harriet Wasserman. Bellow had threatened to leave Daniel home, grumbling about having to rent him a tuxedo, but he relented in the end. It turned out to be a rare harmonious occasion. Adam had T-shirts printed for the whole family with the legend: NOBEL SAVAGE. "It was only light for about an hour and a half a day," recalled Guinzburg. "Everyone was drunk all the time, knocking back little glasses of schnapps. Bellow looked great. It was the one time I saw him really happy."

The week in Stockholm was an exhausting round of lunches and banquets and television interviews. On the morning of December 13, Bellow and Alexandra were put through the "Lucia" ceremony, in which white-clad maidens bearing lit candles burst into their bedroom early in the morning to serenade them while they were still in bed. Bellow smiled gamely for the photographers, but it wasn't a pleasurable occasion. "They came bearing a tray with bad coffee and some buns which they set down on my bathrobe so that I couldn't reach it. And behind them was the press, in force. I scowled, and then my face formed the smile which is obligatory on such occasions."

Bellow was anxious about his speech. When Harriet Wasserman arrived at his hotel suite the following morning to type it for him, he was pale. "Saul was reading from his notes, revising as he spoke," she recalled. "At the same time, he was watching my face to see my reaction." At noon, the speech was released to the press, and Bellow and his amanuensis slipped into the Wintergarden restaurant for lunch, positioning themselves behind a column in the hope of going unnoticed. But the orchestra, decked out in Père Noël hats, struck up "Chicago, Chicago, that toddling town." On Sunday—"the best day for dark reflections"—he gave his speech before an appreciative audience in the Grand Hall in Stockholm's Old Town as a heavy snow fell outside. He was introduced by Professor Karl Ragnar Gierow, who lauded Bellow's heroes for never abandoning "the realm of values in which man becomes human." The official citation was read, and Bellow approached the podium to thunderous applause. Loosening his tie, he smiled at Alexandra in the second row and began to read his speech, speaking "softly and a bit nervously," according to *The New York Times*'s correspondent.

He opened his remarks, as he often did, with a memory out of his youth, recalling his discovery of the novels of Joseph Conrad, a writer who appealed to Bellow "because he was like an American—he was an uprooted Pole sailing exotic seas, speaking French and writing English with extraordinary power and beauty." Out of this doubtful heritage Conrad had created works that celebrated, in the words of his famous preface to *The Nigger of the Narcissus*, "what was fundamental, enduring, essential."

What was striking about Bellow's seventy-minute address was its sense of mission—that writers themselves could awaken from the intellectual torpor that had descended upon civilization and reacquaint that civilization with the higher values it had forsaken. There was something heroic about this impulse to assume responsibility, not to be passive. "Writers are greatly respected," Bellow admitted finally, eschewing the note of grievance that had so often made itself heard in his public pronouncements:

The intelligent public is wonderfully patient with them, continues to read them, and endures disappointment after disappointment, waiting to hear from art what it does not hear from theology, philosophy, social theory, and what it cannot hear from pure science. Out of the struggle at the center has come an immense, painful longing for a broader, more flexible, fuller, more coherent, more comprehensive account of what we human beings are, who we are, and what this life is for. At the center, humankind struggles with collective powers for its freedom; the individual struggles with dehumanization for the possession of his soul. If writers do not come again into the center it will not be because the center is preempted. It is not. They are free to enter. If they so wish.

It was a theme he had sounded almost since the beginning—from his rejected application for assistance from the Rockefeller Foundation when he was living penuriously in Queens in 1951 to his lectures before packed halls at the world's great universities. Only now, as he stood before the world in white tie and tails, he could perhaps reflect with greater confidence on where his own descent into "the lonely regions" had ultimately brought him.

It had been a good year—especially since, as Bellow told Richard Stern, "All I started out to do was show up my brothers. I didn't have to go this far."

26

I pursue my deadline across a calendar-desert. It's fun, of an anxious kind; and so life keeps rushing towards the horizon.

—Bellow to Zita Cogan

"THE AWARD OF THE PRIZE has often marked a point of crisis in the careers of the great American writers," noted the critic Malcolm Bradbury, speaking at a symposium on Bellow at the Free University of Brussels a year after the Nobel ceremony. Previous winners had accomplished little in the wake of their literary apotheosis. It was "a ticket to one's own funeral," T. S. Eliot had noted darkly—a sentiment echoed by other winners, who also invoked the specter of premature senescence.* The Nobel was a hard act to follow.

Bellow regarded the perils of laureateship with equanimity. "I don't think the Prize is going to make much difference," he wrote Ralph Ross on March 22, 1977: "It's been very confusing and delusive, but the delusions aren't hard to shake off. Some of the contemporary literary winners have made wonderful comments about Stockholm. [George] Seferis said it allowed him, after long effort, to be *nobody,* to be unnoticed, as Homer said of Ulysses. The noise dies down, and then you find your scale. If you have any sense, you go back to your trade, and humor is part of my trade."

* "This would be good if I were ready to die or if I were material for the priesthood," John Steinbeck said. "No son of a bitch that ever won the Nobel Prize ever wrote anything worth reading afterwards," Ernest Hemingway said.

One of the burdens of literary anointment was the growing body of critical commentary on Bellow's work. The expansion of higher education in postwar America, combined with the emphasis on scholarly publishing as a requirement of tenure, had created a new academic industry. In 1977, three book-length bibliographies of Bellow appeared. Twenty books about his work were now in print, as were hundreds of essays in many languages, from Lakshmi Kannan's "That Small Voice in Bellow's Fiction" (*Visvabharati Quarterly*) to Eva Manske's "Das Menschenbild im Prosaschaffen Saul Bellows Anspruch und Wirklichkeit" (*Zeitschrift für Anglistik und Amerikanistik*).

Bellow was impatient with this critical outpouring, little of which he bothered to read. Always contemptuous of critics, he could really let himself go with a Nobel under his belt. In a Brandeis University commencement speech, he compared them to deaf piano tuners. Elsewhere, he declared that Richard Poirier, who had written a strident attack on *Herzog*, was "stupid"; the experimental writers Poirier endorsed were "spiritless, etiolated, and the liveliest of them are third-rate vaudevillians." Who would want to be a literary critic, anyway? Bellow wondered. "I'd rather inspect gas mains in Chicago."

All the same, he was polite to scholars. Daniel Fuchs, who had been given the run of Bellow's archive at the University of Chicago library and whose *Saul Bellow: Vision and Revision* became the definitive textual study of the manuscripts, recalled Bellow's wariness when Fuchs first approached him. "He gave me a look that said, 'Are you going to stab me in the back, too?'" But he gradually warmed to the idea, as he often did with scholars in the early stages of their research. And the letters he wrote to those who earned his trust were remarkably candid. "I don't like to read about myself—I recoil from it, heart and bowels," he confided to Fuchs; he wasn't ready to be summed up.

> We haven't gotten to the pith and the nucleus yet. We're seeing the limbs, the heart and belly aren't in the picture yet (etc.) Why so slow? I can't say. Maybe it's the situation, maybe a certain timidity or tardiness or sluggishness or laziness—or *sleep* (Henderson, via Shelley, wants to haunt the spirits' sleep). But you should know that I have learnt (gathered, inferred) one useful thing from you. This is that I've been arguing too much—

debating, infighting, polemicizing. The *real* thing is unfathomable. You *can't* get it down to distinct meaning or clear opinion. Sensing this, I have always had intelligence enough (or the intuition) to put honor between myself and final claims.

In the spring of 1977, Bellow gave the Jefferson Lecture in the Humanities, a two-part talk sponsored by the National Endowment for the Humanities and carrying with it a ten-thousand-dollar honorarium. The first part, entitled "The Writer and His Country," was delivered in Washington on March 30 before a "well-gussied audience," as a reporter for *The Washington Post* described the crowd of more than a thousand. Afterward, there was a dinner in the Benjamin Franklin dining room at the State Department, attended by a host of Washington luminaries, including Joan Mondale, wife of the vice president. (The main course was going to be called Beef Bellow, but it was changed at the last minute to Beef Jefferson to avoid echoes of a Chicago slaughterhouse.) It was, according to the *Post's* breathless account, "the first hot social event of the year."

Sporting a red-and-lavender velvet bow tie to complement his dinner jacket, Bellow sipped from a crystal tumbler of Canadian Club, which he had carried in from prelecture cocktails. It was a strong performance, one of his most eloquent evocations of life in Chicago, "the prairie city with a waterfront." Describing the view from his Sheridan Road aerie, Bellow conjured up its arctic features:

> On this January day, the thermometer is well below zero, and Lake Michigan resembles Hudson Bay, scaly white and gray, with slabs of ice piled offshore by high winds. Oceangoing ships, late in leaving Calumet Harbor, seem to be stuck on the horizon, and their coast guard rescuers also appear to be immobilized. In this weather, Chicago, which has changed so much in the last forty years, looks its old self again in its ice armor of frozen grime, fenders and car doors whitened with salt, smoke moving slowly from the stacks, the fury of the cold shrinking the face and heart as it did in the good old days.

Bellow's genius for the particular images of his youth reached new elegiac heights in the Jefferson lectures. He never tired of contemplating the miracle of his journey from three-dollar rented rooms in the "white-knuckle" city of stockyards and slums to a high-rise overlooking Lake Michigan, with all the abundance it offered, both material and spiritual. That journey, as he saw it, was at once his story and the story of America.

Two days later, on April 1, he delivered the second part of his Jefferson lecture in the Gold Coast Room at the Drake Hotel in Chicago. He gamely tried to play down the pomp and circumstance, noting that it was April Fool's Day and admitting to "a long and rooted prejudice" against lectures. "But here I am. That's life."

Part two began as a meditation on success, inspired by a little anthology that a friend had sent him called *The Bitch Goddess Success*, a collection of aphorisms and anecdotes from famous Americans about the perils of success. (The title was a phrase of William James.) But the lecture soon resumed Bellow's original theme, the uncomplicated joys of the old immigrant Chicago—the Poles and Lithuanians, Greeks and Italians and Serbians clustered together in Humboldt Park as they pursued the American dream. In Bellow's nostalgic view, that dream had been undone by the Immigration Act of 1924, which slowed the arrival of the Europeans whose infusion of culture had made the country great—"carpenters, printers, pastry cooks, sign painters, cobblers"—and supplanted them with an "internal immigration" from Puerto Rico and the South. Half a century later, the city of his childhood had become "devastated Chicago," a city where the crumbling schools were filled with students possessed by "a demonic knowledge of sexual acts, guns, drugs, and of vices which are not vices here." Bellow's perspective on recent American history was ungenerous to minorities who faced greater obstacles to assimilation than he had—less than a generation later, such sentiments were derided for "privileging" white Europeans over other ethnic groups. But that wasn't his intent. As Bellow saw it, the later wave of new arrivals was another threat to his hard-won sense of specialness, another constituency intent upon undermining the fragile foundations of his cultural authority. He was engaged in a turf war: "The streets of Chicago are *mine*." And he wasn't about to give them up without a struggle.

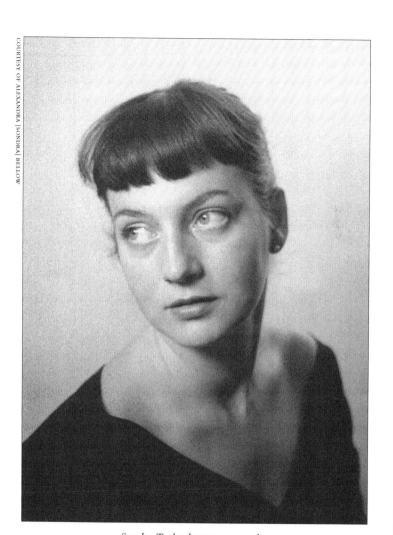

Sondra Tschacbasov, soon to be
the second Mrs. Bellow, in the early 1950s.

*Sondra with the
very young Adam,
ca. 1957.*

*The family romance, part 2:
Bellow with Sondra
and Adam.*

*Bellow (center) with his friends Alfred Kazin
and Ann Birstein (Kazin's wife), in New York.*

*Bellow and his third wife, the former Susan Glassman,
on Martha's Vineyard, summer of 1962.*

Bellow's South Shore Drive residence.

The author of Herzog, *Bellow's passport
to great fame and wealth, 1963.*

Bellow in the late sixties, when he was writing Mr. Sammler's Planet.

*Bellow inverted, in
Aspen, Colorado,
ca. 1969.*

*Bellow and Maggie
Staats on Nantucket,
August 1969.*

ARLETTE JASSEL, BELLOWING AND BALLING (1969), ACRYLIC ON CANVAS, 69" X 106". PHOTO: GREG STALEY

Arlette Landes's free-spirited portrayal of herself, Bellow, Daniel, and Landes's daughter, Bonnie: "He did his own thing, and people danced around him."

Bellow with his three sons—Daniel, Adam, and Gregory—in the late 1970s.

Bellow and Alexandra, on the town in Victoria, British Columbia, early 1982.

John Berryman at work on his Dream Songs
in Ryan's Pub, Dublin, in May 1967,
a few years before his suicide.

Delmore Schwartz, in his Humboldt phase,
in Washington Square Park,
New York, 1961.

Allan Bloom, Bellow's contentious confrère, in the 1980s.

Bellow in London, 1975.

*Barley Alison,
Bellow's longtime editor
at Secker and Warburg.*

*Bellow shaking hands with Sweden's King Karl Gustaf
at a dinner for the 1976 Nobel laureates.*

*John Cheever, speaking at the National Arts Club in 1978, finds
an appreciative audience in Bellow (far right), who is being awarded
the Club's Medal of Honor for Literature.*

*Bellow (right) and Abraham Held at the sixtieth reunion
of the Tuley High School Class of '33.*

ABOVE: *Bellow and his fifth wife, Janis, in Brattleboro, May 27, 1995.* BELOW: *Saul and Naomi Rose Bellow, January 15, 2000.*

PHOTOS BY JILL KREMENTZ

As if to confirm his place in the Chicago scheme of things, Bellow found himself enmeshed in fresh legal complications on several fronts, enabling him to renew his familiarity with the Cook County courthouse. In the summer of 1977, the indefatigable Susan and her lawyers, intent on getting a piece of Bellow's Nobel Prize money, redoubled their efforts to overturn the original divorce agreement. Susan asserted that Bellow had made $461,303 in royalties the year before, in addition to the $160,000 Nobel award, all the while claiming that he was earning something in the neighborhood of $30,000 a year. She wasn't far off; *Humboldt's Gift* was on the bestseller list for nine months, and the paperback rights had been sold to Avon for $175,000. On June 15, 1977, Harriet Wasserman sent Bellow a "bouquet" of foreign royalties that came to $22,692.

Matters were further complicated by the fact that the judge hearing the case was unsympathetic to the defendant. "I don't like that son of a bitch," he complained to one of Bellow's lawyers. "He writes pornography." Susan's lawyers prevailed, extracting an additional five hundred thousand dollars from the beleaguered novelist, plus eight hundred dollars a month in child support until Daniel achieved his majority. BIG ALIMONY BOOST FOR BELLOW EX-WIFE, read the headline in the *Chicago Sun-Times*.

Bellow refused to settle the case, against his lawyer's advice. In September, claiming it was under appeal, he declined to pay the award and was held in contempt of court; when he failed to show up at the hearing and delayed posting a fifty-thousand-dollar bond, the presiding judge sentenced him to ten days in jail. "There's no way in hell he'll ever see the inside of a jail," his lawyer George Feiwell told a reporter from *Time*. "That would be indecorous."

Bellow managed to muster a grim humor about the proceedings. He was "striving manfully with life's problems," he wrote Richard Stern on October 1:

> They will say in the next world, "You certainly went on in good faith, Kid, doing what you were brought up to do. Very respon-

sible. You may have missed a thing or two (of importance) by
sticking to these commitments." But there's nothing to be done
now. I feel a little weaker than I did in the last decade. I don't
recover all my rest in sleep or other forms of rest. I get more and
more restless, to less and less purpose. And I can't keep up with
all the difficulties. The reason I was slow to write to you was
that the court proceedings were hotter and heavier than usual.
Just now, for instance, I am in contempt. I am coming to
Daniel's barmitzvah but I may be arrested in front of KAM next
Saturday despite my truce agreement (for the weekend) with
Susan. The court held me in contempt because—I will tell it in
legal language—pursuant to advice of counsel I refused to
comply with the alimony assessment of the court but appealed
the decision. Until the appeal is formally filed, I am in contempt
(I can't even spell the damn word, there is so much emotional
interference). My lawyers tell me that I won't be handcuffed and
dragged away to alimony row. Such a vile shock, or culmination, might actually reverse the emotional tides and bring me
peace. Who knows?

Bellow remained a free man. Later that month, an appeals court
reversed the judge's decision on the grounds that Bellow's lawyers
had filed for an extension on the bond. "For now, Bellow is spared
the slammer," reported *Newsweek* on October 31. In the end, a
good portion of the money went to Susan's lawyers—after much
wrangling in court, $125,000.* "A lot of lawyers in Chicago got
more out of the Nobel than I did," Bellow remarked acidly. "And
they weren't my lawyers." There was something peculiar about the
intensity and sheer duration of the divorce proceedings. Fighting
in court kept the couple together; the vows they obeyed were vows
of retribution. "They wanted to hurt each other," suggested
Feiwell. "It was a matter of who was going to hurt who the
worst." At Daniel's bar mitzvah, Bellow and Susan danced
joyously with each other; two days later, they were back in court.

Daniel got caught in the middle and was forced to testify. At one
point, Bellow sued for custody on the grounds that Susan was
causing the boy "severe emotional trauma." She had subjected
him to "oppressive and harsh conduct, rendering his life miser-

---

*The jail term was finally voided in 1979, and the alimony reduced to two
thousand dollars a month until Daniel turned eighteen.

able," in the language of the brief submitted to the court. One of Bellow's chief complaints was that Daniel had been sent to a psychiatrist—if it hadn't worked for the father, why should it work for the son? In this dispute, too, the judge ruled against Bellow, maintaining that Daniel had been doing well until he stopped going to the psychiatrist.*

On the stand, Daniel made it clear to the judge that he was in no hurry to go live with his dad. "He was hypercritical: it was always, 'You can't do this; you got it wrong; you messed up.' It got so that I dreaded Sunday"—the one day they spent together each week. Bellow found Daniel's company equally trying. "Now that my ex-wife has moved my son Daniel to West End Avenue my visits to New York will be more frequent," he wrote Al Glotzer in the summer of 1978: "Not pleasant to entertain your kid in hotel rooms, however snazzy, so you may expect me quite soon. I will have need of good adult company."

Adam's mother had also moved to the Upper West Side, following unhappy periods in Westchester and Great Neck; there were two Mrs. Bellows listed in the Manhattan phone book on West End Avenue. (However tough it was being an ex–Mrs. Bellow, the prestige of the name was apparently hard to forgo.) Sondra's post-divorce life had been hard. She worked at a series of unrewarding jobs—editing an engineering journal, working at the Hudson Institute and for a management-consultant firm in New York. "My mother was Hester Prynne and I was little Pearl," Adam recalled of this difficult period. But he had done well, attending Princeton and struggling to find his own way in life. At twenty, he was trying to choose between the two professions his father had considered: anthropology and literature. He had enrolled in a summer writing workshop at Michigan State University—"an incredible opportunity for me to get to know some people who are weird in the same way I am," he reported. The family name was a burden for an aspiring writer. Hoping to remain anonymous, he had registered as Adam Bell, but a secretary mistakenly sent out the student list with his real name.

---

*Concerned about Daniel's asthma attacks, Bellow poured out his heart to Edith Tarcov: "He's very bright and we have distressing conversations. He confesses his troubles naturally. He seems to have inherited from me the feeling that life is a very hard thing to get through."

Adam liked to say that the three sons represented the three marriages that had produced them. Greg, the first son, born of a traditional marriage between young parents, followed his mother into a career of social work and resembled her in other ways as well. He had married young, while still in his twenties, and stayed married. He was the dutiful son. "You know there's nothing that makes a nice Jewish boy like me feel better than making his papa proud of him," he wrote his father in the spring of 1975, reporting on his burgeoning practice in a suburb of San Francisco. Whatever resentment Greg felt about having been left as a boy had long since been resolved—or buried. "I've made my peace with my father," he told Stuart Brent.

Daniel, the third son, bore the scars of his parents' long-running divorce. By his own account, he was in trouble "all the time" as an adolescent, especially after he and his mother moved to New York in 1977. It wasn't until he was sent off to Northfield Mount Hermon, a posh boarding school in the Berkshires, that he began to settle down. "Going away to school saved my life. I'm lucky I'm alive. That whole experience left a lot of scars." Even as a boy, Daniel cultivated a self-protective sarcasm. On a trip to Disneyland, he sent his father a postcard of Goofy with the message "I thought that I would buy a postcard with your picture on it."

Adam was the son closest to Bellow: "He felt I was like his mother. He would take out the family album and linger over the photograph of his mother, saying 'You see how much you resemble her?'" He resembled his father even more; as he grew to maturity, he began to manifest a startling likeness to photographs of Bellow as a young man. Temperamentally, however, he was his father's opposite. Perhaps as a reaction to the domestic chaos of his childhood, Adam had acquired a calm and steady disposition. "I can't see where I'm headed, quite yet," he wrote his father in the summer of 1977, implying that he was in no hurry.

After a summer in Vermont, the Bellows stayed in the East for the academic year 1977–78; Alexandra had a visiting professorship at Brandeis, and the English department seized upon the opportunity to offer her illustrious husband one as well. (At last an English department wanted Bellow!) They rented an apartment in a Cambridge high-rise on the Charles River.

For the moment, Bellow's fourth marriage seemed to be working, despite occasional storms of tension. His uxoriousness was evident in *To Jerusalem and Back,* in which he devoted numerous tender passages to his wife's elegance and European civility. She was also "very sexy," noted several of their friends; the first time Dave Peltz met her, she showed up at the door in a miniskirt and black stockings. His marriage was "the one good thing that was happening," Bellow wrote his friend Hyman Slate, alluding to his many trips (some all the way from Cambridge) to the Cook County courthouse. He referred to Alexandra fondly as "my absent-minded professor." A reporter visiting Bellow one day who happened to overhear a telephone conversation between them detected in Bellow's replies "the voice of a man in love."

About the institution of marriage in general he remained cynical. "Nothing lasts more than a decade," he liked to say. Fidelity was a value he continued to hold in low regard. When his Chicago crony Sam Freifeld claimed that marriage would disappear as an institution, Bellow retorted, "Marriage will remain as a viable institution because a man has to have something to be unfaithful to." Alexandra had laid down the law on this score—"no fucking around," as Dave Peltz put it—and Bellow claimed to be in compliance; he was "monogamous, for once," he told Rosette Lamont. Meanwhile, he was sneaking off for occasional trysts with Maggie Staats.

Bellow tried to follow his wife's work and even hired a mathematics tutor; he was seen boning up on calculus. But he was jealous of Alexandra's independence and resented her mathematician colleagues; there was too much shoptalk, he complained. And when she disappeared into her study for hours, sometimes days at a time or called him up from her office at Northwestern and asked him to do the grocery shopping, he felt abandoned, humiliated by her apparent indifference to the great man that he was. It bothered him that Alexandra ignored the traditional housewifely chores and rarely cooked. Mel Tumin once arrived for lunch in Chicago and found her in the kitchen, scribbling equations on a yellow pad. When Bellow asked her if there was anything to eat, she opened a can of tuna and put out some crackers. "She's very busy," Bellow said dryly. "She's thinking."

There was a competitive edge to their marriage. After Bellow won the Nobel, Alexandra took to saying that there was no Nobel in mathematics because Alfred Nobel's wife had run off with a mathematician—implying that otherwise she might have been a candidate herself. But Bellow noted unchivalrously that most mathematicians did their best work in their twenties. Alexandra may have been his equal, but, as in Orwell's *Animal Farm*, some were more equal than others. By the time he wrote *To Jerusalem and Back*, he was already "getting a little frosty about Alexandra," according to Elisabeth Sifton. "Since I've never understood women anyway, I finally married one who is really a mystery," he said to Dave Peltz, not entirely approvingly.

The nature of the Bellows' marriage was reflected in the arrangement of their Chicago apartment, which was in fact two adjacent apartments with identical layouts, including kitchens and bathrooms. Bellow's study faced the lake; sliding glass doors opened onto a balcony. The walls were lined floor to ceiling with books. His massive antique desk stood in a corner. Bellow typed at a folding card table beside a music stand that held fresh pages of his manuscript. As he wrote, his favorite Mozart operas thundered at high volume over the stereo—"this rapturous singing for me that's always on the edge of sadness and melancholy and disappointment and heartbreak, but always ready for an outburst of the most delicious music."

The Bellows' nest of high culture, perched on the twelfth floor of a high-rise that formed one brick in the wall of luxury buildings stretching all the way from Hyde Park to the North Side, offered a stark contrast to the slums at their back. There were in reality two Chicagos: the Chicago he saw from his apartment on a Sunday morning, "a great expanse of fresh water working under the wind, surf breaking on the beaches, while thousands of automobiles driven by restless spirits who find no peace at home crowd the Outer Drive." And at his back, another Chicago, where old people were robbed and sometimes murdered on the snowy streets, where the old six-flats he'd grown up in were "stripped of salable metals, innards torn out, copper cable chopped to pieces and sold for scrap, windows all smashed, and finally fire and emptiness." Alexandra made a point of checking behind her car in the basement garage of 5901 Sheridan Road before she got in to make sure no one was hiding behind it; Bellow stayed away from the beach and carried a twenty-dollar bill with him in case he was mugged. For once, his paranoia was justified. Poverty was endemic in the city; the welfare population was over a million, and crime was at a new high; Cabrini-Green, a notorious public-housing project just a few miles south and west of the Bellows' apartment, was the site of some of Chicago's most spectacular murders in those years. And such killings weren't always confined to the projects; on one occasion, a woman was abducted from her building on Lake Shore Drive by a carful of young men and murdered in a nearby alley.

Determined to chart the transformation of his beloved city, Bellow embarked in the late seventies on what he called his "Chicago Book." It was intended as a work of reportage, a domestic version of *To Jerusalem and Back*. Once again, he reverted to the habits of his student days, assigning himself a rigorous regimen of books and amassing a file of data: William H. Whyte, Jr.'s *The Organization Man;* the Chicago Housing Authority annual report for 1976; a copy of *The Butcher Workman,* the journal of the meatpacking industry. One folder, bluntly labeled "blacks' criminal activity," contained newspaper clippings about bizarre murder cases, prison riots, and other typical Chicago mayhem (9 SAW OUT OF JAIL TIER; ONE ESCAPES).

William Hunt, Bellow's anthroposophical friend, served as an occasional guide. Hunt was an anomalous compatriot for Bellow. A University of Chicago graduate, he was a poet whose work had appeared in the Chicago-based *Poetry* and other journals. But he was also black and had grown up in the South Side ghetto. He worked as an administrator for social-service organizations in Woodlawn, a black slum that few whites ever penetrated.

Hunt and Bellow spent a good deal of time together while the Chicago book was in progress. They browsed in Great Expectations, an Evanston bookshop in the shadow of the elevated tracks on Sherman Street, near the Northwestern campus, and then adjourned for coffee next door at The Spot. To Hunt, Bellow confided his anguish about things he saw. "He would be moved to tears by the bleakness of the whole damn thing. He really felt that black people were being driven into some kind of mass suicide." When Hunt took him to a school for retarded children on the West Side, Bellow wept at the pathos of the scene.

Brooding in The Spot one afternoon about the violence and self-destructiveness that plagued the ghetto, Bellow remarked to Hunt that "black people aren't like us." Hunt sensed that it had never occurred to Bellow that his light-skinned confidant was black; more probably, Bellow gave Hunt a pass because he identified him as a member of the intelligentsia. That blacks and Latinos had destroyed their habitats, the very neighborhoods he'd loved as a child, was a tragedy in which all colluded. "They took possession of the near-nothing (our old Chicago slum) and annihilated it (brought it to total ruin), in this way asserting the other utter nothingness of their surroundings, and thus reaching the boundaries of literalness," Bellow observed: "Humankind is always involved in some kind of metaphysical enterprise." In his own convoluted, evasive fashion, he was expressing—or trying to express—empathy for the black and Hispanic populations that he felt had ruined Humboldt Park. He resented them for having destroyed the physical monuments of his youth, but he pitied them the nihilism that was their only recourse. Living in squalor, as Bellow saw it, could be interpreted as a means of protest—resisting, Augie March might have said.

Fame hadn't altered Bellow's intense attachment to his past. He still preferred the company of the old Tuley gang. He left tender notes for "Zitochka" (Zita Cogan), informing her that "S. Bellow paid a visit," and he would call up Stuart Brent when he felt like talking Yiddish. (Sometimes Brent got a call at six o'clock in the morning.) He had "a fantastic memory" for his childhood, said Sara Schelley, another Tuleyite. "He could remember all kinds of little details about people"—such as the fact that Schelley's nickname had been "Blondie." Whenever he talked about "the Old Bunch," recalled their classmate Morris Rotman, "his eyes lit up." He felt most comfortable going back to the habits of his adolescence—where he lived emotionally.

Among Bellow's closest friends in the years when he lived on the North Side was Hyman Slate, by then a retired social worker. "The Chicago Book" includes a remarkable portrait of Slate, who was a reader of cerebral works such as Elie Faure's *The Spirit of the Forms,* a terrific chess player who haunted the outdoor chess tables in Lunt Avenue Park, a Hyde Park autodidact able to quote Spinoza and William James. Now Slate lived in a threadbare apartment a few blocks from Bellow, with torn yellow window shades, tatty rugs, and mismatched furniture from the Salvation Army; on the walls were cheap reproductions of Caillebotte, Pissarro, and Toulouse-Lautrec. Bellow looked forward to their "Sunday gabfests." He felt he had much to learn from such friends. One day, when Slate was being lively and talkative, Bellow slumped forward, staring intently at his host, and said, "Just keep talking. I'm taking you in." He was impressed with Slate's fidelity to his wife of forty years and the obvious pleasure they took in each other's company—"the sort of human news that doesn't get into the papers," Bellow noted in a draft of "The Chicago Book."

Bellow confided in Slate, openly discussing "matters of sex, health, and neurosis," as well as money. Slate had known him when he was "Sol," as his old friends pronounced it. "My position is peculiar," he wrote Slate from Vermont in the summer of 1978, "and there are times when I have a pressing need to tell you what it's like. We are the survivors of a band of boys who were putting something of their own together in cultureless Chicago forty years ago. Now we drink tea together of a Sunday afternoon, and I feel the touch again. It would be merely sentimental if we weren't *really* talking. As you yourself have often observed, we *talk,* the subjects are real."

Bellow had been a professor at the University of Chicago for more than fifteen years by now, far longer than he'd been at any other institution. He was a familiar figure on campus, "the white-haired, compact, handsome prince of American literature," as Richard Stern described him, "strolling through Hyde Park in one

of Armando's splendid suits, candy-striped shirt from the Burling-
ton Arcade, Hermès tie, his velvety fedora jaunty with a Patago-
nian eaglet's feather in the braid." He was hard to miss in his
elaborate getup. One faculty wife remembered him walking up
Dorchester "in a complete deerstalker's outfit, including cape and
cane; he looked as though he had walked out of a nineteenth-
century movie."

The Committee on Social Thought was Bellow's home base, but
now that he was a Nobel Prize winner, the English department had
grudgingly invited him to become a member, though he never
attended a department meeting. His fiefdom was the fifth floor of
the Social Science Building, where he occupied a large office and a
tiny room under the eaves that served as a private sanctum.

The aura of high seriousness that surrounded the committee
didn't exempt it from academic politics; it was just as factional as
any other department. Even Bellow's close ally Edward Shils came
to swell the ranks of Bellow's enemies' list. Chief among the father
figures Bellow adopted serially throughout his life, Shils had been
instrumental in bringing Bellow back to Chicago; he had provided
invaluable advice in the revision of *Mr. Sammler's Planet;* he had
offered Bellow a roof over his head when his marriage to Susan
was breaking up.

Bellow had returned the kindness in *Humboldt's Gift,* depicting
Shils, in the person of Professor Richard Durnwald, with generous
affection. "Elderly but powerful, thickset and bald, a bachelor of
cranky habits but a kind man," Durnwald/Shils was the intellectual's intellectual, a man for whom "the only brave, the only
passionate life was a life of thought." In his correspondence with
Shils, Bellow expressed himself with a courtly, stilted decorum,
unconsciously emulating Shils's elaborate Anglophile courtesy.
"We'll have a jolly good time," he wrote Shils, anticipating a
dinner together in London. "We might dine at the Etoile, the
restaurant to which you introduced me and where, as I learned
from reading his memoirs, Malcolm Muggeridge used to dine in
the Thirties." When Bellow sat down to write a letter to Shils,
Augie March gave way to Dr. Johnson: "I shan't be in Chicago for
some weeks yet."

Their feeling for each other was genuine. Shils sent Bellow his
"most affectionate regards," and Bellow replied, "I love you

dearly." But they were both notoriously competitive. "Edward couldn't stand promoting anyone whose books sold more than his did," said a member of the English department. Bellow's fame he managed to endure—perhaps in some small measure identifying himself with it; for most of their colleagues he had only contempt. David Grene he dismissed as an academic politician, always in pursuit of his own ends; Harold Rosenberg was "a free-booting old Trotskyite whose loyalty to anything—except possibly to the memory of his youth in the cafes around Columbia or Union Square or the Village—is not very great." In his book-lined apartment on South Blackstone Avenue, a green eyeshade shielding his eyes, Shils spoke sneeringly of *Partisan Review* intellectuals, fellow professors, novelists, scholars. Few met his exacting standards—not even Bellow, whose immigrant ways he belittled mercilessly (though why Shils, whose father had worked in a Philadelphia cigar factory, considered himself of a different class is something of a mystery). "Saul is the kind of Jew who wears his hat in the house," he said—as opposed to an eyeshade.

Bellow didn't require a precipitating cause to end a friendship. In the case of Shils, its erosion was slow, beginning with their skirmish in the 1970s over Bellow's efforts to promote Edith Hartnett, his "screwee." Shils was also infuriated by a story Bette Howland had published that referred in passing to the contentious relationship between a "dry-as-dust professor" and his crotchety mother who lives on the floor above him—an unmistakable reference to Shils. "He felt personally invaded, and thought it was all Bellow's fault," according to their colleague James Redfield. Bellow attributed the outbreak of mutual hostilities to Shils's condescending manner at an academic conference: " 'This is not really Professor Bellow's cup of tea; he doesn't know what he's talking about.' " By the end of the seventies, the rift between them was final.

In later years, Shils was mordant on the subject of Bellow. He derided Bellow's womanizing ways, putting him down as "a skirt-chaser from Humboldt Park." When October, Nobel month, rolled around a few years after they'd become estranged, Shils warned a colleague on the committee: "Better watch out for Saul today; he's in a bad mood. The Nobel Prize is being announced, and you can't win twice."

Writing to Bellow in the fall of 1976, Shils had brought up a subject that was to have profound reverberations: "I have on several occasions mentioned the name of Allan Bloom, who is a graduate of the Committee on Social Thought and now professor at Toronto. He is probably the best of Leo Strauss's pupils and tends, unfortunately, to be a bit of a fanatic on all the important questions discussed by Strauss. At the same time, I have become informed that he has become a little more polished in his manners and a bit easier to get on with."

Bellow was lukewarm about Bloom's candidacy at first— probably because David Grene, fearing a rival classicist in the department, opposed it.* But the committee desperately needed new blood; the ship was going down, as Shils put it. The anomalous nature of the committee—it was now regarded as something of an academic backwater—scared off potential recruits. Bloom was an ideal candidate. A brilliant professor of philosophy who had been an undergraduate at the university at the height of its Great Books phase in the late 1940s, he had gone on to a professorship at Cornell and produced a scholarly edition of Rousseau's *Émile,* with his own translation. Alienated by the campus unrest at Cornell, where gun-toting black student militants occupied an administration building in 1969, he had sought refuge at the University of Toronto. He had long dreamed of returning to Chicago.

Bloom and Bellow quickly became soul mates. Bloom was fifteen years younger than Bellow and a homosexual, but their affinities outweighed their differences. They were both products of a culture-hungry Jewish immigrant milieu, and raised in the Midwest; Bloom was the child of Jewish social workers in Indianapolis. He was also, like Bellow, a clotheshorse, going about the Gothic campus in bespoke double-breasted suits from Savile Row. An electrifying teacher, he communicated a tremendous passion for ideas, stammering and chain-smoking as he paced up and

---

*Bloom later testified that Bellow had "worked hard" to get him the job, but the two were close friends by then.

down before the class. "He spoke with extraordinary intensity," recalled one of his students. "There were moments of tension in the seminar when he would smoke the lighted end of a cigarette." In the summer of 1978, Bellow lost his closest associate on the committee, his intellectual mentor Harold Rosenberg. On a sweltering July day, he traveled from his Vermont house to a memorial service at the New York Public Library. Mary McCarthy delivered the eulogy, lamenting that now all the "tall pines" were dead—the Italian émigré intellectual Nicola Chiaromonte, Edmund Wilson, Philip Rahv. ("That was her list of ramrods," remarked Saul Steinberg, who was also in the audience.) Bellow resented the imputation that there were no giants left to stride the world of the New York intellectuals. Dwight Macdonald was there, he noted in describing the event to Robert Hivnor, "and so were some other Christmas trees and evergreen dwarfs."

Life was "teaching him a few more lessons," Bellow wrote in January 1978 to Leon Wieseltier, a Junior Fellow at Harvard who later became the literary editor of *The New Republic:*

> I thought I knew corrupt Chicago, the money world, the legal and accounting professions and all their psychological types and all the political parallels—I did, of course, but it was an intelligent person's closet knowledge and fate decided that I should get a finishing course, that I should feel all the fingers on my skin and have my internal organs well squeezed. In its way this is fair enough. I *said* I wanted to know: I claimed that I already knew; and I held positions in the Higher Life, its representative in the Midwest. All that has got to be paid for, and I'm in the process of doing that. There is no other way. It's time consuming, sordid—one is abused, dragged through the schmutz, publicized. But that's one's country, as it is, and that's one's own high-minded self, dedicated to art and wisdom. But then convenience and comfort make us dimwitted, and celebrity threatens to complete one's imbecility. I've seen more than one figure turn into a cork dummy. It might be nice to have a garden of one's own to cultivate at a time like this and let the preposterous world do its preposterous things. I love rose bushes, but I love objectivity even more, and self-objectivity more than any other

type. This makes all the noise, troubling, cheating, vengefulness and money grabbing tolerable and at times even welcome. When I come home, though, or go to the office, I find the books, journals and letters flooding in. I haven't the time to read, much less comment or answer. No sorcerer arrives to bail the apprentice out. When insomnia permits it, I dream of monasteries or hermit's caves. But I'm a Jew, and married—uxorious.

He had been on the road "to make money to pay taxes and also legal fees, as well as accountants and wives, and children's tuitions and medical expenses," he reported to Wieseltier. "The patriarchal list should go on to include menservants and maidservants and camels and cattle. I'd be lucky to get into the end of the procession, among the asses."

Money was as big a problem as ever: Earning more simply made Bellow more vulnerable to Susan's demands. To Owen Barfield on September 19, 1978, he gave a dire account of his circumstances:

I am being deprived by the courts of all my possessions. This morning I suddenly remembered a touching photograph, taken after his assassination, of Gandhi's possessions: sandals, rice bowl, eyeglasses and *dhoti*. Can anyone with more property than that resist the powers of darkness? I make light of it, but the threat is serious. Today I was asked for an inventory of my personal belongings, and I wonder whether the court would hesitate to put them on auction. I manage nevertheless to concentrate daily on the distinctions between the essential and the inessential.

It was a curious association: the much-married, often-divorced novelist identifying with the ascetic apostle of nonviolence. But Bellow saw himself, too, as a martyr.

As his financial situation worsened, he counted increasingly on advances from his publisher to bail him out—and provoked a conflict when it couldn't. He was particularly disenchanted with the way Viking had handled *Humboldt's Gift:* The book was a commercial success, but the physical product was shabby. Bellow had demanded and gotten an unprecedented 17½ percent royalty (normally, the highest a publisher offers is 15 percent); in an effort to recoup its costs, Viking had skimped on the quality of the book's production. The paper was flimsy, the binding glued rather than sewn. Bellow had approved the design, but when Thomas Powers published an article in *The New York Times Book Review* about the deterioration of books and cited *Humboldt* as a prime exhibit, Bellow grew testy, complaining that his book was bound so poorly "it wouldn't stand up on a shelf."

He soon found other reasons to be discontented with Viking, among them Elisabeth Sifton. Rumors had begun to circulate in the house that he felt she didn't "edit enough"—meaning that she didn't pay him enough attention. During the editing of *Humboldt's Gift*, she had been staying home on Mondays to take care of her two young children; Bellow invariably called her there, "punishing me for not being on the bridge of the vessel," as Sifton put it. He expected her to be his "personal courier," she said, and even wanted her to make a special trip to Chicago to pick up the galleys.

Bellow was also disenchanted with Thomas Guinzburg, the head of Viking: He was one of Them—in other words, an Ivy League WASP (who happened to be Jewish). Nor did Guinzburg's austere, laconic manner suit Bellow's need for attention. "Saul wanted to be admired," said Corlies ("Cork") Smith, another Viking editor. "Tom's strong suit was never flattery."

Meanwhile, Erwin Glikes, the editorial director of Harper and Row, had been assiduously courting Bellow, sending him notes and, on one occasion, flying to Chicago. A gracious, courtly refugee from Antwerp, Glikes was an ideal editor for Bellow. Formerly a dean at Columbia, he had been driven from academic life by the political turmoil of the sixties and felt a special affinity with Bellow's Mr. Sammler, heckled in a Columbia lecture hall. "*Sammler* confirmed my sense that Bellow knew everything," Glikes recalled. "He was *our* writer."

Glikes's attentions paid off. In the fall of 1978, Harriet Wasserman invited him to lunch and revealed that Bellow wanted Glikes to publish his new book. Glikes immediately offered a two-book contract for "A Non-Fiction Book About Chicago," as it was described in the contract, and "a Greenwich Village love story" (probably the "Zetland" manuscript). The terms were $400,000 for the first book and $600,000 for the second book, with a 15 percent royalty: a total of $1 million.

Early in December, Glikes, accompanied by Wasserman and Harvey Ginsberg, the editor who had been assigned to work directly with Bellow, flew to Chicago to deliver the contract in person. There was only one hitch, and it nearly proved fatal. Wasserman asked Glikes if it was true that he was about to hire Ted Solotaroff as an editor. "You know, Saul and Ted aren't friendly." Nervous about jeopardizing the deal, Glikes denied that he was hiring Solotaroff, and the contract was duly signed. Glikes got the keys to a brand-new Volvo station wagon as a reward.

Solotaroff, an acolyte of Bellow at the University of Chicago who had made a name for himself as the editor of *New American Review*, was guilty of a major offense: He had written a mildly equivocal review of *Herzog*. Though he found it "a rich book, brimming with wit and thoughtfulness and feeling," he gently chided Bellow for evading some of the issues his outspoken protagonist had raised. "It was ninety percent a love letter, with maybe two objections," recalled Solotaroff. That was two too many, as far as Bellow was concerned.

A few days later, Wasserman called Harper and Row's chairman, Winthrop Knowlton, and announced "with the utmost gravity" that she needed to see him right away. When she arrived at Knowlton's office, she declared that the deal was off because Glikes had lied: He had hired Solotaroff. The contract was amended, becoming a one-book deal, and Glikes was off the case. ("There was much speculation around the house about whether he'd had to give the Volvo back," according to another Harper editor, Ed Burlingame.)

Soon thereafter, Ginsberg left for another house, and Burlingame was appointed Bellow's official "handler." When Solotaroff ran into the company's prize acquisition in the halls a few months later, the atmosphere was "radioactive," recalled Burlingame. Glikes himself was forbidden even to read Bellow's work in progress. "It was one of the most painful things that ever happened to me," Glikes said ruefully. "I wanted to grow old publishing him."*

*Bellow did forgive, but it took time. Years later, Solotaroff invited him to write the introduction to a biography of Bellow's old friend Josephine Herbst and received a cordial note in reply. Glikes, meanwhile, became editor in chief of the

BELLOW LEAVES VIKING, SWITCHES TO HARPER & ROW ran a headline in *The New York Times* on December 12, 1978. "In a surprising move," the story began, "the novelist Saul Bellow has switched to Harper & Row after nine books and 30 years with Viking Press. The Chicago-based Nobel laureate in literature plans to bring out his first book with his new publisher in 1980." Viking had been informed of the change by a letter from Wasserman just before Thanksgiving. Bellow himself wrote a gracious note to Elisabeth Sifton, saying he was sorry to leave Viking: "It's the closest thing to a monogamous relationship that I've had."

Bellow had no comment about his change of publishers, reported the *Times:* He was on his way to Romania. Alexandra's mother was ill. Getting there wasn't easy. Romania was ruled by the iron hand of Nicolae Ceaușescu, and Alexandra's mother, Florica Bagdazar, formerly the minister of health, had fallen afoul of the regime during one of the Communist Party shake-ups of the fifties. To obtain a visa, Bellow had to enlist the help of Senator Daniel Moynihan.

By the time the Bellows got to Bucharest in mid-December, it was nearly too late; Alexandra's mother was in the hospital, hooked up to a respirator. She died a few days after their arrival and was cremated in a freezing-cold mortuary. "You could feel the fires below," Bellow wrote in *The Dean's December*, the novel that emerged from this harrowing experience. "Currents of heat flowed under the floor, but it wasn't the kind of heat you could be warmed by. It came from the openings at the edges of the raised bier, through the metal joints, from under the long bivalve barrel which would close when the coffin sank." It was a painful loss; Alexandra's mother had attended his Nobel ceremony in Stockholm and once spent a convivial week with the Bellows in London. Mrs. Bagdazar wasn't Jewish, but she belonged to that Old World generation of Europeans that reminded Bellow of his parents. She

Free Press, where he hired Adam Bellow—his eventual successor—as an editor. When Glikes encountered his nemesis in the corridors one day, Bellow "couldn't have been more friendly."

was family—and she was a mother, which gave her death a special resonance.

By the end of January, the Bellows were home. It had been an arduous trip, but it had provided Bellow with new material. In the course of its transformation from nonfiction to fiction, "The Chicago Book" became also a "Romanian book," recounting the traumatic sojourn in Bucharest and the death of Alexandra's mother virtually the way they happened. Like Valeria, the valiant old woman in the novel, Alexandra's mother had exemplified a fierce independence of mind that set her at odds with the drab functionaries who gained control of the party after 1956; like Valeria, she had succeeded her late husband as the minister of health and been deposed by the state. For Bellow, an innocent American protected by the indulgence of American democracy, the brutal politics of Eastern Europe provided still another opportunity for reality instruction.

But in fiction as in life, it was events back home that captured his attention. Near the end of his labors, Bellow revisited Division Street for a television documentary about his old neighborhood, in the company of Zita Cogan, Dave Peltz, and Morris Rotman. Shadowed by the TV crew, they tried to locate their old haunts—Ceshinsky's bookstore, Schechter's butcher shop, the Tolstoi Vegetarian Restaurant—but found only burned-out buildings and empty lots. The benches where garment workers had once sat reading Haldeman-Julius Blue Books were now occupied by drug pushers.

The program, "Saul Bellow's Chicago," aired the following spring. Bellow came across as naïve and out of his depth—"pitching 'softball' questions," as an unkindly review in the *Chicago Tribune* put it, to former alderman Thomas Keane and former Cook County jail warden Winston Moore. "What *do* the gang members do?" he asked Moore in a perplexed tone.

Bellow himself wasn't entirely happy with his performance. "No one felt easy," he recalled. Gangs of noisy kids from the neighborhood had crowded around them. "There was nothing to see—two elderly men reminiscing about basketball games in a gymnasium that wasn't even there." The footage with Peltz was cut entirely. "You looked too good," Bellow explained.

Still, there were some affecting moments—memories of his early school days at Sabin, where the teachers stuffed his head with English poetry; of movie nights at the Strand; and of long afternoons in the public library on North Avenue. "I was filled with enthusiasm, high spirits, immense energy, and a sense for the magic of existence."

27

*Someday, when you're inclined to listen, I'll take pleasure in drawing
a freeflowing sketch of what gives with me this decade.*

—Bellow to Hyman Slate, August 19, 1979

IN THE EARLY FALL OF 1979, *The New York Times Book
Review* published a letter that alarmed Mark Harris, who had
been at work on Bellow's biography for more than a decade.
Ruth Miller, his subject's dear friend, was requesting "letters,
documents, anecdotes, personal memoirs and photographs from
his friends and associates" for an "authorized biography" of Saul
Bellow. Miller was quick to assure Harris, when he wrote her an
agitated letter, that she had no such project in mind; she was working on "a canon study of the novels."

Relieved to have the field to himself, Harris prepared to launch
his work in progress with an excerpt in the *Georgia Review*; it was
a chapter about Bellow's ill-fated visit to Purdue in the spring of
1968, illustrated with caricatures by David Levine, the house artist
for *The New York Review of Books*.

In a headnote, Harris explained that "the comedy spread below
is part of a larger work." Bellow was not amused. He had grudgingly given the indefatigable biographer permission to quote from
his letters. ("I don't much mind if you quote me, though my editing finger itches. But I realize it's not right to edit one's own letters.
They are what they are.") But when Harris, always torn between
ingratiating himself with his subject and pushing him, rang up
Bellow to find out his reaction, he got a cold reception. "I thought

I looked like a turd in it," Bellow said of the excerpt. "Bad-tempered. Nasty. Snappish. I don't see myself that way."

"That's because it's not oneself," Harris replied, seeking refuge in the impersonal pronoun. "It's my version of oneself."

"Biography," said Bellow, "is a specter viewed by a specter."

When Harris's book came out in the spring of 1980, Bellow was curtly dismissive. "The Harris book?" he wrote to his Minnesota lawyer John Goetz. "It's as if my arthritis were to turn author and write its own chronicle of one of my joints." Anyway, it wasn't a book about him, he said; it was a book about Mark Harris—which, in a sense, it was. Harris hadn't even tried to write a real biography—he had set out to explore his conflicts as a biographer. All the same, Bellow was stung by the candor of Harris's portrait; it took him years to forgive Richard Stern for his quip that Bellow had two hobbies: "philosophy and fucking." What would Alexandra say?*

Harris flouted the rules of definitive biography, defiantly parading his indifference to names and dates: "For specific facts you must go to a certified public accountant." He was a "Bellow-watcher," a diarist; like Boswell, he wasn't shy about setting up situations in which he could observe his subject. (Harris in fact later edited a condensation of Boswell's papers from the definitive Yale edition.) Boswellian also in his mixture of self-abasement and self-promotion, Harris benefited from the tacit collusion of his "biographee." Professing to be "both flattered and reluctant," Bellow maintained a Johnsonian distance, allowing his biographer to "eavesdrop" even as he fended him off. The result was a literary collaboration—or perhaps collusion—almost self-consciously modeled on that of the most famous biographer and subject in history, only with less sycophancy and more bite. Critics savaged

---

*Harris, meanwhile, continued to make a career out of Bellow. He got written up in *People* on the basis of his decade-long biographical obsession, and he published an article in *The New York Times Book Review* about the indignity of being called up by an editor who wanted Bellow's phone number. He also continued to amorously pursue his subject's third wife, sending her the latest update of his voluminous curriculum vitae ("On the theory that the way to a girl's heart is through her literary sensibilities, I enclose herewith a list of my complete works").

the book when it came out, put off by Harris's willingness to humiliate himself in the name of literary biography, but it afforded a vivid glimpse of his subject.

In the pages of *Saul Bellow, Drumlin Woodchuck,* Bellow emerges as a sardonic, wary figure, at once tolerant and bristling, guarded and open to life. His joke telling, dry wit, and occasional malice are vintage examples of the effervescent humor known in Yiddish as *spritz.* Bellow could never resist a pun, even a bad one: A travel agency is a "travail agency," a synagogue is a "synagogo." When someone ordered a kirsch at dinner, he spoke of "the kirsch of an aching heart." There was a rueful note to his sense of humor—the mixture of "laughter and trembling," a feel for "the comic sense of life," that Bellow identified in his introduction to *Great Jewish Short Stories* as uniquely Jewish. When Harris noted that his landlord had been reading *Henderson the Rain King* but "feeling like Portnoy" (of *Portnoy's Complaint*), Bellow quipped, "He doesn't know whether to travel or masturbate."

As if submitting to biographical scrutiny wasn't a sufficient ordeal, Bellow had to contend with a fictional rendering at the hands of a master: Philip Roth's novella *The Ghost Writer* contained a sympathetic but telling sketch of the great novelist Felix Abravanel. Casting himself in one of his favorite roles, the young literary disciple, Roth reconstructed his momentous encounter with Bellow at the University of Chicago some twenty years before. Roth captured perfectly Bellow's dandy side, his "five-hundred-dollar shantung suit, burgundy silk tie, and gleaming narrow black tasseled loafers." And he captured the elder novelist's playful, ironic side. When an earnest graduate student starts muttering about alienation, Abravanel retorts: "Alienation? Oh, let the other guy be alienated." (It was one of Bellow's favorite remarks.) Roth also got at something deeper: Bellow's guardedness, his unwillingness to be pinned down. "The charm was like a moat so oceanic that you could not even see the great turreted and buttressed thing it had been dug to protect." Joking was a form of guardedness, another way of deflecting intimacy.

Bellow wasn't any happier with Roth's version of him than he was with Harris's. Writing to Daphne Merkin, a young critic who had sent him her negative review of the book in *The New Leader,* he gave heated expression to his displeasure (employing a curiously ambiguous trope that required him to jump through rhetorical hoops to explain himself):

> I agree with your judgement. Mine would have been profaner. I thought it disgusting—a disgusting article, I mean an article of trade. Milton Friedman and Adam Smith would have given it a pass as such but I am not in the *laissez-faire* business. I shouldn't have been surprised that it was so handsomely received and that it sold so well. I wasn't so much astonished by the critical reception as by the book's best sellerdom (perhaps I should have said best sellerhood). The public buys the best plugged books, and that seems to be that. Will it ever rebel, or has it been debauched for good?

He also heard from another fan—Dean Borok, the illegitimate son of his brother Maurice, whose existence Bellow had revealed (at great cost to their relationship) in *The Adventures of Augie March*. Borok craved public recognition of his blood tie to the greatest living novelist in the English language. Bellow wasn't prepared to go that far, but he showed Borok's letter to his brother Sam and wrote his nephew a sympathetic reply:

> Neither of us could form a picture of the life you've led. But that's hardly strange when you think that we have no clear picture of our eldest brother's life, either. He sees none of us, brothers, sister, or his two children by his first marriage, nor their children—neither does he telephone or write. He had no need of us—he has no past, no history. His adopted children do not seem to care for him. His present wife? An enigma. He probably has some money—he's thought about little else all his life. But he's old now—73—and ill—he's had a coronary bypass. I tell you all this to warn you about the genes you seem so proud of. If you've inherited them (it's possible you have) many of them will have to be subdued or lived down. I myself have had some bad going with them.

It was probably a good thing that Bellow couldn't form a picture of Borok's life. A draft dodger who had fled to Canada in the sixties, Borok had become a minor legend in the lower depths of Montreal. He put on all-leather fashion shows at Yuk Yuk's Comedy Club and owned a leather shop that specialized in S&M accessories, Dean's Boutique de Cuir; he was featured in *High Society,* a glossy pornographic magazine, as "Doctor Dean, Madman of Montreal." ("Draft dodger, leatherwear designer, X-rated comedian and 'Gynecologist to the Stars,' Dean Borak [*sic*] is driving Canada crazy. Our northern neighbors rue the day they let this maniac cross the border!")

Borok *had* inherited the Bellow genes. He had the physiognomy—handsome, with wide dark-brown eyes in a broad face. He also had what he called "a literary streak"—he read widely and wrote Algrenesque stories about boxers and nightclub comics, sometimes under the name Dean Belmont, that were erratic but showed definite signs of literary talent. He had never gotten over being abandoned by his father. "The last time I saw my old man, he gave me fifty bucks and told me to get lost," he complained to Bellow. Since then, Borok had led what he described as "a lonely, arduous life," hoping somehow that his familial association with a Nobel Prize winner would redeem him in the world's eyes. For years, he bombarded Bellow with letters of "unbelievable venom and bitterness," he acknowledged. On occasion, he enclosed graphic snapshots of himself performing sex acts with women.

Bellow did not reciprocate the correspondence, but the one letter he wrote to Borok was revealing, for it encapsulated his own credo. "If you can find the right way to do it, perhaps you should write the story of your life," he counseled his wayward nephew: "To get rid of it, as it were. In writing it successfully, you will forgive everyone in the process. Yes, all those who seemed against you will be forgiven. (That's what I would call a successful effort to get one's life down on paper.)" For Bellow, the world was a hostile environment; only writing could salve his wounds. Toward Borok, so obviously a genuine victim, he displayed a magnanimous grace, inviting him to see himself as a writer and to see the act of writing, an exalted but selfish preoccupation, as a means of personal redemption.

Yet for all his singleness of purpose, wisdom had so far eluded Bellow. "Life grows more complex with the years," he lamented to Borok, opening his heart to a relative he'd never met. "I had expected it to be simpler."

In the summer of 1979, Bellow rented a house in West Halifax, Vermont, just north of the Massachusetts border, a corner of the state that he had become increasingly attached to over the previous two summers. He called it his hideaway.

He was badly in need of a respite, he reported to Hyman Slate in July: "When we got here, I discovered that I wasn't so well. It is a beautiful place but I was too tired and dejected to like it. I had no idea that I was in such bad shape. You don't know until you begin to relax the tensions and feel the accumulated fatigue. For two weeks I was extremely depressed—depleted. I couldn't even try to pull myself together. If I took a sleeping pill I paid later with insomnia for the night's sleep I got, so I stopped taking the pills."

Part of the trouble was the whirlwind schedule he kept up. When he wasn't in the countryside, he was on the road: That year, he spoke before an audience of a thousand at the Bernard Horwich/Mayer Kaplan Jewish Community Center in Skokie; gave a reading at the Goodman Theatre downtown (billed as "a rare public appearance"); scribbled autographs at Marshall Field in the Old Orchard shopping mall ("Just say it's for Naomi"); and showed up on the cover of the *Chicago Tribune Magazine* ("A Rare Visit with Chicago's Saul Bellow"). "He would talk to women's groups in Highland Park, the cousin of uncle Louis' sister-in-law," noted Joseph Epstein, who had secured a number of rare visits with the great man.

He also found time for a cameo appearance in Woody Allen's film *Zelig*. Allen, ever alert to intellectual fashion, had persuaded Susan Sontag, Irving Howe, Bruno Bettelheim, and Bellow to offer pseudoerudite commentary on his pliable lead character. Bellow, in slacks and a blue plaid shirt, was comfortable before the camera, discoursing easily on the fictional Zelig phenomenon: "His sickness was also at the root of his salvation; it was his very disorder that made a hero of him."

He had feared that the Nobel would be his passport to obscurity, but the shower of awards and honors showed no sign of abating. He was presented with the International Visitors Center's Gold Medallion, the Scopus Award from the Chicago American Friends of the Hebrew University, and the Malaparte Prize from

Italy. He accepted this deluge of acclaim with dignity. For the benefit of still another journalist, he recalled a Saki story about a very good little girl who earned lots of medals and wore them all: "One day, she and her playmates were frightened by a wolf in the forest. The other children hid and were quiet, but the little girl trembled so much, all her medals clattered and the wolf found her and ate her. Sometimes I wonder if I am exposed to that sort of danger."

Chief among Bellow's numerous official responsibilities in the late seventies and early eighties was serving on the board of the MacArthur "genius" program established by the Chicago-based John D. and Catherine T. MacArthur Foundation to dispense grants to worthy recipients in the arts. The awards were the brain-child of John MacArthur's son, Rod, who had made a fortune of his own by founding a brokerage house for collectors' commemorative plates. MacArthur, who aspired to become a Chicago Medici, was convinced that only large amounts of money could make a difference. His notion was to give out grants of $250,000 to $300,000, depending on the recipient's age, dispensed over a period of five years—enough to provide freedom but not life-transforming wealth, as MacArthur liked to put it. The generosity of the award did make a real difference, and the MacArthur instantly became the most coveted private grant in America.

Potential MacArthur candidates were selected by "nominators," an anonymous panel of distinguished men and women (among them Ralph Ellison, Helen Vendler, and Galway Kinnell), who were paid a thousand dollars a year and were pledged to secrecy. The board consisted of five permanent members and four rotating members of the Prize Fellows Committee; from 1977 to 1982, Bellow was one of the four.* He traveled several times a year to Santa Fe and other pleasant locales for board meetings, and he was notably conscientious, once passing up lunch to read a candidate's book that other members had praised.

*Others on the board during Bellow's tenure included Kenneth Keniston, Jonas Salk, Jerome Weisner, Edward Levi, and Murray Gell-Mann. Bellow provided a withering portrait of Gell-Mann in "Him with His Foot in His Mouth," as Professor Schulteiss, "one of those bragging polymath types who gave everybody a pain in the ass" with his discourses on Chinese cookery or the linguistic affinities between Bantu and Swahili.

During his time on the board, Bellow vehemently opposed candidates he perceived as radical or "trendy." When a member of the committee nominated the militant black poet Amiri Baraka, Bellow—no doubt remembering Baraka/Jones's efforts to install a black-studies curriculum at the University of Chicago—was apoplectic; he tore into Susan Sontag and Edward Said, a critic with a Marxian bent ("We're talking murdered," said a member of the board). He also lobbied strenuously—and successfully—on behalf of his own candidates, notably Cormac McCarthy, William Kennedy, and Bette Howland. "He was more focused on who should get it than on who shouldn't," said Leon Botstein, the president of Bard College and a colleague on the committee. "Saul had an agenda, but the agenda was positive."

Each of his novels, Bellow said, represented "a bulletin on his own condition." By the middle of 1981, he was deeply immersed in his "Chicago Book," now conjoined with a fictional account of his recent trip to Romania. He had started the new version at the beginning of 1980, and by the following summer he was well along. He arrived at Robert Penn Warren's house in Vermont one night with the loose manuscript beside him on the front seat of his car, the pages blown about. "I don't know if it's any good," he confided to the poet Jay Parini, another guest. "It's about Alexandra and me visiting her mother in Bucharest."

Once he'd found the form for a book, Bellow wrote night and day, as if on a deadline. "I wish it was as easy for me as it is for Studs Terkel," he complained to Ralph Ross; Terkel's oral histories were bestsellers. "He has his tape-recorder, but all I have is a fountain pen." On a visit to London in the spring of 1981, Bellow was in a notably foul mood. "Saul's visit has been a nightmare," Barley Alison reported to Ed Burlingame. "He is in a frightful state of exhaustion and feeling persecuted on every side. . . . The burden of his song is that neither I nor Harpers understand that he is 66, a creative writer, a genius etc. and why should *he* care about our cash-flow our schedules etc." Finishing the book wore him out. "This is no youthful fatigue," he wrote Hyman Slate: "I used to bounce back. Now I drag myself outside mornings to sit under the trees. Late summer, fortunately, is very beautiful. There's only the telephone to fear—news of a new lawsuit by Susan. The wicked never let up. The lawyers learn no kindness. My own are as bad as hers, and the moronic inferno is as hot as ever."

Back in Chicago that fall, he attended the fiftieth reunion of the Tuley High School classes of 1931 and 1932.* The event was held on a Saturday night in October at the Fireside Inn in Morton Grove, a venue that reflected the migration of so many Jews of that generation from what had become the inner city to the suburbs. The event was the occasion for "a gigantic dose of nostalgia," as the program for the evening put it. "Fifty years! Where have they all gone?"—the lament of every half-century reunion. As for Bellow's classmates, most of them were either dead or "hidden away in nursing homes, doddering in Florida, dying of Alzheimer's disease in Venice, California," he noted sadly. He was glad to see the ones who remained and "wore his lapel badge just like everyone else," Julius Echeles recalled. Their classmate Belle Myers confessed to Bellow that she'd never been kissed by a Nobel Prize winner before.

Albert Corde, the hero of *The Dean's December,* is a tall, "lanky" academic of Irish-Huguenot descent, one of the hearty, larger-than-life—also physically larger—WASPs who seem to alternate in Bellow's fiction (as Philip Roth noted shrewdly) with guilty, repressed Jews: Augie and Tommy Wilhelm, Henderson and Herzog, Sammler and Citrine. "When I wrote *Augie,* they said I was Augie; when I wrote *Henderson,* they said I was Henderson; when I wrote *Herzog,* they said I was Herzog: How many people can I be?" Bellow asked.

Corde hews even more closely to the facts of his creator's life than Bellow's other autobiographical protagonists: A dean at the University of Chicago, he arrives in Bucharest, Romania, one dreary Christmas with his wife, Minna, to visit her dying mother. Obstructed by a vindictive bureaucrat who refuses them visiting privileges, Minna pleads with various Stalinist officials who are

---

*He had actually graduated in January 1933. Bellow was listed in the program as a "Nobel Laureate in Literature" and identified, for some mysterious reason, as "married to Mildred."

unwilling to forget that her mother is out of favor with the regime. Corde, with his "dreamy tendencies," is no match for these hard-hearted apparatchiks. The Romanian bureaucracy turns out to be another reality instructor, this time in the form of a communist state—big brother as Big Brother.

Brooding in a dreary guest room at his mother-in-law's apartment, Corde leafs through a two-part article that he published in *Harper's* just before his departure, a fierce polemic about Chicago that stirred up a considerable tempest. Corde's exposé of his hometown is written with an almost biblical fervor. Corde is more than just another reformed liberal demanding law and order: He compares the Chicago slums to Passchendaele and the Somme and warns that urban blacks are "a people consigned to destruction, a doomed people." Just as the architects of communism sacrificed whole populations to their ideology, so corporate America had written off a whole class.

The Dean's December revolves largely around accounts of two actual murders that occurred in the city in the late seventies. One involved a young black man, Hernando Williams, who abducted a North Side housewife and locked her in the trunk of his car for thirty-six hours, freeing her just long enough to rape her twice before finally murdering her; in the midst of this ordeal, Williams attended a court hearing on an earlier rape charge. Bellow made this case the centerpiece of Corde's interview with a public defender, whose brisk laying out of the facts is offered up as a contrast to the dean's high-flown speculations on "evil, betrayal, corruption, savagery, sadism"—on the death of civility and the impending death of civilization.

The other news event Bellow drew upon was the murder of a University of Chicago student named Mark Gromer, who was pushed to his death from his third-story apartment on a steamy summer night in 1977, a murder that shocked even crime-hardened Hyde Park residents. After a reward was posted, a prostitute and her pimp were arrested. It was a grisly and protracted case, in the midst of which potential witnesses were shot at by a student radical sympathetic to the defendants. In the novel, Corde becomes entangled in the case—the radical is his nephew, the murderers' lawyer his cousin.

Bellow used these cases to sound a warning—about what, it wasn't entirely clear, but the general sense was that barbarism had invaded the United States and no one was paying attention:

> Again, the *high* intention—to prevent the American idea from being pounded into the dust altogether. And here is our American idea: liberty, equality, justice, democracy, abundance. And here is what things are like today in a city like Chicago. Have a look! How does the public apprehend events? It doesn't apprehend them. It has been deprived of the capacity to experience them. Corde recognized how arrogant he had been. *His* patience was at an end. *He* had had enough. *He* was now opening his mouth to speak. And now, look out.

An honorable mission. But the true subject of "The Chicago Book"—the precipitous downward spiral of an American city—is obscured by Corde's shrill complaints that he is misunderstood. For Bellow, the really compelling drama in *The Dean's December* is the controversy surrounding Corde's articles—a preemptive strike against Bellow's own critics. Time and again, Corde excoriates himself for his own naïveté—a way of condemning in advance those unfeeling enough to challenge his apocalyptic vision of urban America.

Bellow's hostility toward his hero's adversaries, most of whom would have been readily identifiable by their models, seemed pitiless. Of Maxie Detillion, who Bellow himself acknowledged was a portrait of Sam Freifeld, he wrote: "His once handsome nose was beginning to look damaged, cartilages blasted, and as he aged and grew heavier his cheeks thickened, his color darkened; he looked leaden, he lost height, his pelvis widened, his courtroom pacing was slightly lame." Proud of his appearance as one of the Einhorns in *The Adventures of Augie March*, as steatopygous Alec Szathmar in *Humboldt's Gift*, Freifeld was stung to the quick by Bellow's latest depiction of him. "To be loused up by Humboldt was really a kind of privilege," says Charlie Citrine of that "champion detractor" Von Humboldt Fleisher; to be loused up by Bellow, at this late date, was pure bad luck.

Bellow's Tuley sidekick Sydney J. Harris also fell to the novelist's sharp ax—his only discernible crime the banality of his column in the *Chicago Daily News*. (Or could it have been his plagiarism of Bellow's review of *Gone with the Wind* in *The Beacon* in 1937? Bellow could hold a grudge for a long time.)* Harris was so fearful of finding himself in the pages of a Bellow novel that he'd delegated to his wife, Patricia, the job of vetting each new book as it appeared. This time, she ruefully admitted, his number had come up. Dewey Spangler, the columnist who has a warm reunion with Corde in Bucharest and joins his old Chicago pal for long sessions of reminiscence, was a dead ringer for Harris. Spangler is a world-renowned pundit, a Walter Lippmann or James Reston figure; but only in the size of his reputation does he diverge from the bookish boy who had sat at the kitchen table with Bellow composing florid poetry. The portrait of Spangler as a "kinky adolescent who had told preposterous lies, had screaming quarrels with his mother, and wrote violently revolutionary poems" was hard enough to countenance, but Bellow went further and made Spangler an arrogant, fawning blowhard. In a final insulting detail, the journalist wears a colostomy bag, a bodily metaphor for the stuff he writes in his syndicated column.[†]

If he was brutal with his old Chicago cronies, Bellow was notably tender in his portrait of Corde's wife, a likeness of Alexandra. Unlike the gallery of nagging wives and ex-wives who dominate his earlier books, Minna is sensitive, refined, intelligent, a beautiful woman with an international reputation in her field—a "hard" scientist. Her only shortcoming is a certain reserve, a distractedness and inaccessibility that cuts her off from her uxorious husband. "What he minded was her fanatical absorption." Not surprisingly, the most sympathetic character is Corde himself. A visionary, messianic figure, he is the soul of rectitude, a reformed

---

*When his old enemy William Phillips was put up for membership in the august Century Association, Bellow resigned. "My letter was posted on the bulletin board as evidence of my unbelievable effrontery," he reported to Fred Dupee.

†Corde himself (and thus, perhaps, Bellow) was aware that he'd gone over the line. "I'm going to miss something about the man while I gratify my taste for wicked comment," he worries after a particularly malicious assault on Spangler. It was something to worry about. "And God help Spangler whoever he is," wrote Bellow's English publisher, Tom Rosenthal.

womanizer who has been tempered by life, a "moralist of seeing" whose vocation is "to interpret, to pity, to save!"

Curiously, the two victims in the book—Rickie Lester, the student pushed to a terrifying death, and Mrs. Sathers, the young suburban housewife who is abducted and murdered—are submitted to ethical cross-examinations that manage to turn them both into subtle accomplices. Ricky Lester encounters his two eventual murderers in a bar where he's gone in search of kinky sex, leaving his wife alone in their apartment; he invites the whore he brings home to join him in the toilet, "to go down on him while she was shitting." Mrs. Sathers, it emerges, is also a collaborator in her own violent demise. Why didn't she avail herself of the few opportunities she had to escape? According to Corde, she unconsciously gave in to her aggressor. "There must be a sense of complicity in rapes," he theorizes, in conversation with the public defender. "The sex nerves can stream all by themselves. If people think they're going to be murdered anyway when it's over, they may desperately let go." In these two strikingly similar scenarios, the victim becomes a virtual collaborator in the act of victimization.

There was something grotesque in the way Bellow appropriated Mark Gromer's story for his own literary purposes. One reads his interpretation of events against an unpublished memoir by Gromer's wife, Crystal, with a sinking heart: In her account, the full terror of the event—a knife at her throat; the sound of her husband being hurled out the window; her frantic race to the sidewalk below—achieves a primal terror absent from Bellow's fictional narrative: "In my dreams as in my life: I cannot hear the sound of my own screams, but I know when I ceased them. I gave up, in a minute, my life. It was gone from me. I heard the guttural, animal sounds that came from Mark, sounds that began as human but that were filtered by the gag stuffed in his mouth until they were brute utterances. Not him; not human; not him."*

Two new and disturbing elements emerge in this novel: explicit sex and violence. Until now, they had surfaced as rare nightmarish

---

*When Bellow "puts his imagination to work" on the circumstances of Rickie Lester's death, the results are unsatisfying; in the end, all he can come up with is what he calls "the fact of facts": "the kid on the slab, the long soiled feet, the face with the only-just-subtracted expression and the hint of mature knowledge."

moments in Bellow's work: Moses Herzog has a fleeting fantasy of assaulting Madeleine when she asks for a divorce, and in *Humboldt's Gift* the car-bashing Rinaldo Cantabile fantasizes about a threesome involving Citrine and Rinaldo's wife. ("There's a thing the three of us can do together. You lie on your back. She gets on top of you and at the same time goes down on me.") But it wasn't until *The Dean's December* that sex and violence declared their urgency. No longer is the Bellow protagonist a victim; he has become instead a kind of aggressor, taking his anger out on his model's other characters. The lesson to be learned from the fate of Mrs. Sathers and Rickie Lester is: *They were asking for it.* It was as if winning the Nobel had disinhibited Bellow, allowing him to graphically express the rage that in his previous novels had been hidden behind the persona of the unworldly intellectual.

Bellow wasn't entirely unaware of this hitherto submerged theme, which ventured far beyond mere misogyny. Through the voice of Corde, he offered up hints about his own dark impulses. Despite his professorial mien, Corde intimates that he, too, has an unruly sexual appetite—and worse. Is he, the dean wonders, "a gentle soul, or a masked killer?" He compares himself to Hermann in Pushkin's tale "The Queen of Spades," who stalks an old woman in her bedroom, and, acknowledging his latent criminality, to "a longtime sexual offender still on probation." This expression of a Dostoyevskian affinity with the aggressor offered a disquieting glimpse of Bellow's divided nature.

He had been writing a story at the same time as "The Chicago Book," he confided to Ruth Miller, "about a man called Rude, who is in Reichian analysis, and discovers his animal nature, that sexuality and violence go together." In that story, which Bellow broke off to write *The Dean's December*, Rude brings an "ugly tart" to his house for the purpose of acting out his brutal sexual fantasies; in a fit of rage, he goes on a murderous rampage, killing his psychiatrist, the whore, and, finally, himself. "Dear God!" was Miller's comment.

Bellow was apprehensive about the book's reception. "It wasn't the book that was expected of me," he wrote Tom Rosenthal in

December 1981. Writing it had worn him out. He was ready for a change. The English department of the University of Victoria had invited him to spend a semester as a guest lecturer, and he accepted with relief. "Alexandra and I are clearing out for the winter to British Columbia which I look forward to as to a sanitarium," he wrote to Philip Roth on the last day of 1981: "I've warned them in the English Department there that if they run me too hard I may have a breakdown. I'm not pretending, I'm ready for a padded cell. The Dean took it out of me, I wrote it in a kind of fit and I'm left with a peculiar residue that I don't know how to get rid of. I can't even describe it."

The university had arranged for the Bellows to sublet a house on a lake near the outskirts of Victoria. Bellow's official duties were light. He was to give two public lectures and make himself available to students and faculty. No one awaited his arrival more keenly than a part-time member of the faculty who had an office in the building to which Bellow had been assigned. "And now as of January 1982, the great writer would occupy an office one *floor* above the one in which I'd thought, dreamed, agonized, writhed." It was Bellow's loyal correspondent Barnett Singer. Tipped off by his girlfriend, who worked in the library, Singer hunted Bellow in the stacks. Bellow claimed that all he wanted to do in Victoria was keep his critics at bay and "take silent nature walks," but it wasn't easy to avoid his importunate fan, who promptly offered his services as a guide.

Singer's record of Bellow's table talk, published in an obscure Canadian journal, is pitch perfect. As the two of them are crossing a busy road, Singer warns Bellow to look out; he could get killed. "I better *not* get killed," Bellow retorts. "I only came for a rest." Over egg creams at Pagliacci's, an Italian restaurant owned by a friend of Singer, they discuss old movies. "Did you ever get scared at those '20s films?" asks Singer, noting that his own father "saw Lon Chaney in 'Phantom of the Opera' and couldn't sleep for a week." "With a father like mine," says Bellow, "the movies weren't so frightening."

On their last night in Victoria, the Bellows joined Singer for dinner at his girlfriend's apartment. They listened to old jazz recordings by Artie Shaw (another one of Singer's correspondents) and Billie Holiday; Bellow sang "Ol' Man River"—"quite fault-lessly," in Singer's verdict, "though without the verve of a Paul Robeson." But he was preoccupied with their impending depar-ture. "I'm going to have my troubles back in Chicago," he said. He had written a controversial book about the city; the Chicago Establishment was unhappy. He'd have to face the music.

The Dean's December was an act of deliberate provocation. "This is a book of hard knocks. And the language knocks you hard," Bellow said in an interview with Eugene Kennedy, a Chicago writer who was to become a close friend. "It demands your attention, the way a man does when he grabs you by the lapels." The adulatory Kennedy saw Bellow as "a Roman senator musing seriously about the empire's corruption" and compared the novelist's delicate features with "bone china on a sterling silver tray." A journalist named Helen Dudar came away with a distinctly less favorable impression. Her piece in *The Saturday Review of Literature*, "The Graying of Saul Bellow," opened: "At 66, he is our most esteemed novelist. But his new book, 'The Dean's December,' is drab and tired. What happened to the famous Bellow energy?" She described it as "a strange, bleached, autumnal work," "patchy" and "infuriatingly uneven." But she was even harder on its author. Like many others who knew him a good deal better, Dudar noted Bellow's sudden physical transfor-mations, the way he could look "jauntily ageless and vigorous" one minute and "wasted" the next. "He seemed drained, his eyes looking bruised and needy, his small, delicate hands more often quiet than active." For Dudar, *The Dean's December* was the beginning of the end. "It's as if Bellow had agreed to say hello to old age and was now nervously tuned in for the first sound of time's wingèd chariot at the door." She claimed to hear a chorus—herself loudly joining in—gloating, "*Aha, another Nobelist bites the dust.*" It was an unkind piece, and it hurt.

The reviews were almost uniformly negative. A few critics praised the novel, notably Salman Rushdie, who found it "astoundingly well-written." But for the most part, the book came off badly. D. M. Thomas, writing in *The Washington Post*, complained that it was "difficult to make virtue interesting." *The New York Times*'s Christopher Lehmann-Haupt, never a fan, praised the novel's closing scene, in which Corde and Minna visit Mount Palomar, but with a devastating qualification: "I can't honestly swear that I didn't love it because coming to it at last was like not hitting one's head against the wall anymore." And Hugh Kenner, who liked to go as far as he could in the direction of overt anti-Semitism, argued that Corde was "not a Jewish Dean from the Bellow Repertory Company" but a character whose WASP identity failed to disguise the fact that he was modeled after his "fox-faced creator."

The most damaging assessment was by John Updike in *The New Yorker*. Updike had never treated Bellow gently, mocking the hectic pace of *Humboldt's Gift* as "a static of human busyness" and dismissing Charlie Citrine as "a bore."* He didn't go easy this time, either: "The good thing about *The Dean's December* is that it is *by* Saul Bellow. The bad thing about *The Dean's December* is that it is *about* Saul Bellow." Corde was too transparently a mouthpiece for Bellow, in Updike's judgment; the nonfiction book he'd jettisoned obtruded its "papery reality" on the novel. He objected to the "little reassuring compliments" Corde was forever bestowing on himself: "Literature can do with any amount of egoism; but the merest pinch of narcissism spoils the broth."

Bellow blamed his bad reviews on the fact that he'd tackled a taboo subject: race. His critics wanted to see him fail, he told a Chicago reporter; the reviews were sour grapes. "Is he past his prime? Is he gonna fall on his face? Should he hang up his gloves?" He went on the offensive, urging his publishers to run an ad pointing up the controversial nature of the book; why not take the position that it had stirred up a debate? But he was clearly wounded. The reviews constituted a "savage and rather personal" attack, he maintained in a letter to Ed Burlingame; the "New York Review of Books crowd" was up to its old tricks. If Bellow had been looking for a fight, he'd gotten it.

---

*Updike's stealthily cruel reviews of Bellow's novels, which he dismembered one by one in *The New Yorker*, were collectivized by Bellow into "the fastidious goy critics on guard for the Protestant establishment and the genteel tradition." Bellow discerned a subtext in Updike's harsh review of *Humboldt's Gift*: "Isn't it wonderful that he can use English so well considering that it's not his native language?"

The news wasn't all bad. In America, *The Dean's December* was briefly on the bestseller list, rising as high as number six. Melvyn Bragg, whose *South Bank* program on British television reached a wide and discerning audience, had flown to British Columbia with a crew and interviewed Bellow; the show aired in March and generated much favorable press. Bellow also taped three half-hour shows with Dick Cavett.

Even so, the book lost money. Harper and Row "took a huge bath" on it, according to Aaron Asher, now an editor at the firm. Returns—that curse of the book trade, whereby unsold stock is sent back to the publishers—were heavy. The $600,000 advance made back about $160,000 on the trade edition, and subsidiary rights added another $200,000, leaving "at risk" some $240,000. Bellow, to his credit, was concerned about what he described as his "debt" to Harper and Row and raised the possibility of extending the unrecovered advance to his next book, perhaps a collection of short stories and novellas. But the tough reviews and unspectacular sales put him in a foul mood.

"Saul needs a little stroking and buttering up," Barley Alison wrote to Ed Burlingame in September 1982, during Bellow's promotional swing through Europe. Before going on Alain Pivot's popular show, *Apostrophes,* Alison reported, Bellow downed a tumbler of gin, on top of the two gin-and-tonics he'd had at a reception at the Elysée Palace. Afterward, his French publishers took Bellow and his entourage to Hemingway's old hangout, the Brasserie Lipp, where he partook of more gin and wine. "At this stage," Alison confided to Burlingame, "not *apparently* drunk but unlikely to be entirely sober, he laid into me and said that a sale of 15,000 copies odd [in England] was a disgrace after he had worked his guts out for me being interviewed by Melvyn Bragg." His litany of complaints grew more insistent as the night wore on: He was disappointed with the way Harper and Row had marketed the book; he'd been shortchanged by Book-of-the-Month Club; the Swedes were "hopeless." It was all Alison's fault.

The next morning they met for coffee, and no more was said about the matter. The storm had—momentarily—passed.

Bellow had ducked the funerals of Isaac Rosenfeld, Oscar Tarcov, and Delmore Schwartz. Funerals were superfluous; the dead were always with him, he said. But he tended to make exceptions for the famous—either because of their fame or because he hadn't known them as well and could mourn from a greater emotional distance. (Years later, he skipped his old friend Al Glotzer's memorial service in New York on the grounds that he was "too frail" to make the trip, then showed up a few weeks later at the Museum of Modern Art to attend a memorial for Saul Steinberg.) When John Cheever died in the summer of 1982, Bellow came east for his funeral.

In the car to the church with Cheever's family, he was full of foreboding; Nathanael West had been killed in a car crash on the way to a funeral, he reminded Cheever's daughter, Susan. But he delivered a moving eulogy in the crowded church. The two writers hadn't met often, he noted, but they had a deep affinity: "Our friendship, a sort of hydroponic plant, flourished in the air." They weren't rivals but partners in the same imaginative enterprise: "Each of us knew what the other was."

Toward the end of 1981, when Cheever was dying of the lung cancer that would kill him six months later, Bellow had written him a valedictory letter that slipped poignantly in and out of the past tense:

Dec 9, 81
    Dear John:
    Since we spoke on the phone I've been thinking incessantly about you. Many things might be said, but I won't say them, you can probably do without them. What I would like to tell you is this: we didn't spend much time together but there is a significant attachment between us. I suppose it's in part because we practiced the same self-taught trade. Let me try to say it better, we put our souls to the same kind of schooling, and it's this esoteric training which we had the gall, under the hostile stare of exoteric America that brings us together. Yes, there are other, deeper sympathies but I'm too clumsy to get at them. Just now I can offer only what's available. Neither of us had much use for the superficial "given" of social origins. In your origins there

were certain advantages; you were too decent to exploit them. Mine, I suppose, were only to be "overcome" and I hadn't the slightest desire to molest myself that way. I was, however, in a position to observe the advantages of the advantaged (the moronic pride of Wasps, Southern traditionalists, etc.) There wasn't a trace of it in you. You were engaged, as a writer should be, in transforming yourself. When I read your collected stories I was moved to see the transformation taking place on the printed page. There's nothing that counts really except this transforming action of the soul. I loved you for this. I loved you anyway, but for this especially.

Up and down on these rough American seas we've navigated for so many decades we've had our bad trips, too—unavoidable absurdities, dirty weather, but that doesn't count, really. I've been trying to say what does count.

My son Adam who has been visiting us in Chicago, when I told him that I was writing to you wanted me to say that he was charmed by your short book. I was, too.

If it isn't possible for you to come to Chicago I will fly to New York whenever it's convenient for you.

Love, Saul

28

Nobel laureate Saul Bellow and wife No. 4 Alexandria [sic]
are telling it to their divorce attorneys.

—"Kup's Column," *Chicago Tribune,*
February 27, 1986

THE RECEPTION OF HIS BOOKS, positive or negative, had little effect on Bellow's productivity. Even as he was weathering the reviews of *The Dean's December,* he was immersed in a long story entitled "Him with His Foot in His Mouth."

The new work was very different in tone from the novel, which was dominated by the dark, Old Testament voice of Dean Corde. Narrated in the first person by one Herschel ("Harry") Shawmut, a well-known musicologist exiled to British Columbia after a business deal went bad, "HWHFIHM"—as Bellow's publishers referred to it—was comic, Mozartian, at once lighthearted and profound. It showed again Bellow's remarkable versatility. While he explored the same motifs in all his work, he did so in a Heraclitean spirit, never stepping into the same river twice.

Shawmut, apart from the fact that he's "tall," is one of Bellow's most revealing fictional explorations of "that hoard of strange formulations" that was his nature. The title offers a hint of the narrator's affliction: Shawmut is a compulsive wise guy. He can never pass up the chance to deliver a devastating witticism. His most notorious crack, still remembered at the small New England college where it was uttered thirty-five years earlier, was a response to a librarian who remarked innocently of his baseball cap, "Oh, Dr. Shawmut, in that cap you look like an archaeologist." To which the cruel Shawmut replies, "And you look like something I just dug up."

Shawmut's riposte is witnessed by Eddie Walish, a fellow teacher, who later writes out of the blue to tease him about it. Bellow was obviously still brooding about an abusive letter he'd received from his old friend Ted Hoffman after he won the Nobel Prize. Hoffman had been a witness to the original slighting remark—identical to Shawmut's—which Bellow had made to the elderly librarian at Bard, Ada Green, more than thirty years previously. ("Yes, you actually said that, I testify," Hoffman had reminded him. "Five Andrew Jacksons [twenty-dollar bills] in a plain brown wrapper, and I'll promise never to retail it at a cocktail party at which Jason Epstein or Norman Podhoretz are present.") What was curious was the literary use to which Bellow put Hoffman's rambling diatribe. If he had meant to be "querulously affectionate," as he claimed, Hoffman badly misjudged his correspondent. In the story, Bellow eviscerated his hostile correspondent with the same alarming gusto he had applied to Sam Freifeld and Sydney J. Harris in *The Dean's December,* dwelling pitilessly on Hoffman's physical deformities, his limp and curvature of the spine, his "distinctly Jewy" look.* Outwardly "considerate, deferential, civil," Shawmut smolders inwardly with rage. "I overdid things and wiped myself twice where people of better breeding only wiped once," he confesses. "But no such program of betterment could hold me for long. I set it up, and then I tore it down, and burned it in a raging bonfire." Jokes, as Freud demonstrated, are a means by which these suppressed impulses can be expressed—the same could be said of art.

The jokes in "Him with His Foot in His Mouth" *are* funny. When the wife of pompous Professor Schulteiss frets that no one will be learned enough to write her husband's obituary, the mischievous narrator pipes up: "I don't know if I'm qualified, but I'd be happy to do the job." This was a variant on a quip Bellow claimed to have made after a rabbi quoted Leslie Fiedler's lament

---

* "The physical description was clearly me," Hoffman admitted. "I read it standing up in the store; I wasn't about to give him a royalty."

that when he died there would be no one to say kaddish because none of his children knew Hebrew. "If he's willing to die now," Bellow volunteered, "I'll say it for him." For Bellow, jokes were an important form of communication. He was forever calling up Philip Roth or Joseph Epstein for the express purpose of sharing a good one, preferably told at length. His one-liners were legendary. When his second wife, Sondra, complained long after their marriage had ended that Jack Ludwig was "like a steamroller," Bellow rejoined, "But you didn't have to lay down the asphalt." To a student who referred to the Russian Formalist literary critic Mikhail Bakhtin: "Bakhtin, eh? Sounds like a germicide." Upon learning that Thomas Edison was an anti-Semite: "That's why Jews light candles." For Bellow, as for Shawmut, jokes were involuntary, a form of "seizure, rapture, demonic possession, frenzy, *Fatum*, divine madness, or even solar storm—on a microcosmic scale."

Despite Shawmut's weakness for biting rejoinders, he's not entirely heartless. The form of the story is epistolary: It's a letter of apology to Miss Rose, the unfortunate librarian he slandered so many years ago. The tone is conciliatory, even when he's writing about Allen Ginsberg, whose flamboyant homosexuality and revolutionary utterances would ordinarily have been anathema to Bellow. Shawmut admires Ginsberg's "screwball" candor; he's won over by the poet's "purity of heart." Despite his propensity for vicious portraiture, Shawmut is more at peace with himself as he approaches old age, more prone to accept "the whole agreeable openness of things toward the end of the line, the outskirts of the City of Life."

Within a year, Bellow had produced two other long stories— enough to contemplate assembling a collection. "What Kind of Day Did You Have?" which first appeared in *Atlantic Monthly*, was a tour de force of portraiture; anyone who had known Harold Rosenberg would have recognized him instantly in the character of Victor Wulpy, a famous art critic with a majestic, Nasser-like visage who could quote Heidegger by the yard. Wulpy's cerebral discourses on modern history, on the avant-garde's efforts to free itself from the "death grip of tradition" and the "proletarianization" of modern culture, are right out of Rosenberg's *The Tradi-*

tion of the New. Wulpy was "located in the central command post of comprehension."

The other major character in the story, Wulpy's mistress Katrina Goliger, appeared at first to be simply another one of Bellow's tarty shrews, a divorcée from Evanston with "touch-cock" fingers and black ostrich-leather boots. Summoned to Buffalo in the midst of a snowstorm to ferry her eminent and ailing lover back to Chicago, she plays the conventional Bellovian role of handmaiden to genius. But her yearning for the higher life is genuine. An idle suburban housewife and neglectful mother, she struggles with the intricacies of a Wulpy essay on Valéry over lunch at the Old Orchard shopping center; she tries to write a children's book about an elephant trapped on the fifth floor of Marshall Field; she senses that she, too, has been summoned to some larger human destiny, even if it's only to serve Wulpy, the Thinker Prince.*

Him with His Foot in His Mouth was published as a collection in the spring of 1984; it included the title story, "What Kind of Day Did You Have?" "Cousins," and two shorter works: "A Silver Dish," which had appeared in *The New Yorker*, and "Zetland: By a Character Witness," a fragment of the abandoned novel about Isaac Rosenfeld. A loving portrait of Dave Peltz's stormy relationship with his ne'er-do-well immigrant father, "A Silver Dish" was a classic short story: formal, precise, and self-contained. In it, Woody Selbst, presiding at sixty over his aged father's impending death, has to climb into the old man's hospital bed to prevent him from pulling out his IVs. "I wasn't even aware that I had talked about that moment in my relationship with my father," said Peltz.

The last story in the collection, "Cousins," was a leisurely, somewhat long-winded meditation on the durability of family ties. Its garrulous narrator, Ijah Brodsky, a Chicago lawyer and "media personality," is a repository of the idiosyncratic lore Bellow carried

---

*Katrina Goliger contains elements of Bellow's former lover Fran Gendlin, but her primary model was Joan Ullmann Schwartz, Rosenberg's mistress. "I was absolutely enslaved by Harold—willingly enslaved," Schwartz said. Like Goliger in the story, she thought nothing of jumping on a plane to meet Rosenberg at an airport: "But how Saul knew that I helped him take off his shoes"—a detail in the story—"I'll never know."

around in his head: snippets of Hegel and James Whitcomb Riley; the rituals of the Koryak and Chukchee tribes in Siberia; Yiddish jokes and snatches of college drinking songs. Brodsky's relatives, all of them derived from various Gameroffs and Dworkins and Bellows, compose a colorful gallery of human types: cousin Shana, "a kind of human blast furnace" who cooked primitive dishes like calves'-foot jelly in her kitchen on Hoyne Street; Brodsky's grandfather, who had memorized the whole of the Babylonian Talmud; Aunt Tanya the movie buff ("Oy, Clark Gebble, I love him so!"). What unites them is, in Cynthia Ozick's words, "a powerfully recognizable Jewish family feeling—call it, in fact, family love, though it is love typically mixed with amazement and disorder." Bellow was loyal to his own cousins: He kept up with branches of the family in Israel and Montreal and sponsored Russian cousins who came to America. On Sundays, he visited relatives from the Old Country who had settled in Chicago. "The immediate family threw a chill on your exuberance, and you simply turned to the cousins," observes Brodsky's nagging but astute ex-wife. He could idealize them from a distance.

Brodsky's own view is more exalted; it's his Arnoldian aspiration "to long for the best that ever was." His anthropological fascination with kinship has a deep spiritual basis: "This was not an abstract project. I did not learn it over a seminar table. It was a constitutional necessity, physiological, temperamental, based on sympathies which could not be acquired. Human absorption in faces, deeds, bodies, drew me toward metaphysical grounds. I had these peculiar metaphysics as flying creatures have their radar." Shedding Citrine's comic bluster and the willed musings of Corde, Bellow could at last articulate the strange condition of existence that he had been brooding about in print for forty years: "One comprehensive light contained everybody. Among the rest— parents, patriarchs, angels, God—there was yourself." That was the central mystery: one's unscripted, unbidden appearance in the world.

Him with His Foot in His Mouth got enthusiastic reviews, none more so than Ozick's front-page appreciation in *The New York Times Book Review.* "For Saul Bellow, at age 68, and with his Nobel speech eight years behind him, the moment for decoding is now," Ozick announced, in an appraisal radiant with insight. For Bellow, great fame had become "a sort of obscuring nimbus," Ozick argued. His voice was so established that it had become hard to assess his achievement; each new book provoked speculation about his politics, his development as a novelist, the real-life sources of his characters. The new stories defied these conventional responses: What he had accomplished in *Him with His Foot in His Mouth* was nothing less than "to restore the soul to American literature."

Journalists who made the pilgrimage to Chicago—and they were numerous, as always—took note of Bellow's altered mood. D. J. R. Bruckner interviewed Bellow for *The New York Times Magazine* in April 1984 and came away with the impression that his subject had mellowed. "All my axes are hanging on the wall now, unground, and I have no urge to take them down. I seem to be going through some sort of change. I don't know what it is. I suppose I am getting rid of the melioristic and reforming side of myself."

There was "a lot of laughter in the man," Bruckner observed in the course of a leisurely Saturday morning in the Bellows' sunfilled apartment overlooking Lake Michigan. But Bruckner, a former administrator at the University of Chicago who had known his subject for years, came as a fan; others who interviewed Bellow still detected an edge of malice amid his geniality. When a reporter from *The Washington Post* questioned him about feminists' objections to the way he depicted women in his books, he replied sharply: "Well, I'm sorry girls—but many of you *are* like that, very much so. It's going to take a lot more than a few books by Germaine Greer or whatshername Betty Friedan to root out completely the Sleeping Beauty syndrome."* As he grew older, the bones of a deeply conservative, xenophobic vision of life emerged more clearly. Like his anger at blacks, which excepted those who

---

*Years earlier, when he was visiting a class at City College, a woman had asked him, "Why are the female characters in your books such nebulous creatures?" "My dear," Bellow answered, "you should meet the women I have known."

were his friends (Ralph Ellison, William Hunt, Stanley Crouch), Bellow's misogyny was a cultural anachronism for which he almost gleefully refused to apologize. He had never been so outspoken before, he confessed to William Kennedy: "It's an exhibitionistic thing to do, which amuses the public, but I'm getting old enough now not to care. I could have named lots of people. They'll never know how much they've been spared."

Sometimes his candor got him in trouble. The year before, *People* magazine had called him up about Philip Roth, whose *Zuckerman Unbound* had just been published. "Why write three novels that examine one's career as a novelist?" Bellow replied. "Things are bad out there. The knife is at our throats. One can't write books so attentive to one's own trouble." Roth was justifiably sore. "The Good Intentions paving company had fucked up again," Bellow wrote him contritely:

> The young interviewer turned my opinions inside out, cut out the praises and made it all sound like disavowal, denunciation and excommunication. Well, we're both used to this kind of thing, and beyond shock. In agreeing to take the call and make a statement I was simply muddle headed. But if I had been interviewed by an angel for the *Seraphim and Cherubim Weekly* I'd have said, as I actually did say to the crooked little slut, that you were one of our best and most interesting writers. I would have added that I was greatly stimulated and entertained by your last novel, and that of course after three decades I understood perfectly well what you were saying about the writer's trade—how could I *not* understand, or missed suffering the same pains. Still our diagrams are different, and the briefest description of the differences would be that you seem to have accepted the Freudian explanation: a writer is motivated by his desire for fame, money and sexual opportunities. Whereas I have never taken this trinity of motives seriously.

As for journalists, "we can only hope that they will die off as the deerflies do towards the end of August."

Since the sixties, Bellow had become increasingly identified with the neoconservatives who, led by Irving Kristol, had fled the ranks of liberal intellectuals. Bellow was no ideologue and no more willing to ally himself with a political group than he had been in the thirties, when the Trotskyites had dominated political discourse. But he concurred with the main tenets of neoconservative thought: that the Russians posed a threat to American security; that Americans had grown morally lax, a legacy of liberalism and the welfare state; that big government was bad. Over the years, he had affixed his name to letters in *The New York Times* espousing their causes, and he often participated in symposia sponsored by neoconservative organizations. His name adorned the masthead of the Committee for the Free World—founded in 1981 to advance "the struggle for freedom"—which was headed by Midge Decter, the wife of Norman Podhoretz. But he was put off by the shrill rhetoric of Decter's committee. He was especially unhappy when his views were misrepresented by Joseph Epstein, speaking at a committee-sponsored conference at the Plaza Hotel, "Our Country and Our Culture" (a title borrowed from the famous *Partisan Review* symposium held three decades earlier). Epstein attributed to Bellow the belief that American writers "no longer had the great subject"—that only writers who had survived totalitarian regimes had anything to write about. It was a belief that Bellow had expressed but he resented Epstein's formulation of it. The last straw was the special issue of the committee's journal, *Contentions*, in which books that had won the 1983 Pulitzer Prizes were "re-reviewed" in highly disparaging terms. *Is There No Place on Earth for Me?*, Susan Sheehan's portrait of a schizophrenic, was dismissed as "a piece of journalistic detritus from the veneration of insanity"; Alice Walker's *The Color Purple* was "confirmation of the continuing debasement of our literary currency."

On February 7, 1984, Decter heard from Bellow.

> Inquiries and complaints—mainly complaints—having been made about my participation in or sponsorship of your Special Issue of *Confrontations* [sic] ("Winners"), I read the offending number, which I had missed, and although the prize books you attacked seemed squalid enough your own reviews were in such bad taste that it depressed me to be associated with them. I have for some time been struggling with the growing realization that a problem exists: about Nicaragua we can agree well enough but as soon as you begin to speak of culture you give me the willies. I was on the point of dropping from the Committee when

Joseph Epstein last year read a paper in your symposium ascribing to me views I do not hold and pushing me in a direction I wouldn't dream of taking. It was uncomfortable to be misunderstood and misused in [a] meeting of which I was one of the sponsors and even more uncomfortable to see his speech reprinted in *Commentary.* But where there are politics there are bedfellows, and where there are bedfellows there are likely to be fleas, so I scratched my bites in silence. Your Special Issue, however, is different. I can't allow the editors of *Contentions* to speak in my name, or with my tacit consent as board-member, about writers and literature. When there are enemies to be made I prefer to make them myself, on my own grounds and in my own language. *Le mauvais goût mène aux crimes,* said Stendhal [bad taste leads to crime], who was right of course but who didn't realize how many criminals history was about to turn loose.

I am resigning from the board and request that you remove my name from your announcements.

In the late spring of 1984, Bellow received a telephone call from the mayor of Lachine, Quebec, the little town near Montreal where he'd been born sixty-nine years before. M. Descary informed Bellow that the town had decided to rename its public library after him. Would he attend the commemoration of the Saul Bellow Municipal Library on June 10? Bellow wept when he heard the news.

He arrived the day before the ceremony and checked into the Ritz-Carlton on Sherbrooke Street in Montreal. The next morning, escorted by Alexandra, his sister, Jane, his niece Leisha, and a reporter from *People* magazine (not the "crooked little slut" but a young male correspondent), he embarked on a tour of his old haunts. When the limousine pulled up at the door of the two-story redbrick house at 130 Eighth Avenue in Lachine where he was born, Bellow knocked on the door while "men in sweaty T-shirts and their tired-looking wives" observed the scene from neighboring porches. Bellow spoke in French to the woman who came to the door: "I was born here. May I have a look around?" She invited him in, and Bellow happily wandered the cramped rooms, entertaining his entourage with sometimes apocryphal stories about his relatives and the drunken doctor who attended his birth.

By eleven, a crowd had assembled in front of the library at 3100 Saint Antoine Street, a modest edifice surrounded by concrete tenements, a Dunkin' Donuts, a filling station, and a Midas muffler shop. A band played "Chicago," followed by "When the Saints Go Marching In" and—when the guest of honor appeared, in his fedora—"Happy Birthday to You." Today, intoned the master of ceremonies, was a day that would "leave its footprints on the sands of time."

After a brief speech by Descary, who marveled that a writer born in Lachine was now "on top of the world's literary people," Bellow himself spoke. He began in French, describing the "*petite maison*" in which he was born and stressing that all his life he had remained "*vraiment lachinois.*" He was moved—*ému*—by the honor that had been bestowed on him. Then, switching to English, he evoked his earliest memories—of his Indian nursemaid, his uncles and cousins, the storekeepers on Nôtre-Dame, Lachine's main drag ("I remember the drop seat of my rompers being buttoned by Mrs. Dentner after she had sold me two honeymoons for a penny in the grocery"). In the midst of this catalog, the microphone failed; Bellow put it aside and continued on his own, speaking in a hoarse voice weakened by age but still strong:

> I am here as a kind of testimony to the fact that it's possible for a child from Lachine to do some things which have been called—not by me but others—extraordinary. It also fits very well my own resistance to that deterministic philosophy that tells you that the place that you come from makes you absolutely: it does not. The human soul has its own way to declare its own freedom and to develop itself in its own way, and it is not true to say: "Show me where you came from and I'll tell you what you are." That's not the way things really are; we are people capable of freedom, and some of us are even willing to take chances for the sake of freedom: I see the thing that way. It is not necessary to be fully determined by one's surroundings. Your mind and your spirit have their own liberty, and each individual should be loyal to that.

After the unveiling of a plaque by the front door of the library and the presentation of an oil painting of the redbrick house in which he had been born, the guest of honor was shown the display in the library, which featured a huge blown-up photo of Bellow over the front counter, accompanied by the bilingual legend: UN GRAND ÉCRIVAIN NÉ À LACHINE, CONSCIENT DE SES ORIGINES ET ORIENTÉ VERS LA COMPRÉHENSION HUMAINE; AMERICA'S GREAT-EST URBAN NOVELIST, LACHINE-BORN, SLUM-RAISED, STREET-WISE KID, CHICAGO-MADE, WORLD-RENOWNED WRITER. Beside it were photographs of the novelist and his siblings as children; there was Bellow in a Buster Brown haircut and a smocklike shirt.

The ceremony was followed by a luncheon for Bellow at the Maison de Brasseur, a restored brewery on the waterfront. There were sixteen speakers that afternoon, among them Marvin Gameroff and Ruth Wisse, a professor of Yiddish literature at McGill. The mayor presented Bellow with a painting by a local artist of Saint Joseph Boulevard, where Bellow had played as a child. Then everyone sang "Happy Birthday to You" again.

"I was the child and plaything of everyone and I was spared the harsher aspects of family life," Bellow told the assembled guests. The childhood he persisted in remembering as idyllic had left him a confusing legacy, "because affection was not the reality principle and I should have been pursuing some other line—I will probably never be able to make up my mind—all I know is it remains a permanent part of my character and outlook." Lachine was paradise. "I never found it again."

The spring of 1985 was the low point of Bellow's life. His first wife, Anita, died in March. His brother Maurice, who had moved to Thomasville, Georgia, and gone into the antiques business, had liver cancer at the age of seventy-eight; his other brother, Sam, just seventy-four, was on his deathbed at Memorial Sloan-Kettering in New York.

Bellow flew down to see Maurice at the end of April, a month before the end. Over the Memorial Day weekend, Ruth Miller paid a condolence call. Bellow answered the door dressed in "a very dashing well-cut suit with a vest, so sharp, so rich"—it had belonged to Maurice. To Miller, Bellow described his final visit with his brother: "He knew he would never see him again, but they did not say goodbye. Bellow told him that if Maury needed him, he would come, just to call and he would fly down. Well, one night his brother called and said if he meant it, if he wanted to come, now was the time. He had better come now. Before Bellow left for the airport to take the plane, a telephone call came to say Maury was dead. 'So I never went. I have this suit.'"

Sam, meanwhile, had gone home from the hospital to die. His friends sat around his bedside trying to extract contributions to his favorite charities—"to the synagogue, the yeshiva, an old people's home, to this, to that," in Miller's words. When Bellow came to visit, his brother said, "As we began so are we ending. You were there at the beginning. You're here now. It's all on you afterwards." It was purgatory, Bellow said, to witness the disintegration of his family.

Sam died on June 3, just three weeks after Maurice. Bellow attended his service at the Hebrew Theological College in Skokie and sat shiva with the family. "I suppose it's unnatural to grieve so much but I've so often been accused of unnatural inclinations that it doesn't greatly concern me," Bellow wrote to Barley Alison later that summer. "It's hard enough to be oneself, natural or not."

To add to this catalog of woes, Bellow himself was turning seventy. As the date drew near, he became "obsessed" with its significance, according to Aaron Asher. He was "even more prickly than usual," Asher warned his colleagues at Harper and Row in a memo. "As you know, he wants no congratulations or any other acknowledgment of this event." When the *Saul Bellow Journal,* an academic journal published in Michigan, put together a seventieth-birthday issue in his honor, he pretended to take no notice of it.

There was one small celebration, a joint seventieth-birthday party that Gerald Freund, the former director of the MacArthur Foundation, gave at his New York apartment for Bellow and Alfred Kazin, whose birthday was June 5. Bellow still hadn't forgiven Kazin for his churlish review of *Mr. Sammler's Planet,* but Freund thought "it would be nice to bring them together." Instead, the birthday boys got into a big argument about politics. While Bellow had moved to the right, Kazin had remained faithful to the spirit of his youthful radicalism; if he was no longer a socialist, he still considered himself a freethinker true to his working-class origins. But their friendship went back a long way, so they tried to make it a cordial evening, if only for the sake of the past. By dessert, however, they were squabbling about Israel, the politics of *The New Republic*, Leon Wieseltier's articles on Hannah Arendt. When Bellow made the case that Franco had saved Jews, Kazin objected bitterly. "I was a Trotskyite when you were writing for Luce," Bellow retorted. Somehow they got onto the subject of *The New York Times*. Kazin said he was troubled by the conservative line the paper seemed to be taking on Israel, and Bellow blew up. "How can you call a paper conservative that publishes Anthony Lewis?" (Lewis was the most uncompromising liberal on the op-ed page.) Bellow left early, without saying goodbye. It was "an ugly scene," Kazin admitted. They never spoke to each other again.

The dedication page of *Him with His Foot in His Mouth* reads "For my dear wife, Alexandra."* Bellow's friends were convinced his fourth marriage would last. His other three wives, in the commonly held view, were all from the same mold: domineering mother-substitutes without their own developed talents or careers. Alexandra, the European-born mathematician, was of a wholly different order. To all appearances, the couple was deeply in love. At the Montreal home of Ruth Gameroff, they ate off the same plate, holding hands and staring into each other's eyes.

But all was not as tranquil as it seemed. In her biography, Ruth Miller provides an account of a tense weekend with the Bellows in Vermont in the early eighties. They seemed happy at first: Bellow was "cheerful," Alexandra was "beautiful, warmhearted, caring." Solicitous about her husband's diet, she removed the skin from his chicken. At once formal and affectionate, they addressed each other as "my dear." "The whole scene, I thought, was like something out of Bonnard." It wasn't long before cracks began to show in this domestic idyll. In the day's mail was a fan letter for Bellow from a young woman who had enclosed a photograph of herself in a short skirt and a tight red sweater. Bellow picked it up and studied it several times in the course of the evening. Meanwhile, Alexandra had received an article about her parents that upset her.

*In the title story, meanwhile, Bellow kills off the wife: "Death has taken Gerda out of circulation, and she has been wrapped up and put away for good."

But when Bellow pressed her to "articulate her miseries," she begged off and tried to excuse herself; she was tired. The conversation grew awkward. Miller left them sitting in silence.

The next morning, she found Bellow in the kitchen, looking "ghastly, worn and grim." He and Alexandra had quarreled. Alexandra didn't like being stuck away in Vermont; she found Bellow "sardonic and self-centered and oblivious of her feelings." She resented the way he had put pressure on her to stay up with their guest when she had wanted to go to bed. Bellow had grievances, too: for instance, Alexandra's refusal even to consider buying a house in Vermont. And she was too involved in her work. After Bellow had dropped everything and accompanied her to Romania, he charged, she had returned to their apartment in Chicago and gone straight to her study: "They had lived like strangers in the same house. When she had gotten sick, he had nursed her and done everything, everything, and she had not acknowledged what he was doing for her. She had taken no interest at all in what he was doing."

There was some truth to Bellow's complaints. It was almost with pride that Alexandra proclaimed her ignorance of his work. Bellow responded by disparaging hers. "You can have your research assistants at Secker's check this out for you at Cambridge or Oxford: the power of even the ablest mathematicians begins to decline in the third decade," he wrote Barley Alison after things began to go visibly wrong: "Alexandra is now in her fifties. She may enjoy trotting around to congresses where she is sure of a warm welcome because she is pretty and, thanks to me, well-heeled also. She can stand the young prodigies to lunch, but she has little to contribute to the proceedings. She told me with heavy emphasis not many months ago that for a long time she had not been able to obtain significant results in her researches, and that it was ALL MY FAULT." He also let on to Barley that he suspected Harriet Wasserman was secretly in love with him. "He now believes that Harriet's fantasy life is that Alexandra will leave him and she'll look after him in his old age as the 5th Mrs Bellow," Barley reported to Ed Burlingame.

Bellow was willing to share the blame for their difficulties. His fanatic concentration on *The Dean's December* had clearly taken a toll: "Emanations from my convulsed inner self were hard to take. I turned into a beast. Nothing else mattered. I was soaring, but to Alexandra it was offensive." And the book itself created problems. Bellow fretted that he couldn't write, that she inhibited him. But the book he did write was an unnervingly authentic portrait of a woman to whom he was still married. It was highly flattering, praising Alexandra's Old World manners, her intelligence, her *pudeur;* but it also turned on her the novelist's unsparing eye for physical detail. With pitiless candor, Bellow chronicled his wife's thinness and pallor; in a shocking image, he compared her to Corde's dying mother, recalling "the wasted mummy look of her last days." A private person, Alexandra felt "violated."

Age was also a factor. While Bellow grew older, his successive wives remained the same age; as each one approached her forties, she was replaced by one a decade younger—an innovative way of arresting the aging process. Alexandra was now well beyond that disconcerting marker.

Bellow wasn't oblivious to his own deficiencies as a husband and lover. In one of his confiding letters to Hyman Slate, he recalled a writer in Paris—probably Arthur Koestler—who had described him as having "bureaucratic tendencies." He had organized his life around "a single purpose," according to this observer: writing. "There *was* one other drive," Bellow noted, "the sexual one, but even that presently gave way. My erotic life was seriously affected, too, in that I directed my self with a kind of executive indiscriminateness—without a proper interest in women." They were there for the cursory satisfaction of his own sexual and emotional needs.

The final parting from Alexandra was acrimonious. As Bellow told it, he had arrived back from Vermont and was standing in the living room with his suitcase when she announced that she wanted a divorce. She had put red tags on his possessions. To Stuart Brent, he described in lurid detail how she had stormed about the apartment, slamming doors. The four bathrooms were employed to dramatic effect: "She used the first bathroom to get dressed, the second to put on her lipstick; the third to put on her stockings, shoes and gloves; then she came out of the fourth and said, 'You used me for your fucking novels and you drained me dry; go ahead and sue me. I want you out of the house in 24 hours.'" It sounds more like a speech that a wife in *Humboldt's Gift* would deliver than a declaration from the refined Alexandra Tulcea.

Bellow seemed to have no idea why Alexandra had thrown him out. "He was pretty broken up about it," recalled William Hunt. The decision had been entirely Alexandra's, Bellow maintained: "I wasn't the architect." To Helen Garrie, Bellow's account of the breakup of his fourth marriage was identical to the account he'd given of the breakup of his second marriage twenty-five years before, when he'd blamed Sondra for emotional neglect. "If I'd had a tape recorder, it would have been the same story."

If Alexandra had been the architect, she gave no indication; in her own accounts of their split, she was as unhappy as Bellow. "It is sad, very sad, heartbreaking, but it's a fact of life," she wrote Barley Alison the following spring. She didn't allocate blame. As Alison put it to Ed Burlingame: "Her line was, roughly speaking, 'it is better to have loved and lost than never to have loved at all.'" She could no longer make him happy, she explained to Alison. She was grateful for the time they'd spent together. "It had to happen sometime."

Bellow would have none of it. That he, too, was unhappy in the marriage was immaterial: The way he saw matters, it was always the wife who left. Alexandra had "done one of her most exquisite snowjobs" on Alison. "You are one of a regiment of friends whom she has entirely convinced that I wanted to divorce her," he replied sarcastically: "It all makes excellent sense: two brothers die, I turn seventy, and then I put myself out on the street. Do you know this anecdote about the Duke of Wellington? He is approached on the street by a gentleman who asks, 'Sir, are you Mr. Jones?' Wellington answers, 'Sir, if you can believe *that,* you can believe anything.'"

His tone was immoderately bitter in the months that followed. Writing Alison in the spring of 1986 to alert her that he was coming over to give a talk to PEN, he admitted that the changes in his life were "lamentable" and offered to have a "chat" with her about Alexandra. "Like one of the more forbidding tales in Herodotus, that will be, the one in which the severed head of a defeated prince is plunged into a tub of blood by the barbarian who has killed him. A little of that will go a long way." And could she please not have any office parties for him? "I am in no mood to face your personnel—all those pretty girls whose reward is to gaze upon celebrities."

He wasn't entirely immune to the charms of "pretty girls," according to Lord Weidenfeld, who was often summoned to Bellow's hotel room to "sit by the side of his bed while he kvetched about this one and that one." Bellow was "sweet and touchingly vulnerable in his self-pity," his former publisher recalled, but also "overtly carnal. He wore his marital and extra-marital affairs on his sleeve." Before one of Lord Weidenfeld's posh dinner parties, his author would "screen the female guest list for availability." Sometimes he got up from the table and called one of the many young women he encountered in the corridors of Secker and Warburg, inviting her to "come 'round."

Philip Roth, who was living in London with the actress Claire Bloom, had a more sympathetic impression of Bellow in the spring of 1986: "He was very lonely. He was seventy; he had to start all over again. . . . Claire and I took him with us to hear the Borodin String Quartet play Shostakovich. If he wasn't depressed enough, we were going to help him out with the three last string quartets. They're not designed to lift your spirits; they organize your misery. So we went to Festival Hall. Saul was very silent; he didn't say anything about the concert, which was astonishingly beautiful."

On top of his other woes, Bellow was haunted by the death of Bernard Malamud, who had dropped dead of a heart attack in March. Malamud was only a year older than Bellow. In the taxi on the way to the concert with Roth and Bloom, he stared gloomily out the window and said—alluding to his triadic description of Roth, Malamud, and himself as the Hart, Schaffner, and Marx of American literature—"Well, Schaffner's gone." What would his own old age be like? He worried about dying alone in the street.

In an effort to forestall this dire scenario, Bellow paid a call on his old Tuley girlfriend Eleanor Fox, who was divorced herself and lived on Lake Shore Drive. She felt he wanted "to start something." He took her out to dinner at the Palmer House and floated the thesis that a psychiatrist had once told him he'd never finished working through their relationship. Fox was unconvinced. "I wasn't going to be one of the five."

As Bellow's divorces went, his fourth one was amicable. Alexandra got a cash settlement of one hundred thousand dollars and the double apartment on Sheridan Road. Bellow moved back to an apartment in the bunkerlike high-rise on Dorchester where he and Alexandra had lived before the move to the North Side.

Some months later, he told Richard Stern that he'd figured out what was wrong with *The Dean's December:* He'd been too easy on Alexandra.

29

Bellow, at this point in his career, has sat atop the American literary heap longer than anyone else since William Dean Howells.

—JOHN UPDIKE,
The New Yorker, May 1, 1989

I N JANUARY 1986, Bellow flew to New York for the PEN Congress, a huge international gathering of writers convened to discuss "The Writer's Imagination and the Imagination of the State." For nearly a week, at panels, cocktail parties, and press conferences, several hundred writers from all over the world gossiped, drank, and debated the role of the writer. For Bellow, the congress provided a forum from which to put forth his increasingly conservative political views.

He was out of sympathy with the popular culture that, in his view, drowned out serious art in America. Public life in the United States, he said on many occasions, was noisy, farcical, "a mass of distractions." But he had even less patience with left-wing writers who attacked it. In a panel discussion at the Essex House, he got embroiled in a controversy with the German novelist Günter Grass.

Bellow started off the proceedings with a speech that was "maddening for its frigid superiority," according to Rhoda Koenig, the literary correspondent of *New York* magazine. "In America, we didn't start very high, and we didn't rise very high, either," he noted archly, disparaging the leveling tendencies of American democracy. In France, the artist still had some association, however tenuous, with the aristocratic tradition. What did America have to offer its citizens? Little in the way of culture, perhaps, but at least it provided a measure of social stability. "We have shelter, health, protection, and a certain amount of security against injustice."

It was this last claim that Grass challenged. "A walrus-shaped figure in full worker's-intellectual kit who slumped forward aggressively, clutching his pipe," as Koenig described him, Grass was spoiling for a fight. "There are places in the U.S. where some *don't* have shelter, don't have food," he admonished Bellow. The South Bronx, for instance, which Grass had seen with his own eyes. What about those citizens? Nadine Gordimer, Breyten Breytenbach, and Robert Nozick, who were also onstage, tried to calm the waters, but when Bellow rose to defend himself, he roiled them again. "No intelligent writer is devoid of political feelings," he said. "On the other hand, one must not get megalomaniacal notions of the powers of writers. What did the Feuchtwangers and the Romain Rollands and the Brechts achieve in containing the power of Hitler or Stalin? They were turned inside out and made to look like idiots." When Salman Rushdie protested that the panelists had abdicated "the task of imagining America's role in the world," Bellow answered sharply, "Tasks are for people who work in offices." In his report on their acrimonious encounter, *Time*'s reporter praised Bellow for his "patient grace." Others in the audience were more aware of his combativeness. "The man looks as if he was born sneering," commented Robertson Davies.

Though Bellow delivered his message in a harsh tone, it was more than a curmudgeonly rant. In his late essays and lectures, he returned to a powerful and deeply felt (and often reiterated) theme: that art occupies a high place in the spectrum of human activity. "Literature exists because writers believe in spiritual powers of personality and individuality," he stated in a talk the following year at Bennington College. It was their access to the soul that ratified their unique status. Since the Enlightenment, civilization had come to overvalue the role of the conscious, deliberative mind; now, more than ever, the imagination mattered: "We can no longer derive our summations from the definitions of humankind set by enlightened democracy. These have been used up entirely. Those of us who are called, or call ourselves, artists must turn again to the sources of our permanent strengths, to the stronghold of the purest human consciousness. Only the purest human consciousness, art consciousness, can see us through this time of nihilism."

Whether it was literature itself or merely the sense of his own special status as a writer that was being threatened, Bellow sounded increasingly besieged by the technological transformations of modern life. In an address given to celebrate the Whiting Awards, a recently instituted annual prize bestowed on young and promising writers, he railed against television, the proliferation of cable stations, the new habit of switching from channel to channel. He quoted from *The Art of Reading Books* by Johann Adam Bergk, a disciple of Rousseau: "Instead of responding passively to the text, you should throw yourself into it. You should seize its meaning and apply it to your own life."

That Bellow's argument on behalf of the primacy of art had its roots in his lifelong struggle to prove himself in the eyes of his "philistine" father and brothers doesn't invalidate it. At the core of his neoconservatism was the belief—seldom stated, perhaps seldom even grasped—that *all* forms of authority, including intellectual authority, were suspect. Intellectuals had misjudged the staying power of capitalism and the malevolence of communism. "They had misdiagnosed the problem," as Ruth Wisse wrote: "Bourgeois society was never so flawed as was their dream of a new kind of human being who could transcend it." The perfectibility of man was a myth.

Bellow, on the threshold of old age, manifested symptoms common to his time in life: irritability, resentment of change, and a bewilderment over the new, expressed as a defiant celebration of the old. But his themes were remarkably constant: When he thundered against the tyranny of consensus—what Harold Rosenberg referred to as "the herd of independent minds"—he was staking a claim for his own autonomy, his calling, his very identity. And taking on all those who threatened it.

Already testy, Bellow had been virtually in open warfare with his publishers ever since the publication of *Him with His Foot in*

His Mouth. They were stingy with advertisements, he complained; they didn't print enough copies. "You're publishing this book as if it's a collection of short stories," he rebuked Ed Burlingame.* Burlingame organized a luncheon for Bellow and reviewers from the major publications. Too late: Bellow had already decided that Burlingame was "a bottom-line type"—a mystifying allegation, since he was also convinced that Burlingame didn't know how to sell books.

Burlingame had another mark against him: Like his predecessor Cork Smith, who had briefly been Bellow's editor at Viking, he was a New England WASP. But his main failing was a phantom one: Bellow thought him insufficiently attentive. One day, Harriet Wasserman called him up and said, "Saul will never speak to you again." What infraction had Burlingame committed now? He had failed to call Bellow to commiserate about a negative review "in the Hartford Courant (or it may have been the Sacramento Bee)." Since he hadn't called, he must have agreed with the review. Burlingame was perplexed by this urgent need for solidarity: "He already had so many medals he could hardly stagger under the weight of them."

By the beginning of 1986, matters had reached the point where Barley Alison alerted Burlingame that Bellow was about to jump ship. In a last-ditch effort to placate his prize author, Burlingame offered to fly out to Chicago. Bellow replied frostily on February 4:

> Dear Ed,
>   It's good of you to offer to fly to Chicago. I don't think that such a trip would make much difference. Several times I came to discuss *Him with His Foot in His Mouth* with you, and each time I was made to feel that I was entreating Harper & Row to do right by me. It seems that all my suggestions and requests were referred to your marketing people, who simply rejected them. Not once did you do what I asked. I couldn't help feeling that I had placed myself in a humiliating position and I could only conclude that in your view I had written my books for nobody but your marketing experts. I wouldn't want to go through such treatment again.

*But it *was* a collection of short stories. And it *had* been advertised widely, including a costly full-page ad in *The New York Times Book Review*.

The letter was signed, "Yours without rancor, Saul."

On February 12, Burlingame reported to Alison: "It is an impossible task to reassure or to please him, for he is so convinced—fuelled by Harriet's provocations—that his publishers are incompetent rascals, bent on cheating and mistreating him. . . . Our problems with Harriet worsen every week. She is utterly impossible to do business with and she seizes every opportunity to create worry on his part, so that her role as watchdog and defender is magnified."

Nine months later, on November 25, 1986, an item announcing Bellow's latest move appeared in *The New York Times*. "Eight years and two books after moving to Harper & Row, Saul Bellow has a new publisher: William Morrow & Company."

There was something melancholy about Bellow finding himself on his own again, divorced from both his publisher and his wife, at the age of seventy-one, living again in Hyde Park, in the same building on Dorchester where he'd lived before his divorce. His apartment was on the eleventh floor, two floors below his old residence, with a view through picture windows of the grand-columned Museum of Science and Industry, its vast parking lot jammed with yellow school buses and, beyond it, Lake Michigan—so arctic in winter, Bellow joked, that "you half-expected to see a polar bear out on the ice." The familiar antique rolltop desk with his mother's passport in the drawer had been installed in the living room, along with his broccoli-colored couch, a glass-topped coffee table, and an Eames chair by the window. There were books everywhere: *Crime and Punishment; The Orphic Vision: Seer Poets from Novalis to Rimbaud; The Golem: Mystical Tales from the Ghetto of Prague; Eros and Magic in the Renaissance* by Ioan P. Couliano; a volume of Thucydides (in David Grene's translation) open on a reading stand.

There were four Nobelists in the building: the economist George Stigler, the physicist S. Chandrasekhar, the economist Milton Friedman, and—as it said beside the doorbell that buzzed visitors in through the locked iron gate—S. Bellow. But he was strangely isolated. In London, he lived the life of an international literary celebrity, dining with V. S. Naipaul and Isaiah Berlin. In Paris, he drank with Samuel Beckett at the Pont-Royal. But in Chicago, he often dined alone, on "a piece of fish" from Burhop's. Morris Philipson, a novelist and the editor in chief of the University of Chicago Press, was out walking with his young son in Hyde Park one day when they encountered Bellow, whom Philipson introduced as "a very famous novelist." "If he's so famous," said the boy as they walked away, "how come he looks so sad?"

On one of his frequent trips to New York, in the spring of 1987, Bellow had an emotional meeting with Isaac Rosenfeld's son, George. Now living in the Bronx, George had gone to medical school and, like his father, engaged in a long flirtation with Reichianism; along the way, he had jettisoned his father's name and taken his mother's—Sarantakis—shortening it to Sarant. He was in his early forties, a shy, sweet-natured man who was clearly struggling with the legacy of his chaotic upbringing and his father's early death. They met at the Lotos Club on East Sixty-sixth Street near Central Park; Bellow often stayed there when he was in New York. Sarant waited self-consciously in the elaborate club with its circular marble staircase, velvet drapes, and wood-paneled walls—"underdressed, overweight, and not knowing how it would go."

Finally, Bellow appeared. They shook hands and hugged, then settled down to reminisce about Isaac and Vasiliki, who was now retired and living in Hawaii. Isaac had been a doting father, Bellow told the still-bereft son. "Saul said at some point that he felt that the two things that Isaac wanted more than anything else was Vasiliki's love and my love."

Sarant invited Bellow to come and speak at Einstein Medical College, where he was on the staff, but Bellow gently put him off. He was busy; he didn't know what he'd say; he no longer needed a stage. "I'd only do it for you."

"I was so moved by this that I started to cry," Sarant recalled: "I was a little embarrassed and said 'I'm sorry.' He said 'that's ok' and I saw that he was crying too. Tears rolled down his cheeks and he looked away. It was a very moving afternoon. I have the feeling that it had to happen and that it was important certainly for me but also for him. There was a bond between us and a closeness. I really felt him and was so deeply moved and touched. I felt how much he really did love my parents and also felt how terribly lonely he is."

Seven years later, Sarant died of a heart attack. He was forty-eight—a decade older than his father had been when he dropped dead in his furnished room on Walton Street.

After four marriages, Bellow was forced to acknowledge his shortcomings as a husband, but he continued to cast himself in the role of victim. To Keith Botsford, who had also gone through several wives, he offered an account of his own marital history that was at once engaging in its modesty and revealing in its lack of insight: "I think nothing but karma can explain the ridiculous and self-mutilating things that I did in the course of my life. I lived for many years with a woman"—Sondra—"who didn't really care in the slightest for me. How did I get into that, why did I do that and what sort of blindness was it that made it possible? It's very curious to speculate on that." Then, with a laugh: "I'm not absolutely stupid except about myself."

Living alone had considerable drawbacks. Bellow had "a detestation of solitude," said Botsford. "He has never, ever been alone." Women came and went from the apartment on Dorchester with unabated frequency. "Saul's schmuck is like a dowser," cracked Stuart Brent. Both new and old flames were recruited to fill the gap left by Alexandra's departure. Monique Gonthier arrived from Paris to interview him for a French magazine. Zita Cogan, who had been in love with Bellow since their Tuley days and who kept prominently displayed on her bookshelves copies of his books inscribed "the second-story man" and "second-story Bellow from Humboldt Park"—a reference to Bellow's habit of climbing the back staircase to her family's kitchen—came to him with a proposition: "If you're not married by the time you're 78, I'll take care of you if you'll take care of me." It sounded fine to him, Bellow said.

Then he found Janis. In fact, she had been on the scene for several years; as early as February 1984, the name of Janis Freedman, identified as "Secretary to Saul Bellow," had appeared on a letter dictated to Ruth Miller. Freedman was a graduate student in the Committee on Social Thought, writing her dissertation on Dostoyevsky. She came from Toronto, where her father was a psychiatrist, and had enrolled in the department expressly to study with Bellow; she was twenty-five when they met—forty-four years his junior.

Where Alexandra represented a diversion from what could be called the generic Bellow wife—"motherly, nice Jewish women," as one of his friends described her precursors—Freedman conformed to the type. It was easy to make fun of Bellow's repetitive marital scenarios. ("There are some people where you don't even bother to learn the wives' names," sniped Gore Vidal.) But if outwardly she resembled the Jewish-mother figures Bellow seemed drawn to throughout his life, Freedman possessed distinctive qualities. Austere and willfully plain, "a Jewish/Amish woman," as one of their friends described her, she was also selfless and untemperamental. It was Freedman, Bellow told his friends, who would "see him through." Nadine Nimier, when she heard about the new woman in Bellow's life, exclaimed, "*Ah! la veuve* [the widow]."

By the spring of 1987, Freedman had become a permanent fixture on the scene. When Bellow traveled to Israel in April for a conference on his work, a correspondent noted, "He was also joined by his former student, Janice Friedman [*sic*], young and attractive and alert. Dark-haired and dark-eyed, with a Roman nose, Janice Friedman could have been mistaken for Bellow's daughter. One waggish conferee referred to her as 'Bellow's Abishag.'"

In the spring of 1987, Bellow's political convictions leaped back into the public consciousness by an unlikely route: the publication of *The Closing of the American Mind*, a book by his friend and colleague Allan Bloom. Though younger than Bellow by fifteen years, Bloom was the latest—and last—of his intellectual mentors, succeeding Harold Rosenberg and Edward Shils in the role of Great Books tutor.

The Bloom/Bellow partnership was already legendary in Hyde Park. The literature course they team-taught drew crowds. Standing together before a rapt audience in the Social Sciences Building auditorium, they worked their way through Proust and Céline, Flaubert and Dickens, Gide and Joyce, and "The Brothers Manischewitz" (as they called *The Brothers Karamazov*). "There always seemed to be a large emotional charge in those exchanges," recalled one of their students. "Many of us sat on the edge of our seats when the big guns began to go off." (Not everyone was so impressed: Another, less reverential student described them as Don Quixote and Sancho Panza, tilting at intellectual windmills.)

The legend was local until Bellow persuaded Bloom to write down the harsh comic tirades about the corruption of the American university with which he entertained Hyde Park dinner parties. "These were things I'd been saying to friends for a long time," Bloom recalled. "You know, writing them down late at night for my own amusement." Bellow strong-armed Harriet Wasserman, who had set up shop on her own, into representing his voluble colleague and agreed to write an introduction. In the late spring of 1986, Bloom delivered an eloquent, densely theoretical manuscript on the decline and fall of higher education. His publisher, Simon and Schuster, ordered up a first printing of ten thousand copies. Within weeks of Christopher Lehmann-Haupt's rave review in the daily *New York Times* on March 11, 1987, the book had risen to the top of the *Times*'s bestseller list. By the end of the year, it had sold half a million copies.

One of the more lasting and destructive legacies of the turbulent sixties, in Bloom's view, was the emergence of cultural relativism: the notion that all cultures are equal, that truth is a social construct employed to maintain the hegemony of those in power. The latest pedagogic trends on campus—black studies, women's studies, deconstruction, the rehabilitation of German philosophy in the neo-Marxist guise of Herbert Marcuse—represented nothing less than an assault on the values for which a classical education stood. "The real community of man," Bloom argued, "is the community of those who seek the truth, of the potential knowers."

In his foreword to *The Closing of the American Mind*, Bellow quoted these words approvingly, endorsing Bloom's Platonic defense of elitism and giving it a characteristic Bellovian twist. For Bellow, the issues Bloom raised had everything to do with the fundamental right of intellectuals to steer an independent course;

the book was a gallant expression of resistance to conformity. When Bloom spoke of our dependence on "history and culture," he meant not that we should repudiate what those forms of knowledge had to teach us but that we should form our own judgments as to their meanings in our lives. "There was not a chance in the world that Chicago, with the agreement of my eagerly Americanizing extended family, would make me in its image," Bellow wrote, making of Bloom's book still another occasion to rehearse the circumstances that had shaped his own life. "Before I was capable of thinking clearly, my resistance to its material weight took the form of obstinacy." He refused to become, as he put it, "the product of an *environment.*" Once again, the need to subvert determinism—put another way, to deny dependency—was paramount.

So intent was Bellow upon distancing himself from any cause or doctrine that he was reluctant to become identified publicly with the phenomenon he'd brought into being. He didn't begrudge Bloom his success. "You couldn't ask for a better friend," said Bloom, before and after he ascended to celebrity status. Bellow seemed genuinely without jealousy and counseled Bloom on how to weather sudden fame: "It's like going through the Inferno without Vergil as a guide."* But their dual stardom made him uneasy. When Bellow learned that *The New York Times Magazine,* which had commissioned a profile of Bloom, was contemplating putting the two of them together on the cover, he dispatched Harriet Wasserman to the magazine's offices to demand that the editors leave him out of the picture and even tried to get his photograph removed from the *Times* archives on the grounds that it made him look "like a herring that had been left out in the rain too long." In his version of the incident, Bellow claimed that he didn't want to steal the limelight from Bloom. But some friends put forth another theory: Bellow wished to avoid the negative criticism Bloom was generating, especially from the liberal press. Others speculated that Bloom's open if undeclared homosexuality made him nervous. In the end, Bloom was featured alone on the cover.

---

*Edward Shils, by contrast, was apoplectic about "that book." When Bloom organized a symposium on "The Decline of the West," Shils joked that it should have been called "The Decline of the West Side."

Bellow's skittishness about journalists never stopped him from saying what was on his mind. In the course of an interview with the reporter from the *Times* who'd been assigned to write about Bloom, Bellow uttered what was to become one of the most controversial remarks of that politically turbulent era: "Who is the Tolstoy of the Zulus? The Proust of the Papuans? I'd be glad to read him." This challenge to "politically correct" academics who insisted that all cultures were equal was delivered with the self-delighting laugh, head thrown back, that accompanied his funniest one-liners. But for years afterward, the comment—often misquoted—was trotted out by old leftists and outraged defenders of multiculturalism as an egregious example of reactionary tendencies. "My heart sank with each fresh report of Bellow's contempt for the lower orders," wrote Alfred Kazin sanctimoniously.

The more scrutiny his work received, the more Bellow claimed to be made uncomfortable by it. "I often feel like a beaver gnawing wood in a stream surrounded by Forest Service placards describing the life and habits of the beaver," he complained to Malcolm Cowley about the Viking Critical Library edition of *Herzog*. And he professed to be no fan of the *Saul Bellow Journal*, which gave him an "in-memoriam" chill: "I'm not about to order my cenotaph." One of his favorite images, offered up in numerous interviews, was of the bushes and trees he'd seen in Japan, draped with fortunes obtained for a penny at temples and attached to the branches for good luck: He likened his own oeuvre to those shrubs. Yet he read every word of the *Saul Bellow Journal,* and worthy disciples were encouraged rather than turned away.*

None was more ardent than Martin Amis, who became one of the keenest expositors of Bellow's work—and, eventually, a close friend. The son of Kingsley Amis, young Amis had acquired preco-

---

*His correspondence with a Montreal scholar, Ann Weinstein, starkly reveals his contradictory attitude toward students of his work. On one occasion, he wrote her, "I do not exaggerate when I say that reading about myself drives me up the wall—yes, and across the ceiling too." On another, praising a paper she'd written: "What a mountain needs to make it delectable is to have wild fauna dancing on it."

cious fame as a novelist in his own right, publishing in his twenties a series of slim, well-crafted books that in a British way resembled Bellow's early efforts. By his thirties, Amis had graduated to big, ambitious novels such as *Money*, which had the sprawl and ardor of *Augie March* combined with Bellow's love of the vernacular. They had met in 1983, when Amis interviewed Bellow for *The Observer;* within a few years, Amis himself had become profile material. When a writer for *The New York Times Magazine* called up Bellow for a quote on Amis, Bellow compared him to Flaubert and Joyce. For his part, Amis considered Bellow the preeminent novelist of his time; Augie, he wrote in his admiring foreword to the Everyman's Library edition of *The Adventures of Augie March,* was "a figure of Shakespearian solidity, rendered with Dickensian force."

Their mutual appeal was no mystery. Amis was from a broken home; his parents had divorced when he was twelve. The pompous and competitive Kingsley displayed little interest in his son's work and was in the habit of confiding his indifference to journalists. Bellow served as a convenient surrogate writer-father.* With Martin Amis, he could enjoy the gratifications of a mentor-disciple relationship without the conflicts that inevitably arise between fathers and sons. By the time he'd reached his mid-thirties, Amis had his own cultural authority and was grateful for the elder writer's attention but not dependent on it.

Bellow was aware that being the son of a world-famous novelist was a burden and a liability. "You didn't have the freedom to be no one," he wrote Adam after he had graduated from Princeton and was trying to figure out what to do with his life. But paternal guidance was seldom forthcoming. When Daniel, the youngest boy, went off to Paris, Dave Peltz asked Bellow what he was going to do there: "Fuck his brains out, presumably," Bellow replied dismissively.

If being a son was hard, being a father was apparently even harder. "A parent is a fetish for children to pound nails in," Bellow liked to say. He found Nathan Asch's memoir of his father, the

---

*It was more than a figure of speech. After Amis's father died, he records in his memoir, *Experience*, he told Bellow, "You'll have to be my father now."

novelist Sholem Asch, distasteful—or, perhaps, as Joseph Epstein has suggested, it provoked guilt about his own failings as a father. In the memoir, Asch gives a painful description of the emotional neglect he suffered at his father's hands; Bellow read it as just another son airing his grievances. Anyway, *he* was the son; there wasn't room for another.

More than one hundred scholars from all over the world showed up at the University of Haifa in April 1987 to read papers such as "Finding the Middle Ground: A Study of Bellow's Philosophical Affinity with Emerson in *Humboldt's Gift*" and "The End of Enlightenment: Bellow's Universal View of the Holocaust in *Mr. Sammler's Planet.*" "If I have to listen to another word of this I think I'm going to *die*," Bellow muttered as he ducked out of a session on *Herzog*. But he had a good time, too. It wasn't only academics who attended: The Israeli novelists A. B. Yehoshua and Amos Oz gave talks, as did Amis and Allan Bloom.

Amis's talk was a lucid exposition of Bellow's forthcoming novel, *More Die of Heartbreak*. Bellow's debut with William Morrow was scheduled for publication in June 1987; Amis, who possessed an advance proof, had pored over its dense mysteries and made the novel perhaps clearer than it was. The title derives from a statement made by its hero, Benn ("Benno") Crader, a world-renowned botanist: Dilating on the impact of the Chernobyl disaster, Crader maintains that more people still die of heartbreak than of radioactivity. But the experience of having your heart broken also helps you to live: "Perhaps one of the many, many things the new novel has to say," observed Amis, "is that you *need* heartbreak, to keep you human."

The novel is narrated not by Crader—a departure for Bellow, who generally put his books in the hands of studious, Bellow-like protagonists—but by his nephew, Kenneth Trachtenberg, a professor of Russian literature enmeshed in an intense, "devouring" relationship with his distinguished uncle. (Could it have been this deep emotional connection between a younger and an older man that spoke so compellingly to Amis?) Crader, the book's hero, is a brilliant bumbler, visionary in his grasp of the big picture but hapless in romance. He "had the magics," his nephew attests, "but as a mainstream manager he was nowhere." His second wife is "more difficult, more beautiful, more of a torment" than the first. As for the incidental women in Crader's life, they're high-strung, temperamental dames intent on snaring the famous scientist and making trouble; he's "dredged in floury relationships by ladies who could fry him like a fish if they had a mind to."

Crader's deficiencies in the human sphere are made up for by his capacities as a thinker. Like Ijah Brodsky in "Cousins," he's an avid reader of philosophy, anthropology, the literature of travel; one of his favorite books is Admiral Byrd's *Alone*. Yet he's also, in true Bellovian fashion, obsessed with his own past. Gazing up at the Ecliptic Circle Electronic Tower, a monolithic skyscraper that dominates the horizon of the unnamed "Rustbelt metropolis" where he lives, Crader muses, "My old life is lying under it: my mother's kitchen, my father's bookshelves, the mulberry trees." Once again, the brutal modern world was seen as an instrument of destruction, eradicating all traces of the old. Bellow's own house on LeMoyne was literally gone, the building he'd grown up in replaced by an empty lot. Like Herzog mourning his idyllic early life in the Jewish slums of Montreal ("All he'd ever wanted was there"), Crader yearns for the lost Eden of his childhood. His old life is his real, authentic emotional life.

Bellow wrote *More Die of Heartbreak* in just six months, and it showed. Even by his standards, the novel is digressive, its convoluted plot an afterthought. The characters are lost in a fog of discourse. For pages at a time, the garrulous uncle-nephew team perform a convoluted duet. "Kenneth and Benn, a pair of jabbering, irresolute dreamers from a city that never existed, look like the end of the line," wrote Terrence Rafferty in *The New Yorker*.

More Die of Heartbreak earned the wide coverage and respectful treatment to which Bellow had become accustomed—yet another front-page review in *The New York Times Book Review*, full-page ads, "rare" interviews in the press. It was on the bestseller list for thirteen weeks. But it sold fewer than seventy thousand copies in hardcover, and Dell, publisher of the paperback edition, sold less than half of its six-hundred-thousand printing. The reviews were distinctly halfhearted. *Time*, in recent years a convert to Bellow, weighed in with dutiful praise ("crackles with intelligence and wit"); but most reviewers were baffled, to put the matter politely. Leon Wieseltier, writing in *The New Republic*, praised the novel's high-minded pursuit of the contemplative life while dismissing it as "a sorry tale of male self-pity."

A former disciple himself, Wieseltier may have been unnerved by Bellow's portrait of the fawning Kenneth Trachtenberg, but his criticism wasn't far off the mark. That Bellow had trouble writing sympathetically about women was a matter of public record by now. Even Harold Bloom, no feminist, dismissed Bellow's female characters as "absurdities, third-rate pipe-dreams." *More Die of Heartbreak* features a veritable gallery of grasping and pathetic women. In the arms of his hateful wife, Matilda—an even less flattering version of Susan Glassman than her previous fictional incarnations—Crader fantasizes about strangling her. Here, Bellow's rage against women, so disturbingly manifest in *The Dean's December*, reaches a new low.

Ruth Miller, who visited Bellow when he was in the midst of writing *More Die of Heartbreak*, gained a private glimpse into the more benign aspects of his thinking. He had always had a project, he told her, a quest for meaning, for the essence of things. He read her a revealing passage from Proust in which the narrator, gazing out the window of a train, is struck by his lack of feeling for nature. How, if he had the soul of an artist, could he be so unmoved by the sight of flowers in a field, "for can one hope to transmit to the reader a pleasure that one has not felt?"

For Bellow, Miller surmised, it wasn't the natural world from which he felt closed off; it was people. "As he was glancing through Proust, he was describing what I felt to be his paradox as a writer. His job was to observe, to see, to take note of every detail, but that very act of taking notice prevented him from making a sympathetic connection with the essence. To observe was the task of the writer, and to empathize was the act of the man."

In the end, Crader goes off alone to Antarctica, to live in the wintry dark and study lichens. As Miller noted tersely, "It is a sad book."

Ken Trachtenberg says: "The greater your achievement, the less satisfactory your personal and domestic life will be." This was

Bellow's paradox in the spring of 1987. At seventy-one, he was still a whirlwind of restless energy. From Haifa he flew to France, following a frenetic itinerary that left him depleted. "I stripped my thread," he told an audience at the Montreal Council of Foreign Affairs in the middle of May, offering a bizarrely candid account of his recent travels and travails:

That is to say, "I screwed it." I became very tired and went to take a holiday in Europe. I ended up by flying from place to place and tried to catch up with the train from Avignon to Lyon which was determined to leave me behind and then I got on to the railroad station in Lyon and asked where the hotel where I had a reservation was located. . . . I shot up in an elevator to the 48th floor and there I found myself sealed in one of these modern hotel rooms where you couldn't even open a window, where you could scarcely breathe and I thought, "This is Lyon: Is this the holiday where I regrow my depleted tissues?" The answer was No and flying around from place to place was all a big mistake and then I came back to the U.S. I land in Boston. I go to Vermont. I drive up to Lachine because it is impossible for me to refuse an invitation by M. Descary [the mayor of Lachine] and so here I am still on the run, on the lam, so to speak, and one of these days, I am going to withdraw from all this and I hope I'm going to be able to bear the tranquility without falling apart. That is the one thing which really threatens a man.

For Bellow, Augie March's effort to "sit in [his] own nature" remained an elusive ideal. His rambling narrative in Montreal made him sound more like a fugitive—"on the lam, so to speak"— than a pilgrim in quest of spiritual enlightenment.

Though he visited new destinations in these years—notably the hill towns of Tuscany—for the most part Bellow *re*visited, haunting the places that had formed his character. Montreal continued to exert a powerful attraction. During his trip there in the spring of 1987, the Jewish community showed up in force to greet its famous native. "It was a holiday for a whole sector of the city, a great event," said Ruth Wisse. Bellow made the rounds, calling on Willie Greenberg, his next-door neighbor from almost seventy years before, and on the Gameroffs. The keenness of his memory astonished those who came to hear him. While Bellow was being interviewed at the Jewish Public Library, a man introduced himself as a person from the old neighborhood. Bellow questioned the man closely about where he'd lived, then began to describe his interlocutor's father, his uncle, everyone in his household, "as if it had all been yesterday."

On the way to the airport, Bellow asked Wisse to drive him to Lachine. He wanted to stop in and see Louis Gameroff, who still had a hat shop on Nôtre-Dame.

30

The big artists, big minds, didn't peter out like average guys.
—SAUL BELLOW, *"What Kind of Day Did You Have?"*

I N THE SPRING OF 1988, Bellow had a new publisher—or
rather, an old publisher. Disenchanted with William Morrow,
he had returned to Viking. He also had a new work in
progress, a novella called *A Theft*. Its main character, Ithiel Regler,
is a Washington power broker, a worldly "behind-the-scenes operator" who's always jetting off somewhere on a glamorous secret
assignment—"in the Persian Gulf, with a Japanese whiskey firm
looking for a South American market, with the Italian police
tracking terrorists." Regler's outward features—from the green
Jaguar he drove to the wife who literally cleaned him out, leaving
behind an empty house—belonged to Bellow's friend Walter
Pozen, a lawyer and former advisor to Robert Kennedy. ("He
kicked the crap out of my second wife," Pozen remarked about the
book.) But the portrait of Regler was larger-than-life; think-tank
maven, White House gadfly, he could have been "the Gibbon or
the Tacitus of the American Empire." In Regler, Bellow created an
idealized version of himself as a Hegelian world-historical figure,
Henry Kissinger–like in his grasp of "the big picture," a man who
gave off an aura of "power, danger, secrecy" that made him irresistible to women.

One woman in particular, Clara Velde, the novel's main character, finds "Teddy" so compelling that other men pale in compari-

son. "He outclassed everybody, it seemed to her," Bellow wrote of Velde's long-standing attachment to the globe-trotting Regler. Modeled closely on Maggie Staats (now, after several marriages, Maggie Simmons), his intermittent girlfriend over several decades, Velde was "a rawboned American woman," a blonde from the Bible Belt who maintains a chaotic household on Fifth Avenue and is said to be "the czarina of fashion writing." Like Regler and Velde, Bellow and Simmons had remained close through several marriages apiece. "We were in many ways made for each other, Saul and I," Simmons said wistfully.

The central incident in *A Theft* was drawn from an episode in Simmons's life: A ring that Bellow had bought for her was stolen by her au pair's Haitian boyfriend and, after many complicated negotiations, returned. In itself, it was a commonplace episode; what made the book fresh was the narrative voice. Bellow had never told a story through the eyes of a woman before. The trouble was that while Velde's breezy, knowing references to Armani, Lacroix, and Sonia Rykiel comported with her identity as a fashion czarina, her monologues sounded like Bellow. No gender change could disguise his preoccupations with the World-Spirit and the role of personal emotion in the sphere of public life. As Bellow approached seventy-five—his "great old age," he liked to say—the voice that had established him as such a forceful presence in modern American literature was hard-pressed to register new tonalities.

A Theft was an awkward length—just over one hundred pages. *The New Yorker* and *Vanity Fair* both turned it down on the grounds that it was too long. One editor asked Bellow to cut it. "But one can't do with a story what one does with sliced salmon, in order to give the reader a taste," he told a reporter from *The New York Times*. To protect his honor, Bellow came up with an innovative solution: He would publish it as a paperback. It was a daring idea—publishers were still convinced that only hardcover sales could recoup steep advances—and it got a lot of press coverage. "One detects that the Nobel Laureate, never shy about promulgating his opinions through his fictional characters, rather enjoys the chance to explain the motivation behind this month's appearance of *A Theft* between jaunty orange paperback covers bearing the Penguin logo and a $6.95 price," noted a reporter for *People*. Bellow made his case with numbers: He aspired to an audience larger than the one he generally reached, which he variously estimated at somewhere between 100,000 and 250,000. Why should "titanic bestsellers" dominate the market? Why shouldn't Saul Bellow, too, have a million readers?

The book appeared in March 1989, and Bellow's publishers deemed their "bold" experiment a great success. "It had a spectacular reception, and we sold many more copies in paper than we would have in hardcover," an unnamed executive told Adam Begley, *The New York Observer*'s publishing correspondent. But it wasn't reviewed as prominently as Bellow's books normally were. *The New York Times Book Review* failed to give it the usual front-page coverage, while *The New Yorker* and *The New York Review of Books* grouped it with books by other writers, unheard-of for a work by Bellow.

The reviews were lukewarm at best. John Updike, who had an unnerving capacity for getting at a book's deficiencies, remarked on the novel's "aggressive breathlessness" and "gossipy tone, as if fictional characters were a subdivision of the rich and famous." With magisterial condescension masquerading as generosity, Updike acknowledged Bellow as "our most exuberant and melodious postwar novelist." Even this thin performance at times "flared into an arresting vividness," but not often enough to save it. The book was "skimpy," Updike complained—the same adjective used by Robert Towers in *The New York Review of Books*. In the end, *A Theft* sold about one hundred thousand copies out of the quarter million that had been printed—a disappointing figure.

Bellow was outwardly stoic. "I've lived long enough not to be edgy about my reputation," he told a British journalist, adopting an Olympian tone. But he was furious about the reviews. The critics were "*a pritchek on my tuches*," he said to Stuart Brent—a prick on my ass. He was hurt when he peered in the window of Brent's bookshop and didn't see his new book on display. "Do you think I'm losing my audience?" he asked.

As if to reassure himself of his value, Bellow put up for auction at Sotheby's the manuscript of *Mr. Sammler's Planet*. He removed the notebooks, typescripts, and galleys of the novel from the

Regenstein Library at the University of Chicago, where his papers were on deposit, and had them appraised by Andreas Brown of the Gotham Book Mart. Brown estimated the manuscript's value at between sixty thousand and one hundred thousand dollars. In the event, the New York Public Library obtained it for sixty-six thousand. "I could have wished for a higher price," Bellow, clearly disappointed, told a reporter from *The New York Times*. What he didn't know was that the money had come from Sam Goldberg, a New York lawyer who was an old friend of his. When the reporter asked what he would do with the money, Bellow said, "I have the thought to endow a chair in some university for a writer." He never did.

Seven months later, he was back with a second novella, *The Bellarosa Connection*. He found the brief form congenial; he no longer had the stamina for long books, he confided to Adam. And he liked getting into print fast. A paperback novella was more like a long story in a magazine than a book. *The Bellarosa Connection*, like *A Theft* a Penguin original with a $6.95 cover price, sold about the same number of copies.

But if Bellow made few inroads in his efforts to achieve a wider audience, the second book was a great improvement over its predecessor. It was a strange, idiosyncratic work. The ruminative unnamed narrator, who directs a vaguely defined institution called the Mnemosyne Institute in Philadelphia, is an elderly Jew, the son of Russian immigrants, who now lives alone in a vast, lavishly furnished house. As he looks back over his life, he finds himself dwelling on the fate of Harry Fonstein, a distant relative, and his wife, Sorella, memorable chiefly for her bulk. Sorella is not merely a large woman: She is monumentally large, "a mountain of lipoids," "biologically dramatized in waves and scrolls of tissue"; her overworked heart, challenged to supply blood to "so extensive an organism," undertakes with each beat "a bold operation, bigger than the Turkish waterworks."

The Polish-born Harry is also afflicted with a physical anomaly, less sensational than his wife's but equally significant: One of his legs is shorter than the other, and he wears an orthopedic boot. This handicap would have doomed him instantly in the Nazi death camps had he not managed to escape during the war to Italy, where he was saved by the efforts of the real-life impresario Billy Rose—the Bellarosa of the title—who financed an underground operation to smuggle Jews out of Europe. The story centers around Harry's subsequent attempts to thank Billy Rose for saving his life and Rose's adamant refusal to meet him.

Bellow had only a brief encounter with the real Rose, on a trip to Jerusalem, but it wasn't hard to conjure up a character out of the legend; Rose was "already nine-tenths fictionalized," he told a writing class at the University of Florida. "He was a creature who had excreted a legend about himself. Beneath it all was a sad little guy who was very unhappy with himself. Blue. There are many people of that kind." Andrew Gordon, a member of the class, suspected their illustrious guest was offering a veiled self-description.

Whatever affinity Bellow had with Rose, a lyricist, nightclub owner, and tabloid columnist right out of the pages of Damon Runyon, was strictly biographical; they were both sons of Jewish immigrants, much married (Rose, too, had five wives), ambitious to make a name for themselves in the arts. But it was the septuagenarian narrator, death-haunted and alone, who spoke for Bellow. In the course of the story, the narrator impulsively decides to track down the Fonsteins, only to discover that they're both dead, along with everyone else who figured in the Billy Rose saga. His job is to remember them: "If you have worked in memory, which is life itself, there is no retirement except in death."

Bellow was proud of his phenomenal memory, the way he could quote Sydney J. Harris's high-school poetry by the yard and rattle off the names of all his grammar-school teachers in Chicago sixty years before. But he was aware that his capacity for remembering the past was sometimes a substitute for preserving it. Incapable of establishing deep emotional ties with the people who had meant the most to him, he "put them in storage," in "a mental warehouse." As he wrote of the narrator in *The Bellarosa Connection*: "If he loved them, then how could he find it in his heart to check them in his locker and lose the key? When he tries to find these people he loves so much, they've all been filed away. If you live long enough, you'll do this to people. You say, 'Yes, I've got them inside me.'"

In the book, the narrator relates a terrible dream he had, in which he was struggling to climb out of a deep pit:

> Despair was not principally what I felt, nor fear of death. What made the dream terrible was my complete conviction of error, my miscalculation of strength, and the recognition that my forces were drained to the bottom. The whole structure was knocked flat. There wasn't a muscle in me that I hadn't called on, and for the first time I was aware of them all, down to the tiniest, and the best they could do was not enough.

And what was the nature of this devastating revelation? "I was being shown—and I was aware of this in sleep—that I had made a mistake, a lifelong mistake: something wrong, false, now fully manifest."

The Bellarosa Connection was the book Bellow had been longing to write ever since *The Victim* over forty years before, the book that finally grappled with the issue of how an American Jew should respond to the Holocaust. Over the years, Bellow had expressed regret that while the catastrophe of the death camps had been unfolding in Europe, he had been living out the ambitious hopes of his generation in America. Like the narrator of his new book, he condemned himself as innocent, frivolous, "an immature unstable Jewish American" who had knocked around Greenwich Village picking up Bennington girls in the midst of a world-historical event that redefined forever what it meant to be human: "You were equal, you were strong, and here you could not be put to death, as Jews *there* had been." But it "suffocated" him to dwell on the Holocaust. "I didn't want to think of the history and psychology of these abominations, death chambers and furnaces," protests the narrator of *The Bellarosa Connection*.

In a letter to Cynthia Ozick written in the late 1980s, Bellow offered a concise account of his own dilemma as a "Jewish" writer:*

> It's perfectly true that "Jewish writers in America" (a repulsive category!) missed what should have been for them the

---

*The occasion was a review of Ozick's novel *The Messiah of Stockholm* by Robert Alter, in which Alter criticized Ozick for not dealing directly with the Holocaust.

central event of their time, the destruction of European Jewry. I can't say how our responsibility can be assessed. We (I speak of Jews now and not merely writers) should have reckoned more fully, more deeply with it. Nobody in America seriously took this on and only a few Jews elsewhere (like Primo Levi) were able to comprehend it at all. The Jews as a people reacted justly to it. So we have Israel, but in the matter of "higher" comprehension—well, the mental life of the century having been disfigured by the same forces of conformity that produced the Final Solution, there were no minds *fit* to comprehend. And intellectuals like Alter are trained to expect and demand from art what intellect is unable to do. (Following the foolish conventions of high-mindedness.) All parties then are passing the buck and every honest conscience feels the disgrace of it.

I was too busy becoming a novelist to take note of what was happening in the forties. I was involved with "literature" and given over to preoccupations with art, with language, with my struggle on the American scene, with claims for the recognition of my talent or, like my pals of the *Partisan Review*, with modernism, Marxism, New Criticism, with Eliot, Yeats, Proust etc.—with anything except the terrible events in Poland. Growing slowly aware of this unspeakable evasion I didn't even know how to begin to admit it into my inner life. Not a particle of this can be denied. And can I really say—can anyone say—what was to be done, how this "thing" *ought* to have been met? Since the late forties I have been brooding about it and sometimes I imagine that I can *see* something. But what such broodings may amount to is probably insignificant. But I can't even begin to say what responsibility any one of us may bear in such a matter, in a crime so vast that it brings all Being into judgment. To assess and assign responsibility as Alter seems to do (as if he were referring to an understandable phenomenon) is a mistake, to say the least. "Metaphysical aid" as someone says in *Macbeth* (God forgive the mind for borrowing from such a source in this connection) would be more like it than "responsibility"; intercession from the spiritual world, assuming that there is anybody here capable of being moved by powers nobody nowadays takes seriously. Everybody is so "enlightened." By ridding myself of a certain amount of enlightenment I can at least have thoughts of this nature. I entertain them at night while rational censorship is sleeping. Revelation is, after all, at the heart of Jewish understanding, and revelation is something you can't send away for. You can't be ordered to procure it. Alter, when he talks about our "obligations" puts himself into the field of procurement and "procurement" is a bureaucratic concept.

That he may have failed to comprehend the fathomless depths of human evil haunted Bellow always; but there was perhaps another, more personal motif in the "merciless brutality" revealed to Fonstein in his dream: the recognition that, in some unspecified yet profoundly troubling way, his creator had fallen short. In the dream, the narrator is the victim, unable to absorb the blows that life deals out. But he also suffers a deep sense of personal failure: "I couldn't call on myself, couldn't meet the demand, couldn't put out."

Janis Freedman had been ever more visible in Bellow's life since their trip to Israel in the spring of 1987. They spent that summer together in Vermont, and when Bellow went to the White House early in the new year to receive an award from President Reagan, Freedman was by his side. By then, she had moved into the apartment on Dorchester, and Bellow was again contemplating marriage. After four wives, it wasn't something he did lightly; there were intense discussions about the advisability of such a move with Maggie Simmons, who, if she couldn't marry Bellow herself, could at least judge the suitability of other potential wives. In the end, he decided to take another chance.

They married in August 1989. Bellow was seventy-four and Janis was thirty-one.

Some of Bellow's friends thought it was a *shonda*—a scandal. How could he marry such a young woman, practically a girl, at his age? And what did she gain? She would give up her childbearing years to an elderly man, only to end up his nursemaid. To Adam Bellow, Janis Freedman was the last in a succession of mother figures, the legacy of his father's overly dependent relationship with a mother who died before he achieved independence from her. "My father needed to be taken care of," said Adam—and that need accounted for his many marriages.

Outwardly, Janis seemed docile and demure, comfortable in the role of dutiful wife. On a campus visit, she accompanied Bellow everywhere. "When he spoke before [Padgett] Powell's class, she sat dutifully, hands folded, like Nancy Reagan listening to a speech by the Gipper," one student recalled. At a summer picnic in Vermont, Bellow asked Janis to fetch his cap from the car, and as she trotted off he said, with only the slightest tone of irony, "There's a good wife."

But she was a more substantial young woman than she may have appeared to be to those who saw only her youth. She was herself a formidable scholar; invited by the Committee on Social Thought to lecture, she gave a talk on Flaubert that Bellow pronounced "a real triple feature." Her essays and reviews, which turned up in *Partisan Review,* were informal, lively, and direct, if somewhat edgily defensive. "No doubt there will be a bitchy review in one of the 'literary' papers by a militant defender of the feminist faith," she wrote of a later Philip Roth novel, defending him against anticipated charges of sexism. "After that the morally righteous will have to go back to the newspapers for their daily outrage-fix."

Her main work, though, was to nurture and protect her distinguished husband. To friends, it was evident that they were close in a way Bellow had never been with his other wives. He could still be irascible, but Janis possessed the emotional resilience to weather his moods. "Her devotion to him—her delight in him—is so heartfelt," Philip Roth observed. "When he says something funny, she says, 'He's always like that.' It's like the delight you take in your child."

In the fall of 1989, Bellow accepted an invitation from Boston University to teach there for a semester. He and Janis set up house in a furnished apartment owned by the university on Bay State Road, beside the Charles River. They liked Boston. It was a civilized city, with stately homes and tree-lined boulevards, and the Bellows were a popular couple. Bellow's speaking appearances around town drew large crowds. Speaking at the Kennedy School in Cambridge, he filled the hall. And when he gave a reading at the Tremont temple in Boston on a rain-swept evening in November, a big crowd turned out despite the weather and greeted him with tremendous applause. Bellow read from "A Silver Dish."

Early in the new year, he spoke to a reporter from The Boston Globe. He was in a reflective mood as he considered his "twilight" years: "Before I was embattled. Narcissism changes as you get older. In 10 or 15 years I'll be dead. I won't be here to make a fuss. I won't be here to guard my republic with a sword. As you get older, you become more impersonal yourself." It was a revealing comment: Narcissism changes; it doesn't disappear.

That sad fact of old age, the dwindling of one's ranks, was now upon Bellow. The deaths of friends had become a regular event. "Life is running a lot thinner," he lamented. He delivered a moving eulogy for Sydney J. Harris and attended the funeral of Edith Tarcov in New York. Then Sam Freifeld died. The two Tuleyites had never patched things up after Bellow's acrimonious divorce from Susan, but he took the news hard. When Marilyn Mann, Freifeld's second wife, encountered Bellow at a performance of *The Dybbuk* in Skokie not long afterward, he was "visibly shaken," she recalled. "They're really going," he told her.*

In his conversation, old age was a persistent theme. He was "too old to fly" back and forth across the Atlantic, he told Daniel Fuchs, explaining his reluctance to attend a conference on his work in Heidelberg. Life was almost over for him, he had taken to saying; the last act was at hand. "Do you think I'll live ten more years?" he plaintively asked Stuart Brent.

He was moderate in his appetites, a great tea-drinker, and he was on a regimen devised by Dr. Harry B. Demopoulos—the famous "Dr. D." whose vitamin "Performance Packs" were popular among movie stars and business moguls. There was no medical evidence for Dr. D.'s claim that his pills offered protection against "free radicals"—atoms with unpaired electrons, which can damage cells—but this didn't stop Bellow from blurbing *Formula*

---

*He was a selective mourner. When Irving Howe died, Bellow wrote to Al Glotzer, "I didn't think well of his talents or of his plans for personal advancement. I can't say that he succeeded in combining Socialism and Jewishness with any sort of originality. As an editor of Dissent, he struck me as rather quaint, like an old-fashioned lady who still cans her tomatoes in August." He was annoyed that Howe had given him "a cold nod" at Edith Tarcov's funeral.

for Life, a book to which Dr. D. contributed, as a cure for "the premature slipping away of vital mental powers."

Jonathan Rosen, a young writer who came to Chicago to interview him for the *Forward,* found Bellow in good shape. He showed up for lunch in "a brown fedora, a silk suit threaded with red and blue, a red and white bow tie, a pink shirt and pink socks." Bellow was in an expansive mood, reminiscing about how his father used to read aloud from the old Yiddish *Forward* at the dinner table and giving his views on "the crisis culture," the excess of media stimulation that had put Americans under stress: "Hearing him think aloud is like hearing a famous tune from the radio suddenly sung in person. It may not be the national anthem but it is still a familiar part of the culture—an American song, optimistic in spite of itself."

He still cut a vigorous figure around town, dropping in at the mayor's office at city hall and lunching at the Bismarck Hotel, a celebrated pols' hangout down the street. In the company of his friend Eugene Kennedy, he "mooched around," attending hearings of the city council—"the greatest show on earth," Kennedy called it—and showing up at the office of the Chicago Crime Commission; a photograph of the two "notables" appeared in the commission's journal, *Searchlight.*

There was a certain innocence about their forays into the notorious underworld of Chicago politics. When the two writers decided to embark on an investigative story about a mob figure reputed to have made illicit donations to one of Alderman Edward Vrdolyak's failed mayoral campaigns, a lawyer crony of Bellow warned him off the case: "He thought we were a couple of dumbbells," as Bellow put it ruefully.

But he did more than dabble in local politics. When there was a principle at issue, he could be courageously outspoken. A case in point came in the furor over Steven Cokeley, a black demagogue on the city council who made public statements in the late eighties claiming that a conspiracy of Jewish doctors was spreading AIDS in the black community. After Eugene Kennedy was attacked in the *Chicago Tribune* for an editorial he had written denouncing Cokeley, Bellow defended his friend in a long, eloquent letter to the paper. (To its credit, the *Tribune* featured it on the editorial page.) Speaking out against Cokeley's "illiterate mob incitement" had been a brave act, Bellow argued, not a betrayal of the city's interests. "Does no one remember Stalin and his 'Jewish doctors' plot? Has everyone forgotten Hitler?"

Bellow's letter in the *Tribune* was datelined "Brattleboro, Vt." After renting a house in West Halifax, a secluded hamlet near Brattleboro, for several summers, he had built a house of his own, deep in the woods outside of Jacksonville, a tiny town near the Massachusetts border. Completed in 1989, it was a large, salmon-colored dwelling, two stories high, in a plain neocolonial style; Bellow had no architect, relying on a local builder. He liked the area, he said, because it reminded him of Lachine and of the summers he'd spent as a child in Valleyfield, Quebec. And he liked the remoteness of his plot of land, tucked away on a dirt road that wound past ponds with pink lilies and old white-clapboard farmhouses. Pointing to a little cemetery in the woods a mile down the road from his house, he would gloat, "My nearest neighbors!"

Bellow's sense of exclusion, so powerful to begin with, was exacerbated by his physical distance from the centers of cultural influence. He had a litany of grievances: *The New Yorker* had turned down his talk on Mozart; the editor of *The New York Times Book Review* didn't like his work because she was "a feminist." He was tartly—sometimes brutally—dismissive of other writers. Reading Nadine Gordimer, he remarked, was "like gagging on a Kotex." He no longer made any pretense of keeping up. He hadn't read the critic James Wolcott's praise for *The Bellarosa Connection* in *Vanity Fair*; he didn't buy the Sunday *New York Times*: "My eyes are on eternity."

Still, he wasn't entirely cut off from the centers of power during his long summers in Vermont. There were daily phone dispatches from the culture front—Stanley Crouch calling with gossip from New York, Allan Bloom calling from Chicago to fulminate about the *New York Times* op-ed page. Videocassettes of the evening news arrived from Chicago, courtesy of Eugene Kennedy. Nor did he lack for visitors. He had persuaded Walter Pozen to build a house in West Halifax, and they met for coffee every morning when

Pozen was in residence. Most weekends, the house was filled with guests: Bette Howland, Zita Cogan, Martin Amis, sons, and grandchildren. William Kennedy arrived from Albany one day in a white stretch limousine that amazed the citizens of Jacksonville as it negotiated the tortuous and muddy back roads; with him was Jack Nicholson, who owned the film rights to *Henderson the Rain King*.

The country life agreed with Bellow. There was a garden in the front yard that he and Janis tended and a swimming hole out back, as well as a writing studio where Bellow worked in the mornings. In the afternoons, he picked raspberries in the woods and bicycled on the dirt roads. The only real hazard was the local black-bear population—when he and Janis were out in the woods, they parked their Range Rover by the side of the road and put Mozart on the tape deck at high volume to scare them off. On one unnerving occasion, a bear clambered onto the porch of Bellow's studio and peered at him through the screen door. "I was writing a story. He watched me. I watched him. He was thinking it over." Finally, the bear ambled off, and Bellow got back to work.

Bellow's rural wardrobe was a curious amalgam of farmer and dandy. He showed up at the post office or the Jacksonville general store in a worn, multipocketed jacket and khakis, sporting a railroad cap or, sometimes, a bandanna; but he also had on polished black leather shoes with red tassels. Around his neck he wore an ascot—bow ties were banished for the summer. He looked well in the country, rested and fit. His face was wrinkled, and he had grown slightly hard-of-hearing, but he was still vigorous enough to dig up boulders around the property, heavy labor that he kept up until his eighties.

Vermont was a refuge from the hard streets of Hyde Park, which had grown harder over the years. When he and Janis were in Chicago, Bellow felt like a prisoner in his fortress on Dorchester, unable to walk freely in the neighborhood where he'd spent most of his years over the last half century. Chicago had become a "barred and gated city," he complained to Zita Cogan, who lived in a Mies van der Rohe high-rise on the lake and had also grown cautious about going out, especially at night. Bellow was anxious if Janis was even a few minutes late getting home; sometimes he didn't leave the apartment for days at a time.

In May 1990, about one hundred of Bellow's friends and relatives received an invitation to his seventy-fifth birthday party, to be held on Saturday, June 9, at Le Petit Chef in West Dover, Vermont, a few miles from the Bellows' summer home in Jacksonville. The RSVP card was to be sent care of Janis's parents in Toronto: "Mum's the word. It's a SURPRISE."

Janis was determined to assemble an inclusive guest list. John Auerbach traveled all the way from Israel; Al Glotzer and Zita Cogan were part of the entourage from Chicago; there was a Russian cousin from Riga; Maggie Simmons; Eleanor Clark; Harriet Wasserman; Saul Steinberg, who flew in from the Hamptons by helicopter; and three generations of family members, including Dan and Adam, nieces, nephews, and grandchildren.* Janis had taken over the Inn at Marlboro for the guests, so she invited the innkeeper to the party, along with a local architect and the Bellows' groundskeeper.

The guests had been instructed to arrive a half hour early and were herded into a back room to wait. Janis had told Bellow that she didn't feel like cooking that night and persuaded him to take her out to dinner. When they walked into the restaurant at seven, "Whammo! great screams and cheers," as one of the guests remembered the moment. Bellow seemed genuinely surprised. He gazed around the room at the faces that composed a collective portrait of his life, and his face grew red. "It was very Chekhovian," said Philip Roth. "People got up and burst into tears and sat down." The cousin from Riga gave a toast in Yiddish; Bellow sang a Yiddish song; Maggie Simmons wept. The meal was lavish— champagne, smoked salmon, and a birthday cake made of Belgian chocolate. It was a happy event, but also melancholy—"a lot of shaky old men with very young wives," Vicki Lidov, the widow of Arthur Lidov, noted bitterly.

Early in October, Mayor Richard M. Daley threw a belated seventy-fifth birthday party for Bellow at the Art Institute, to

---

*Gregory, who had just been east to visit colleges with his daughter, skipped the occasion.

acknowledge the major public role he had played in the city's life. Allan Bloom, who had flown in from Paris for the occasion, was the master of ceremonies. There were tributes and a rousing medley of Bellow's favorite opera tunes, sung by a "whalish woman and a double whale" in white tie and tails whose "thrilling, room-bursting notes"—in Richard Stern's comic description—enthralled the guests. The mayor spoke—"very awkward and touching," Stern recalled. It was a more civilized era than the one in which Bellow had grown up. The mayor's father, Richard J. Daley, had made a point of displaying his contempt for high culture. This mayor was different; he was an enthusiastic sponsor of the arts and a friend to the city's cultural institutions. Bellow had returned the favor, traveling around the city with Daley during his mayoral campaign in 1989 and speaking at his inauguration. "Saul is to Chicago what Balzac was to Paris," said Bloom. "He has always understood that even if you are on your way from Becoming to Being, you still have to catch the train at Randolph Street."

A month later, he received a medal from the National Book Foundation "for distinguished contribution to American letters," at the fortieth anniversary ceremony of the National Book Awards' annual gala. *Publishers Weekly* described Bellow's acknowledgment speech as "a short, rather peevish address" in which he managed to disparage both writers and editors, who constituted the major portion of his audience that night. "Not everyone who writes books is a writer," he said; "good writers grow scarcer with every decade." Bellow seemed to find the business of receiving honors a chore: He had won so many medals, he complained, that he felt like a Russian general. He was greeted by a standing ovation when he rose to speak, reported the correspondent for *PW*, "but finished to considerably milder applause."

He also spoke at an evening in honor of the Czech president and playwright Václav Havel at the Cathedral of St. John the Divine. It was a glittering occasion, attended by Barbara Walters, Henry Kissinger, and other important people. Lewis Lapham, the editor of *Harper's*, offered a cutting account of the proceedings. "Bellow was glad to know that when Havel was in prison, he had remembered to read Bellow's novel *Herzog*. As a reward for Havel's intelligence and taste, Bellow had brought an autographed copy of the novel which he hoped the obviously perceptive president of Czechoslovakia would accept as a token of his esteem." At the dinner afterward, Bellow was so intent on meeting Havel that he presented himself at the president's table, copy of *Herzog* in hand.

In England to give a lecture at Oxford, Bellow had a private lunch with Margaret Thatcher at 10 Downing Street. "It didn't go tremendously," admitted George Walden—the minister of higher education and a friend of Allan Bloom—who had arranged the meeting. The prime minister was tired and talked too much. "What I wanted to ask you, Mr. Bellow," she began, "was about blacks in Chicago. Now, I've always felt . . ." And she proceeded to deliver a twenty-minute monologue. "She didn't need me," Bellow said. "She answered her questions herself."

The praise and attention he received somehow never felt like the right amount to him: It was either too little or too much. When Stuart Brent wrote in one of the newsletters he sent to regular patrons of his Michigan Avenue bookstore that Bellow was "the greatest writer since Tolstoy," he couldn't understand why Bellow was offended. Studs Terkel explained: "He thinks he's greater than Tolstoy."

Bellow fully expected biographies of him to be written. "My father would be very unhappy if he thought no one was going to write his biography," said his son Adam. But not yet. "I still consider myself a growing tree, and I'm not ready for the sawmill." Biographers, he said in a memorable image, were "the shadow of the tombstone falling across the garden."

There was also the issue of privacy. "Can't I retain my poor porous figleaf?" he said plaintively. And there were others to consider. "*I* don't give a damn," he insisted. "It's really for Janis's sake. It hurts her to read about all this. She doesn't think I should do it." When one of his most persistent chroniclers, Ann Weinstein, tried to interview his relatives in Montreal, he drew the line. She didn't need his permission to write about him, he stressed: "You no more require blessing from me than any anthropologist gets from a tribe of Eskimos." All the same, it "distressed" him to be an object of research, and she must leave his relatives out of it.

"They have never seen me as a celebrity, they think of me as a kid, and I greatly prefer the latter to the former."

But his own tacit collusion with biographers made it harder to fend them off. No sooner had the indefatigable Mark Harris dropped from sight than Ruth Miller, Bellow's friend for half a century, prepared to weigh in with *Saul Bellow: A Biography of the Imagination*. It was a curious hybrid, part biography, part academic *explication de texte*. Bellow had given Miller complete access to the vast archive of his papers in the Regenstein Library, a collection to which he added frequently. He had invited her into his life, knowing that after their long talks she went home and wrote down the best approximation she could manage of what he'd said. He urged his publishers to allow Miller to quote from his work without charge. He even sent her copies of letters he deemed significant.

Miller described herself as "one of Bellow's girls"—whether in the literal sense or not is a question that elicits conflicting testimony. In any event, they were close; Miller had grown up in the same West Side of Chicago milieu as Bellow, in the same period, and he referred to her as "my closest literary confidante for fifty years." When he signed a contract with Harper and Row for a collection of his nonfiction writings, it was with the condition that Miller edit it.* When Sigmund Koch, a professor of psychology at Boston University, subjected him to an eight-hour "research interview" as part of a project on artistic genius, Bellow insisted that Miller join him before the camera. And when she showed him the final draft in Vermont during the summer of 1990, he embraced her and said it was "the best book, bar none, written about him."

But at the last moment, when the manuscript had already been typeset, he suddenly changed his mind. The book was too personal. "She couldn't resist the gossip," he complained. It had been his understanding that Miller was going to write about his books; instead, she'd written about his books in the context of his life. As the book made its way from manuscript to bound galleys,

---

*That book, provisionally titled "Occasional Pieces," never appeared, though Miller assembled it. A different version, put together by Bellow himself, was published several years later under the title *It All Adds Up*.

he grew increasingly skittish: He didn't want his sons' names mentioned; he objected to references to his clothes. "He got nervous and panicked," said Michael Denneny, Miller's editor at St. Martin's Press. "He didn't want this, he didn't want that. He behaved like a cranky old man; he was used to getting his way." Denneny, a former Bellow student in the Committee on Social Thought, hoped he would be able to mediate between subject and biographer. It wasn't to be. (Did Bellow recall his skirmish with Denneny, who had tried to intervene on behalf of campus militants in the sixties?) In the end, Bellow denied Miller permission to quote from his letters or papers and enlisted a lawyer to make sure he got his way. When the book appeared in March 1991, it was full of monotonous paraphrases; the long excerpts from Bellow's letters to Owen Barfield and others that had been in the bound galleys were gone.

In her preface, Miller wrote: "I understand that Bellow disagrees with much of what I say in this book and, I am told, now denies having said many of the things I quite clearly recall him saying, things I often recorded in my journal at the time." But it wasn't so much what he said as her version of how he said it that offended him. He didn't like the way he sounded in the book— and, in truth, Miller did have a tin ear. She made Bellow sound earnest and solemn ("My soul goes into this work I do"); the play-fulness and sparkle of his conversation, captured so vividly by Mark Harris, was nowhere in evidence. "Between the time she'd left my apartment and the time she got home, she forgot what I'd said, so she made it up herself," he complained. If he'd been wary of biographers before, he was bristlingly suspicious now. The book was "crude and gross," he maintained, "dumb, vulgar, seedy." He'd been "burned." After Miller's book came out, he ordered his archive closed to scholars unless they had obtained his express permission to use it.

He suffered further biographical embarrassment over Joseph Epstein's story "Another Rare Visit with Noah Danzig." From the number of letters in his first and last name to the distinguishing physical characteristics—Danzig's "hooded" eyes and "thin, high-bridged nose," his sexual vanity, even his Volvo—the figure was utterly recognizable as Bellow. Like Bellow himself in his fictional self-portraits, Epstein made Danzig "tall" and—a gratuitously insulting variant from the truth—"quite bald"; in all other respects, he stayed close to the facts. Even the jokes Danzig told were Bellow's. So were the women in his life. Epstein's account of his promiscuous hero's problematic love life got close to the heart of the matter:

> Fame, especially artistic fame, can be a splendid aphrodisiac, and Noah seemed to want to take advantage of his resources in this line whenever possible. But I was often surprised to discover how unambitious he was on this front, despite a persistent flirtatiousness. He just didn't seem to get, at least in my view, dollar value. His fame ought to have brought him dazzling and fascinating women, but among the seven or eight he coupled with during the time I knew him, all had rather emphatic flaws: they were hopelessly neurotic or shy or witless or idiotically subservient to him. He seemed to be searching for uncritical adoration, but was unable to find even that. No wonder Noah Danzig couldn't create convincing women—he knew so few.

The only thing missing from the story was any sympathy for Danzig. Like Bellow's own portraits of ex-friends, it was satire untempered by generosity. Perhaps the flaw was Epstein's motive: He was getting revenge for a crony. "Maybe twenty or thirty people in the world ever knew that I was the model for Morty Feldman in *Hochfelder's Revenge*," the narrator writes of his unflattering cameo role in one of Noah Danzig's novels—about the same number who would have been able to identify the model for Magnasco, the pushy art critic in *Humboldt's Gift* who turns Humboldt over to the police ("overweight, round-faced, young in calendar years only, steady, unflappable, born to make progress in cultural New York"), as Epstein's good friend, the art critic Hilton Kramer.

Bellow dismissed the story as "gross, moronic, and clumsily written." "I could do worse to them, but it wouldn't amuse me," he wrote to Ruth Wisse. *Them*, not *him*: Bellow was convinced—not without reason—that Epstein was part of a group, loosely identifiable as "the *Commentary* crowd," that had it in for him. Kramer and Epstein were the leaders. They were both public neoconservatives, a designation Bellow eschewed; they were both critics, a vocation that he regarded with considerable distrust; and they were both regular contributors to *Commentary,* yet another strike against them. The magazine's editors, Norman Podhoretz and his deputy, Neal Kozodoy, were on Bellow's enemies list. "Norman and Kozodoy have decided that I don't exist!" Bellow complained to Wisse. "They review Gore Vidal and ignore me."*

In the fall of 1991, Viking issued a collection of three "tales" entitled *Something to Remember Me By;* it included *A Theft, The Bellarosa Connection,* and the title story, which had first appeared in *Esquire* the year before. In it, Bellow again revisited the event that he regarded as the central trauma of his life: his mother's death in the winter of 1933.

In the story, it was a freezing winter, just like the "frightful January" recalled by Herzog. The now elderly narrator, Louie (a name perhaps intended to commemorate Bellow's own recently deceased cousin, Louie), is thinking back to the time in his long-ago adolescence when his mother died. Until that terrible and momentous time, he had lived a typical second-generation Chicago Jewish boyhood: hanging around Hammersmark's bookstore, working for a florist, necking in the park with his high-school girlfriend, reading T. S. Eliot at the kitchen table late at night. In the story's key episode, Louie delivers flowers to a wake and comes away haunted by the image of a dead girl laid out in her coffin. Seeking solace, he drops in at his brother-in-law's dental office on Argyle (where Bellow's own brother-in-law had an office), only to stumble upon a naked woman on the examining table in the adjoining doctor's office. "The cells of my body were like bees, drunker and drunker on sexual honey." After he succumbs to the woman's advances and accompanies her to her room, she throws his clothes out the window to a partner waiting in the alley below, forcing

---

*If only they had. In the July 1993 issue of *Commentary,* Kramer published a dismissive essay about Bellow, noting that he had "dropped out of the Bellow fan club" when *Humboldt's Gift* was published—without mentioning his own unflattering appearance in the book. Bellow combed through the letters column hunting for replies in his defense but found none. "They must be killing them in the office," he concluded.

him to find his way home in a borrowed dress. "In short, you got mixed up with a whore and she gave you the works," comments the bartender in the speakeasy where the hapless boy seeks refuge. The pathos of the situation is leavened by gentle humor: The bartender offers to help Louie out with carfare if he'll take home a drunk from the bar—a comic reversal of fortune: "Instead of a desirable woman, I had a drunkard in my arms."

The real irony goes deeper; Louie's grief over his mother is intensified by his pressing sexual needs, in pursuit of which he succeeds—like so many of Bellow's characters—in becoming a victim, humiliated by a prostitute in his moment of greatest vulnerability. And as Louie hurries home, the other compelling theme of Bellow's childhood emerges: He knows that if his father beats him, it will mean that his mother is still alive; otherwise, he would be too distracted by his own grief to bother. In this way, Bellow managed to turn his father's abuse into something positive, a sign that tragedy had—even if only momentarily—been averted. Pain was converted into pleasure.

Alternating with these violent and traumatic scenes were touchingly gentle ruminations on the unfathomable fact of death. "I had had only the anonymous pages in the pocket of my lost sheepskin to interpret it to me," Louie muses, referring to a decrepit philosophy book that he carries with him on his floral delivery rounds: "They told me that the truth of the universe was inscribed into our very bones. That the human skeleton was itself a hieroglyph. That everything we had ever known on earth was shown to us in the first days after death. That our experience of the world was desired by the cosmos, and needed by it for its own renewal." Nothing can explain the deep mystery of individual existence—the life that briefly animates the dying mother, the father who beats his wayward son, the kindly bartender and the whore, only to be extinguished forever. "Well, they're all gone now, and I have made my preparations." Louie ends his tale, apostrophizing his own son: "I haven't left a large estate, and this is why I have written this memoir, a sort of addition to your legacy." It's an ending as quietly elegiac as that of Joyce's "The Dead."

In a gracious introduction to the trilogy, Bellow praised brevity, offering up one of his favorite quotations, from the nineteenth-century English clergyman and wit Sydney Smith: "Short views, for God's sake, short views!" Especially in this day and age, Bellow wrote, when the world was inundated with distracting data—"cable TV, politicians, entertainers, academics, opinion makers, porn videos, Ninja turtles"—you have to grab readers by the lapels if you want to hold their attention.

Critics noted and applauded this "Chekhovian brevity," as one critic described it. John Sutherland, writing in *The Times Literary Supplement,* called the title story "a gem." In the space of thirty-five pages, Bellow had managed to capture the greedy sexual hunger of adolescence, the bewildering obliteration worked by time, and the regret for life's squandered opportunities. Sutherland predicted that "Something to Remember Me By" would stand high in Bellow's achievement "when the final reckoning comes." And he added: "The tone of the tale implies that the author does not think that such reckoning will be too long delayed."

Perhaps not; but as he moved into the second half of his eighth decade, Bellow showed few signs of slowing down. On October 25, 1991, despite protestations that he was "persona non grata" at Harvard—apparently the honorary degree he'd received didn't count—he went to Cambridge to celebrate the inauguration of Neil Rudenstine's presidency, sharing the stage with Seamus Heaney, Toni Morrison, and the cellist Yo-Yo Ma. Sporting a brilliant peacock-blue bow tie, he read for nearly an hour from "Something to Remember Me By," interrupted by much laughter and applause.

Six weeks later, he was in Florence, giving a talk on his beloved Mozart at the Teatro Comunale. It was a bravura performance, animated by Bellow's deep familiarity with the life and works of his favorite composer, whose operas had thundered on his hi-fi as he wrote his books. "What is attractive about Mozart is that he is an individual," Bellow told the rapt audience. "He learned for himself (as in 'Così Fan Tutte') the taste of disappointment, betrayal, suffering, the weakness, foolishness and vanity of flesh and blood, as well as the emptiness of cynicism. In him we see a person who has only himself to rely on." Thus did even Mozart become another version of Augie March.

His remarks about Mozart's utter indifference to his surroundings also had personal resonance. The only thing that mattered to Mozart, Bellow asserted, was his work. The composer changed residence eleven times within a single decade. Bellow quoted Einstein: "Mozart as a man was nowhere truly at home: neither in Salzburg, where he was born, nor in Vienna, where he died." The originality that came from "God-knows-what source" exacted a price. The cost of art was high. The consistency of Bellow's themes is striking. Art as an expression of freedom, the loneliness of the artist, the persistence of "snubs and defeats"—they were the same near the end of his life as at the beginning.

In April 1992, he attended a conference on "Intellectuals and Social Change in Central and Eastern Europe" at Rutgers University. Bellow spoke on "Transcending National Boundaries." Sponsored by *Partisan Review,* the conference took him back to his own literary beginnings, when the relationship between politics and literature had been the subject of ardent debate. Among those in attendance were Joseph Brodsky and Czeslaw Milosz; the Hungarian novelist and essayist György Konrád; Norman Manea, a Romanian writer who had been forced into exile; Ralph Ellison; and Susan Sontag.

On a panel with Ellison, Milosz, and Brodsky, Bellow appeared frail and tired. "In the middle of the night, I woke my wife, and she kindly agreed to take some notes for me," he explained to the sparse but reverential audience. They were notes about the limits and opportunities afforded by "the American experience," which offered "unexampled prosperity, comfort, and consumerism, together with the terrible threat of instability, disharmony, and spiritual misery." In the realm of freedom, America had delivered on the promise of its original revolution, but it had failed to address the spiritual needs of its citizens. Behind the Iron Curtain, the curtailment of freedom gave freedom meaning; in the West, where you could say and do anything, "freedom was something of a joke." The collapse of communism was an event to be celebrated, but it also meant that the West would be forced to confront the emptiness of its own values: "That's the picture that came to me in the night."

Bellow's mainstay in these years was Allan Bloom, who lived next door in the Cloisters. Bloom was a wealthy man now, enjoy-

ing the substantial profits from his surprise bestseller. In his roomy
twelfth-story apartment, surrounded by Persian carpets, Chinese
chests, Hermès porcelain, and a priapic Greek sculpture he'd
picked up in Paris for "only" five thousand dollars, Bloom sat in a
silky Japanese robe fielding phone calls from disciples all over the
country, supplying fresh evidence of the decline of the American
university.

It was a sadly brief moment of glory. In the fall of 1990, Bloom
fell ill with a mysterious ailment that was at first diagnosed as
Guillain-Barré syndrome. No one came out and said what many
suspected: that Bloom had AIDS. (A frequenter of the sex empori-
ums of North Halsted Street, Bloom confessed to Edward Shils
that he "couldn't keep away from boys.") The following spring,
Bellow canceled a long-planned trip to Paris in order to care for his
friend. "Saul was my salvation," Bloom attested. "He was there
every day. Sometimes I hallucinated. We watched a show on Jewish
comedians."

Sustained by the cartons of Marlboros that he had dispatched
Janis to bring him, Bloom dictated his last book, *Love and Friendship*, a diffuse but impassioned ramble through the books he and
Bellow had taught over the previous twelve years: *Pride and Prejudice, Madame Bovary, Anna Karenina, The Red and the Black*.
For Bloom, the deepest theme of these disparate books was the
imaginative transformation wrought by the workings of eros in
our lives. "The necessity in love and friendship is that of nature,"
he summed up in a moving epilogue. "Once entered in this world,
we are free of all other constraints, but the power of the beloved or
the friend over our whole being does not itself admit of free choice
in the usual use of the term, and there seems to be no act of the will
involved. We simply walk into a magnetic field and are drawn by
it."

The book appeared posthumously. On October 7, 1992, Bloom
died of "peptic-ulcer bleeding, complicated by liver failure,"
according to a university press release. He was sixty-two. At the
memorial service, held in the Piser Chapel on the North Side,
Bellow was among the speakers who eulogized the beloved teacher
before a grieving throng of colleagues, friends, and disciples—"a
hundred young men in elegantly tailored dark suits," as one of the

mourners described the turnout. "It was like a yeshiva," remarked James Redfield.

After Bloom's death, Chicago seemed more desolate than ever to Bellow. "Every time I walk out the door I have to go by the house," he told Hillel Fradkin, a young scholar who had worked closely with Bloom on his final book. Eager to get away, he and Janis made the postponed trip to Paris. They sublet an apartment on the Left Bank from the poet William Jay Smith and visited with Bellow's old Chicago friends who had long ago settled in Paris, H. J. Kaplan and Julian Behrstock. But Bellow was haunted, as he wandered the familiar neighborhoods where he'd lived more than forty years before, by the shade of his beloved friend.

In the early nineties, Boston University began making aggressive overtures to Bellow. John Silber, the president of the university, had lured two other Nobelists to BU, Derek Walcott and Elie Wiesel. An outspoken conservative who shared Bloom's conviction that American universities had been taken over by left-wing ideologues, Silber was politically compatible with Bellow; they had known each other since 1970, when Silber was an administrator at the University of Texas and Bellow was editing *Anon* with Keith Botsford. Silber had since recruited Botsford to Boston, along with two of Bellow's other friends from that era: the classicist William Arrowsmith, whom he had first met at Princeton, and the French literature scholar Roger Shattuck. And Boston appealed to the Bellows after their experience in Paris, where they had gotten used to walking the streets without fear; Boston, they fancied, would be a kind of American Paris, a city where you didn't have to huddle behind locked doors.

At first, Bellow denied the rumors that he was contemplating a change of address. He was furious when "Kup" ran an item in his column speculating about the significance of a lengthy two-part interview Bellow had given to *Bostonia*, Botsford's university-funded journal. Did this mean the Chicago novelist was Boston bound? "Just asking." Kup, as usual, had good information. In the spring of 1993, Bellow accepted Silber's offer. He would join the faculty of BU beginning in the fall semester.

Bellow's friends were stunned. "Who will you have to talk Yiddish with?" demanded Stuart Brent. "Not those *farshtinkener goyim*" in Boston. How could he forsake the city that had shaped his character, provided him with a literary identity? To his millions of readers around the world, Bellow and Chicago were virtually synonymous.

Some of his friends suggested that he felt neglected by the university to which he'd given so many years. As a professor emeritus since 1985, Bellow had to contend with the diminished status that was the lot of retired professors, Nobel Prize winners or not. It bothered him that the university wouldn't give him a full-time secretary. Moreover, he had only a modest pension, and BU was prepared to pay him a star's salary: $155,000 a year to teach two classes. Dave Peltz offered another explanation for the move: "fresh adoration."

Bellow maintained that Boston was closer to Vermont, and he wanted to spend more time there. But there was perhaps an even more compelling motive for pulling up stakes: To stay in Chicago, a city of ghosts and aging friends, was to face his own mortality. Confronted with a fate he couldn't alter, he did what he had done all his life: He left. He often spoke of his relationship with Chicago as a marriage. Going to Boston was merely repeating a pattern.

In Chicago—despite his protestations that he lived there in obscurity—Bellow's departure was news. Eugene Kennedy wrote a column lamenting the move, and John Blades, who unofficially covered "the Bellow beat" for the *Chicago Tribune*, produced a dispatch under the headline BELLOW LEAVING CHICAGO IN BODY BUT NOT IN SPIRIT. Blades found Bellow in "buoyant spirits" when he called him for a quote. He denied that he bore the University of Chicago any ill will. For thirty years, he'd had "a wonderful time," he maintained: "I thought I was due for a change. Lots of people leave Chicago in my time of life, and nobody thinks anything of it." Blades also got a quote from Mayor Daley, who lamented the departure of "a good friend" and expressed the hope that Bellow would keep a voting address in Chicago.

Over the Memorial Day weekend, Bellow attended the sixtieth reunion of his Tuley High School class at the Radisson Hotel in Lincolnwood. Their ranks had inevitably thinned since the fiftieth reunion, but 125 graduates of the class of '33 turned up. Toward the end of lunch, Bellow rose and gave a brief speech in praise of his teachers. He wore an unpressed light-gray suit; a lime-green bow tie, alarmingly askew; and over the suit, a windbreaker. On this occasion, he looked his years.

After lunch, he got in a taxi and headed for O'Hare. He was on his way to Boston.

31

*I have begun in old age to understand just how oddly we all are put
together. We are so proud of our autonomy that we seldom if ever realize
how generous we are to ourselves, and just how stingy with others.
One of the booby traps of freedom—which is bordered on all sides by
isolation—is that we think so well of ourselves. I now see that I have
helped myself to the best cuts at life's banquet.*

—SAUL BELLOW, *"Ralph Ellison in Tivoli,"*
Partisan Review, fall 1998

*Beyond the age of eighty the perspectives of a lifetime wither and shrink
like all else. You feel that your mortal car is straddling the median line
and the righthand wheels are rumbling in* this *world with the other
two in a different one.*

—SAUL BELLOW, *"All Marbles Still Accounted For"*

I N BOSTON, the Bellows settled into a university-owned apartment on Bay State Road, overlooking busy Storrow Drive and the Charles River and close to Fenway Park, a few doors down from where they'd lived in the fall of 1989. "Just look for the Citgo sign," Bellow directed visitors. "Baronial ceilings and staircase, the polished wooden floors and plush rugs make it feel like the private chambers of a British palace," noted one of the many reporters who trooped to Bellow's door for an account of his latest transition. Yet like all his residences, it had a temporary feel about it, the heavy antiques scattered forlornly about the long, empty room. For Bellow, it was "almost too grand."

His office, on the sixth floor, in the department of theology, was equally makeshift. "His solid brown desk was old, the windows behind it somewhat grimy," wrote John Blades in the *Chicago Tribune*. "There were no couches to sink into, no paintings on the walls, just two flimsily framed pieces of paper: one his National Book Award for 'Herzog,' the other the Harold Washington Literary Award. There were three black filing cabinets, one wall of books and four cardboard boxes on the worn purple carpet. It felt like the office of a cheap detective." The author came off better than his surroundings: "Drinking tea in the twilight shadows of his townhouse, Bellow might be a dethroned and exiled potentate looking back on the ruins of a fallen empire. But his words, though often regretful, are neither lachrymose nor bitter. If there's any lingering sadness, he conceals it behind a distant smile, which often turns to hearty laughter." He still wrote every morning, he told the reporter, working from nine-thirty until one-thirty or two—"Then I'm just washed out for the rest of the day."

The Bellows had plenty of friends to visit: Monroe Engel and the Bells, Daniel and Pearl, in Cambridge; William Phillips, who had moved *Partisan Review* up to Boston, under the sponsorship of Boston University;* and Bellow's sidekick of four decades, Keith Botsford. But he missed his old home: In the BU corridors, he was often spotted in a faded University of Chicago baseball cap.

By November, he was back in Chicago to attend the unveiling of a bust of himself at the recently opened Harold Washington Library. Speaking before an audience of two hundred, including Mayor Daley, Bellow graciously conferred his approval on the bronze sculpture by Sara Miller, a local real-estate agent who had turned her hand to art late in life; Bellow had sat for her one afternoon just before his departure, allowing her to measure his head while he watched a Bulls game on TV. "My brother always said I'd be a bust," he joked. As for the statue, he quipped to a reporter, "I'm sorry Picasso wasn't around to do one of me with two noses. For one nose, it's fine."

He clearly welcomed the attention. As he approached his eightieth birthday, Bellow was troubled increasingly by the suspicion that he was becoming obsolete. His literary generation, the New York intellectuals who had helped bring the Jewish immigrant experience into the American mainstream, was no longer as significant a force in the culture as it had once been. Other, younger writers from other traditions and backgrounds and ethnic groups—Robert Stone, Toni Morrison, Amy Tan—now occupied center stage. "I had no idea our time would be so brief," Bellow

---

*Phillips had been rehabilitated by the sheer fact of his survival; there weren't enough contemporaries left to squander too many friendships on old feuds.

noted sadly. Most of the old *Partisan Review* gang was gone by now, and he felt his own readership had dwindled. "I had a cheering section once—no longer."

He continued to give talks, packing the hall at the Ninety-second Street Y in New York, where he read from *The Bellarosa Connection.* In the summer of 1994, he participated in a round-table discussion at BU, "The State of Letters," with Joseph Brodsky, Seamus Heaney, Christopher Ricks, and Derek Walcott. His rhetoric had grown ever more heated. On one occasion, he launched into a Bloomian polemic against the legacy of the avant-garde "artists who make packages of bridges and monuments by covering them in wrapping paper; or the beneficiaries of Federal Arts projects whose idea of art is to pass out their government cash to poor Mexicans." He made no secret of his distaste for mass entertainment. "Is rap music in any respect a folk art?" he asked rhetorically. "Can we rank the appetite for Nintendo or rock and rap CDs or Mortal-Kombat video games with the literary passions of an earlier time?" Literature was over because Saul Bellow was over.

Yet his reputation was stronger than ever. In the spring of 1994, *The Sunday Times* of London had published the results of a poll it had undertaken of Britain's leading writers and critics. "Who is the greatest living novelist writing in English?" the editors asked, noting that the recent deaths of Anthony Burgess, William Golding, and Graham Greene had depopulated the literary landscape. Were there any Grand Old Men (or Women) of Letters left? Bellow came out ahead, with ten mentions, followed by Updike with eight, and Muriel Spark with five.* Among those putting Bellow at the top was Salman Rushdie, who maintained that if any book deserved to be labeled the Great American Novel, it was *The Adventures of Augie March.*†

---

*Others cited were Philip Roth, Anthony Powell, V. S. Naipaul, and Jeanette Winterson, who nominated herself.

†Four years later, when an august board of scholars and writers that included Daniel Boorstin, William Styron, and Arthur Schlesinger, Jr., was convened under the auspices of the Modern Library to select the one hundred greatest novels of the twentieth century, *Henderson* occupied the twenty-first spot, *Augie* the eighty-first.

It wasn't only in fiction that Bellow had distinguished himself. That spring, Viking brought out a collection of his essays under the title *It All Adds Up* that provided an impressive exhibit of his nonfiction over the years. Subtitled *From the Dim Past to the Uncertain Future,* it was a lean and highly readable volume; he had culled a rigorous selection from the extensive prose he'd published over a half century. Missing were any of his book reviews from the forties or his early essays on American writers, but most of the important journalism was there and the best of his public lectures, along with five examples of a genre that he was increasingly called upon to produce these days: the eulogy. Bellow was a master of the commemorative art, sketching his dead friends' characters with a few salient details: Isaac Rosenfeld gesturing "like a Russian-Jewish intellectual, a cigarette between two fingers"; Allan Bloom in his Japanese robe. He was equally adept at the large generality, summing up the spirit of an age in a few deft strokes. In an essay written originally for *Forbes,* "There Is Simply Too Much to Think About," he returned again to the theme of modern distractedness that had long occupied him. Knowledge, once the possession of an elite, had become a mass phenomenon purveyed by "artists of information," he argued, referring to the TV anchormen whose version of reality had come to dominate the collective consciousness. But he was more bemused than alarmed by these developments. "When you have completed your self-education and mastered your trade, you are likely to find that your time has run out," he wrote in his introduction, paraphrasing Henry James. It is that note of humility that makes Bellow's occasional journalism so appealing.

It All Adds Up was more an elegiac summing-up than a polemical exercise, and reviewers responded generously to its even tone. "Saul Bellow has shaped and compelled the modern imagination," wrote Malcolm Bradbury on the front page of the London *Sunday Times*'s book section on September 11, 1994, expressing the general view. "It is notable that a novelist who began work in the 1940s, dominated the 1950s, outraged the 1960s, won Nobel acclaim in the 1970s, quietened, but did not cease writing in the 1980s, should occupy this magical position. But the homage is justified."

Toward the end of March 1994, Bellow came to New York to participate in a panel discussion on anti-Semitism at the Ninety-second Street Y. On the morning of the event, he gave an interview to David Remnick, a staff writer for *The New Yorker* (and later its editor). They met at the Lotos Club, where Remnick found Bellow "out of sorts." Asked how it was going in Boston, the novelist answered wearily, "Not so hot. I feel the rupture. Janis does, too. I felt that I had given Chicago the best years of my life, as they say in divorce court"—a curious metaphor, given the fact that it was Bellow who had left the city. (But then, it was Bellow who had left most of his marriages.) He wasn't much charmed by New York either. Upper Broadway was overrun with drug dealers and panhandlers, "some foreign writer's invention of an American slum."

Bellow had other reasons for his dour mood. He was taking a lot of heat, as one of his Chicago characters might have put it. Earlier that spring, *The New York Times Magazine* had published an excerpt from a forthcoming memoir by Brent Staples, a member of the *Times*'s editorial board, about growing up poor and black. The son of an alcoholic truck driver, Staples had beaten the odds (his drug-dealer brother was murdered) and had entered the University of Chicago as a graduate student in psychology. He didn't have an easy time of it. In the *Times* piece, he described the terrorizing effect that he, a tall and powerful-looking black, had on the whites huddled in their academic ghetto surrounded by black slums. Walking the dark, empty streets of Hyde Park, Staples was identified as a menace by the color of his skin—not a fervent admirer of Bellow's work who could quote long passages of the novels from memory but a mugger from the other side of the Midway. Intimidated by Bellow's immense reputation and angered by the harsh description of the black pickpocket in *Mr. Sammler's Planet* who exposes his "large, tan-and-purple uncircumcised thing" to the helpless Sammler, Staples took to haunting the entrance to Bellow's gated fortress on Dorchester. "I wanted to trophy his fear." One night, the young future author bagged his prey:

I turned out of 58th Street and was passing in front of the Cloisters when I saw him: a little man in an overcoat, hurrying along
the sidewalk about twenty yards ahead of me. . . . He threw
back a glance, wisps of white hair flying, then picked up his
pace. He showed surprising bounce getting up the stairs. When
I reached the tower, I saw only his shoe disappearing through
the gate.

Bellow was outraged by Staples's depiction of him as a cowardly
victim; he even had Walter Pozen call the *Times* and threaten legal
action. But the piece struck a nerve. Bellow was "obsessed with
black-Jewish relations," according to Richard Stern. "He couldn't
leave it alone." To friends, he went on about how many credit
cards the government of Chicago had issued to black city workers,
and he was troubled by the phenomenon of the Chicago-based
black nationalist Louis Farrakhan. "There is this sort of attitude
among the blacks," he told Remnick, responding to Farrakhan's
anti-Semitic outbursts: "'Whatever else we may be, whatever
handicaps we may labor under, we are, nevertheless, not Jews.'"

Still, it made him nervous to get embroiled in these volatile
issues. When Remnick brought up the subject of racial politics,
Bellow "winced" and said he hoped there was "an undangerous
way" to talk about it: "There's a certain tangible, palpable fear of
putting your foot in it now." There were blacks you could talk to,
he stressed, citing Ralph Ellison, Stanley Crouch, and William
Julius Wilson; but when blacks resorted to blaming their people's
failure to rise on "a Jewish conspiracy," dialogue was no longer
possible.

To Remnick, Bellow insisted that he would continue speaking
out despite efforts to intimidate him. "I write as I write. If I'm
going to take heat because of it—well, that's the name of the
game." But his anxiety was manifest. Just two weeks before his
interview with Remnick, he had published an op-ed piece in the
Times that seemed designed to placate his critics. Entitled
"Papuans and Zulus," it addressed the controversy Bellow had
stirred up with his notorious remark, "Who is the Tolstoy of the
Zulus? The Proust of the Papuans? I'd be glad to read him."
Bellow sought to rebuff the subsequent characterizations of him as
racist. "Nowhere in print, under my name, is there a single refer-

ence to Papuans or Zulus. The scandal is entirely journalistic in origin, the result of a misunderstanding that occurred (they always do occur) during an interview. I can't remember who the interviewer was." But he did recall, a paragraph later, that it was "a telephone interview" (it was in fact conducted in his University of Chicago office) and that "immediately" after it he had remembered that "there was a Zulu novel after all: 'Chaka' by Thomas Mofolo, a profoundly, unbearably tragic book about a tribal Achilles who had with his own hands cut down thousands of people, including his own pregnant wife." Bellow had read it in his student days, in translation.

Yet he had been accused of "contempt for multiculturalism and defamation of the third world." Why him? "I am an elderly white male—a Jew, to boot. Ideal for their purposes." Bellow had meant no harm, he insisted; he had once been a student of anthropology, and he was simply trying to draw a distinction between literate and preliterate societies. His critics were Stalinist—determined to prosecute anyone who disagreed with them. When he was growing up, Americans had been allowed to exercise a sense of humor about sensitive ethnic issues: "We were still able to kid ourselves." But now "rage" had taken over: "The rage of rappers and rioters takes as its premise the majority's admission of guilt for past and present injustices, and counts on the admiration of the repressed for the emotional power of the uninhibited and 'justly' angry. As a onetime anthropologist, I know a taboo when I see one. . . . We can't open our mouths without being denounced as racists, misogynists, supremacists, imperialists or fascists."

That Bellow himself felt compelled to disavow or temper his remark about the Zulus was seen by some neoconservatives as evidence that he, too, had caved in to the pressures of the liberal establishment. And in truth, there was something "phony" about his recantation, as Peter Prescott noted in *The New York Times Book Review:* How could anyone who had read Bellow's novels be surprised that he would say such a thing? But his impulse to put distance between himself and his funny if ill-considered jest was also in keeping with his lifelong resistance to classification. Despite his contempt for academic liberals, "swingers" who ingratiated themselves with the cultural trends of the sixties, Bellow didn't think of himself as a conservative. He had remained, in his own equivocal description, "some sort of liberal." The trouble was that liberalism had become "mindless medallion-wearing and placard-bearing." Political correctness, he told a reporter, posed "a serious threat to political health, because where there is free speech without any debate what you have is a corruption of free speech, which very quickly becomes demagogy. It's a bad moment in the history of the country."

The old political questions, the ones that had enlivened the discourse of the *Partisan Review* gang, were still very much present to his imagination. Introducing an anthology of fiction from the magazine that William Phillips brought out around this time, Bellow harked back to the revolutionary fervor that had been the rage in his Greenwich Village days, when he and his literary cronies hungered for "action, change, transformation." He liked to reminisce about those days with Al Glotzer, who was still producing essays on the Comintern well into his eighties. Writing to congratulate his fellow Tuleyite on the publication of his book about Trotsky, Bellow remarked:

> I have observed that most people are incapable of altering their early beliefs. Most, I've noticed, think of their first education as a sort of investment made during their best, most vital years. Many of the Marxists I've known are unwilling to give up the labor they put into mastering difficult texts. They tend to hang on to the very end.

He admired the fact that Glotzer wasn't "immobilized in the drops of Marxist amber that fell on so many of us in the forest primeval of Revolution," and that he hadn't succumbed to "political Alzheimer's."

The panel discussion at the Ninety-second Street Y in the spring of 1994 offered Bellow a convenient public platform for the expression of these views. But when the moment came, he was reluctant to speak out. Joined on the stage by Cynthia Ozick, the English critic John Gross, and William Phillips, who was now close to ninety and still vigorous with his Yeatsian flowing white hair, Bellow told the same stories he'd told over and over—about reading Spengler as a boy, his conversation with Agnon, Henry

James's disdain for Lower East Side Jews in *The American Scene.* He seemed more concerned with his legacy than with current events. "The record will show what the twentieth century made of me and what I made of the twentieth century," he declared to the full house in a quavering voice. When a member of the audience raised the volatile issue of black anti-Semitism—"a hot subject on a cool evening," as Phillips described it—Bellow was distinctly skittish. The subject had "been under a taboo for so long" that he was reluctant to discuss it. "With lights shining in my eyes I don't think I should actually tell you what I think of these things." When the evening drew to a close and the crowd headed toward the exits, he looked relieved.

A month later, he was off to Sint Maarten in the West Indies with Janis, hoping to finish the novel he'd been working on for the previous two years, "All Marbles Still Accounted For," the ruminations of an octogenarian "about some of the questions which never stop gnawing the heart of humankind," as Bellow described it. It very nearly turned out to be his last trip anywhere.

One night, after a dinner of red snapper, Bellow became violently ill and passed out in the bathroom of their rented apartment on the beach. Janis managed to get him on a plane to Boston, but he was so ill he had to lie down in the aisle. In Boston, an ambulance met him at the airport and rushed him to the intensive-care unit of Boston University Medical Center. For three weeks, he lay in a coma, an IV in his arm and an oxygen mask over his face. "I had some brilliant hallucinations, so great that what I was writing dwindled by contrast with these visions," he recalled. Janis was by his side every minute; she slept in the hospital and didn't change her clothes for a week. She wrote down every dosage of heparin, lifted his oxygen mask to swab his mouth. At first, the doctors thought he had Legionnaires' disease or dengue fever. It turned out he had heart failure and double pneumonia caused by ciguatera poisoning from eating contaminated shellfish. "I was given up for dead. The doctors told me so themselves."

Two years later, Bellow provided a vivid and detailed account of his illness to a convention of doctors in Chicago: "To put matters plainly, I had to decide whether I should or should not make efforts to recover. I had for long weeks been unconscious, my body was wasted—unrecognizable. My sphincters were haywire. I could not walk. It's humiliating to an old man to find he can't dress himself or feed himself or get around independently." Then, switching to the second person and finally to the first, as if struggling to confront the experience directly: "People begin to pass you and you are not even able to raise your voice to stop them. My days were a morass of negligence. I was demoralized and drifting and losing heart in slackness and disorder. I've never been so ill before. It was my first time as an old man." At one point, he clambered out of bed with tubes and needles attached and crashed to the floor, like Woody Selbst's dying father in "A Silver Dish." The nurses had to put him in a restraining vest.

His recovery was nothing short of miraculous. It had truly been, as he said in later years, "a Lazarus experience." For the next few weeks, he was on a walker and had to be held up in the shower. "I'm afraid I'll fall over when I pull my pants on in the morning, and I feel wobbly walking," he confided to a reporter. James Wood, the literary critic of *The New Republic,* met him at a dinner and was stunned by the degree of Bellow's enfeeblement: "He could hardly lift a salad bowl." Four months after he got out of intensive care, he was back in the hospital for a gall-bladder operation. But he was determined to survive, just as he had clung to life as a child in a Montreal hospital: "The choice I made at eight remained effective seventy years later."

His illness had taken a toll. The following summer, he replied to Richard Stern, who had congratulated him on a story in *Esquire:* "When I got out of the hospital (crawled out) last winter I ran a test or two—naturally—to see whether there was a charge still in the batteries. And of course repetitions—deploying the old troops—wouldn't do."

The story that Stern was referring to, "By the St. Lawrence," appeared in July 1995. Written two months after Bellow's recovery, it concerned an old man by the name of Rob Rexler who had been born, as Bellow had, in Lachine, of Russian immigrant parents. The latest in a distinguished line of brainy intellectual protagonists, Rexler is a historian who has written about "cosmopolitan Berlin, about nihilism, decadence, Marxism, national socialism." Like his author, he has just recovered from a near-fatal illness and has decided to go see Lachine again. In the story, a Chekhovian masterpiece of poignance and economy, Rexler hires a chauffeur-driven Mercedes to conduct him to his birthplace, a low brick house surrounded by vacant lots, after which he strolls down to the Saint Lawrence River to revisit old haunts: "So many landmarks were gone. The tiny synagogue had become a furniture warehouse."

Against the backdrop of this single episode, Bellow rehearsed the history of his own near-fatal illness as a child, converting his bout with pneumonia into polio but otherwise remaining faithful to his early brush with death, and to his second encounter many decades later: "He had been unconscious under the respirator for an entire month. . . . Intensive-care nurses had told him that the electronic screens monitoring his heart had run out of graphs, squiggles and symbols at last and, foundering, flashed out nothing but question marks."

Interspersed with these premonitions of mortality is the memory of an episode from his adolescence—the day Rexler, age seven or eight, had gone for a ride with his cousin Albert and been left in the car for hours while Albert disappeared into a white-pillared bungalow from which the boy noticed women coming and going. Then he remembers going to visit the dying Albert years later (much as Bellow had gone to visit Sam Gameroff on his deathbed) and finding him weakened by leukemia: "In the upside-down intravenous flask a pellucid drop was about to pass into his spoiled blood. If other things could be as clear as that fluid."

In his late years, Bellow spent more and more time in Vermont, stretching the summer months to include May and September and driving up with Janis on vacations. Vermont was "The Good Place," as he liked to call it, a refuge from the stresses of urban life, which can be particularly oppressive to the elderly. It also had the feel of home. (The only other home Bellow had ever owned was the old mansion in Tivoli.) In Boston, the Bellows had moved into a house in suburban Brookline. But the house, a rental owned by the university, was oddly situated, adjacent to gritty Beacon Street, where streetcars made their grinding clatter, and just down the street from an auto-repair shop. Bellow's indifference to his domestic surroundings had rarely been more starkly displayed than in this tastefully if sparely furnished stucco house in a nondescript neighborhood.

Its aura of transience was offset by the stolidity of Bellow's Vermont establishment. What he liked best about Vermont was the quiet. It was peaceful in the woods, miles from the nearest town. "When the birds awaken you, you open your eyes on the massed foliage of huge old trees," he wrote in a paean to his rural bower: "Should the stone kitchen be damp, as it may be even in July, you bring wood up from the cellar and build a fire. After breakfast you carry your coffee out to the porch. The dew takes up every particle of light. . . . And when you walk down to the pond, you may feel what the psalmist felt about still waters and green pastures."

For his eightieth birthday, on June 10, 1995, Janis gave him a party at the house in Vermont with all three sons and their children.

Among the many journalists who beat a path to Bellow's door was a writer on assignment for *The Sunday Times Magazine* of London, Bryan Appleyard. His profile, accompanied by a brooding photograph of his subject, appeared on the cover of the May 21, 1995, issue; the headline read ANGRY OLD MAN. "Bellow is 80 on June 10 and his face has taken on the look of Buster Keaton's in old age—deep-eyed, wispy-haired, lined and replete with lived life," wrote Appleyard. In the interview, Bellow came across as only intermittently angry. He railed against *The New York Times* for running in its Sunday magazine a mildly critical piece on the new intellectual right—and featuring his son Adam, editor in chief of the conservative-leaning Free Press, in a group photograph on the cover: "The ideals and principles of the 1960s are the permanent ideals of the New York Times." But for the most part, he was in a tolerant and reflective mood, commenting with a certain bemusement on his happily married state ("I got lucky this time"), his fortunate survival, and the role of religion in his life. "In truly serious moments when I'm not being frivolous or ironic, I really do feel a turning toward God in some way," he said. "I'm gullible about spirituality; I have a weakness for it."

The terms in which Bellow described his religious impulses—weakness and gullibility—were equivocal at best. But as he passed the threshold of old age, his yearning to believe began to overshadow the innate skepticism that had made him such a dilatory student of Owen Barfield. Even now, it was no conventional god that received his attention but an Emersonian version of the "soul"—the god that resides within oneself. "I think the first thing to do is to locate your soul and find out what it has to suggest," he told a reporter. "The farther you get away from the promptings of your soul, the more trouble you're in." But he also claimed to believe in a higher being that he referred to, with only a trace of irony, as the Great One. When Melvyn Bragg asked him, on the BBC's *South Bank Show,* if he believed in God, he answered firmly yes. And when another interviewer, Jack Miles (who later wrote the classic *God: A Biography*), asked if he prayed, Bellow answered that he did. Pushed to describe the manner of his prayer, he described it as "a casual checking in at universe headquarters, at night, as I pull up the covers."

In the end, religious feeling, for Bellow, was engendered less by a belief in God than by fear and bafflement over his own death. Was this really a club he couldn't refuse to join? "The scientific rationality of death is that it's simple annihilation, obliteration," he said.

> The body returns to the sphere of Matter. I have my doubts about the scientific view. There are some people who are so interesting, so clever, so gentle, so beautiful that it's impossible to accept that death will annihilate them. Someone is missing who used to be there. You are forced by your scientific outlook to accept their death as natural. Something in me can't accept that. I rebel. So I think of them as if they were still alive. Then I wonder when I die how their memory will continue.

Like Henderson, who tried to communicate with his dead mother and father by playing the violin, Bellow could never quite believe that the dead were truly and utterly dead.

"What does old age avail," wrote Delmore Schwartz, "but the best seats at the funerals of friends?" Every month seemed to bring news of another death in Bellow's circle. Back in the spring of 1994, he had mourned the passing of Ralph Ellison. "I loved Ralph, and this came as a blow," he told a reporter from *The New York Times*. Bellow was almost too choked up to talk: "When you get to be this age, it comes to you with the regularity of a drum tattoo." Hyman Slate died, too. A few months later, it was Zita Cogan, who was soon followed by Yetta Barshevsky Shachtman, the class orator and high-school crush.

Bellow's eulogy for Yetta, read by a friend at her service, was a moving ode to the passing of his generation: "There is something radically mysterious in the specificity of another human being which everybody somehow responds to. Love is not a bad word for this response." Evoking memories of Yetta's family on Spaulding Avenue, just around the corner from the Bellows', more than sixty years before, he conjured up images of her father, a carpenter whose "jalopy was filled with saws and sawdust"; her orthodox grandfather, "a short bent man with a beard that seemed to have rushed out of him and muffled his face"; and of Yetta herself, whose "militant, urgent" valedictory speech had electrified the class of '32. Bellow dwelled lovingly on the physiognomic details that distinguished Yetta from everyone else on the planet—her "Jewish beauty," "the small genetic accident that made one of her eyes seem oddly placed"—details that contributed to "the power of being Yetta."

He tried to make his peace with the dead and the soon-to-be dead. When Edward Shils, afflicted with cancer, was dying in the winter of 1994, Bellow asked to visit him. Like Isaac Braun in his story "The Old System," imploring his estranged sister to let him visit her on her deathbed, Bellow longed for a reconciliation, if only to acknowledge the transience of all human passions and endeavors. ("One after another you gave over your dying," Braun thinks. "One by one they went. You went. Childhood, family, friendship, love were stifled in the grave.") It was no use. Shils refused to see him.

The book he was writing reflected—as his books always did—his current preoccupations, which were now centered almost

582 | JAMES ATLAS

entirely around old age and death. "All Marbles Still Accounted For" concerned an elderly gentleman by the name of Hilbert Faucil, the wealthy publisher of a national tabloid with the Jabberwockian name *Brillig's Bulletin*. Returning from a trip around the world to visit his sister in Miami (Bellow's own sister, Jane, lived there), Faucil is first seen "shuffling" through Miami International Airport, sockless, a visor over his eyes. Badgered by customs officials, who call him "grandpa," he imagines answering them, "I've been in outer space, among the stars. This trip was arranged by Arthur C. Clarke. I wasn't as old as you see me when I left. Those time-warps do it to you. And now please don't bug me. I just stepped off a flying saucer that landed way out in the tall grass and I've had a long hot walk."

Faucil is a typically introspective Bellovian hero, devoted to "reviewing the basic, the deepest, the finest layers of our feelings." Like Bellow, he has suffered a devastating illness and survived. His descriptions of being in a coma in intensive care, with his girlfriend Chickie by his side, and of the hell of emergency rooms possess a hallucinatory vigor. But the book—or what remains of it—is also very funny. Venturing onto Collins Avenue, Faucil remarks that it looks "as if all the hospitals, nursing homes and mental institutions in Dade County had discharged their patients at the same moment." Lying in his hospital bed, he has a dream about his ex-wife, Vila—his "sixties wife"—who proposes that the couple freeze themselves through cryogenics and wake up in the twenty-second century, when people will live to be two hundred years old. "It's the only chance for our marriage," she argues. Faucil responds: "If I could be induced to marry you perhaps I could also be talked into being frozen for a century."

Just before Christmas 1995, Bellow returned to Chicago to give a talk at the university. Richard Stern, who hadn't seen him in several years, found him diminished but with his aura still intact. "I'd say Saul is about 75% of what he was a dozen years ago, maybe a bit less," Stern reported. "It varies. When we were alone, he was much of the old Saul, inquisitive, full of memories. . . . But this true Pharaoh of the imagination always assigns the little slave

Saul the job of hauling great intellectual boulders up to build a pyramid." His lecture, portentously titled "Literature in a Democracy: From de Tocqueville to the Present," was piled high with the usual references to Alexandre Kojève and Nietzsche, Wyndham Lewis and Dostoyevsky, until, Stern wrote, "the speech tottered and fell." Bellow's frailty was evident to the crowd of a thousand packed into Mandel Hall. He spilled a glass of water on the manuscript, lost his place, and kept muttering, "I'm not an intellectual." When he ended with the simple words, "That's all I've got," the applause was thunderous. THE BOTTOM LINE: CHICAGO LOVES BELLOW AND BELLOW LOVES CHICAGO, the *Tribune*'s headline summed up the event. For Bellow, naturally, it wasn't enough. "You're not lionized when you live here, only when you're a visitor," he complained to the paper's reporter.

Just after the new year he was off again, flying to Miami for Dan's wedding at the fabled Coral Gables Biltmore; his bride, Heather, was the daughter of a Miami physician. There was some anxiety about how Bellow and Susan would respond to being in each other's proximity after all these years, and Bellow was "a little sticky" the night before the wedding, one of the guests recalled: "He didn't come to the party Susan gave, claiming he hadn't been invited." But at the ceremony itself, he stood beside his third ex-wife, and the party afterward was festive. There was also an ex-girlfriend in attendance, who got drunk and made a spectacle of herself. Another guest, Margo Howard—the daughter of the advice columnist Ann Landers—described it as "a color war with wedding cake."

In April, Bellow flew to New York by himself to give a talk at Queens College. "This was my first solo journey and I regretted leaving Janis behind," he wrote Al Glotzer. "I am like you in my boyish rejection of elderliness (antiquity: why not come right out with it). You pack a snowball on a winter day and imagine taking a belly flop on *your* sled as we all used to do back in the beautiful twenties—I was ten years old in 1925. All that remains is the freshness of the impulse."

The old books continued to exert their magic spell. The living room of his house in Vermont was strewn with classics—Southey's life of Nelson, Hobbes's translation of Thucydides, *The Brothers*

Karamazov. At BU, he taught a course called "The Ambitious Young Man," going back to *Père Goriot, The Red and the Black, Great Expectations, Crime and Punishment, Sister Carrie,* and *The Great Gatsby.* But he tried to stay contemporary. He taught a course in new fiction, assigning Denis Johnson's *Resuscitation of a Hanged Man,* Philip Roth's *Operation Shylock,* Martin Amis's *Money.* Leon Wieseltier, visiting Bellow in Vermont, spotted on his bed the galleys of a new novel by David Foster Wallace, and he gave a blurb to Padgett Powell's *Edisto Revisited.* "I got tired of having people say to me, You old timers, you never pay attention to younger writers."

He also found the time and energy to start another literary journal. In the tradition of *The Noble Savage* and *Anon, News from the Republic of Letters* was a tabloid, published irregularly ("as often as we have good enough material to fill it"). On the masthead as coeditor was Bellow's longtime collaborator Keith Botsford. *News from the Republic of Letters* was not a sophisticated publication; it had the look of a college lit magazine, illustrated with artistic woodcuts and photographs, and featuring no advertisements and lots of white space. The contents felt a little hoary— Bellow's recycled lectures; a "Notebook" by Botsford, writing under the pseudonym "Pierre Bayle," author of a satirical seventeenth-century dictionary; and nepotistic contributions from the editors' stable of pals and ex-lovers—but it was still a brave effort, saucily irreverent and willfully oblivious to its own belatedness. A statement on the contents page read: "If you would like to acquire your citizenship, Saul Bellow and Keith Botsford welcome your adherence." And if not, not. The print run hovered around a thousand copies. "When I hear the literary fire bell ringing I stagger to my feet like an old fire horse," Bellow wrote Philip O'Connor, whose *Memoirs of a Public Baby* he had admired, offering up a terrific image of his unquenchable and lifelong passion.

He could still make news. On February 14, 1996, *The New York Times* carried a brief story in its publishing column headlined BELLOW MAKES A CHANGE. It wasn't a change of editors (or wives) this time but of agents. After twenty-five years, the paper reported, he was deserting Harriet Wasserman "to join the growing group of writers flocking to sign up with Andrew Wylie." A highly effective agent who commanded big advances for his clients and resuscitated their backlists, Wylie had amassed an impressive roster of clients, including Philip Roth, Norman Mailer, Salman Rushdie, and Susan Sontag. With Hamlet-like irresolution, Bellow denied that he was contemplating a change and even managed to cast himself in his favorite role: *He* was the victim; his agent was leaving him. To one of his foreign publishers, he scribbled an anguished note: "Harriet has cast me into outer darkness and no longer communicates with me." Meanwhile, he was instructing his lawyer to inform Wasserman that he had gone with Wylie.

Harriet Wasserman's own book, which appeared within a year of her dismissal, was a curious addition to the growing shelf of Bellow biography. Unable to decide whether her memoir was an homage or an act of revenge, she told embarrassing stories about the man for whom she had functioned, in Bellow's description, as "coach, manager, and trainer" for a quarter of a century—he was indifferent to his children and pathetically insecure about his work; he pocketed royalties that should have gone through her office; he was snappish, irritable, vain—while at the same time fawning over her client, "a man of genius, of high art and moral vision, an original thinker who has reached the pinnacle of his craft." Whatever its literary deficiencies, and apart from its rich store of anecdotes, *Handsome Is* portrays, more vividly than any other first-person account, the depth of Bellow's inconstancy. Ruminating on his mother's death, he says to Wasserman: "She didn't leave me; I left her." His failure to mourn, in other words, amounted to a desertion of the dead. No one could ever leave Bellow; he would leave them first, obviating the possibility of abandonment.

Wasserman's book was a late contribution to Bellow's public image as a fickle, contrary old man, vain and hypochondriacal; one wonders what revelations were contained in the pages razored out of the galleys circulated to reviewers by its publisher, a marginal house named Fromm International. It was an image Bellow did his best to maintain. He gave a blistering *Playboy* interview, sounding off indiscriminately at English departments ("the

profession has decided that we're better off without literature");
young writers ("Nowadays when a young man thinks of becoming
a writer, first he thinks of his hairstyle and then what clothes he
should wear and then what whiskey he's going to endorse"); California ("like an artificial limb the rest of the country doesn't really
need"); Bill Clinton ("a yuppie, a playboy . . . basically unseri-
ous"); and other writers (Nabokov was "a cold narcissist"; Gore
Vidal was "a good writer, he's just not as good as he thinks he is").
The tone of his remarks was heavy-handed, angry, and largely
devoid of wit; Bellow was out to settle scores. Of Truman Capote,
who had once suggested that Jews ought to be stuffed and put in
museums, he said: "That's where the little fairies like that really
belong, in Auschwitz on the general's staff, in the Auschwitz
barracks with a swagger stick." Liz Smith, quoting the best bits
from the interview, headlined her gossip column in the *New York
Post* SAUL BELLOWS HIS BILE.

In other ways, he had mellowed. Once a fugitive from the rigors
of family life, he now enjoyed having his children and grandchildren around him. ("Even they look a little wrinkled from time to
time," he joked to Al Glotzer.) He had grown more dependent on
his family. It pleased him that Dan had gotten a job as an editor at
The Rutland Herald and lived nearby with his new wife; he was
crushed when they moved to Seattle in the spring of 1998. Adam
was also a frequent visitor, arriving at the house in Vermont for
long summer vacations with his two children in tow. Having left
his job at the Free Press, he had at last set out on a career as a
writer and signed a lucrative contract for a book on nepotism. He
would work out his patriarchal issues in print.

Janis proved to be the wife Bellow had always longed for: steadfast, undemanding, utterly devoted to his needs. "Like any elderly
great man, Saul requires that his basic work be done for him,"
Richard Stern noted; and Janis was glad to do this work, considering it her chosen role in life to be the great man's guardian. She
had made sacrifices, subjugating her career to his, but her devotion
was unwavering, and he depended on her as he had never
depended on any of his previous wives. "He always wants to know
what I think, but I'm not really there to criticize," she told a
reporter, commenting on Bellow's practice of reading his work in

progress aloud. "It's not so much a reaction he wants as the sound of it being read aloud."

Susan, too, remained a presence in his life. She had taken to showing up at Bellow-related events—a talk by Daniel Bell about the New York intellectuals, a reading by Brent Staples. Bellow's long medical ordeal depressed her. She "couldn't imagine life without him," she told her friend Joan Schwartz. Shockingly, she was the first to go. On December 17, 1996, Susan died suddenly of an aneurysm in her apartment on West End Avenue. She was sixty-three. A heavy smoker with a family history—her father and grandfather had died young—she had been fatalistic about her health, convinced that she would come to a premature end. But it was a devastating blow to those who loved her. "She truly was the most radiant beauty I have ever seen," recalled Judith Barnard, a childhood friend: "People literally gasped when she entered a room. Her death was a shock."

When Dan broke the news to his father over the phone, Bellow wept. "Tell your mother I'm sorry," he said brokenly, the present tense a haunting reminder that it was too late to apologize. The funeral was held at K.A.M. Isaiah Israel Congregation in Hyde Park. Bellow offered to make the trip, but Dan thought it would be too much for him: "I didn't want to lose both my parents in the same weekend."

Bellow's work in progress, "All Marbles Still Accounted For," was eventually supplanted by a new novel, *The Actual,* about another "elderly gent" (as Bellow had taken to describing himself) "in the late phase of maturity": Harry Trellman, a dealer in "antiquities" who, like the author himself, had returned to Chicago after the war because of "unfinished emotional business." Trellman is another of Bellow's "first-class noticers," a reader of Jowett's *Plato* still trying to "crack the cipher" of reality, unable "to rid himself of the habit of watching for glimpses of higher capacities and incipient powerful forces." Like many of Bellow's other protagonists, Harry is "large."

The novel takes place during the course of a single morning and afternoon and features two other main characters: Sigmund Adletsky, an aged millionaire who has retained Trellman as an advisor, and Trellman's high-school sweetheart, Amy Wustrin, a divorcée who is the Adletskys' interior decorator. Trellman's attachment to Wustrin is reminiscent of Bellow's preoccupation with Eleanor Fox: "Half a century of feeling is invested in her, of fantasy, speculation and absorption, and imaginary conversation." He recognizes that he is entering his "final years," "a period of 'mature acceptance,' reconciliation, open-handedness, general amnesty," and this recognition colors his memory, tempering with nostalgia the disappointment of unrequited love: "There were still kitchens with onions and potato peels in the sink, and streetcars grinding on the rails." Even at this late date, after the passage of nearly seven decades, Bellow was transforming the pain of his early years in Chicago into a 1920s idyll. *The Actual,* he told a reporter, was a story "about the tenacity of early affections." The Northwest Side of his long-vanished youth, teeming with the ghosts of old lovers and friends whose aging he could forever postpone by resurrecting them in his imagination, was Bellow's utopia.

In the last scene, Trellman and Wustrin make a trip to the cemetery to attend to the reburial of her husband, Jay, and Trellman proposes to her, acknowledging that "it's not the best moment for a marriage offer." He doesn't want to miss a second chance.

It's a surprising finale, unprepared for by anything that's gone before; and its suddenness points up the sketchy, unfinished quality of the narrative—marred, like all of Bellow's later work, by improvisation and haste. But for all its quirkiness and plot-deficient meandering through scenes the narrator couldn't possibly have witnessed, *The Actual* has a certain pathos, even heroism. At eighty-one, the man who often said that he wrote as involuntarily as birds sang was still producing music. He hadn't written *The Actual* to display his wisdom, Bellow confessed, but "to prove a point: that I could still do it."

He was fully conscious of both the limits and the privileges afforded by old age. To James Wood, one of the most generous and sensitive appraisers of his work, he wrote a moving account of his situation:

> I had, a fanatical or enraged reader, studied over many decades gallery after gallery of old men in novels and plays and I thought

I knew all about them. But to be one is full of surprises. Let me see: there is Oedipus at Colonus, there is the old sculptor from Ibsen's When We Dead Awaken, there is of course King Lear, and also old Duncan in Macbeth and Polonius in Hamlet, and there are Jonathan Swift's Struldbruggs, the repulsive and unkillable old, there is old Count Bolkonsky in War and Peace, there is Father Zossima in The Brothers K, there is Gerontion, and Yeats in his final years. But all of this business about crabbed age and youth tells you absolutely nothing about your own self. . . . I can't even begin to say what it's really like.

Essentials, when I can find them, are the first order of business. Not a chance of course of "fulfilling" myself before I am called away but I do my damndest—hacking away at the penultimate words in the hope of grasping you-know-what. At last!

That he had accomplished something of a feat in producing a novel at all didn't spare him from the critics. When it came out from Viking in the late spring of 1997, the reviews were mixed. David Gates, writing in *Newsweek,* called the novel "thin gruel, with featureless characters and tin-ear dialogue," and even James Wood described the book as "slight . . . a ricochet from a talent that has already hit many targets." But Alfred Kazin, who had been reviewing Bellow's novels for nearly as long as Bellow had been writing them, found the novelist "sharp as ever," and Louis Begley, in *The New York Times Book Review,* called *The Actual* "the work of a great master still locked in unequal combat with Eros and Time." As Martin Amis, whose own maturing work had been so strikingly shaped by his mentor's idiom (he referred to Saul as "Soul"), put it: "Late Bellow has given way to Even Later Bellow."

When critics chose to put his work in a larger context, the news wasn't so good. Sven Birkerts, writing in *The New York Observer,* delivered himself of a long essay whose thesis was evidenced by the drawing that accompanied it, a cartoonist's rendering of Roth, Bellow, Mailer, and Updike as dinosaurs roaming a primeval forest. (Bellow was a pterodactyl.) It was entitled "Twilight of the Great Literary Beasts: Roth, Mailer, Bellow Running out of Gas." Birkerts wrote: "There comes a moment—it is scored in the evolving grain of things—when the balance between a father and son draws up even, holds for an instant, and then begins its slow tipping in the new direction." For Birkerts, the direction in which Bellow had begun to tip was unambiguously down.

He still gave interviews. He spoke to Mel Gussow of *The New York Times*, whose profile, accompanied by a photograph of the author standing beside the bookshelves in his BU office, appeared in the paper on May 26, 1997. And he still got out and about, especially after he had a pacemaker installed. In Toronto, he gave the Allan Bloom Memorial Lecture. "A spry and tidy man in a turquoise green shirt and thin-striped jacket, Bellow looked like a healthy fifty-five year old," noted a correspondent for *LRC: The Literary Review of Canada*. "He seemed invigorated by the prospect of reading to the large audience of more than three hundred that showed up that night." He loved returning home to Canada. Writing to Shulamis Yelin, who had sent him a collection of her stories about growing up in Jewish Montreal early in the century, Bellow reveled in her evocation of "those marvelous years" and the "nostalgic ecstasy" her book had induced. So powerful was the draw of his childhood that he devoted considerable effort, on a subsequent visit to the town of his birth, to locating Ezra Davis, the "roomer" in his family's house in Chicago more than seventy years before who had retired to a Montreal nursing home; he would have been close to one hundred by now. Not surprisingly, Davis was deceased.

On June 12, 1997, two days after his eighty-second birthday, Bellow attended a ceremony at the National Portrait Gallery in Washington at which a portrait of the novelist was unveiled. Donated by friends, it showed the guest of honor in an open-necked shirt, looking contemplative and relaxed. The portraitist was Sarah Yuster, from Staten Island. A cake with candles was brought out and "Happy Birthday to You" was sung, much to Bellow's embarrassment. "If this were a restaurant I would walk out," he grumbled. But he seemed gentle and somewhat chastened. "Life has a certain sweetness, and so does Bellow," reported David Streitfeld in *The Washington Post*. The speakers "tried to turn him into a marble bust while he sat in front of them," recalled Richard Stern, who described his old friend as "a bit fragile and osteoporotic but Jesus, when he got up and spoke for five minutes the marble dissolved and there was the unique *mensch*." In his speech, Bellow graciously deflected the notion that he was even remotely a media star. "Instead of fans chasing me in the street, I have people who deeply and earnestly appreciate my labors," he said, quoting the Bible: "See the man who is diligent in his work. He shall stand before kings." Then he gestured toward his portrait. "We don't have kings in a democracy, but this will do for me."

For Bellow, old age was as much an interesting phenomenon as an affliction. "Death's a challenge," he told a reporter from *The Sydney Morning Herald* with his innate resilience and optimism. "I've got to summon the guts to face it. I'm not in a flap. I'm curious." If he was Lear-like, it was less the doleful Lear than the elegiac Lear of act 5, unprotestingly resigned to senescence—"a foolish fond old man." He wasn't "a bred-in-the-bone curmudgeon," he insisted, extending forgiveness even to his critics. On the matter of John Updike, who had long been a torment to him, both as a critic and as the creator of Henry Bech, a Jewish novelist with signally unattractive traits, he had finally arrived at indifference: "He's welcome to the glory. I don't care. I've lived long enough not to be edgy about my reputation. It goes when you have the Lazarus experience—all the vanities take a beating then." And when a reporter asked him if he thought Norman Mailer deserved a Nobel Prize, he answered comically, "Well, I'd give it to him—if he had anything to trade."

He kept up with modern life, installing answering machines in his two homes ("Please leave your message, which we are panting to hear"); he signed petitions in *The New York Times* ("Only Ground Troops Will End Ethnic Cleansing in Kosovo"); made public appearances (a Hemingway conference at the Kennedy Library in Boston; a memorial service for Ralph Ellison at the Ninety-second Street Y); wrote essays (for the *Chicago Tribune*, *National Review*, *The New York Times*'s "Writers on Writing" series). He flogged *News from the Republic of Letters* on National Public Radio and corresponded with old friends, reminiscing about their Chicago days and stirring up old rivalries; to Dave Peltz, who had submitted a story to Bellow's journal, he wrote a stingy rejection letter ("your story toils on and you deal with problems nobody wants to hear about"). He compared himself to the Notre Dame song:

> Cheers, cheers for Old Notre Dame
> Listening to the drunkards mumble her name.
> Send somebody out for gin
> Don't let a sober person in.
> We stagger on but we never fall.

He was clear-eyed about his own achievements. "One of my weaknesses as a writer is that I was far too modest in my choice of subjects," he told the interviewer from *Playboy*. "If I were going to invest my talent more profitably I should have had more ambitious themes than I allowed myself to have." And when his interlocutor invited him to comment on Joyce Carol Oates's assessment of him as a genius "off the scale of even Truman Capote, Thomas Pynchon or Thomas Wolfe," Bellow replied: "I tend to agree with her, but Lenin said, when describing what happened in Russia in 1917, 'The power was lying in the street, I just picked it up.'" Then he laughed. He felt himself to be a "winner," he confessed, but a winner who had fallen far short of his capabilities: "I did the best that I could be expected to do." As for the way he'd conducted his life, he knew he was no model of virtue. He liked to quote Socrates' declaration that the unexamined life wasn't worth living, adding "but sometimes the examined life makes you wish you were dead." He said it with only the slightest of smiles.

He continued to turn out occasional brief commentaries for *News from the Republic of Letters*. One issue featured a "riposte" by Bellow to a story by Jack Miles. Miles's contribution, a parable entitled "The Nihilist and the Inventor," was about a privileged young rock musician from Silicon Valley who decides that life has no meaning and retreats to a cabin in the northern California woods. The story disturbed Bellow, for whom the soul—and the possibility of an afterlife—were more than abstract concepts. And what about the Holocaust? Were not the "cancelled years" of six million souls a rebuke to the easy nihilism of Miles's bourgeois Californian? He invoked to great effect the doomed Claudio in Shakespeare's *Measure for Measure*, claiming that

> The weariest and most loathed worldly life
> That age, ache, penury, and imprisonment

Can lay on nature, is a paradise
To what we fear of death.

Death, apparently, would have to wait. In the fall of 1999, Bellow made yet another pilgrimage to his Canadian birthplace, visiting such old haunts as Schwartz's deli, where he ordered a Montreal delicacy known as the smoked-meat sandwich, and showing Janis the street in the Jewish quarter where he'd lived eighty years before. The family home was gone, replaced by a warehouse; the only shop he recognized was Berson's, the tomb-stone maker. Dapper in a bow tie and pink striped shirt, he gave a reading at a Montreal synagogue and took questions from the audience. Asked how it was that he had such a good memory, Bellow brought down the house with his answer: "I forget." He also spoke at the Saul Bellow Municipal Library in Lachine. "Bellow was never more human, loveable, humble, appreciative, giving," reported his indefatigable scribe, Ann Weinstein, who drove him around town. The best way of fending off death, he told the relatives, old friends, and local Bellow enthusiasts gathered at the library, was to have unfinished business that one feels compelled to complete. He was coming to the end of a new book, he said, joking that it would be "like all the others—about women who wear out after three or four kids."

There was another work in progress. Janis, at forty and after five miscarriages, was visibly pregnant. How did he do it? an elderly gentleman present at the library event wondered aloud. "Practice, practice, practice," Bellow replied.

The baby, Naomi Rose, was born on December 23, 1999.

By the end of 1999, Bellow was nearly finished with the novel that he'd been hard at work on for the last two years. Entitled *Ravelstein*, it was a powerful story of friendship between a charis-matic homosexual teacher facing death—based on Allan Bloom, as Bellow acknowledged freely to reporters, reversing his lifelong habit of denying his characters' real-life sources—and an admiring foil who goes through a life-threatening episode of his own. *Ravelstein* was a startling achievement, the most compelling book Bellow had written in years. *The Actual* and *A Theft* had been thin performances—understandably so, in light of Bellow's advancing age; few fiction writers have produced novels of any length in their late years. At eighty-four, Bellow was capable of bringing to completion a manuscript that, at 234 pages, was not only longer than anything he'd written in the previous decade but a work of great originality.

Ravelstein is a biographical portrait in the manner of Macaulay's essay on Boswell's *Johnson*—a book that the narrator, Chick (a name that suggests innocence, even infantility), admits to having read in "a purple fever." Of Chick himself very little is said; for once, the focus is almost entirely on a subject who isn't some version of Bellow. Like Charlie Citrine, the survivor of his poet-buddy Humboldt, Chick serves as a presiding intelligence, a shrewd interpreter of his doomed, geniusy friend Abe Ravelstein, an academic philosopher who has written—at Chick's instigation—a "spirited, intelligent, warlike" book denouncing American higher education and gotten instantly rich when it became a surprise best-seller. Bellow's evocation of Bloom's physical presence is masterly: the chain-smoking, the shaking hands, the neighing stammer, the shiny bald crown. And he was just as unsparing about his friend's self-destructive bent, his oblivious devotion to fine wine and rich food: "He treated his body like a vehicle—a motorbike that he raced at top speed along the rim of the Grand Canyon." For Ravelstein, as for Bloom, money "is something to be thrown from the back of a speeding train"; his life—or what remains of it—is an orgy of conspicuous consumption: Armani suits, Vuitton luggage, gold Montblanc pens. His apartment is crammed with pricey goods: Oriental carpets, classical figurines, Lalique chandeliers. His dynamism is scarcely slowed by impending mortality: Italian opera blasts from his state-of-the-art CD player, Chicago Bulls' games flit across the big-screen TV. Laid out in the intensive-care unit, he orders a new BMW with customized features from his hospital bed—a memorable moment in Bloom lore—and has to be carried down and deposited in the passenger seat for his final ride home.

Like Bloom, who became a significant force among American conservatives after he published *The Closing of the American Mind*, Ravelstein is an ideological power broker. From his tele-phonic "command post," he keeps up with former students who have gone on to occupy high places in Washington; he's invited to the Reagan White House and Mrs. Thatcher's Downing Street. He leads "a large-scale mental life." It's notable that, for all his resistance to biography—a prejudice he expressed with increasing stridency—Bellow demonstrated a deep familiarity with the classics of the genre, from Plutarch and Aubrey to Johnson's life of the poet Richard Savage, all of whom he mentions in *Ravelstein* as models. He worked hard at his portrait of Bloom, laying out his friend's "fundamental assumptions": the belief in the "soul," the hunger for a passionate life, the devotion to the best that has been thought and said. "If these are left out of my account of his life we'll see only his eccentricities or foibles, his lavish, screwy purchases, his furnishings, his vanities, his gags, his laugh-paroxysms, the *marche militaire* he did as he crossed the quadrangle in his huge fur-lined coat of luxurious leather." What makes *Ravelstein* such a satisfying work of biographical portraiture is the balance it strikes between the particular characteristics that Johnson considered essential to life-writing and the representative traits that make Ravelstein a subject worthy of sustained attention. Like Humboldt, he's both an exceptionally vivid human being and a figure through whom the author can explore the America that produced him—immigrant-fueled, materialistic, raised up to celebrity by "the vast hydraulic forces of the country."

The book's subplot—salvaged from the manuscript of "All Marbles Still Accounted For"—concerns Chick's marriage to Rosamund, a graduate student of Ravelstein, and features a bitter portrait of Bellow's marriage to Alexandra, which disintegrated into mutual acrimony. Here Bellow reverted to the one-sided account that mars all his marital self-portraits, depicting Alexandra in the person of Vela, a cold, emotionally ungenerous professor of physics who is too wrapped up in her work to pay sufficient attention to her husband. ("In the morning she would slam out of the house.") He also stuck in a lengthy digression about his own recent brush with death: how Janis—in the novel, Rosamund—got him on the plane after the near-fatal dinner in Sint Maarten, slept in his hospital room for weeks, spoon-fed him, monitored his medicines, and finally pulled him through. "Rosamund kept me from dying." He lived, Chick hypothesizes, because he had to write his account of Ravelstein: "I am a great believer in the power of unfinished work to keep you alive."

For Bellow, writing *Ravelstein* was a mission. "The rule for the dead is that they should be forgotten," Chick observes near the end of the book. "After burial there is a universal gradual progress toward oblivion. But with Ravelstein this didn't altogether work. He claimed and filled a more conspicuous space." He leaves the reader with a last image of the great thinker, dressing to go out, putting on his five-thousand-dollar suit, smoking, tying his tie, listening to *Carmen*, polishing his bald head with a handkerchief. The book ends: "You don't easily give up a creature like Ravelstein to death." It was Bellow's greatest act of literary portraiture.

His capacity for provoking controversy was still robust. In January 2000, three months before the novel was scheduled to appear, *The Toronto Star* ran an item noting its imminent publication. Taking up Bellow's broad public hints that his main character was based on Bloom—"It's treated as fiction," he'd told a reporter from *The Washington Post*—the *Star* made the reasonable deduction that the novel was in fact a kind of biography, in which "Bellow reveals for the first time that Bloom was a homosexual." This would not have been news to Bloom's friends; Bloom's homosexuality had even found its way into scholarly footnotes. But the American press got hold of the item in the *Star,* and within two days the equation of Ravelstein and Bloom was firmly established: Journalists all over America were announcing that—as the New York *Daily News* put it—Bellow had "outed" Bloom. Bellow went further: Speaking by phone to a writer from *The New York Times,* he confirmed as fact a disclosure in the novel: Bloom had died of AIDS. "You didn't hear that from me," he had said a few years before, when asked to confirm the cause of Bloom's death. In the novel, he not only stated it but offered intimate details about the persistence of sexual hunger in the face of imminent death. Sitting bony-legged in his Japanese robe, Ravelstein confesses that he still gets "hot" and masturbates to relieve his desire. "I'm fatally polluted," he confides to Chick. On one occasion, he recruits a black youth from the neighborhood to satisfy him, insisting that he practices "safe sex."

The details were shocking, and Bellow's willingness to vouch for their veracity quickly raised the stakes. Now—in addition to the news that Bloom, a vociferous conservative, had been homosexual—there was a moral issue: Did Bellow have the right to make such matters public? "Allan would be spinning in his grave," claimed Harriet Wasserman; and even Bellow admitted to "a feeling" that Bloom would have minded his candor. But he also maintained that Bloom had asked him to write a memoir that was, in the words of the novel, "without softeners or sweeteners." He was simply doing what he had always done: using whatever material was at hand. Art, as always, came first.

But did it? Unnerved by the gathering storm of protest—even as intellectual pundits rushed to defend him, praising his courage in celebrating what the openly homosexual journalist Andrew Sullivan described as Bloom's reverence for "the erotic life"—Bellow backpedaled furiously. Having previously refused to be interviewed by *The New York Times Magazine* on the subject of *Ravelstein,* he reversed himself and summoned a reporter to Boston. Reverting to his "Proust of the Papuans" strategy—say what you please, then deny what you've said while expressing remorse for having said it—he offered a convoluted explanation. On the one hand, he stressed, the novel was "testimony to my *feeling* for Bloom"; on the other, he fretted, perhaps he had "crossed the line."

To further complicate matters, there appeared to be some question about whether Bloom *had* died of AIDS. Nathan Tarcov, the son of Bellow's old friend Oscar as well as Bloom's medical executor, issued a flat denial. Bloom's doctor, Nicholas Davidson, insisted the cause of death was "pretty much irrelevant." Bloom was "in heart failure, kidney failure. The body was winding down." The death certificate, equally indeterminate, attributed the immediate cause to "gastrointestinal bleed" and "duodenal ulcers (probably)"—but AIDS is rarely given as the official cause of death. In all likelihood, Bloom died of complications from HIV rather than full-blown AIDS. "For a long time, I thought I knew what Allan died of, and then I discovered other things that didn't jibe with that, so I really can't say now," Bellow told the reporter from the *Times*. In the finished book, he altered explicit references in the galleys to Ravelstein's disease: He excised the words "from H.I.V." from the phrase "And not only his death from H.I.V. but a good many other deaths as well." The sentence "Abe was taking the common drug prescribed for AIDS" had become "Abe was taking the common drug prescribed for his condition."* Did these modest evasions atone for Bellow's transgression? And was the book a transgression at all, or was it rather the fulfillment of a deathbed promise? As Andrew Patner, a former student of Bloom, wrote in the *Chicago Sun-Times Book Week,* "Only two people know what promise Bloom extracted from Bellow about a posthumous book, and one of them is dead."

Ravelstein was published on April 24 to enthusiastic reviews. Writing in *The New York Times Book Review,* which featured Bellow on the cover, Jonathan Wilson found the novel "a cause . . . for celebration." So did Sven Birkerts, who only three years before had dismissed Bellow as a dinosaur in the pages of *The New York Observer.* "I cashiered him out," he confessed in *Esquire,* recalling an afternoon he'd spent interviewing Bellow for a Boston literary journal, *The Agni Review.* "Saul Bellow, I thought: one of the greats, done now." But *Ravelstein* had surprised Birkerts: It was "full of heart and wisdom." Bellow had "hit his number again." In every sense: By May, *Ravelstein* was on the bestseller list.

Wilson, author of a book on Bellow (*On Bellow's Planet: Readings from the Dark Side*), noted that *Ravelstein* was his "most Jewish novel." There's no confusion about the ethnic identity of Chick and Ravelstein: They brood fraternally on Jewish history, Jewish soul, the fate of Israel, the survival of the Jewish people despite Hitler's efforts to wipe them off the map. Even more significant, Chick's older brother is named Shimon, a notable alteration

---

*Christopher Hitchens, writing in *The Nation,* noted that Bellow had also removed a passage alluding to Ravelstein's dalliances with "barely legal boys of African-American provenance." How would such a proclivity, Hitchens wanted to know, square with Bloom's attack on black militants in *The Closing of the American Mind;* or, more troublingly, with the antihomosexual bias of the Straussian theorists who had made Bloom their hero? A good question.

from *The Adventures of Augie March,* in which Augie's brother is named Simon. "Behind the addition of that Hebraizing 'h' is a long rounding of the bases in American fiction." The drama of assimilation had ended happily, Wilson intimated (he didn't need to spell out the implications): Jewish-American had become American. So thorough was the transformation, so confident the survivors of Bellow's generation, those once-hyphenated intellectuals and writers who had struggled to achieve selfhood in the New World, that they could now acknowledge their origins without apology—indeed, in triumph.

Toward the end of 1997, Bellow had appeared on a BBC television show with Martin Amis, who had flown over to America and interviewed him at the Lotos Club. How did he feel about death? Amis wondered, getting straight to the point. "There are moments in the day when I feel as if I'm looking back at life from the beyond; I've reckoned with death for so long that I look at the world with the eyes of someone who's died," Bellow replied. Then he read, in his elderly, quavering voice, a page from his new novel in progress: "What I have to say, all I have to say, is that I count on seeing the dead—my dead. When I die they will be waiting for me. I don't anticipate, nor do I visualize any actual settings. I can't tell you what my father will say or my mother and brothers and friends. Very possibly they will all tell me things I badly need to be told."

The last scene in the program was shot in Boston. As he and Bellow sit by the window of a coffee shop, Amis asks his mentor if he believes in the afterlife. Bellow thinks for a long moment before giving his answer: "Well, it's impossible to believe in it because there's no rational ground. But I have a persistent intuition, and it's not so much a hope because it would be better to be blotted out entirely—call it love impulses. What I think is how agreeable it would be to see my mother and my father and my brothers again—to see again my dead. But then I think, 'How long would these moments last?' You still have to think of eternity as a conscious soul. So the only thing I can think of is that in death we might become God's apprentices and have the real secrets of the universe revealed to us."

ACKNOWLEDGMENTS

Biography is a collective enterprise. The writer of fiction sits in a room alone, configuring a story out of his imagination. The biographer assembles his tale out of the materials of his subject's life: letters, journals, manuscripts, and above all the testimonies of friends and enemies, spouses and siblings, disciples and mentors—all those whose paths and the subject's crossed in life. What would we know of Dr. Johnson today had it not been—of course—for Boswell but also for the record of his extraordinary character left by such vivid witnesses as Johnson's close friend Mrs. Hester Thrale Piozzi?

In the lengthy and elaborate process of writing a biography, the biographer comes to know the ancillary figures almost as well as he knows the subject. How much more intense this experience of knowing becomes when the subject is still living or only recently dead and thus surrounded by a throng of those who recall him as he was in the flesh. "We know how few can portray a living acquaintance, except by his most prominent and observable particularities, and the grosser features of his mind," remarked Dr. Johnson, "and it may be easily imagined how much of this little knowledge may be lost in imparting it, and how soon a succession of copies will lose all resemblance of the original." The closer we are to those details, before the subject has receded into the shadows of history, the better chance we have of making him come alive.

My first biography, of Delmore Schwartz, was a happy ordeal—the oxymoron reflects the loneliness of the writer's life (especially that of a young writer, as I was at the time), the struggle to master a craft, the physical and mental demands involved in cobbling a huge, untidy array of data into a coherent narrative, and the keen pleasure of getting to know so many of the remarkable people who had known Schwartz. In the course of my labors on that biography, I made friends for life, not least among them Schwartz's executor, Dwight Macdonald, a great critic and master of American prose who taught me most of what I know about how to write. I never knew Schwartz—he died when I was still a teenager—but I saw him through the eyes of others so attuned to the nuances of his character that he eventually became as real to me as if I had known him myself.

In the case of Bellow, I *do* know the man. I talked with him on numerous occasions; I corresponded with him; I even dined with him, like Boswell with Johnson at the Mitre. Whether this firsthand experience resulted in a portrait any more accurate or revealing than my portrait of Schwartz is for others to determine; but I can say with assurance that I immersed myself more deeply in his life than I ever did in Schwartz's. In the earlier work, I was a historian, a chronicler, an archivist, putting together a portrait largely from hearsay. Here, my proximity to the life I was writing was so close (so suffocating, Bellow might have said) that it recalled the scene in his early novel *The Victim*, where Leventhal, the beleaguered hero, is forced to carry his double, his tormenter, Allbee, on his back; there were moments when I wondered if I was living my own life at all.

But there were many other moments—so many that writing this book became one of the great experiences of my life—when I found myself in a rich, often bewilderingly complex relation with people whom I would never have known had it not been for Saul Bellow. In a protracted project such as this, one longs to get to the end—not only to be done, to move on, to embark on the next project, but to arrive at the occasion of giving thanks. As I sat at the dinner tables of various hospitable interlocutors, set up shop in their studies to copy correspondence onto my battered laptop, even slept in their guest rooms, I marveled at my acquaintance with an ever-widening circle of friends, family, and associates of my subject, whose peripatetic and dazzling passage through the world has attracted such a memorable populace in its wake.

Where else to begin but Chicago, where Zita Cogan, Bellow's friend from his Tuley days, provided me bed and board in Hyde Park and became in time my own friend; I wish she had lived to read this acknowledgment. Other friends of Bellow, notably Marshall and Doris Holleb, Stuart Brent, David Peltz, and the late Albert Glotzer, became like family to me, occupying the place once occupied by my own dispersed Chicago family. So did John Blades of the *Chicago Tribune*, who offered me unlimited access to a spare bedroom in my hometown of Evanston and treated me like his own son. Abel Swirsky, a Tuleyite of Bellow's generation, did archival research at the school—now Roberto Clemente High School—and went over my chapter on those years while plying me with cold cuts in a North Side deli. The late Allan Bloom (how often, sadly, I find it necessary to use that adjective), whom I first came to know when I went to Chicago on assignment for *The New York Times* to write a magazine profile of him, also ended up a friend. Bellow's Hyde Park crony Richard Stern, a Boswellian explainer of the great man to the general public, kept me company through the long weeks I spent poring over Bellow's papers in the Regenstein Library at the University of Chicago. My childhood friend Charles Dawe, a counterpart to Bellow's Tuley cronies, welcomed me into his home; Susan Freifeld, the daughter of Bellow's friend Sam, renewed an acquaintance dating back to high school; Joseph Epstein permitted our bond as "Chicago boys" to conquer ideological differences. I've rarely felt more at home anywhere than I did sitting in a booth with Joe at the Olympia Coffee Shop in downtown Evanston. Scott Turow, another "Chicago boy," and his wife, Annette, also provided welcome companionship.

Edward Shils, a distinguished sociologist at the University of Chicago for half a century who played a significant role in Bellow's life, also played a significant role in mine. Shils overcame his distaste for what he imagined were my politics and devoted immense time and effort to my chaotic manuscript. It was over dinner in a Chinese restaurant on Cermak Road that, remembering the tonic effect of Dwight Macdonald's pitiless and caustic commentary in the margins of my apprentice biography, I invited Shils to concentrate his tough-minded, unsentimental, even at times brutal intellect on my work in progress. He responded with a sixteen-thousand-word memo, dictated in his final illness, that I kept by my side as I worked through a revision; by then, it was a voice from the grave. In a rare departure from his daunting principles of scholarly propriety, Shils urged me to leave him out of my book entirely, since he had become estranged from Bellow. But he could no more be a phantom in this narrative than he could in the history of *Mr. Sammler's Planet*, which he helped shape. Edward, I violate your wishes with a clear conscience and give thanks.

Following in Bellow's footsteps, I traveled to Montreal, the town of his youth, where I was welcomed by Ann Weinstein, an indefatigable researcher into the remotest ancestral corners of my subject's past. Ann took me on a tour of Bellovian haunts, arranged a lunch with M. Descary, the mayor of Lachine, and invited members of Montreal's Jewish community to her home. As I fell asleep in her guest bedroom one night, she was still stuffing material from her vast Bellow archive under the door. Three years later—biographers measure time in years, if not decades—Ruth Wisse, then a professor at McGill, now the first professor of Yiddish literature at Harvard, invited me to lecture and offered me the hospitality of her home.

I would like to think that writing this biography was my own idea, but the truth is that it had numerous proponents. Georges Borchardt was among the first to suggest I undertake a project that seemed to me untenable at the time; Kate Medina, my smart and kindhearted editor at Random House, assured me it could be done and made sure it was; she and her then-assistant, Meaghan Rady, skillfully line-edited my elephantine manuscript and made cuts that shed no blood; her Random House colleagues Harold Evans, Jason Epstein, and Joni Evans also provided both emotional and material support. Others at Random House oversaw the book through the final stages of production: Frankie Jones helped assemble the photographs and assisted in a thousand other details, as did Carol Schneider and Tom Perry; Timothy Mennel copyedited the final manuscript with the zeal of a conductor presiding over an unruly orchestra, noting every contradiction and discrepancy in my eight-hundred-page manuscript and improving it beyond measure.

During the decade I spent on this book, I had to work at other jobs; not even as munificent a publisher as Random House can underwrite a literary biography on its own. My primary anchor was *The New York Times*, whose generous editors allowed me the luxury of coming and going over the years: Edward Klein, who recruited me to *The New York Times Magazine;* James Greenfield, Jack Rosenthal, and Adam Moss, who tolerated my unpredictable hours; and Joseph Lelyveld, who granted me a leave of absence. After I migrated to *The New Yorker,* Tina Brown made possible—and *fun*—the writer's life. Deb Garrison presided with patience and grace over the excerpt that appeared there—and then, in an act of unprecedented literary heroism, read over and edited the entire manuscript; Ann Stringfield, of the fabled checking department, produced an oasis of accuracy in the desert of guesswork that even the most meticulous biographer produces in the end; Bill Buford commissioned and shaped the first excerpt from the book, in *Granta*, and later goaded me to publish the journal chronicling my complex relationship with my subject in *The New Yorker*. My friend and agent Andrew Wylie made sure I was kept financially afloat; he also read my manuscript, chapter by chapter, as I wrote it, and his encouragement meant more to me than I can say. I would also like to thank Robert Silvers, the distinguished coeditor of *The New York Review of Books*, for encouraging me to write an essay on Isaac Rosenfeld and for asking a question that lingered in my mind: "Is this part of a longer work?" Robert McCrum, former editorial director of Faber and Faber, was another influential voice; when I mentioned to him, over a drink at the Groucho Club in London, that I was contemplating this book, his enthusiasm became a catalyst. That was in 1988.

Many institutions supported this project over the years. For financial assistance I would like to thank Joel Conarroe, the president of the Guggenheim Foundation, and G. Thomas Tanselle; Philip Roth, Joyce Carol Oates, and the late Alfred Kazin for recommending me to the foundation; Lynne V. Cheney, then chairman of the National Endowment for the Humanities; Hillel Fradkin of the Lynde and Harry Bradley Foundation in Milwaukee; Irving Kristol, who recommended me to the Manhattan Institute, which sponsored the Bradley grant; William Hammett and Lawrence Mone, successive presidents of the Manhattan Institute, for making me a part of their intellectual community; and my dear friends Kenneth and Evelyn Lipper, whose generous foundation came to my aid. Ken has transformed my life in marvelous ways; by inviting me to be his partner in the Lipper/Viking series of brief biographies known as the Penguin Lives, he made it possible for me to work full-time at my passion and gave me a secure anchor in a volatile world. The late Gerald Freund, who in his lifetime held just about every post of importance in the world of foundations and philanthropy, offered me helpful advice on the nuances of procuring grants.

Librarians also played a necessary role in the making of this book, and I'd like to thank the following: Alice Schreyer, Daniel Meyer, and the late Robert Rosenthal of the Rare Book and Manuscripts Collection at the Regenstein Library, University of Chicago; Mark Piel of the New York Society Library, where I was offered a quiet refuge for months at a time; Dr. Alice Birney at the Library of Congress in Washington, D.C., who provided me with copies of Bellow's correspondence with Ralph Ellison and Philip Roth before they were officially cataloged; Patrick Quinn, University Archivist, for his tireless tracking down of publications from Bellow's Northwestern days; Kenneth A. Lohf and Bernard Crystal of the Rare Books and Manuscripts Library at Columbia University; Allen Lathrop of the Berryman Collection at the University of Minnesota, for the letters to John Berryman; Levi D. Phillips of the Department of Special Collections of the University of California, Davis; Susan Bryntesen, of the University of Delaware Library, for navigating me through the Mark Harris papers; Nancy MacKechnie, Curator of Rare Books and Manuscripts, Vassar College, for correspondence between Mary McCarthy and Hannah Arendt; Joy Weiner and Mimi Bolling of the New York Public Library, for Bellow's correspondence with *The New Yorker*; and Harold Oakhill of the Rockefeller Archive Center in Pocantico Hills, North Tarrytown, New York. The late Dr. Lola Szladits, a curatorial legend, warmly greeted me when I showed up at the Berg Collection of the New York Public Library to inaugurate my research, long before I even had a book contract in hand. Also, Tina Schneider, reference librarian at the Ohio State University at Lima, assisted with fact-checking.

I relied heavily on biographers, editors, and scholars who generously shared with me their research: Sam Tanenhaus, the biographer of Whittaker Chambers, provided insights into Bellow's ill-starred interview with Chambers at *Time*; Joseph Blotner, the biographer of Robert Penn Warren, sent me transcripts of his interviews with Warren; Mark Shechner of the University of New York at Buffalo loaned me papers and correspondence of Isaac Rosenfeld; David Gates of *Newsweek* put in my hands the magazine's substantial file on Bellow assembled for a cover story by Jack Kroll and the late Walter Clemons (Clemons also gave me the transcript of his long interview with Bellow); Henry Kisor, book editor of the *Chicago Sun-Times*, introduced me to its morgue; Andreas Brown furnished me his detailed inventory of Bellow's papers on deposit at the Regenstein Library at an early stage in my work; Michael Wreszin, the biographer of Dwight Macdonald, supplied copies of Bellow's letters to Macdonald; Macdonald's son Michael supplied photographs of Bellow; Ned Polsky put me on the trail of an old flame of Bellow; Rosie Alison sent me the correspondence between her aunt, Barley Alison, and Bellow, and wrote a brief memoir of Alison; Andrew Gordon, who observed Bellow in a classroom at the University of

Florida, provided me with a lively description of the event; John Haffenden steered me to the Bellow/Berryman letters at the University of Minnesota; Bernard Richards provided me with correspondence in the Library of the Jewish Theological Seminary of America; Mark Staebler of the University of Puerto Rico interviewed Professor Bernard Lockwood and other university faculty members; William Roth entertained me in Princeton and handed over a remarkable sheaf of letters chronicling Bellow's early misadventures with Colt Press. George Plimpton underwrote one of my first research trips to Chicago, assigning me to interview Richard Stern for *The Paris Review.* Keith Botsford and Jerrold Hickey, the founding and current editors of *Bostonia*, made available to me an invaluable archive of photographs from Bellow's family album. My research assistants, Sydney Johnson and Camille Sweeney, were inexhaustible in their search for undiscovered Bellow troves. Adam Kirsch, my assistant at the Lipper/Viking Penguin "Lives" project—and an accomplished literary critic in his own right—labored to make my sometimes impressionistic citations credible.

A number of pioneering Bellovians saved me from months of arduous research by going where no scholars had gone before. Gloria Cronin and Leila Goldman, editors of the *Saul Bellow Journal*, furnished me with back issues and put me on their subscription list. Daniel Fuchs, the author of *Saul Bellow: Vision and Revision*, shared with me correspondence and memories of Bellow over lunch in a seedy Chinese restaurant on upper Broadway. I have many other miscellaneous debts: to Karen Zydron in Scott Turow's office, who performed an extensive document search of Chicago court records; Raymond L. Gillmore, who located Bellow's WPA essays in the vast archive of the Illinois State Historical Library in Springfield; Gordon Grant, who read and summarized the Bellow papers in the Harry Ransom Humanities Research Center at the University of Texas, Austin; Michael Milman, who ensured access to Bellow's papers in the offices of Viking Press; Ben Yagoda, the official historian of *The New Yorker*, who shared Bellow-related findings with me; and Keith Opdahl, who provided me with an annotated version of his essay on Bellow in the *Dictionary of Literary Biography*. Jay Parini provided me with documents from the files of the Salzburg Seminar in American Studies, Schloss Leopoldskron, Salzburg, Austria, pertaining to Bellow's stay there. I would also like to thank Virginia Avery, who copyedited the manuscript twice while I continued to revise it. (I hope my maddening delays and interventions played no role in her decision to retire.)

Then there were my predecessors in the field, Mark Harris and Ruth Miller, whose biographical forays paved the way for my own. Harris directed me to his valuable papers at the University of Delaware, and Miller sent me copies of Bellow's letters to her and to Owen Barfield. Barnett Singer, the author of an unpublished memoir of Bellow, kindly shared with me his literary hero's correspondence and "talked Bellow" on a number of pleasant occasions.

The list of those I interviewed or corresponded with is long and sometimes melancholy; many who gave assistance of various kinds are dead, among them Julian Behrstock, Walter Blair, Paul Carroll, Catharine Carver, Eleanor Clark, Ezra Davis, Leon Edel, Ralph Ellison, Sam Freifeld, Nathan Gould, Erwin Glikes, John Goetz, Clement Greenberg, Milton Hindus, Irving Howe, James Laughlin, Harry Levin, Arthur Lidov, William Maxwell, Moody Prior, George Reedy, Edouard Roditi, Ralph Ross, Lyn Rotblatt, Yetta Barshevsky Shachtman, Karl Shapiro, Peter Shaw, Evelyn Shrifte, Hyman Slate, Saul Steinberg, Edith Tarcov, Diana and Lionel Trilling, Mel Tumin, Eliseo Vivas, and Alan Williams. Of these, I mourn most keenly for Dr. George Sarant, the son of Isaac Rosenfeld, who, by loaning me his father's papers, started me on the path to Bellow. George became my friend—I was devastated when his life was cut short by a heart attack.

Fortunately, the living are more numerous: Lionel Abel, Alice Adams, Ellen Adler, Mortimer Adler, Woody Allen, Martin Amis, Bryan Appleyard, Aaron Asher, Morris August, David Bazelon, Miles Beermann, Daniel Bell, Gregory Bellow, Sondra Bellow, Eleanor Bergstein, Barnet Berkin, Paul Bernick, Simon Michael Bessie, Ann Birstein, Helen Garrie Bishop, Wayne Booth, Dean Borok, Keith Botsford, Leon Botstein, Robert Boyers, Stuart Brent, Robert Brustein, Edward Burlingame, Stanley Burnshaw, Susan Cheever, Toby Cole, Janet Coleman, Edward Cone, Marion Cumpiano, Midge Decter, Jack Delano, Michael Denneny, Barbaralee Diamonstein, Barbara Dupee, Julius Echeles, Dr. Albert Ellis, Monroe Engel, Candace Falk, Ann Farber, George Feiwell, Leslie Fiedler, Beverly Fields, Eileen Finletter, Frances FitzGerald, Milton Friedman, Marvin Gameroff, Louise Gans, Leslie Garis, Frances Gendlin, Ben Gerson, Louise Glück, Herbert Gold, David Goldknopf, Arlette Jassel Goldstein, Monique Gonthier, Rockwell Gray, Martin Greenberg, Willie Greenberg, Crystal Gromer, Thomas Guinzburg, Donald Hall, Patricia Harris, Edith Hartnett, Anthony Hecht, Virginia Heiserman, Abe Held, Gertrude Himmelfarb, Robert Hivnor, Edward Hoagland,

Sandra Hochman, Lynn Hoffman, Ted Hoffman, William Humphrey, William Hunt, Robert Johnson, Max Kampelman, Ruth Kane, H. J. Kaplan, Roger Kaplan, Arno Karlen, William Karush, Mrs. Charles Kauffman (Jane Bellow), Pearl Kazin, Eugene Kennedy, William Kennedy, Hilton Kramer, Rosette Lamont, Anita Landa, Rudy Lapp, R. W. B. Lewis, Victoria Fischman Lidov, Leo Litwak, Marilyn Mann, Herbert and Mitzi McCloskey, John McCormick, Molly McQuade, Dr. Paul Meehl, Arthur Miller, Vivian Missner, Belle and Miriam Myers, John Nathan, Cynthia Ozick, Cora Passin, Herbert Passin, Constance Perin, William Phillips, Barbara Hanson Pierce, Norman Podhoretz, Walter Pozen, Dr. Chester Raphael, Piers Paul Read, James Redfield, Charles Reich, Jesse Reichek, Carlin Romano, Patia Rosenberg, Vasiliki Rosenfeld, Tom Rosenthal, William Roth, Edward Rothstein, Morris Rotman, Sara Schelley, Arthur Schlesinger, Jr., Joan Ullmann Schwartz, Margaret Shafer, Judith Shavrein, Jason Shinder, Sam Shulman, Ben Sidran, Shirley Sidran, Philip Siegelman, Elisabeth Sifton, Eleanor Fox Simmons, Maggie Simmons, Eileen Simpson, Louis Simpson, Corlies ("Cork") Smith, Douglas LaRue Smith, Deborah Solomon, Ted Solotaroff, Aviva Sorkin, Leo Spiegel, Brent Staples, Jerome Stone, William and Rosalyn Targ, Shirley Teper, Dr. A. Boyd Thomes, Rosalyn Tureck, Leonard Unger, Gore Vidal, George Walden, Dr. William and Edith Wanamaker, Andrews Wanning, Harriet Wasserman, Lord Weidenfeld, Theodore Weiss, Leon Wieseltier, Elsa Zion, and Steven Zipperstein.

If I have omitted anyone deserving of acknowledgment and thanks, the omission is inadvertent; memory—as any biographer knows—is fallible.

During the composition of this book, my children, Molly and William, grew up. They were two and six when I began, twelve and sixteen when I finished; they spent their entire childhoods hearing about Saul Bellow and viewing with alarm the rising stack of pages on my desk. My wife, Anna, whose sorry fate it has been to be married to a writer, remained steadfast throughout and gave the manuscript a discriminating final read that notched it up. She bore with me through my first biography, yet when I wavered about the feasibility of this project, it was she who urged, "I think you should write it whether he wants you to or not."

Finally, I'd like to thank the Bellows. In the writing of this book, Adam and Daniel, sons two and three, became good friends. They never stood in the way of my project, even when it must have been confusing and, at times, painful for them to learn facts about their own lives from a stranger. Saul Bellow, a noted biographobe, eventually became reconciled, or at least resigned, to my presence in his life. He saw me at regular intervals, provided access to documents, offered me tea and dinner, and—this is key—never interfered in what I wrote, or even asked to read it. In a lecture, Bellow once spoke of "that freedom to approach the marvelous which cannot be taken from us, the right, with grace, to make the most of what we have." Freedom is Bellow's primary theme, and freedom is what he gave me.

Toward the very end of my project, Bellow asked me what I had learned, and I answered with a quote from Henry James: "Never say you know the last word about any human heart." Which doesn't mean you can't learn a great deal from its study: When I remarked to Bellow, over dinner at Le Petit Chef in Vermont on a hot summer night, what an interesting life he'd had, he responded dryly, "I'm glad I haven't lived in vain."

NOTES

Most scholars look upon others in their field as threats, potential tres-
passers on their turf, but I am grateful to have been preceded by a
legion of diligent researchers who performed the thankless labor of
compiling bibliographies of Bellow's published work. In the last three
decades, the tide of books and articles about Bellow has turned to a
flood—there now exist several full-length books devoted to chronicling the secondary sources. I have relied most heavily on the indispensable *Saul Bellow: An Annotated Bibliography* by Gloria L.
Cronin and Blaine H. Hall (New York: Garland Publishing, 1987)
and on Marianne Nault's *Saul Bellow: His Works and His Critics, An
Annotated International Bibliography*, Garland Reference Library of
the Humanities, vol. 59 (New York: Garland, 1977). The most
comprehensive interview with Bellow, an eight-hour series of video-
taped interviews, was conducted by Sigmund Koch of Boston University; entitled "Research Conversations with Saul Bellow," these are
now in the Boston University Aesthetics Research Archive. In addition, I relied on the following books and articles: Gloria Cronin and
Ben Siegel, eds., *Conversations with Saul Bellow* (Jackson, Miss.:
University of Mississippi Press, 1994); B. A. Sokoloff and Mark
Posner, *Saul Bellow: A Comprehensive Bibliography* (Folcroft, Pa.:
Folcroft, 1972); Leslie Field and John Z. Guzlowski, "Criticism of
Saul Bellow: A Selected Checklist," *Modern Fiction Studies* (spring

1979); Joe W. Kraus, "Interviews with Saul Bellow," *Bulletin of Bibliography* 50:3; and Edith Tarcov, ed., *The Portable Saul Bellow* (New York: Viking, 1974). Most of Bellow's published stories, essays, and reviews can be readily found in these sources; otherwise they are cited in my notes.

Bellow's letters have been gathered from many sources; where there is no citation, the reader can assume I'm quoting from a letter in the recipient's hands. Otherwise, the institution or library that holds it is cited. With the exception of the typescript and notebooks of *Mr. Sammler's Planet*, Bellow's manuscripts are on deposit at the Rare Book and Manuscripts Collection of the Regenstein Library at the University of Chicago, along with a significant archive of notebooks, papers, and miscellaneous documents pertaining to his life and work; the catalog alone runs to more than one hundred pages. Unless otherwise noted, all quotations from and references to unpublished work derive from the Bellow Papers. Uncited quotations from Bellow are from my own interviews with him; quotations from other sources, unless attributed in the notes, are also from personal interviews. In a few instances, I have left sources anonymous at their requests. To avoid citational clutter, I have not listed every quotation from fugitive newspaper clippings; unless otherwise indicated, these clips are from the morgues of *The New York Times*, the *Chicago Tribune*, the *Chicago Sun-Times*, and *Newsweek*.

CHAPTER 1

3   "Starting Out in Chicago," *The American Scholar* 44.1 (winter 1974–75).

5   The Edmund Wilson quotation is from "Hull-House in 1932," in *The American Earthquake* (New York: Farrar, Straus & Giroux, 1958).

5   For details about the history of Chicago literary life, I relied on the following: Emmett Dedmon, *Fabulous Chicago* (New York: Atheneum, 1981); Bernard Duffey, *The Chicago Renaissance in American Letters: A Critical History* (East Lansing, Mich.: Michigan State College Press, 1954); and Carl S. Smith, *Chicago and the Literary Imagination: 1880–1920* (Chicago: University of Chicago Press, 1984).

6   Edward Shils's interpretation of Bellow was made in a letter to me: March 30, 1994. For background on the Belos' lives in

Russia, I consulted Salo Baron's indispensable *The Russian Jew under Tsars and Soviets* (New York: Macmillan, 1964); Mark Zborowski and Elizabeth Herzog's *Life Is with People: The Culture of the Shtetl* (New York: Schocken, 1988); and Irving Howe's classic *World of Our Fathers: The Journey of the East European Jews to America and the Life They Found and Made* (New York: Harcourt Brace Jovanovich, 1976).

6   Bellow's characterizations of his father are from an unpublished manuscript in the Bellow Papers, excerpted in "Memoirs of a Bootlegger's Son," *Granta* 41 (autumn 1992).

7   "I am not yet part of that family": Bellow to Ruth Miller, quoted in *Saul Bellow: A Biography of the Imagination.*

8   My portrait of Bellow's early life in Canada relied heavily on the notes and clippings and miscellaneous data collected by Ann Weinstein. I also drew upon the following sources: Shulamis Yelin, *Shulamis: Stories from a Montreal Childhood* (Montreal: Vehicule Press, 1983); Michael Greenstein, "Saul Bellow's Roots," *Viewpoints* 19.6 (1991). Newspaper articles: David M. Alpern, "Montreal Magnifique," *The Jewish Week,* December 18, 1987; Janice Arnold, "Lachine to Name Library in Honor of Saul Bellow," *The Canadian Jewish News,* June 7, 1984; Stanley Asher, "Landmarks of Montreal Jewry," *The Gazette* (Montreal), October 22, 1995; Sheila Fischman, "Saul Wanders Streets of His Montreal Past," *The Montreal Star,* May 3, 1976; Dusty Vineberg, "Last Vestiges of a Ghetto," *The Montreal Star,* January 24, 1972.

8   Bellow himself has written and talked a great deal about his Canadian roots: Saul Bellow, "On Jewish Storytelling," *Jewish Heritage* (winter 1964–65); see also his moving introduction to *Great Jewish Short Stories* (New York: Dell, 1963); "Why the Persecution of the Jews?" *Commentator* (Toronto) 8.1 (January 1964); and two interviews: "Bellow on Himself and America," *The Jerusalem Post Weekly,* July 6, 1970, and a taped talk given to the Montreal Council of Foreign Affairs on May 14, 1987, a transcript of which was provided by Ann Weinstein.

9   Marvin Gameroff of Stowe, Vermont, provided background on his relatives the Gameroffs.

10   "The trunks my parents traveled with were exotic": Cathleen Medwick, "A Cry of Strength: The Unfashionably Uncynical Saul Bellow," *Vogue,* March 1982.

10   "*Jenke, shpil epes*": interview with Willie Greenberg.

14 Review of *Adventures of Mottel, the Cantor's Son:* "Laughter in the Ghetto," *The Saturday Review of Literature*, May 30, 1953.

14 Leon Edel's quotation is from "Marginal *Keri* and Textual *Chetiv*: The Mythic Novel of A. M. Klein," in *The A. M. Klein Symposium*, ed. Seymour Mayne (Ottawa: University of Ottawa Press, 1975), cited in Michael Greenstein, "Bellow's Canadian Beginnings," *Saul Bellow Journal* 7.1 (winter 1988).

15 Letter to the biblical scholar Stephen Mitchell: June 22, 1991 (courtesy of Albert Glotzer).

17 "the topography of scars": interview with Shirley Teper.

18 For information about Bellow's relatives the Dworkins and their early days in Chicago, I'm indebted to Louis Dworkin's daughter, Vivian Missner, and to Jerome Stone.

CHAPTER 2

20 My portrait of Chicago in the 1920s is drawn from a number of sources, primarily Melvin G. Holli, ed., *My Ethnic Chicago* (Grand Rapids, Mich.: William B. Eerdmans, 1977); Irving Cutler, *The Jews of Chicago: From Shtetl to Suburb* (Urbana: University of Illinois Press, 1996); Seymour Jacob Pomrenze, "Aspects of Chicago Russian-Jewish Life," in *The Chicago Pinkas*, ed. Simon Rawidowicz (Chicago: College of Jewish Studies, 1952); Hyman L. Meites, ed., *History of the Jews of Chicago* (Chicago: Jewish Historical Society of Illinois, 1924); William Adelman, *Pilsen and the West Side: A Tour Guide* (Chicago: Illinois Labor History Society, 1983); and "The Jews of Illinois," *The Reform Advocate*, May 4, 1901.

20 Bellow's own vivid account of his early life in Chicago is drawn primarily from his unpublished memoir, entitled in typescript "The Chicago Book," in the Regenstein Library archives. He also wrote numerous essays on this key period in his life, some of them unpublished drafts of lectures on deposit at the Regenstein Library, others published: "Literature in the Age of Technology," *Harper's* (August 1974); "A Matter of the Soul," address to the fourth international congress of the Institute of Verdi Studies, *Opera News* (January 11, 1975); "Skepticism and the Depth of Life," in *The Arts and the Public: Essays by Saul Bellow*, eds. James E. Miller, Jr., and Paul D. Herring

(Chicago: University of Chicago Press, 1967); "A World Too Much with Us," *Critical Inquiry* 2.1 (1975); and "A Writer from Chicago," *The Tanner Lectures on Human Values,* vol. 3, ed. Sterling M. McMurrin (Salt Lake City: University of Utah Press, 1982), which reproduces a good deal of the material intended for "The Chicago Book." Bellow also dealt extensively with his Chicago youth in the Jefferson Lectures, sponsored by the National Endowment for the Humanities and delivered in Washington, D.C., on March 30, 1977, and in Chicago on April 1, 1977. These invaluable lectures are available in Bellow's collection of nonfiction prose, *It All Adds Up: From the Dim Past to the Uncertain Future* (New York: Viking Penguin, 1994). In addition, see two uncollected newspaper articles: "A Writer Looks at Chicago Culture, 'This Furious Spirit Which Builds Up and Pulls Down,'" *Chicago Daily News,* November 11–12, 1972; and "Mr. Sugarman's Pledge of Allegiance," *Chicago Tribune,* August 25, 1996.

21   For memories of the period, I have relied on my own interviews with Bellow, and with Dave Peltz, Stuart Brent, Rosalyn Tureck, Eleanor Fox, Irving Letchinger, William Karush, Jane (Bellow) Kauffman, Morris Rotman, Albert Glotzer, Sam Freifeld, Ezra Davis, Nathan Gould, Zita Cogan, Yetta Barshevsky Shachtman, and numerous friends of my own family.

21   There also exists in the Regenstein Library a remarkable collection of taped interviews with Fred Glotzer, Sydney J. Harris, and other Chicagoans who knew Bellow; it was compiled by D. J. R. Bruckner. In addition, see Beatrice Michaels Shapiro, "Humboldt Park: Jews Who Lived There Remember Their Old Neighborhood," *JUF News,* September 1989.

24   The description of Tureck's stimulating effect on other students is from an account Bellow gave to Richard Stern.

27   The quotation from *The Sabinite* is from a copy in the possession of Paul ("Isadore") Bernick, who also supplied the graduation program of Murray F. Tuley High School, January 23, 1933.

27   Bellow's portrait of Isaac Rosenfeld was first published in *Partisan Review,* fall 1956, then revised and expanded as the foreword to Isaac Rosenfeld, *An Age of Enormity: Life and Writings in the Forties and Fifties,* ed. Theodore Solotaroff (Cleveland: World Publishing, 1962), and reprinted in *Preserving the Hunger: An Isaac Rosenfeld Reader,* ed. Mark Shechner

(Detroit: Wayne State University Press, 1988). See also James
Atlas, "Golden Boy," *The New York Review of Books*, June
29, 1989; Steven J. Zipperstein, "The First Loves of Isaac
Rosenfeld," *Jewish Social Studies* 15.1–2 (fall/winter 1998–
99); and Bonnie Lyons, "Isaac Rosenfeld," in *Dictionary of
Literary Biography*, vol. 28. Rosenfeld's novel, *Passage from
Home* (Cleveland: World Publishing, 1946), was reprinted by
Markus Weiner Publishing in 1988. Bellow spoke about the re-
lationship between Rosenfeld and "Zetland" in his interview
with D. J. R. Bruckner, "A Candid Talk with Saul Bellow," *The
New York Times Magazine*, April 15, 1984.

27 The best portrait of the Tuley years is Bruce Cook's profile,
"Saul Bellow: A Mood of Protest," *Perspectives on Ideas and
the Arts*, February 12, 1963. See also Walter Clemons and Jack
Kroll, "America's Master Novelist: An Interview with Saul Bellow," *Newsweek*, September 1, 1975.

28 The book with Bellow's inscription is from the collection of
Charles M. and Arlene Newman; Newman's father was a member of the same Chicago synagogue as Bellow's brother Sam.

29 Bellow's recollections of Sydney J. Harris are from the "Memorial Speech for Sydney J. Harris," typescript supplied by Sol
Rosen. Other memories of the Tuley gang can be found in a
profile of Sam Freifeld by Alan Gross, "I'm an Honest, Decent,
Sensitive, and Unprincipled Fellow," *Chicago Magazine*, December 1979; and in James Atlas, "His Kind of Town, Chicago
Is," *Vanity Fair*, May 1987.

34 "Something to Remember Me By" was first published in *Esquire*, July 1990, and was the title story of a trilogy of late stories (New York: Viking, 1991).

35 "the one she called *moi kresavitz*": interview with Rosette Lamont.

35 Death certificate: Chicago Public Records.

CHAPTER 3

38 On Bellow's time at Crane, see "In the Days of Mr. Roosevelt,"
Esquire, December 1983; reprinted in *It All Adds Up*.

39 My portrait of the University of Chicago during the Hutchins
era draws on Molly McQuade, ed., *An Unsentimental Education: Writers and Chicago* (Chicago: University of Chicago

Press, 1995); Harry S. Ashmore, *Unseasonable Truths: The Life of Robert Maynard Hutchins* (Boston: Little, Brown, 1989); Mary Ann Dzuback, *Robert M. Hutchins: Portrait of an Educator* (Chicago: University of Chicago Press, 1991); William H. McNeill, *Hutchins' University: A Memoir of the University of Chicago, 1929–1950* (Chicago: University of Chicago Press, 1991); and Thomas Wakefield Goodspeed, *A History of the University of Chicago: The First Quarter-Century* (Chicago: University of Chicago Press, 1972 [1916]). See also Edward Shils, "Some Academics, Mainly in Chicago," *The American Scholar* 50 (1981); and Hugh Dalziel Duncan, "The Search for a Middle Ground: I," in *Culture and Democracy* (Totowa, N.J.: Bedminster Press, 1965).

40 Isaac Rosenfeld, "Journal of a Generation," *The New Republic*, January 11, 1943, reprinted in *An Age of Enormity.*

40 Copies of *Soapbox* were supplied by the Northwestern University Archives, Evanston.

40 "Don't you forget what happened to Lyova": "Marx at My Table," *The Guardian*, April 10, 1993.

41 Irving Howe refers to the Yiddish version of "Prufrock" in his memoir, *A Margin of Hope* (New York: Harcourt Brace Jovanovich, 1982); the actual quotation is from a letter from Jerry Greenfield to George Sarant (December 13, 1993).

41 Irving Kristol, "Memoirs of a Trotskyist," *The New York Times Magazine*, January 23, 1977. See also Daniel Bell, *Marxian Socialism in the United States* (Princeton, N.J.: Princeton University Press, 1952).

41 Interview with David Bazelon; see also his collection, *Nothing but a Fine Tooth Comb: Essays in Social Criticism* (New York: Simon and Schuster, 1969).

42 The "Prowst" story is from Maurice's daughter, Lyn Rotblatt.

43 William Barrett, *The Truants: Adventures among the Intellectuals* (Garden City, N.Y.: Anchor/Doubleday, 1982).

43 Letters to Oscar Tarcov are in the possession of his son, Nathan Tarcov.

43 "I'm like my poor father": letter to Ruth Miller.

44 Details of Bellow's cross-country trip were supplied by Bellow and Herbert Passin, supplemented by "In the Days of Mr. Roosevelt."

46 Allan Bloom, *The Closing of the American Mind* (New York: Simon and Schuster, 1987).

46   Bellow's grades at the University of Chicago: Official Academic
      Record, the Office of the University Registrar.

47   Walter Blair recalled his impressions of Bellow for me; Norman
      Maclean's disparagement comes from Bellow himself.

47   The story of the accident at the Carroll Coal Company is from
      an unsigned interview with Martha Duffy, "Some People Come
      Back Like Hecuba," *Time*, February 9, 1970.

47   Bellow's grades at the University of Wisconsin: University of
      Wisconsin–Madison Division of Archives.

47   My portrait of Northwestern is based on Harold F. Williamson
      and Payson S. Wild, *Northwestern University: A History,
      1850–1975* (Evanston: Northwestern University Press, 1976).
      For information about Evanston, I relied on Ira J. Bach, *A
      Guide to Chicago's Historic Suburbs* (Chicago: Swallow
      Press/Ohio University Press, 1981).

48   "There were plenty of renegades": interview with Dr. Donald
      H. Atlas.

49   Diana Trilling, "Lionel Trilling: A Jew at Columbia," in Lionel
      Trilling, *Speaking of Literature and Society* (New York: Har-
      court Brace Jovanovich, 1989); also see Diana Trilling's mem-
      oir, *The Beginning of the Journey* (New York: Harcourt Brace,
      1994). A useful general account of this issue can be found
      in Susanne Klingenstein, *Jews in the American Academy,
      1900–1940: The Dynamics of Intellectual Assimilation* (New
      Haven: Yale University Press, 1991).

49   The description of William Frank Bryan is from Moody Prior.

49   For an account of Bellow's relationship to anthropology, see
      Judie Newman, "Saul Bellow and Social Anthropology," in
      Saul Bellow at Seventy-five: A Collection of Critical Essays, ed.
      Gerhard Bach, Studies and Texts in English, no. 9 (Tübingen:
      G. Narr, 1991). Bellow's remarks on the subject are from his in-
      terview with Nina Steers, "Successor to Faulkner?" *Show*, Sep-
      tember 1964.

49   On Melville Herskovits, including his recommendation of Bel-
      low: Melville J. Herskovits Papers, University Archives, North-
      western University Library. Also see Herskovits's own book,
      The Myth of the Negro Past (Boston: Beacon Press, 1958).

51   That Bellow's story was "not good enough" for publication in
      The Daily Northwestern was recounted to me by Julian Behr-
      stock. "Pets of the North Shore" appeared in the paper on
      April 1, 1936.

52   "I wanted to break with everybody": interview with Terry
      Gross, *Fresh Air,* National Public Radio, October 4, 1989.

53   Information about Edward Hungerford is from the Northwest-
      ern University Archives, Evanston, supplemented by an inter-
      view with Beverly Fields.

53   Helen Jaffe's recollections are from a television documentary,
      "Saul Bellow's Chicago," WMAQ, Chicago, March 27, 1981.

54   Details of Anita Goshkin's family past were provided by Greg-
      ory Bellow.

55   "John Paul," "Northwestern Is a Prison," *The Beacon: Chi-
      cago's Liberal Magazine* 1.1 (April 1937); copies of *The Bea-
      con* were supplied by Patricia Harris.

56   Bellow's letters to James T. Farrell are in the James T. Farrell
      Collection, Special Collections Room, Van Pelt Library, Uni-
      versity of Pennsylvania, Philadelphia.

56   Eliseo Vivas shared with me his impressions of Bellow and
      Rosenfeld at the University of Wisconsin.

56   Rosenfeld's letters to Oscar Tarcov were provided by Rosen-
      feld's biographer, Steven J. Zipperstein of Stanford University.

57   Bellow's reminiscences of Goldenweiser are in Harvey Breit, "A
      Talk with Saul Bellow," *The New York Times Book Review,*
      September 20, 1953.

57   "In my innocence, I had decided to become a writer": in *Twen-
      tieth Century Authors* (New York: H. W. Wilson, 1955).

CHAPTER 4

58   Bellow's comments on Dreiser are from Steve Neal, "The Quin-
      tessential Chicago Writer," *Chicago Tribune Magazine,* Sep-
      tember 6, 1979; his review of F. O. Matthiessen's book,
      "Dreiser and the Triumph of Art," appeared in *Commentary,*
      May 1951.

59   Shils's observation is from a letter to me, March 30, 1994.

60   "a crazy scribbler": "Starting Out in Chicago."

60   The story of Bellow's father threatening to shoot him was re-
      layed to me by David Peltz.

60   Bellow's recollections of Novinson are from "The Chicago
      Book."

61   Bellow's grades: Official Academic Record, the Office of the
      University Registrar, University of Chicago.

61 Bellow chronicled the atmosphere of this period of unemployment in "The Writer and the Welfare State" (n.d.; in Regenstein Library); in "A World Too Much with Us," *Critical Inquiry* (autumn 1975); and in "Perils for Literature," *Chicago Sun-Times Book Week*, September 11, 1968.

62 Bellow's reading list at the Pestalozzi-Froebel Teachers College was supplied by Ruth Miller.

63 On the Federal Writers' Project: Leslie F. Orear and Alan H. Stein, "Writers as Workers: A Fifty-year Retrospective of the Illinois Writers Project, 1935–1939," Illinois Labor Historical Society; *Illinois: A Descriptive and Historical Guide* [1939], American Guide Series (New York: Hastings House, 1974); "Dear Jerre," letters to Jerre Mangione (author of *The Dream and the Deal* [Boston: Little, Brown, 1972]), *Pennsylvania Gazette*, November 1975. On Bellow and the WPA, see also Joyce Illig, "An Interview with Saul Bellow," *Publishers Weekly*, October 22, 1973.

64 For the relationship between Trotsky and the intellectuals, see Alexander Bloom, *Prodigal Sons: The New York Intellectuals and Their World* (New York: Oxford University Press, 1986), and Alan M. Wald, *The New York Intellectuals: The Rise and Decline of the Anti-Stalinist Left from the 1930s to the 1980s* (Chapel Hill: University of North Carolina Press, 1987). Also see Albert Glotzer, *Trotsky: Memoir and Critique* (Buffalo: Prometheus Books, 1989); and Bellow's "Writers, Intellectuals, Politics: Mainly Reminiscence" in *The National Interest*, spring 1993 (reprinted in *It All Adds Up*).

67 For the trip down South in 1940, see Saul Bellow, *Summations,* the Bennington Chapbooks in Literature, Lecture no. 9, May 12, 1987.

68 Graham Greene's description of Taxco is from Norman Sherry, *The Life of Graham Greene*, vol. 1: 1904–1939 (New York: Viking Penguin, 1989).

68 Bellow's Mexican interlude is based on interviews with Bellow and Herbert Passin.

69 For a vivid account of Trotsky's last days in Mexico, see Alain Dugrand, *Trotsky in Mexico, 1937–1940* (Manchester, England: Carcanet Press, 1992).

71 For the early history of *Partisan Review,* I relied on Ruth R. Wisse, "The New York (Jewish) Intellectuals," *Commentary,* November 1987; William Phillips, *A Partisan View: Five Dec-*

ades of the Literary Life (New York: Stein and Day, 1983); Neil Jumonville, *Critical Crossings: The New York Intellectuals in Postwar America* (Berkeley and Los Angeles: University of California Press, 1991); Thomas Bender, *New York Intellect: A History of Intellectual Life in New York City from 1750 to the Beginnings of Our Own Time* (Baltimore: Johns Hopkins University Press, 1987); Howe, *World of Our Fathers;* and *Creators and Disturbers: Reminiscences by Jewish Intellectuals of New York,* drawn from conversations with Bernard Rosenberg and Ernest Goldstein (New York: Columbia University Press, 1982).

75   Ruth Miller, apparently preparing half a century in advance for her role as Bellow's first biographer, compiled a list of the books on his shelf in 1939.

76   The archives of the Vanguard Press, including Bellow's correspondence with James Henle and Evelyn Shrifte, are in the Columbia University Library; see also Guy Henle, "Vanguard Press: Sixty-two Influential Years," *Columbia Library Columns* 40.1 (November 1990).

76   Correspondence from Bellow's first agent, Maxim Lieber, is in the files of *Story* magazine, Firestone Library, Princeton University.

79   Philip Rahv to F. W. Dupee: Dupee Papers at the Low Library, Columbia University.

79   Michael Wreszin shared with me copies of the Bellow–Macdonald correspondence; the originals are among Macdonald's papers in the Beinecke Rare Book and Manuscript Library at Yale University, New Haven. See also Wreszin, *A Rebel in Defense of Tradition: The Life and Politics of Dwight Macdonald* (New York: Basic Books, 1994).

CHAPTER 5

81   The quotations from Rosenfeld's journal are in Shechner, *Preserving the Hunger.*

81   Shils's characterization of Vasiliki was made to me.

82   Harold Rosenberg's essay "On the Fall of Paris" was published in *Partisan Review,* November/December 1940; see also H. J. Kaplan, "Paris Letter," *Partisan Review,* May/June 1945.

82   Alfred Kazin's description of postwar New York is from *Our New York,* with David Finn (New York: Harper and Row,

1989); his portrait of Bellow is in *New York Jew* (New York: Alfred A. Knopf, 1978); Bellow's rebuttal is in his two-part interview with Keith Botsford, "A Half Life: An Autobiography in Ideas," *Bostonia*, November/December 1990 and January/February 1991.

84   "Possibly the pride": letter to Kazin, the Berg Collection, New York Public Library.

85   Archives of the John Simon Guggenheim Memorial Foundation, New York.

85   Review of *The World of Sholom Aleichem*: "Laughter in the Ghetto," *The Saturday Review of Literature* 36 (May 30, 1953).

85   Sydney J. Harris: interview with D. J. R. Bruckner, the Regenstein Library.

86   Lionel Abel, *The Intellectual Follies: A Memoir of the Literary Venture in New York and Paris* (New York: W. W. Norton, 1984).

86   Tumin's recollections: "Homage to Saul Bellow," a speech Tumin gave at the presentation of the Jewish Heritage Award for Excellence in Literature by B'nai B'rith, Philadelphia, March 3, 1968; copy provided by Tumin.

87   Janet Richards, *Common Soldiers: A Self-Portrait and Other Portraits* (San Francisco: Archer Press, 1979).

88   Wallace Markfield, "Isaac Rosenfeld," entry in *Contemporary Authors*, vol. 3. (Detroit: Gale Research, 1981–).

89   Bellow reminisced about his reviewing days in remarks made on October 31, 1985, at the Whiting Foundation Writers' Program ceremony, the Morgan Library, New York City; text provided by Gerald Freund.

89   John U. Nef, *The Search for Meaning: Autobiography of a Nonconformist* (Washington, D.C.: Public Affairs, 1973).

89   On the culture of *Time* in those days, see W. A. Swanberg, *Luce and His Empire* (New York: Scribner's, 1972); on Whittaker Chambers, see Sam Tanenhaus's comprehensive biography, *Whittaker Chambers: A Biography* (New York: Random House, 1997).

91   Dana Tasker's letter to Ik Shuman, August 13, 1943, is in the *New Yorker* Records, Manuscripts and Archives section, New York Public Library.

92   Herman Kogan, *The Great EB* (Chicago: University of Chicago Press, 1958). On Adler's project, see Mortimer Adler, *Philoso-*

pher at Large: An Intellectual Autobiography, 1902–1976 (New York: Macmillan, 1977).

96 Hemingway's influence on Bellow: Bellow, "Hemingway and the Image of Man," review of *Ernest Hemingway*, by Philip Young, *Partisan Review*, May/June 1953; also Allan Chavkin, "Fathers and Sons: 'Papa' Hemingway and Saul Bellow," *Papers on Language and Literature* 19.4 (1983).

98 M.A. and Ph.D.: interview with Maggie Simmons, "Free to Feel," *Quest*, February/March 1979.

99 Reviews of *Dangling Man*: Delmore Schwartz, "A Man in His Time," *Partisan Review*, May/June 1944; John Chamberlain, "Books of the Times," *The New York Times*, March 25, 1944; Kenneth Fearing, "Man Versus Man," *The New York Times Book Review*, March 26, 1944; Irving Kristol, *Politics*, June 1944; "Introspective Stinker," *Time*, May 8, 1944; Edmund Wilson, "Doubts and Dreams: *Dangling Man* under a Glass Bell," *The New Yorker*, April 1, 1944.

CHAPTER 6

100 Diana Trilling, "Fiction in Review," *The Nation*, April 15, 1944.

101 William Targ, *Indecent Pleasures: The Life and Colorful Times of William Targ* (New York: Macmillan, 1975).

104 Bellow's letter to Jean Stafford is among her papers in the Rare Books Room, University Libraries, University of Colorado at Boulder; letters to Sam Freifeld are in the possession of his daughter, Susan; the letter to James T. Farrell is at the University of Pennsylvania.

108 Kazin's portrait of Lidov is in *New York Jew*.

109 John Lehmann's correspondence with Bellow is in the Harry Ransom Humanities Research Center, the University of Texas, Austin.

109 Bellow's review of *The Journey Home*: "Four Novels," *Commentary*, December 1945.

111 The most vivid portrait of Rahv is by Mary McCarthy in Philip Rahv, *Essays on Literature and Politics, 1932–1972*, ed. Arabel J. Porter and Andrew J. Dvosin (Boston: Houghton Mifflin, 1978).

112 Daniel Bell, "The Position of the Intellectual Jew," *Jewish Frontier Anthology* (New York: Jewish Frontier, 1945).

113 George Sarant lent me Rosenfeld's journals when I was researching my essay on Rosenfeld.

114 For information on the University of Minnesota in these years, I'm indebted to Joseph Blotner for the text of his interview with Robert Penn Warren, supplemented by his *Robert Penn Warren: A Biography* (New York: Random House, 1997); Blotner also shared with me an interview with Warren in the archives of the Robert Penn Warren Oral History Project at the University of Kentucky, Lexington. Bellow's letters to Warren are at the Beinecke Library at Yale. For a general account of life at the University of Minnesota in those years, see Max Kampelman, *Entering New Worlds: The Memoirs of a Private Man in Public Life* (New York: HarperCollins, 1991). I also drew upon the recollections of Robert Hivnor and Ralph Ross, as well as an unpublished memoir by Douglas LaRue Smith.

CHAPTER 7

120 Bellow's description of Madrid is from "Spanish Letter," *Partisan Review*, March/April 1948.

121 "keeping his acne down" and "To the Sancho Panza": interview with Robert Johnson.

127 "The Jewish Writer and the English Literary Tradition: A Symposium, Part 2," *Commentary*, October 1949. See also Mark Shechner, "Jewish Writers," *The Harvard Guide to Contemporary Writing*, ed. Daniel Hoffman (Cambridge, Mass.: Harvard University Press, 1979); Mark Shechner, "Down in the Mouth with Saul Bellow," in *After the Revolution: Studies in the Jewish-American Imagination* (Bloomington: Indiana University Press, 1987); and Harold Rosenberg, "Jewish Identity in a Free Society," in *Discovering the Present: Three Decades in Art, Culture, and Politics* (Chicago: University of Chicago Press, 1973); and L. H. Goldman, "The Holocaust in the Novels of Saul Bellow," *Modern Language Studies* 16.1 (1986).

128 "That's how I view my own Jewishness": See "Americans Who Are Also Jews," *Jewish Digest*, April 1977. See also Bellow, "Why the Persecution of the Jews?"

128 "to write about American life": Chirantan Kulshrestha, "A Conversation with Saul Bellow," *Chicago Review* 23 (fall 1972).

130 Reviews of *The Victim:* Diana Trilling, "Fiction in Review," *The Nation,* January 3, 1948; Elizabeth Hardwick, "Fiction Chronicle," *Partisan Review,* January/February 1948; Charles Poore, "Books of the Times," *The New York Times,* November 22, 1947; "Suffering for Nothing," *Time,* December 1, 1947.

131 "I'll lather you": interview with Douglas LaRue Smith.

135 Correspondence from Frank Taylor is in Low Library, Columbia University.

CHAPTER 8

137 Bellow's account of postwar life in Paris is drawn largely from "My Paris," *The New York Times Magazine,* part 2: *The Sophisticated Traveler,* March 13, 1983; and from "The French as Dostoyevsky Saw Them," *The New Republic,* May 23, 1955, reprinted as the foreword to Feodor M. Dostoevsky, *Winter Notes on Summer Impressions* (New York: Criterion, 1955). Kaplan's remark is also quoted in this article.

138 Bellow's correspondence with Monroe Engel is from the files of Viking Press, New York.

139 "built a very sizable section of Newark, New Jersey": interview with H. J. Kaplan.

140 "a cemetery": interview with Vivian Missner.

141 Abel, *Intellectual Follies.*

142 Phillips, *Partisan View.*

142 H. J. Kaplan, "Paris Letter," *Partisan Review,* May/June 1945.

142 The one surviving chapter of "The Crab and the Butterfly" appeared under the title "The Trip to Galena" in *Partisan Review,* August 1950.

143 "I was terribly depressed": Keith Opdahl, "Saul Bellow," *Dictionary of Literary Biography,* vol. 28 (Detroit: Gale Research, 1978–).

143 "bothering the life": interview with Julian Behrstock.

144 "I had a room in Paris": Bellow's letter to John Lehmann, in the Harry Ransom Humanities Research Center, the University of Texas, Austin.

146   William Barrett, "New Innocents Abroad," *Partisan Review,* autumn 1949.

152   "Address by Gooley MacDowell to the Hasbeens Club of Chicago" appeared in *Hudson Review,* summer 1951; "A Sermon by Doctor Pep" appeared in *Partisan Review,* May 1949.

156   On Bellow's Salzburg visit: interview with Ted Hoffman; Archives of the Salzburg Seminar in American Studies, Schloss Leopoldskron, Salzburg, Austria; Thomas H. Eliot and Lois J. Eliot, *The Salzburg Seminar* (Ipswich, Mass.: Ipswich Press, 1987).

CHAPTER 9

161   "Saul Bellow is back from Paris": Isaac Rosenfeld Papers, Regenstein Library, University of Chicago.

163   Telephone interview with Dr. Chester Raphael.

163   "The trouble with Paul Goodman": Journals of Isaac Rosenfeld, Regenstein Library.

163   "The Freudians had their own Thermidor": Botsford interview, *Bostonia,* part 2. Kazin's account of Rosenfeld's Reichian phase is in *New York Jew;* the description of Bellow's Reichianism comes from interviews with David Bazelon and Dr. George Sarant.

164   "There were women": interview with Victoria Lidov.

165   "The Wrecker," *New World Writing No. 6* (New York: New American Library, 1954).

167   Archives of the Rockefeller Foundation, Pocantico Hills, North Tarrytown, N.Y.

170   Albert Halper, *This Is Chicago: An Anthology* (New York: Holt, 1952). A. J. Liebling, *Chicago: The Second City* (New York: Alfred A. Knopf, 1952).

173   Archives of the American Academy of Arts and Letters, New York.

173   Archives of Yaddo, Saratoga Springs, N.Y.

173   On Princeton: Russell Fraser, *A Mingled Yarn: The Life of R. P. Blackmur* (New York: Harcourt Brace Jovanovich, 1981); Eileen Simpson, *Poets in Their Youth* (New York: Random House, 1982); and James Atlas, *Delmore Schwartz: The Life of an American Poet* (New York: Farrar, Straus & Giroux, 1977). Also Carlos Baker, "Bellow's Gift," *Theology Today,* January

1976, and the two biographies of John Berryman: Paul Mariani, *Dream Song: The Life of John Berryman* (New York: Morrow, 1990), and John Haffenden, *The Life of John Berryman* (Boston: Routledge and Kegan Paul, 1982).

175 Adam Bellow, typescript of personal memoir; for the early days of Sondra's courtship with Bellow, see Adam Bellow, "When My Parents Were in Love," *Talk*, October 1999.

177 "Out of Bounds": Regenstein Library.

178 "buckshoe humanists": Howe, *Margin of Hope.*

180 "Our Country and Our Culture: A Symposium," *Partisan Review*, May/June 1952.

181 Philip Rahv's major essay on Henry James is in *Literature and the Sixth Sense* (Boston: Houghton Mifflin, 1969); Delmore Schwartz's essays on Dos Passos and Hemingway are collected in *Selected Essays of Delmore Schwartz*, ed. Donald A. Dike and David H. Zucker (Chicago: University of Chicago Press, 1970).

181 "*Our* forests, Alfred?": Norman Podhoretz, *Making It* (New York: Random House, 1967).

182 Trilling's prediction was found among John Marshall's notes in the Rockefeller Foundation Archives, Pocantico Hills, North Tarrytown, N.Y.

CHAPTER 10

183 Diana Trilling, "Speaking of Books," *The New York Times Book Review*, June 15, 1952; John Aldridge, ibid., June 22, 1952.

184 Bellow's correspondence with Lionel Trilling is in Low Library, Columbia University.

184 Review of *Invisible Man*: "Man Underground," *Commentary*, June 1952.

186 "How I Wrote Augie March's Story": *The New York Times Book Review*, January 31, 1954.

190 On Bellow's borrowings from Daniel Mannix, see Eusebio L. Rodrigues, "Augie March's Mexican Adventures," *Indiana Journal of American Studies* 8 (1978); and D. W. Gunn, *American and British Writers in Mexico* (Austin: University of Texas Press, 1974). I also drew upon a telephone interview with Daniel Mannix; a letter from Mannix elaborating on our conversation (November 13, 1991); and a letter to me from Keith Jennison.

191 Irving Howe's description of *Augie*'s style is in *World of Our Fathers.*

192 On Bellow's translation of "Gimpel the Fool": In addition to Howe's account, I owe certain details to a conversation with Harvey Shapiro. The story was published in *Partisan Review,* May/June 1953, and reprinted in *A Treasury of Yiddish Stories,* ed. Irving Howe and Eliezer Greenberg (New York: Viking, 1954).

193 Karl Shapiro, *The Younger Son* (Chapel Hill: Algonquin Books, 1988).

193 Philip Toynbee, "To Be a Good Man," *The Observer,* October 24, 1976.

193 Bellow's letter to Bernard Malamud: *The Bernard Malamud Society Newsletter* 5 (fall 1995).

CHAPTER 11

196 The fictional portraits of Bard: Mary McCarthy, *The Groves of Academe* (New York: New American Library, 1952); Michael Rubin, *A Trip into Town* (New York: Harper and Row, 1961).

197 "At Bard, Literature": interview with Elsa Heister Zion.

197 Information about Bard comes from the files of the college; also an article by Keith Botsford, "Saul Bellow: Made in America," *The Independent Weekend,* February 10, 1990. Bellow's observations are from Botsford's interview with him in *Bostonia,* part 2.

197 Al Ellenberg, a student of Bellow's at Bard, wrote about that period in "Saul Bellow Picks Another Fight," *Rolling Stone,* March 4, 1982.

197 "river people": interview with Andy Dupee.

197 On Chanler Chapman: Edmund Wilson provided a sketch of Chapman in *The Thirties* (New York: Farrar, Straus & Giroux, 1980). My account of him is supplemented by a letter from Joseph R. Hixson, a subsequent tenant at Sylvania Farms.

198 Reviews of *Augie:* Robert Gorham Davis, "Augie Just Wouldn't Settle Down," *The New York Times Book Review,* September 20, 1953; Harvey Curtis Webster, "Quest Through the Modern World," *The Saturday Review of Literature,* September 19, 1953; "What Makes Augie Run?" *Time,* September 21, 1953;

Anthony West, "A Crash of Symbols," *The New Yorker,* September 26, 1953; Norman Podhoretz, "The Language of Life," *Commentary,* October 1953.

199 Bellow's correspondence with Katharine White is in the archives of *The New Yorker* at the New York Public Library.

200 My account of the controversy surrounding Podhoretz's review is based on interviews with Bellow, Podhoretz, William Phillips, Clement Greenberg, and Martin Greenberg, who worked in the magazine's office at the time.

201 Trilling's letter to Pascal Covici is in the Viking files, New York. His published opinions of *The Adventures of Augie March* are in "A Triumph of the Comic View," *The Griffin* (September 1953), and in his introduction to the Modern Library edition of the novel (1965).

204 Bellow's review of Joyce Cary's novel appeared in *The New Republic,* February 22, 1954. His most pointed comments about Eliot are in an interview conducted by Rockwell Gray, Harry White, and Gerald Nemanic, *Triquarterly* 60 (1984).

206 Bellow's correspondence with his father is in the Regenstein Library, as is Rosenfeld's congratulatory letter to Bellow.

210 On the negotiations over the National Book Award: letter to me from Leon Edel.

211 English reviews: Kingsley Amis, *The Spectator,* May 21, 1954; J. B. Priestley, "A Novel on the Heroic Scale," *Sunday Times* 9 (May 1954); V. S. Pritchett, "That Time and That Wilderness," *The New Statesman,* September 28, 1962.

211 Delmore Schwartz's journal entry about Bellow: *Portrait of Delmore: Journals and Notes of Delmore Schwartz, 1939–1959,* ed. Elizabeth Pollet (New York: Farrar, Straus & Giroux, 1986).

213 "I often feel, when I'm writing": Bellow's remark to Louis Sidran was passed on to me by Sidran's son, Ben.

213 Rosenfeld to Bellow: Regenstein Library.

214 "will not attend": letter from Selena Berkin Bellow in the possession of Ann Weinstein.

CHAPTER 12

217 "in a setting of pines, ticks and sun": letter to Reginald Cook, Special Collections, Starr Library, Middlebury College, Middlebury, Vermont.

217 Hannah Arendt/Mary McCarthy letters: Special Collections, Vassar College Library (August 10, 1954); McCarthy's letter to Bowden Broadwater is also at Vassar. See Carol Brightman, *Writing Dangerously: Mary McCarthy and Her World* (New York: Clarkson Potter, 1992). Fran Kiernan, another biographer of McCarthy, shared with me the transcript of her interview with Bellow.

217 Bellow's comments on McCarthy were made to the author and to Keith Botsford in his two-part *Bostonia* interview.

218 "You could see the electricity starting up": interview with Alfred Kazin.

219 "It's true that my name won't go down": interview with Lyn Rotblatt.

219 "You could look up in the library": interview with Lyn Rotblatt.

220 Bellow recalls his father's unwillingness to be a pal in a letter to Robert Penn Warren; Abram's letters to Bellow are in the Regenstein Library.

221 Abram's obituary: *Chicago Sun-Times*, May 3, 1955.

222 Bellow's letters to Mark Harris are among the Mark Harris Papers at the University of Delaware Library, Newark.

222 Miller, *Saul Bellow*.

222 "Illinois Journey," *Holiday*, September 1957.

224 Covici's letters to Bellow are in the Viking files, New York; Bellow's letters to Covici are at the Harry Ransom Humanities Research Center, University of Texas, Austin.

226 "Theatre Chronicle," *Partisan Review*, May/June 1954; the letter to Delmore Schwartz is in the *Partisan Review* files, Boston University; his letter to Henry Volkening is in the files of Russell and Volkening, New York; the letter to Karl Shapiro is from the files of *Poetry* magazine, Chicago.

227 Bellow's letters to John Berryman are in the Manuscripts Division, the University of Minnesota Library, Minneapolis.

227 "The University as Villain," *The Nation*, November 16, 1957.

228 Bellow's letter to Louis Simpson is in Simpson's papers at the Library of Congress, as is his side of an extensive correspondence with Ralph Ellison; his letter to Granville Hicks is in the Hicks papers at Syracuse University, Syracuse, New York.

228 "Distractions of a Fiction Writer," in *The Living Novel: A Symposium*, ed. Granville Hicks (New York: Macmillan, 1957).

232 The account of Arthur Miller's time in Reno is from his autobiography, *Timebends: A Life* (New York: Grove, 1987), and from my interview with Miller.

CHAPTER 13

234 The portrait of Rosenfeld in his last years is from Bellow's foreword to Rosenfeld's posthumous collection, *An Age of Enormity;* Wallace Markfield's entry in *Contemporary Authors;* and my own interviews with Bellow.

235 Bellow's letter to Gertrude Buckman was provided by Andreas Brown.

236 "He combined all the reticence": letter from Bellow to Mark Shechner, September 30, 1975.

236 "victim literature": Gordon Lloyd Harper, "The Art of Fiction: Saul Bellow," *The Paris Review,* winter 1966; reprinted in *Writers at Work: Third Series,* ed. Alfred Kazin (New York: Viking, 1967).

238 Dr. Tamkin's Reichianism: Eusebio L. Rodrigues, "Reichianism in *Seize the Day,*" in *Critical Essays on Saul Bellow,* ed. Stanley Trachtenberg (Boston: G. K. Hall, 1979). See also Daniel Fuchs, *Saul Bellow: Vision and Revision* (Durham, N.C.: Duke University Press, 1984).

240 The manuscripts of *Seize the Day* are at the Harry Ransom Humanities Research Center, University of Texas, Austin.

240 "One parent or another": Maxwell Geismar, "Saul Bellow: Novelist of the Intellectuals," in *American Moderns: From Rebellion to Conformity* (New York: Hill and Wang, 1958).

240 "for he emerges": Leslie Fiedler, "Saul Bellow," *Prairie Schooner* 31 (1957); reprinted in *Saul Bellow and the Critics,* ed. Irving Malin (New York: New York University Press, 1967).

240 Louis Simpson, *North of Jamaica* (New York: Harper and Row, 1972).

241 "given [him] asylum": letter to Sam Freifeld.

241 "We're going to have a child": interview with Sondra Bellow.

241 "I poured my life's blood": Botsford interview, *Bostonia,* part 1.

241 "We may have to drill a new one": letter to Ruth Miller.

242 "My wife had *had* it with artists": Botsford interview, *Bostonia,* part 2.

242   "I hate painters": interview with Hilton Kramer.
243   "none too hot, either": letter to Alfred Kazin.

CHAPTER 14

245   The Bellow–Stern correspondence is in the Regenstein Library.
245   *The Journals of John Cheever*, ed. Robert Gottlieb (New York: Alfred A. Knopf, 1991).
246   Saul Bellow, "A Tribute to John Cheever," *The New York Review of Books*, February 17, 1983. Cheever's citation is in the archive of the American Academy and Institute of Arts and Letters, New York. See also Scott Donaldson, *John Cheever: A Biography* (New York: Random House, 1988).
246   Bellow's letters to Philip Rahv are in the files of *Partisan Review*, Boston University.
246   Brendan Gill, "Long and Short," *The New Yorker*, January 5, 1957; Alfred Kazin, "In Search of Light," *The New York Times Book Review*, November 18, 1956; Leslie Fiedler, "Some Footnotes on the Fiction of '56," *The Reporter*, December 13, 1956.
247   Bellow's letter to Granville Hicks is among Hicks's papers at the Syracuse University Library, Syracuse, New York; I also heard testimony on the Smith College "hassle" from William Maxwell and Brendan Gill.
248   My account of Bellow's confrontation with Faulkner is from Donald Hall's engaging memoir, *Their Ancient Glittering Eyes: Remembering Poets and More Poets* (New York: Ticknor and Fields, 1992), supplemented by several conversations with Hall; Bellow's letter to Faulkner is in the Special Collections Department, Alderman Library, University of Virginia, Charlottesville. He also referred to this episode in a speech he delivered, "Alone in Mixed Company," at the PEN/New England awards ceremony at the John F. Kennedy Library, Boston; reprinted in *The Boston Globe*, May 19, 1996.
250   "Motion stirs my sometimes sluggish imagination": letter to Ruth Miller. "That g-d book": letter to Pascal Covici, Harry Ransom Humanities Research Center, University of Texas, Austin.
252   Foreword to John Berryman, *Recovery* (New York: Farrar, Straus & Giroux, 1973); first published in *The New York Times Book Review*, May 27, 1973.

253 Philip Roth, *The Ghost Writer* (New York: Farrar, Straus & Giroux, 1979). Bellow's review of *Goodbye, Columbus*: "The Swamp of Prosperity," *Commentary*, July 1959.

254 "And that was the beginning of Saul's *tsuris*": interview with Philip Roth.

CHAPTER 15

255 "tear up his life": interview with Fran Gendlin.

256 "a sweet, mouselike person": interview with Elsa Heister Zion.

257 Jack Ludwig's writings: *Above Ground* (Toronto: New Canadian Library, McClelland and Stewart, 1968); see also his story "Confusions: Thoreau in California," *The Noble Savage* 1, March 1960.

258 "There are no concessions in God's circus": interview with Alfred Kazin.

258 "Jack was offering amorous advice": interview with Lynn Hoffman.

258 "some other chick in the chickenyard": interview with Ralph Ellison.

259 "We were embarrassed": interview with Patricia Harris.

260 "The Sealed Treasure," *The Times Literary Supplement*, July 1, 1960.

CHAPTER 16

262 Bellow's letters to Josephine Herbst are in the archives of *New World Writing* at the Beinecke Rare Book and Manuscript Library at Yale University, New Haven.

263 "The worse my personal disasters became": David D. Galloway, "An Interview with Saul Bellow," *Audit-Poetry* 3 (1963).

263 "patched things up": letter to Pascal Covici, Harry Ransom Humanities Research Center, University of Texas, Austin.

265 "Letter to Doctor Edvig," *Esquire*, July 1963.

265 "melancholic," "a depressive temperament": Jay Nash and Ron Offen, "Saul Bellow," *The Literary Times*, December 1964.

266 a "Goldoni comedy": Botsford interview, *Bostonia*, part 1.

268 Bellow's application to the Ford Foundation is in the foundation's American Literary Manuscripts Collection, New York.

269 "Deep Readers of the World, Beware!" *The New York Times Book Review,* February 15, 1959.

270 Bellow's borrowing from Chanler Chapman: letter to Joseph R. Hixson.

272 "an astonishing feat of creative synthesis": Fuchs, *Saul Bellow, Vision and Revision.* For a discussion of Reichianism in *Henderson the Rain King,* see Eusebio L. Rodrigues, "Bellow's Africa," *American Literature* 43.2 (May 1971).

272 Dr. Paul Schilder, *The Image and Appearance of the Human Body* (New York: International Universities Press, 1950).

273 Carlos Baker, "To the Dark," *The New York Times Book Review,* February 22, 1959.

274 Bellow's interpretation of *Henderson* is in a letter to Richard Stern.

274 "Henderson—the absurd seeker of high qualities": Steers, "Successor to Faulkner?"

275 Reviews of *Henderson:* Charles Rolo, "Reader's Choice," *The Atlantic Monthly,* March 1959; Orville Prescott, *The New York Times,* February 23, 1959; Elizabeth Hardwick, "A Fantastic Voyage," *Partisan Review,* spring 1959; Richard Stern, "Henderson's Bellow," *Kenyon Review* 21.4 (1959); Harvey Swados, "Bellow's Adventures in Africa," *The New Leader,* March 23, 1959. English reviews: Malcolm Bradbury, "Saul Bellow's *Henderson the Rain King,*" *The Listener,* January 30, 1964; Margaret Drabble, "A Myth to Stump the Experts," *The New Statesman,* March 26, 1971.

276 Henry Miller's letter is in the Viking files, New York.

276 Bellow complained about the reception of *Henderson* in letters to Pascal Covici and William Phillips; the letter to Phillips is in the *Partisan Review* archives, Boston University.

277 "He's not supposed to let me out of his sight": interview with Eugene Kennedy.

277 My sketch of Nelson Algren is based on Bettina Drew's biography, *Nelson Algren: A Life on the Wild Side* (New York: Putnam, 1989). See also John Raymer, "A Changing Sense of Chicago in the Works of Saul Bellow and Nelson Algren," *Old Northwest,* April 4, 1978.

277 For Bellow's relationship with Josephine Herbst, I depended on Elinor Langer, *Josephine Herbst: The Story She Could Never Tell* (Boston: Little, Brown, 1984).

278 My description of Bellow's effort to intervene on behalf of Delmore Schwartz is from interviews conducted with James

Laughlin and Elizabeth Pollet for my biography of Schwartz; the quotation in the footnote is from a letter Bellow wrote to Laughlin. Bellow also described this episode in a letter to Schwartz's first wife, Gertrude Buckman, in the possession of Andreas Brown.

278 Bellow's letter to Harvey Swados—including his vision of *The Noble Savage*—is in the Archives and Manuscripts Department, University Library, University of Massachusetts at Amherst.

279 *The Noble Savage*, a Meridian Periodical. The complete run numbered five issues: March and October 1960; April and October 1961; October 1962.

280 Bellow's letters to Ludwig and Botsford are in the *Noble Savage* archive at Beinecke Library, Yale University; his letters to Mark Harris are in the Harris Papers at the University of Delaware, Newark.

281 *Like You're Nobody: The Letters of Louis Gallo, 1961–1962, plus Oedipus-Schmoedipus, the Story That Started It All* (New York: Dimensions Press, 1966).

CHAPTER 17

285 Ludwig's letters to Bellow are in the Regenstein Library.

287 "a *devoradora des hombres*": transcript of Bellow's interview with Fran Kiernan.

287 Arendt/McCarthy correspondence: Vassar College Library, Poughkeepsie, New York.

288 Bellow's reference to the novel that became *Herzog* is in a letter to Pascal Covici; his letters to Marshall Best are in the files of Viking, New York.

290 "In much the same way": "Starting Out in Chicago."

290 Theodore Solotaroff, "A Vocal Group: The Jewish Part in American Letters," *The Times Literary Supplement*, November 6, 1959.

290 Leslie Fiedler, "On the Road; Or the Adventures of Karl Shapiro," *Poetry* 96 (April–September 1960).

291 Bellow's letters to Bernard Richards are in the research library of the Jewish Theological Seminary of America, New York; Richards's letters are in the Regenstein Library.

291 *Great Jewish Short Stories.*

292 Richard Poirier, "*Herzog,* or Bellow in Trouble," in *Saul Bellow: A Collection of Critical Essays,* ed. Earl Rovit (Englewood Cliffs, N.J.: Prentice, 1975).

294 Botsford's letter to Bellow is in the Regenstein Library.

295 "nightly bed-time reading": Daniel Fuchs, "Bellow and Freud," *Studies in the Literary Imagination* 17.2 (1984); see also Robert Boyers, "Literature and Culture: An Interview with Saul Bellow," *Salmagundi* 30 (summer 1975), which contains Bellow's most extensive statement of his views on Freud.

295 On Albert Ellis, see Daniel N. Wiener, *Albert Ellis: Passionate Skeptic,* foreword by Paul Meehl (New York: Praeger, 1988).

295 "high-smelling farts": interview with Joseph Epstein.

295 "I talk people out of their bullshit": interview with Dr. Albert Ellis; Bellow's assessment of his treatment with Ellis was made in an interview with me.

297 Ted Hoffman's appraisal of Bellow is from a letter to me.

298 "He met these women": interview with Ann Birstein.

298 "well-born": interview with Rosette Lamont; see also Rosette C. Lamont, "Bellow Observed: A Serial Portrait," *Saul Bellow Journal* 4.2 (summer 1985).

300 "Don't make me ashamed": Greg's letter is among the letters of Oscar Tarcov; Bellow sent it to Tarcov, seeking advice. Bellow gave his side of the story in a letter to Tarcov.

301 "The world *is* sound somewhere": letter to John Goetz.

301 F. W. Dupee's recollections are in a letter to Dwight Macdonald, supplied by Michael Wreszin.

301 "It's funny": interview with Gore Vidal.

301 "What's a jungle bunny like you": interview with Edward Rothstein.

CHAPTER 18

303 "to study skin-diving": letter to David Peltz.

303 Bellow's letter to Josephine Herbst: archives of *New World Writing,* the Beinecke Rare Book and Manuscript Library, Yale University, New Haven.

304 On Bellow in Puerto Rico: interviews with Bernard Lockwood, Joan McMurray, and Thomas Noel conducted by Mark Staebler. See also William Kennedy, "If He Doesn't Have a True Word to Say, He Keeps His Mouth Shut," *Esquire,* February

1982; reprinted in *Riding the Yellow Trolley Car: Selected Nonfiction* (New York: Viking, 1993).

305 Bellow's letter to Ludwig was quoted in the first bound galley (later suppressed) of Miller, *Saul Bellow: A Biography of the Imagination.*

307 "You are not *my* tough friend": Miller, *Saul Bellow: A Biography of the Imagination.*

307 Stern's minatory letter is among Bellow's papers at the Regenstein Library.

309 Mark Harris, *Saul Bellow, Drumlin Woodchuck* (Athens, Ga.: University of Georgia Press, 1980).

310 "The Riddle of Shakespeare's Sonnets," *The Griffin*, June 1962.

310 My account of Bellow's time at Wagner College is from Susan Dworkin, "The 'Great Man' Syndrome: Saul Bellow and Me," *Ms.*, March 1977.

312 Bellow's Hopwood Lecture, "Where Do We Go from Here? The Future of Fiction," was printed in the *Michigan Quarterly Review* 1.1 (1962); reprinted in Malin, *Saul Bellow and the Critics.*

312 "Literature," *Encyclopaedia Britannica*, 1963. See also *Imaginative Literature 1: From Homer to Shakespeare*, by Mortimer J. Adler and Seymour Cain, preface by Saul Bellow (Chicago: Encyclopaedia Britannica, Inc., 1963).

313 "Facts That Put Fancy to Flight," *The New York Times Book Review*, February 11, 1962.

313 "Literary Notes on Khrushchev," *Esquire*, March 1961.

314 Bellow described the intention behind *Herzog* in a television interview: "Saul Bellow Tells (Among Other Things) the Thinking Behind 'Herzog,'" *Chicago Tribune*, January 24, 1965, a condensed transcript from the Chicago television show *Book Beat*, with Robert Cromie. See also Norman Glubok, "Success Diverts Saul Bellow," *Chicago Daily News*, February 20, 1965.

315 Bellow's letter to Herbert Gold is in Low Library, Columbia University.

316 Edward Levi: interview with D. J. R. Bruckner, the Regenstein Library.

317 Edmund Wilson, *The Sixties* (New York: Farrar, Straus & Giroux, 1993).

317 Bellow on Kennedy: "Aria," *The Noble Savage* 5, October 1962.

CHAPTER 19

318 "When people ask whether I have roots here": John Blades, "Bellow Leaving Chicago in Body but Not in Spirit," *Chicago Tribune*, May 25, 1993.

319 "the art life": "Skepticism and the Depth of Life," in Miller and Herring, *Arts and the Public.*

319 Malcolm Cowley, "Who's to Take the Place of Hemingway and Faulkner?" *The New York Times Book Review,* October 7, 1962.

319 "You're next": Richard Stern, "Bellow's Gift," *The New York Times Magazine,* November 21, 1976.

321 Susan's letter to Margaret Shafer is among the Bellow letters in Shafer's possession.

322 Bellow's movie reviews appeared in *Horizon* (September and November 1962, March 1963).

323 Hellman's remarks on Bellow the playwright are recounted in a letter from Bellow to William Phillips; also a letter to the author from Joan Mellen, one of Hellman's biographers.

325 A copy of Bellow's letter to Sondra dated September 30, 1962, is in the files of John Goetz.

329 Reviews of *Herzog:* Julian Moynahan, "The Way up from Rock Bottom," *The New York Times Book Review,* September 20, 1964; V. S. Pritchett, "King Saul," *The New York Review of Books,* October 22, 1964; Philip Rahv, "Bellow the Brain King," *The New York Herald Tribune Book Week,* September 20, 1964; John Aldridge, "The Complacency of Herzog," in *Herzog: Text and Criticism,* ed. Irving Howe (New York, Viking, 1976); Richard Poirier, "Bellows to *Herzog,*" *Partisan Review,* spring 1965. See also Norman Podhoretz, "The Adventures of Saul Bellow," *Doings and Undoings* (New York: Farrar, Straus & Giroux, 1964).

330 Thomas Meehan, "Off the Couch by Christmas," *The New Yorker,* January 9, 1965.

330 Pete Hamill, "A Look at Saul Bellow, Writer at the Top," *The New York Herald Tribune,* September 27, 1964; Gerald Nachman, "A Talk with Saul Bellow," *New York Post,* October 4, 1964.

331 For a thorough account of the fate of *The Last Analysis,* see Marilyn Stasio, *Broadway's Beautiful Losers* (New York: Delacorte, 1972); Joe Anthony's observation about Bellow is from this source. The richest trove of information about Bellow's ca-

reer in the theater is the archive of Toby Cole, housed at the library of the University of California, Davis.

332 Edward Hoagland's recollections are in "The Job Is to Pour out Your Heart," *The New York Times Book Review,* October 4, 1981.

332 Reviews of *The Last Analysis:* Howard Taubman, "'Last Analysis' of Saul Bellow Arrives," *The New York Times,* October 3, 1964; Walter Kerr, "Bellow's 'Last Analysis,'" *The New York Herald Tribune,* October 3, 1964; Robert Brustein, "Saul Bellow on the Drag Strip," *The New Republic,* October 24, 1964. See also Robert Gutwillig, "Talk with Saul Bellow," *The New York Times Book Review,* September 20, 1964; and Marc Saporta, "Saul Bellow: le véritable écrivain?" *Le Figaro Littéraire,* no. 1193, March 17, 1969.

CHAPTER 20

334 "I received two or three thousand letters": "The Thinking Behind *Herzog,*" *Book Beat,* interview with Robert Cromie.

337 "I'm not just a flower girl": interview with Rosette Lamont.

337 "Have you read *Herzog?*": interview with John Goetz.

338 "I'm Valentine Gersbach": interview with Corlies Smith.

338 "It's very hard": Sanford Pinsker, "Saul Bellow in the Classroom," *College English* 34 (1973).

338 "Maybe he is": interview with Herbert and Mitzi McCloskey.

338 Theodore Solotaroff, "Saul Bellow: The Lines of Resistance," *The Red Hot Vacuum* (New York: Atheneum, 1970).

338 Stanley Edgar Hyman, "Seize the Moon," *The New Leader,* December 8, 1969.

339 The publishing history of *Herzog* is from the Viking files, New York.

339 "Novelist Saul Bellow Gives Home in Tivoli to Bard College," *Poughkeepsie Journal,* January 20, 1965.

340 Lewis Nichols, "In and Out of Books," *The New York Times Book Review,* January 10, 1965.

340 Jack Ludwig, "The Wayward Reader," *Holiday,* February 1965.

341 "Art is not the Mayor's dish": "Some Questions and Answers: An Interview with Myself," *The New Review* 2.18 (1975).

341 Joseph Epstein, "Another Rare Visit with Noah Danzig," *Commentary*, October 1990.

342 "Gloria Steinem Spends a Day in Chicago with Saul Bellow," *Glamour*, July 1965.

343 Alfred Kazin, "My Friend Saul Bellow," *The Atlantic Monthly*, January 1965.

344 On Bellow's visit to the Johnson administration White House: Eric F. Goldman, "The White House and the Intellectuals," in *The Tragedy of Lyndon Johnson* (New York: Alfred A. Knopf, 1969); Howard Taubman, "White House Salutes Culture in America," *The New York Times*, June 15, 1965; Pierre Dommergues, "Rencontre avec Saul Bellow," *Preuves* 17.191 (January 1967).

347 Letter from Robert Hatch to Dwight Macdonald, July 14, 1965; copy in the possession of Michael Wreszin.

349 Bellow's letter to Jack Leggett is in Low Library, Columbia University.

350 Mark Harris's journal is in the library of the University of Delaware, Newark.

351 Bellow's letters to Toby Cole are in the library of the University of California, Davis.

352 Nabokov on Bellow: Vladimir Nabokov, *Selected Letters, 1940–1977*, ed. Dmitri Nabokov and Matthew J. Bruccoli (London: Vintage, 1990).

353 Walter Kerr, "Saul Bellow's 'Under the Weather,'" *The New York Times*, October 28, 1966; Edith Oliver, *The New Yorker*, November 5, 1966.

353 Bellow's letters to Harold Rosenberg were given to the author by Rosenberg's daughter, Patia; his essay "A Comment on Form and Despair" appeared in *Location* 1 (summer 1964).

354 Nathan A. Scott, *Three American Moralists: Mailer, Bellow, Trilling* (Notre Dame: University of Notre Dame Press, 1973).

355 See also "The Enemy Is Academe," *Publishers Weekly*, July 19, 1966; "Bellow Belabors Literary Intelligentsia," *Montreal Star*, June 25, 1966, a transcript of his PEN remarks; and Henry Brandon, "Writer versus Readers," *The Sunday Times* (London), September 18, 1966.

355 Morris Dickstein, "For Art's Sake," *Partisan Review*, fall 1966.

356 "American Fiction: the Postwar Years, 1945–1965," *Chicago Sun-Times Book Week*, September 26, 1965.

356 "*Paris Review* interview": "The Art of Fiction," *The Paris Review* 9.36 (1966).

357   "The Arts and the Public," draft of an unpublished lecture, the
       Regenstein Library.

357   The story of the shoes is from Lamont, "Bellow Observed."

CHAPTER 21

358   Sondra's letters: files of Marshall Holleb.

360   My account of Susan Glassman's response to the end of her
       marriage to Bellow is from Harris, *Saul Bellow, Drumlin
       Woodchuck;* also a letter to me from Judith Barnard.

360   "You've been a real Klondike": unpublished essay by Susan
       Glassman Bellow, courtesy of Daniel Bellow.

362   *Single* 1.1 (August 1973).

363   "He felt he had unfinished business": interview with Adam Bel-
       low.

368   Information about Bellow's divorce from Susan is based on the
       files of two Chicago lawyers, Marshall Holleb and Miles Beer-
       mann; also *Susan Bellow v. Saul Bellow,* no. 66D-19472, court
       records of Cook County, Illinois, supplied by Marianne Nault.

370   Bellow's dispatches from the Six-Day War: *Newsday,* "After
       the Battle: Troops, Sightseers," June 9, 1967; "In Israel's Eyes,
       It's a Crazy World," June 12, 1967; "Sinai's Savage Sun Fits Its
       Scenery," June 13, 1967; "A Look O'er Jordan," June 16,
       1967.

370   Some of these reports were later incorporated into the text of
       To Jerusalem and Back.

371   "People here go out at five": letter to Richard Stern.

CHAPTER 22

372   Reviews of *Mosby's Memoirs:* Ivan Gold, *The New York Times
       Book Review,* November 3, 1968; Charles Thomas Samuels,
       "Action and Idea in Saul Bellow," *The Atlantic Monthly,* No-
       vember 1968; Jack Richardson, "Chasing Reality," *The New
       York Review of Books,* March 13, 1969. Theodore Solotaroff's
       review is in his collection, *The Red Hot Vacuum.*

374   For my account of the events at San Francisco State, I relied on
       a letter from Leo Litwak; the recollections of Kay House are in
       a letter to Mark Harris in his archive at the University of

Delaware, Newark, along with the clipping from the *San Francisco Chronicle* and the transcript of the confrontation.

377 Clifford Geertz, *After the Fact: Two Countries, Four Decades, One Anthropologist* (Cambridge, Mass.: Harvard University Press, 1995).

379 "You forget, Lillian": interview with Naomi Goodman.

380 "an armistice, a moratorium": letter to Maggie Staats Simmons.

380 The journal of Leslie Garis is in the possession of the author.

381 Sondra's letters to Bellow are in the Regenstein Library; Bellow's letter to Sondra is quoted in the first bound galley of Miller, *Saul Bellow, A Biography of the Imagination*.

381 Ludwig, *Above Ground*.

383 George Weidenfeld's recollections of Bellow in London were made in an interview with me and in his autobiography, *Remembering My Good Friends* (London: HarperCollins, 1994).

384 "My *yideneh* is here": interview with Alfred Kazin.

384 Heinz Kohut, *How Does Analysis Cure?* (Chicago: University of Chicago Press, 1984).

386 Alice Albright Hoge, "Saul Bellow Revisited, at Home and at Work," *Chicago Daily News*, February 18, 1967.

386 "so openly Bellow's mind now": Alfred Kazin, "Though He Slay Me . . . ," *The New York Review of Books*, December 3, 1970; see also Kazin's "The Earthly City of the Jews," in his *Bright Book of Life: American Novelists and Storytellers from Hemingway to Mailer* (Boston: Little, Brown, 1973).

387 "a secession from the life of the mind": "The Young Lack Faith in Leaders," *Chicago Sun-Times*, November 30, 1967.

389 "a Nazi of the intellect": interview with Judith Shavrein.

390 On Marek Edelman, see John Maclean, "Fears Arise for Warsaw Ghetto Hero," *Chicago Tribune*, December 22, 1981.

390 The manuscript of *Sammler*, with Edward Shils's annotations, is in the Berg Collection of the New York Public Library; see also Keith Cushman, "Mr. Bellow's *Sammler*: The Evolution of a Contemporary Text," *Studies in the Novel* 7 (1975).

392 "*Sammler* isn't even a novel": letter to Daniel Fuchs.

392 "*Sammler* is the superego's book": Mark Shechner, "Down in the Mouth with Saul Bellow," *American Review* 23 (1975).

393 Reviews of *Mr. Sammler's Planet*: John Bayley, "More Familiar Than Novel," *The Listener*, July 9, 1970; Alison Lurie, "The View from the Moon," *The New Statesman*, July 10, 1970;

Kazin, "Though He Slay Me . . ."; Joseph Epstein, *The New York Times Book Review,* May 9, 1971. See also Hugh Kenner, "Bellow: A Wry Laugh at High Moments," *Baltimore Sun,* October 30, 1978.

CHAPTER 23

398   Jane Howard, "Mr. Bellow Considers His Planet," *Life,* April 3, 1970.

398   Bellow's visit to Purdue is chronicled in Harris, *Saul Bellow, Drumlin Woodchuck;* also see his correspondence in the Harris archive at the University of Delaware, Newark.

398   "Culture Now: Some Animadversions, Some Laughs," *Modern Occasions,* winter 1971.

399   "out of sheer decency": *Anon* (Austin, Texas), December 1970, "published by the Kolokol Press for the editor [Keith Botsford] with the anonymous collaboration for this issue of, among others, Saul Bellow, Mark Harris & Roger Shattuck." Copy provided by Keith Botsford.

400   "Saul Bellow on America and American Jewish Writers," *Congress Bi-Weekly,* part 1, October 23, 1970; part 2, December 4, 1970.

401   Shlomo Grodzensky, "Firm in the Void," *Jewish Frontier,* March 1977.

401   "a survivor's soliloquy": Kazin, *New York Jew.*

403   "We learned from him": Mel Tumin, "Homage to Saul Bellow."

405   "This rich university": letter to Benjamin Nelson in Low Library, Columbia University.

405   Semon Strobos, "Saul Bellow As Professor," *Saul Bellow Journal* 6.1 (winter 1987).

406   "Would you walk into an opera in the middle of an act?": interview with Edward Rothstein.

409   *Sammler* aftermath: Marc Chavannes, "Bellow Searches for Order and Harmony within Man," *Chicago Sun-Times Showcase,* September 12, 1971; Harriet Heyman, "Q & A with Saul Bellow," *The Chicago Maroon* 80.34 (February 4, 1972); and Art Weinberg, "Revolt from the Adult World," *Women's Wear Daily,* December 12, 1968.

412 Epstein, "Another Rare Visit with Noah Danzig."

413 "Saul was the ass": interview with Joseph Epstein.

413 Bellow's description of Harriet Wasserman and her account of their very brief affair is from her memoir, *Handsome Is: Adventures with Saul Bellow* (New York: Fromm, 1997).

414 *Last Analysis* revival: Stasio, *Broadway's Beautiful Losers.*

415 Bellow's letter to Irving Kristol is in the archives of *The Public Interest*, the State Historical Society of Wisconsin, Madison.

417 For a description of Monk's House, see Leonard Woolf's autobiography, *Downhill All the Way* (New York: Harcourt, Brace, and World, 1967).

419 "Literature in the Age of Technology," in *Technology and the Frontiers of Knowledge*, Frank K. Nelson Doubleday Lecture Series (Garden City, N.Y.: Doubleday, 1975).

420 Bellow's letter to Trilling is in Low Library, Columbia University; Trilling's reply is in the Regenstein Library.

423 My account of Alexandra Tulcea's mathematical career is from Miller, *Saul Bellow: A Biography of the Imagination.*

CHAPTER 24

424 Berryman's letter to Bellow is quoted in Bellow's foreword to *Recovery*; his letter about *Herzog* is quoted in Mariani, *Dream Song.*

429 On Bellow's use of Schwartz, see Keith Botsford, "What's Wrong with Modern Fiction?" *The Sunday Times* (London), January 12, 1975, in which Bellow openly acknowledges Schwartz as the model for Humboldt; Robert Robinson, "Saul Bellow at 60," *The Listener*, February 13, 1975.

430 Dwight Macdonald's letter was written to Mark Shechner, who shared it with me.

430 Excerpts from *Humboldt's Gift* appeared in *Playboy*, January 1974, and *Esquire*, December 1974.

434 "I HEARD the words": letter in the Harris papers at the University of Delaware, Newark.

436 Rudolf Steiner, *The Boundaries of Natural Science* (Spring Valley, N.Y.: Anthroposophic Press, 1983).

437 Bellow spoke extensively of his interest in Steiner in his interview with Melvyn Bragg, "'Off the Couch by Christmas,' Saul Bellow on His New Novel," *The Listener* 93 (November 20, 1975).

437 Roger Shattuck, "A Higher Selfishness?" *The New York Review of Books*, September 18, 1975.

437 "Secretary Kissinger and Danny Kaye": Saul Bellow, "An Interview with Myself," *New Review* 2.18 (1975).

438 Bellow's description of his meeting with Henry Kissinger is in *To Jerusalem and Back*.

438 Owen Barfield, *Saving the Appearances: A Study in Idolatry* (Middletown, Conn.: Wesleyan University Press, 1988 [1957]); see also Herbert J. Smith, "*Humboldt's Gift* and Rudolf Steiner," *Centennial Review* 12 (1978).

439 Copies of Bellow's letters to Owen Barfield are in the possession of Ruth Miller; Barfield's letters to Bellow are in the Regenstein Library.

440 "Vela had a stiff upper lip": *Ravelstein* (New York: Viking Penguin, 2000).

440 Barley Alison's papers are in the Secker and Warburg archive at the University of Reading; my account of her life is drawn largely from an informative letter written to me by her niece Rosie Alison.

442 Walter Clemons and Jack Kroll, "America's Master Novelist: An Interview with Saul Bellow," *Newsweek*, September 1, 1975.

442 Karyl Roosevelt, "Saul Bellow Is Augie, Herzog and Henderson—and of Course the Hero of His Latest Book," *People*, September 8, 1975.

442 Barnett Singer, "Looking for Mr. Bellow," *Jewish Dialog* (Toronto), Hanukkah 1982.

444 Reviews of *Humboldt's Gift*: Richard Gilman, "*Humboldt's Gift*," *The New York Times Book Review*, August 17, 1975; Jack Richardson, "A Burnt-Out Case," *Commentary*, November 1975; John Aldridge, "Saul Bellow at 60: A Turn to the Mystical," *The Saturday Review of Literature*, September 6, 1975; John Updike, "Draping Radiance with a Worn Veil," in *Hugging the Shore* (New York: Alfred A. Knopf, 1983).

445 Carlin Romano, "An Interview with Saul Bellow," *Nassau Literary Review*, fall 1975.

CHAPTER 25

449 Louis Simpson, "The Ghost of Delmore Schwartz," *The New York Times Magazine*, December 7, 1975.

452 Dana Gioia, "Meeting Mr. Cheever," *Hudson Review* 39.3 (1986).

452 "Wreathed in vapor": *The Letters of John Cheever*, ed. Benjamin Cheever (New York: Simon and Schuster, 1988), letter of June 1, 1962.

453 Bellow's legal troubles: No. 61454, First District (4th Division), 40 Ill. App. 3D 442, July 14, 1976; No. 77-1788, First District (4th Division), 72 Ill. App. 3D 608, May 17, 1979.

454 Irving Howe, "People on the Edge of History—Saul Bellow's Vivid Report on Israel," *The New York Times Book Review*, October 17, 1976.

454 "*You're* the original thinker": archives of *The New Yorker*, the New York Public Library.

456 "I'm under the covers with Jane Austen": Wasserman, *Handsome Is*.

456 On the Nobel: Joseph Berger, "Bellow: Still Delighted, Still Skeptical," *New York Post*, November 15, 1976; Jan Rhodes, "Bellow Wins Nobel; Makes 2 for UC," *The Chicago Maroon* 86.15 (October 25, 1976); Timothy McNulty, "Saul Bellow: 'Child in Me Is Delighted,'" *Chicago Sun-Times*, October 22, 1976. See also Blake Morrison, "So You Want to Win a Nobel Prize," *The New York Times Magazine*, October 1, 1995; Richard Stern, "Bellow's Gift," *The New York Times Magazine*, November 22, 1976; Herbert Mitgang, "Saul Bellow Taking Laureateship Lightly," *The New York Times*, November 14, 1976.

457 "I have scarcely begun to master my trade": *Newsweek* files, New York.

457 "At this rate, my heirs will get it in a day or two": quoted in Miller, *Saul Bellow: A Biography of the Imagination*.

458 "Hey, Solly": interview with David Peltz.

458 Edward Shils's disparaging remark was reported to me by Allan Bloom.

459 Mitgang, "Saul Bellow Taking Laureateship Lightly."

461 The text of Bellow's Nobel speech was published under the title *The Nobel Lecture* (New York: Targ Editions, 1979) and reprinted in *It All Adds Up*.

CHAPTER 26

463 Malcolm Bradbury, "Saul Bellow and the Nobel Prize," *Journal of American Studies* 11.1 (1977).

464   See also Leslie Field, "Saul Bellow and the Critics: After the Nobel Award," *Modern Fiction Studies*, 1979.

464   Bellow's animadversions on Richard Poirier were made in an interview with Michiko Kakutani, "A Talk with Saul Bellow: On His Work and Himself," *The New York Times Book Review*, December 13, 1981.

465   Bellow's "Jefferson Lectures" are reprinted in *It All Adds Up*.

465   Henry Mitchell, "Orbiting Mr. Bellow's Planet," *The Washington Post*, March 31, 1977.

467   On Bellow and Susan's protracted divorce settlement: Edward I. Stein, "Today's Institute Report," *Daily Law Bulletin*, August 10, 1976; Theodore R. Postel, "Property Settlement Is Vacated 3½ Years Later," *Daily Law Bulletin*, December 10, 1976; "Notes on People," *The New York Times*, October 20, 1977.

470   "I thought that I would buy a postcard"; "I can't see where I'm headed": the Regenstein Library.

471   "my absent-minded professor": Al Ellenberg, "Saul Bellow Picks Another Fight," *Rolling Stone*, March 4, 1982.

472   "his favorite Mozart operas": "Mozart: Work Transformed into Play," *Bostonia*, spring 1992.

473   Bellow's observations on Chicago in this period are from drafts of "The Chicago Book," published in a very altered form in "A Writer from Chicago," in *The Tanner Lectures on Human Values*.

475   "the white-haired, compact, handsome prince": Richard Stern, *One Person and Another: On Writers and Writing* (Dallas: Baskerville, 1993).

476   "in a complete deerstalker's outfit": interview with Virginia Heiserman.

477   Shils's characterizations of his colleagues are from conversations with and a letter to me.

477   "Better watch out for Saul today": conversation with Allan Bloom.

479   "He spoke with extraordinary intensity": Clifford Orwin quoted in James Atlas, "Chicago's Grumpy Guru," *The New York Times Magazine*, January 3, 1988.

479   Mary McCarthy's eulogy of Harold Rosenberg was published in *The New York Times*: "Ideas Were the Generative Force of His Life," May 6, 1979.

481   "the deterioration of books": Thomas Powers, "Will Glue Outlast Auden?" *The New York Times Book Review*, November 21, 1976.

482 Solotaroff's offending review of *Herzog*: "Napoleon Street and After," *Commentary*, December 1964.

484 Herbert Mitgang, "With Bellow in Chicago," *The New York Times Book Review*, July 6, 1980.

484 "Saul Bellow's Chicago," channel 5, Chicago, March 27, 1981.

484 "No one felt easy": letter to David Peltz.

CHAPTER 27

486 Mark Harris, "Saul Bellow at Purdue," *Georgia Review* 32.4 (1978); "Of Cars, Woodchucks and Being Bellow's Boswell," *The New York Times Book Review*, November 4, 1984.

486 The conversation between Bellow and Harris is on a tape in the Harris Papers at the University of Delaware, Newark.

489 Dean Borok shared with me his letters from Bellow, along with press clippings about his variegated career in Canada and copies of stories he wrote under the pseudonym Dean Belmont.

492 Saki story: Leah Garchik, "Bellow's 'Less Easy to Bother Nowadays,'" *San Francisco Chronicle*, January 2, 1983.

492 My portrait of the MacArthur awards is based on reporting I did for "I Dream of Genius," *Vanity Fair*, November 1986.

494 The program from the fiftieth reunion of Tuley High School was provided by Paul Bernick.

497 Bellow's letter to Dupee is in Low Library, Columbia University; see also a letter from Russell Lynes, a member of the board, in Bellow's archive at the Regenstein Library.

497 "And God help Spangler": copy of a letter to Bellow in the Secker and Warburg archive.

498 Crystal Gromer provided me with a copy of her unpublished memoir.

499 "Dear God!": Miller, *Saul Bellow: A Biography of the Imagination*.

500 Singer, "Looking for Mr. Bellow."

501 Eugene Kennedy, "Bellow Awaits Heat from Novel of 'Hard Knocks,'" *Chicago Tribune Book World*, January 10, 1982; Helen Dudar, "The Graying of Saul Bellow," *The Saturday Review of Literature*, January 1982.

501 Reviews of *The Dean's December*: Salman Rushdie, "The Big Match," *The New Statesman*, April 2, 1982; D. M. Thomas, "Saul Bellow's Darkening Vision," *Washington Post Book*

World, January 10, 1982; Hugh Kenner, "From Lower Bellowvia: Leopold Bloom with a Ph.D.," *Harper's,* February 1982; John Updike, "Toppling Towers Seen by a Whirling Soul," *The New Yorker,* February 22, 1982.

503 Bellow's three-part interview with Dick Cavett aired on May 12–14, 1982.

503 Financial details about Bellow's advances and Barley Alison's letters to Ed Burlingame are from the files of Harper and Row, New York.

504 My account of Cheever's funeral is from an article by Paul L. Montgomery in *The New York Times,* June 24, 1982; see also Donaldson, *John Cheever: A Biography.* Bellow's letter to Cheever was provided by Donaldson.

CHAPTER 28

508 "Bakhtin, eh? Sounds like a germicide": letter to me from Doug Thomson.

510 Cynthia Ozick, "Farcical Combat in a Busy World," *The New York Times Book Review,* May 20, 1984; reprinted in *Saul Bellow: Modern Critical Views,* ed. Harold Bloom (New York: Chelsea House, 1986).

511 D. J. R. Bruckner, "A Candid Talk with Saul Bellow," *The New York Times Magazine,* April 15, 1984.

511 "My dear": letter from Bellow to Gene S. Kupferschmid.

512 Bellow on Roth: Andrea Chambers, "Portnoy's Creator Would Like It Known: His Books Are Novels, Not Confessionals," *People,* December 19, 1983.

513 The quotations from *Contentions* are from a special issue of the newsletter entitled "Winners," October 1983, published by the Committee for the Free World.

513 Bellow's letter to Midge Decter was provided by Decter.

514 On Bellow in Lachine: Joshua Hammer, "Saul Bellow Returns to Canada, Searching for the Phantoms That Shaped His Life and Art," *People,* June 25, 1984; Ann Weinstein, "Bellow's Reflections on His Most Recent Sentimental Journey to His Birthplace," *Saul Bellow Journal* 4.1 (1985). Weinstein also provided me with a videotape of the event in Lachine.

516 My account of the deaths of Bellow's brothers is from Miller, *Saul Bellow: A Biography of the Imagination,* and from my interview with Lyn Rotblatt.

518 Fight with Kazin: Alfred Kazin, *A Lifetime Burning in Every Moment* (New York: HarperCollins, 1996).

521 "I wasn't the architect": Atlas, "His Kind of Town, Chicago Is."

521 "Her line was, roughly speaking": letter from Barley Alison to Edward Burlingame, Harper and Row files, New York.

522 Lord Weidenfeld's recollections of Bellow in London are from *Remembering My Good Friends* and from an interview with me.

CHAPTER 29

524 Rhoda Koenig, "At Play in the Fields of the Word: Alienation, Imagination, Feminism, and Foolishness at PEN," *New York*, February 3, 1986. See also Richard Stern, "Penned In," *Critical Inquiry* 13 (autumn 1986); "Some Members of the Congress," *Critical Inquiry* 14 (summer 1988); reprinted in *One Person and Another.*

525 Bennington speech: Saul Bellow, *Summations.*

526 Text of Bellow's remarks at the Whiting Award ceremony, October 31, 1985. For other readings of this time, see Edwin McDowell, "Bellow Visits New York for Rare Public Reading," *The New York Times,* January 19, 1985; Lisa Lednicer, "An Evening with Saul Bellow," *Jewish Post and Opinion,* April 30, 1986.

527 "in the Hartford Courant": letter from Ed Burlingame to Barley Alison, Secker and Warburg archive, University of Reading; Bellow's letter to Burlingame is in the files of Harper and Row, New York.

529 "a very famous novelist": Harris, *Saul Bellow, Drumlin Woodchuck.*

529 George Sarant's account of his visit with Bellow is from a letter to me.

530 "I think nothing but karma can explain": Botsford interview, *Bostonia,* part 2.

530 "If you're not married:" note among the private papers of Zita Cogan.

531 Bloom, *The Closing of the American Mind;* Atlas, "Chicago's Grumpy Guru."

533 "like a herring": interview with Harvey Shapiro.

534 "My heart sank": Kazin, *A Lifetime Burning in Every Moment.*

534 Bellow's letter to Malcolm Cowley is in the Viking files.

535 Bellow on Amis: Mira Stout, "Martin Amis: Down London's Mean Streets," *The New York Times Magazine,* February 4, 1990; of Amis's numerous writings on Bellow, the most important pieces are included in *The Moronic Inferno* (New York: Viking, 1987) and *Visiting Mrs. Nabokov and Other Excursions* (London: Jonathan Cape, 1993).

536 "If I have to listen to another word of this": interview with Allan Bloom.

537 Reviews of *More Die of Heartbreak:* Terrence Rafferty, "Hearts and Minds," *The New Yorker,* July 20, 1987; William Gaddis, "An Instinct for the Dangerous Wife," *The New York Times Book Review,* May 24, 1987; Leon Wieseltier, "Soul and Form," *The New Republic,* August 31, 1987.

538 "absurdities, third-rate pipe-dreams": Harold Bloom, interview of Saul Bellow, *The Paris Review,* spring 1991.

539 The text of Bellow's talk before the Montreal Council of Foreign Affairs was provided by Ann Weinstein.

CHAPTER 30

542 Andrea Chambers, "At 73, Nobel Laureate Saul Bellow Decides He Wants to Be a Paperback Writer," *People,* March 27, 1989.

543 Reviews of *A Theft:* John Updike, "Nice Tries," *The New Yorker,* May 1, 1989; Robert Towers, "Mystery Women," *The New York Review of Books,* April 27, 1989.

543 Sotheby's: Rita Reif, "Bellow Auctioning Off 'Sammler' Manuscript," *The New York Times,* May 5, 1988.

546 "You were equal": Philip Gillon, "Bellow's Credo," *The Jerusalem Post Weekly,* December 24, 1974.

549 "When he spoke before [Padgett] Powell's class": letter to me from Andrew Gordon.

549 "There's a good wife": personal observation.

549 "a real triple feature": reported to me by Richard Stern.

549 Janis Freedman, review of Philip Roth, *Sabbath's Theater,* in *Partisan Review,* fall 1995.

550 "'twilight' years": Marian Christy, "'Twilight Years' Have Mellowed 74-year-old Nobel Prize Winner," *The Boston Globe*, January 1, 1990; I also depended on a letter from Brian McLaughlin, who organized the reading at the Tremont temple.

551 Jonathan Rosen, "Saul Bellow's Seven Layers," *Forward*, November 16, 1990.

551 Eugene Kennedy, "Anti-Semitism in Chicago: A Stunning Silence," *The New York Times*, July 26, 1988; Bellow, "Voice of the People: Face the Truth of Racial Turmoil," *Chicago Tribune*, August 14, 1988; Fred Barnes, "Race and Politics in Chicago," *The New Republic*, April 10, 1989.

553 "barred and gated city": interview with Zita Cogan.

554 See also Jerry Nemanic, "Politicians Sing of Bellow's Gift to Fiction, City," *Chicago Tribune*, October 9, 1990; John Blades, "Birthday Salute," *Chicago Tribune*, October 4, 1990.

555 My account of the evening in honor of Václav Havel is from Lewis Lapham, "Play on Words," *Harper's*, May 1990; also from conversations with Janet Malcolm and Rebecca Sinkler.

556 Lunch with Margaret Thatcher: George Walden, *Lucky George: Memoirs of an Anti-Politician* (London: Allen Lane/Penguin Press, 1999).

556 "greater than Tolstoy": interview with Stuart Brent.

556 "My father would be very unhappy": conversation with Adam Bellow.

556 "not ready for the sawmill": John Blades, "Spare Bellow the Premature Dissections," *Chicago Tribune*, March 2, 1990.

556 "the shadow of the tombstone": interview with Eugene Kennedy.

556 "Can't I retain my poor porous figleaf?": James Atlas, "The Shadow in the Garden," *The New Yorker*, June 26–July 3, 1995.

557 "my closest literary confidante for fifty years": letter to me from Ruth Miller; "the best book, bar none, written about him": entry from Miller's journal.

558 Epstein, "Another Rare Visit with Noah Danzig."

559 "gross, moronic, and clumsily written": letter to Ruth Wisse.

562 John Sutherland, "Miss Ferguson's Twitching Ferule," *The Times Literary Supplement*, November 6, 1992.

562 Bellow's "Mozart" lecture: "The Talk of the Town," *The New Yorker*, December 23, 1991; "Mozart: Work Transformed into Play," *Bostonia*.

563 "Intellectuals and Social Change in Central and Eastern Europe," *Partisan Review*, fall 1992.

563 "In the middle of the night": my notes of the proceedings.

564 "Saul was my salvation": Bloom in conversation with Richard Stern.

564 Allan Bloom, *Love and Friendship* (New York: Simon and Schuster, 1993).

565 Irv Kupcinet, "Kup's Column," *Chicago Sun-Times*, November 20, 1990.

566 Blades, "Bellow Leaving Chicago in Body but Not in Spirit"; see also Charles Storch, "Bellow's Defection No Match for Affection from Hometown," *Chicago Tribune*, November 9, 1993.

CHAPTER 31

568 "His solid brown desk": John Blades, "Bellow in Boston: Why Our Finest Novelist Abandoned Chicago," *Chicago Tribune Magazine*, June 19, 1994; and "Bellow in Boston: Saul Bellow Finds Chicago Is a Nice Place to Be a Visitor," *Chicago Tribune*, December 31, 1995; also Blades's notes of his interview.

570 "The State of Letters: A Conversation," conference at the University Playwrights' Theatre, reprinted in *Bostonia*, summer 1994.

570 Nicolette Jones, "The Order of Merit," *The Sunday Times* (London), March 13, 1994.

571 "There Is Simply Too Much to Think About," *Forbes*, September 14, 1992.

571 Malcolm Bradbury, "Being There," *The Sunday Times* (London), September 11, 1994.

572 David Remnick, "Mr. Bellow's Planet," *The New Yorker*, March 23, 1994; see also M. R. Montgomery, "Bellow on Boston? Don't Ask," *The Boston Globe*, April 23, 1996.

572 Brent Staples, *Parallel Time: Growing Up in Black and White* (New York: Pantheon, 1994).

573 "Papuans and Zulus," *The New York Times*, March 10, 1994; Bellow made the original remark during the course of an interview with me on December 16, 1987. See Atlas, "Chicago's Grumpy Guru."

574 Peter Prescott, "Mr. Bellow's Planetoid," *The New York Times Book Review,* April 10, 1994; Hilton Kramer, "Saul Bellow, Our Contemporary," *Commentary,* June 1994.

575 *Sixty Years of Great Fiction from Partisan Review,* ed. William Phillips (Boston: Partisan Review Press, 1996).

575 "Is There a Cure for Anti-Semitism? A Symposium," *Partisan Review,* summer 1994.

576 "The View from Intensive Care," *News from the Republic of Letters* 1; excerpted in *Harper's,* September 1997.

577 "I'm afraid I'll fall over": Desmond O'Grady, "Intimations of Mortality," *The Jerusalem Post,* July 11, 1997.

577 "He could hardly lift a salad bowl": letter to me from James Wood.

578 "Vermont: The Good Place," in *It All Adds Up.*

579 Bryan Appleyard, "Angry Old Man," *The Times* (London), May 21, 1995.

580 *South Bank Show,* BBC-TV, March 28, 1982.

580 Jack Miles, "Saul Bellow's Life Is an Open Book," *Los Angeles Times,* March 30, 1989.

581 William Grimes, "Did Ralph Ellison Leave a Second Classic?" *The New York Times,* April 20, 1994.

581 "In Memory of Yetta Barshevsky," September 22, 1996, privately printed. Copy supplied by Albert Glotzer.

582 Stern made his observations on Bellow's condition in a letter to me.

583 Sabrina L. Miller, "Bellow's Return: It All Adds Up," *Chicago Tribune,* December 7, 1995.

583 Dan Bellow's wedding was described in Margo Howard, "Hell's Bells," *Boston Magazine,* September 1996.

584 Mary B. W. Tabor, "Bellow Makes a Change," *The New York Times,* February 14, 1996; Frank Bruni, "The Literary Agent as Zelig," *The New York Times Magazine,* August 11, 1996; Celia McGee, "Harriet Wasserman Tells All about Bellow in New Memoir," *The New York Observer,* December 23–30, 1996.

585 Bellow interview with *Playboy,* May 1997; Liz Smith, "Saul Bellows His Bile," *New York Post,* April 21, 1997. See also *The Independent,* January 25, 1992.

587 "Tell your mother I'm sorry": interview with Joan Ullmann Schwartz.

589 Reviews of *The Actual:* David Gates, "The Heavy Hitters Are Up," *Newsweek,* April 28, 1997; James Wood, "Essences Ris-

ing," *The New Republic*, June 16, 1997; Alfred Kazin, "Struggles of a Prophet," *The New York Review of Books*, June 26, 1997; Louis Begley, "Old Flames and Trillionaires," *The New York Times Book Review*, May 25, 1997; Martin Amis, "Hitting His Stride," *Los Angeles Times Book Review*, June 8, 1997.

589   Sven Birkerts, "Twilight of the Great Literary Beasts: Roth, Mailer, Bellow Running out of Gas," *The New York Observer*, October 13, 1997.

590   Late interviews with Bellow: Mel Gussow, "For Saul Bellow, Seeing the Earth with Fresh Eyes," *The New York Times*, May 26, 1997; Jeet Heer, "Saul Bellow and the *Schmoes*," *LRC: The Literary Review of Canada* 5.6 (June 1996); Hillel Italie, "The New Adventures of Saul Bellow," *Chicago Sun-Times*, May 4, 1997. See also "Saul Bellow at Eighty: An Interview and Tributes," *Salmagundi*, spring–summer 1995.

590   Bellow at the National Portrait Gallery: David Streitfeld, "A Jolly Good Fellow: The Author, in Person and Paint, at Portrait Gallery," *The Washington Post*, June 12, 1997; also a letter to me from Richard Stern.

591   "Death's a challenge": Desmond O'Grady, "Intimations of Mortality," *The Sydney Morning Herald*, May 27, 1997.

591   Late writings: "Hidden Within Technology's Empire, a Republic of Letters," *The New York Times*, October 11, 1999; "The Next Chapter," *National Review*, January 24, 2000.

594   "money 'is something to be thrown'": Bellow, "Allan Bloom," in *It All Adds Up*.

596   David Streitfeld, *The Washington Post*, May 23, 1999; "Spotlight: Bellow Biography on Hold Again," *The Toronto Star*, January 24, 2000; Rush and Molloy, New York *Daily News*, January 26, 2000; Dinita Smith, "A Bellow Novel Eulogizes a Friendship," *The New York Times*, January 27, 2000.

597   D. T. Max, "With Friends Like Saul Bellow," *The New York Times Magazine*, April 16, 2000.

597   Laura Kipnis provided me with the information on Bloom's death certificate. In *Bound and Gagged: Pornography and the Politics of Fantasy in America* (New York: Grove Press, 1996), Kipnis writes that "it was fairly common knowledge around the University of Chicago campus that Bloom was gay. . . . Given that his public pronouncements and political affiliations seemed in conflict with his personal life, this was of some local interest. Thus inevitably, rumors swept the campus that he'd

died of AIDS not, as the university announced, of bleeding ulcers."

598   Christopher Hitchens, "Bloom's Way," *The Nation*, May 15, 2000; see also Hitchens, "The Egg-Head's Egger On," *London Review of Books*, April 27, 2000.

598   Andrew Patner, "Allan Bloom, Warts and All," *Chicago Sun-Times Book Week*, April 16, 2000.

598   Jonathan Wilson, "Bloom's Day," *The New York Times Book Review*, April 23, 2000.

598   Sven Birkerts, "The Last Titan," *Esquire*, April 2000; see also Birkerts, "A Conversation with Saul Bellow," *The Agni Review* 46 (1997).

599   "Saul Bellow's Gift," *Bookmark*, BBC-TV, August 1, 1998.

INDEX

Abel, Lionel, 82, 86, 140, 141, 142,
    145, 226
Above Ground (Ludwig), 381–83
"Acatla" (Bellow) (unpubl.), 70–71
Ackroyd, Peter, xii
Actual, The (Bellow), 587–89,
    593–94
Adams, Alice, 172, 226
Adams, Henry, 127, 205
Adams, J. Donald, 250–51
"Address by Gooley MacDowell to the
    Hasbeens Club of Chicago"
    (Bellow), 152
Adler, Mortimer, 72, 92, 261, 403
Adorno, T. W., 390
"Adventurers, The" (Bellow)
    (unpubl.), 104
Adventures of Augie March, The
    (Bellow), 185–96
  American identity in, 194, 290
  autobiographical elements in, 44*n*,
    45, 146, 187–89, 386, 494
  critical responses to, 169, 182, 193,
    196, 198–204, 206–7, 209, 210,
    211, 394, 429, 570
  family members as models for char-
    acters in, 12, 190, 489
  friends portrayed in, 87, 145, 190,
    212–13, 496
  high-cultural allusions in, 186
  Jewish atmosphere in, 192–93, 240,
    599
  length of, 186
  Mexico chapter in, 70, 190–91

  neighborhood characters in, 20,
    145, 189–90, 274
  opening sentence of, xi, 185, 189
  original title of, 301
  Paris experiences in, 137, 138, 386
  philosophical themes in, 168
  prose style of, 144, 153, 156–57,
    175, 185–87, 191–92, 193–94,
    200, 202, 240, 245, 319, 434,
    535
  publication of, 144, 153, 180, 182,
    195–96, 339, 535
  sales of, 206
  SB's assessments of, 157, 169, 193,
    323
  writing process and, 143–44, 145,
    147, 153, 156–58, 167, 169, 171,
    175–76, 180, 185–86, 195, 339
Agee, James, 89, 322
Agnon, S. Y., 291–92, 401, 451, 575
Aldridge, John, 183–85, 228, 329–30,
    444–45
Aleichem, Sholem, 14
Alexander III, Czar of Russia, 21
Algren, Nelson, 44, 63, 64, 77, 151,
    170, 199, 277, 342, 409, 431
Alison, Barley, 440–41, 493, 503, 517,
    519, 521, 527, 528
Alison, Rosie, 441
Allan Bloom Memorial Lecture, 590
Allen, Woody, 491
"All Marbles Still Accounted For"
    (Bellow) (unpubl.), 568, 576, 582,
    587, 595

Alter, Robert, 546*n*, 547, 548
"Americans Who Are Also Jews"
    (Bellow), 128
Amichai, Yehuda, 400
Amis, Kingsley, 211, 534, 535
Amis, Martin, 534–35, 536, 553, 584,
    589, 599
Anderson, Sherwood, 5, 63–64, 76,
    156, 181, 185, 202, 448
Anon, 407–8, 565, 584
"Another Rare Visit with Noah Danzig"
    (Epstein), 341–42, 558–59
Anthony, Joseph, 327–28, 331, 332,
    333
Anthroposophical Society, 436, 437
anti-Semitism:
    of academic English departments,
        115, 178, 204
    in black community, 551–52, 573,
        576
    of French intellectuals, 455
    of literary establishment, 204–5,
        247, 452–53, 502, 586
    in literature, 127, 204, 248–49
    of Spengler, 25
Appleyard, Bryan, 579
Arendt, Hannah, 82, 196, 217, 287,
    389, 408, 518
Aristotle, 82, 261, 420
Arnold, Matthew, 205, 227–28, 433,
    510
Arrowsmith, William, 565
Art of Reading Books, The (Bergk), 526
"Arts and the Public, The" (Bellow),
    357
Asch, Nathan, 535–36
Asch, Sholem, 536
Asher, Aaron, 259, 267, 293, 298–99,
    309, 503, 517
Astor, Mrs. Vincent, 400
Atkinson, Brooks, 172–73
Aubrey, John, 595
Auden, W. H., 82, 173, 195, 438
Auerbach, Erich, 312–13, 406
Auerbach, John, 447, 554
August, Charlie and Morris, 20, 189
Auschwitz, 289, 401, 586

Babel, Isaac, 191, 401
Bagdazar, Florica, 483–84
Bair, Deirdre, xiv
Baker, Carlos, 178, 179, 273, 281
Bakhtin, Mikhail, 508

Balanchine, George, 317
Baldwin, James, 141
Balzac, Honoré de, 5, 154, 186, 193,
    312, 444, 555
Banach, Stefan, 423*n*
Baraka, Amiri (LeRoi Jones), 374,
    387, 493
Bard College, 196–97, 198, 207–8,
    216, 235, 267, 301, 339, 408
Barfield, Owen, 438–39, 447, 480,
    558, 580
Barnard, Judith, 587
Baroja y Nessi, Pío, 120
Barrett, William, 43, 112, 142, 146–47
Barshevsky, Yetta, *see* Shachtman,
    Yetta Barshevsky
Barthelme, Donald, 311
Barzun, Jacques, 195
Bataille, Georges, 141
Baudelaire, Charles-Pierre, 110, 137
Baum, L. Frank, 25
Bayley, John, 393
Bazelon, David, 41, 65–66, 98, 106,
    108, 111, 169
Beach, Joseph Warren, 114, 116
Beacon, The, 55–56, 75, 497
Beauvoir, Simone de, 141–42, 154
Beckett, Samuel, xiv, 58, 403, 529
Begley, Adam, 543
Begley, Louis, 589
Behrstock, Julian, 51, 82, 139, 144,
    148, 411, 565
Bell, Daniel, 107, 112, 142, 181, 239,
    569, 587
Bell, Pearl, 569
Bellarosa Connection, The (Bellow),
    544–46, 552, 560, 570
Bellow, Abraham (Abram) (SB's
    father):
    businesses of, 6, 7, 10, 13, 17–18,
        31, 47, 175
    Chicago move of, 18, 19
    death of, 221–22, 239, 241
    emigration of, 7, 22–23, 120
    as father, 8, 215, 219, 220, 238,
        500, 561
    finances of, 10, 13, 17, 23, 31, 47,
        241, 242
    jobs of, 18, 23, 30–31
    literary and musical interests of, 6,
        10–11, 17, 551
    marriages of, 6, 7, 42
    physical appearance of, 6–7, 12, 22

political beliefs of, 40–41, 551
as raconteur, 13
religious observances by, 14, 21, 115
SB's conflicts with, 32, 43, 60,
    115–16, 220–21, 457
on SB's writing career, 60, 115–16,
    206, 221, 457
temperament of, 6, 9–10, 22, 32,
    43, 60, 220
Bellow, Adam Abraham (SB's son),
    505, 544
author's writings on, xiv, 609–10
birth of, 251, 327
childhood of, 257, 259, 262, 269,
    282, 285, 292–93, 300, 305, 309,
    325, 328, 347, 348, 358, 361,
    371, 377, 381, 382, 392, 469
as editor, 483*n*, 579, 586
at family events, 554
physical appearance of, 470
profession chosen by, 469, 470
on SB's biography, 556
SB's fame and, 460, 469, 535
on SB's marriages, 548
travels of, 415, 441
as writer, 586
Bellow, Alexandra Ionescu Tulcea (SB's
    fourth wife):
academic career of, 422, 423,
    439–40, 446, 452, 456, 470, 519
family background of, 422, 483–84
fictional portrayals of, 423, 440,
    497, 520, 523, 595
homes of, 456, 472, 473, 519, 523
as mathematician, 423, 440, 441,
    453, 471, 472, 519
physical appearance of, 422, 471,
    518, 519, 520
SB's marriage to, 422–23, 440, 461,
    471–72, 487, 506, 518–21, 523,
    530, 531, 595
SB's work and, 423, 493, 519–20
travels of, 438, 440, 453, 459, 493,
    500, 514
Bellow, Anita Goshkin (SB's first wife),
    120
death of, 516
in divorce settlement, 177, 180, 209,
    214, 215, 222, 223, 224, 229–30,
    232, 300, 302
education of, 3, 53, 61, 215–16
employment of, 61, 67, 75, 85, 153,
    166, 300

family background of, 54, 102, 109
fictional portrayals of, 54, 96, 166*n*,
    237*n*
homes of, 61, 85–86, 93, 104, 108,
    115, 147
as mother, 92, 102
physical appearance of, 54
political views of, 54, 86
remarriage of, 229
SB's marriage to, 54, 57, 63, 68, 69,
    85–86, 88, 90, 91–92, 105,
    116–17, 118, 123–24, 141, 148,
    164, 166, 170, 172, 173–74, 216,
    229, 264, 385
SB's work and, 123, 368
travels of, 67, 68, 69, 136, 147, 155
Bellow, Daniel Oscar (SB's son), 587
on author's biography of SB, xiv,
    609–10
birth of, 327
career of, 586
childhood of, 348, 360, 380, 427,
    460, 467, 468–69, 470, 535
at family events, 554
marriage of, 583
Bellow, Fannie Gebler (SB's step-
    mother), 42, 221
Bellow, Gregory (SB's son), 221
birth of, 102, 105
career of, 470
childhood of, 109, 115, 116, 118,
    123, 147, 170, 174, 177, 214–15,
    216, 218, 232, 243, 262, 300,
    302, 348, 360*n*, 457
at family events, 554*n*
marriage of, 470
SB's relationship with, 470
Bellow, Heather (SB's daughter-in-
    law), 583
Bellow, Jane (Zelda) (SB's sister), *see*
    Kauffman, Jane Bellow
Bellow, Janis Freedman (SB's fifth
    wife), 556, 564, 568
background of, 530–31
birthday parties arranged by, 554,
    579
fictional portrayal of, 595
homes of, 549, 553, 565, 572
as mother, 593
SB's marriage to, 548–49, 556, 576,
    579, 583, 586–87
scholarship of, 530–31, 549
travels of, 565, 576, 578

Bellow, Liza (Lescha) Gordin (SB's
mother), 470
Abram Bellow's work and, 17, 23,
30–31
Chicago move of, 18, 19
death of, 27–29, 66, 548, 560, 585
emigration of, 7, 10
family background of, 7, 10, 175
marriage of, 6, 7
as mother, 7, 8, 9, 385, 444
name changed by, 7
religious observance of, 14
self-improvement stressed by, 24
Bellow, Maurice (SB's brother), *see*
Bellows, Maurice
Bellow, Naomi Rose (SB's daughter),
593
Bellow, Samuel (SB's brother), *see*
Bellows, Samuel
Bellow, Saul (SB):
on aging, 550, 552, 568, 571, 577,
582, 583, 588–89, 592, 593
alienation from American mainstream felt by, 50, 51, 133, 228,
229, 409, 433–34, 524–26, 533,
570
ambition of, 41, 42, 46, 59, 61, 68,
82, 97–98, 101, 107, 185, 449,
457, 458–59
American identity of, 53, 65,
128–29, 145–47, 159, 182, 194,
290, 291, 292, 369, 401
anthropology studies of, 49–51,
56–57, 61, 72–73, 272
on anti-Semitism, 16, 25, 127, 178,
204–5, 247–49, 359, 455, 502n,
552, 586
author's relationship with, xii–xiii,
xiv, 43n, 602, 610
awards/honors received by, 210,
293, 339, 340–41, 356, 357, 378,
399–400, 403, 409, 418, 451,
452, 453–63, 472, 476, 491–92,
514–16, 548, 555, 562, 568, 569,
590
biography resisted by, xii–xiii, xiv, 9,
43n, 60n, 364, 365–66, 486–88,
556–58, 595, 610
birthday celebrations of, 554–55, 579
birth of, 8–9
Canadian early youth of, 10–18, 78,
145–46, 212, 300, 338n, 514–16,
539–40, 577, 590, 593

career progress of, 70, 71, 73,
76–80, 83, 101, 105, 107,
169–70, 182, 206–7, 229, 276,
312, 319, 329, 330–31, 332, 356,
393–94, 510–11, 524, 569–70
celebrity of, 276, 312, 330–31, 334,
341–42, 355–57, 364, 366, 415,
424, 442, 460, 474, 477, 479,
491–92, 522, 556, 591
Chicago departure of, 566–67, 569,
572
childhood hospitalization of, 12,
15–17, 28, 143, 577, 578
childhood of, 10–37, 60, 78, 143,
145–46, 212, 218, 292, 300,
338n, 385, 402, 458–59, 484–85,
500, 514–16, 537, 539–40, 548,
551, 560, 561, 577, 583, 593
correspondence style of, 104–5, 106,
162, 212, 224–25, 281–82,
409–10, 476
domestic demands vs. work efforts
of, 104, 109, 147, 164, 243,
250, 255, 262–63, 392–93,
519–20
duality of, 114, 153, 238, 250, 451,
499
education of, 30, 38, 46–47, 48–51,
53–55, 56–57, 60, 61, 72–73,
84–85, 260–61, 485, 494, 531
on expressive freedom, 72, 107,
226–27, 295, 422, 462, 515, 526,
532–33, 563, 610
family background of, xi, 6–15, 32,
109, 120, 127, 175, 242, 294,
321, 444, 446–47, 510
family estrangement felt by, 16–17,
43–44, 59, 74, 107, 229, 252,
404–5, 434, 489, 526
fans' relationships with, 442–44,
500–501, 518
as father, 102–3, 172, 215, 241,
308, 326, 362, 407, 579; *see also*
Bellow, Adam Abraham; Bellow,
Daniel Oscar; Bellow, Gregory;
Bellow, Naomi Rose
on feminism, 511, 552
finances of, 13, 45, 60, 61, 66, 70,
78, 90, 101, 107–8, 114, 116,
131, 132, 134, 138, 153–55,
166–67, 168, 169–70, 196, 210,
217, 219, 220, 224, 232, 233,
241–42, 250, 252, 268, 300, 302,

339, 368–69, 372, 378–79, 404,
405, 411, 453, 457, 467–68, 480,
481, 503, 544
first employment of, 3, 31, 45, 154
foundation grants received by,
134–35, 136, 153, 155, 157,
167–68, 173, 222, 233, 275,
288–89
friendships of, 27, 41–42, 113–14,
123, 212–13, 246, 249–50,
257–59, 327, 366–67, 403, 413,
428–29, 432–33, 447, 451,
474–75, 504–5, 517–18, 531,
533, 534–35, 550, 569
friends' work promoted by, 226,
277–78, 279, 280, 281, 365, 408
health of, 12, 15–17, 103, 123, 124,
180, 491, 550–51, 553, 576–77,
578, 583, 587, 590
high-school years of, 26, 27–37,
458–59, 474–75, 494, 530,
566–67
on Holocaust, 126, 127, 388–90,
536, 544–45, 546–48, 592
homes of, 3–4, 11, 20, 23, 31, 42,
45, 53, 56, 61, 85–86, 93, 104,
108–9, 115, 116, 124, 138, 151,
155, 161, 166, 197, 209–10, 216,
217, 222, 233, 241–42, 282, 300,
303, 315, 320, 347, 348–49, 360,
361, 371, 384, 388, 411, 456,
471, 472–73, 491, 519, 523, 528,
549, 552–53, 565, 568, 572,
578–79, 583
on homosexuals, 150, 508, 533
interviews of, 341–42, 438, 441–42,
448, 457, 501, 503, 511, 534,
550, 551, 557, 579–80, 585–86,
590, 592, 599
on Israel, 369–71, 446–48, 454–55,
518
Jewish identity of, 21, 53, 54, 59,
114–15, 123, 127–29, 146, 178,
192–93, 204–5, 228, 240, 246,
247–49, 289–92, 311, 329, 369,
400–401, 458, 477, 480, 488,
502, 546–48, 574, 598–99
linguistic background of, 13, 14, 26,
456
linguistic skills of, 121, 192, 292,
514, 515
literary agents of, 76, 101, 153, 315,
413–14, 584–85

literary executor for, 413
literary influences on, 25–26, 29,
31, 58–60, 63–64, 66, 73, 75–76,
83, 97, 186, 191–92, 583–84
literary magazines of, 267, 278–81,
293–94, 305, 309, 360, 407–8,
565, 584, 591
marriages of, 103, 164, 165,
173–75, 307–8, 325, 362,
411–12, 480, 520; *see also*
Bellow, Alexandra Ionescu Tulcea;
Bellow, Anita Goshkin; Bellow,
Janis Freedman; Bellow, Sondra
Tschacbasov; Bellow, Susan
Alexandra Glassman
memory acuteness of, 60, 402, 474,
539–40, 545, 593
military service of, 78, 80, 91, 93,
103, 105, 106
on mundane realism vs. high
culture, 71–72
musical instruments played by, 17,
24, 62, 179, 211, 273, 302
name altered by, xiv, 8, 52–53, 75,
237
in New York literary milieu, 83–84,
88–89, 107, 108, 110–12, 233,
318–19, 328–29
Nobel Prize awarded to, xii, 5–6,
128, 319*n*, 446, 453–54, 455–63,
472, 476, 477, 483, 499
others' fictional portrayals of,
207–8, 245, 253, 341–42,
381–82, 412–13, 488–89,
558–59
outsider mentality of, 32, 50, 64–65,
133, 137, 139, 145–46, 193, 248,
292, 341, 345, 355
physical appearance of, 12, 29, 53,
84, 87, 88, 101, 116, 189, 207–8,
246, 299, 312, 331, 342–43, 359,
401, 403–4, 442, 443, 452, 456,
459, 470, 475–76, 488, 490, 501,
516, 529, 551, 553, 558–59, 567,
579, 590
political attitudes of, 32–33, 40–41,
52, 55, 56, 65–66, 69, 83, 85,
110, 121–22, 142, 248, 313, 341,
343–44, 345–47, 386–87, 398,
400, 401, 407, 408, 412, 447–48,
454, 455, 511–14, 517–18,
524–26, 531, 534, 551–52, 563,
574–76

Bellow, Saul (*cont'd*):
  professional discipline of, 46,
    75–76, 103, 138, 142, 144, 159,
    171, 259, 315, 327, 347, 407,
    417, 427, 457, 569
  psychiatry and, 263–65, 294–96,
    324, 384–86, 522
  racial views of, 50, 76, 273, 301,
    344, 387, 388, 400, 409, 474,
    495, 502, 511–12, 572–74
  Reichianism and, 162–65, 211
  religious training of, 13–14, 15–16,
    21, 128
  reserve maintained by, 88, 113, 341,
    488
  romantic relationships of, 24, 33–34,
    53–54, 86–88, 113, 121, 123–24,
    134, 141, 148, 149, 171–72,
    175–77, 214, 218, 254, 257, 282,
    286–87, 296–99, 306–9, 312,
    349–51, 360–63, 366, 377, 379,
    380–81, 383, 384, 385, 387–88,
    393, 402, 406, 412–13, 414,
    416–17, 422–23, 471, 477, 487,
    522, 530–31, 542, 559, 588
  rural life enjoyed by, 300, 315,
    552–53, 578, 579
  self-dramatizing of, 43, 414
  separation from family undergone
    by, 15, 16–17
  solitude avoided by, 250, 530
  spiritual beliefs of, 73, 436–37,
    438–40, 448, 510, 561, 580–81,
    599
  sports activities of, 28–29, 404
  student radicals and, 374–77,
    386–87, 391, 398
  teaching skills of, 131, 156, 171,
    207, 304, 309–11, 405–6,
    531–32, 584
  on technological innovations, 419,
    437, 526
  theatrical agent of, 418–19
  travels of, 44–45, 66–69, 118–23,
    124, 136–42, 145–51, 153–59,
    170, 172, 186, 222–23, 284–90,
    303–4, 359, 379, 383–84,
    392–93, 395–97, 400, 415–18,
    438, 440, 441, 451, 453, 459,
    483–84, 503, 539, 562, 565, 576,
    582, 583
  university-faculty positions of, 39,
    62, 70, 78, 89, 114–16, 118, 131,
    154, 159–60, 161, 166–67, 173,
    196, 197, 216, 227, 244, 250,
    251–52, 259, 263, 268, 269, 302,
    304, 309–10, 312, 315–17, 322,
    355, 369, 405–7, 470–71,
    475–76, 500, 549, 565–66
  U.S. naturalization of, 78
  vocational commitment of, 57,
    58–59, 64, 69–70, 75, 85, 118,
    132, 185–86, 188–89, 228–29,
    265, 313, 433, 444, 457, 464–65
  wardrobe of, 53, 342–43, 383, 443,
    452, 465, 476, 488, 516, 551,
    553, 567, 590
  wit of, 41, 49, 83, 212, 342, 343,
    417, 459, 488, 507, 508, 569, 591
  younger generation estranged from,
    397–99, 569–70, 584, 589–90
Bellow, Saul, writing of:
  on artists in American society,
    433–34, 444, 448–50, 524–26
  autobiographical elements in, 12,
    16, 44*n*, 45, 61, 82, 86, 88, 91,
    93, 96, 102–3, 143, 146, 153,
    171, 172, 187–88, 189, 216,
    218–20, 237–38, 263, 274, 285,
    314–15, 336–38, 340, 375, 386,
    409–10, 411, 427–28, 449, 493,
    494–95, 497–98, 502, 506–8,
    536–37, 541–42, 545, 560–61,
    577–78, 581–82, 593, 595–96
  book reviews, 53–54, 58, 85, 89,
    108, 109, 166, 184, 204, 254,
    310, 322, 497, 571
  burlesque plot developments in, 274
  on Chicago, xi, 4, 5, 6, 20, 22, 31,
    107, 193–94, 318, 319, 320, 321,
    336, 373, 435–36, 465–66,
    472–73, 495, 501
  commencement addresses, 3, 464
  critical responses to, 99, 100, 101,
    129–30, 169, 172–73, 182, 193,
    196, 198–204, 206–7, 209,
    210–11, 275–76, 329–30, 332–33,
    337*n*, 340, 342, 353, 356,
    372–73, 374, 391, 392, 393–94,
    397, 399*n*, 409–10, 429, 444–45,
    449–51, 454, 455, 464–65, 482,
    501–2, 506, 510–11, 527, 535,
    536, 537–38, 543, 560*n*, 562,
    570, 571, 589–90, 591, 598
  on death, 16, 17, 561, 580–81, 591,
    593, 595, 596, 599

dedications in, 86, 176, 518
in early youth, 26, 29, 30, 45, 48,
    51–52, 53, 54, 60
elder-statesman persona in, 435,
    497–98
essays, 48, 51, 131, 260–61, 310,
    312–13, 419–22, 557, 571, 592
eulogies, 571, 581
feminist criticisms of, 337n, 511
film reviews, 322
film rights to, 367, 418–19, 553
foreign editions of, 109n, 211, 440
high-culture references in, 71, 97,
    186, 271, 454–55, 541, 583, 587
humor in, 76, 133–34, 143, 204,
    250–51, 263, 325, 411, 435, 445,
    506–8, 582
images of sex and violence in, 498–99
journal articles, 48, 53, 210, 222,
    226, 243, 359, 408, 437–38
lectures, 60, 128, 155–56, 170,
    172, 245, 292, 312, 354–55,
    357, 359, 374–76, 398–99,
    400–401, 419, 446, 461–62,
    465–66, 524–26, 549, 555,
    562–63, 570, 583, 590
in library archives, xiii, 259, 339,
    344, 464, 544, 557, 558, 611, 612
literary criticism, 226, 260, 269–70,
    312–13, 353–55, 448, 461
manuscript auction of, 543–44
memoirs, xiii, 3
moral sensibility in, 372–73,
    409–10, 435
mother's death in, 35–36, 240,
    338n, 429, 560, 561
others' experiences appropriated for,
    190–91, 431–32
philosophical topics in, 52, 75, 98,
    143
plays, 163, 172, 282, 287, 310,
    322–25, 327–28, 331–33,
    351–53, 414–15
popular milieu vs. high culture in,
    xi, 71–72, 191
prose style of, xi, 14, 52, 55–56,
    70–71, 75, 93–94, 96, 129, 144,
    151–53, 156–57, 175, 185–87,
    191–92, 193–94, 200, 202, 240,
    245, 246, 257, 260, 319, 329,
    372, 373, 434–35, 502, 543, 588
protagonists' monologues in,
    152–53, 391–92

publication of, 73, 74, 76–79, 85,
    92, 93, 117–18, 132, 135–36,
    144, 151, 153, 180, 182, 195–96,
    224–25, 230–31, 233, 323, 329,
    333, 339, 372, 440, 444, 454,
    480–83, 508, 509, 526–28, 534,
    536, 537, 541, 542–43
real models for fictional characters
    in, ix, xii, 11–12, 22, 27, 33–34,
    54, 84, 96, 110–11, 145, 166n,
    173, 174, 177, 190, 198, 208,
    212–13, 236–37, 242, 255,
    258–59, 264, 270–71, 283, 298,
    325, 335, 337–38, 349, 368, 381,
    382, 390, 396, 397, 423, 427,
    428–33, 434, 440, 444, 449, 476,
    492n, 496–97, 507, 508–9, 520,
    523, 542, 545, 559, 560n, 593,
    594–95, 596–98
research process of, 359, 448
sales of, 101–2, 105, 109, 117–18,
    131–32, 155, 206, 252, 276,
    338–39, 503, 527, 537, 543
scholarship on, 464, 517, 534, 536,
    598
self-absorbed protagonists in,
    73–74, 87, 88
self-assessments of, 78–80, 98–99,
    107, 127–28, 129, 130–31, 169,
    193, 236, 246, 269, 313, 323,
    333, 353–54, 392, 441, 443,
    448–49, 592, 593
short stories, 50, 51–52, 73–75, 79,
    80, 101, 151–53, 210, 318,
    372–74, 492n, 506–11, 560–62,
    577–78
sibling relationships in, 74, 133, 219
social criticism, 419, 448–50,
    461–62, 495–96, 573–74
unpublished manuscripts, xiii,
    70–71, 76, 77–79, 90, 104, 110,
    142–43, 147, 171, 174, 218–20,
    427
vindication of personal wrongs in,
    91, 336–37, 368
writing process and, 79–80, 85, 92,
    103–4, 116, 117, 143–44, 147,
    156–58, 185, 186, 195, 230, 250,
    259, 262–63, 264–65, 278, 289,
    313–14, 327, 328, 339, 359, 407,
    426–27, 434, 448, 472, 476, 484,
    493–94, 500, 519–20, 537, 544,
    553, 569, 576, 586–87, 593

Bellow, Saul, writing of (*cont'd*):
  Yiddish influences on, 14, 128, 192,
    335
  see also individual works
Bellow, Sondra (Alexandra) (Sasha)
    Tschacbasov (SB's second wife):
  on Bard College, 197
  Catholicism of, 176–77, 214
  divorce settlement of, 283, 289,
    292–93, 300–301, 302, 304, 337,
    358, 379–80, 381, 382
  employment of, 175, 176, 469
  family background of, 175, 177, 242
  fictional portrayals of, 177, 209,
    242, 287, 381, 382–83
  homes of, 209, 241, 242, 259, 309
  Ludwig's affair with, 255–56, 257,
    263, 264, 266–67, 282, 284,
    305–6, 314, 381, 382–83, 508
  as mother, 241, 243, 251, 259,
    268–69
  physical appearance of, 175, 176,
    255, 256
  SB's relationship with, 175, 176,
    180, 209, 214, 218, 222, 229,
    230, 233, 242–43, 255, 256–57,
    259, 262, 263, 264, 267–68, 275,
    282–84, 296, 297–98, 307, 325,
    521, 530
  on SB's work, 175–76, 250, 257
  scholarship of, 175, 256–57, 268,
    282
  social life of, 208, 209, 256
Bellow, Susan Glassman (SB's third
    wife):
  death of, 587
  divorce settlement of, 368, 381,
    410–11, 451, 452, 457, 467–69,
    494, 550
  family background of, 299, 321
  fictional portrayals of, 350*n*, 368,
    433, 538
  homes of, 320, 348–49, 411
  literary aspirations of, 322
  as mother, 326, 327, 360, 468–69
  physical appearance of, 254, 299,
    587
  SB's relationship with, 299, 307,
    308–9, 315, 322, 325–26, 348,
    349, 358, 360, 365, 468, 476,
    583, 587
  on SB's work, 321–22, 368, 433
  social life of, 317, 347

Bellows, Charlie, 42
Bellows, Maurice (Moishe) (Movscha)
    (SB's brother), 221, 302
  in business, 12, 42, 45, 107, 190,
    404
  childhood of, 7, 12, 220
  children of, 190, 368, 404, 489, 490
  death of, 516–17
  emigration of, 7
  financial success of, 13, 31, 219,
    367, 404
  legal problems of, 367–68
  name of, 10*n*, 42
  philistinism of, 42, 242
  physical appearance of, 42, 53, 242
  real-estate success of, 12, 107, 404
  in SB's fiction, 190
  SB's hand-me-downs from, 53, 87,
    516, 517
  SB's job with, 3, 45
  on SB's writing career, 42, 328, 339,
    457
Bellows, Nina (SB's sister-in-law), 460
Bellows, Samuel (Schmule) (SB's
    brother), 221, 489
  in business, 12, 42, 47, 107, 219
  childhood of, 7, 8, 12, 404
  death of, 516, 517
  education of, 31
  financial success of, 12, 13, 107,
    404
  in Jerusalem, 446–47
  nursing homes owned by, 13, 323,
    453*n*
  religious observances of, 404
  on SB's finances, 210, 219, 241*n*
  on SB's unworldliness, 43–44
  surname changed by, 42
Belo (surname), *see individuals named*
    Bellow, Bellows
Benjamin, Walter, 419–20, 421
Bennett, Arnold, 128
Berghof, Herbert, 347, 351
Bergk, Johann Adam, 526
Bergstein, Eleanor, 312
Berle, Milton, 331
Berlin, Isaiah, 529
Bernanos, Georges, 4
Bernick, Isadore, 28, 41
Bernstein, Leonard, 317
Berryman, John, 90, 176, 267
  alcohol problems of, 179, 213–14,
    424, 425

death of, 424–26, 430*n*, 433
marriages of, 179, 278, 308, 424
poems of, 179, 226–27, 279, 243,
    395, 424, 455
SB's friendship with, 179, 424–25
SB's letters to, 243, 250, 259, 294,
    300, 322, 326, 327
SB's writing admired by, 203, 424,
    429
teaching positions of, 179, 233,
    251*n*, 252, 424
Bessie, Simon Michael, 197
Best, Marshall, 231, 288–89, 292
Bettelheim, Bruno, 491
biography, ix–xi, 601–2
Birkerts, Sven, 589–90, 598
Birstein, Ann, 211, 217
black-Jewish relations, 551–52, 573,
    576
Blackmur, R. P., 173, 178
Blades, John, 566, 568–69
Blair, Walter, 46–47, 49, 384
Blake, William, 271, 300
Blau, Herbert, 309
Bloom, Allan, 556, 570
    books written by, 46, 531, 532–33,
        564, 565, 598*n*
    celebrity of, 533, 634
    death of, 564–65, 596–98
    family background of, 478
    fictional portrayal of, 593, 594–95,
        596–98
    homosexuality of, 150, 478, 533,
        564, 596–97
    lecture in honor of, 590
    physical appearance of, 478, 571,
        594
    on SB's Chicago connection, 555
    SB's friendship with, 150, 390, 478,
        531, 533, 552, 555, 563–64, 597
    on SB's writing, 536
    on university faculty, 478–79,
        531–32
Bloom, Claire, 522
Bloom, Harold, 538
Blotner, Joseph, 417*n*
Bluecher, Heinrich, 196, 408
Boas, Franz, 49, 50, 51
Böhme, Jakob, 97
Böll, Heinrich, 418
Booker Prize, 415
Book-of-the-Month Club, 195–96,
    441, 503

Boorstin, Daniel, 570*n*
Booth, Wayne, 328
Borok, Dean, 190, 489–90
Borushek, Grisha, 24
Boston Adventure (Stafford), 104–5
Boston University, 549, 557, 565–66,
    568–69, 570, 583
Boswell, James, x–xi, 281, 443, 487,
    594, 601
Botsford, Keith, 215, 569
    background of, 208
    as literary-magazine editor, 278,
        280, 293–94, 407, 447*n*, 565,
        584
    on Ludwig, 209
    SB's fictional portrayal of, 208, 430,
        431
    SB's letters to, 215, 251, 257, 267,
        269, 282, 289, 293, 297, 302,
        304, 310
    on SB's marriages, 215, 298, 308,
        530
    university-faculty positions of, 267,
        302, 407, 565
    as writer, 208, 280, 294
Botstein, Leon, 493
Bowen, Catherine Drinker, 346
Bradbury, Malcolm, 275*n*, 463, 571
Bragg, Melvyn, 503, 580
Brandeis University, 464, 470–71
Brecht, Bertolt, 82, 525
Breit, Harvey, 207, 248
Brent, Stuart, 456, 470, 474, 520, 530,
    543, 550, 556, 566
Breytenbach, Breyten, 525
Briggs, Asa, 417
Brightman, Carol, 405
Broadwater, Bowden, 217, 286
Brodsky, Joseph, 563, 570
Brooks, Cleanth, 247
Brooks, Van Wyck, 173
Brown, Andreas, 544
Brown, Norman O., 390
Browne, Sir Thomas, 152
Brownell, Sonia, 150, 383
Broyard, Anatole, 412, 444, 445
Broyard, Sandy, 412
Bruckner, D. J. R., 511
Brustein, Robert, 331, 333, 347
Bryan, William Frank, 49, 54
Buckman, Gertrude, 235
Bülow, Bernhard von, 121
Buñuel, Luis, 322

Burckhardt, Jacob, 186
Burgess, Anthony, 570
Burlingame, Edward, 414, 482, 493,
    502, 503, 519, 521, 527–28
Burnshaw, Stanley, 175, 202
Burton, Richard, 272
Butler, Samuel, 227
"By the St. Lawrence" (Bellow),
    577–78

Caballero, Jiminez, 120
Caesar, Sid, 323
Caffí, Andrea, 144–45, 390
Cahan, Abraham, 59
Calder, Alexander, 346
Caldwell, Erskine, 76
Cameron, Angus, 304
Camp, Walter Chauncey, 28
Camus, Albert, 141, 142
Canetti, Elias, 454
Capote, Truman, 135, 142, 150, 459,
    586, 592
"Car, The" (Bellow), 79
Carlyle, Thomas, 28n
Carroll Coal Company, 42, 47, 206,
    221, 229, 241n
Carter, Jimmy, 460
Carver, Catherine, 440
Cary, Joyce, 204
Casbah, the, 164, 174
Cather, Willa, 5
Cavett, Dick, 503
Céline, Louis-Ferdinand, 140, 532
Century Association, 315, 497n
Cermak, Anton, 62
Cervantes, Miguel de, 122, 202, 312
Chagall, Marc, 453n
Chamberlain, John, 99
Chambers, Whittaker, 90
Chambrun, Jacques, 101
Champion, D'arcy Lyndon (Jack), 68,
    191
Chandrasekhar, S., 528
Chapman, Chanler, 197–98, 208, 209,
    270–71
Chapman, John Jay, 197
Chapman, Olivia, 198
"Charm and Death" (Bellow)
    (unpubl.), xiii
Cheever, Frederico, 452
Cheever, John, 245–46, 315, 410, 452,
    458, 504–5
Cheever, Susan, 410, 504

Chekhov, Anton, 193, 562
Chiaromonte, Nicola, 479
Chicago, Ill.:
    Bellow family move to, 18–20
    cultural atmosphere in, 4–6, 24–25,
        31, 319, 357, 403, 555
    Humboldt Park area of, 20–21, 30,
        31, 402, 435, 466, 474
    Hyde Park neighborhood of,
        320–21, 572
    Jewish population of, 21, 436
    1968 Democratic convention in, 378
    poverty in, 472–74
    SB's characterizations of, xi, 4, 5, 6,
        20, 22, 31, 107, 193–94, 318,
        319, 320, 321, 336, 373, 402,
        435–36, 465–66, 472–73, 495,
        501
    SB's departure from, 566–67, 569,
        572
    socialist politics in, 32, 33, 402
    television documentary on, 484–85
    writers in, 5, 170, 367, 555
Chicago, University of, 38–40, 59, 84,
    253, 254
    Committee on Social Thought, 39,
        89, 92, 316–17, 386, 389, 405–7,
        476, 478, 531, 549, 558
    establishment of, 38
    Great Books curriculum of, xi, 39,
        66, 92, 143, 478
    Hyde Park neighborhood of,
        572–73
    Jewish enrollment in, 38–39
    Northwestern vs., 48–49, 53
    political atmosphere at, 39–40, 41,
        386
    SB on faculty of, 315–17, 369, 405,
        475–76, 566
    SB's archive at, xiii, 259, 339, 344,
        464, 544, 557, 612
    student activism at, 377n, 386
    undergraduate classes at, 46–47,
        116
"Chicago Book, The" (Bellow)
    (unpubl.), 19, 20, 22, 32, 473,
    475, 484, 493, 496, 499
    see also *Dean's December, The*
Chicago Public Library, 25–26
Chicago Symphony, 24
"Children of Darkness, The" (Bellow)
    (unpubl.), 133
Chilton, Nola, 447

Cieslakiewicz, Ted, 29
Clark, Eleanor, 103, 245, 317, 554
Clarke, John, 267, 302, 309
Clemons, Walter, 441–42
Clinton, Bill, 586
Closing of the American Mind, The
    (Bloom), 46, 531, 532–33, 594,
    598*n*
Cogan, Herman, 378
Cogan, Zita, 34, 46, 378, 463, 474,
    484, 530, 553, 554, 581
Cohen, Arthur A., 267, 293
Cokeley, Steven, 551–52
Cole, Toby, 331, 332, 351, 359,
    414–15, 418–19
Coleridge, Samuel Taylor, 75, 167
Colt Press, 77–78
Commentary, 58, 127, 166, 184, 254,
    444, 514, 559–60
Committee for a Sane Nuclear Policy
    (SANE), 344
Committee for the Free World,
    513–14
Common Soldiers (Richards), 87
"Confessions of Moses Herzog, The"
    (Lamont), 334
Congress of Racial Equality (CORE),
    344
Connolly, Cyril, ix, 150
Conrad, Joseph, 273, 458*n*, 461
Conroy, Jack, 64
Contentions, 513–14
"Conversion of the Jews, The" (Roth),
    253
Cooper, James Fenimore, 454*n*
Corelli, Marie, 138
Coudich Castle, 45
Couliano, Ioan P., 528
"Cousins" (Bellow), 50, 110, 509–10,
    537
Covici, Pascal (Pat), 210, 232
    death of, 339–40
    magazine project opposed by, 267
    physical appearance of, 224
    SB's letters to, 212, 224–26, 230,
      252, 255, 263, 275, 276, 277,
      282, 286, 288, 289
    SB's relationship with, 201, 224–26,
      231, 250, 329, 339–40
    SB's work praised by, 261
    on Sondra Bellow, 255, 268
    on Susan Bellow, 368
Covici, Pascal, Jr., 460

Cowley, Malcolm, 77, 137, 173,
    198–99, 224, 534
"Crab and the Butterfly, The" (Bellow)
    (unpubl.), 136, 142–43, 147, 167,
    220
Crane, Hart, 433
Crane, R. S., 49
Crane Junior College, 38
Cromie, Robert, 334
Crouch, Stanley, 512, 552, 573
cultural relativism, 532–33, 534
Culture and Democracy (Duncan), 39
"Culture Now" (Bellow), 398–99
Cummings, E. E., 156, 202

Daitch (Bellow family's boarder),
    11–12, 218
Daley, Richard J., 341, 378, 458, 555
Daley, Richard M., 554–55, 566
Dangling Man (Bellow), 80, 93–100,
    236, 319
    American idiom in, xi
    autobiographical elements in, 61,
      82, 86, 88, 93, 96, 117, 188, 386
    critical responses to, 95, 99, 100,
      112, 118, 129, 130, 337*n*, 394
    literary themes of, 96–97
    models for fictional characters in,
      12, 96, 166*n*
    philosophical discussions in, 52, 143
    prose style of, 93–94, 129, 153,
      245, 246, 373
    publication of, 85, 92, 93, 132
    sales of, 101–2, 105, 109, 117–18,
      131
    SB's assessments of, 98–99, 107, 236
    writing process and, 85, 92
d'Arms, Edward (Chet), 167–68
Davidson, Nicholas, 597
Davies, Robertson, 525
Davis, Constance, 51*n*
Davis, Ezra, 20, 24, 25, 590
Davis, Robert Gorham, 198
Dean's December, The ("The Chicago
    Book") (Bellow), 493–503
    autobiographical elements in,
      494–95, 497–98, 502
    critical responses to, 499–500,
      501–2, 506
    expressive prose style in, 98, 153
    misogynist facets of, 498–99, 538
    models for fictional characters in,
      423, 496–97, 507, 520, 523

Dean's December, The (cont'd):
murder cases in, 495–96, 498
protagonist of, 153, 189, 494, 506
Romanian scenes in, 483, 484, 493,
494–95
sex and violence in, 498–99
writing process and, 493–94, 500,
519–20
Decline of the West, The (Spengler), 25
Decter, Midge, 513
Defoe, Daniel, 192, 405
Delano, Jack, 303
Demopoulos, Harry B., 550–51
Dempsey, David, 210
den Haan, Izaak, 171
Denneny, Michael, 386, 558
Dennis, Nigel, 89
Depression, the, 30, 38, 43, 44, 62–63
Desani, G. V., 408
Descary, M., 514, 515, 539
de Toledano, Ralph, 212
Dewey, John, 93
Dickens, Charles, 127, 186, 193, 202,
419, 427, 448, 532, 535
Dickstein, Morris, 355
Diderot, Denis, 97, 145, 391
Dilling, Elizabeth, 48
Dinesen, Isak, 322
"Distractions of a Fiction Writer"
(Bellow), 228
Dole, N. H., 53
Donat, Alexander, 389
"Don Juan" (Bellow) (unpubl.), 171,
286
Donne, John, 300
"Dora" (Bellow), 151
Dos Passos, John, 63, 71, 121, 198,
207, 307
Dostoyevsky, Fyodor, 236, 322, 531,
583
antiheroes of, 167, 499
on French bourgeoisie, 138–39
on Gogol's influence, 254
as SB's literary model, 58, 76, 92,
97, 125*n*, 130, 186
in SB's teaching curriculum, 304,
532
social models from, 73, 85, 167
Victim plot derived from, 125*n*, 130
Drabble, Margaret, 275*n*
Dreiser, Theodore:
career disappointments of, 58
Chicago backgrounds in, 5, 58, 95
and ending of *Seize the Day,* 239*n*
naturalism of, 58, 203, 277
SB's admiration of, 83, 185, 448
in SB's teaching curriculum, 156,
207, 304
social issues in, 448
Dubnow, Simon, 76
Duchamp, Marcel, 307
Dudar, Helen, 501
Dumont, Margaret, 215
Duncan, Hugh Dalziel, 39
Dupee, Andy, 302
Dupee, Fred W., 79, 196–97, 209,
301–2, 497*n*
Durkheim, Emile, 49
Dworkin, Louis, 18, 19, 140
Dworkin, Rose, 19, 20
Dworkin, Susan, 310, 311

"Eagle, The" (Bellow), 191
Eban, Abba, 448
Echeles, Julius "Lucky," 403, 494
Edel, Leon, x, 14, 72, 210
Edelman, Marek, 390
Edison, Thomas, 508
Ehrlich, Stanton, 368, 369
Eichmann, Adolf, 398
Einstein, Albert, 413, 563
Eisenhower, Dwight, 248, 303
"11:30 A.M. The Gambler" (Bellow),
74
Eliade, Mircea, 316, 422
Eliot, T. S., 350
American identity of, 454*n*
biography of, xii
on Jews, 48, 127, 204, 205
as modernist, 354, 420, 448
at Monk's House, 418
on Nobel Prize, 463
in *Partisan Review,* 71, 73
self-definition of, 128
Yiddish version of, 41
Ellenberg, Al, 207, 314
Ellis, Albert, 295–96
Ellison, Ralph:
death of, 581, 591
in literary social circles, 89, 180
on Ludwig, 258
SB's friendship with, 301, 512, 573,
581
SB's letters to, 229, 233, 241, 252,
257, 260, 285, 304
Sondra Bellow's letters to, 256*n*, 264

at Tivoli house, 256*n*, 260, 301, 304
university teaching positions of,
179, 316
writings of, 184, 185, 267, 279,
356*n*
Ellmann, Richard, x–xi, 350
Emerson, Ralph Waldo, 202, 205,
536, 580
Encyclopaedia Britannica, 92–93, 101,
312
Engel, Monroe, 180, 569
on *Augie March,* 153, 156–57
SB's letters to, 138, 144, 147, 155,
160
SB's lodgings and, 155, 164
at Viking, 135, 138, 201
Engels, Friedrich, 76
Epstein, Jason, 507
Epstein, Joseph, 423, 491, 508, 536,
558–60
on American culture, 367, 513, 514
on Chicago, 367
fictional portrayal of SB by, 341–42,
412–13, 558–59
on SB's physical appearance, 403–4
on SB's writing, 387, 393–94
Esquire, 265, 307, 313, 314, 315, 351,
397, 430, 577
Essays in Our Changing Order
(Veblen), 38
Eternal Husband, The (Dostoyevsky),
125*n*
Evanston, Ill., 47–48

"Facts That Put Fancy to Flight"
(Bellow), 313
Fadiman, Clifton, 196
Fagin, N. Bryllion, 172
Falk, Candace, 386
Farber, "Buzz," 310–11
Farber, Leslie, 86
Farber, Manny, 322
Farber, Marjorie (Midge), 86–87, 279
Farrakhan, Louis, 573
Farrar, Straus & Giroux, ix
Farrell, James T., 77
autobiographical facets in work of,
63
background of, 59–60
as journal contributor, 71
naturalistic style of, 55, 59, 202
other Chicago writers vs., 170, 277
in Paris, 142

SB's assessments of, 55, 59, 131
SB's letters to, 56, 106–7
as Trotskyite, 68
Fast, Howard, 76
"Father-to-Be, A" (Bellow), 102–3,
215, 326
Faulkner, William, 55, 131, 156, 181
Camus on, 142
death of, 356
in Japan, 417
political involvements of, 248–49
SB's work vs., 275*n*
Southern background of, 4, 241,
415
Fawcett, 339
Fearing, Kenneth, 99
Federal Writers' Project, 63–64
Feiffer, Jules, 279, 298
Feiwell, George, 348, 467, 468
Ferber, Edna, 248
Ferlinghetti, Lawrence, 303
Feuchtwanger, Lion, 525
Fiedler, Leslie, 326, 507
on homosexual literary themes, 301
on Jewish writers, 183, 193, 290–91
on literary anti-Semitism, 127
on Princeton faculty, 178, 179
on Rosenfeld, 113
SB's letters to, 204, 212, 214, 216,
222
on SB's literary associates, 233
on SB's work, 193, 240, 247
on Twain, 301
Fielding, Henry, 191, 202, 251, 312
Fitzgerald, F. Scott, 50, 83, 145, 156,
205, 356*n*
Fitzgerald, Robert, 179
Flaubert, Gustave:
on chaos, 255
on French life, 154
as literary model for SB, 31, 58, 76,
125, 129, 185, 186, 188, 193
Rahv on, 99, 300
revision process of, 117
on rural life, 300
in SB's teaching curriculum, 170,
304, 405, 406, 532
Forbes, Frederick E., 272
Ford, Gerald, 437, 457, 458
Ford Foundation, 201*n*, 268, 275,
284, 288–89
Forster, E. M., 269
Fortsch, Edouardo, 120

Fowles, John, 415
Fox, Eleanor, 26, 33–34, 36, 350n,
    522, 588
Fradkin, Hillel, 565
Franco, Francisco, 121, 156, 518
Fraser, Antonia, 415
Fraser, Russell, 178
Frederick, John T., 53, 63
Freedman, Janis, *see* Bellow, Janis
    Freedman
Free Press, 579, 586
Freifeld, Judy, 90
Freifeld, Rochelle, 90
Freifeld, Sam, 114
    death of, 550
    family finances of, 30
    on Gregory Bellow, 215
    on marriage, 471
    in military service, 90
    on SB's divorce negotiations, 368,
        369, 451, 550
    SB's fictional portrayal of, 368, 430,
        431, 496, 507
    SB's fictional portrayals of family of,
        145, 190
    SB's friendship with, 70, 106, 195,
        212, 220, 235, 259, 367, 368,
        369, 451, 550
    SB's letters to, 88, 89–90, 106, 120,
        139, 159, 173, 206, 214, 221,
        223, 230, 232, 241, 255, 264,
        359, 411
Frelk, Ray, 29
Freud, Sigmund, 162, 271, 308, 338n,
    420, 507, 512
Freund, Gerald, 517
Friedan, Betty, 511
Friedman, Milton, 5–6, 457, 489, 528
Frost, Robert, x, 260, 364
Fuchs, Daniel, 143, 295, 390, 392,
    428, 429, 464, 550
Fulbright, William, 438

Gallo, Louis, 280–81, 303, 442, 540
Gameroff, Marvin, 363, 516
Gameroff, Max, 7, 8, 9, 10, 67
Gameroff, Rosa Bellow, 7, 8, 9, 10
Gameroff, Ruth, 8, 9, 518
Gameroff, Sam, 8, 11, 578
García Lorca, Federico, 120, 149, 210
García Lorca, Francisco, 120
Garis, Leslie, 380, 381
Garrie, Helen, 297, 308, 413, 521

Gates, David, 589
Gauss, Christian, 179
Gauss Seminars, 178–79
Gay, Peter, 200
Geertz, Clifford, 377n
Geismar, Maxwell, 240
Geist, Eileen and Stanley, 141
Gell-Mann, Murray, 492n
Gendlin, Fran:
    background of, 384
    SB's fictional portrayal of, 509n
    SB's letters to, 396, 397, 415–16
    SB's relationship with, 384, 393,
        402, 413, 416, 418, 422, 453
    on SB's work, 386
    on Shils, 390
    as writer, 413
Genesis, Book of, 13–14
George III, King of England, 317
Gestalt psychology, 238
Ghost Writer, The (Roth), 245, 253,
    488–89
Gibbon, Edward, 541
Gide, André, 71, 532
Gierow, Karl Ragnar, 461
Gill, Brendan, 246, 247, 329, 349
Gilman, Richard, 444
Gingiss, Benjamin, 367
Ginsberg, Allen, 508
Ginsberg, Harvey, 482
Gioia, Dana, 452
Glassman, Frank, 315
Glassman, Susan, *see* Bellow, Susan
    Glassman
Glikes, Erwin, 481–82
Glotzer, Albert:
    Chicago youth of, 32, 402
    death of, 504
    leftist politics of, 32, 68, 575
    Russian family background of, 32
    SB's friendship with, 67, 81, 212,
        402, 469, 504, 554
    SB's letters to, 402, 550n, 583,
        586
    as Trotsky's bodyguard, 32, 68–69
Glotzer, Fred, 21, 24, 26, 34, 36–37
Glück, Louise, 380–81
Goethe, Johann Wolfgang von, x, 71,
    97, 145, 158, 204, 437
Goetz, John, 283, 305, 337, 449, 487
Gogol, Nikolai, 25, 75, 254, 313,
    403
Gold, Edith, *see* Hartnett, Edith Gold

Gold, Herbert:
    on Ralph Ellison, 260, 301
    marriages of, 406, 411
    in Paris, 141, 142, 147, 148
    SB's letters to, 169, 315, 322
    on SB's residences, 147, 166
    on SB's romantic involvements, 147,
        148, 257, 266
    writings of, 142, 267, 279
Gold, Ivan, 372
Goldberg, Sam, 377, 544
Goldenweiser, A. B., 57
Goldenweiser, Alexander, 57
Golding, William, 570
Goldman, Eric, 344, 345
Goldsmith, Oliver, 317
"Golub" (Bellow) (unpubl.), 161, 174,
    177
Gonthier, Monique, 412, 530
"Gonzaga Manuscripts, The"
    (Bellow), 122, 185*n*, 210
Goodman, Paul, 73, 78, 89, 162, 163
Gordimer, Nadine, 525, 552
Gordon, Andrew, 545
Gordon, Caroline, 317
Gordon, Liza, 446
Gordon, Nota, 446, 447
Gornick, Vivian, 337*n*
Goshkin, Anita, *see* Bellow, Anita
    Goshkin
Goshkin, Sonya, 4, 174
Gould, Nathan, 33, 76, 402
Grant, Cary, 437
Grass, Günter, 524, 525
Great Jewish Short Stories, 291–92,
    488
Green, Ada, 507
Green, Henry, 150
Greenberg, Clement, 73, 112, 201
Greenberg, Eliezer, 192
Greenberg, Martin, 129
Greenberg, Willie, 13, 17, 539
Greene, Graham, 68, 383–84, 570
Greer, Germaine, 511
Grene, David, 316–17, 366, 386, 405,
    407, 477, 478, 528
Grodzensky, Shlomo, 401
Gromer, Crystal, 498
Gromer, Mark, 495, 498
Gross, John, 575
Groves of Acadame, The (McCarthy),
    196
Gruner, Louise, 208

Guggenheim Fellowships:
    SB's applications for, 9, 71, 85, 100,
        106–7, 109–10, 132, 133, 153,
        155, 157, 167, 168, 218
    SB's receipt of, 134–35, 136, 222
    SB's recommendations on, 410
Guinzburg, Harold, 161, 224, 231,
    460
Guinzburg, Thomas, 460, 481
Gussow, Mel, 590

Hagen, Uta, 347
Haifa, University of, 536
Haldeman-Julius Blue Books, 25
Hall, Donald, 248
Halper, Albert, 170
Hamill, Pete, 330, 349
Hamilton, Ian, xii
Hamlet, 30, 279–80, 589
Handsome Is (Wasserman), 585
Hanson, Barbara, 347–48
Hardwick, Elizabeth, 130, 275, 308,
    317
Hardy, Thomas, 114, 186
Harold Washington Library, 569
Harper and Row, 197, 414, 481–83,
    493, 503, 517, 526–28, 557
Harper's, 420, 421
Harper's Bazaar, 195
Harris, Mark:
    biography of SB attempted by, xii,
        364–66, 442, 486–88, 557, 558
    as fiction writer, 222, 281, 410
    in journal collaboration, 408
    Purdue seminar organized by, 398,
        399
    on SB as father, 360
    SB's letters to, 222, 284, 374, 376,
        377, 381, 398, 409, 410–11
    on SB's romantic relationships, 284,
        309, 350, 360
    on SB's writing, 281, 372, 374
Harris, Patricia, 497
Harris, Sydney Justin, 29, 37, 55, 56,
    85, 458–59, 496–97, 507, 545,
    550
Hartnett, Edith Gold, 148, 406, 411,
    477
Harvard University, 562
Hatch, Robert, 347
Havel, Václav, 555–56
Hawthorne, Nathaniel, 170, 186, 207,
    454*n*

Hayek, Friedrich von, 316
Heaney, Seamus, 562, 570
Hearst, William Randolph, 40
Hebrew University, 400, 446, 451, 491
Hecht, Anthony, 196, 208, 247, 257,
    258, 349, 361
Hecht, Ben, 151
Heidegger, Martin, 273, 508
Heifetz, Jascha, 24
Heine, Heinrich, 292
Heister, Elsa, 198, 207, 257
Heller, Joseph, 303
"Hell It Can't, The" (Bellow), 52
Hellman, Lillian, 282, 323, 328, 347
Hemingway, Ernest, 55, 178, 181, 591
    anti-Semitism of, 50, 205
    background of, 4
    death of, 356
    heroic public image of, 96–97, 185
    Nobel Prize awarded to, 97, 463n
    prose style of, 83, 329
    in SB's teaching curriculum, 156
    travels of, 137, 145, 503
    as war correspondent, 121, 370
Henderson the Rain King (Bellow),
    269–76, 315n, 488
    anthropology sources of, 272, 395
    critical response to, 275–76, 281,
        356, 394, 570n
    film rights to, 553
    models for fictional characters in,
        198, 270–71
    mortality confronted in, 273–74, 580
    opera based on, 418
    prose style of, 260, 319, 435
    protagonist in, 189, 198, 270–71,
        273, 274, 494
    Reichian concepts in, 272–73
    sales of, 268, 276
    satirical aspects of, 271–72
    SB's assessment of, 269, 313, 464
    title of, 269
    writing process and, 230, 243, 250,
        255, 259, 261, 262, 263, 264–65,
        339
Henle, James:
    Anita Bellow's letters to, 122, 123
    on authors' livelihoods, 101–2
    on Guggenheim application, 106,
        107, 132
    SB's letters to, 89, 93, 98, 104, 105,
        109, 110, 114, 115, 124, 129,
        130, 131–32, 224

    as SB's publisher, 92, 117–18,
        131–32, 135–36
    Vanguard run by, 76–77
Henry, O., 25
Herbert, George, 454
Herbst, Josephine, 76, 262, 267, 269,
    277–78, 279, 303, 482n
Herodotus, 92, 521
Hersey, John, 173, 344, 346
Herskovits, Melville J., 49–50, 54,
    272, 336
Herzog (Bellow), 334–42, 555–56
    autobiographical elements in, 16, 30,
        35, 146, 172, 258–59, 262, 263,
        264, 265, 285, 294, 296, 297, 308,
        314, 325, 326, 328, 330, 336–38,
        340, 375, 386, 429, 494, 560
    Bellow family history in, 17, 32, 33,
        35, 36, 43, 336, 337, 429, 560
    critical responses to, 329–30, 337n,
        338, 340, 342, 356, 394, 399n,
        424, 464, 482, 536, 568
    epistolary elements in, 334–35
    imagery of sexual violence in, 499
    models for fictional characters in,
        12, 22, 54, 166n, 177, 255,
        258–59, 264, 283, 298, 335,
        337–38
    opening sentence of, 335
    philosophical topics in, 143, 330
    portrayals of wives in, 54, 166n,
        177, 242, 255, 325, 337, 381, 382
    prose style of, 434, 442
    publication of, 265, 314, 315, 329,
        339, 534
    satirical quality of, 314
    SB's assessment of, 353–54
    success of, 330, 333, 334, 338–39,
        340–41, 348, 356, 365, 368–69,
        429
    title choices on, 335
    writing process and, 313–14, 315,
        318, 326, 328, 329, 368
Hess, Thomas, 354
Hicks, Granville, 99, 228, 247
Himmelfarb, Gertrude, 54, 84
"Him with His Foot in His Mouth"
    (Bellow) (story), 492n, 506–8,
    518n
*Him with His Foot in His Mouth and
    Other Stories* (Bellow) (collec-
    tion), xiii, 509, 510–11, 518,
    526–27

Hindus, Milton, 453*n*
Hitchens, Christopher, 598*n*
Hitler, Adolf, 65, 67, 93, 140, 295–96,
    440, 446, 525
Hivnor, Robert, 124, 150, 158, 159,
    180, 218, 226, 408, 425, 479
Hoagland, Edward, 279, 332
Hobbes, Thomas, 92, 316, 583
Hochman, Sandra, 297, 308
Hodgson, Marshall, 316
Hoffman, Lynn, 210
Hoffman, Ted, 156, 170, 180, 196,
    210, 226, 256, 297, 507
Hoffmann, E. T. A., 298
Hofstadter, Richard, 376
Holiday, 222, 224, 260
Holleb, Doris, 348
Holleb, Marshall, 348, 353, 358, 368,
    372, 378–79, 422
Holmes, Oliver Wendell, Jr., 346
Holocaust, 126–27, 205, 289, 387,
    388–90, 401, 536, 546–48, 592
Homer, 186, 463
Honig, Edwin, 408
Hoover, Herbert, 30
Hopkins, Harry, 64
Horizon, 150, 322, 407
House, Kay, 376
Howard, Jane, 398
Howard, Margo, 583
Howe, Irving, 71, 340, 491
    death of, 550*n*
    Pound's award opposed by, 248
    on Rosenfeld, 81, 113
    on SB's prose style, 14, 191
    SB's work reviewed by, 454, 455
    university jobs of, 178, 181
    on Yiddish, 14, 192
Howells, William Dean, 524
Howland, Bette, 311, 360–61, 379,
    406, 413, 431, 477, 493, 553
Hudson Review, The, 195
Hugo, Victor, 419, 444
Humboldt Park, 20, 21, 30, 31, 402,
    435, 466, 474
Humboldt's Gift (Bellow), 426–38, 439
    on American indifference to artists,
    433–34, 444, 448–50
    autobiographical elements in, 16,
    75, 280, 314, 318, 378, 411, 424,
    427–28, 434, 449
    characters based on family members
    in, 12

Chicago evoked in, 435–36
    critical responses to, 436, 444–45,
    449–51, 452, 454, 536, 560*n*
    on death, 424
    Delmore Schwartz as model for title
    character of, ix, 84, 173, 429–30,
    434, 444, 449
    female characters in, 337*n*, 368,
    411, 521
    friends portrayed as characters in,
    33–34, 208, 236, 337*n*, 349, 350,
    368, 427, 428–33, 476, 496, 559,
    560*n*
    plot absurdities of, 274, 435
    Princeton faculty described in, 173,
    178
    prose style of, 434–35, 502
    publication of, 430, 438, 444,
    480–81
    Ravelstein vs., 594, 595
    SB's assessments of, 435, 441
    sexual images in, 499
    Steiner's spiritual beliefs in, 436–37
    two stories in, 427–28
    writing process and, 236, 426–28,
    434, 438, 481
Humphrey, Hubert, 116
Humphrey, William, 209
Hungerford, Edward, 49, 53
Hunt, William, 436, 473–74, 512, 521
Hutchins, Robert Maynard, 39, 55,
    84, 92, 116, 320
Hutchinson, Pearse, 226
Huxley, Aldous, 29
Hyman, Stanley Edgar, 338, 373*n*

Ibsen, Henrik, 46, 58, 589
Ickes, Harold L., 55
*Image and Appearance of the Human
    Body, The* (Schilder), 272
Imperial Baking Company, 18, 23,
    30–31
"In Dreams Begin Responsibilities"
    (Schwartz), 71, 324*n*
Invisible Man (Ellison), 184, 199,
    356*n*
Ionesco, Eugène, 307
Israel, 369–71, 446–48, 454–55, 518
It All Adds Up (Bellow), 557*n*, 571

Jaffe, Helen, 53
Jaffe, William, 49
Jamar, Pia, 171

James, Henry, 71, 170, 198, 240, 445,
    571, 610
    Americans abroad observed by, 142,
        199
    critical literature on, 73, 181, 454*n*
    expatriate life of, 154, 403
    immigrants disliked by, 204, 205,
        576
    writing process of, 262
James, William, 271, 466
James Joyce (Ellmann), x–xi
Jarrell, Randall, 110, 179
Jean Paul (Johann Paul Friedrich
    Richter), 48
Jefferson Lectures in the Humanities,
    3, 465–66
Jennie Gerhardt (Dreiser), 156, 239*n*
"Jew in the American Novel, The"
    (Fiedler), 183
"Jewish Writer and the English Liter-
    ary Tradition, The," 119, 127
Jews:
    in academia, 49, 114–15, 178, 181
    as American writers, 59, 72, 126,
        127–29, 169, 182, 183, 193, 194,
        247–48, 290–91, 329, 502,
        546–48, 598–99
    assimilation of, 400–401
    black relations with, 551–52, 573,
        576
    English literary tradition and, 49,
        54, 59, 114–15, 127, 248–49
    in Holocaust, 126–27, 289, 546–47
    in Israel, 446–48, 455
    linguistic versatility of, 292
    in Russia, 6, 21, 32, 407
    storytelling tradition of, 291
John D. and Catherine T. MacArthur
    Foundation, 492–93
Johnson, Denis, 584
Johnson, Eyvind, 453
Johnson, Lyndon B., 46, 341, 344–47,
    359
Johnson, Robert, 122, 123
Johnson, Samuel, x–xi, 111, 145, 317,
    405, 443, 487, 595, 601
Jones, James, 145, 312, 412
Jones, LeRoi, *see* Baraka, Amiri
Joyce, James, 58, 251, 458*n*
    biography of, x–xi
    in comic tradition, 202
    Dublin locale of, 6, 186
    literary influence of, 71, 99

    as modernist, 354, 448
    Moses Herzog character of, 335*n*
    in SB's teaching curriculum, 386,
        405, 417, 532
    SB's work influenced by, 74, 76, 97,
        186, 335*n*, 561
    Stephen Dedalus character of, 74,
        188
Jung, Carl, 271

Kafka, Franz, 52, 71, 94, 125, 171,
    235, 373
Kahn, E. J., 453*n*
Kannan, Lakshmi, 464
Kant, Immanuel, 71, 102, 391, 417
Kaplan, Celia, 140
Kaplan, Harold, 79, 81–82, 120, 138,
    139–41, 155, 170, 565
Karlen, Arno, 311
Karush, William, 28
Kauffman, Jane (Zelda) Bellow, 221,
    582
    on Abram Bellow's conflicts with
        SB, 60, 457
    childhood of, 7, 10, 12, 23, 36, 218
    fictional portrayal of, 218
    job of, 31
    marriage of, 42
    name of, 10*n*
    at SB's honorary ceremonies, 460,
        514
Kaye, Danny, 437
Kazin, Alfred:
    on Jewish-American writers, 128,
        453*n*
    on Lidov, 108
    literary career of, 83–84, 89, 181,
        247
    on New York culture, 82
    politics of, 407, 517, 518, 534
    on Rosenfeld, 84, 164
    SB's friendship with, 83, 211, 217,
        410, 517–18
    SB's letters to, 84, 98, 99, 136, 154,
        155, 190, 203, 222, 250, 255,
        328, 340, 343
    on SB's personality, 83, 84, 88, 101,
        343
    on SB's romances, 218, 402
    on SB's writing, 110, 130, 185, 246,
        329, 386, 392, 393, 409–10, 451,
        517, 589
    on Schloss Leopoldskron, 156

on sexual mores, 87
on White House intellectual
    contacts, 317
on Wiesel, 401
Kazin, Pearl, 108, 200, 209, 212, 215,
    239, 243, 257
Keane, Thomas, 484
Keats, John, 29, 30, 238
Kees, Weldon, 89
Keniston, Kenneth, 492n
Kennedy, Eugene, 501, 551, 552, 566
Kennedy, Jacqueline, 359
Kennedy, John F., 303, 317
Kennedy, Joseph P., 359
Kennedy, Robert F., 359, 541
Kennedy, William, 303, 304, 493, 512,
    553
Kenner, Hugh, 502
Kerr, Walter, 332–33, 353, 415
Keynes, John Maynard, 387, 390–91
Khrushchev, Nikita, 313
Kierkegaard, Søren, 110, 261
King Lear, 589, 591
"King Solomon" (Rosenfeld), 234
Kinnell, Galway, 492
Kipling, Rudyard, 4–5
Kirchner, Leon, 418
Kissinger, Henry A., 437, 438, 555
Kline, Reamer, 339
Klonsky, Milton, 89
Klopfer, Donald, 248
Knowlton, Winthrop, 482
Koch, Sigmund, 557
Koenig, Rhoda, 524, 525
Koestler, Arthur, 71, 141, 147, 520
Kogan, Herman, 92
Kohut, Heinz, 384–86
Kollek, Teddy, 448
Konrád, Gyorgy, 563
Korda, Michael, 101n
Kozodoy, Neal, 560
Kramer, Hilton, 278, 299, 559–60
Krim, Seymour, 279
Kristol, Irving, 41, 99, 387, 415, 512
Kunitz, Stanley, 345
Kupcinet, Irv, 341, 506, 565

Lachine, Quebec, 8, 9, 11, 514–16,
    540, 577, 578, 593
Lamont, Rosette:
    background of, 298
    on SB's divorce, 411
    SB's fictional portrayal of, 337

SB's relationship with, 298–99, 301,
    302, 357, 393, 413
    on SB's romances, 300, 306–7, 471
    writings of, 307, 334, 408
Landers, Ann, 583
Landes, Arlette, 361–62, 379, 383,
    384, 405
Langer, Elinor, 278
Lapham, Lewis, 555–56
Last Analysis, The (Bellow):
    dramatic action of, 323–25
    productions of, 310, 327–28,
        331–33, 351, 352, 353, 414–15
    on psychoanalysis, 294, 324
    reviews of, 332–33, 353
    title choices for, 322–23
    writing process and, 287, 299, 310,
        322–23, 327
Laughlin, James, 77, 201n, 430
Lawrence, D. H., 110, 170, 188, 374,
    458n
    marriage of, 256
    in Mexico, 66, 67
    as SB's literary model, 66, 73, 76,
        83, 185
    in SB's teaching curriculum, 170,
        267
Lawrence, Frieda, 256
"Leaving the Yellow House" (Bellow),
    223
Leggett, Jack, 349
Lehmann, John, 109n, 149, 150, 151,
    169, 288
Lehmann-Haupt, Christopher, 501–2,
    532
Leites, Nathan, 61
LeMay, Peter, 436
Lenin, V. I., 40–41, 76, 592
Leonard, John, 458
Leskov, Nikolai, 419
Lesley, Leonard, 172
Letchinger, Irving, 28
Levene, Sam, 331, 333, 414
Levi, Edward, 316, 492n
Levi, Primo, 547
Levin, Harry, 72, 217, 342n
Levin, Meyer, 59, 170
Levine, Ann, 308
Levine, David, 486
Lévi-Strauss, Claude, 72n
Lévy-Bruhl, Lucien, 49
Lewis, Anthony, 518
Lewis, R. W. B., 175, 176, 178, 307

Lewis, Sinclair, x, 4, 52
Lewis, Wyndham, 76, 354, 448, 583
Lewisohn, Ludwig, 59
Lidov, Arthur, 108–9, 114, 190, 554
Lidov, Victoria, 108–9, 114, 554
Lieber, Bart, 124
Lieber, Maxim, 76
Liebling, A. J., 170, 453*n*
Life of Samuel Johnson (Boswell), x–xi
"Literary Notes on Khrushchev"
    (Bellow), 313
"Literature in a Democracy" (Bellow),
    583
"Literature in the Age of Technology"
    (Bellow), 419
Litwak, Leo, 374, 375
Lockwood, Bernard, 304
Lolita (Nabokov), 352, 356*n*
"Looking for Mr. Bellow" (Singer),
    442–43
"Looking for Mr. Green" (Bellow),
    373
Lowell, Robert, 105, 179, 317,
    344–45, 346, 347, 424, 433
Lowry, McNeil, 268
Luce, Henry, 89, 518
Ludwig, Jack, 226, 230, 241, 330
    at Bard College, 208–9, 233
    fictional portrayal of, 314, 335,
        337–38
    as literary-magazine editor, 267,
        278, 280, 293, 305
    physical appearance of, 208
    SB's friendship with, 209, 230, 256,
        257, 258–59, 263, 267, 285, 288,
        293, 304–6
    on SB's work, 209, 340
    Sondra Bellow's affair with, 255–56,
        258, 263, 264, 266–67, 282, 283,
        284, 305–6, 314, 365, 381,
        382–83, 508
    teaching positions of, 208–9, 263,
        267, 301, 340, 381, 451
    as writer, 226, 257–58, 280, 381–83
Ludwig, Leah, 230, 256, 266
Lurie, Alison, 393

Ma, Yo-Yo, 562
Mabley, Jack, 341
MacArthur, Rod, 492
MacArthur awards, 492–93
Macbeth, 30, 324, 547, 589
McCarthy, Cormac, 493

McCarthy, Mary, 326, 389, 405, 479
    Bard colleagues portrayed by, 196,
        197
    on eastern European tour, 284,
        286–87
    marriages of, 11, 286
    in Paris, 142
    Rahv depicted by, 111–12
    SB on writing of, 217–18, 438
    on SB's work, 210
McCloskey, Herbert, 149
    Abram Bellow's visit with, 115, 116
    European travels of, 118, 119
    on Rosenfeld, 243, 429
    on SB's marriages, 123, 166, 229,
        307, 411
    SB's teaching job arranged by, 114,
        131
    at University of Minnesota, 114
McCloskey, Mitzi, 149, 229
    Abram Bellow's visit with, 115
    European travels of, 118, 119
    on Rosenfeld, 243
    on SB's family background, 120
    on SB's marriages, 123, 124, 237*n*,
        307, 411
McCormick, John, 170, 171
Macdonald, Dwight, 79, 80, 112, 169,
    322, 346, 347, 430, 479, 602
McGehee, Ed, 124
Machiavelli, Niccolò, 208
MacKenzie, Rachel, 231, 454
Maclean, Norman, 47
MacNeice, Louis, 288
Madame Bovary (Flaubert), 405
Mailer, Norman, 194, 310, 330, 340,
    356*n*, 585, 589, 591
Making It (Podhoretz), 182
Malamud, Bernard, 172, 193, 194,
    290, 291*n*, 292, 329, 356*n*, 522
Maloff, Saul, 346
Malraux, André, 317, 408
Mandelstam, Osip, 341
Manea, Norman, 563
Mann, Marilyn, 259, 550
Mann, Theodore, 414
Mann, Thomas, 72, 76, 99
Mannix, Daniel, 190–91
Mannix, Jule, 190–91
Mansfield, Katherine, 256
Manske, Eva, 464
Marcuse, Herbert, 390, 532
Markels, Bobby, 296–97

Markfield, Wallace, 89
Marlowe, Christopher, 73, 127
Marsh, Peggy, 223
Marshall, John, 167–68, 182
Martinson, Harry, 453
Marx, Groucho, 215
Marx, Karl, 41*n*, 45, 76, 110, 111, 329, 391
"Marx at My Table" (Bellow), 45
Marxism, 41, 64–65, 110, 141–42, 313, 420, 532, 575
Matthiessen, F. O., 58, 156
Maugham, W. Somerset, 101*n*
Maupassant, Guy de, 25, 170
Maurois, André, 458
Mauss, Marcel, 49
Maximilian, Anita, 176, 242
Maxwell, William, 247
Mayer, Milton S., 55
Mead, G. H., 93
Mead, Margaret, 156
Measure for Measure, 592–93
Meehan, Thomas, 330*n*
Meehl, Paul, 263–65, 266, 283, 285, 294, 296
Meir, Golda, 402
Meites, H. L., 19
Melville, Herman, 76, 186, 202, 207, 387
"Memoirs of a Bootlegger's Son" (Bellow) (unpubl.), 218–20
Mencken, H. L., 5, 48
Menotti, Gian Carlo, 352
Mercader, Ramón ("Jacson"), 69
Meredith, George, 114
Meridian (publisher), 267, 309
Merkin, Daphne, 488–89
Merman, Ethel, 151
"Mexican General, The" (Bellow), 74–75, 778
Milano, Paolo, 176, 299, 357
Miles, Jack, 580, 592
Miller, Arthur, 194, 224, 232–33, 237, 317, 341, 407
Miller, Henry, 78, 142, 154, 171, 202, 276, 458
Miller, Karl, 288
Miller, Ruth:
    on Abram Bellow, 220, 222
    background of, 220, 557
    book on SB written by, xiv, 486, 557–58
    on deaths of SB's brothers, 516–17

SB's letters to, 223, 229, 232, 244, 320, 327, 328, 348, 369, 409, 425, 449–51, 499, 530
    on SB's romantic partners, 86, 296, 381, 422–23, 518–19
    on SB's writing, 450, 538
    writing career of, 226, 279
Miller, Sara, 569
Mills, C. Wright, 101
Mills, Ralph J., 316
Milosz, Czeslaw, 141, 563
Milton, John, 30, 186, 243
Mimesis (Auerbach), 313, 406
Minnesota, University of:
    cold climate of, 251–52
    English department of, 114–15, 251, 302
    humanities department of, 116, 251
    Jewish faculty members at, 115
    SB's friends at, 115, 252, 263
    SB's teaching positions at, 114, 116, 118, 131, 154, 216, 227, 251, 263, 268, 302, 309–10
Mishakoff, Mischa, 24
Mishima, Yukio, 322
Mississippi Freedom Summer, 344
Mitchell, Stephen, 15, 16
Mitgang, Herbert, 459
Mizener, Arthur, 210
Moby-Dick (Melville), 269
Modern Language Association, 340
Moe, Henry Allen, 134, 155, 167
Mofolo, Thomas, 574
Mondale, Joan, 465
Monk, Samuel Holt, 114
Monk's House, 417–18
Monroe, Marilyn, 232, 276–77
Montale, Eugenio, 453
Montreal, Jewish neighborhood of, 11, 15, 539–40, 590
Moore, Winston, 484
Morante, Elsa, 158
Moravia, Alberto, 158
More Die of Heartbreak (Bellow), 319, 435, 536–38
Morris, Wright, 267, 374, 376, 458
Morrison, Toni, 562, 569
"Mosby's Memoirs" (Bellow) (story), 392
Mosby's Memoirs (Bellow) (story collection), 372–74
Mostel, Zero, 331, 352, 453*n*

Moynahan, Julian, 329
Moynihan, Daniel Patrick, 483
Mozart, Wolfgang Amadeus, 156, 211, 222, 454, 472, 552, 562–63
"Mr. Katz, Mr. Cohen, and Cosmology" (Bellow), 74, 75
Mr. Sammler's Planet (Bellow), 386–94
    critical responses to, 373*n*, 391, 392, 393, 394, 397, 409–10, 517
    dissident students in, 376, 386, 391, 481
    expressive prose style of, 98, 434
    Holocaust addressed in, 388–90, 536
    manuscript auction price of, 543–44
    models for characters in, 208*n*, 390
    as polemic, 386, 391–92
    protagonist in, 189, 387, 390, 409–10
    publication of, 387, 393
    racial attitudes in, 50, 388, 409, 572
    SB's assessment of, 392, 443
    sexual liberation critiqued in, 387–88
    Shils's suggestions on, 390–91, 476, 603–4
    writing process and, 390–91, 392–93, 434
"Mr. Wollix Gets an Honorary Degree" (Bellow), 408
Muggeridge, Malcolm, 476
Murry, John Middleton, 256
Myers, Belle, 494
Myth of the Negro Past, The (Herskovits), 49

Nabokov, Vladimir, 315, 352, 356*n*, 586
Naipaul, V. S., 529, 570*n*
Nathan, John, 417
National Book Awards, 210, 252, 340, 409, 452, 555, 568
National Institute of Arts and Letters, 246, 314
National Portrait Gallary, 590
Nef, John U., 89
Nelson, Ben, 338
neoconservatism, 512–13, 526, 560, 574–75
New American Library, 339
New Directions, 77
New Review, 437

New School for Social Research, 83, 244, 250, 257, 268
News from the Republic of Letters, 584, 591, 592
New York, intellectual culture in, 82–83, 88–89, 110, 180–82, 318–20, 355, 399
New Yorker, The, 279, 452–53
    rejections from, 231, 267, 542
    reviews of SB's work in, 99, 199–200, 246, 247, 452, 502, 543
    SB's writing published in, 180, 182, 195, 372, 509
New York Jew (Kazin), 84, 101, 156, 402
New York Public Library, 544
New York University, 159–60, 161, 251, 399–400
Nichols, Lewis, 340
Nichols, Mike, 298, 351
Nicholson, Jack, 553
Nietzsche, Friedrich, 71, 261, 583
"Nihilist and the Inventor, The," (Miles), 592
Nimier, Nadine Raoul-Duval, 140–41, 363, 412, 415, 531
Nimier, Roger, 141
"9 A.M. Without Work" (Bellow), 73–74
Nobel, Alfred, 472
Nobel Prize, xiii, 5–6, 319*n*, 446, 453–54, 455–63, 472, 477
Noble Savage, The, 278–81, 291*n*, 293–94, 300, 305, 309, 317, 345, 360, 365, 407, 584
Norris, Frank, 5
Northwestern University, 47–51, 53, 54–55, 259
Notebooks of Malte Laurids Brigge (Rilke), 97
"Novel from Hawthorne to the Present, The" (Bellow), 170
novels, American decline of, 183–85, 228, 419*n*
Nozick, Robert, 525

Oasis, The (McCarthy), 111–12
Oates, Joyce Carol, 592
O'Connor, Philip, 584
O'Hara, John, 55
Olay, Maxim, 402
"Old System, The" (Bellow), 363, 374, 392, 581

Oliver, Edith, 353, 453n
Oliver Twist (Dickens), 127
Olmsted, Frederick Law, 321
O'Neill, Eugene, 55, 56
"On the Platform" (Bellow), 101
"Orange Soufflé" (Bellow), 351, 352
Orwell, George, 121, 150, 383, 472
"Out from Under" (Bellow), 351, 352
"Out of Bounds" (Bellow), 177
Oz, Amos, 536
Ozick, Cynthia, 510–11, 546, 575

Paley, Grace, 298
"Papuans and Zulus" (Bellow),
    573–74
Parini, Jay, 493
Paris, cultural milieu of, 137–42,
    154–55
Parkman, Francis, 181
Partisan Review, 547
    circulation of, 71
    cultural symposia sponsored by,
        180–81, 513, 563
    editors of, 79, 399n
    on European modernist literature,
        71
    offices of, 83, 569
    SB's work published in, 73, 74, 78,
        85, 153, 169, 192, 195, 226,
        230–31, 236, 323, 568
    social/intellectual circle of, 64, 107,
        111–12, 139, 141, 150, 176, 182,
        205, 233, 317, 322, 477, 570
Passage from Home (Rosenfeld), xiii,
    112, 194
Passin, Cora, 57, 67, 69
Passin, Herbert, 20, 44–45, 54, 57, 67,
    68–69, 70
Pasternak, Boris, 341
Patner, Andrew, 598
Pavese, Cesare, 408
Pegler, Westbrook, 55
Peltz, David, 484
    African travels of, 395, 396, 397
    on Algren, 277
    career of, 213
    Chicago boyhood of, 22, 32, 34n
    father of, 509
    fictional portrayals of, 396, 397,
        427, 430–33, 509
    on Jewish background, 32, 290
    on Minnesota, 252
    play production backed by, 353

on Rosenfeld, 459
on SB's Chicago departure, 566
on SB's dislike of solitude, 250
SB's letters to, 276, 327, 328, 331,
    379, 417, 431–33, 441, 535
on SB's literary ambitions, 46, 459
on SB's romantic partners, 166, 299,
    321, 349, 422, 423, 471, 472
on sexual mores, 34n
story written by, 591–92
Penguin Books, 105, 108
Penn, Arthur, 330
Perelman, S. J., 453n
Peretz, I. L., 401
Pestalozzi-Froebel Teachers College,
    62, 70, 78
"Pets of the North Shore" (Bellow),
    51
Philipson, Morris, 529
Phillips, Edna, 142, 150
Phillips, William, 310
    in Europe, 142, 150
    on Koestler, 147
    on panel with SB, 575, 576
    at *Partisan Review*, 71, 111, 112,
        399n, 569, 575
    physical appearance of, 575
    SB's fictional portrayal of, 111
    SB's resentment of, 497n
    on SB's writing, 196, 201
    on Sontag, 399
Piozzi, Hester Thrale, 601
Pivot, Alain, 503
Plato, 260, 261, 532
Playboy, 374, 430, 431, 585–86, 592
"Pleasures and Pains of Playgoing"
    (Bellow), 210
Plutarch, 92, 400
Podhoretz, Norman, 182, 200–201,
    407, 507, 513, 560
Poe, Edgar Allan, 433
Poirier, Richard, 257, 330, 342, 399n,
    464
Pollet, Elizabeth, 180, 451
Ponge, Francis, 141
Poore, Charles, 130
Pope, Alexander, 431
Popkin, Zelda, 109
Poster, Herbert and William, 111
Pound, Ezra, 58, 77, 127, 137, 204,
    248–49, 354, 448
Powell, Anthony, 288, 570n
Powell, Padgett, 549, 584

Powers, Thomas, 481
Pozen, Walter, 405, 418, 456, 552–53, 573
Praz, Mario, 156
Prescott, Orville, 275
Prescott, Peter, 397, 574
Priestley, J. B., 211, 288
Princeton University, 173, 177–79, 196
Prior, Moody, 49
Pritchett, V. S., 211, 275*n*, 329, 359
Proffer, Carl, 352*n*
Proust, Marcel, 74, 76, 140, 251, 260, 448, 449, 458*n*, 532, 538
Pryce-Jones, David, 438, 439, 440
Puerto Rico, University of, 267, 302, 303–4
Pulitzer Prize, 131, 452
Purdue University, 398–99, 486
Pushkin, Aleksandr, 6, 499
Pynchon, Thomas, 279, 592

Rabin, Yitzhak, 448
Rafferty, Terence, 537
Rahv, Philip, ix, 246
  on European literary tradition, 71, 99
  fictional portrayal of, 111–12
  on large cultural ideas, 110
  literary criticism by, 181, 279, 454*n*
  politics of, 328–29
  romantic involvements of, 111, 175, 479
  on rural life, 300
  on SB's writing, 79, 329
"Ralph Ellison in Tivoli" (Bellow), 568
Random House, 135, 136
Raoul-Duval, Nadine, *see* Nimier, Nadine Raoul-Duval
Raphael, Chester, 162–63, 165, 166, 272, 295
Ravelstein (Bellow), 593–99
  Allan Bloom depicted in, 593–95, 596–98
  autobiographical elements in, 595–96
  critical reception of, 598–99
  press controversy over, 596–97
  as SB's "most Jewish novel," 598–99
Readers' Subscription, 195, 202
Reagan, Ronald, 548, 595
Recovery (Berryman), 425, 426

Redfield, James, 406, 407, 477, 565
Reedy, George, 46
Regenstein Library, 557
Reich, Charles, 20
Reich, Rebecca, 20
Reich, Wilhelm, 73, 162, 163, 164, 234, 239*n*, 272, 295
Reichek, Jesse, 142
Reichianism, 162–64, 165, 234, 238–39, 257, 385
Reinhardt, Max, 156
Remnick, David, 572, 573
Retort, 74
Richards, Bernard G., 291*n*
Richards, Janet, 87, 88
Richardson, Jack, 444
Richter, Johann Paul Friedrich, *see* Jean Paul
Ricks, Christopher, 570
Riesman, David, 188
Riggs, Tom, 174, 179, 180
Rilke, Rainer Maria, 97, 137
Rockefeller, David, 317
Rockefeller, John D., 38
Rockefeller Foundation, 167–68, 173, 179, 379, 462
Roethke, Theodore, 172, 179, 455
Róheim, Géza, 72–73
Rolo, Charles, 275
Rolland, Romain, 25, 525
Romano, Carlin, 445
Romanoff, Harry, 62
Roosevelt, Franklin Delano, 32–33, 62–63, 64, 66, 67
Roosevelt, Karyl, 427, 442
Root, Robert K., 178
Roscoe, John, 272
Rose, Billy, 545
Rosen, Jonathan, 551
Rosenberg, Harold, 181, 279, 526
  death of, 479
  as intellectual mentor, 112, 353, 390, 479, 531
  on Paris, 82, 138
  SB's fictional portrayal of, 508–9
  Shils on, 477
Rosenfeld, George (George Sarant), 529–30
Rosenfeld, Isaac, 106
  as author, xiii, 40, 63, 81, 85, 96, 98, 112, 159, 213, 234, 235, 279
  Chicago boyhood of, xiii, 84, 236
  children of, 155, 236, 529

death of, xiii, 215, 235–36, 239,
  243, 327, 378, 425, 430*n*, 504
education of, 40, 56, 81
family background of, 28, 41–42
finances of, 89
in high school, 27, 28
in literary circles, 82, 83, 88–89,
  108, 110, 112–13
marriage of, 81, 113, 164, 174, 234,
  529
on New York, 81, 121, 155
physical appearance of, 28, 29, 84,
  235, 571
political interests of, 40, 41
Reichian therapy of, 162, 163, 164,
  165, 234, 272, 529
SB's career and, xiii, 81, 112–13,
  159, 161, 213, 243, 429, 459
SB's fictional portrayals of, xiii, 27,
  110, 236, 428–29, 509
SB's friendship with, xiii, 27, 29, 41,
  56, 113–14, 159–60, 161–62,
  165, 206–7, 212, 235–36, 243,
  428–29, 529
teaching positions and, 213, 235,
  251*n*
wit of, 41, 45
Rosenfeld, Sam, 235
Rosenfeld, Vasiliki Sarantakis, 81, 82,
  83, 162, 174, 234, 235, 243, 428,
  529
Rosenthal, Raymond, 164
Rosenthal, Tom, 460, 497*n*, 499
Ross, Barney, 112
Ross, Ralph, 252
  humanities programs chaired by,
    159, 251, 263
  on Ludwig, 266–67, 305
  on Rosenfeld, 161
  SB's letters to, 302, 304, 312,
    313–14, 322, 425, 463, 493
  on SB's marriage, 266–67, 283
Rosten, Leo, 384
Rosten, Norman, 339
Roszak, Theodore, 419
Rotblatt, Lynn Bellows, 190, 337, 368,
  404
Roth, Philip, 458, 500, 508, 554,
  570*n*, 585, 589
  fictional portrayal of SB by, 245,
    253, 488–89
  as Jewish writer, 290, 291*n*, 292,
    363

on SB as biography subject, ix, xi
SB as model for, 253–54
SB on work of, 254, 290, 312, 512,
  522, 584
on SB's protagonists, 494
on SB's wives, 254, 299, 412, 549
Roth, William, 77–78, 79
Rothko, Mark, 317
Rotman, Morris, 474–75, 484
Rousseau, Jean-Jacques, 186, 312,
  334, 478, 526
Rubin, Michael, 207–8
Rudenstine, Neil, 562
Runyon, Damon, 545
Rushdie, Salman, 501, 525, 570, 585
Russell and Volkening, 413–14
Russia, Jews in, 6, 21, 32, 407
Rutgers University, 563

Sabin Junior High School, 27
Said, Edward, 493
St. Martin's Press, 558
Saint-Simon, Louis de Rouvroy, duc
  de, 71
Saki (H. H. Munro), 492
Salas, Floyd, 375
Salazar, Leandro, 75
Salinger, J. D., xii, 291*n*, 312, 356*n*
Salk, Jonas, 492*n*
Salzburg Seminar in American Studies,
  156, 170–71
Samuel, Maurice, 85
Sandburg, Carl, 5, 224, 364
"Sand-Man, The" (Hoffmann), 298
SANE (Committee for a Sane Nuclear
  Policy), 344
Sansom, William, 171
Sapir, Edward, 163
Sarant, George (Rosenfeld), 529–30
Saroyan, William, 202
Sartre, Jean-Paul, 141, 142, 250, 271,
  273, 455, 456
Saturday Review of Literature, The,
  68, 238
Saul Bellow (Fuchs), 464
Saul Bellow (Miller), 557–58
Saul Bellow, Drumlin Woodchuck
  (Harris), xii, 364, 486–88
Saul Bellow Journal, 517, 534
Saul Bellow Municipal Library,
  514–16, 593
Savage, Richard, 595
Schaller, George, 395

Schapiro, Lillian, 379
Schapiro, Meyer, 83, 112, 379
Schelley, Sara, 474
Schenk, Bebe, 86
Schilder, Paul, 272–73
Schiller, Friedrich von, 132
Schimmel, Harold, 455
Schlesinger, Arthur, Jr., 319, 570n
Schloss Leopoldskron, 155, 156
Schopenhauer, Arthur, 27
Schorer, Mark, x
Schwab, Dave, 26
Schwartz, Delmore, 79, 205
    on aging, 581
    author's biography of, ix, x, xii, 602
    critical success of, 84
    death of, 425, 429, 430n, 504, 602
    literary criticism by, 181
    marriages of, 180, 235, 451
    as model for SB's fictional charac-
        ters, ix, 84, 173, 174, 236–37,
        429–30, 434, 444, 449
    on New York, 82
    at *Partisan Review,* 226, 322
    on Pound's anti-Semitism, 248
    on Princeton faculty, 173, 178, 179
    publishers of, 77
    on Rahv, 111, 112
    SB's friendship with, 210–11, 278,
        429
    on SB's work, 95, 203, 429
    self-destructiveness of, 179, 180,
        213, 278, 429
    writings of, 71, 84, 194, 324n
Schwartz, Joan Ullmann, 366, 431,
    509n, 587
Schwartz, Jonas, 283, 337
Scott, Hazel, 68, 70
Scott, Nathan, 354
Scott, Sir Walter, 193
Scott, Walter Dill, 48
"Sealed Treasure, The" (Bellow), 260
Secker and Warburg, 440, 520
Seferis, George, 463
Seidel, Toscha, 24
Seize the Day (Bellow), 236–40
    autobiographical elements in, 216,
        237–38, 386
    Bellow family history in, 36
    critical responses to, 240, 246–47,
        252, 269, 356, 394
    dramatization of, 351
    funeral scene in, 239

hotel setting in, 176
    models for fictional characters in,
        166n, 214, 236–37
    publication of, 230–31, 233, 236,
        246, 267
    sales of, 252
    SB's assessment of, 246
    tight composition of, 240, 319, 369
    title of, 230n
    writing process and, 243, 313
"Sermon by Doctor Pep, A" (Bellow),
    152–53
Shachtman, Max, 33
Shachtman, Yetta Barshevsky, 33, 581
Shafer, Margaret, 321, 326, 348
Shakespeare, William, 30, 46–47, 49,
    75, 97, 127, 186, 279–80, 310,
    312, 535, 592–93
Shannon, Nellie, 246
Shapiro, Karl, 119, 171–72, 193, 226,
    290–91
Shattuck, Roger, 408, 437, 565
Shavrein, Judy, 389, 413
Shaw, Artie, 323, 500
Shaw, George Bernard, 46
Shaw, Peter, 267
Shawn, William, 199–200, 231, 452
Shechner, Mark, 392
Sheehan, Susan, 513
Sheen, Fulton J., 177
Shelley, Percy Bysshe, 30, 271, 437,
    464
Shils, Edward, 415, 455
    in academic politics, 386, 406, 407
    on Allan Bloom, 533n, 564
    death of, 581
    as model for fictional characters,
        390, 476
    Mr. Sammler's Planet edited by,
        390–91, 476, 603–4
    on Nobel Prize, 458
    SB's friendship with, 6, 360, 390,
        395, 418, 476–78, 531, 581, 603
    on SB's realism, 72
    on SB's romances, 361, 406
    at University of Chicago, 39, 316,
        386, 406, 407, 476, 477
Shrifte, Evelyn, 77, 102
Shuman, Ik, 91
Sidran, Ben, 378
Sidran, Ezra, 378
Sidran, Louis, 213, 377–78
Sidran, Shirley, 378

Siegelman, Philip, 266, 305
Sifton, Elisabeth, 452, 472, 481, 483
Silber, John, 565
Silk, Dennis, 455
Silone, Ignazio, 71, 158, 458
"Silver Dish, A" (Bellow), 396, 509,
 549, 577
Silvers, Robert, 345
Simmons, Eleanor Fox, 26, 33–34, 36,
 350n, 522, 588
Simmons, Maggie Staats, 370, 554
 background of, 350
 fictional portrayal of, 349, 350,
 351, 542
 as literary executor, 413
 physical appearance of, 350
 SB's romantic involvement with,
 349, 350–51, 358, 360, 361, 362,
 371, 377, 379, 380, 383, 384,
 386, 393, 471, 542, 548
 travels of, 353, 392
Simpson, Eileen, 179, 180
Simpson, Louis, 211, 217, 228, 233,
 240, 449–51
Sinaiko, Herman, 407
Sinatra, Frank, 277
Sincerity and Authenticity (Trilling),
 419–21
Sinclair, Upton, 5, 142, 448, 449
Singer, Barnett, 442–44, 500–501
Singer, Isaac Bashevis, 192, 453, 454
Singer, Richard G., 162
Sister Carrie (Dreiser), 58, 62
Six-Day War, 369–71, 402
"Skepticism and the Depth of Life"
 (Bellow), 60, 354–55
Slate, Hyman, 281, 282, 471, 475,
 486, 491, 493, 520, 581
Smith, Corlies, 481, 527
Smith, David, 346
Smith, Henry Nash, 114
Smith, Liz, 586
Smith, Sydney, 561–62
Smith, William Jay, 565
Smyth, Joseph Hilton, 68, 70
socialism, 32, 33, 64–66
Socrates, 592
Solotaroff, Theodore, 290, 327, 338n,
 372–73, 482
Solzhenitsyn, Aleksandr, 312, 407
"Something to Remember Me By"
 (Bellow) (story), 34, 35, 36, 318,
 560–61, 562

Something to Remember Me By
 (Bellow) (collection), 560–62
Sontag, Susan, 374, 399, 491, 493,
 563, 585
Sophocles, 316
Southey, Robert, 583
Spark, Muriel, 570
Spender, Stephen, 150, 288, 383
Spengler, Oswald, ix, 25, 575
Spiegel, Leo, 114, 151
Spiegel, Nancy, 151
Spoleto Festival, 352
Staats, Maggie, *see* Simmons, Maggie
 Staats
Stafford, Jean, 104–5, 377
Stalin, Joseph, 33, 40, 64, 65, 69, 341,
 401, 440, 525, 552
Staples, Brent, 572–73, 587
"Starting Out in Chicago" (Bellow), 3,
 30
Stasio, Marilyn, 414
Stead, Christina, 458
Stein, Gertrude, 137
Steinbeck, John, 142, 224, 249, 319,
 377, 457, 463n
Steinberg, Saul, 141, 371, 395–96,
 397, 479, 504, 554
Steinem, Gloria, 342, 356
Steiner, George, 359
Steiner, Rudolf, 73, 436–37, 438, 439,
 440, 448
Stendhal, 67, 88, 99, 154, 185, 188,
 304, 355, 381, 454, 514
Stern, Richard, 254, 555
 on black-Jewish relations, 573
 on Harris biography of SB, 365
 SB described by, 475–76, 582–83
 on SB's aging, 582–83, 586, 590–91
 SB's friendship with, 366–67, 413,
 456, 487
 SB's letters to, 245, 269, 273, 282,
 314, 318, 335, 377, 380, 393,
 407, 417, 430n, 453, 457, 462,
 467, 577
 on SB's romantic involvements, 307,
 377, 523
 on SB's work, 271n
 on university faculty, 253, 316
 writing by, 279, 408, 456
Stevens, Roger L., 327, 331
Stigler, George, 528
Stone, Robert, 569
Strachey, Lytton, 387

Straus, Roger W., ix
Strauss, Leo, 478, 598*n*
Stravinsky, Igor, 208
Streitfeld, David, 590
Strobos, Semon, 405, 406
Student Project for Amity among
    Nations (SPAN), 120
Studs Lonigan (Farrell), 59, 63
Styron, William, 199, 328, 412, 570*n*
Sugarman, Joey, 32–33
Sullivan, Andrew, 597
Sutherland, John, 562
Swados, Harvey, 100, 198, 276,
    278–79, 287, 345
Swift, Jonathan, 48, 192, 406, 589
Swinburne, Algernon Charles, 31
Sykes, Gerald, 210
Sylvania Farms, 197, 198

Tacitus, 92, 541
Tan, Amy, 569
Tarcov, Edith, 29, 54, 327, 389, 422,
    451, 469*n*, 550
Tarcov, Nathan, 597
Tarcov, Oscar, 43, 388, 597
    Chicago boyhood of, 29, 41
    death of, 326–27, 378, 504
    Rosenfeld's letters to, 56, 166
    SB's letters to, 44, 117, 148, 161,
        294, 326
    writings of, 213, 226, 326–27
Targ, William, 101
Tasker, Dana, 89, 90, 91
Tate, Allen, 73, 84, 141, 159, 205, 317
Taubman, Howard, 333
Taylor, Frank, 135, 136
Taylor, Harold, 349
Teitelbaum family, xi
Tennyson, Alfred, Lord, 271
Terkel, Studs, 96, 493, 556
Texas, University of, 407, 408, 565
Thatcher, Margaret, 556, 595
Theft, A (Bellow), 351, 541–43, 544,
    560, 593–94
"There Is Simply Too Much to Think
    About" (Bellow), 571
"This Is the Way We Go to School"
    (Bellow), 48
Thomas, D. M., 501
Thomas, Dylan, 172, 214
Thomes, A. Boyd, 266, 426
Thompson, Hunter, 303
Thompson, John, 211

Thompson, Lawrance, x
Thoreau, Henry David, 202
Thorp, Willard, 178
"Thoughts of Sergeant George Flavin,
    The" (Bellow), 151
Thucydides, 92, 583
Time, 89–90, 391
Tindall, William York, 335*n*
Tocqueville, Alexis de, 260, 583
To Jerusalem and Back (Bellow), 446,
    447, 452, 454–55, 471, 472
Tolstoy, Leo, 25, 236, 251, 419, 458*n*
    life of, 57, 250
    as literary model, 53, 76, 186, 260,
        556
    in SB's teaching curriculum, 304,
        405
Tomalin, Claire, 412
To the Finland Station (Wilson),
    64*n*–65*n*
Towb, Harry, 353
Towers, Robert, 543
Toynbee, Philip, 193, 415
Tragic Generation, 179
"Transcending National Boundaries"
    (Bellow), 563
Trilling, Diana, 49, 100, 101, 130,
    131, 182, 183, 228
Trilling, Lionel, 71, 72, 195
    on American cultural poverty, 228,
        419–20
    Anglophilia of, 228
    career of, 49, 181, 227–28, 421
    novel of, 194
    SB's criticism of, 131, 419–22
    SB's letters to, 184, 188, 420–21
    on SB's writing, 182, 201–3
Trip to Town, A (Rubin), 207–8, 209
"Triumph of the Comic View, A"
    (Trilling), 202–3
Trotsky, Leon, 32, 33, 40, 52, 64, 65,
    68–69, 74, 75, 162, 575
Tschacbasov, Sondra, *see* Bellow,
    Sondra Tschacbasov
Tulcea, Alexandra Ionescu, *see* Bellow,
    Alexandra Ionescu Tulcea
Tuley, Murray F., 27
Tuley High School, xiii, 26, 27–28, 29,
    30, 33–34, 38, 474, 494, 566–67
Tuley Review, The, 27, 28, 29, 30, 33
Tumin, Mel, 86, 101, 169, 179, 214,
    219, 403, 471
Tureck, Rosalyn, 24

Turgenev, Ivan, 185, 365
Twain, Mark, 114, 192, 202, 301,
    454*n*
"Two Morning Monologues"
    (Bellow), 73–74, 77, 318

Ulysses (Joyce), 186, 198, 270, 335*n*,
    340, 382*n*, 405
Under the Weather (Bellow), 351–53
Unger, Leonard, 115
"University as Villain, The" (Bellow),
    227, 355
Updike, John, 312, 433, 502, 524,
    543, 570, 589, 591
Uris, Leon, 291*n*

Van Doren, Mark, 173, 344
Van Gelder, Robert, 85, 89
Vanguard Press, 76–77, 92, 105,
    117–18, 129, 132, 135–36, 224
Vanity Fair, 508, 542
Van Vechten, Carl, 154
Veblen, Thorstein, 38
Vendler, Helen, 492
Verne, Jules, 415
"Very Dark Trees, The" (Bellow)
    (unpubl.), 76, 77–79, 92, 147, 220
Victim, The (Bellow), 124–32, 319,
    602
  anti-Semitism as theme in, 125–27,
    130, 388, 546
  autobiographical elements in, 91,
    386
  critical responses to, 129–39, 167,
    394
  dedication of, 176
  dramatization of, 172–73
  philosophical topics in, 143, 188
  plot of, 125
  prose style of, 153, 246
  publication of, 117, 124–25, 224
  sales of, 131–32, 135
  SB's assessment of, 98, 236
  writing process and, 104, 114, 115,
    117, 118, 119, 123
Victoria, University of, 500
Vidal, Gore, 150, 301, 327, 378, 531,
    560, 586
Vietnam War, 344, 345–46, 347
Views from a Window (Simpson), 217
Viking Press, 186, 383–84, 589
  advances paid by, 136, 196, 224,
    233, 250, 268, 339, 372

  book sales reported by, 330
  film rights negotiated with, 367
  production quality of, 124–25,
    480–81
  publisher of, 161, 224
  royalty payments from, 206, 210
  SB's departure from, 481, 483
  SB's editors at, 135, 138, 201,
    224–25, 231, 261, 329, 339, 452,
    481, 527
  SB's return to, 541
  SB's works reissued by, 224, 451,
    534
Virgil, 186
Vivas, Eliseo, 56
Volkening, Henry, 101, 153, 159, 225,
    226, 315, 413
Vrdolyak, Edward, 551

Wagner College, 310–12, 360
Wakefield, Dan, 279
Walcott, Derek, 570
Wald, George, 400
Walden, George, 556
Walker, Alice, 513
Walker, Nancy, 351
Wallace, David Foster, 584
Walters, Barbara, 555
Wanning, Andrews, 302
Warren, Robert Penn, 43, 116, 124,
    186, 251*n*, 317, 398, 458, 493
  SB's letters to, 170, 195, 210, 372
  on SB's work, 115, 117, 129–30,
    169
Wasserman, Harriet, 554
  as Allan Bloom's agent, 532, 597
  memoir by, 585
  publisher changes and, 481, 482,
    483, 527, 528
  as SB's agent, 413–14, 467, 533,
    584, 585
  SB's friendship with, 414, 519
  SB's Nobel Prize and, 456, 460, 461
Waugh, Evelyn, 273
Weber, Max, 71
Webster, Harvey Curtis, 198
Weidenfeld, George, Lord, 288, 315*n*,
    383, 440, 522
Weill, Yellow Kid, 238
Weinstein, Ann, 534*n*, 556, 593
Weisner, Jerome, 492*n*
Weiss, Theodore, 196, 231, 258
Wellington, duke of, 521

Wells, H. G., 128, 199, 317, 391
"Wen, The" (Bellow), 351, 352–53
West, Anthony, 199–200
West, James, 286
West, Nathanael, 504
West, Rebecca, 19, 199
Weybright, Victor, 108
"What Are Writers Doing in the
     Universities?" (Bellow), 374
"What Kind of Day Did You Have?"
     (Bellow), 508–9, 541
"Where Do We Go from Here?"
     (Bellow), 312
White, Katharine, 199–200, 453
Whiting Awards, 526
Whitman, Alden, 448, 449
Whitman, Walt, 152, 202, 205, 271,
     454*n*
"Who Breathes Overhead" (Bellow),
     132
Whyte, William H., Jr., 473
Wiesel, Elie, 307, 401
Wieseltier, Leon, 479–80, 518, 538,
     584
Wilde, Oscar, 4, 31, 55, 442
William Morrow (publisher), 528,
     536, 541
Williams, Hernando, 495
Williams, Tennessee, ix, 317
Williams, William Carlos, 170
Wilson, Edmund, 71
     anti-Semitism of, 205
     as biographical subject, ix–x
     on Chicago, 5, 107
     Mary McCarthy's marriage to, 111,
          479
     physical appearance of, 65*n*
     at Princeton, 179
     publisher of, 78
     SB on work of, 65*n*, 107, 279
     SB's writing reviewed by, 99, 110,
          205
     on Trotsky, 64*n*–65*n*
     at White House events, 317, 344
Wilson, Harold, 437
Wilson, John T., 457
Wilson, Jonathan, 598–99
Wilson, William Julius, 573
Wilt, Napier, 49
Winter Notes on Summer Impressions
     (Dostoyevsky), 138–39, 140
Winters, Shelley, 352, 353
Winterson, Jeanette, 570*n*

Wisconsin, University of, 47, 54, 55,
     56–57
Wiseman, Joseph, 414
Wisse, Ruth, 516, 539, 540, 559, 560
Wolcott, James, 552
Wolfe, Thomas, 76, 127, 196, 211,
     592
Wolfe, Tom, 419*n*
Wolfe, Winifred, 367
Wolff, Helen, 347
Wolfson, Victor, 109
Wood, James, 577, 588–89
Woolf, Leonard, 417–18
Woolf, Virginia, 76, 129, 417–18
Wordsworth, William, 22, 90, 271
"Work of Art, A" (Bellow) (unpubl.),
     351
Works Progress Administration
     (WPA), 62–63, 70
Wouk, Herman, 291*n*
"Wrecker, The" (Bellow), 165, 172
Wright, Frank Lloyd, 321
Wright, Richard, 63, 142, 145, 170,
     277
"Writer and His Country, The"
     (Bellow), 465–66
Wrzecionkowski, Casimir, 29
Wylie, Andrew, 584–85

Yaddo, 173, 244, 245–46
Yagoda, Ben, 453*n*
Yeats, William Butler, 58, 114, 354,
     589
Yehoshua, A. B., 400, 536
Yelin, Shulamis, 590
Yerkes, Charles T., 5
Yiddish language, 14
Young Communist League, 40, 56, 64
"Young Eccentric, A" (Bellow),
     133–34
Young People's Socialist League
     (YPSL), 33, 41
Yuster, Sarah, 590

Zangwill, Israel, 14
Zelig, 491
"Zetland" (Bellow) (unpubl.), 110–11,
     163, 236, 428–29, 481
     published fragment of, 27, 509
Zimmer, Mary, 51*n*
Zola, Emile, 76, 137, 170, 448
Zuckerman Unbound (Roth), 512
Zuluf, Mahmud Abu, 455

ABOUT THE AUTHOR

JAMES ATLAS is the author of *Delmore Schwartz: The Life of an American Poet,* which was nominated for a National Book Award in 1978; *The Great Pretender,* a novel; and *Battle of the Books: The Curriculum Debate in America.* A former editor of *The New York Times Magazine* and staff writer for *The New Yorker,* he is the founding editor of the Lipper/Viking Penguin Lives series of brief biographies. He lives in New York City with his wife, the psychiatrist and writer Anna Fels, and their two children.

ABOUT THE TYPE

This book was set in Sabon, a typeface designed by the well-known German typographer Jan Tschichold (1902–1974). Sabon's design is based on the original letterforms of Claude Garamond and was created specifically to be used for three sources: foundry type for hand composition, Linotype, and Monotype. Tschichold named his typeface for the famous Frankfurt typefounder Jacques Sabon, who died in 1580.